FIND IT FAST

Preparing for the Free-Response Questions on the AP® English Language Exam

Ideas in Argument

Building Skills and Understanding

Ideas in Argument

Building Skills and Understanding

for the AP® English Language Course

John R. Williamson
Model Laboratory School at
Eastern Kentucky University, KY

Mary Jo Zell
Keller High School, TX

Elizabeth Davis
College Station High School, TX

bedford, freeman & worth
high school publishers

Boston | New York

Senior Vice President, Humanities, Social Sciences, and High School: Chuck Linsmeier
Executive Program Director, High School: Ann Heath
Executive Program Manager, High School Humanities: Nathan Odell
Development Editor: Jeff Ousborne
Editorial Assistant: Meghan Kelly
Director of Media Editorial: Adam Whitehurst
Media Editor: Gina Forsythe
Executive Marketing Manager, High School: Lisa Erdely
Assistant Marketing Manager, High School: Tiffani Tang
Senior Director, Content Management Enhancement: Tracey Kuehn
Senior Managing Editor: Michael Granger
Senior Manager of Publishing Services: Andrea Cava
Content Project Manager: Matt Glazer
Senior Workflow Project Manager: Jennifer Wetzel
Production Supervisor: Brianna Lester
Director of Design, Content Management: Diana Blume
Interior Design: Heather Marshall, Periwinkle Design Studio
Cover Design: William Boardman
Illustration Coordinator: Janice Donnola
Illustrations: Ron Weickart
Director, Rights and Permissions: Hilary Newman
Text Permissions Project Manager: Elaine Kosta, Lumina Datamatics, Inc.
Photo Permissions Project Manager: Richard Fox, Lumina Datamatics, Inc.
Director of Digital Production: Keri deManigold
Lead Media Project Manager: Jodi Isman
Copyeditor: Melissa Brown Levine
Composition: Lumina Datamatics, Inc.
Cover Images: nantonov/Getty Images (brush stroke); klikk/Getty Images (fountain pen); narvikk/Getty Images (typewriter); Ollustrator/Getty Images (color wheel); Imo/Getty Images (book); pedrosala/Getty Images (musical score); dottedhippo/Getty Images (butterflies); bgblue/Getty Images (abstract background); Juliasv/Getty Images (compass); David Malan/Getty Images (young woman); Fotofeeling/Getty Images (elephant); Photographs in the Carol M. Highsmith Archive, Library of Congress, Prints and Photographs Division (Statue of Liberty, Brooklyn Bridge, U.S. Capitol); goktugg/Getty Images (trumpet); WLADIMIR BULGAR/Getty Images (laboratory glassware); Radoslav Zilinsky/Getty Images (scales)
Printing and Binding: Transcontinental

Library of Congress Control Number: 2021944103

ISBN 978-1-319-35663-7 (Student Edition)
ISBN 978-1-319-41881-6 (Teacher's Edition)

Printed in Canada.
2   3   4   5   6   26   25   24   23   22

Acknowledgments

Text acknowledgments and copyrights appear at the back of the book on pages T-1–T-4, which constitute an extension of the copyright page. Art acknowledgments and copyrights appear on the same page as the art selections they cover.

AP® is a trademark registered by the College Board, which is not affiliated with, and does not endorse, this product.

For information, write: Bedford, Freeman & Worth High School Publishers, 120 Broadway, 25th Floor, New York, NY 10271 hsmarketing@bfwpub.com

To those who taught and inspired us
and
to those who teach and inspire others

From the Authors

Greetings,

Ideas in Argument develops critical readers and thoughtful writers. It was created to support both students and teachers. We're excited for you to see it because we believe it's exactly what students need to be successful!

Ideas in Argument

- is **completely aligned** to the units in the AP® English Language and Composition Course and Exam Description;
- sequences and **spirals the skills across the units** in a way that **builds students' confidence** and success;
- includes contemporary **engaging and inspiring texts** that students will love to read, and favorites that teachers love to teach;
- presents **rhetorical reading and analytical writing workshops** that actually teach **the craft of argument**;
- builds critical thinking skills about **cultural ideas that stimulate conversations and take students beyond the classroom into real-world arguments**;
- contains **organizers, charts, and tips** that help students understand and practice the rhetorical skills and concepts that matter most;
- is written in a voice that **speaks to students**;
- provides **test-taking strategies** along with **practice questions in every unit**.

We are committed to helping all students succeed. So, we've shared what's been successful for us. We hope *Ideas in Argument* will support teachers and guide students as they become stronger analytical readers and persuasive writers. We'd love to hear from you as you discover *Ideas in Argument*.

Keep up the great work!

John R. Williamson   Mary Jo Zell   Elizabeth Davis

About the Authors

Steve Lemon

John R. Williamson

John R. Williamson is the Dean of K–12 Programs and Superintendent of Model Laboratory School at Eastern Kentucky University where he also continues to teach both AP® English courses. Prior to this role, John served as the Vice President of Curriculum, Instruction, and Assessment for the College Board's AP® Program, where he led the transformation of all thirty-eight AP® courses and exams, including both AP® English Language and AP® English Literature. For more than twenty years, John has led workshops across the country as an AP® faculty consultant. Additionally, he has experience as a reader and table leader for both AP® English Exams. John has taught courses at all high school levels, as well as both undergraduate and graduate courses in composition, rhetoric, linguistics, and literature.

Steve Lemon

Mary Jo Zell

Mary Jo Zell currently serves as the English Department Chair at Keller High School in Keller, Texas, where she teaches AP® English Language, AP® English Literature, and Dual Credit English. She is also an adjunct professor at Tarrant County Community College. She has been a reader and table leader for the AP® English Language Exam for over twenty years. She served on the AP® English Literature Instructional Design Team and is an AP® faculty consultant for both AP® English Language and AP® English Literature who has conducted national workshops and summer institutes.

Steve Lemon

Elizabeth Davis

Elizabeth Davis has taught English for more than three decades for Round Rock Independent School District and College Station Independent School District, where she also served as English Department Chair for many years. She has been a reader for the AP® English Language Exam and served on the AP® Literature Instructional Design Team. For more than twenty years, she has served as an AP® faculty consultant, conducting workshops in both AP® English Language and AP® English Literature.

Advisory Board

Willard Jones

Stephanie M. Carter
McCracken HS, KY

Kacie Smith

Kacie Smith
Liberty HS, TX

Emily Valaitis

Emily Valaitis
Naperville North HS, IL

Courtesy of Jim Jordan and Sacred Heart Cathedral Preparatory

Jim Jordan
Sacred Heart Catholic
Prepatory, CA

Darrin Pollock

Darrin J. Pollock
Walton Verona HS, KY

Sherry Wynn Perdue

Sherry Wynn Perdue
Oakland University, MI

Tracy Rankin

Tracy Rankin
Keller ISD, TX

Lauren Jones

Lauren Jones
Fallbrook Union HS, CA

Acknowledgments

We are grateful to all who made this project possible:

To Nathan Odell, our editor, who believed in this project and brought it to life; Jeff Ousborne, our developmental editor, who polished our prose; Matt Glazer, our content project manager, whose keen eye kept us consistent; Lisa Erdely, our marketing manager, who found just the right ways to share our book; and the entire team at Bedford, Freeman & Worth for bringing this book to market and supporting us every step of the way.

To Erick Collings who helped us find a voice that speaks to students and reminded us just how important those early years of teaching are, Brandon Abdon who developed AP®-style multiple-choice questions, and Lauren Tyra who created graphics that made the abstract more concrete.

To the hundreds of you who evaluated early proposal materials and completed market surveys that helped guide the direction of this project. Our thanks in particular to our reviewers: Jennifer Couling, Nancy Dickinson, Lauren Djigo, Christi Gervasi, Randy Gingrich, Laura Hensley, Lauren Jones, Jim Jordan, Nathan Lamar, Jennifer Manuel, Sherry Wynn Perdue, Elizabeth Siegfried, Laurie Skop, Kellye Statz-Simon, Emily Valaitis, David Waselko, Erik Witherspoon, and Deon Youd.

To all those who have been in our workshops and fellow AP® readers and consultants who shared favorite texts, instructional strategies, and nuggets of wisdom.

To our students, both past and present, who taught us more about teaching than any book or professor could, and who were the first who saw these workshops and texts and gave them the student seal of approval.

To our friends and colleagues who provided feedback, support, and mentorship: Trevor Packer, Jay McTighe, David McFaddin, Brian Robinson, Terry Redican, Christopher Budano, Chris Heiert, Sally Guadagno, Patti Azzara, Tina Rose, Hephzibah Roskelly, Kris Vogel, and Lara Leigh Ewing.

And, most importantly, to our families who provided encouragement when we really needed it and who made sacrifices so that we could share our ideas with you: Rob, Sophie, Sam, Mickey, Josh, Kaitlyn, Nick, Hannah, Margot, Jaime, Paul, Jeanne, Jessica, Lynn, and Robert. Thank you!

An Introduction to *Ideas in Argument*

A Clear Pathway to Success

In his role as Vice President of Curriculum, Instruction, and Assessment for the College Board's AP® Program, John R. Williamson, this book's lead author, spearheaded the transformation of all thirty-eight AP® courses, including AP® English Language and Composition. At the heart of this transformation are carefully constructed skill units broken into Big Ideas that represent a strategic pathway to building skills and achieving success on the AP® Exam.

Deeply Aligned to the AP® Units. Now, for the first time, a complete textbook program puts those ideas into practice, turning the AP® units into a clear pathway to success in the AP® English Language and Composition course. *Ideas in Argument* has nine units, with instruction and practice deeply aligned to the AP® Course Framework. In addition to guiding students to success, this structure will also make it easy to use the resources found on AP® Classroom, such as Personal Progress Checks, released AP® Exam Items, AP® Daily videos, and more.

How Does a Unit Work?

Each unit is divided into sections with color coding to match the AP® Course Description:

- Reading and Analysis Workshops
- Ideas in American Culture
- Composition Workshops
- Preparing for the AP® Exam

Unit at a Glance

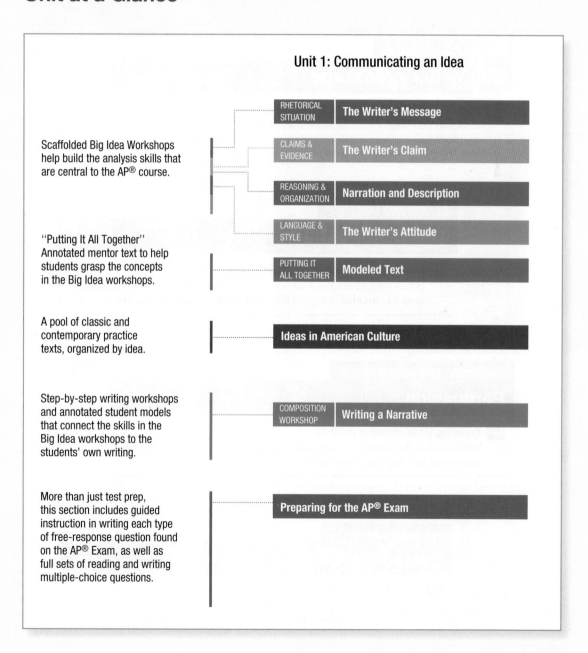

Unit 1: Communicating an Idea

Scaffolded Big Idea Workshops help build the analysis skills that are central to the AP® course.

RHETORICAL SITUATION	The Writer's Message
CLAIMS & EVIDENCE	The Writer's Claim
REASONING & ORGANIZATION	Narration and Description
LANGUAGE & STYLE	The Writer's Attitude

"Putting It All Together" Annotated mentor text to help students grasp the concepts in the Big Idea workshops.

| PUTTING IT ALL TOGETHER | Modeled Text |

A pool of classic and contemporary practice texts, organized by idea.

Ideas in American Culture

Step-by-step writing workshops and annotated student models that connect the skills in the Big Idea workshops to the students' own writing.

| COMPOSITION WORKSHOP | Writing a Narrative |

More than just test prep, this section includes guided instruction in writing each type of free-response question found on the AP® Exam, as well as full sets of reading and writing multiple-choice questions.

Preparing for the AP® Exam

Focused Workshops on the Big Ideas

Each unit begins with four brief workshops in argument and rhetorical analysis, keyed to the Big Ideas and Enduring Understandings of the course and color coded for ease of navigation. Each of these workshops includes content, instruction, and guided practice with a high-interest practice text.

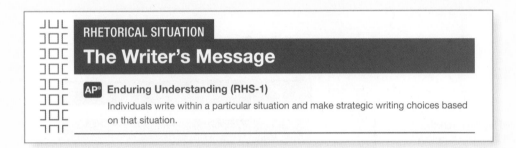

RHETORICAL SITUATION
The Writer's Message

AP Enduring Understanding (RHS-1)

Individuals write within a particular situation and make strategic writing choices based on that situation.

CLAIMS AND EVIDENCE
The Writer's Claim

AP Enduring Understanding (CLE-1)

Writers make claims about subjects, rely on evidence that supports their reasoning, and often acknowledge or respond to other, possibly opposing, arguments.

REASONING AND ORGANIZATION
Persuasion

AP Enduring Understanding (REO-1)

Writers guide understanding of a text's line of reasoning and claims through that text's organization and integration of evidence.

LANGUAGE AND STYLE
Syntactical Choices for Effect

AP Enduring Understanding (STL-1)

The rhetorical situation informs the strategic stylistic choices that writers make.

Putting It All Together

After each series of workshops, the book takes a moment to step back and model how the skills of the unit can be used to analyze a text. This is done through a modeled annotation of a mentor text.

Unifying Idea	2008 Election Victory Speech	Rhetorical Choices	Effects of Choices
hope for change	The road ahead will be long. Our climb will be steep. We may not get there in one year, or even one term, but America—I have never been more hopeful than I am tonight that we will get there. I promise you: We as a people will get there.	definition: line of reasoning (trait/ characteristic) pronoun reference	defining the challenges ahead through analogy—climbing a hill uses "I" and "you" to establish that his role is different from the audience's role, but both will help achieve change
hope for change	What began 21 months ago in the depths of winter must not end on this autumn night. This victory alone is not the change we seek—it is only the chance for us to make that change. And that cannot happen if we go back to the way things were. It cannot happen without you.		
hope for change	So let us summon a new spirit of patriotism; of service and responsibility where each of us resolves to pitch in and work harder and look after not only ourselves, but each	definition: line of reasoning (trait/ characteristic)	defining a new spirit of patriotism by identifying its traits of service and responsibility

Ideas in American Culture—Uncovering the Ideas within the Arguments

Decades of experience as writing teachers and AP® Exam leaders showed the authors of *Ideas in Argument* that one secret ingredient was both the key to success on the exam and often missing in lower-scoring essays: ideas.

It's not enough to just discuss a topic. To be successful, students need to express an *idea* about that topic. That's why ideas are at the core of every unit in *Ideas in Argument*. After the Big Idea workshops come two Ideas in American Culture sections that explore some of the ideas and contexts that inform our cultural conversation. With a brief introduction to foreground and contextualize the ideas, and an Idea Bank to help students make relevant and contemporary connections, this section is all about critical thinking and guiding students to the next level of analysis and argument.

IDEAS IN AMERICAN CULT

had helped defend the colonies during the conflict. But the colonists viewed these policies as unfair and illegitimate "taxation without representation," as they had no voice in Parliament. After the British enacted a tax on tea in 1773, Bostonians raided three British ships and dumped over 92,000 pounds of British tea into the Boston harbor. In retribution, the harbor was closed, which punished the entire city. Soon, the American Revol

America's fight for freedo
from slavery and the civil righ
Harvey Milk's "You've Got to
envisions a democracy that is
most of us have witnessed ma
from injustice and inequality
Black Lives Matter, protests o
the United States has not alw
African Americans and wome
basic voting rights. But the h
gradual — expansion of demo
dom, justice, and equality will
as well.

Speech to the Virginia Convention

Patrick Henry

THE TEXT IN CONTEXT

In 1775, in the midst of political debate about whether to prepare for war or find a peaceful resolution with Britain, the Virginia House of Burgesses held a convention. After listening to other delegates, Patrick Henry (1736–1799), the first governor of Virginia, gave a speech that ultimately persuaded Virginia to prepare for the fight against Britain.

Pictorial Press Ltd/Alamy Stock Photo

REUTERS/Shannon Stapleton

▲
The Women's March is a founda
oppression against women throu
women and men all over the wo
American history.
———
What characteristics do the pe
American revolutionaries?

No man thinks more highly than I do of the patriotism, as well as abilities, of the very worthy gentlemen who have just addressed the House. But different men often see the same subject in different lights; and, therefore, I hope it will not be thought disrespectful to those gentlemen if, entertaining as I do opinions of a character very opposite to theirs, I shall speak forth my sentiments freely and without reserve. This is no time for ceremony. The question before the House is one of awful moment to this country. For my own part, I consider it as nothing less than a question of freedom or slavery; and in proportion to the magnitude of the subject ought to be the freedom of the debate. It is only in this way that we can hope to arrive at truth, and fulfill the great responsibility which we hold to God and our country. Should I keep back my opinions at such a time, through fear of giving offense, I should consider myself as guilty of treason towards my country, and of an act of disloyalty toward the Majesty of Heaven, which I revere above all earthly kings.

Mr. President, it is natural to man to indulge in the illusions of hope. We are apt to shut our eyes against a painful truth, and listen to the song of that siren till she transforms us into beasts. Is this the part of wise men, engaged in a great and arduous struggle for liberty? Are we disposed to be of the number of those who, having eyes, see not, and, having ears, hear not, the things which so nearly concern their temporal salvation? For my part, whatever anguish of spirit it may cost, I am willing to know the whole truth; to know the worst, and to provide for it.

I have but one lamp by which my feet are guided, and that is the lamp of experience. I know of no way of judging of the future but by the past. And judging by the past, I wish to know what there has been in the conduct

Practice Texts That Build Understanding and Context

Within the two Ideas in American Culture sections, you'll find paired texts that explore those ideas. These often include a classic text and a contemporary text, or two voices that present different perspectives on the idea to spark conversation.

For those of you whose AP® English Language course also happens to be an **American Literature** course, you'll find that many of the foundational texts and essential voices are here organized chronologically and put in conversation with more recent voices to show just how the ideas of the past continue to resonate.

Composition Workshops—Applying AP® Skills to Writing

One of the things that make AP® English Language so unique is that all of the key skills apply not only to reading and analysis but also to student writing. That's why in each unit of *Ideas in Argument* you will see a one-to-one correlation between what's taught in the Big Idea workshops and what's taught in the Composition Workshop. This is an example of that correlation from Unit 2:

Reading Skill	Writing Skill
Considering the Audience	Appealing to an Audience
Relevant and Sufficient Evidence	Selecting Relevant Evidence
Persuasion	Developing a Line of Reasoning
Syntax for Effect	Creating Emphasis through Syntax

Annotated Student Models

To give students a clear example of the skill in practice, each Composition Workshop includes an annotated student model that is a published work.

Phones Create Barriers between Peers
Kalindi Desai

The following student example is an editorial published in the College Station High School newspaper the *Catamount* in 2016. With the help of the marginal notations, discuss the writer's use of evidence, rhetorical strategies, line of reasoning, and call to action to persuade her audience.

The ability to communicate with people through cell phones and social media is a technological discovery that has made it easier than ever to interact with people from many areas of the world. We can talk to our friends that live miles away at any time, see what our favorite celebrities are up to, or keep up with whatever news is going around. But with this advance comes a downfall. People have become too afraid to talk to others about issues in person because confrontation scares them since our generation is so used to confronting others behind their thumbs through a cell phone screen.

writer includes context for the argument

introduces problem: people are afraid of face-to-face conversation

It's the easier option. You don't feel bad calling someone names if you can't see their face or allow them to retaliate in person. We seem to always be taking the easier route. The one that won't make us feel like horrible people for spreading rumors and forming lies about people that are based on assumptions.

reason: (opposing viewpoints) online communication is easier

Friend issues are highly common in high school due to changing personalities. With these friend issues comes confrontation. Our generation has somehow been brainwashed into thinking that it's okay to communicate over text about serious problems that could possibly hurt someone's feelings.

reason: friend issues arise with online communication

Preparing for the AP® Exam

Instruction in Writing Free-Response Essays

This invaluable section is more than just test prep items. It's a detailed guide to writing for the AP® Exam. Each Preparing for the AP® Exam section begins with a mini-workshop on a key AP® Exam writing skill, such as the following:

	Essay Type	Key Skill
Unit 1	Rhetorical Analysis	Writing and Supporting a Defensible Thesis
Unit 2	Argument	Establishing a Line of Reasoning
Unit 3	Synthesis	Incorporating Evidence from Sources
Unit 4	Rhetorical Analysis	Writing Commentary
Unit 5	Argument	Creating Unity and Coherence
Unit 6	Synthesis	Synthesizing Evidence from Sources
Unit 7	Rhetorical Analysis	Explaining Significance
Unit 8	Argument	Acknowledging and Responding to Opposing Arguments
Unit 9	Synthesis	Demonstrating Complexity

AP®-Style Multiple-Choice Reading Questions

Every unit also includes a set of multiple-choice reading questions to help students practice reading for rhetoric, argument, and understanding.

PREPARING FOR THE AP® EXAM
Multiple-Choice Questions: Reading

AP®-Style Multiple-Choice Writing Questions

Each unit includes a full set of multiple-choice writing questions to help students deeply familiarize themselves with this new type of assessment.

PREPARING FOR THE AP® EXAM
Multiple-Choice Questions: Writing

What Else Will You Find in This Program?

Throughout the book, you'll find thoughtful features to help students navigate the text and do well on the exam.

Diverse, High-Interest Readings and Student Writing Examples

In addition to classic works from authors like Henry David Thoreau and Rachel Carson, we've included a wealth of contemporary and diverse voices like Trevor Noah, Edward Snowden, Kamala Harris, Kareem Abdul-Jabbar, J. D. Vance, Harvey Milk, Bryan Stevenson, Ta-Nehisi Coates, Mindy Kaling, and more.

Rachel Carson	Trevor Noah	Edward Snowden	Bryan Stevenson	Mindy Kaling
©Erich Hartmann/ Magnum Photos	Jeff Schear/Getty Images	Gary Miller/ Getty Images	Jared Siskin/ Getty Images	FOX/ Getty Images

It's essential that students see themselves in the texts and authors represented in their textbooks. That's why each unit also includes **a published work written by a student**. These op-eds, college admissions essays, and essay contest winners help students see themselves as writers too.

At-a-Glance Reference Charts

Throughout *Ideas in Argument*, you'll find color-coded reference charts and instructional graphics that help students understand the effects of a writer's rhetorical choices.

RHETORICAL SITUATION		
Component	**Definition**	**Key Questions**
Writer	A writer is the author or creator of a text. The writer is a source who presents a perspective shaped by his or her background or context.	Who exactly is the writer, and what is his or her relationship to the subject? What values and beliefs does the writer hold about the subject? What is the writer's relationship to the situation? To the audience?
Message	The message is the writer's claim that is developed with reasoning and evidence.	What is the writer's claim? In other words, what idea or perspective does he or she have on the subject?
Purpose	The purpose is what the writer hopes to accomplish within a text.	What does the writer hope to accomplish? - To persuade or elicit change through a call to action - To narrate - To inform - To evaluate Why did the writer create this text for this particular audience?

AP® Skills Practice and Graphic Organizers

There are opportunities throughout the book to practice the skills and often in an approachable and structured way. In addition, printable graphic organizers can be found throughout the book wherever you see the Handout Icon .

 SKILLS PRACTICE | LANGUAGE AND STYLE **Analyzing Syntax**

In this informative and impassioned televised address, George W. Bush employed strategic syntactical choices to engage the American people toward a unified call to action. You may use the following graphic organizer as you read and find examples of the following syntactical techniques and consider the effect they had on President Bush's message and on his audience as you answer the questions after the text.

Analyzing Syntax

Rhetorical Devices	Definition	Examples and Effect
Repetition	Repeating or recurrence of a word, phrase, sentence, or other element	
Juxtaposition	Contrasting ideas, scenes, settings, images, or other elements	
Parallel Structure	Repeating words or phrases in the same grammatical structure	
Rhetorical Question	Posing a question that is expected to be considered but not answered literally	
Antithesis	Contrasting ideas in parallel grammatical structure	
Fragment	Expressing a broken thought or only part of a sentence intentionally	
Simple Sentence	Expressing a complete thought consisting of a subject and verb	

Key Point Boxes Help Students See the Big Picture

At the start of each Big Idea workshop are brief Key Point boxes that focus students on an important takeaway for the workshop as they read the instructions.

KEY POINT

Writers craft sentences in ways that not only engage their readers but also convey their message.

Insider AP® Tips on How to Do Well on the AP® Exam

Ever wondered what the people who score the AP® Exam are looking for? Ever wonder what tips and tricks they tell their students? Now you know. AP® Insider Tips give you access to all the tidbits the *Ideas in Argument* authors share with their students.

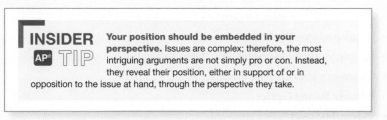

INSIDER AP® TIP

Your position should be embedded in your perspective. Issues are complex; therefore, the most intriguing arguments are not simply pro or con. Instead, they reveal their position, either in support of or in opposition to the issue at hand, through the perspective they take.

Student and Teacher Support Materials

Annotated Teacher's Edition

This all-in-one guide to planning, pacing, and teaching with *Ideas in Argument* includes the following:

- Planning and Pacing Guides
- Detailed Alignment to the AP® Course and Exam Description
- Lesson Overviews
- Reading Comprehension Check Questions
- Instructional Strategies and Differentiation
- Strategies and Activities for Differentiation
- Annotations That Are Aligned to Rhetorical Concepts
- Answers to All Questions
- Alignment to AP® Classroom Resources

Student Workbook

All of the graphic organizers and note-taking tools in this book are available for students to work with in the Student Workbook. Make learning handy and active with this essential tool. The Student Workbook is available in print or as hand-outs on the book's digital platform.

ELL Essential Guide

These guides to vocabulary, context, and understanding cover each page of the book, providing detailed support for English Language learners or any learner who needs additional support.

Teacher's Resource Materials

Available digitally, and embedded as links in the Teacher's Edition e-book, are a whole range of useful teaching materials, including the following:

- Reproducible Graphic Organizers
- Image Analysis Workshops
- Sample Student Essays and Annotated Rubrics
- Classroom Instructional Posters
- Editable Pacing Guides
- Videos/Podcasts
- Lexile Text Complexity Measures
- Professional Development Videos
- And more!

LearningCurve | Learning Curve Adaptive Quizzing
macmillan learning

Our Learning Curve adaptive quizzing engine will guide students to mastery of the course concepts. This first-ever Learning Curve for AP® Language will build understanding of rhetoric and argument principles.

Digital Options | More Than Just an E-book

Ideas in Argument is available on our fully interactive digital platform. On this platform, students can read, highlight, and take notes on any device, online or offline. You have the ability to assign every question from the book, as well as supplemental quizzes and activities, and students' results automatically sync to your gradebook. You can also access the Teacher's Resource Materials, test bank, adaptive quizzing, and more.

Assessment | High-Quality AP®-Style Items

Almost 1,000 **AP®-style multiple-choice and free-response questions** to help students prepare for the AP® Exam are available on our digital platform and the ExamView® Assessment Suite. They include

- Reading comprehension checks
- Unit mini-AP®-style assessments
- A mid-year AP®-style Exam
- A full-length AP®-style practice exam

The ExamView Test Generator lets you quickly create paper-, internet-, and LAN-based tests. Tests can be created in minutes, and the platform is fully customizable, allowing you to enter your own questions, edit existing questions, set time limits, and incorporate multimedia. To discourage plagiarism and cheating, the test bank can scramble answers and change the order of questions. Detailed result reports feed into a gradebook.

Brief Contents

Contents

UNIT 1

Communicating an Idea

UNIT 2

Appealing to an Audience

UNIT 3

Understanding Context

UNIT 4

Analyzing Purpose

COMPOSITION WORKSHOP: Writing a Definition Argument

UNIT 5

Creating Coherence

UNIT 6

Establishing and Evaluating Credibility

UNIT 7

Comparing Perspectives

COMPOSITION WORKSHOP: Writing an Evaluation Argument Using Comparison/Contrast   587

PREPARING FOR THE AP® EXAM   602

UNIT 9

Joining the Conversation

COMPOSITION WORKSHOP: Writing a Multimodal Argument   767

PREPARING FOR THE AP® EXAM   785

Ideas in Argument

Building Skills and Understanding

Muhammad Hamed/Reuters

UNIT
1

Communicating an Idea

Writers communicate ideas. They do this by creating *texts*, which can mean anything from a story to an article, from a podcast to a painting to share their ideas with others. Through these texts, writers communicate a message, which conveys their ideas and perspectives on a subject. That message is created to appeal to a specific audience. At its core, that is rhetoric: creating a text that conveys a message designed to influence an audience.

In the image at the beginning of this unit, a Syrian refugee speaks to her friends about ending child marriage among Syrian refugees, an issue that is important to her. The most powerful messages come from those who are passionate about their ideas. This passion drives writers to tell stories, make arguments, engage in conversations, participate in debates, share their opinions, and convey their attitudes through the language that they choose. To share their ideas effectively, writers have to use these elements and others deliberately and strategically.

UNIT GOALS

	Unit Focus	Reading, Analyzing, and Interpreting	Writing
Big Idea: Rhetorical Situation	**The Writer's Message**	Describe the writer's message in a text.	Develop a message that conveys an idea.
Big Idea: Claims and Evidence	**The Writer's Claim**	Describe the writer's claim in a text.	Develop a thesis statement.
Big Idea: Reasoning and Organization	**Narration and Description**	Explain how a writer develops an idea through narration.	Write a personal narrative.
Big Idea: Language and Style	**The Writer's Attitude**	Explain how words convey a tone.	Choose words to connect with an audience to convey an idea or perspective.
Ideas in American Culture	• **Colonization and Exploration** • **Faith and Doubt**	Explain how the ideas of colonization, exploration, faith, and doubt are reflected in classic and contemporary American texts.	
Preparing for the AP® Exam	• **Free Response: Rhetorical Analysis** • **Multiple Choice**	Analyze rhetorical choices in classic and contemporary nonfiction texts.	Develop a thesis with a defensible claim and support it with textual evidence in a rhetorical analysis.

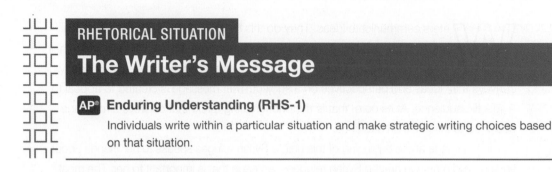

The Writer's Message

AP **Enduring Understanding (RHS-1)**

Individuals write within a particular situation and make strategic writing choices based on that situation.

KEY POINT

Writers create texts to share their ideas and perspectives on important subjects.

We write primarily to share ideas. Rather than merely focusing on a subject, effective writers focus on ideas: abstract concepts such as progress, democracy, and sustainability, for instance. That is true for famous writers like William Shakespeare and Maya Angelou, whose works explore ideas like love, jealousy, vengeance, and greed, among many other concepts; but it's true for all of us, as well.

Throughout this book, you are going to focus on ideas that matter. So, as you read about specific subjects, you will be challenged to go beyond a basic understanding of the issue at hand, and instead examine the importance and significance of the underlying idea. In other words, you will explore the ideas in arguments.

From Idea to Message

Ideas are important because they are more universal than just a single subject. For example, an essay focused exclusively on the subject of soccer and its details would probably have limited appeal, except to fans of the sport. In contrast, an essay that used the subject of soccer (a player, a match, a personal experience) to explore the idea of persistence would appeal to a broader audience. These readers could then reflect on the specific details of soccer in the context of the writer's larger purpose: to convey a message about persistence.

In nonfiction writing, a writer's message is often called the **claim**. The formal statement of that claim is called the **thesis**. A message is the unique idea and perspective that a writer conveys about a topic. This unifying idea is the thread that the writer uses to stitch the entire argument together. Because others may express different perspectives about a subject, the writer's message may be up for debate. Understanding the writer's idea and perspective about a subject is necessary to understand his or her overall message. This is what teachers mean when they ask you to read figuratively. As you read or listen to a writer's message, identify the abstract idea that unifies his or her message.

The Rhetorical Situation

When you read a text, whether it's an assigned reading or an article that interests you, remember that it was created by a real person writing for a real audience with a real purpose at a specific time. In other words, think about the **rhetorical situation**. For example, a senior class president who delivers a commencement speech at graduation would primarily be addressing fellow classmates. The **writer** (sometimes referred to as a *speaker*) may want this **audience** to reflect on shared experiences, or he or she may want to inspire classmates and give them advice about the future. This person was prompted, inspired, or even provoked by internal or external circumstances to write a speech. We call these elements and circumstances the **context**.

Along with the writer's personal background, this context shapes the motivation for creating the text, which is called the **exigence**. For example, a student may write a letter to school administrators asking them to provide more parking spaces for students. He became frustrated when day after day, he had to park blocks away from the school. This motivation, or exigence, will influence the writer's **message**: his or her perspectives and ideas. In turn, the message will be influenced by the writer's general **purpose**, whether that is to inform, persuade, or evaluate. The writer achieves this purpose by creating a text such as a speech, an email, a video, or an essay. All of these components are interconnected. Change the audience, for instance, and the writer will likely need to adjust the message. Together, these components comprise the rhetorical situation.

RHETORICAL SITUATION		
Component	**Definition**	**Key Questions**
Writer	A writer is the author or creator of a text. The writer is a source who presents a perspective shaped by his or her background or context.	Who exactly is the writer, and what is his or her relationship to the subject? What values and beliefs does the writer hold about the subject? What is the writer's relationship to the situation? To the audience?
Message	The message is the writer's claim that is developed with reasoning and evidence.	What is the writer's claim? In other words, what idea or perspective does he or she have on the subject?
Purpose	The purpose is what the writer hopes to accomplish within a text.	What does the writer hope to accomplish? - To persuade or elicit change through a call to action - To narrate - To inform - To evaluate Why did the writer create this text for this particular audience?
Exigence	The exigence is the part of a rhetorical situation that inspires, stimulates, or provokes writers to create a text.	What specifically has prompted or motivated this particular writer to create this text?
Context	All texts are created within the writer's context, including the time, place, and occasion.	What is the specific circumstance or occasion? What historical, political, social, and/or cultural event is this particular situation or context embedded within?
Audience	The audience of a text has shared as well as individual beliefs, values, needs, and backgrounds.	Who is the intended audience? What beliefs or values do they likely hold about the subject?

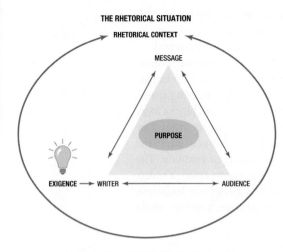

THE RHETORICAL SITUATION

RHETORICAL CONTEXT

MESSAGE

PURPOSE

EXIGENCE → WRITER ←→ AUDIENCE

The Rhetorical Triangle

In his book *The Art of Rhetoric*, the Greek philosopher Aristotle (384–322 B.C.E.) first expressed how these rhetorical components are interrelated. He created the Aristotelian Triangle to illustrate these relationships.

The **writer** and **audience** are in a situation (**context**) where they are connected through a common subject. This situation creates motivation (**exigence**) for the writer to convey a unifying idea through a text (**message**) and engage the **audience** (**purpose**). Writers usually know who their audience is before they write a text: their backgrounds, beliefs, and values. This relationship between the writer and audience affects the rhetorical choices they make when developing an argument.

INSIDER
AP® TIP

Thesis statements need a controlling idea. A thesis statement must be more than a provable fact. An effective thesis statement makes a claim: it expresses an idea and a perspective about that idea. By doing this, the writer establishes a defensible claim that will serve as the controlling idea that unifies the argument.

AP® SKILLS PRACTICE | RHETORICAL SITUATION
Creating a Message

Think of a situation where you are trying to convince or persuade someone. Describe your message. Consider your subject, perspective, and unifying idea.

Subject What is the literal subject?	
Perspective What is your position on the subject?	
Unifying Idea What larger idea are you advancing about the subject?	
Message What is the writer's message for the audience?	

RHETORICAL SITUATION

History Will Remember Your Actions

Queen Elizabeth II

Buckingham Palace via AP

THE TEXT IN CONTEXT

Queen Elizabeth II (b. 1926) has served as monarch of the United Kingdom and fifteen other Commonwealths since 1952. As the longest reigning monarch of Great Britain, she has led through public and private turmoil, including World War II, the Cold War, and the death of Princess Diana. In April 2020, shortly after the outbreak of the coronavirus pandemic, England's Queen Elizabeth II delivered a televised address to the nation. Other than her annual message each Christmas Day, this speech is only the fifth televised address she has delivered since being crowned Queen of England in 1952.

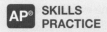 **SKILLS PRACTICE** | RHETORICAL SITUATION
Describing the Rhetorical Situation

As you read, use the following graphic organizer to identify and describe the components of the rhetorical situation. You'll be asked to consider how the components influence the writer's message.

Describing the Rhetorical Situation

Component	Questions for Consideration	Significance for This Text
Writer (or Speaker)	Who is the writer? What is his or her role? What values and beliefs does the writer hold about the subject? What is the writer's relationship to both the situation and the audience?	
Context	In what circumstance was this text created? What is going on historically? Politically? Socially? Culturally?	

(continued)

Component	Questions for Consideration	Significance for This Text
Exigence	What is the writer's relationship to the context?	
	What has motivated the writer to create this text?	
Audience	Whom is the writer addressing in this text?	
	What is that audience's background? How do they likely feel about the subject?	
Purpose	Why did the writer create this text for this audience? What is he or she trying to do?	
Message	What is the writer's message for this audience?	

History Will Remember Your Actions

I am speaking to you at what I know is an increasingly challenging time.

A time of disruption in the life of our country: a disruption that has brought grief to some, financial difficulties to many, and enormous changes to the daily lives of us all.

I want to thank everyone on the NHS front line, as well as care workers and those carrying out essential roles, who selflessly continue their day-to-day duties outside the home in support of us all.

I am sure the nation will join me in assuring you that what you do is appreciated and every hour of your hard work brings us closer to a return to more normal times.

I also want to thank those of you who are staying at home, thereby helping to protect the vulnerable and sparing many families the pain already felt by those who have lost loved ones.

Together we are tackling this disease, and I want to reassure you that if we remain united and resolute, then we will overcome it.

I hope in the years to come everyone will be able to take pride in how they responded to this challenge.

And those who come after us will say the Britons of this generation were as strong as any.

That the attributes of self-discipline, of quiet good-humoured resolve and of fellow-feeling still characterise this country.

The pride in who we are is not a part of our past, it defines our present and our future.

The moments when the United Kingdom has come together to applaud its care and essential workers will be remembered as an expression of our national spirit; and its symbol will be the rainbows drawn by children.

Across the Commonwealth and around the world, we have seen heart-warming stories of people coming together to help others, be it through delivering food parcels and medicines, checking on neighbours, or converting businesses to help the relief effort.

And though self-isolating may at times be hard, many people of all faiths, and of none, are discovering that it presents an opportunity to slow down, pause and reflect, in prayer or meditation.

It reminds me of the very first broadcast I made, in 1940, helped by my sister. We, as children, spoke from here at Windsor to children who had been evacuated from their homes and sent away for their own safety.

Today, once again, many will feel a painful sense of separation from their loved ones. 15

But now, as then, we know, deep down, that it is the right thing to do.

While we have faced challenges before, this one is different.

This time we join with all nations across the globe in a common endeavour, using the great advances of science and our instinctive compassion to heal.

We will succeed—and that success will belong to every one of us.

We should take comfort that while we may have more still to endure, better days will return: we will be with our friends again; we will be with our families again; we will meet again. 20

But for now, I send my thanks and warmest good wishes to you all.

RHETORICAL SITUATION

1. What is the **context** of this speech?

2. Who is the **writer**, and what is her role or position?

3. How does the writer's relationship with her **audience** affect her **exigence**?

4. Who is the **audience**? What is Queen Elizabeth's **message** for this specific audience? How does the message of the speech communicate a relationship between writer/speaker, **purpose**, and audience?

5. The **purpose** and the **message** are critical to the effect of this speech. What is the purpose? What is the message? How are they different?

The Writer's Claim

AP **Enduring Understanding (CLE-1)**

Writers make claims about subjects, rely on evidence that supports their reasoning, and often acknowledge or respond to other, possibly opposing, arguments.

KEY POINT

A claim expresses an idea and a perspective on a subject that serves to unify the argument.

As you read fictional narratives, you may have to infer a writer's message by making sense of literary elements such as metaphor and symbol. But nonfiction writers usually make their messages about the idea more explicit. These explicit statements — called thesis statements — are claims that express a perspective and an idea about their subject.

Everything's an Argument

Advertisements. Tweets. Photographs. Speeches. Artwork. Movies. Video games. Narratives. In a world with so many complex perspectives and ideas, *anything* can be an argument.

An argument conveys a writer's **position** — that is, his or her **perspective** and idea — about a subject. When writers state their idea about a subject, they make a **claim**. Claims justified by **reasons** that are supported with **evidence** are the key components of an effective argument.

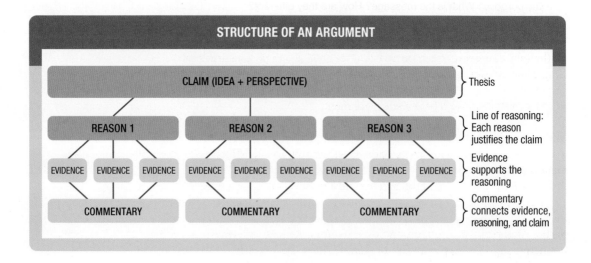

But lively and engaging arguments convey more than a simple "pro" or "con" position about a subject. As most issues are complex, writers need to take in a wide range of perspectives and considerations. So good writers rarely take unqualified "black-and-white" positions with their arguments. Still, effective claims should be strong and provocative. They should require support, justification, and defense rather than being a statement of facts or an obvious general truth.

The Writer's Perspective

Arguments convey an idea and a perspective on a subject. We often use the term *argument* for everyday personal conflicts. You have a position; your "opponent" takes the opposite side. You might argue with a friend about politics, or music, or where to go on a Friday night. You might argue with a teacher about a grade or with your parents about your summer travel plans. Sometimes, arguments can be emotional because the issues are important to you.

Arguments are also common in an academic context. But rather than engaging in personal conflicts, scholars, students, policy experts, informed citizens, and others usually use argumentation to share their perspectives, reasoning, and new conclusions with others. Given the complexity of issues — especially with regard to government and public policies — these arguments allow for constructive debate on important issues.

The Writer's Thesis

Most effective writers argue their position by establishing their perspective on a subject. This is called the writer's claim. Consider the following examples, which illustrate the difference between a position and a perspective:

Everyone should recycle.

This could be the primary thesis in an argument. Although it expresses a position on the subject of recycling, it doesn't provide an idea or a perspective about recycling. Now, consider this thesis that conveys the primary claim of an argument:

Recycling leads to a healthier environment.

In this statement, the writer's subject is recycling. She claims that recycling leads to a healthier environment. In this case, healthier is the perspective, and environment is the unifying idea. As you can see, the most compelling **thesis statements** provide claims that include both an idea and a perspective about a subject.

In most nonfiction texts, writers state their claims in an explicit thesis statement. They might place this statement at different points in the text, depending on the rhetorical situation, among other factors. As you read essays and other nonfiction arguments, you'll want to identify the writer's position on the subject. But perhaps more important, you'll want to understand the writer's claim. In other words, be sure to identify both the writer's idea and perspective about that subject.

Some Arguments Are Better Than Others

The quality of an argument depends mainly on the quality and relevance of the evidence that the writer uses to support, explain, or defend the claim. Writers may draw on many different types of evidence, including the following:

TYPES OF EVIDENCE	
Fact	a truth known by actual experience or observation, something known to be true
Anecdote	a brief account of a particular incident or event
Analogy	a comparison based upon similar features of two things
Statistic	a numerical fact or set of data
Example	an instance used to illustrate
Detail	a piece of information
Illustration	a picture, photograph, diagram, cartoon, chart, artwork, infographic, or other visual
Expert opinion	testimony that comes from a credible source in a particular field
Personal observation	something that the writer has seen
Personal experience	something that the writer has firsthand knowledge of
Testimony	a statement made by someone who has experience but not necessarily as an expert
Experiment	an observation generated under a controlled condition

INSIDER
AP® TIP

Narratives are arguments. Writers create stories — autobiographical and otherwise — to illustrate different perspectives on issues. These narratives draw upon figurative language to express their messages and meaning. As readers, we interpret and uncover that meaning. While this meaning is called *theme* in fiction, in nonfiction we call this meaning the writer's claim.

 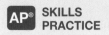

AP® SKILLS PRACTICE | CLAIMS AND EVIDENCE
Developing a Claim

Consider a subject such as pets, music, or video games. Craft a thesis statement that contains a claim (perspective and idea) and takes a position.

Thesis Statement		
	Claim	
Subject	Perspective + Unifying Idea	

Why We Crave Horror Movies

Stephen King

Scott Eisen/Getty Images

THE TEXT IN CONTEXT

Stephen King (b. 1947) is one of America's most prolific writers of horror stories, including bestsellers like *Carrie* (1974), *Cujo* (1981), and *The Outsider* (2018). His books have also been adapted into iconic films such as *The Shining* (1980), *The Shawshank Redemption* (1994), and *It* (2017). In this 1981 essay about the persistent popularity of the horror genre, he explores the reasons readers are drawn to these films and stories.

AP® | **SKILLS PRACTICE** | CLAIMS AND EVIDENCE
Describing the Thesis of an Argument

As you read the following essay by Stephen King, look for his thesis statement. Identify the subject and his claim (both the perspective and the idea). Record the different types of evidence King uses to defend his overall argument.

Identifying Thesis and Supporting Evidence		
Subject	**Claim**	
	Perspective + Unifying Idea	
	Evidence	

Why We Crave Horror Movies

I think that we're all mentally ill; those of us outside the asylums only hide it a little better—and maybe not all that much better, after all. We've all known people who talk to themselves, people who sometimes squinch their faces into horrible grimaces when they believe no one is watching, people who have some hysterical fear—of snakes, the dark, the tight place, the long drop . . . and, of course, those final worms and grubs that are waiting so patiently underground to play their part in the great Thanksgiving table of life: what once ate must eventually be eaten.

When we pay our four or five bucks and seat ourselves at tenthrow center in a theater showing a horror movie, we are daring the nightmare.

Why? Some of the reasons are simple and obvious. To show that we can, that we are not afraid, that we can ride this roller coaster. Which is not to say that a really good horror movie may not surprise a scream out of us at some point, the way we may scream when the roller coaster twists through a complete 360 or plows through a lake at the bottom of the drop. And horror movies, like roller coasters, have always been the special province of the young; by the time one turns forty or fifty, one's appetite for double twists or 360-degree loops may be considerably depleted.

We also go to reestablish our feelings of essential normality; the horror movie is innately conservative, even reactionary. Freda Jackson as the horrible melting woman in *Die, Monster, Die!* confirms for us that no matter how far we may be removed from the beauty of a Robert Redford or a Diana Ross, we are still light-years from true ugliness.

And we go to have fun.

Ah, but this is where the ground starts to slope away, isn't it? Because this is a very peculiar sort of fun, indeed. The fun comes from seeing others menaced—sometimes killed. One critic has suggested that if pro football has become the voyeur's version of combat, then the horror film has become the modern version of the public lynching.

It is true that the mythic "fairy-tale" horror film intends to take away the shades of grey (which is one reason why *When a Stranger Calls* doesn't work; the psycho, well and honestly played by Tony Beckley, is a poor schmuck beset by the miseries of his own psychoses; our unwilling sympathy for him dilutes the

film's success as surely as water dilutes Scotch); it urges us to put away our more civilized and adult penchant for analysis and to become children again, seeing things in pure blacks and pure whites. It may be that horror movies provide psychic relief on this level because this invitation to lapse into simplicity, irrationality and even outright madness is extended so rarely. We are told we may allow our emotions a free rein . . . or no rein at all.

If we are all insane, then sanity becomes a matter of degree. If your insanity leads you to carve up women like Jack the Ripper or the Cleveland Torso Murderer, we clap you away in the funny farm (except neither of those two amateur-night surgeons were ever caught, heh-heh-heh); if, on the other hand, your insanity leads you only to talk to yourself when you're under stress or to pick your nose on your morning bus, then you are left alone to go about your business . . . though it is doubtful that you will ever be invited to the best parties.

The potential lyncher is in almost all of us (I exclude saints, past and present, but then, most or all saints have been crazy in their own ways), and every now and then, he has to be let loose to scream and roll around in the grass. Our emotions and our fears form their own body, and we recognize that it demands its own exercise to maintain proper muscle tone. Certain of these emotional "muscles" are accepted—even exalted—in civilized society; they are, of course, the emotions that tend to maintain the status quo of civilization itself. Love, friendship, loyalty, kindness—these are all the emotions that we applaud, emotions that have been immortalized in the bad couplets of Hallmark cards and in the verses (I don't dare call it poetry) of Leonard Nimoy.

When we exhibit these emotions, society showers us with positive reinforcement; we learn this even before we get out of diapers. When, as children, we hug our rotten little

5

10

puke of a sister and give her a kiss, all the aunts and uncles smile and twit and cry, "Isn't he the sweetest little thing?" Such coveted treats as chocolate-covered graham crackers often follow. But if we deliberately slam the rotten little puke of a sister's fingers in the door, sanctions follow — angry remonstrance from parents, aunts, and uncles; instead of a chocolate-covered graham cracker, a spanking.

But anti-civilization emotions don't go away, and they demand periodic exercise. We have such "sick" jokes as, "What's the difference between a truckload of bowling balls and a truckload of dead babies?" (You can't unload a truckload of bowling balls with a pitch-fork . . . a joke, by the way, that I heard originally from a ten-year-old.) Such a joke may surprise a laugh or a grin out of us even as we recoil, a possibility that confirms the thesis: If we share a brotherhood of man, then we also share an insanity of man. None of which is intended as a defense of either the sick joke or insanity but merely as an explanation of why the best horror films, like the best fairy tales, manage to be reactionary, anarchistic, and revolutionary all at the same time.

My agent, Kirby McCauley, likes to relate a scene from Andy Warhol's film *Bad* — and he relates in the fond tones of the confirmed horror-movie buff. A mother throws her baby from the window of a skyscraper; we cut away to the crowd below and hear a loud splat. Another mother leads her son through the crowd and up to the mess (which is obviously a watermelon with seeds removed), points to it, and says, to the effect, "That's what will happen to you if you're bad!" It's a sick joke, like the one about the truckload of dead babies — or the one about the babes in the wood, which we call "Hansel and Gretel."

The mythic horror movie, like the sick joke, has a dirty job to do. It deliberately appeals to all that is worst in us. It is morbidity unchained, our most base instincts let free, our nastiest fantasies realized . . . and it all happens, fittingly enough, in the dark. For those reasons, good liberals often shy away from horror films. For myself, I like to see the most aggressive of them — *Dawn of the Dead*, for instance — as lifting a trap door in the civilized forebrain and throwing a basket of raw meat to the hungry alligators swimming around in that subterranean river beneath.

Why bother? Because it keeps them from getting out, man. It keeps them down there and me up here. It was Lennon and McCartney who said that all you need is love, and I would agree with that.

As long as you keep the gators fed.   15

1. Consider the title of the essay: "Why We Crave Horror Movies." How does King answer the question in the title? King begins the text with a **thesis** but waits until the end of his essay to present his claim. What is the idea of the **claim**, and what is the **perspective** of the claim?

2. King uses various types of **evidence**. Choose one example and discuss the effect of this evidence. How effectively does it support his claim?

3. Reread paragraph 13. List the **evidence** in this paragraph and discuss how this evidence supports the **ideas** and **perspectives** in King's original **claim**.

Narration and Description

 Enduring Understanding (REO-1)

Writers guide understanding of a text's line of reasoning and claims through that text's organization and integration of evidence.

KEY POINT

Narratives present descriptions and details that build to a tension or conflict, ultimately revealing insights about the human experience.

Writers can convey their ideas and messages in many ways, from novels and speeches to advertisements and videos. Regardless of the medium (how the message is delivered), we can classify texts based on the writer's purpose: narrative, persuasive, expository, and evaluative. Narrative texts tell a story, persuasive texts call for a change or an action, and expository texts explain things. All of these are arguments in their own way. In this unit, we'll focus on narration. Narrative appeals to audiences because everyone loves a good story, regardless of whether the narrative is nonfiction — such as an autobiography describing the writer's experiences — or fiction — such as a fable that ends with a moral.

Everyone Loves a Good Story

What makes a certain book, TV series, or video game popular? What makes a comedy special funny? What makes a movie trailer memorable? The secret to engaging an audience isn't just telling a good story. Rather, it's in the ideas that the story conveys. There has to be a point. Good stories tell us something interesting about life or the world — the human experience.

From the earliest human history, people have been telling stories to entertain listeners, teach lessons, and share universal truths through specific experiences. When a person shares an experience through a story, we connect with the storyteller. While we may not have had the exact same experience as that person, we can understand the underlying feeling or idea. By the end of a story, writers often come to an understanding about themselves or the world around them. That revelation communicates the writer's perspective about an idea (their claim).

So, What Makes a Good Story?

Good stories might be funny or serious, touching or tragic, or all of these things at once. They may bring tears or even haunt readers for the rest of their lives. There's no formula for the perfect story. But good stories allow the audience to connect with the writer on a personal level.

Writers build a connection with their audience one detail at a time. They relate sensory details, illustrate ideas, and use other elements of narrative. They choose details carefully, selecting only the ones that help convey their overall message or idea. Remember: not all details are important. Even in a nonfiction narrative, some details are completely factual, while others may be exaggerated, simplified, or changed so that the writer can make a larger point about an idea.

Conflict Matters

Writers use narratives to express ideas and convey messages. One way they do this is by exploring conflicts, which may be caused by tensions, questions, or problems. If there is no conflict, there is no story. In fiction, of course, good stories require a plot to engage the reader. For example, murder mysteries and television crime shows often focus on the question: "Who done it?" But this principle applies to nonfiction writing too. In a college application essay, your narrative might answer questions such as, "What is an obstacle that you have faced, and what did you learn from overcoming it?" In a narrative, the characters or forces in conflict often represent values or perspectives on an idea. The resolution of this conflict will tell us a lot about the ideas behind the story, and the writer's perspective on them. For instance, if you are writing a story about missing the bus and that conflict is resolved by getting a ride from a friend, that might tell us something about the value of our relationships, or simply that life is sometimes just a matter of luck.

How should a story begin? Some narratives begin at the beginning — "Once upon a time" — while others begin in the middle of the action. Where a writer begins narrating the tale affects how the audience understands the story.

Writers also set up contrasts and shifts to help convey their ideas. Contrasts show emphasis. For example, a writer might emphasize one character's virtue by intentionally including a corrupt figure in the narrative. Shifts, on the other hand, communicate a change in understanding or insight. For example, a writer might narrate an experience that changed his or her attitude, behavior, or understanding. When such shifts are sudden revelations, we call them **epiphanies**.

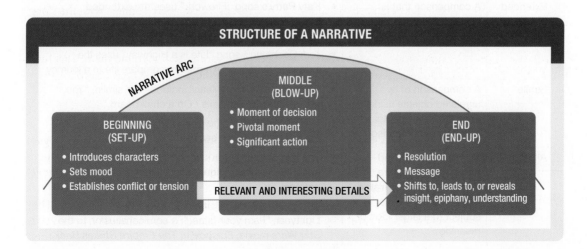

STRUCTURE OF A NARRATIVE

NARRATIVE ARC

**BEGINNING
(SET-UP)**
• Introduces characters
• Sets mood
• Establishes conflict or tension

**MIDDLE
(BLOW-UP)**
• Moment of decision
• Pivotal moment
• Significant action

RELEVANT AND INTERESTING DETAILS

**END
(END-UP)**
• Resolution
• Message
• Shifts to, leads to, or reveals insight, epiphany, understanding

It's All in the Details

In narratives, writers may use concrete objects to represent abstract ideas or evoke an image in the reader's mind. We call these representations **figurative language**. To understand figurative language, the audience must make the connection between the concrete object and the abstract idea or image and think about why the writer made that connection.

FIGURATIVE LANGUAGE		
Figurative Language	Rhetorical Effect	Examples from Popular Culture
Symbol	A concrete object that represents an idea or value	• Valentine's Day hearts symbolize the idea of love. • Captain America's shield symbolizes strength, resiliency, and the obligation to protect others.
Image	Language that expresses a sensory experience, such as sound, sight, smell, touch, or taste	• Brand names often use imagery, such as Juicy Couture clothes, Krispy Kreme donuts, and Trident Splash gum, to associate appealing ideas with a product.
Motif	Several recurring related symbols or images that create a pattern to reinforce an idea	• The "Imperial March" musical motif in *Star Wars* reinforces Darth Vader's dreadful power. • In *The Hunger Games*, fire is a recurrent motif that reinforces ideas such as power and defiance.
Metaphor	A comparison of two unrelated objects that assigns ideas to the points of comparison	• Pharrell Williams's song "Happy" uses the metaphor "I'm a hot air balloon that could go to space" to highlight the singer's joy. • The book *Twilight* presents the relationship between Edward the vampire and Bella the human girl as a lion falling in love with a lamb: a comparison that suggests a predator falling in love with its prey.
Extended Metaphor	A comparison that is sustained throughout a text	• Katy Perry's song "Firework" uses the extended metaphor of fireworks to urge a person to "own the night / Like the Fourth of July." • Tom Cochrane's song "Life Is a Highway" uses the extended metaphor of a road to compare life to a journey.
Simile	A comparison of two unrelated objects using *like* or *as* that assigns ideas to the point of comparison	• Taylor Swift's song "Mean" includes the simile, "You, with your voice like nails / On a chalkboard." • In *Harry Potter and the Sorcerer's Stone*, a character's eyes glint "like black beetles."
Allusion	An indirect or implied reference to literature, culture, religion, or history that connects a writer's subject to a larger idea or meaning	• The title of Lady Gaga's song "Judas" alludes to a treacherous biblical figure and suggests themes of betrayal. • In *Toy Story 2*, the villainous Emperor Zurg tells Buzz Lightyear, "I am your father": a comical allusion to the *Star Wars* movie, *Episode V: The Empire Strikes Back*.

INSIDER

Shifts reveal insights. Looking at a shift may help to reveal a new understanding or insight. This strategy may be especially helpful when analyzing narratives to understand a writer's epiphany.

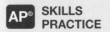 **SKILLS PRACTICE** | REASONING AND ORGANIZATION
Analyzing the Narrative

Think of a movie or streamed show that you've seen recently. Use the organizer that follows to record the arc of the story and elements of the story line. Then identify specific or concrete details associated with the three aspects of the narrative. Describe how these details could take on a larger symbolic or figurative meaning.

Analyzing Narrative Structure		
	Questions to Ask	Concrete Details and Their Figurative Meaning
The Set-Up (Beginning)	Who is telling the story? What details establish the problem, tension, or conflict?	
The Blow-Up (Middle)	What are the values or ideas represented by each side of the conflict?	
The Wrap-Up (End)	How is the conflict resolved? What does the narrator come to realize?	

The Jacket

Gary Soto

Chris Felver/Getty Images

THE TEXT IN CONTEXT

Gary Soto (b. 1952) is a poet, novelist, and activist who was born and raised in Fresno, California. Soto's works often focus on his personal and cultural identity as *Chicano*: a person born in the United States to Mexican immigrant parents. He is the writer of dozens of books, including *A Summer Life* (1990), a memoir of his childhood. In the following personal narrative, which is taken from that book, Soto reflects on his experiences growing up Latino in Fresno during the late 1950s and early 1960s.

 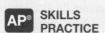

AP® SKILLS PRACTICE	REASONING AND ORGANIZATION **Analyzing a Narrative**

As you read Gary Soto's personal narrative, "The Jacket," use the graphic organizer that follows to record details of the story that will help you understand his message. The details of the story should help you discover what Soto comes to realize because of his experience. How is this idea relevant to people other than Soto?

Analyzing Narrative Structure		
	Questions to Ask	**Concrete Details and Their Figurative Meaning**
The Set-Up (Beginning)	Who is telling the story? What details establish the problem, tension, or conflict?	
The Blow-Up (Middle)	What are the values or ideas represented by each side of the conflict?	
The Wrap-Up (End)	How is the conflict resolved? What does the narrator come to realize?	

The Jacket

My clothes have failed me. I remember the green coat that I wore in fifth and sixth grades when you either danced like a champ or pressed yourself against a greasy wall, bitter as a penny toward the happy couples.

When I needed a new jacket and my mother asked what kind I wanted, I described something like bikers wear: black leather and silver studs with enough belts to hold down a small town. We were in the kitchen, steam on the windows from her cooking. She listened so long while stirring dinner that I thought she understood for sure the kind I wanted. The next day when I got home from school, I discovered draped on my bedpost a jacket the color of day-old guacamole. I threw my books on the bed and approached the jacket slowly, as if it were a stranger whose hand I had to shake. I touched the vinyl sleeve, the collar, and peeked at the mustard-colored lining.

From the kitchen mother yelled that my jacket was in the closet. I closed the door to her voice and pulled at the rack of clothes in the closet, hoping the jacket on the bedpost wasn't for me but my mean brother. No luck. I gave up. From my bed, I stared at the jacket. I wanted to cry because it was so ugly and so big that I knew I'd have to wear it a long time. I was a small kid, thin as a young tree, and it would be years before I'd have a new one. I stared at the jacket, like an enemy, thinking bad things before I took off my old jacket whose sleeves climbed halfway to my elbow.

I put the big jacket on. I zipped it up and down several times, and rolled the cuffs up so they didn't cover my hands. I put my hands in the pockets and flapped the jacket like a bird's wings. I stood in front of the mirror, full face, then profile, and then looked over my shoulder as if someone had called me. I sat on the bed, stood against the bed, and combed my hair to see what I would look like doing something natural. I looked ugly. I threw it on my brother's bed and looked at it for a long time before I slipped it on and went out to the backyard, smiling a "thank you" to my mom as I passed her in the kitchen. With my hands in my pockets I kicked a ball against the fence, and then climbed it to sit looking into the alley. I hurled orange peels at the mouth of an open garbage can and when the peels were gone I watched the white puffs of my breath thin to nothing.

I jumped down, hands in my pockets, and in the backyard on my knees I teased my dog, Brownie, by swooping my arms while making birdcalls. He jumped at me and missed. He jumped again and again, until a tooth stuck deep, ripping an L-shaped tear on my left sleeve. I pushed Brownie away to study the tear as I would a cut on my arm. There was no blood, only a few loose pieces of fuzz. . . . Dog, I thought, and pushed him away hard when he tried to bite again. I got up from my knees and went to my bedroom to sit with my jacket on my lap, with the lights out.

That was the first afternoon with my new jacket. The next day I wore it to sixth grade and got a D on a math quiz. During the morning recess Frankie T., the playground terrorist, pushed me to the ground and told me to stay there until recess was over. My best friend, Steve Negrete, ate an apple while looking at me, and the girls turned away to whisper on the monkey bars. The teachers were no help: they looked my way and talked about how foolish I looked in my new jacket. I saw their heads bob with laughter, their hands half-covering their mouths.

Even though it was cold, I took off the jacket during lunch and played kickball in a thin shirt, my arms feeling like Braille from goose bumps. But when I returned to class

5

I slipped the jacket on and shivered until I was warm. I sat on my hands, heating them up, while my teeth chattered like a cup of crooked dice. Finally warm, I slid out of the jacket but a few minutes later put it back on when the fire bell rang. We paraded out into the yard where we, the fifth graders, walked past all the other grades to stand against the back fence. Everybody saw me. Although they didn't say out loud, "Man, that's ugly," I heard the buzz-buzz of gossip and even laughter that I knew was meant for me.

And so I went, in my guacamole jacket. So embarrassed, so hurt, I wouldn't even do my homework. I received Cs on quizzes, and forgot the state capitols and the rivers of South America, our friendly neighbor. Even the girls who had been friendly blew away like loose flowers to follow the boys in neat jackets.

I wore that thing for three years until the sleeves grew short and my forearms stuck out like the necks of turtles. All during that time no love came to me—no little dark girl in a Sunday dress she wore on Monday. At lunchtime I stayed with the ugly boys who leaned against the chain link fence and looked around with propellers of grass spinning in our mouths. We saw the girls walk by alone, saw couples, hand in hand, their heads like bookends pressing air together. We saw them and spun our propellers so fast our faces were blurs.

I blame that jacket for those bad years. I blame my mother for her bad taste and her cheap ways. It was a sad time for the heart. With a friend I spent my sixth-grade year in a tree in the alley, waiting for something good to happen to me in that jacket that became my ugly brother who tagged along wherever I went. And it was about that time I began to grow. My chest puffed up with muscle and,

strangely, a few more ribs. Even my hands, those fleshy hammers, showed bravery through the cuffs, the fingers already hardening for the coming fights. But the L-shaped rip on the left sleeve got bigger, bits of stuffing coughed out from its wound after a hard day at play. I finally Scotch-taped it closed, but in rain or cold weather the tape peeled off like a scab and more stuffing fell out until that sleeve shriveled into a palsied arm. That winter the elbows began to crack and whole chunks of green began to fall off. I showed the cracks to my mother, who always seemed to be at the stove with steamed up glasses, and she said there were children in Mexico who would love that jacket. I told her that this was America and yelled that Debbie, my sister, didn't have a jacket like mine. I ran outside, ready to cry, and climb the tree by the alley to think bad thoughts, and breathe puff white and disappear.

But whole pieces still casually flew off my jacket when I played hard, read quietly, or took a vicious spelling test at school. When it became so spotted that my brother began to call me "camouflage," I flung it over the fence into the alley. Later, however; I swiped the jacket off the ground and went inside to drape it across my lap and mope.

I was called to dinner: steam shriveled my mother's glasses as she said grace; my brother and sister with their heads bowed made ugly faces at their glasses of powdered milk. I gagged too, but eagerly ate rips of buttered tortilla that held scooped up beans. Finished, I went outside with my jacket across my arm. It was a cold sky. The faces of clouds were piled up, hurting. I climb the fence, jumping down with a grunt. I started up the alley and soon slipped into my jacket, that green ugly brother who breathed over my shoulder that day and ever since.

10

REASONING AND ORGANIZATION

1. Soto uses **figurative language** to describe the jacket and emphasize its significance. What **symbolic** meaning(s) does the jacket seem to have? Explain the significance of Soto's use of the jacket to create an **extended metaphor**.

2. What **imagery** does Soto use in "The Jacket"? Identify two related examples of imagery and then describe how this **motif** further conveys Soto's message.

3. In his conclusion, Soto's perspective seems to undergo a shift. What is the shift? How does it suggest an **epiphany** or a new understanding on the part of the narrator?

⨆⨅⨆
⨞⨉⨛
⨞⨉⨛
⨞⨉⨛
⨞⨉⨛
⨞⨉⨛
⨅⨅⨆

LANGUAGE AND STYLE

The Writer's Tone

AP Enduring Understanding (STL-1)

The rhetorical situation informs the strategic stylistic choices that writers make.

KEY POINT

Writers choose words and create sentences in ways that help them convey an attitude about a subject— called the tone.

When you boil it down, writing is about making language choices. Writers use language to convey their perspectives and ideas about a subject. The specific word choices they make, called **diction**, are not just a way of delivering the message: they can also reveal the writer's feelings and attitudes toward the subject. So as we read, we need to think about the words that a writer has chosen, as this language creates images and conveys feelings and attitudes. Ultimately, those feelings and attitudes reveal a writer's perspective.

Writers Convey Attitude

Writers reveal their attitudes toward their subjects through diction and writing style, which is called **tone**. The writer's tone can express anger, sarcasm, optimism, or seriousness, much like our tone of voice when we speak. The tone of a text is conveyed through the writer's word choices and writing style. *Diction* refers to a writer's choice of words. Recall that all words have **denotations** (relatively neutral dictionary definitions) and **connotations** (sensory, emotional, or cultural associations) that constitute their meaning. For example, the words *old, ancient, outdated, vintage, decrepit,* and *venerable* all have similar denotations, but a wide variety of connotations. Good writers know the emotional and cultural weight of the words that they choose, along with correct dictionary definitions. Finding the exact word can be difficult, but when writers choose the most precise language, they reduce confusion and sharpen their ability to connect with their audience.

Writers also convey their attitude through sensory language that creates **imagery** in the minds of readers. When you read, you should pay attention to the specific words a writer chooses. Review the following pairs of words and consider how their connotations affect meaning:

angry	livid	bright	smart	energetic	hyper
sleep	slumber	crowd	mob	cold	icy

Now review the following example. Each of the possible choices to complete the sentence has a similar denotation. But notice how each verb changes the meaning by evoking a different visual impression:

The stray cat _____ out of moving traffic.

ran	darted	scurried	charged
to move at a speed faster than a walk	to move somewhere suddenly and rapidly	to move hurriedly with short, quick steps	to move forward as if to assault
	implies moving quickly with precision, purpose, and urgency (as one might throw a dart)	implies a small animal is moving quickly and perhaps secretively	implies moving quickly with confidence and possibly aggression

As these images can have positive or negative associations, writers use them to connect with — and persuade — their audiences. You can often achieve the most precise meaning and the most suitable imagery by considering words across a tonal scale:

Least Intense   **Most Intense**
Disturbed   *Upset*   *Angry*   *Infuriated*   *Enraged*

Shifts in Tone

Readers can sense a writer moving from one attitude to another merely from a change in diction and imagery. The shift may also be signaled by a structural or stylistic choice. Consider the following examples, which work at the level of sentence structures, punctuation, transitional words, and paragraphs.

MARKERS OF RHETORICAL SHIFTS	
Sentence Structure	• A short, simple sentence or fragment that stands alone • A rhetorical question
Punctuation Mark	• The use of a less frequent punctuation mark, such as a colon :, dash —, or parentheses ( )
Transition Word	• A transition word illustrating a contrast, such as *however, or, but,* or *although*
Paragraphing	• A change in idea represented by a paragraph often with a contrasting transition word • A short paragraph among other longer paragraphs • A single-sentence paragraph

INSIDER AP® TIP

Tone is an effect. A writer's language reveals the tone. Writers do not *use* tone — instead, their tone is conveyed through their rhetorical choices.

AP® SKILLS PRACTICE | **LANGUAGE AND STYLE** **Using Precise Diction**

Choose an emotion, such as happy, sad, or scared, and create a tonal scale of at least three words for that emotion from least intense to most intense. Then draw or pick an emoji for each of the words.

Least Intense		Most Intense

The World Doesn't Love You
Trevor Noah

Jeff Schear/Getty Images

THE TEXT IN CONTEXT

The following is an excerpt from *Born a Crime*, a 2016 memoir written by comedian and *Daily Show* host Trevor Noah (b. 1984). Noah is the mixed-race son of a Swiss father and a Black South African mother. In this autobiographical account, Noah recounts growing up during (and after) South African apartheid: the country's system of racial classification and discrimination that existed from 1948 to the early 1990s.

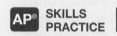 **SKILLS PRACTICE** | LANGUAGE AND STYLE
Describing Tone

As you read the narrative, identify where Noah's tone shifts. Create a table illustrating Noah's diction before and after this shift. How does Noah's diction reveal a shift in tone? Considering his shift in tone, what is his overall claim?

Identifying Shifts in Tone

Words before the Shift	Words after the Shift
Tone Before	Tone After
Claim	

The World Doesn't Love You

My mom never gave me an inch. Anytime I got in trouble it was tough love, lectures, punishment, and hidings. Every time. For every infraction. You get that with a lot of black parents. They're trying to discipline you before the system does. "I need to do this to you before the police do it to you." Because that's all black parents are thinking from the day you're old enough to walk out into the street, where the law is waiting.

In Alex[andria], getting arrested was a fact of life. It was so common that out on the corner we had a sign for it, a shorthand, clapping your wrists together like you were being put in handcuffs. Everyone knew what that meant.

"Where's Bongani?"

Wrist clap.

"Oh, s***. When?"   5

"Friday night."

"Damn."

My mom hated the hood. She didn't like my friends there. If I brought them back to the house, she didn't even want them coming inside. "I don't like those boys," she'd say. She didn't hate them personally; she hated what they represented. "You and those boys get into so much [trouble]," she'd say. "You must be careful who you surround yourself with because where you are can determine who you are."

She said the thing she hated most about the hood was that it didn't pressure me to become better. She wanted me to hang out with my cousin at his university.

"What's the difference if I'm at university 10 or I'm in the hood?" I'd say. "It's not like I'm going to university."

"Yes, but the pressure of the university is going to get you. I know you. You won't sit by and watch these guys become better than you. If you're in an environment that is positive and progressive, you too will become that. I keep telling you to change your life, and you don't. One day you're going to get arrested, and when you do, don't call me. I'll tell the police to lock you up just to teach you a lesson."

Because there were some black parents who'd actually do that, not pay their kid's bail, not hire their kid a lawyer—the ultimate tough love. But it doesn't always work, because you're giving the kid tough love when maybe he just needs love. You're trying to teach him a lesson, and now that lesson is the rest of his life.

• • •

One morning I saw an ad in the paper. Some shop was having a clearance sale on mobile phones, and they were selling them at such a ridiculous price I knew Bongani and I could flip them in the hood for a profit. This shop was out in the suburbs, too far to walk and too out-of-the-way to take a minibus. Fortunately my stepfather's workshop and a bunch of old cars were in our backyard.

I'd been stealing Abel's junkers to get around since I was fourteen. I would say I was test driving them to make sure they'd been repaired correctly. Abel didn't think that was funny. I'd been caught many times, caught and subjected to my mother's wrath. But that had never stopped me from doing anything.

Most of these junkers weren't street legal. 15 They didn't have proper registrations or proper number plates. Luckily, Abel also had a stack of old number plates in the back of the garage. I quickly learned I could just put one on an old

car and hit the road. I was nineteen, maybe twenty, not thinking about any of the ramifications of this. I stopped by Abel's garage when no one was around, picked up one of the cars, the red Mazda I'd taken to the matric dance, slapped some old plates on it, and set off in search of discounted cell phones.

I got pulled over in Hillbrow. Cops in South Africa don't give you a reason when they pull you over. Cops pull you over because they're cops and they have the power to pull you over; it's as simple as that. I used to watch American movies where cops would pull people over and say, "You didn't signal" or "Your taillight's out." I'd always wonder, *Why do American cops bother lying?* One thing I appreciate about South Africa is that we have not yet refined the system to the point where we feel the need to lie.

"Do you know why I pulled you over?"

"Because you're a policeman and I'm a black person?"

"That's correct. License and registration, please."

When the cop pulled me over, it was one of 20 those situations where I wanted to say, "Hey, I know you guys are racially profiling me!" But I couldn't argue the case because I was, at that moment, actually breaking the law. The cop walked up to my window, asked me the standard cop questions. Where are you going? Is this your car? Whose car is this? I couldn't answer. I completely froze.

Being young, funnily enough, I was more worried about getting in trouble with my parents than with the law. I'd had run-ins with the cops in Alexandra, in Soweto, but it was always more about the circumstance: a party getting shut down, a raid on a minibus. The law was all around me, but it had never come down on me, Trevor, specifically. And when you haven't had much experience with the law, the law appears rational. . . .

Your parents, on the other hand, are not rational at all. They have served as judge, jury, and executioner for your entire childhood, and it feels like they give you a life sentence for every misdemeanor. In that moment, when I should have been scared of the cop, all I was thinking was . . . *I'm in so much trouble when I get home.*

The cop called in the number-plate registration and discovered that it didn't match the car. Now he was really on my case. "This car is not in your name! What's going on with these plates?! Step out of the vehicle!" It was only then that I realized. . . . *Now I'm in real trouble.* I stepped out of the car, and he put the cuffs on me and told me I was being arrested on suspicion of driving a stolen vehicle. He took me in, and the car was impounded.

The Hillbrow police station looks exactly like every other police station in South Africa. They were all built by the same contractor at the height of apartheid—separate nodes in the central nervous system of a police state. If you were blindfolded and taken from one to the other, you probably wouldn't even know that you'd changed locations. They're sterile, institutional, with fluorescent lights and cheap floor tile, like a hospital. My cop walked me in and sat me down at the front booking desk. I was charged and fingerprinted.

In the meantime, they'd been checking out 25 the car, which wasn't going well for me, either. Whenever I borrowed cars from Abel's workshop, I tried to take the junkers rather than a real client's car; I thought I'd get in less trouble that way. That was a mistake. The Mazda, being one of Abel's junkers, didn't have a clear title of ownership. If it had had an owner, the cops would have called the owner, the owner would have explained that the car had been dropped off for repairs, and the whole thing would have been sorted out. Since the car

didn't have an owner, I couldn't prove I hadn't stolen it. . . .

. . . Not only could I not prove I hadn't stolen the car, I couldn't prove I hadn't murdered someone for it, either. The cops were grilling me. "You kill anyone to get that car, boy? Eh? You a killer?"

I was in deep, deep trouble. I had only one lifeline: my parents. One call would have fixed everything. "This is my stepfather. He's a mechanic. I borrowed his car when I shouldn't have." Done. At worst I'd get a slap on the wrist for driving a car that wasn't registered. But what would I be getting at home?

I sat there in the police station—arrested for suspicion of grand theft auto, a plausible suspect for carjacking or murder—and debated whether I should call my parents or go to jail. With my stepfather I was thinking, *He might actually kill me.* In my mind that was an entirely realistic scenario. With my mother I was thinking, *She's going to make this worse. She's not the character witness I want right now. She won't help me.* Because she'd told me she wouldn't. "If you ever get arrested, don't call me." I needed someone sympathetic to my plight, and I didn't believe she was that person. So I didn't call my parents. I decided I didn't need them. I was a man. I could go it alone. I used my call to phone my cousin and told him not to tell anyone what had happened while I figured out what to do—now I just had to figure out what to do.

I'd been picked up late in the afternoon, so by the time I was processed it was close to lights-out. I was spending the night in jail, like it or not. It was at that point that a cop pulled me aside and told me what I was in for.

The way the system works in South Africa 30 is that you're arrested and held in a cell at the police station until your bail hearing. At the hearing, the judge looks at your case, hears arguments from the opposing sides, and then he either dismisses the charges or sets bail and a trial date. If you can make bail, you pay and go home. But there are all sorts of ways your bail hearing can go wrong: You get some court-appointed lawyer who hasn't read your case and doesn't know what's going on. Your family can't pay your bail. It could even be that the court's backed up. "Sorry, we're too busy. No more hearings today." It doesn't matter the reason. Once you leave jail, you can't go back to jail. If your situation isn't resolved that day, you go to prison to await trial. In prison you're housed with the people awaiting trial, not with the general population, but even the awaiting-trial section is incredibly dangerous because you have people picked up for traffic violations all the way up to proper hardened criminals. You're stuck there together, and you can be there for days, weeks, maybe months. It's the same way in America. If you're poor, if you don't know how the system works, you can slip through the cracks, and the next thing you know you're in this weird purgatory where you're not in prison but you're not not in prison. You haven't been convicted of any crime, but you're still locked up and can't get out.

This cop pulled me aside and said, "Listen, you don't want to go to your bail hearing. They'll give you a state attorney who won't know what's going on. He'll have no time for you. He'll ask the judge for a postponement, and then maybe you'll go free or maybe you won't. Trust me, you don't want to do that. You have the right to stay here for as long as you like. You want to meet with a lawyer and set yourself up before you go anywhere near a court or a judge." He wasn't giving me this advice out of the goodness of his heart. He had a deal with a defense attorney, sending him clients in exchange for a kickback. He handed me the attorney's business card, I called him,

and he agreed to take my case. He told me to stay put while he handled everything.

Now I needed money, because lawyers, as nice as they are, don't do anything for free. I called a friend and asked him if he could ask his dad to borrow some money. He said he'd handle it. He talked to his dad, and the lawyer got his retainer the next day.

With the lawyer taken care of, I felt like I had things under control. I was feeling pretty slick. I'd handled the situation, and, most important, Mom and Abel were none the wiser.

When the time came for lights-out a cop came and took my stuff. My belt, my wallet, my shoelaces.

"Why do you need my shoelaces?"

"So you don't hang yourself."

"Right."

Even when he said that, the gravity of my situation still wasn't sinking in. Walking to the station's holding cell, looking around at the other six guys in there, I was thinking, *This is no big deal. Everything's gonna be cool. I'm gonna get out of this.* I thought that right up until the moment the cell door clanged shut behind me and the guard yelled, "Lights out!" That's when I thought, *Oh s***. This is real.*

• • •

The day of my hearing came. . . . I was hand-cuffed and put in the back of a police van and driven to the courthouse to meet my fate. In South African courts, to minimize your expo-sure and your opportunities for escape, the holding cell where you await your hearing is a massive pen below the courtroom; you walk up a set of stairs into the dock rather than being escorted through the corridors. What happens in the holding cell is you're mixed in with the people who've been in prison awaiting trial for weeks and months. It's a weird mix, everything from white-collar criminals to guys picked up on traffic stops to real, hardcore criminals covered with prison tattoos. It's like the cantina scene from *Star Wars*, where the band's playing music and Han Solo's in the corner and all of the bad guys and bounty hunters from all over the universe are hanging out—a wretched hive of scum and villainy, only there's no music and there's no Han Solo.

I was with these people for only a brief window of time, but in that moment I saw the difference between prison and jail. I saw the difference between criminals and people who've committed crimes. I saw the hardness in people's faces. I thought back on how naive I'd been just hours before, thinking jail wasn't so bad and I could handle it. I was now truly afraid of what might happen to me. . . .

I didn't know where to go.

I looked over at the colored corner. I was staring at the most notorious, most violent prison gang in South Africa. I looked like them, but I wasn't them. I couldn't go over there doing my fake gangster s*** and have them discover I was a fraud. No, no, no. That game was over, my friend. The last thing I needed was colored gangsters up against me.

But then what if I went to the black corner? I know that I'm black and I identify as black, but I'm not a black person on the face of it, so would the black guys understand why I was walking over? . . . Because going to the black corner as a perceived colored person might piss off the colored gangs even more than going to the colored corner as a fake colored person. Because that's what had happened to me my entire life. Colored people would see me hanging out with blacks, and they'd confront me, want to fight me. I saw myself starting a race war in the holding cell.

"Hey! Why are you hanging out with the blacks?"

"Because I am black." 45

"No, you're not. You're colored."

"Ah, yes. I know it looks that way, friend, but let me explain. It's a funny story, actually. My father is white and my mother is black and race is a social construct, so. . . ."

That wasn't going to work. Not here.

All of this was happening in my head in an instant, on the fly. I was doing crazy calculations, looking at people, scanning the room, assessing the variables. *If I go here, then this. If I go there, then that.* My whole life was flashing before me—the playground at school, the *spaza* shops in Soweto, the streets of Eden Park, every time and every place I ever had to be a chameleon, navigate between groups, explain who I was. It was like the high school cafeteria, only it was the high school cafeteria from hell because if I picked the wrong table I might get beaten or stabbed. . . . I'd never been more scared in my life. But I still had to pick. Because racism exists, and you have to pick a side. You can say that you don't pick sides, but eventually life will force you to pick a side.

That day I picked white. They just didn't 50 look like they could hurt me. It was a handful of average, middle-aged white dudes. I walked over to them. We hung out for a while, chatted a bit. They were mostly in for white-collar crimes, money schemes, fraud and racketeering. They'd be useless if anyone came over looking to start trouble; they'd get their a**** kicked as well. But they weren't going to do anything to me. I was safe.

Luckily the time went by fairly quickly. I was in there for only an hour before I was called up to court, where a judge would either let me go or send me to prison to await trial. As I was leaving, one of the white guys reached over to me. "Make sure you don't come back down here," he said. "Cry in front of the judge; do whatever you have to do. If you go up and get sent back down here, your life will never be the same."

Up in the courtroom, I found my lawyer waiting. My cousin Mlungisi was there, too, in the gallery, ready to post my bail if things went my way.

The bailiff read out my case number, and the judge looked up at me.

"How are you?" he said.

I broke down. I'd been putting on this tough-guy facade for nearly a week, and I just couldn't do it anymore.

"I-I'm not fine, Your Honor. I'm not fine."

He looked confused. "What?!"

I said, "I'm not fine, sir. I'm really suffering."

"Why are you telling me this?"

"Because you asked how I was."

"Who asked you?"

"You did. You just asked me."

"I didn't say, 'How are you?' I said, 'Who are you?' Why would I waste time asking 'How are you?'! This is jail. I know everyone is suffering down there. If I asked everyone 'How are you?' we'd be here all day. I said, 'Who are you?' State your name for the record."

"Trevor Noah."

"Okay. Now we can carry on."

The whole courtroom started laughing, so then I started laughing, too. But now I was even more petrified because I didn't want the judge to think I wasn't taking him seriously because I was laughing.

It turned out that I needn't have been worried. Everything that happened next had been arranged beforehand. He presented my case. I had no priors. I wasn't dangerous. There were no objections from the opposing side. The judge assigned my trial date and set my bail, and I was free to go.

I walked out of court and the light of day hit my face and I said, "Sweet *Jesus*, I am never going back there again." It had been only a

week, in a cell that wasn't terribly uncomfortable with food that wasn't half bad, but a week in jail is a long, long time. A week without shoelaces is a long, long time. A week with no clocks, with no sun, can feel like an eternity. The thought of anything worse, the thought of doing real time in a real prison, I couldn't even imagine.

• • •

I drove with Mlungisi to his place, took a shower, and slept there. The next day he dropped me back at my mom's house. I strolled up the driveway acting real casual. My plan was to say I'd been crashing with Mlungisi for a few days. I walked into the house like nothing had happened. "Hey, Mom! What's up?" Mom didn't say anything, didn't ask me any questions. I was like, *Okay. Cool. We're good.*

I stayed for most of the day. Later in the afternoon we were sitting at the kitchen table, talking. I was telling all these stories, going on about everything Mlungisi and I had been up to that week, and I caught my mom giving me this look, slowly shaking her head. It was a different look than I had ever seen her give before. It wasn't "One day, I'm going to catch you." It wasn't anger or disapproval. It was disappointment. She was hurt.

"What?" I said. "What is it?"

She said, "Boy, who do you think paid your bail? Hmm? Who do you think paid your lawyer? Do you think I'm an idiot? Did you think no one would tell me?"

The truth came spilling out. Of course she'd known: the car. It had been missing the whole time. I'd been so wrapped up in dealing with jail and covering my tracks I'd forgotten that the proof of my crime was right there in the yard, the red Mazda missing from the driveway. And of course when I called my friend and he'd asked his dad for the money for the lawyer, the dad had pressed him on what the money was for and, being a parent himself, had called my mother immediately. She'd given my friend the money to pay the lawyer. She'd given my cousin the money to pay my bail. I'd spent the whole week in jail thinking I was so slick. But she'd known everything the whole time.

"I know you see me as some crazy old bitch nagging at you," she said, "but you forget the reason I ride you so hard and give you so much s*** is because I love you. Everything I have ever done I've done from a place of love. If I don't punish you, the world will punish you even worse. The world doesn't love you. If the police get you, the police don't love you. When I beat you, I'm trying to save you. When they beat you, they're trying to kill you."

LANGUAGE AND STYLE

1. The text begins with **connotative diction**. Give an example of the connotative words in the first few paragraphs and explain how the connotation conveys Noah's perspective.

2. Paragraph 22 includes a shift. Identify the shift and the **metaphor** the writer uses to describe the shift.

3. The **transitions** are clear in the narrative. Identify the shift to the middle of the narrative or the end of the narrative and explain the effect of the shift.

4. Toward the end of the text, Noah writes, "The truth came spilling out." Explain the shift in **diction** prior to the epiphany and the diction the writer uses to reveal his epiphany.

5. What is the **tone** of the text? Give examples of word choice, both **connotative** and **denotative** words, that reveal the tone.

⅃⊔⅃
⊐⊐⊏
⊐⊐⊏
⊐⊐⊏
PUTTING IT ALL TOGETHER
Modeled Text

Why I, a Heterosexual Teenage Boy, Want to See More Men in Speedos
Noah Spencer

THE TEXT IN CONTEXT

The following essay, written by high school student Noah Spencer was published by the *New York Times* in 2014. Spencer was one of ten winners in the newspaper's student editorial contest.

Unifying Idea	Why I, a Heterosexual Teenage Boy, Want to See More Men in Speedos	Rhetorical Choices	Effects of Choices
gender equality	The *Sports Illustrated* Swimsuit edition recently celebrated its 50th birthday. As an 18-year-old heterosexual male, I was happy to join in the festivities. However, one section of the magazine left me feeling something less than festive.	context and exigence	writer shares initial perspective that he enjoys the special issue
	It wasn't the "Legends" section, featuring former models old enough to be my mother, nor the controversial photographs of Barbies in bathing suits (though that was pretty creepy). What upset me was the "Athletes" (pp. 196–205). Just two summers ago, I had watched Alex Morgan, star of the U.S. women's national soccer team, seize victory over the Canadian team in the Olympic semifinals with a gorgeous, heart-wrenching (for a Canadian) header in the 120th minute. Now I saw her posing seductively in a blue bikini, lumped together with dolls both plastic and flesh.	metaphor	compares models to Barbies: unrealistic expectations of beauty
		transitions	transitions clarify timing of the writer's experiences
		imagery	plastic and flesh connect to Barbie metaphor, and other models

Unifying Idea	Why I, a Heterosexual Teenage Boy, Want to See More Men in Speedos	Rhetorical Choices	Effects of Choices
gender equality	It wasn't Morgan (or WNBA star Skylar Diggins or surfer Anastasia Ashley) posing in the magazine that spawned my guilt. An athletically refined body is a source of great beauty and has cultural significance. In fact, my issue with the "Athletes" section wasn't with what it actually contained, it was with what it left out: Morgan et al.'s male counterparts.	transition	signals a shift from details/context to argument
	Nowhere in this edition, nor in its forty-nine predecessors, was a male athlete photographed. By having exclusively female athletes model in scarce clothing, S.I. belittles their athletic accomplishments and serves to increase the gender inequality that is so widespread in sports.	message	writer criticizes featuring only female athletes which objectifies them
	Start typing "Alex Morgan" into YouTube and its first suggestion is "Alex Morgan hot"; click that and the top video on the page is one uploaded by "Sports Illustrated Swimsuit." (By contrast, the first suggestion that YouTube generates for "Cristiano Ronaldo," another world-class, attractive soccer player, is "Cristiano Ronaldo skills.") I can only imagine how dispiriting it must be for young girls who dream of becoming athletes to realize that even if they score a game-winning goal in the Olympics, their legacy will be more concerned with how they looked doing it.	evidence	examples contrast the treatment of male and female athletes
gender equality	According to the *New York Times*, the S.I. Swimsuit edition reaches millions of people worldwide. It has the power to influence readers' views of the athletes they feature. Currently, this power is being used to objectify women, but it doesn't have to be		

Unifying Idea	Why I, a Heterosexual Teenage Boy, Want to See More Men in Speedos	Rhetorical Choices	Effects of Choices
	that way. My proposed solution is that *Sports Illustrated* rebrand their swimsuit issue to be similar to *ESPN the Magazine*'s "Body Issue," focusing solely on athletes, male and female. By presenting the issue in this egalitarian method, athletes' bodies are celebrated for their beauty and S.I. is once again distributing magazines that are sports-related. Most importantly, the issue would no longer be contributing to the gender divide in sports,	]—thesis	*writer expresses his idea for a more equitable representation of male and female athletes*
	which would allow me to ogle Alex Morgan in good conscience.	]— exigence	*writer concludes by stating interest again*

Works Cited

Vega, Tanzina. "A New Swimsuit Issue Feature." The *New York Times*, 10 Feb. 2013.

North, Anna. "Put Ryan Lochte in the Sports Illustrated Swimsuit Issue." BuzzFeed, 12 Feb. 2013.

"Alex Morgan Body Painting—Swim Daily." YouTube, 2 July 2013.

Sports Illustrated 2014 Swimsuit Edition.

IDEAS IN AMERICAN CULTURE
Colonization and Exploration

Although European explorers are sometimes credited with "discovering" America, Native Americans had lived on these continents for thousands of years. Indeed, long before Christopher Columbus spotted the Virgin Islands in 1493 or the *Mayflower* arrived in 1620, indigenous peoples had established thriving cultures. The story of European settlement and expansion is — in many ways — a story of ruthless conquest, as natives were often forcibly displaced from their territories. But this convergence of "Old World" Europe with the American "New World" also set the stage for a new nation: a vast country based on new and noble ideals.

We can see the origins of this hope and idealism in the many reasons that Europeans came to the New World. Some ambitiously sought new trade routes. Others hoped to find gold, silver, ample land for cash crops, and opportunities for a better life. Still others emigrated to escape religious persecution and seek religious freedom. These ideas of ambition, independence, and freedom of thought and worship gave rise to the belief that America was an exceptional place — or, as colonial governor John Winthrop said, a "city on a hill" — and Americans were exceptional people. William Bradford cemented this concept with his eyewitness history *Of Plymouth Plantation* (p. 39), in which he recounts firsthand the journey of the Pilgrims on the *Mayflower* and the beginnings of the new colony.

Captain John Smith landed in Jamestown, Virginia, in 1607, which marked the beginning of the southern colonies in North America. Unlike the Pilgrims,

IDEA BANK

Assimilation
Colonization
Conflict
Cooperation
Culture
Discovery
Exploitation
Exploration
Governance
Hardship
Hope
Journey
Opportunity
Persecution
Perseverance
Pilgrimage
Settlement
Slavery
Survival
Work Ethic

Bayes, Alfred Walter (1858–1903) (after) IVAN LAWRENCE ESQ./Private Collection/Bridgeman Images

▲
This nineteenth-century painting by Alfred Walter Bayes depicts *Mayflower* passengers who are about to embark on their arduous journey to the new world. In 1620, separatists from the Church of England left the only home they knew to seek religious freedom.

Despite the hardships and adversity, why do modern people continue to explore?

these English immigrants came to America primarily for economic opportunity. In the case of Jamestown, the Virginia Company offered settlers 50 acres of land each. But establishing and maintaining these large agricultural settlements created a demand for imported enslaved labor and thus began a struggle for the soul of the nation that still echoes today. Between 1618 and 1620, approximately 50,000 enslaved Africans were brought to Jamestown and forced to work in a new plantation economy that would eventually dominate the South. By the time the transatlantic slave trade ended in 1807, over 12 million Africans had been brought to the Americas in chains.

As we look back on American history, it's startling to see that some of the earliest ideas, ideals, and conflicts remain powerfully influential today. The United States still struggles with its history of white supremacy, political inequality, and racial conflict. This dark legacy reminds us of the enormous human costs that can attend exploration and colonialization. For example, we can hear some of the lost legends and historically marginalized voices of Native Americans in N. Scott Momaday's "The Way to Rainy Mountain" (p. 46).

The lure of discovery and the powerful attraction of new frontiers remain invigorating. We still dream of human missions to other planets. We eagerly watch SpaceX launches and follow the NASA rovers that gather information on Mars. We also continue to explore the earth, from the Amazon rain forests to the depths of the Mariana Trench in the Pacific Ocean. Researchers in various fields pursue discoveries, as well, whether in the form of lifesaving vaccines, surprising revelations in quantum physics, or fresh approaches to challenges, such as climate change and political polarization. We also continue the struggle to reach the ideals held by the country's early settlers. Many politicians, including President Ronald Reagan and President Barack Obama, have used the phrase "city on a hill" to evoke the wonder, hope, and freedom associated with America.

▲
Into the Wild is a 1996 nonfiction book by Jon Krakauer, and a 2007 movie starring Emile Hirsch (shown here). The story recounts the adventures and ultimate death of Christopher McCandless after a two-year journey that ended with him living in an abandoned bus in the Alaskan wilderness.

How is the spirit of adventure and exploration alive today?

from Of Plymouth Plantation

William Bradford

THE TEXT IN CONTEXT

The following historical journal account was written in 1651 by William Bradford (1590–1657), an English Puritan separatist who emigrated to Plymouth, Massachusetts, on the *Mayflower* in 1620. Later, he was one of the forty-one passengers who signed the Mayflower Compact and served as the first elected governor of Plymouth from 1621 to 1656. This journal excerpt recounts several events of the first thirty years (1620–1651) of the Plymouth colony.

Stillman Rogers/Alamy Stock Photo

Of Their Voyage and How They Passed the Sea; and of Their Safe Arrival at Cape Cod

September 6. These troubles being blown over, and now all being compact together in one ship, they put to sea again with a prosperous wind, which continued divers days together, which was some encouragement unto them; yet, according to the usual manner, many were afflicted with seasickness. And I may not omit here a special work of God's providence. There was a proud and very profane young man, one of the seamen, of a lusty, able body, which made him the more haughty; he would alway be contemning the poor people in their sickness and cursing them daily with grievous execrations; and did not let to tell them that he hoped to help to cast half of them overboard before they came to their journey's end, and to make merry with what they had; and if he were by any gently reproved, he would curse and swear most bitterly. But it pleased God before they came half seas over, to smite this young man with a grievous disease, of which he died in a desperate manner, and so was himself the first that was thrown overboard. Thus his curses light on his own head, and it was an astonishment to all his fellows for they noted it to be the just hand of God upon him.

After they had enjoyed fair winds and weather for a season, they were encountered many times with crosswinds and met with many fierce storms with which the ship was shroudly shaken, and her upper works made very leaky; and one of the main beams in the midships was bowed and cracked, which put them in some fear that the ship could not be able to perform the voyage. So some of the chief of the company, perceiving the mariners to fear the sufficiency of the ship as appeared by their mutterings, they entered into serious consultation with the Master and other officers of the ship, to consider in time of the danger, and rather to return than to cast themselves into a desperate and inevitable peril. And truly there was great distraction and difference of opinion amongst the mariners themselves; fain would they do what could be done for their wages' sake (being now near half the seas over) and on the other hand they were loathe to hazard their lives too desperately. But in examining of all opinions, the master and others affirmed they knew the ship to be strong and firm under water; and for the buckling of the main beam, there was a great iron screw the passengers brought out of Holland, which would raise the beam into his place; the which being done, the carpenter and master affirmed that with a post put under it, set firm in the lower deck and otherways bound, he would make it sufficient. And as for the decks and upper works, they would caulk them as well as they could, and though with the working of the ship they would not long keep staunch, yet there would otherwise be no great danger, if they did not overpress her with sails. So they committed themselves to the will of God and resolved to proceed.

In sundry of these storms the winds were so fierce and the seas so high, as they could not bear a knot of sail, but were forced to hull for divers days together. And in one of them, as they thus lay at hull in a mighty storm, a lusty young man called John Howland, coming upon some occasion above the gratings was, with a seele of the ship, thrown into sea; but it pleased God that he caught hold of the topsail halyards which hung overboard and ran out at length. Yet he held his hold (though he was sundry fathoms under water) till he was hauled up by the same rope to the brim of the water, and then with a boat hook and other means got into the ship again and his life saved. And though he was something ill with it, yet he lived many years after and became a profitable member both in church and commonwealth. In all this voyage there died but one of the passengers, which was William

Butten, a youth, servant to Samuel Fuller, when they drew near the coast.

But to omit other things (that I may be brief) after long beating at sea they fell with that land which is called Cape Cod; the which being made and certainly known to be it, they were not a little joyful. After some deliberation had amongst themselves and with the Master of the ship, they tacked about and resolved to stand for the southward (the wind and weather being fair) to find some place about Hudson's River for their habitation. But after they had sailed that course about half the day, they fell amongst dangerous shoals and roaring breakers, and they were so far entangled therewith as they conceived themselves in great danger; and the wind shrinking upon them withal, they resolved to bear up again for the Cape and thought themselves happy to get out of those dangers before night overtook them, as by God's good providence they did. And the next day they got into the Cape Harbor, where they rid in safety. . . .

Being thus arrived in a good harbor, and brought safe to land, they fell upon their knees and blessed the God of Heaven who had brought them over the vast and furious ocean, and delivered them from all perils and miseries thereof, again to set their feet on the firm and stable earth, their proper element. . . . ⁵

• • •

But here I cannot but stay and make a pause, and stand half amazed at this poor people's present condition; and so I think will the reader, too, when he well considers the same. Being thus passed the vast ocean, and a sea of troubles before in their preparation (as may be remembered by that which went before), they had now no friends to welcome them nor inns to entertain or refresh their weatherbeaten bodies; no houses or much less towns to repair to, to seek for succor. It is recorded in Scripture as a mercy to the Apostle and his shipwrecked company, that the barbarians showed them no small kindness in refreshing them, but these savage barbarians, when they met with them (as after will appear), were readier to fill their sides full of arrows than otherwise. And for the season it was winter, and they that know the winters of that country know them to be sharp and violent, and subject to cruel and fierce storms, dangerous to travel to known places, much more to search an unknown coast. Besides, what could they see but a hideous and desolate wilderness, full of wild beasts and wild men—and what multitudes there might be of them they knew not. Neither could they, as it were, go up to the top of Pisgah to view from this wilderness a more goodly country to feed their hopes; for which way soever they turned their eyes (save upward to the heavens) they could have little solace or content in respect of any outward objects. For summer being done, all things stand upon them with a weather-beaten face, and the whole country, full of woods and thickets, represented a wild and savage hue. If they looked behind them, there was the mighty ocean which they had passed and was now as a main bar and gulf to separate them from all the civil parts of the world. If it be said they had a ship to succor them, it is true; but what heard they daily from the master and company? But that with speed they should look out a place (with their shallop) where they would be, at some near distance; for the season was such as he would not stir from thence till a safe harbor was discovered by them, where they would be, and he might go without danger; and that victuals consumed apace but he must and would keep sufficient for themselves and their return. Yea, it was muttered by some that if they got

not a place in time, they would turn them and their goods ashore and leave them. Let it also be considered what weak hopes of supply and succor they left behind them, that might bear up their minds in this sad condition and trials they were under; and they could not but be very small. It is true, indeed, the affections and love of their brethren at Leyden was cordial and entire towards them, but they had little power to help them or themselves; and how the case stood between them and the merchants at their coming away hath already been declared.

What could now sustain them but the Spirit of God and His grace? May not and ought not the children of these fathers rightly say: "Our fathers were Englishmen which came over this great ocean, and were ready to perish in this wilderness; but they cried unto the Lord, and He heard their voice and looked on their adversity," etc. "Let them therefore praise the Lord, because He is good: and His mercies endure forever." "Yea, let them which have been redeemed of the Lord, shew how He hath delivered them from the hand of the oppressor. When they wandered in the desert wilderness out of the way, and found no city to dwell in, both hungry and thirsty, their soul was overwhelmed in them. Let them confess before the Lord His loving kindness and His wonderful works before the sons of men."

The Starving Time
But that which was most sad and lamentable was, that in two or three months' time half of their company died, especially in January and February, being the depth of winter, and wanting houses and other comforts; being infected with the scurvy and other diseases which this long voyage and their inaccommodate condition had brought upon them. So as there died sometimes two or three of

a day in the foresaid time, that of one hundred and odd persons, scarce fifty remained. And of these, in the time of most distress, there was but six or seven sound persons who to their great commendations, be it spoken, spared no pains night nor day, but with abundance of toil and hazard of their own health, fetched them wood, made them fires, dressed them meat, made their beds, washed their loathsome clothes, clothed and unclothed them. In a word, did all the homely and necessary offices for them which dainty and queasy stomachs cannot endure to hear named; and all this willingly and cheerfully, without any grudging in the least, showing herein their true love unto their friends and brethren; a rare example and worthy to be remembered. Two of these seven were Mr. William Brewster, their reverend Elder, and Myles Standish, their Captain and military commander, unto whom myself and many others were much beholden in our low and sick condition. And yet the Lord so upheld these persons as in this general calamity they were not at all infected either with sickness or lameness. And what I have said of these I may say of many others who died in this general visitation, and others yet living; that whilst they had health, yea, or any strength continuing, they were not wanting to any that had need of them. And I doubt not but their recompense is with the Lord.

But I may not here pass by another remarkable passage not to be forgotten. As this calamity fell among the passengers that were to be left here to plant, and were hasted ashore and made to drink water that the seamen might have the more beer, and one in his sickness desiring but a small can of beer, it was answered that if he were their own father he should have none. The disease began to fall amongst them also, so as almost half of their company died before they went away, and many of their officers and lustiest men, as the boatswain, gunner, three quartermasters, the cook and others. At which the Master was something strucken and sent to the sick ashore and told the Governor he should send for beer for them that had need of it, though he drunk water homeward bound.

But now amongst his company there was far another kind of carriage in this misery than amongst the passengers. For they that before had been boon companions in drinking and jollity in the time of their health and welfare, began now to desert one another in this calamity, saying they would not hazard their lives for them, they should be infected by coming to help them in their cabins; and so, after they came to lie by it, would do little or nothing for them but, "if they died, let them die." But such of the passengers as were yet aboard showed them what mercy they could, which made some of their hearts relent, as the boatswain (and some others) who was a proud young man and would often curse and scoff at the passengers. But when he grew weak, they had compassion on him and helped him; then he confessed he did not deserve it at their hands, he had abused them in word and deed. "Oh!" (saith he) "you, I now see, show your love like Christians indeed one to another, but we let one another lie and die like dogs." Another lay cursing his wife, saying if it had not been for her he had never come this unlucky voyage, and anon cursing his fellows, saying he had done this and that for some of them; he had spent so much and so much amongst them, and they were now weary of him and did not help him, having need. Another gave his companion all he had, if he died, to help him in his weakness; he went and got a little spice and made him a mess of meat once or

10

twice. And because he died not so soon as he expected, he went amongst his fellows and swore the rogue would cozen him, he would see him choked before he made him any more meat; and yet the poor fellow died before morning.

Indian Relations

All this while the Indians came skulking about them, and would sometimes show themselves aloof off, but when any approached near them, they would run away; and once they stole away their tools where they had been at work and were gone to dinner. But about the sixteenth of March, a certain Indian came boldly amongst them and spoke to them in broken English, which they could well understand but marveled at it. At length they understood by discourse with him, that he was not of these parts, but belonged to the eastern parts where some English ships came to fish, with whom he was acquainted and could name sundry of them by their names, amongst whom he had got his language. He became profitable to them in acquainting them with many things concerning the state of the country in the east parts where he lived, which was afterwards profitable unto them; as also of the people here, of their names, number and strength, of their situation and distance from this place, and who was chief amongst them. His name was Samoset. He told them also of another Indian, whose name was Squanto, a native of this place, who had been in England and could speak better English than himself.

Being, after some time of entertainment and gifts dismissed, a while after he came again, and five more with him, and they brought again all the tools that were stolen away before, and made way for the coming of their great Sachem, called Massasoit. Who,

about four or five days after, came with the chief of his friends and other attendance, with the aforesaid Squanto. With whom, after friendly entertainment and some gifts given him, they made a peace with him (which hath now continued this twenty-four years) in these terms:

1. That neither he nor any of his should injure or do hurt to any of their people.

2. That if any of his did hurt to any of theirs, he should send the offender, that they might punish him.

3. That if anything were taken away from any of theirs, he should cause it to be restored; and they should do the like to his.

4. If any did unjustly war against him, they would aid him; if any did war against them, he should aid them.

5. He should send to his neighbors confederates to certify them of this, that they might not wrong them, but might be likewise comprised in the conditions of peace.

6. That when their men came to them, they should leave their bows and arrows behind them.

After these things he returned to his place called Sowams, some forty miles from this place, but Squanto continued with them and was their interpreter and was a special instrument sent of God for their good beyond their expectation. He directed them how to set their corn, where to take fish, and to procure other commodities, and was also their pilot to bring them to unknown places for their profit, and never left them till he died.

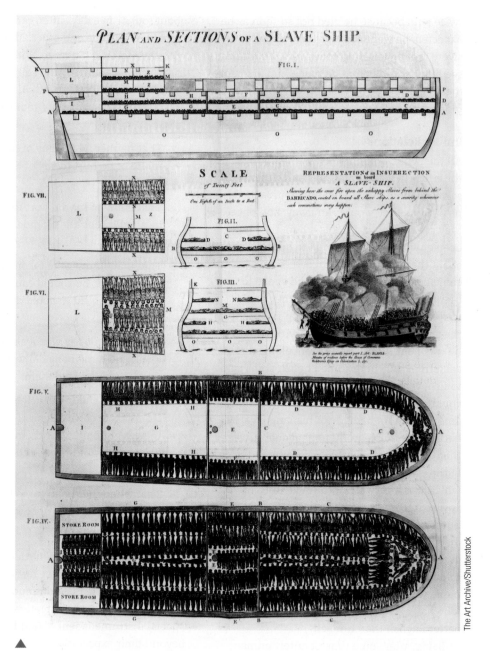

The Art Archive/Shutterstock

▲

This image is a diagram and description of the Liverpool-based slave trade ship, *Brookes*. The diagram shows that this ship can stow far more Africans than was legally regulated. This diagram was used by Thomas Clarkson as evidence against slave trade and was instrumental in the British Abolition of the Slave Trade Act in 1807.

The first enslaved people were brought to America in 1619, just a year before Bradford's journal. What does this picture reveal about the conditions of these enslaved people?

RHETORICAL SITUATION

1. In the first paragraph, Bradford introduces an idea. What is that idea, and what is the **writer's perspective** on that idea?

2. The **writer** and the **audience** share beliefs, values, and ideas. Give an example of this shared belief and discuss how the belief would influence the audience.

3. What is the **context** of this text? Why is it necessary to understand this moment in time in this text?

CLAIMS AND EVIDENCE

4. Describe the details Bradford uses as **evidence** to support the idea in the **claim**.

5. Bradford includes personal experience, testimony, and stories as **evidence** in his narrative. How effectively do they support his claim(s)?

REASONING AND ORGANIZATION

6. The text is a **narrative** chronicle that presents similar conflicts in the beginning, middle, and end of the text. What are these conflicts? In each instance, how is the conflict resolved?

7. Reread the section "Of Their Voyage and How They Passed the Sea; and of Their Safe Arrival at Cape Cod." Give an example of description that includes sensory **details**. What do these details reveal about the Pilgrims?

LANGUAGE AND STYLE

8. Bradford's direct emotional involvement in the narrative contributes to the **tone**. Give an example from the text that illustrates the writer's tone.

9. How do the **connotations** of specific words in the text illustrate the writer's attitude? Give an example and discuss.

10. Reread the treaty. Is the **diction** balanced? Are all components of the treaty fairly written with equality and balance in mind?

IDEAS IN AMERICAN CULTURE

11. Many Pilgrims believed in a religious *typology*: the idea that the events and hardships they experienced were parallel to those in the Bible. How does *Of Plymouth Plantation* reflect this idea and illustrate this biblical context?

PUTTING IT ALL TOGETHER

12. *Of Plymouth Plantation* was written as a historical account of the Pilgrims' voyage from Bradford's memory. How does Bradford's account contribute to the complexity of the idea, message, and purpose?

from The Way to Rainy Mountain

N. Scott Momaday

Photo © Philippe Matsas/Opale/Bridgeman Images

THE TEXT IN CONTEXT

The following is an excerpt from the memoir *The Way to Rainy Mountain*, which was published in 1969 by Pulitzer Prize–winning author N. Scott Momaday (b. 1934). Growing up in Arizona, Momaday was steeped in the culture of his Native American heritage. The book recounts the history of the Kiowa Tribe from their beginnings in Montana to their settlement in Rainy Mountain, Oklahoma. In this narrative excerpt, Momaday discovers his Kiowa roots and recounts his later pilgrimage to his grandmother's grave in the region of Rainy Mountain, a prominent landmark for the Kiowa Tribe.

A single knoll rises out of the plain in Oklahoma, north and west of the Wichita Range. For my people, the Kiowas, it is an old landmark, and they gave it the name Rainy Mountain. The hardest weather in the world is there. Winter brings blizzards, hot tornadic winds arise in the spring, and in summer the prairie is an anvil's edge. The grass turns brittle and brown, and it cracks beneath your feet. There are green belts along the rivers and creeks, linear groves of hickory and pecan, willow and witch hazel. At a distance in July or August the steaming foliage seems almost to writhe in fire. Great green and yellow grasshoppers are everywhere in the tall grass, popping up like corn to sting the flesh, and tortoises crawl about on the red earth, going nowhere in the plenty of time. Loneliness is an aspect of the land. All things in the plain are isolate; there is no confusion of objects in the eye, but *one* hill or *one* tree or *one* man. To look upon that landscape in the early morning, with the sun at your back, is to lose the sense of proportion. Your imagination comes to life, and this, you think, is where Creation was begun.

I returned to Rainy Mountain in July. My grandmother had died in the spring, and I wanted to be at her grave. She had lived to be very old and at last infirm. Her only living daughter was with her when she died, and I was told that in death her face was that of a child.

I like to think of her as a child. When she was born, the Kiowas were living the last great moment of their history. For more than a hundred years they had controlled the open range from the Smoky Hill River to the Red, from the headwaters of the Canadian to the fork of the Arkansas and Cimarron. In alliance with the Comanches, they had ruled the whole of the southern Plains. War was their sacred business, and they were among the finest horsemen the world has ever known. But warfare for the Kiowas was preeminently a matter of disposition rather than of survival, and they never understood the grim, unrelenting advance of the U.S. Cavalry. When at last, divided and ill-provisioned, they were driven onto the Staked Plains in the cold rains of autumn, they fell into panic. In Palo Duro Canyon they abandoned their crucial stores to pillage and had nothing then but their lives. In order to save themselves, they surrendered to the soldiers at Fort Sill and were imprisoned in the old stone corral that now stands as a military museum. My grandmother was spared the humiliation of those high gray walls by eight or ten years, but she must have known from birth the affliction of defeat, the dark brooding of old warriors.

Her name was Aho, and she belonged to the last culture to evolve in North America. Her forebears came down from the high country in western Montana nearly three centuries ago. They were a mountain people, a mysterious tribe of hunters whose language has never been positively classified in any major group. In the late seventeenth century they began a long migration to the south and east. It was a journey toward the dawn, and it led to a golden age. Along the way the Kiowas were befriended by the Crows, who gave them the culture and religion of the Plains. They acquired horses, and their ancient nomadic spirit was suddenly free of the ground. They acquired Tai-me, the sacred Sun Dance doll, from that moment the object and symbol of their worship, and so shared in the divinity of the sun. Not least, they acquired the sense of destiny, therefore courage and pride. When they entered upon the southern Plains they had been transformed. No longer were they slaves to the simple necessity of survival;

they were a lordly and dangerous society of fighters and thieves, hunters and priests of the sun. According to their origin myth, they entered the world through a hollow log. From one point of view, their migration was the fruit of an old prophecy, for indeed they emerged from a sunless world.

Although my grandmother lived out her long life in the shadow of Rainy Mountain, the immense landscape of the continental interior lay like memory in her blood. She could tell of the Crows, whom she had never seen, and of the Black Hills, where she had never been. I wanted to see in reality what she had seen more perfectly in the mind's eye, and traveled fifteen hundred miles to begin my pilgrimage. 5

Yellowstone, it seemed to me, was the top of the world, a region of deep lakes and dark timber, canyons and waterfalls. But, beautiful as it is, one might have the sense of confinement there. The skyline in all directions is close at hand, the high wall of the woods and deep cleavages of shade. There is a perfect freedom in the mountains, but it belongs to the eagle and the elk, the badger and the bear. The Kiowas reckoned their stature by the distance they could see, and they were bent and blind in the wilderness.

Descending eastward, the highland meadows are a stairway to the plain. In July the inland slope of the Rockies is luxuriant with flax and buckwheat, stonecrop and larkspur. The earth unfolds and the limit of the land recedes. Clusters of trees, and animals grazing far in the distance, cause the vision to reach away and wonder to build upon the mind. The sun follows a longer course in the day, and the sky is immense beyond all comparison. The great billowing clouds that sail upon it are shadows that move upon the grain like water, dividing light. Farther down, in the land of the Crows and Blackfeet, the plain is yellow.

Sweet clover takes hold of the hills and bends upon itself to cover and seal the soil. There the Kiowas paused on their way; they had come to the place where they must change their lives. The sun is at home on the plains. Precisely there does it have the certain character of a god. When the Kiowas came to the land of the Crows, they could see the dark lees of the hills at dawn across the Bighorn River, the profusion of light on the grain shelves, the oldest deity ranging after the solstices. Not yet would they veer southward to the caldron of the land that lay below; they must wean their blood from the northern winter and hold the mountains a while longer in their view. They bore Tai-me in procession to the east.

A dark mist lay over the Black Hills, and the land was like iron. At the top of a ridge I caught sight of Devil's Tower upthrust against the gray sky as if in the birth of time the core of the earth had broken through its crust and the motion of the world was begun. There are things in nature that engender an awful quiet in the heart of man; Devil's Tower is one of them. Two centuries ago, because they could not do otherwise, the Kiowas made a legend at the base of the rock. My grandmother said:

Eight children were there at play, seven sisters and their brother. Suddenly the boy was struck dumb; he trembled and began to run upon his hands and feet. His fingers became claws, and his body was covered with fur. Directly there was a bear where the boy had been. The sisters were terrified; they ran, and the bear after them. They came to the stump of a great tree, and the tree spoke to them. It bade them climb upon it, and as they did so it began to rise into the air. The bear came to kill them, but they were just beyond its reach. It reared against the tree and scored the bark all around with its claws. The seven sisters were borne into the sky, and they became the stars of the Big Dipper.

From that moment, and so long as the legend lives, the Kiowas have kinsmen in the night sky. Whatever they were in the mountains, they could be no more. However tenuous their well-being, however much they had suffered and would suffer again, they had found a way out of the wilderness. 10

My grandmother had a reverence for the sun, a holy regard that now is all but gone out of mankind. There was a wariness in her, and an ancient awe. She was a Christian in her later years, but she had come a long way about, and she never forgot her birthright. As a child she had been to the Sun Dances; she had taken part in those annual rites, and by them she had learned the restoration of her people in the presence of Tai-me. She was about seven when the last Kiowa Sun Dance was held in 1887 on the Washita River above Rainy Mountain Creek. The buffalo were gone. In order to consummate the ancient sacrifice—to impale the head of a buffalo bull upon the medicine tree—a delegation of old men journeyed into Texas, there to beg and barter for an animal from the Goodnight herd. She was ten when the Kiowas came together for the last time as a living Sun Dance culture. They could find no buffalo; they had to hang an old hide from the sacred tree. Before the dance could begin, a company of soldiers rode out from Fort Sill under orders to disperse the tribe. Forbidden without cause the essential act of their faith, having seen the wild herds slaughtered and left to rot upon the ground, the Kiowas backed away forever from the medicine tree. That was July 20, 1890, at the great bend of the Washita. My grandmother was there. Without bitterness, and for as long as she lived, she bore a vision of deicide.

Now that I can have her only in memory, I see my grandmother in the several postures that were peculiar to her: standing at the wood stove on a winter morning and turning meat in a great iron skillet; sitting at the south window, bent above her beadwork, and afterwards, when her vision failed, looking down for a long time into the fold of her hands; going out upon a cane, very slowly as she did when the weight of age came upon her; praying. I remember her most often at prayer. She made long, rambling prayers out of suffering and hope, having seen many things. I was never sure that I had the right to hear, so exclusive were they of all mere custom and company. The last time I saw her she prayed standing by the side of her bed at night, naked to the waist, the light of a kerosene lamp moving upon her dark skin. Her long, black hair, always drawn and braided in the day, lay upon her shoulders and against her breasts like a shawl. I do not speak Kiowa, and I never understood her prayers, but there was something inherently sad in the sound, some merest hesitation upon the syllables of sorrow. She began in a high descending pitch, exhausting her breath to silence; then again and again—and always the same intensity of effort, of something that is, and is not, like urgency in the human voice. Transported so in the dancing light among the shadows of her room, she seemed beyond the reach of time. But that was illusion; I think I knew then that I should not see her again.

Houses are like sentinels in the plain, old keepers of the weather watch. There, in a very little while, wood takes on the appearance of great age. All colors wear soon away in the wind and rain, and then the wood is burned gray and the grain appears and the nails turn red with rust. The windowpanes are black and opaque; you imagine there is nothing within, and indeed there are many ghosts, bones given up to the land. They stand here and there against the sky, and you approach them for a longer time than you expect. They belong in the distance; it is their domain.

Once there was a lot of sound in my grandmother's house, a lot of coming and going, feasting and talk. The summers there were full of excitement and reunion. The Kiowas are a summer people; they abide the cold and keep to themselves, but when the season turns and the land becomes warm and vital they cannot hold still; an old love of going returns upon them. The aged visitors who came to my grandmother's house when I was a child were made of lean and leather, and they bore themselves upright. They wore great black hats and bright ample shirts that shook in the wind. They rubbed fat upon their hair and wound their braids with strips of colored cloth. Some of them painted their faces and carried the scars of old and cherished enmities. They were an old council of warlords, come to remind and be reminded of who they were. Their wives and daughters served them well. The women might indulge themselves; gossip was at once the mark and compensation of their servitude. They made loud and elaborate talk among themselves, full of jest and gesture, fright and false alarm. They went abroad in fringed and flowered shawls, bright beadwork and German silver. They were at home in the kitchen, and they prepared meals that were banquets.

There were frequent prayer meetings and great nocturnal feasts. When I was a child I played with my cousins outside, where the lamplight fell upon the ground and the singing of the old people rose up around us and carried away into the darkness. There were a lot of good things to eat, a lot of laughter and surprise. And afterwards, when the quiet returned, I lay down with my grandmother and could hear the frogs away by the river and feel the motion of the air. 15

Now there is a funeral silence in the rooms, the endless wake of some final word. The walls have closed in upon my grandmother's house. When I returned to it in mourning, I saw for the first time in my life how small it was. It was late at night, and there was a white moon, nearly full. I sat for a long time on the stone steps by the kitchen door. From there I could see out across the land; I could see the long rows of trees by the creek, the low light upon the rolling plains, and the stars of the Big Dipper. Once I looked at the moon and caught sight of a strange thing. A cricket had perched upon the handrail, only a few inches away from me. My line of vision was such that the creature filled the moon like a fossil. It had

gone there, I thought, to live and die, for there, of all places, was its small definition made whole and eternal. A warm wind rose up and purled like the longing within me.

The next morning I awoke at dawn and went out on the dirt road to Rainy Mountain. It was already hot, and the grasshoppers began to fill the air. Still, it was early in the morning, and the birds sang out of the shadows. The long yellow grass on the mountain shone in the bright light, and a scissortail hied above the land. There, where it ought to be, at the end of a long and legendary way, was my grandmother's grave. Here and there on the dark stones were ancestral names. Looking back once, I saw the mountain and came away.

Shane Brown Photography

▲

This photograph was taken on set during the filming of the documentary *Return to Rainy Mountain*, a 2017 adaptation of Momaday's novel *The Way to Rainy Day Mountain*. The image shows N. Scott Momaday (right), his daughter Jill Momaday (center), and "Uncle Luke" Toyebo (left), a Kiowa Tribe elder.

What does this image suggest about Native American culture today?

RHETORICAL SITUATION

1. Who is the **writer**? What does the writer share with the **audience**?

2. What is the **exigence** of the text? Explain how the **context** and **exigence** contribute to the **purpose**.

CLAIMS AND EVIDENCE

3. What type of **evidence** does Momaday use to develop his **claim**?

4. How do the **details** of his grandmother's story contribute to the purpose of the text?

REASONING AND ORGANIZATION

5. What is the **thesis**? How does the writer support this thesis?

6. How do the related **images** that create a **motif** contribute to the **message**?

LANGUAGE AND STYLE

7. Momaday uses **imagery** and **symbols** to express larger ideas. Identify examples of **imagery** and other figurative language and describe how Momaday uses these choices to convey his **tone**.

8. What is the **tone** of the text? Explain how this tone contributes to the overall **message**.

IDEAS IN AMERICAN CULTURE

9. This text resonates with the memory and history of the Kiowa Tribe. Explain how Momaday's journey is a personal pilgrimage.

PUTTING IT ALL TOGETHER

10. The figurative language and symbols work to create a powerful message about tradition and culture. Explain how the figurative language contributes to the complexity of Momaday's message.

IDEAS IN AMERICAN CULTURE
Faith and Doubt

IDEA BANK

Accusation

Belief

Devotion

Doubt

Faith

Fear

Grace

Guilt

Hysteria

Judgment

Mortality

Persecution

Redemption

Religion

Revival

Salvation

Simplicity

Sin

Suspicion

Wrath

The Pilgrims and Puritans who settled Massachusetts each held distinctive religious views. For example, the Puritans wanted to remain in the Church of England but practice a reformed version of Christianity away from the corruptions of English society. In contrast, the Pilgrims were religious separatists who found the church irredeemable and had left it altogether. But these two groups also shared many values and convictions. Both Pilgrims and Puritans believed in predestination: the idea that an all-powerful God offered salvation to a small group of Christians called the elect, who were saved by God's mercy alone. Both groups strived for modesty, simplicity, and practicality in their worship and in their lives.

For both Pilgrim and Puritan settlers, this faith was inseparable from daily life. They feared the vast, strange, and dangerous wilderness that surrounded them. Likewise, they were often fearful of outsiders, whether neighboring colonists with different religious views or the indigenous peoples who already inhabited the region. They also feared their God and lived with the terror of eternal damnation. Their fears could turn inward, as well, whether in terms of individual self-reflection or suspicions within their own communities. The Salem Witch Trials (1692–1693) are probably the most infamous example. During this mass

© Peabody Essex Museum/Bridgeman Images

▲

This painting is *The Trial of George Jacobs*, which depicts a courtroom scene during the Salem Witch Trials.

Look closely at the portrayal of the people in the courtroom: their reactions, gestures, expressions, and attitudes. Where in the painting do you see faith? Where do you see doubt?

hysteria, hundreds of people — overwhelmingly women — were accused of witch-craft. The subsequent trials led to the execution of twenty-two individuals. While many of those responsible for this persecution later repented, the idea of a "witch hunt" still connotes suspicion and doubt today.

The Puritan religion continued to play a primary role in American life. Beginning in the 1730s, for example, the "Great Awakening" swept through the thirteen colonies. This religious revival was a call for a revitalized faith and a renewed focus on the individual relationship with God. During this movement, Jonathan Edwards delivered his famous sermon "Sinners in the Hands of an Angry God" (p. 54).

The fabric of religious faith, stretching back to the seventeenth and eighteenth centuries, remains strong in American life today: the United States is the most religious of all the industrialized Western democracies. Indeed, America is home to more Christians and Jewish people than any other single country, as well as to growing populations of other religions, such as Islam. Of course, American history contains strong threads of religious skepticism too. But the intense Puritan anxiety about personal salvation has persisted well beyond the colonial era. For example, we can see it in Langston Hughes's "Salvation" (p. 59), which narrates an intense experience of religious disillusionment. These ideas of faith and doubt apply well beyond the sphere of organized religion. Americans have also placed their faith in institutions and ideals, including technology, progress, democracy, hard work, education, science, the government, and the American dream.

Over the past several decades, however, Americans have witnessed increasing skepticism toward institutions. For example, according to the Pew Research Center, public trust in government is at an all-time low, with only 40 percent of Americans believing that the rights and liberties of all are respected. What has shaken American faith and trust? Many factors have contributed to it, especially recent historical events, such as the September 11 attacks, the war in Iraq, the financial crisis of 2008, and the COVID-19 pandemic.

In the 1950s, Senator Joseph McCarthy accused hundreds of people, including government officials, of being communists, leading to hearings called before the House Committee on Un-American Activities.

This political event has been called a "witch hunt" similar to the Salem Witch Trials in the seventeenth century. What examples can you think of that are modern-day witch hunts?

Bettmann/Getty Images

from Sinners in the Hands of an Angry God

Jonathan Edwards

Art Images/Getty Images

THE TEXT IN CONTEXT

A Puritan theologian, philosopher, and minister, Jonathan Edwards (1703–1758) preached the following sermon on July 8, 1741, in Enfield, Connecticut, a town that — until that day — had little interest in the Great Awakening and few religious conversions as part of the revival. This powerful religious movement swept through New England from 1730–1755. Drawing upon his own interest in science and observation of the natural world, Edwards's writings sought to illustrate God's masterful design as it could be seen in nature.

So that thus it is that natural men are held in the hand of God, over the pit of hell; they have deserved the fiery pit, and are already sentenced to it; and God is dreadfully provoked, his anger is as great toward them as to those that are actually suffering the executions of the fierceness of his wrath in hell, and they have done nothing in the least to appease or abate that anger, neither is God in the least bound by any promise to hold them up one moment; the devil is waiting for them, hell is gaping for them, the flames gather and flash about them, and would fain lay hold on them, and swallow them up; the fire pent up in their own hearts is struggling to break out; and they have no interest in any Mediator, there are no means within reach that can be any security to them. In short, they have no refuge, nothing to take hold of; all that preserves them every moment is the mere arbitrary will, and uncovenanted, unobliged forbearance of an incensed God.

The use of this awful subject may be for awakening unconverted persons in this congregation. This that you have heard is the case of every one of you that are out of Christ. That world of misery, that lake of burning brimstone, is extended abroad under you. There is the dreadful pit of the glowing flames of the wrath of God; there is hell's wide gaping mouth open; and you have nothing to stand upon, nor anything to take hold of; there is nothing between you and hell but the air; it is only the power and mere pleasure of God that holds you up.

You probably are not sensible of this; you find you are kept out of hell, but do not see the hand of God in it; but look at other things, as the good state of your bodily constitution, your care of your own life, and the means you use for your own preservation. But indeed these things are nothing; if God should withdraw his hand, they would avail no more to keep you from falling than the thin air to hold up a person that is suspended in it.

Your wickedness makes you as it were heavy as lead, and to tend downward with great weight and pressure toward hell; and if God should let you go, you would immediately sink and swiftly descend and plunge into the bottomless gulf, and your healthy constitution, and your own care and prudence, and best contrivance, and all your righteousness, would have no more influence to uphold you and keep you out of hell than a spider's web would have to stop a fallen rock. . . .

The wrath of God is like great waters that are dammed for the present; they increase more and more, and rise higher and higher, till an outlet is given; and the longer the stream is stopped, the more rapid and mighty is its course when once it is let loose. It is true, that judgment against your evil works has not been executed hitherto; the floods of God's vengeance have been withheld; but your guilt in the meantime is constantly increasing, and you are every day treasuring up more wrath; the waters are constantly rising, and waxing more and more mighty; and there is nothing but the mere pleasure of God that holds the waters back, that are unwilling to be stopped, and press hard to go forward. If God should only withdraw his hand from the floodgate, it would immediately fly open, and the fiery floods of the fierceness and wrath of God would rush forth with inconceivable fury, and would come upon you with omnipotent power; and if your strength were ten thousand times greater than it is, yea, ten thousand times greater than the strength of the stoutest, sturdiest devil in hell, it would be nothing to withstand or endure it.

The bow of God's wrath is bent, and the arrow made ready on the string, and justice bends the arrow at your heart, and strains the bow, and it is nothing but the mere pleasure of God, and that of an angry God, without any promise or obligation at all, that keeps the arrow one moment from being made drunk with your blood. Thus all you that never passed under a great change of heart, by the mighty power of the Spirit of God upon your souls; all you that were never born again, and made new creatures, and raised from being dead in sin, to a state of new, and before altogether unexperienced light and life, are in the hands of an angry God. However you may have reformed your life in many things, and may have had religious affections, and may keep up a form of religion in your families and closets, and in the house of God, it is nothing but his mere pleasure that keeps you from being this moment swallowed up in everlasting destruction. However unconvinced you may now be of the truth of what you hear, by and by you will be fully convinced of it. Those that are gone from being in the like circumstances with you see that it was so with them; for destruction came suddenly upon most of them; when they expected nothing of it, and while they were saying, Peace and safety: now they see that those things on which they depended for peace and safety were nothing but thin air and empty shadows.

The God that holds you over the pit of hell, much as one holds a spider, or some loathsome insect over the fire, abhors you, and is dreadfully provoked: his wrath toward you burns like fire; he looks upon you as worthy of nothing else but to be cast into the fire; he is of purer eyes than to bear to have you in his sight; you are ten thousand times more abominable in his eyes than the most hateful venomous serpent is in ours. You have offended him infinitely more than ever a stubborn rebel did his prince; and yet it is nothing but his hand that holds you from falling into the fire every moment. It is to be ascribed to nothing else, that you did not go to hell the last night; that you was suffered to awake again in this

5

world, after you closed your eyes to sleep. And there is no other reason to be given why you have not dropped into hell since you arose in the morning, but that God's hand has held you up. There is no other reason to be given why you have not gone to hell, since you have sat here in the house of God, provoking his pure eyes by your sinful wicked manner of attending his solemn worship. Yea, there is nothing else that is to be given as a reason why you do not this very moment drop down into hell!

O sinner! Consider the fearful danger you are in: it is a great furnace of wrath, a wide and bottomless pit, full of the fire of wrath, that you are held over in the hand of that God, whose wrath is provoked and incensed as much against you as against many of the damned in hell. You hang by a slender thread, with the flames of divine wrath flashing about it, and ready every moment to singe it, and burn it asunder; and you have no interest in any Mediator, and nothing to lay hold of to save yourself, nothing to keep off the flames of wrath, nothing of your own, nothing that you ever have done, nothing that you can do, to induce God to spare you one moment. . . .

It is *everlasting* wrath. It would be dreadful to suffer this fierceness and wrath of Almighty God one moment; but you must suffer it to all eternity. There will be no end to this exquisite horrible misery. When you look forward, you shall see a long forever, a boundless duration before you, which will swallow up your thoughts and amaze your soul; and you will absolutely despair of ever having any deliverance, any end, any mitigation, any rest at all. You will know certainly that you must wear out long ages, millions of millions of ages, in wrestling and conflicting with this almighty merciless vengeance; and then when you have so done, when so many ages have actually been spent by you in this manner, you will know that all is but a point to what remains. So that your

punishment will indeed be infinite. Oh, who can express what the state of a soul in such circumstances is! All that we can possibly say about it gives but a very feeble, faint representation of it; it is inexpressible and inconceivable: For "who knows the power of God's anger?"

How dreadful is the state of those that are daily and hourly in the danger of this great wrath and infinite misery! But this is the dismal case of every soul in this congregation that has not been born again, however moral and strict, sober and religious, they may otherwise be. Oh, that you would consider it, whether you be young or old! There is reason to think, that there are many in this congregation now hearing this discourse that will actually be the subjects of this very misery to all eternity. We know not who they are, or in what seats they sit, or what thoughts they now have. It may be they are now at ease, and hear all these things without much disturbance, and are now flattering themselves that they are not the persons, promising themselves that they shall escape. If we knew that there was one person, and but one, in the whole congregation that was to be the subject of this misery, what an awful thing would it be to think of! If we knew who it was, what an awful sight would it be to see such a person! How might all the rest of the congregation lift up a lamentable and bitter cry over him! But, alas! Instead of one, how many is it likely will remember this discourse in hell? And it would be a wonder if some that are now present should not be in hell in a very short time, even before this year is out. And it would be no wonder if some persons that now sit here, in some seats of this meetinghouse, in health, quiet, and secure, should be there before tomorrow morning. Those of you that finally continue in a natural condition, that shall keep out of hell longest, will be there in a little time! Your damnation does not slumber; it will come swiftly and, in all probability, very suddenly

10

upon many of you. You have reason to wonder that you are not already in hell. It is doubtless the case of some whom you have seen and known that never deserved hell more than you, and that heretofore appeared as likely to have been now alive as you. Their case is past all hope; they are crying in extreme misery and perfect despair. But here you are in the land of the living and in the house of God, and have an opportunity to obtain salvation. What would not those poor damned hopeless souls give for one day's opportunity such as you now enjoy!

And now you have an extraordinary opportunity, a day wherein Christ has thrown the door of mercy wide open, and stands in calling and crying with a loud voice to poor sinners; a day wherein many are flocking to him, and pressing into the kingdom of God. Many are daily coming from the east, west, north, and south; many that were very lately in the same miserable condition that you are in are now in a happy state, with their hearts filled with love to him who has loved them and washed them from their sins in his own blood, and rejoicing in hope of the glory of God. How awful is it to be left behind at such a day! To see so many others feasting, while you are pining and perishing! To see so many rejoicing and singing for joy of heart, while you have cause to mourn for sorrow of heart, and howl for vexation of spirit! How can you rest one moment in such a condition? . . .

The Washington Post/Getty Images

▲

The image depicts a current revival on the National Mall in Washington, DC. Today, these gatherings are an integral part of evangelical and charismatic Christianity.

How are contemporary revivals and the Puritan experience similar, and how are they different? Do contemporary revivals have the same purpose and effect? Explain your response.

RHETORICAL SITUATION

1. Who is the **writer**? Who is the **audience**? How might this audience respond to Edwards's text?

2. In the first paragraph of the sermon, the **writer** begins with an idea that resonates throughout the sermon. What is the idea?

CLAIMS AND EVIDENCE

3. The writer makes many **claims** throughout the sermon. Identify a claim. Then indicate both the idea and the **perspective** communicated by the claim.

4. What **evidence** does Edwards use to support his claim? What effect does this variety of evidence have on his audience?

REASONING AND ORGANIZATION

5. What are some **images** that are repeated throughout the sermon? Why did he choose those images for this audience?

6. Explain how the **motif** created by these related images contributes to Edwards's **message**.

LANGUAGE AND STYLE

7. Edwards uses **diction**, **imagery**, and **figurative language** to describe the strength of God. Choose one example and explain its effects.

8. Identify the shift near the end of the sermon. What **transition** indicates this shift? Explain the effect of this shift.

9. What is the **tone** of the sermon? What does it suggest about the writer's attitude toward his subject?

IDEAS IN AMERICAN CULTURE

10. The Puritans believed that the elect were chosen by God to live a godly life. This sermon appeals to both the congregation's desire to live a pure life and their fear of failing to live that life. Explain how this sermon speaks to the hopes and fears of Puritan society.

PUTTING IT ALL TOGETHER

11. What is Edwards's purpose? Explain how Edwards's use of figurative language strengthens his argument and achieves his purpose.

Salvation
Langston Hughes

THE TEXT IN CONTEXT

Langston Hughes (1902–1967) remains one of America's most renowned writers and poets, his name almost synonymous with the Harlem Renaissance in American literature. His first acclaimed poem "The Negro Speaks of Rivers" was published when he was just twenty-one years old. Hughes was raised by his mother and grandmother after his parents divorced when he was a very young boy. After his grandmother's death, he and his mother moved around a great deal, eventually living in Cleveland. In the excerpt from Chapter 3 of his memoir *The Big Sea*, Hughes reflects on a churchgoing experience he had as a young teenager.

Robert W. Kelley/Getty Images

I was saved from sin when I was going on thirteen. But not really saved. It happened like this. There was a big revival at my Auntie Reed's church. Every night for weeks there had been much preaching, singing, praying, and shouting, and some very hardened sinners had been brought to Christ, and the membership of the church had grown by leaps and bounds. Then just before the revival ended, they held a special meeting for children, "to bring the young lambs to the fold." My aunt spoke of it for days ahead. That night I was escorted to the front row and placed on the mourners' bench with all the other young sinners, who had not yet been brought to Jesus.

My aunt told me that when you were saved you saw a light, and something happened to you inside! And Jesus came into your life! And God was with you from then on! She said you could see and hear and feel Jesus in your soul. I believed her. I had heard a great many old people say the same thing and it seemed to me they ought to know. So I sat there calmly in the hot, crowded church, waiting for Jesus to come to me.

The preacher preached a wonderful rhythmical sermon, all moans and shouts and lonely cries and dire pictures of hell, and then he sang a song about the ninety and nine safe in the fold, but one little lamb was left out in the cold. Then he said: "Won't you come? Won't you come to Jesus? Young lambs, won't you come?" And he held out his arms to all us young sinners there on the mourners' bench. And the little girls cried. And some of them jumped up and went to Jesus right away. But most of us just sat there.

A great many old people came and knelt around us and prayed, old women with jet-black faces and braided hair, old men with work-gnarled hands. And the church sang a song about the lower lights are burning, some poor sinners to be saved. And the whole building rocked with prayer and song.

Still I kept waiting to see Jesus.

Finally all the young people had gone to the altar and were saved, but one boy and me. He was a rounder's son named Westley. Westley and I were surrounded by sisters and deacons praying. It was very hot in the church, and getting late now. Finally Westley said to me in a whisper: "Goddamit, I'm tired o' sitting here. Let's get up and be saved." So he got up and was saved.

Then I was left all alone on the mourners' bench. My aunt came and knelt at my knees and cried, while prayers and songs swirled all around me in the little church. The whole congregation prayed for me alone, in a mighty wail of moans and voices. And I kept waiting serenely for Jesus, waiting, waiting—but he didn't come. I wanted to see him, but nothing happened to me. Nothing! I wanted something to happen to me, but nothing happened.

I heard the songs and the minister saying: "Why don't you come? My dear child, why don't you come to Jesus? Jesus is waiting for you. He wants you. Why don't you come? Sister Reed, what is this child's name?"

"Langston," my aunt sobbed.

"Langston, why don't you come? Why don't you come and be saved? Oh, Lamb of God! Why don't you come?"

Now it was really getting late. I began to be ashamed of myself, holding everyone up so long. I began to wonder what God thought about Westley, who certainly hadn't seen Jesus either, but who was now sitting proudly on the platform, swinging his knickerbockered legs and grinning down at me, surrounded by deacons and old women on their knees praying. God had not struck Westley dead for taking his name in vain or for lying in the temple. So I decided that maybe to save further trouble, I'd better lie, too, and say that Jesus had come, and get up and be saved.

So I got up.

Suddenly the whole room broke into a sea of shouting, as they saw me rise. Waves of rejoicing swept the place. Women leaped in the air. My aunt threw her arms around me. The minister took me by the hand and led me to the platform.

When things quieted down, in a hushed silence, punctuated by a few ecstatic "amens," all the new young lambs were blessed in the name of God. Then joyous singing filled the room.

That night, for the first time in my life but one—for I was a big boy twelve years old—I cried, in bed alone, and couldn't stop. I buried my head under the quilts, but my aunt heard me. She woke up and told my uncle I was crying because the Holy Ghost had come into my life, and because I had seen Jesus. But I was really crying because I couldn't bear to tell her that I had lied, that I had deceived everybody in the church, and hadn't seen Jesus, and that now I didn't believe there was a Jesus any more, since he didn't come to help me.

In this season it is well to remember that the hope of our world rests on faith. Through faith our forefathers—men of varied faiths—built this country. And only through faith can we, in our turn, build confidently for the future.

Faith is a family matter, too . . . and with it goes the responsibility for helping our children prepare for tomorrow's world.

Massachusetts Mutual Life Insurance Company
ORGANIZED 1851
Springfield, Massachusetts

▲

Norman Rockwell, an American painter and illustrator, is known for his depictions of everyday life. Many of his illustrations are featured in advertisements for Mass Mutual Life Insurance. In this 1960 ad, a family is kneeling at church.

———

The language of the advertisement relies on faith: in our "forefathers," family, and future. What does the advertisement reveal about the role of faith in America's culture?

RHETORICAL SITUATION

1. Who is the **writer**? How does his relationship with God affect the text?

2. What is the writer's **message**? Does the message remain relevant today? Why or why not?

CLAIMS AND EVIDENCE

3. The writer uses personal testimony as **evidence**. Explain the effect of the testimony.

4. What is the **perspective** presented in the text? How does the perspective of young Langston Hughes differ from the congregation's? Explain how these perspectives contribute to the complexity of the message.

REASONING AND ORGANIZATION

5. How does Hughes's personal experience create and support the **message**?

6. What is the **narrative** arc of this account? What is the tension or conflict? Describe the beginning, middle, and end of the narrative.

LANGUAGE AND STYLE

7. What is the **tone** of the text? How does the writer's **diction** contribute to this tone?

8. Describe the language in paragraph 14. Explain how the **connotations** of specific words contribute to the writer's message.

IDEAS IN AMERICAN CULTURE

9. Hughes recalls a moment in church that many Christians have experienced. Explain how the ideas of faith and fear influence the behaviors of both Hughes and the congregation. How do these ideas work to create a message that still applies today?

PUTTING IT ALL TOGETHER

10. How does Hughes's experience — and his organization of that experience in the text — shape his message and influence his readers?

COMPOSITION WORKSHOP
Writing a Narrative

Personal narratives are autobiographical accounts of specific events in our lives. But for a personal story to engage readers effectively, it must convey an insight that a wider audience can identify with. In effective narratives, writers select details that reveal this insight and help communicate a message to the audience. For most writers, insight into an experience often comes with time and reflection. Getting some perspective on the event not only allows the writer to describe and narrate with more objectivity but also provides an opportunity for the writers to understand the true importance of an experience or event. In this workshop, you will have the opportunity to develop a narrative that shares insight about a significant event in your own life.

KEY POINT

When developing ideas through narration, writers offer details about real-life experiences and offer reflections and insights on the significance of those experiences.

from This I Believe
Brighton Earley

The following student model of a personal narrative was written as a submission to the long-running *This I Believe* program on National Public Radio by Brighton Earley, a senior at Immaculate Heart High School in Los Angeles. She is editor in chief of her school newspaper and founder and editor of a student literary/arts magazine.

Every Friday night the cashier at the Chevron gas station food mart on Eagle Rock Boulevard and Avenue 40 offers us a discount on all the leftover apples and bananas. To ensure the best selection possible, my mother and I pile into our 20-year-old car and pull up to the food mart at 5 p.m. on the dot, ready to get our share of slightly over-ripe fruits.

details and connotative language about the car and the store engage the audience

Before the times of the Chevron food mart, there were the times of the calculator. My mother would carefully prop it up in the cart's child seat and frown as she entered each price. Since the first days of the calculator's appearance, the worry lines on my mother's face have only grown deeper.

writer begins with history of shopping activities

Today, they are a permanent fixture. Chevron shopping started like this: One day my mother suddenly realized that she had maxed out almost every credit card, and we needed groceries for the week. The only credit card she hadn't maxed out was the Chevron card, and the station on Eagle Rock Boulevard has a pretty big mart attached to it.

writer shares moments that serve as the basis for the narrative controlling idea of flexibility is first introduced —

Since our first visit there, I've learned to believe in flexibility. In my life, it has become necessary to bend the idea of grocery shopping. My mother and I can no longer shop at real grocery stores, but we still get the necessities.

writer provides details about the conflict and conveys her attitude

Grocery shopping at Chevron has its drawbacks. The worst is when we have so many items that it takes the checker what seems like hours to ring up everything. A line of anxious customers forms behind us. It's that line that hurts the most—the way they look at us. My mother never notices—or maybe she pretends not to.

writer continues with details that show a shift from information to emotion (discomfort/ embarrassment)

I never need to be asked to help the checker bag all the items. No one wants to get out of there faster than I do. I'm embarrassed to shop there, and I'm deathly afraid of running into someone I know. I once expressed my fear of being seen shopping at Chevron to my mother and her eyes shone with disappointment. I know that I hurt her feelings when I try to evade our weekly shopping trips.

And that is why I hold on to the idea of flexibility so tightly.

writer concludes with her claim that flexibility allows a person to overcome difficulties and to have hope

I believe that being flexible keeps me going—keeps me from being ashamed of the way my family is different from other families. Whenever I feel the heat rise to my face, I remind myself that grocery shopping at a gas station is just a twist on the normal kind of grocery shopping. I remind myself that we won't always have to shop at Chevron—that just because at this point in my life I am struggling does not mean that I will always struggle. My belief in flexibility helps me get through the difficult times because I know that no matter what happens, my mother and I will always figure out a way to survive.

 YOUR ASSIGNMENT

Imagine that you have been invited to share a meaningful personal experience in a vlog. To prepare, consider a pivotal event (or a series of events) in your life that led to one of the following experiences:

- You first came to believe something that you still believe today.
- You stopped believing something that you previously held to be true.

Make sure that your organization and style reflect the intensity of the moment, as well as the importance of the idea.

In this workshop, you will work through the steps of pre-writing, drafting, and publishing a multiparagraph personal narrative in which you recount the moment that led you to this realization.

Your narrative should include

- a clear message connected to an idea that conveys an understanding or insight;
- a narrative arc that includes a beginning, middle, and end;
- a defensible thesis statement with supporting evidence; and
- carefully selected diction that conveys a tone.

RHETORICAL SITUATION Creating a Message

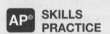 **Enduring Understanding (RHS-1)**

Individuals write within a particular situation and make strategic writing choices based on that situation.

In your personal narrative, your goal is to communicate your understanding or message, not just write "what happened." For example, if you simply recall the sequence of events of a day at an amusement park, your narrative will have little point—and little effect on your readers. But if you focus on how you turned your fear of riding roller coasters into exhilaration when you finally rode one, you express a broader message to the audience about confronting fears. In this moment, you (the writer), your audience, and your message work together as elements of the rhetorical situation.

AP® SKILLS PRACTICE	RHETORICAL SITUATION **Creating a Message**

Reflect on moments in your life that resulted in a new understanding and then choose a unifying idea and perspective and draft the message that you want to communicate in your narrative. For example, in Brighton Earley's narrative, she recounts her experiences with shopping at Chevron to communicate that flexibility helped her overcome her difficulties.

If you are having trouble getting started, try to recall moments in your life when you had the following experiences, which often lead to new insights:

- You learned a new skill.
- You had a thrilling adventure.
- You lost a family member or friend.
- You made a new friend.
- You overcame a fear.

Just remember that your message and your narrative account of the experience must align.

Message with Unifying Idea	Related Experiences

REASONING AND ORGANIZATION   Creating Unity

AP® Enduring Understanding (REO-1)

Writers guide understanding of a text's line of reasoning and claims through that text's organization and integration of evidence.

When you write a personal narrative, you will find it helpful to begin with the end in mind: that is, you should think about the unifying idea that will control your story and your message. This unifying idea will guide your narrative; it will also underlie your claims and your message. The idea anchors the relevant details of the narrative to the claim. Let's return to the previous bulleted prompts and connect them to ideas:

- You learned a new skill: perseverance
- You had a thrilling adventure: confidence
- You lost a family member or friend: grief
- You made a new friend: acceptance
- You overcame a fear: courage

If you share a story about overcoming your fear of roller coasters, for instance, your idea is *courage*, not *roller coasters*. So your audience does not need to know every detail from your day, only those directly associated with courage and the message about facing your fear.

In later units, we will explore different approaches to organizing arguments. For the personal narrative, focus on presenting the events and the details in chronological order. This organization allows you to build suspense leading up to your realization. So the beginning of the narrative will introduce the situation and conflict (the set-up); the middle will explore the conflict or problem, including specific details to develop the story (the blow-up); the ending will resolve the conflict and share your deeper understanding (the wrap-up).

 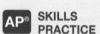 **SKILLS PRACTICE** | REASONING AND ORGANIZATION
Establishing a Unifying Idea

1. Using your message from the previous activity, identify your unifying idea.
2. Record details and notes from your experience in the proper column. Notes should contain both events and reflections on the events.

Message:		
Unifying Idea:		
The Set-Up (Beginning)	The Blow-Up (Middle)	The Wrap-Up (End)

CLAIMS AND EVIDENCE Developing and Supporting a Thesis

AP Enduring Understanding (CLE-1)

Writers make claims about subjects, rely on evidence that supports the reasoning that justifies the claim, and often acknowledge or respond to other, possibly opposing, arguments.

Because you have experienced — and reflected on — the events in your narrative, you know your message and unifying idea. In other words, you know what you've learned as a result of your experience. Personal narratives often begin with the writer sharing the details of the experience and then conclude with a claim. As this form of writing is subjective and complex, the major claim may be implied rather than stated directly. Remember: whether it is an explicit epiphany or more of a subtle suggestion, you must have a claim. Without this element, your narrative is a diary entry. But if your details and evidence lead readers to connect with an idea (e.g., overcoming a fear, experiencing independence), then you will be able to engage your audience and express your message.

Sample Thesis Statements	Effectiveness
Going to Disneyland was a fun vacation.	INEFFECTIVE: It has no reference to an idea or message; it only focuses on the experience.
There are many reasons we should face our fears.	INEFFECTIVE: The phrase *many reasons* is vague; it names an idea but does not include a message or a reference to the experience.
When we allow courage to guide our actions rather than fear, we often discover the depth of our true potential.	EFFECTIVE: It relates to the idea (courage). It connects the experience (facing fear) and the message.

Once you have established your thesis, you need to include specific evidence for support. In a personal narrative, evidence connects the specific details of the story to the message. You will include details that help you convey the idea and perspective of your claim. These details are relevant because they specifically help your audience focus on your key message. That means you will probably have to leave out many more details than you include. But if you have a clear understanding of your claim and message, keep both in mind: they will help you select the necessary details by limiting your focus.

So review your notes from your planning of the set-up, the blow-up, and the wrap-up. You can share your specific evidence using anecdotes, analogies, examples, details, illustrations, personal observations, or personal experiences. Just make sure each supports the claim and message.

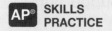

AP® SKILLS PRACTICE | CLAIMS AND PRACTICE
Developing and Supporting a Thesis

As you continue the process, review the message and unifying idea that you wish to convey to your audience, along with the notes about your pivotal moment that you brainstormed on page 66.

Write a thesis that includes your idea and message on a subject.

Record details that are relevant to your unifying idea and message, which you can use as evidence.

Identifying Thesis and Supporting Evidence

Subject	Claim Perspective + Unifying Idea
	Evidence

LANGUAGE AND STYLE Conveying an Attitude

AP® Enduring Understanding (STL-1)

The rhetorical situation informs the strategic stylistic choices that writers make.

With your idea and message clear, and your evidence selected, it is time for you to show, not just tell your story. To do this, you must evoke the experience for the audience with well-chosen details and vivid language that guide readers to the final claim.

How is this done? Every writer's voice is distinctive, so no single rule applies to all writers and all rhetorical situations. But evocative personal narratives usually include strong verb choices, striking figurative language, and vivid imagery. Similarly, your audience should have a clear sense of your attitude (sincere, positive, somber, comic) from the tone of your writing. If your readers can infer your attitude from your rhetorical choices, they are more likely to understand your message. Consider the following two sentences:

Telling: I was so scared when I got on the roller coaster.

Showing: As my heart pounded and my legs shook like wet noodles, I inched toward the rocket of doom, terrified that this would be my first and last adventure in the Magic Kingdom.

In the first sentence, the writer simply tells the audience she was scared. With only denotative, imprecise language. The writer does not convey the intensity of the experience. In fact, readers have no idea whether she was excited or upset about being afraid of the ride. However, in the "showing" sentence, the writer vividly re-creates the moment by including connotative diction (*inched, terrified*), images (*heart pounded, legs shook*), and figurative language (*like wet noodles, rocket of doom*). These rhetorical choices show that the writer's fear was real — and perhaps even evokes similar fears in the reader.

SKILLS PRACTICE | LANGUAGE AND STYLE
Conveying an Attitude

Draft the details of your narrative. Start by writing a few "telling" sentences as notes and then revise them to include "showing" language. When you are finished with your draft, it should include the precise details of your experience in the beginning and middle of your narrative while providing more reflective language related to your message in the conclusion. Check to make sure that all your details and insights not only connect to your unifying idea but also convey your intended message.

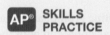

SKILLS PRACTICE | PUTTING IT ALL TOGETHER
Revising and Editing a Narrative

Peer Revision Checklist: Revising and Editing a Narrative		
Questions to Consider	Unit One Focus Skills	Comment on the Effectiveness and/or Make a Suggestion
Does the claim in the introduction or conclusion convey the writer's message and connect it to an idea that serves to unify the narrative?	*Narrative*	
Are the details of the narrative arranged in an appropriate order for the audience?	*Details connected to idea*	
Are all the details the writer included relevant to the unifying idea? Do the details in the story lead to insight and reflection that convey a deeper understanding of the idea?	*Message*	
Has the writer crafted the narrative with effective diction that conveys the writer's tone and attitude?	*Diction for attitude connotation/ denotation*	
Is the writing free of errors in spelling, punctuation, capitalization, and other writing conventions?	*Punctuating syntactical features*	

⌐⌐⌐
⌐⌐⌐
⌐⌐⌐   PREPARING FOR THE AP® EXAM
⌐⌐⌐   **Free-Response Question:**
⌐⌐⌐   **Rhetorical Analysis**
⌐⌐⌐

Writing and Supporting a Defensible Thesis

When you take the Advanced Placement® English Language and Composition Exam, one of the free-response questions, commonly known as the rhetorical analysis question, will require you to read a nonfiction text and explain how the writer employs rhetorical strategies to develop a message. This workshop will take you through the first steps of completing this task.

→ **Step One: Annotate the Passage Based on a Unifying Idea**

Before you begin to write, you must first understand the writing prompt and what it is asking you to do. Then, you will read the passage and take notes on both the writer's rhetorical choices and the writer's purpose and message.

A rhetorical analysis prompt has <u>two</u> important tasks:

1. to describe the writer's message and
2. to explain how the writer conveys that message through his or her choices.

In the exam's prompt wording, you will see the following common elements:

- Background or context on the rhetorical situation
- An instruction for you to write an essay that requires you to
  - analyze the writer's rhetorical choices
  - explain how the rhetorical choices connect to the writer's purpose or message

Let's look at an example and break down the prompt:

Prompt:

background/context — Writing at the age of seventy-seven, Benjamin Franklin (1706–1790) recounts his experience as a twenty-two-year-old seeking to live a life without fault and full of virtue. In the following excerpt from ***The Autobiography,*** Franklin details his plan for moral perfection. Read

writing task — the passage carefully. Write an essay that analyzes **Franklin's rhetorical choices** and explains how they develop **his message about striving for**

writer's message — **perfection.**

In your response, you should do the following:

- Respond to the prompt with a thesis that analyzes the writer's rhetorical choices.
- Select and use evidence to develop and support your line of reasoning.
- Explain how the evidence supports your line of reasoning.
- Demonstrate an understanding of the rhetorical situation.
- Use appropriate grammar and punctuation in your argument.

Read the passage once to record notes related to a unifying idea you have identified. You will notice that the idea is often suggested in the prompt. Focus on the writer's unifying idea and message in the passage. When annotating, you should underline or highlight words, phrases, or parts of the text that relate to the unifying idea and the writer's claim (idea and perspective), rather than merely identifying all the rhetorical devices a writer uses.

In order to respond effectively to the prompt, you will need to explain *how* the rhetorical choices a writer makes helps him or her convey the message to the intended audience. In your annotations, you should not only label a writer's choices but also record the effects of the choices. You will see this method demonstrated for you in each unit of this book through modeled texts.

 INSIDER AP TIP   **Your annotations should be guided by an idea.** For one effective method of annotating a text, you can use the left margin for recording observations about the idea and message. Then, use the right margin for noting rhetorical choices and their effects.

→ **Step Two: Develop a Defensible Claim with a Unifying Idea**

Once you have annotated the passage, you will begin to plan your essay. To do this, you need a clear defensible thesis statement that conveys the writer's idea and message. It may also connect to the writer's rhetorical choices. Your close-reading notes will inform your choices in developing your thesis statement. Your goal is to analyze how the writer's choices convey the message, so review the possible evidence you might incorporate as you plan your analysis.

A word of caution: a thesis statement that does not relate the writer's message is not defensible. Consider this thesis statement:

Ineffective: In his "I Have a Dream" speech, Martin Luther King Jr. uses rhetorical devices to relate his message.

In this example, the student writer does not relate the message or explain how it is conveyed.

Consider these templates to help you compose a **defensible thesis statement**:

Thesis Templates	Model Thesis Statements from Martin Luther King Jr.'s Famous "I Have a Dream" Speech
[The writer] [strong verb for analysis] [message related to the idea].	By contrasting the current state of discord in the country with his dream for a better future in America, Martin Luther King Jr. **contends** that the only way the U.S. can achieve peace is by eradicating its racial discrimination and hatred.
[Writer] in order to [strong verb for analysis] that [message related to the idea].	Martin Luther King Jr. contrasts the current state of discord in the country with his dream for a better future in America to **argue** that the only way America can achieve peace is to eradicate its racial discrimination and hatred.
In his/her speech/letter/essay, [writer] [strong verb for analysis] [message related to idea].	In his pivotal speech, Martin Luther King Jr. **asserts** that the only way to achieve the dream of peace in this country is for Americans to work together to end racial discrimination and hatred.

STRONG VERBS TO CONVEY A WRITER'S PURPOSE

affirms	eulogizes	proves
appeals	highlights	provokes
argues	illustrates	questions
asserts	implores	realizes
claims	insists	reflects
challenges	memorializes	represents
complains	opposes	reveals
contends	persuades	reminds
convinces	pleads	urges
emphasizes	proposes	

With your thesis statement established, you can generate reasons to support your claim. For the rhetorical analysis task, these reasons are often guided by the writer's strategies; therefore, examine your annotations for the overarching strategies in the passage. For example, does the writer contrast something or shift from one idea to another? Does the writer pose a question and answer it or describe a problem and offer a solution? You will group your evidence to support reasons by examining how the writer builds his or her argument to support the overall message. Consider the following example.

Thesis:

In his pivotal speech, Martin Luther King Jr. **asserts** that the only way to achieve the dream of peace in this country is for Americans to work together to end racial discrimination and hatred.

Reason One	Reason Two
Martin Luther King Jr. includes historical evidence to illustrate the painful effects of racial discrimination.	Martin Luther King Jr. draws upon figurative representations to encourage Americans to end the hatred and seek peace for the good of all Americans.

→ **Step Three: Choose Relevant Evidence**

With your claim and reasons in order, you can begin choosing and organizing your evidence into the appropriate supporting (or body) paragraphs. Within each paragraph, select evidence to support your reason and the unifying idea within your claim. In other words, evidence should be used as part of your commentary to explain the rhetorical function or effect in relation to the claim. Evidence should not merely illustrate or exemplify isolated rhetorical devices.

In the model reasons from Step Two, for instance, you will select evidence that supports the reasons directly. While King's speech has many interesting rhetorical features, for this analysis, you will include examples of historical evidence from the speech to support King's first reason related to the effects of discrimination. For the second body paragraph, you will include evidence of figurative language to support King's vision for the future. If your evidence supports your reasons and your reasons support your thesis, your organization will contribute to a unified analysis.

When using textual evidence, you may summarize, paraphrase, or use direct quotation. When you quote directly from the passage, you should embed the text using short phrases rather than quoting a large chunk of text. Note the three examples here of incorporating text within a paragraph.

Examples from Martin Luther King Jr.'s "I Have a Dream" Speech	Notes on Effectiveness
"I have a dream that my four little children will one day live in a nation where they will not be judged by the color of their skin but by the content of their character."	INEFFECTIVE: *Merely drops the full quotation in the paragraphs*
In his speech, **Reverend King says,** "I have a dream that my four little children will one day live in a nation where they will not be judged by the color of their skin but by the content of their character."	ADEQUATE: *Provides a signal phrase for the readers to introduce the quotation*

(continued)

Examples from Martin Luther King Jr.'s "I Have a Dream" Speech	Notes on Effectiveness
In his speech, Reverend King incorporates contrast when he expresses his dream that one day his children and all Black citizens will no longer be judged by the **"color of their skin"** but instead considered for the **"content of their character."**	EFFECTIVE: *Embeds short phrases from the speech and weaves them grammatically to achieve fluency*

→ **Step Four: Develop Your Commentary**

Including evidence to support your reasons is not enough. You will need to explain its relevance which means linking it to the idea in your claim. In subsequent units, you will practice writing effective commentary.

PREPARING FOR THE AP® EXAM

The following prompt is an example of a rhetorical analysis free-response question. Practice the skills you have learned in this workshop to complete the following:

1. Write a **thesis statement** in response to the prompt for *The Autobiography* by Benjamin Franklin.

2. Make a list of **evidence** from the passage that will both support your thesis statement and connect to Franklin's idea and **message**.

3. Briefly explain how each piece of **evidence** connects to the idea in your **claim**.

Prompt:
Writing at the age of seventy-seven, Benjamin Franklin (1706–1790) recounts his experience as a twenty-two-year-old seeking to live a life without fault and full of virtue. In the following excerpt from *The Autobiography*, Franklin details his plan for moral perfection. Read the passage carefully. Write an essay that analyzes Franklin's rhetorical choices and explains how they develop his message about striving for perfection.

In your response, you should do the following:

- Respond to the prompt with a thesis that analyzes the writer's rhetorical choices.

- Select and use evidence to develop and support your line of reasoning.

- Explain how the evidence supports your line of reasoning.

- Demonstrate an understanding of the rhetorical situation.

- Use appropriate grammar and punctuation in your argument.

from The Autobiography of Benjamin Franklin
Benjamin Franklin

It was about this time I conceiv'd the bold and arduous project of arriving at moral perfection. I wish'd to live without committing any fault at any time; I would conquer all that either natural inclination, custom, or company might lead me into. As I knew, or thought I knew, what was right and wrong, I did not see why I might not always do the one and avoid the other. But I soon found I had undertaken a task of more difficulty than I had imagined. While my care was employ'd in guarding against one fault, I was often surprised by another; habit took the advantage of inattention; inclination was sometimes too strong for reason. I concluded, at length, that the mere speculative conviction that it was our interest to be completely virtuous, was not sufficient to prevent our slipping; and that the contrary habits must be broken, and good ones acquired and established, before we can have any dependence on a steady, uniform rectitude of conduct. For this purpose I therefore contrived the following method. . . .

. . . I proposed to myself, for the sake of clearness, to use rather more names, with fewer ideas annex'd to each, than a few names with more ideas; and I included under thirteen names of virtues all that at that time occurred to me as necessary or desirable, and annexed to each a short precept, which fully express'd the extent I gave to its meaning.

These names of virtues, with their precepts, were:

1. Temperance.
Eat not to dullness; drink not to elevation.

2. Silence.
Speak not but what may benefit others or yourself; avoid trifling conversation.

3. Order.
Let all your things have their places; let each part of your business have its time.

4. Resolution.
Resolve to perform what you ought; perform without fail what you resolve.

5. Frugality.
Make no expense but to do good to others or yourself; i.e., waste nothing.

6. Industry.
Lose no time; be always employ'd in something useful; cut off all unnecessary actions.

7. Sincerity.
Use no hurtful deceit; think innocently and justly, and, if you speak, speak accordingly.

8. Justice.
Wrong none by doing injuries, or omitting the benefits that are your duty.

9. Moderation.
Avoid extremes; forbear resenting injuries so much as you think they deserve.

10. Cleanliness.
Tolerate no uncleanliness in body, cloaths, or habitation.

11. Tranquillity.
Be not disturbed at trifles, or at accidents common or unavoidable.

12. Chastity.
Rarely use venery but for health or offspring, never to dulness, weakness, or the injury of your own or another's peace or reputation.

13. Humility.
Imitate Jesus and Socrates.

. . . I made a little book, in which I allotted a page for each of the virtues. I rul'd each page with red ink, so as to have seven columns, one for each day of the week, marking each column with a letter for the day. I cross'd these columns with thirteen red lines, marking the beginning of each line with the first letter of one of the virtues, on which line, and in its proper column, I might mark, by a little black spot, every fault I found upon examination to have been committed respecting that virtue upon that day.

My scheme of Order gave me the most trouble; and I found that, tho' it might be practicable where a man's business was such as to leave him the disposition of his time, that of a journeyman printer, for instance, it was not possible to be exactly observed by a master, who must mix with the world, and often receive people of business at their own hours. Order, too, with regard to places for things, papers, etc., I found extremely difficult to acquire. I had not been early accustomed to it, and, having an exceeding good memory, I was not so sensible of the inconvenience attending want of method. This article, therefore, cost me so much painful

5

attention, and my faults in it vexed me so much, and I made so little progress in amendment, and had such frequent relapses, that I was almost ready to give up the attempt, and content myself with a faulty character in that respect, like the man who, in buying an ax of a smith, my neighbour, desired to have the whole of its surface as bright as the edge. The smith consented to grind it bright for him if he would turn the wheel; he turn'd, while the smith press'd the broad face of the ax hard and heavily on the stone, which made the turning of it very fatiguing. The man came every now and then from the wheel to see how the work went on, and at length would take his ax as it was, without farther grinding. "No," said the smith, "turn on, turn on; we shall have it bright by-and-by; as yet, it is only speckled." "Yes," said the man, "*but I think I like a speckled ax best.*" And I believe this may have been the case with many, who, having, for want of some such means as I employ'd, found the difficulty of obtaining good and breaking bad habits in other points of vice and virtue, have given up the struggle, and concluded that "a speckled ax was best." . . .

The Danger of a Single Story
Chimamanda Ngozi Adichie

My mother says that I started reading at the age of two, although I think four is probably close to the truth. So I was an early reader, and what I read were British and American children's books. [1]

I was also an early writer, and when I began to write, at about the age of seven, stories in pencil with crayon illustrations that my poor mother was obligated to read, I wrote exactly the kinds of stories I was reading: All my characters were white and blue-eyed, they played in the snow, they ate apples, and they talked a lot about the weather, how lovely it was that the sun had come out. [2]

Now, this despite the fact that I lived in Nigeria. I had never been outside Nigeria. We didn't have snow, we ate mangoes, and we never talked about the weather, because there was no need to. My characters also drank a lot of ginger beer, because the characters in the British books I read drank ginger beer. Never mind that I had no idea what ginger beer was. And for many years afterwards, I would have a desperate desire to taste ginger beer. But that is another story. [3]

What this demonstrates, I think, is how impressionable and vulnerable we are in the face of a story, particularly as children. Because all I had read were books in which characters were foreign, I had become convinced that books by their very nature had to have foreigners in them and had to be about things with which I could not personally identify. Now, things changed when I discovered African books. There weren't [4] many of them available, and they weren't quite as easy to find as the foreign books.

But because of writers like Chinua Achebe and Camara Laye, I went through a mental shift in my perception of literature. I realized that people like me, girls with skin the color of chocolate, whose kinky hair could not form ponytails, could also exist in literature. I started to write about things I recognized. [5]

Now, I loved those American and British books I read. They stirred my imagination. They opened up new worlds for me. But the unintended consequence was that I did not know that people like me could exist in literature. So what the discovery of African writers did for me was this: It saved me from having a single story of what books are. [6]

I come from a conventional, middle-class Nigerian family. My father was a professor. My mother was an administrator. And so we had, as was the norm, live-in domestic help, who would often come from nearby rural villages. So, the year I turned eight, we got a new house boy. His name was Fide. The only thing my mother told us about him was that his family was very poor. My mother sent yams and rice, and our old clothes, to his family. And when I didn't finish my dinner, my mother would say, "Finish your food! Don't you know? People like Fide's family have nothing." So I felt enormous pity for Fide's family. [7]

Then one Saturday, we went to his village to visit, and his mother showed us a beautifully patterned basket made of dyed raffia that his [8] brother had made. I was startled. It had not occurred to me that anybody in his family could actually make something. All I had heard about them was how poor they were, so that it had become impossible for me to see them as anything else but poor. Their poverty was my single story of them.

Years later, I thought about this when I left 9 Nigeria to go to university in the United States. I was 19. My American roommate was shocked by me. She asked where I had learned to speak English so well, and was confused when I said that Nigeria happened to have English as its official language. She asked if she could listen to what she called my "tribal music," and was consequently very disappointed when I produced my tape of Mariah Carey.

She assumed that I did not know how to use 10 a stove.

What struck me was this: She had felt sorry 11 for me even before she saw me. Her default position toward me, as an African, was a kind of patronizing, well-meaning pity. My roommate had a single story of Africa: a single story of catastrophe. In this single story, there was no possibility of Africans being similar to her in any way, no possibility of feelings more complex than pity, no possibility of a connection as human equals.

1. The writer's account of her mother stating she "started reading at the age of two" (paragraph 1) supports which of the following claims about the one story?
   (A) It is often backed up by facts.
   (B) It rarely affects people from outside the United States.
   (C) It particularly affects children because they are so impressionable.
   (D) It can only be noticed by people who experience international travel.
   (E) It may not be harmful.

2. In paragraph 5, the writer mentions writers Chinua Achebe and Camara Laye in order to
   (A) disprove the claim that Africans are not civilized.
   (B) demonstrate the importance of reading writers who tell stories about things people can recognize from their own life.
   (C) show the effect of quoting an authority in a text.
   (D) argue that Nigerians do read literature and books, despite the Western perception that they do not or cannot.
   (E) explain why most Western stories include only limited perspectives on Africa.

3. In paragraph 6, the writer recalls that she "loved those American and British books" and that they "stirred [her] imagination" in order to
   (A) contrast the images of the writer's trip to Mexico.
   (B) emphasize the dangers of one story.
   (C) prove the power stories have to damage people.
   (D) show that the story always gets more respect than the storyteller, despite the story's origin.
   (E) demonstrate the effects of books encountered early in life.

4. In order to demonstrate that anyone of any age is susceptible to the dangers of hearing one story about others, the writer references which of the following personal experiences?
   (A) Her mother reading her stories as a child (paragraph 2)
   (B) Her "mental shift" from reading writers like Chinua Achebe and Camara Laye (paragraph 5)
   (C) What she heard about Fide's village from her mother (paragraph 7)
   (D) Her family's visit to Fide's village (paragraphs 7 and 8)
   (E) Her experience with her college roommate (paragraphs 9–11)

5. Which of the following best describes the writer's purpose for including the anecdote about her college roommate in paragraphs 9–11?
   (A) She wishes to avoid discussing the problems that Nigerians face and only mention the things that are successful.
   (B) She is attempting to encourage other people to travel beyond their home country in order to better understand people from different backgrounds.
   (C) She is trying to suggest that Nigeria is as advanced and progressive as any non-African country.
   (D) She wants to demonstrate her roommate's ignorance and unwillingness to educate herself beyond what she had learned from Western stories.
   (E) She seeks to demonstrate how others can be affected by "one story" and the consequences of accepting the "one story" as the complete reality.

6. Which of the following best describes the writer's exigence in the passage for her concerns about one story?
   (A) Visiting the village where her family's house boy — Fide — lived.
   (B) Finally leaving Nigeria.
   (C) Finally getting to taste ginger beer and realizing it was not something she was supposed to enjoy.
   (D) Coming to the United States and realizing that her roommate's perspective of Africans had been shaped by the Western stories she had heard about Africa.
   (E) Exposure to African writers like Chinua Achebe and Camara Laye.

7. The passage makes use of all of the following types of evidence EXCEPT
   (A) Personal experience
   (B) Anecdotes
   (C) Examples
   (D) Experiments
   (E) Personal observations

8. In the passage, the writer makes which of the following claims about one story?
   (A) The British and American books she read saved her from the narrow-minded perspective of a single story.
   (B) Developing an authentic perspective on cultures and countries relies on understanding the one story told about them and how that story represents them and their world.
   (C) One story reflects the kind of paradise that cultures and countries want other people to see.
   (D) One story supports stereotypes that may be true but are incomplete because the one story often fails to represent the complexities and nuances of the world it depicts.
   (E) Having one story can unify and dignify all of humanity under a common narrative.

9. The writer is primarily concerned with
    addressing which of the following issues?
    (A) Though it is easy for us to accept one
        story about a place or a people, there is
        never just one story to be told.
    (B) A single story is easier for the people to
        accept.
    (C) Despite the importance of hearing more
        than one story, we eventually need to
        settle on one story to accept.
    (D) Concerns she has for children in her
        native Nigeria who may not have access
        to the same British stories to which she
        had access as a child.
    (E) Education around the world does little
        to help students understand experiences
        beyond their own.

PREPARING FOR THE AP® EXAM
Multiple-Choice Questions: Writing

The passage below is a draft.

(1) Ancient myths and stories of Greece and Rome have given contemporary American English many terms. (2) For example, the term *Trojan Horse* — a trick used by the Greeks to invade and destroy the city of Troy — is now a term for a computer virus that tricks the user into downloading it only to then attack the computer. (3) But it is not just the Greeks and the Romans who have influenced our language. (4) Understanding the various origin stories of these terms can help us also know where those terms came from and possibly even better understand ourselves.

(5) A term finds its way into English from another language because it describes something that English has trouble describing with few words. (6) *Avatar* is one such term. (7) Even before the 2009 film *Avatar* was one of the biggest money-making films of all time, the word was familiar to gamers and social media users who created digital figures to represent themselves. (8) This term is thousands of years old and comes from Hindu India, where it refers to a god that comes to earth in human form. (9) Having borrowed this from Hindu culture, we can now use one term to capture the entire idea of creating a form that allows you to interact in another world.

(10) Fans of Halloween and certain horror movies will be familiar with another example of a common term in contemporary American English. (11) *Zombie*, a term for creatures once living but now wandering the earth as "living dead," emerged in the seventeenth century from a religion practiced by enslaved Africans in Haiti. (12) However, the term may be centuries older and from further away. (13) It likely evolved from the much older Bantu culture of central Africa and their term *nzambi*, the name for a creator

god and a term for the dual nature of a person's soul: both living and dead in the earthly life and afterlife. (14) Again, a culture and language far removed from English has found a way to express a very complex idea with a simple term.

(15) There really is not a way to briefly explain these ideas in English, so these terms and others like them have been borrowed and have now become a part of everyday American English. (16) When we better understand these words, then we better understand their meaning.

1. The writer is considering adding the following sentence after sentence 3.

   A study by the publishers of the Oxford English Dictionary found that, while 90 percent of English comes from just a few other places, including Greece and Rome, 10 percent comes from languages and cultures that many of us are much less familiar with.

   Should the writer add this sentence after sentence 3?

   (A) Yes, because it provides expert testimony in support of the idea developed by the rest of the passage.
   (B) Yes, because it provides statistics that expand on the idea expressed in sentence 3 and that will develop throughout the passage.
   (C) Yes, because it limits the number of terms being addressed, which narrows the focus of the passage.
   (D) No, because it includes statistics that have not been verified.
   (E) No, because it fails to explain why 10 percent of words are important to the development of the passage.

2. Which version of the underlined text in sentence 4 (reproduced below) provides the most effective claim to set up the discussion that follows in the passage?

    Understanding the various origin stories of these terms can help us also know where those terms came from and possibly even better understand ourselves.

    (A) (as it is now)
    (B) define these terms based on English usage
    (C) plan how to preserve English
    (D) resist cultural changes to English
    (E) understand the cultures that gave them to us

3. In sentence 5 (reproduced below), the writer wants to add the phrase "as many linguists have pointed out" to the beginning of the sentence, adjusting capitalization as needed.

    A term finds its way into English from another language because it describes something that English has trouble describing with few words.

    Should the writer make this addition?

    (A) Yes, because it provides an additional perspective to set up a counterargument.
    (B) Yes, because it acknowledges an expert source beyond the writer.
    (C) Yes, because it introduces a key figure in the development of the passage's argument.
    (D) No, because it introduces new evidence that requires an adjustment to the paragraph's line of reasoning.
    (E) No, because it fails to consider the rhetorical situation of the argument.

4. The writer would like to introduce the information in sentence 13 (reproduced below) in a way that best relates it to the argument presented in the passage.

    It likely evolved from the much older Bantu culture of central Africa and their term nzambi, *the name for a creator god and also a term for the dual nature of a person's soul: both living and dead in the earthly life and afterlife.*

    Which of the following versions of the underlined portion of sentence 13 best supports this goal?

    (A) (as it is now)
    (B) Historical accounts seem to show that it evolved from other African words, but those accounts are unclear about the term *nzambi*.
    (C) *Nzambi* was an African word.
    (D) *Zombie* likely evolved from the word *nzambi*.
    (E) Linguists are at odds over the significance of the term and whether it relates at all to the term *nzambi*.

5. The writer is considering revising sentence 16 (reproduced below) to more clearly state an effective claim that provokes interest, requires a defense, and aligns with other statements in the passage.

When we better understand these words, then we better understand their meaning.

Which of the following best accomplishes this goal?

(A) (as it is now)
(B) Languages are complex and the way they borrow terms from other languages can indicate a lot about the failures of a language's speakers.
(C) When we better understand other cultures and the languages they speak, then we learn how those cultures think about the world we all share.
(D) Developing empathy for those who are not like us depends on seeking to better understand their experiences and ideas.
(E) When we better understand the origin stories of such terms, then we also better understand ourselves and the people and cultures we borrowed them from.

Ollie Millington/Getty Images

UNIT

2

Appealing to an Audience

n Unit 1, you learned that writers create messages to share their ideas and perspectives with an audience. This relationship between writer and audience is part of the rhetorical situation. In this unit, we'll look more closely at the tools writers use to influence and appeal to their audiences.

When we see an issue that calls for change or action, we begin the process of persuasion. We start to think about how to change people's minds or inspire people to act. This means we must understand the rhetorical situation and use it to our advantage. We need a clear purpose, an intended audience, relevant evidence to support our claims, and a well-crafted message to inspire the audience to listen and act. The most persuasive writers take all of these elements into account: the writing situation provides guideposts for crafting an argument that both fulfills its purpose and suits the specific audience.

UNIT GOALS

	Unit Focus	Reading, Analyzing, and Interpreting	Writing
Big Idea: Rhetorical Situation	**Considering the Audience**	Explain how a writer appeals to a particular audience's background and values.	Analyze an audience's background and values to relate, connect, or influence a specific audience.
Big Idea: Claims and Evidence	**Relevant and Sufficient Evidence**	Identify evidence that supports a specific line of reasoning.	Select evidence that supports the writer's claim (i.e., idea and perspective).
Big Idea: Reasoning and Organization	**Persuasion**	Evaluate the effectiveness of inductive and deductive logic.	Write a persuasive argument for a specific audience, purpose, and context.
Big Idea: Language and Style	**Syntactical Choices for Effect**	Explain how a writer uses rhetorical devices of syntax to emphasize ideas and information.	Employ syntactical choices to emphasize ideas and information.
Ideas in American Culture	• **Reason and Revolution** • **Patriotism and Democracy**	Explain how the ideas of reason, revolution, patriotism, and democracy are reflected in classic and contemporary American texts.	
Preparing for the AP® Exam	• **Free Response: Argument** • **Multiple Choice**	Analyze rhetorical choices in classic and contemporary nonfiction texts.	Develop a thesis statement and line of reasoning for an argument essay.

Considering the Audience

AP **Enduring Understanding (RHS-1)**

Individuals write within a particular situation and make strategic writing choices based on that situation.

KEY POINT

Writers make choices in an attempt to appeal to an audience's emotions, reason, or to establish their own credibility.

Consider this situation. Your junior prom is Saturday night. Your friends are going to a local diner afterward, and you want to join. However, you typically have a curfew of 11:00 P.M., so you need to convince your parent or guardian to extend your curfew. You have a motivation, a goal, and an audience.

You think about how to persuade your audience. Depending on whom you are asking, you might offer to help around the house, point out that you have always abided by the curfew, or even give reassurances that you will be safe and responsible. In short, you make specific choices that will help you achieve your goal (extending your curfew) depending on your audience. Indeed, this is exactly what writers do when they develop their arguments.

Writers Know Their Audience

When writers develop a text, they will consider and analyze their **audience** — particularly its values, beliefs, needs, and background. This analysis helps a writer make better choices about how to relate to that audience's beliefs and values. When considering audience, writers might ask themselves questions such as: What is my relationship to the audience? Do they know me?

- How does this audience likely feel about the issue?
- What does the audience already know about the issue? What additional information does the audience need to better understand the issue?
- What values and beliefs does this audience likely hold about the issue?

Rhetorical Appeals

Whether arguing or persuading, writers try to motivate or connect to their audience through **appeals**. In the study of rhetoric, there are three primary appeals, which are often called by their Greek names: ethos, logos, and pathos. To convince or relate to an audience, writers establish their **credibility (ethos)**, develop their **reasoning (logos)**, and influence the audiences' **emotion (pathos)**. In **persuasive** arguments especially, writers often make direct appeals to the emotions of their audience.

Writers create these different appeals by choosing certain words, sentence structures, stories, examples, details, and other evidence that they believe will relate to the audience. These choices may appeal to an audience's emotions or logic, or help the writer build his or her credibility. For a specialized audience familiar with the topic, a writer might use complex data to support a claim and specialized vocabulary to show expertise within a field. But for a more general audience, the same writer might use an emotionally powerful story and simpler language to achieve the same goals. Of course, writers can use a combination of these strategies, as well, depending on the rhetorical situation and the audience.

RHETORICAL APPEALS		
Appeal	**Rhetorical Effect**	**Common Techniques**
Pathos — Appeal to Emotion	When writers pull on the heartstrings of their audience, they are attempting to persuade them by engaging some aspect of the audience's emotions or senses. When persuading, writers attempt to move an audience toward a specific action or belief.	Allusions Anecdote Connotations Examples Figurative language Imagery Repetition Sensory details
Logos — Appeal to Logic	Appeals to logos engage the audience's sense of reasoning or logic, attempting to rationalize his or her perspective or idea to the audience. Writers appeal to logos by making clear, detailed arguments.	Allusions Analogies Anecdote Charts Examples Expert sources Facts Graphs Statistics Personal testimony Repetition Research Syntax
Ethos — Appeal to Credibility	A strong ethical appeal can build rapport and earn the trust of an audience. A writer's background, character, status/position, or association are all means by which he or she implicitly attempts to persuade the audience of his or her credibility. Writers can also associate themselves with the audience by highlighting shared values.	Concession Facts Personal testimony Refutation Statistics Sincerity Use of credible and reliable sources Writer's authority and experience

THE RHETORICAL APPEALS

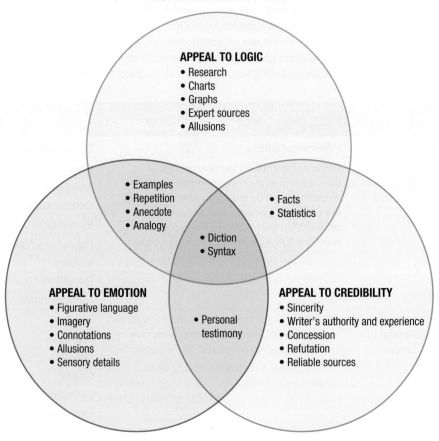

APPEAL TO LOGIC
- Research
- Charts
- Graphs
- Expert sources
- Allusions

- Examples
- Repetition
- Anecdote
- Analogy

- Facts
- Statistics

- Diction
- Syntax

APPEAL TO EMOTION
- Figurative language
- Imagery
- Connotations
- Allusions
- Sensory details

- Personal testimony

APPEAL TO CREDIBILITY
- Sincerity
- Writer's authority and experience
- Concession
- Refutation
- Reliable sources

INSIDER AP® TIP

Pronouns reveal relationships. In some arguments, writers associate themselves with their audiences by using "We" and "Us." In other arguments, writers separate themselves from their audience by using "You." When analyzing a text, it is important to understand the writer's relationship to his or her audience.

 **AP® SKILLS PRACTICE** | RHETORICAL SITUATION
Appealing to an Audience

Consider a rhetorical situation (like the curfew example at the beginning of this unit) you have experienced. Now, analyze your intended audience, considering their background, beliefs, and values. What rhetorical choices would you make to achieve your goal with that audience? How would you attempt to appeal to them?

Appeal	Common Techniques	Examples and Rhetorical Effect
Pathos — Appeal to Emotion	Allusions Anecdote Connotations Examples Figurative language Imagery Repetition Sensory details	
Logos — Appeal to Logic	Allusions Analogies Anecdote Charts Examples Expert sources Facts Graphs Personal testimony Repetition Research Statistics Syntax	
Ethos — Appeal to Credibility	Concession Facts Personal testimony Refutation Statistics Sincerity Use of credible and reliable sources Writer's authority and experience	

I Will Not Be the Last
Kamala Harris

Alex Wong/Getty Images

THE TEXT IN CONTEXT

In November 2020, Kamala Harris (b. 1964) was elected the first female vice president of the United States. The daughter of immigrant parents, Harris is of South Asian and African American descent. After earning an undergraduate degree from Howard University and completing law school at the University of California, she began a career in politics at the Alameda County (CA) district attorney's office. She served as district attorney for San Francisco before being elected in 2010 as California's first female, first African American, and first South Asian American attorney general. In 2016, she was elected to the U.S. Senate. The following remarks were delivered on November 7, 2020, as part of her victory speech for vice president.

  RHETORICAL SITUATION
Analyzing Rhetorical Appeals

As you read the following speech, use the graphic organizer to note the types of appeals Kamala Harris employs to engage her audience.

Analyzing Rhetorical Appeals		
Appeal	Common Techniques	Examples and Their Rhetorical Effect
Pathos — Appeal to Emotion	Allusions	
	Anecdote	
	Connotations	
	Examples	
	Figurative language	
	Imagery	
	Repetition	
	Sensory details	
Logos — Appeal to Logic	Allusions	
	Analogies	
	Anecdote	

	Charts	
	Examples	
	Expert sources	
	Facts	
	Graphs	
	Statistics	
	Personal testimony	
	Repetition	
	Research	
	Syntax	
Ethos — Appeal to Credibility	Concession	
	Facts	
	Personal testimony	
	Refutation	
	Statistics	
	Sincerity	
	Use of credible and reliable sources	
	Writer's authority and experience	

I Will Not Be the Last

Good evening. So, Congressman John Lewis, before his passing, wrote: "Democracy is not a state. It is an act." And what he meant was that America's democracy is not guaranteed. It is only as strong as our willingness to fight for it, to guard it and never take it for granted. And protecting our democracy takes struggle. It takes sacrifice. But there is joy in it, and there is progress. Because we the people have the power to build a better future.

And when our very democracy was on the ballot in this election, the very soul of America at stake, and the world watching, you ushered in a new day for America. . . .

. . . Thank you for turning out in record numbers to make your voices heard.

And I know times have been challenging, especially the last several months — the grief, sorrow and pain, the worries and the struggles. But we've also witnessed your courage, your resilience and the generosity of your spirit.

For four years, you marched and organized for equality and justice, for our lives, and for our planet. And then, you voted. And you delivered a clear message. You chose hope, unity, decency, science and, yes, truth.

You chose Joe Biden as the next president of the United States of America. . . .

. . . We are so grateful to Joe and Jill for welcoming our family into theirs on this incredible journey. And to the woman most responsible for my presence here today—my mother, Shyamala Gopalan Harris, who is always in our hearts.

When she came here from India at the age of 19, she maybe didn't quite imagine this moment. But she believed so deeply in America where a moment like this is possible. And so, I'm thinking about her and about the generations of women—Black women, Asian, White, Latina, Native American women who throughout our nation's history have paved the way for this moment tonight. Women who fought and sacrificed so much for equality and liberty and justice for all, including the Black women who are often, too often, overlooked, but so often prove that they are the backbone of our democracy. All the women who worked to secure and protect the right to vote for over a century: 100 years ago with the 19th Amendment, 55 years ago with the Voting Rights Act and now, in 2020, with a new generation of women in our country who cast their ballots and continued the fight for their fundamental right to vote and be heard.

Tonight, I reflect on their struggle, their determination and the strength of their vision—to see what can be, unburdened by what has been. And I stand on their shoulders. And what a testament it is to Joe's character that he had the audacity to break one of the most substantial barriers that exists in our country and select a woman as his vice president.

But while I may be the first woman in this office, I will not be the last, because every little girl watching tonight sees that this is a country of possibilities. And to the children of our country, regardless of your gender, our country has sent you a clear message: Dream with ambition, lead with conviction and see yourselves in a way that others may not simply because they've never seen it before, but know that we will applaud you every step of the way. . . . 10

RHETORICAL SITUATION

1. Harris begins with a quotation from John Lewis. How does this **appeal** to her **audience**?

2. Who is Harris's **audience**? What values does Harris share with her audience?

3. How does Harris connect to her audience through the **appeals** of logic, emotion, and credibility? Give a specific example of each and explain the effect of each appeal for her audience.

4. What is Harris's **message** specifically for young women? How does Harris's **ethos** qualify her to offer this message?

Relevant and Sufficient Evidence

AP® Enduring Understanding (CLE-1)

When writers make claims about subjects, they rely on evidence that supports their reasoning and justifies those claims. They often acknowledge or respond to counterarguments as well.

As writers attempt to achieve their purpose, they make strategic choices about what evidence will resonate with a particular audience. This includes choosing the specific type of evidence — and the amount of evidence — best suited to that audience. Whether you're listening to your favorite podcast, watching a documentary, or scrolling through TikTok, you often hear unsubstantiated statements such as, "Research shows . . . ," "According to the internet . . . ," and "They say . . . " In fact, many media influencers and authority figures use these appeals regularly.

Why do you believe some sources and not others? Why are you often frustrated when those in authority say, "Because I said so"? Why are rumors so prevalent and frustrating? Because these are unsubstantiated claims. Many people offer opinions without providing reasons or evidence.

KEY POINT

Writers strategically and purposefully select relevant and sufficient evidence to support their argument for a particular audience.

Supporting the Argument

Critical thinkers question unsupported or vacuous claims. They understand that arguments are **valid** when they are justified through logical reasons and that arguments become stronger and more credible when the reasoning is supported through compelling evidence. Writers may use a variety of types of evidence in their arguments, and effective writers carefully select evidence that will appeal to their audience and is appropriate for the context.

Certainly, writers choose **evidence** primarily to support their reasons. Writers choose the best evidence to achieve their purpose with a *particular audience*. Based on a writer's specific audience, he or she may use evidence to

- illustrate, clarify, or exemplify;
- establish a mood;
- create an association; or
- amplify or emphasize a point.

When using evidence from other sources, writers need to give credit by citing the original writer or creator. Not only does this practice attribute the credit appropriately but it also serves to establish the writer's own **credibility**.

INFORMATION THAT CAN BECOME EVIDENCE		
Analogies	Experiments	Personal Experiences
Anecdotes	Expert Opinions	Personal Observations
Details	Facts	Statistics
Examples	Illustrations	Testimonies

Relevant Evidence

In order for a claim to be proven true, it has to be supported and defended with **relevant evidence**. Just because evidence is related to your topic does not make it relevant. Evidence becomes relevant when a writer connects and explains its significance and relevance to the line of reasoning for a particular audience. As writers develop arguments to convey their perspectives, they select evidence based on not just what supports their perspective and line of reasoning, but also what they believe their specific audience will find persuasive.

Sufficient Evidence

There must also be **sufficient evidence** to support each reason in the line of reasoning. Sufficient evidence refers to the quantity and quality appropriate for the argument. While there is no magic formula for the amount of evidence needed for any given argument, a writer should select multiple pieces of evidence to effectively support their argument based on the audience and context.

When you read, hear, or view an argument, you should look for the reasoning and evidence the writer uses to support his or her claim. Evidence can take many forms, and effective writers draw on information that is appropriate and relevant for the audience and situation.

Typical Evidence

Many times, if it's too good to be true, it probably is. **Typical evidence** is evidence that is representative of a population or issue. While some pieces of evidence may be shocking or surprising, writers should rely on a balanced, impartial judgment to determine if their evidence is plausible. Moreover, when writers select evidence from data with a small sample size, or when they rely entirely on an outlying perspective, their use of evidence is unethical and unsubstantiated.

Accurate Evidence

Incorrect (or fallacious) evidence cannot effectively support a claim. **Accurate evidence** is verifiable, meaning other credible sources can check that it is correct. Accurate evidence often indicates the practices, procedures, or experiences that led to its creation so others can verify the details.

While all evidence should be accurate, not all evidence must be recent in order to be accurate. For example, an article on climate change requires evidence from the most recent scientific studies in order to be accurate; however, a study on the works of William Shakespeare could draw upon evidence that was written hundreds of years ago and still be accurate.

As you evaluate the effectiveness of an argument, you should consider the evidence. Some readers use the STAR mnemonic as they evaluate and select evidence for their arguments.

EVALUATING EVIDENCE	
Sufficient	Is there enough evidence to support each reason? Is there enough to be convincing?
Typical	Is the evidence plausible and representative of the issue? Is the evidence reasonable?
Accurate	How recent should the evidence be in order to be accurate? Is the evidence relatable, recent, and accurate?
Relevant	Is the information relevant to the reason and claim, not just the topic? Does the evidence connect to the claim?

INSIDER **Writers strategically include and exclude evidence.** Even though a writer may share the same message with multiple audiences, that writer doesn't necessarily use the exact same evidence with every audience. Considering what is excluded is as important as recognizing what is included.

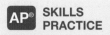

SKILLS PRACTICE | CLAIMS AND EVIDENCE
Selecting Evidence for an Audience

Think about the same claim you might make to two different audiences. Then, think about the two different audiences. Make a list of the information you could use as evidence. Considering the two different audiences, identify which evidence would be appropriate for each of them.

Claim:	
Audience A:	Audience B:
Evidence:	Evidence:

Give the Kids a Break

Steve Rushin

V.J. Lovero/Getty Images

THE TEXT IN CONTEXT

Steve Rushin (b. 1966), journalist and 2005
Sportswriter of the Year, is a regular contributor
to sports magazines such as *Sports Illustrated*.
According to a study by the Center on Education
Policy at George Washington University, between
2001 and 2006, one-third of elementary schools
did not offer daily recess for any grades. In response to this national trend, Rushin
published the following editorial in *Sports Illustrated*, December 2006.

AP® SKILLS PRACTICE | CLAIMS AND EVIDENCE
Connecting Evidence and Audience

As you read Rushin's argument, make note of the evidence he uses to support
his reasons and claim. Considering his audience, how might the evidence appeal
to that audience?

Connecting Evidence to an Audience

Reason	Evidence	Effect (Appeal) to an Audience

Give the Kids a Break

Four square and seven years ago we had recess: 20 minutes, twice a day, of Darwinian contests whose very names— king of the hill, capture the flag, keep-away, dodgeball—screamed survival of the fittest. After all, monkey in the middle isn't just a playground game; it describes the chain of human evolution.

Most of these games were passed down like heirlooms. They crossed continents and centuries with only small modifications, surviving into the modern age with names such as duck, duck, goose; Mother, may I; and Miss Mary Mack. Ancient Greeks jumped rope, Caesar's subjects played a form of jacks, and blindman's bluff was played in the court of Henry VIII. Pity, then, that none of these games may survive the decade, and for one deeply depressing reason: Red rover, red rover, recess is over.

Or it is for many children. According to the National PTA, nearly 40% of U.S. elementary schools "have either eliminated or are considering eliminating recess." Twenty to 30 percent of schools offer 15 or fewer minutes of daily recess. Lifers at Leavenworth get more time in the exercise yard. And the U.S. Department of Education reports that 7% of all U.S. first- and second-graders—and 13% of all sixth-graders—get no recess whatsoever.

How ever did this happen to the fabled fourth R? For starters, increased preparation for standardized tests mandated by No Child Left Behind leaves little time for recess. That legislation was passed by Congress, which through Sunday had spent 138 days in recess during this session, safe in the knowledge that eight-year-olds can't vote. In fairness to school administrators, no one should have to choose between childhood ignorance and childhood obesity. But there are lots of other reasons for the recess recession.

One is fear of injury. Willett Elementary School in Attleboro, Mass., has been roundly ridiculed for banning tag and other so-called chase games. But similar bans were imposed long ago by many other schools in places such as Spokane; Cheyenne, Wyo.; and suburban Charleston, S.C. Attleboro merely fell in line behind them. Trouble is, life is a chase game. At my elementary school every recess ended like Round 8 of a prizefight: with a bell, the mending of cuts and at least two parties forced to sit in a corner.

That kind of unsupervised play literally left its mark on me. The scar on my forehead? I hit a pipe while playing tag in the basement. My left front tooth? Knocked out by a thrown baseball as I daydreamed in the park. And those were just the accidents, independent of the teenage Torquemadas who intentionally inflicted all manner of torture. There were no junior high Geneva Conventions, and so almost everyone endured noogies, wedgies, swirlies, snuggies, sudsies, melvins, wet willies, pink bellies, Indian burns, Russian haircuts and Hertz doughnuts—and a litany of other poetic means of coercion.

That was then, this is now. Last year a 15-year-old boy in Gold Hill, Ore., was charged with offensive physical touching for giving a 13-year-old boy a purple nurple. And therein lie two other reasons that recess is receding: 1) playground bullies and 2) fear of lawsuits over injuries incurred on school grounds. In Maine one school canceled recess for eighth-graders in an effort to end bullying, which is a little like scalping in an effort to end dandruff.

It's a jungle out there, but you'll be hard pressed on most playgrounds to find a jungle gym, or monkey bars, or stainless-steel slides that in the summer months sizzle like a fajita skillet. Many seesaws are built with

5

springs instead of the fulcrums that allowed one kid to jump off at the bottom, causing the other to drop abruptly, as if down an elevator shaft. And every piece of bubble-wrapped playground equipment—excuse me, playscape equipment—is festooned with labels that warn of deadly consequences for the smallest misuse.

If all of this has you saying, "Give me a break," you've just voiced a universal human need. We all need a break. Some Teamsters get two 15-minute breaks per shift, the Supreme Court is in recess from July to October, and the third Thursday of every June is National Recess at Work Day, whose founder,

Rich DiGirolamo, suggests that adults drop whatever they're doing next June 21 and "play tag and dodgeball, jump rope and eat watermelon."

Surely seven-year-olds deserve to do the same. And so National Recess Week was observed in September, with Recess Rallies in schools around America. The PTA and the Cartoon Network are sponsoring a Rescuing Recess campaign. Something called the American Association for the Child's Right to Play is also eager to resuscitate recess. All of them agree with G.K. Chesterton, who wrote, "Earth is a task garden; heaven is a playground." 10

CLAIMS AND EVIDENCE

1. What is Rushin's **claim**? Explain how the **evidence** supports the claim.

2. The writer gives three **reasons** for the problem. Indicate the three reasons. Describe the **evidence** that supports the reasons.

3. Choose one piece of **evidence**. How is that evidence relevant to the **reason** and the **claim**, not just the topic?

4. Rushin's text is persuasive. What is his literal and figurative **call to action**?

5. Rushin ends the text with more **evidence**. How does it affect his **argument**?

Persuasion

AP® Enduring Understanding (REO-1)

Writers guide understanding of a text's line of reasoning and claims through that text's organization and integration of evidence.

A writer's message is only effective if it achieves his or her purpose with an audience. That means the message must reach, affect, influence, or appeal to his or her intended audience. Some writers have a goal of trying to call an audience to act — to do something or stop doing something. In this unit, you'll examine ways writers appeal to their audiences in an effort to persuade them.

KEY POINT

Persuasive arguments may be organized inductively or deductively and include a call to action for the audience.

Persuasive Arguments Call for Action

Persuasion starts with a purpose. As speakers and writers observe and experience the world around them, they are moved to make changes in others' attitudes and behaviors. While all writers make arguments, not all writers attempt to persuade. Argumentation and persuasion are similar concepts, but a key difference is that persuasive texts call an audience to action. That is, the writer calls his or her audience to act — to do something or stop doing something.

The potential for persuasion exists all around us — our homes, our schools, our communities, our country, and our world. It is at the heart of our political and legal systems and serves as the basis for advertising campaigns in commercials and social media. In your life, persuasion may look different than a politician's moving speech, an impassioned op-ed, or a glossy advertising campaign. However, whether the audience consists of friends, teachers, and parents or a trial jury, an eager consumer, or prospective voters, persuasion works similarly.

As you've learned, writers share their ideas and perspectives about topics or issues through the claims they make. But writers can't just make claims without having reasons to justify and evidence to support them. When you consider the audience you're trying to address, the order that you present your information could influence the degree to which they continue to listen to or hear your argument.

Imagine that you are making a speech to a group of your friends to support a particular student council candidate. You and your friends may have similar beliefs, so you may begin by saying that this candidate ought to win. You may then offer a few reasons that you know your friends will agree with. This seems simple, right? But what if you are trying to convince a group of students who are unlikely to support your candidate? In that case, you may begin by giving specific reasons that illustrate points of concern that resonate with your new audience. Then, finally get to the point of support for that candidate. In both instances, the reasons you gave supported your overall claim, which remained the same. Even though your over-all perspective or claim didn't change, the reasons and sequencing of those reasons likely did. The reasons and their sequence are called the **line of reasoning**.

Establishing a Line of Reasoning

Writers must justify their claim or thesis with reasons and support the reasons with evidence: details, facts, anecdotes, or even other sources. They must also provide an explanation of how the evidence supports their claim. As the evidence accumulates, so does the support for that particular line of reasoning. This explanation of connecting the evidence with the reasons and ultimately with the writer's claim is considered the writer's line of reasoning. If the line of reasoning is logical and justifies the writer's claim, then the argument is considered valid.

Because the ordering of each reason within the line of reasoning may affect how well a particular audience within a specific context accepts the writer's message, writers must think carefully about how they organize a text or argument.

Induction and Deduction

Writers use **induction** or **deduction** to organize their reasons and claims based on their audience and context. Inductive reasoning moves from specific observations to broad generalizations, while deductive reasoning begins with a broad generalization followed by specific observations.

INDUCTION

CONTEXT
QUESTION

REASON 1
EVIDENCE
COMMENTARY

REASON 2
EVIDENCE
COMMENTARY

REASON 3
EVIDENCE
COMMENTARY

CLAIM AND CALL TO ACTION

DEDUCTION

CONTEXT
CLAIM

REASON 1
EVIDENCE
COMMENTARY

REASON 2
EVIDENCE
COMMENTARY

REASON 3
EVIDENCE
COMMENTARY

CALL TO
ACTION

INSIDER AP® TIP

Audiences have expectations. The way an argument is constructed is contingent on the audience's expectations. In general, writers in the natural and social sciences convey knowledge through induction. In contrast, writers in the humanities and the arts construct knowledge through deduction.

For example, a call to action is often found at the end of a persuasive text. The call to action may be the writer's thesis. This organization is considered inductive. Induction is frequently used when the audience likely doesn't have the same position as the writer, or the writer doesn't know the audience's perspective on the topic or subject. To convince his or her audience, the writer will provide the reasons first, leading to the claim or call to action in the conclusion.

Conversely, when a writer believes the audience shares common beliefs and may be willing to accept his or her perspective, the writer may begin with the thesis or call to action. This organization is called deduction. When using deduction, a writer presents his or her claim and then lays out his or her reasons.

 **SKILLS PRACTICE** | REASONING AND ORGANIZATION
Establishing a Line of Reasoning

Think about your message or claim from the previous workshop. What reasons would you use to justify your claim for that audience? How would you organize your argument? With induction or deduction? Why did you make that choice?

Audience	
Claim	
Line of Reasoning	
Organization and Rationale	

Why Diversity Is Necessary for Democracy
Tenzin Namgyal

THE TEXT IN CONTEXT

When she wrote this 2019 essay, Tenzin Namgyal was a junior at Bard High School Early College in Queens, New York. It ultimately appeared on Students 4 Social Change, a website and network that promotes civic engagement in secondary students. An avid writer who is passionate about social issues, including the rights of immigrants and women, Namgyal graduated from high school and attends Stanford University.

Tenzin Namgyal

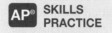 **SKILLS PRACTICE** | REASONING AND ORGANIZATION
Analyzing Organization

As you read her argument, identify the reasons Namgyal uses to persuade her audience. Then consider whether she uses inductive or deductive organization to engage her audience and call them to action. Why do you think she chose this logic?

Analyzing Organization

Audience	
Claim	
Line of Reasoning	
Organization and Rationale	

Why Diversity Is Necessary for Democracy

New Members of Congress

On January 3rd, 2019, the newest members of the House and Senate were sworn in. This incoming class is reported to be the most diverse in history—in both race and gender. Forty of the politicians are women, and sixty are men, which is the smallest gender disparity in American history. Additionally, there are at least twenty-five members of the House who are people of color. For the first time, two Native American women, Sharice Davids and Debra Haaland, were elected to Congress, with Davids also being the first openly LGBT person elected to represent the state of Kansas. Ilhan Omar and Rashida Tlaib are the first two Muslim American women to be elected, and Omar is both the first congresswoman to wear a headscarf and the first woman of color to be elected to represent Minnesota. Even though the American government has more women in it than ever before, and has made large strides towards equality, there is still a long way to go in terms of diversity. In order for this country to be fairer, politicians need to be from all backgrounds and ethnicities.

More Than Just Race

Although racial diversity is extremely important, the incoming congressmen and women are also diverse in several other ways. For instance, they all come from a variety of backgrounds, some even from ones that have nothing to do with politics. There are teachers and doctors, professional athletes, and veterans. They have a multitude of life experiences, which will aid them greatly during their term, as they have held occupations similar to that of many Americans. Citizens will be able to relate to politicians more, lowering levels of distrust. Moreover, because these government officials all have different experiences, they will have varying perspectives on legislation and such, and may be able to point out any possible flaws in the number of bills that are proposed.

The Importance of Representation

Representation is an issue that was fought for even before this country was founded, and is one that is still fought for this very day. To truly make America great, politicians from all classes, races, and backgrounds must be elected. This ensures that everyone has a voice, and that there are people within our government working actively to prevent anyone from struggling the same way they have. The hardships officials have suffered gives them more initiative to incite change within their communities, and make our country a better place overall. Furthermore, representation encourages children from underrepresented backgrounds, because it ultimately proves to them that they can do anything they want to, regardless of their skin color or their class.

Always Room for More

Congress is as diverse as ever, but there is always room for more. For example, almost all forty of the women were Democrats, and the new Republican officials were predominantly white males. This may have to do with the specific ideals of each party, but there should be a significant amount of diversity in both, because Americans of different ethnicities and backgrounds may vote for either. To guarantee a more inclusive future, children should be motivated to become engaged in politics. They should learn about current events in school, and understand thoroughly how the decisions made by the government affects them and their family's daily life. Students from underserved areas should use the adversity they have overcome as inspiration to become involved in activism. Speaking out, and having your thoughts heard, is the most crucial part of the democratic process, and the way to make sure every voice is heard is by electing officials who have experienced similar difficulties during their lifetime.

REASONING AND ORGANIZATION

1. What is Namgyal's **claim**?

2. Namgyal uses a **line of reasoning** to support her **thesis** in this speech. Identify the **reasons** she includes to support her thesis.

3. Is this speech organized **inductively** or **deductively**? Explain why this is effective.

4. Namgyal's **line of reasoning** offers details and **reasons** that connect and build to her conclusion. Why are these choices so powerful to her **audience**?

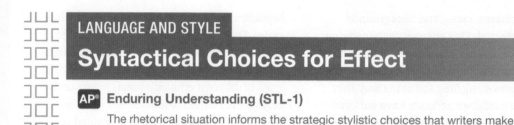
Syntactical Choices for Effect

AP® **Enduring Understanding (STL-1)**

The rhetorical situation informs the strategic stylistic choices that writers make.

> **KEY POINT**
>
> Writers craft sentences in ways that not only engage their readers but also convey their message.

The way a writer communicates a message to an audience can affect how well the audience receives the message. So, writers strategically craft sentences, repeat words or phrases, pose questions, and contrast or connect sentences in a way that emphasizes ideas or asks their audience to reflect. These are deliberate, strategic choices that writers make in an attempt to achieve their purpose with a specific audience.

Syntax Is Part of the Writer's Craft

Consider the following sentences from Thomas Paine's *The American Crisis* (1776). His purpose was to inspire his American audience to fight for their independence from England, even if they had to struggle through hardship and setbacks. He introduces his argument by writing:

> These are the times that try men's souls. The summer soldier and the sunshine patriot will, in this crisis, shrink from the service of their country; but he that stands by it now, deserves the love and thanks of man and woman.

These engaging lines have a rhythm, balance, and power that reinforce his message to his audience. He achieves this effect, in part, through **syntax**: the specific arrangement of words and phrases to create well-formed sentences.

Writers make **syntactical choices** deliberately, with their audience in mind. Have you ever heard a speech in which the speaker asked a question and then paused? The speaker wasn't waiting for a verbal answer from the audience. Rather, he or she paused so that members of the audience could formulate their own answers. Some speakers or writers repeat the same phrase or sentence multiple times. Through this repetition, they intend for their audience to remember that point. And some writers use the same grammatical structure—for example, two simple sentences back-to-back. All of these syntactical choices are intended for some effect, such as emphasis, reflection, or contrast.

Syntactical Moves

Engaging an audience happens sentence by sentence. Effective writers craft sentences (or syntax) intentionally with a goal of connecting with their audience. Some sentences resonate with different audiences differently. However, all writers use syntax to emphasize their ideas.

Sentences may set up contrasts, while others make comparisons. Some sentences may repeat, while others may pose questions. The placement of a sentence within a paragraph or within an essay influences the effect it has on the audience.

Often, the function of the sentence connects to the content of the speech. For example, many times, parallel sentences will function to balance the sentence both grammatically and contextually. We often see this in functions of contrast (**juxtaposition** and **antithesis**) and comparisons (**parallel structure**). Functions of contrasts are also present in syntactical structures like the **rhetorical question**, which directly links the content to the audience. Finally, **repetition** can connect content to emphasize the noun, adjective, adverb, or pronoun. Pay attention to the structure and notice the content; how does the function support the content?

Effective use of syntactical choices allows ideas to be described, clarified, and emphasized. Ultimately, the syntactical choices a writer makes must be strategic in a way that allows him or her to further his or her purpose and message. Keep in mind that merely identifying the type of syntax is not sufficient. What's important is to analyze why a writer made a specific syntactical choice. In other words, what effect does that type of syntax and placement within the overall argument have on the reader in terms of the writer communicating his or her message?

The following table illustrates some common syntactical choices frequently used by persuasive writers to emphasize a particular point to achieve a particular tone.

INSIDER **AP® TIP**

Syntactical choices are for function, not frills. Writers purposefully and strategically craft sentences for effect. Varied sentence structure is not the goal; however, by using meaningful construction, writers achieve variety.

SYNTACTICAL EFFECT

Syntactical Choice	Example	Possible Effect	Questions to Ask
Repetition Repeating or recurrence of a word, phrase, sentence, or other element	"What lies behind us and what lies before us are tiny compared to what lies within us." — Ralph Waldo Emerson	Emphasizes or reinforces an idea or concept often related to the writer's purpose	Why does the writer repeat this particular word, phrase, or sentence? Why does it occur where it does?
Juxtaposition Contrasting ideas, scenes, settings, images, or other elements	"I have a dream that my four little children will one day live in a nation where they will not be judged by the color of their skin but by the content of their character." — Martin Luther King Jr.	Sets up a contrast or comparison of concepts	How did the writer create the juxtaposition (e.g., use of transitions, coordination)? Why does the writer juxtapose these particular ideas?
Parallel Structure Repeating words or phrases in the same grammatical structure	"That government of the people, by the people, and for the people . . ." — Abraham Lincoln	Creates a sense of balance by placing emphasis on the grammatical element that is parallel	Why does the writer want the reader to notice these grammatical elements in particular?
Rhetorical Question Posing a question that is expected to be considered but not answered literally	"But what is government itself but the greatest of all reflections on human nature?" — James Madison	Asks the reader to reflect, contemplate, or consider a concept or idea	What effect does the placement of the rhetorical question have on the message?
Antithesis Expressing contrasting ideas in parallel grammatical structure	"Ask not what your country can do for you, but what you can do for your country." — John F. Kennedy	Provides emphasis on one idea by contrasting it with another	What ideas are being contrasted? What effect do these contrasting ideas have on the audience?
Fragment A broken thought or only part of a sentence	"Silence. The cold rain falling. And the smell of blue electricity blowing under the locked door." — Ray Bradbury	Emphasizes an idea by focusing on a particular phrase or part of a sentence	Why did the writer use only part of a sentence, such as only giving the subject or only giving an exclamation?
Simple Sentence A complete thought consisting of a subject and verb	"Love was on the move. "Mercy was on the move. "God was on the move." — Bono	Placing a simple sentence by itself, especially among other longer or complex sentences, often emphasizes the idea in that sentence	Where are the short, simple sentences? Why are they placed in that location? What idea is being emphasized?

 **SKILLS PRACTICE** | LANGUAGE AND STYLE
Syntax for Effect

Think about the audience you identified in the previous workshop. Which syntactical moves (e.g., parallel structure, rhetorical questions, repetition, juxtaposition) would you use in an argument to convince that audience?

Audience	
Claim	
Syntactical Move and Example	
Syntactical Move and Example	
Syntactical Move and Example	

Address to the Nation on September 20, 2001
George W. Bush

Everett Collection Historical/Alamy Stock Photo

THE TEXT IN CONTEXT

On September 20, 2001, in his first year of an eight-year presidency, George W. Bush (b. 1946) delivered the following speech before the joint houses of Congress. Our forty-third president vowed to pursue terrorists around the world and praised the American people for their courage and unity. The speech was televised to the American people who had nine days earlier, on September 11, 2001, experienced the first terrorist attacks on U.S. soil. Al Qaeda, an Islamic terrorist group, hijacked commercial airplanes, crashing two into the World Trade Center in New York, one into the Pentagon, and one making a failed attempt at the nation's capital, crashing in Shanksville, Pennsylvania. In these attacks, 2,977 Americans lost their lives and over 25,000 were injured. The following is an excerpt of President Bush's speech.

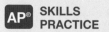 | LANGUAGE AND STYLE
Analyzing Syntax

In this informative and impassioned televised address, George W. Bush employed strategic syntactical choices to engage the American people toward a unified call to action. You may use the following graphic organizer as you read and find examples of the following syntactical techniques and consider the effect they had on President Bush's message and on his audience as you answer the questions after the text.

Analyzing Syntax		
Rhetorical Devices	**Definition**	**Examples and Effect**
Repetition	Repeating or recurrence of a word, phrase, sentence, or other element	
Juxtaposition	Contrasting ideas, scenes, settings, images, or other elements	
Parallel Structure	Repeating words or phrases in the same grammatical structure	
Rhetorical Question	Posing a question that is expected to be considered but not answered literally	
Antithesis	Contrasting ideas in parallel grammatical structure	
Fragment	Expressing a broken thought or only part of a sentence intentionally	
Simple Sentence	Expressing a complete thought consisting of a subject and verb	

Address to the Nation on September 20, 2001

Mr. Speaker, Mr. President Pro Tempore, members of Congress, and fellow Americans, in the normal course of events, presidents come to this chamber to report on the state of the union. Tonight, no such report is needed; it has already been delivered by the American people.

We have seen it in the courage of passengers who rushed terrorists to save others on the ground. Passengers like an exceptional man named Todd Beamer. And would you please help me welcome his wife Lisa Beamer here tonight?

We have seen the state of our union in the endurance of rescuers working past exhaustion. We've seen the unfurling of flags, the lighting of candles, the giving of blood, the saying of prayers in English, Hebrew, and Arabic.

We have seen the decency of a loving and giving people who have made the grief of strangers their own. My fellow citizens, for the last nine days, the entire world has seen for itself the state of union, and it is strong.

Tonight, we are a country awakened to danger and called to defend freedom. Our grief has turned to anger and anger to resolution. Whether we bring our enemies to justice or bring justice to our enemies, justice will be done. . . . 5

On September the 11th, enemies of freedom committed an act of war against our country. Americans have known wars, but for the past 136 years they have been wars on foreign soil, except for one Sunday in 1941. Americans have known the casualties of war, but not at the center of a great city on a peaceful morning.

Americans have known surprise attacks, but never before on thousands of civilians.

All of this was brought upon us in a single day, and night fell on a different world, a world where freedom itself is under attack.

Americans have many questions tonight. Americans are asking, "Who attacked our country?"

The evidence we have gathered all points to a collection of loosely affiliated terrorist organizations known as al Qaeda. They are some of the murderers indicted for bombing American embassies in Tanzania and Kenya and responsible for bombing the USS *Cole*. . . . 10

Al Qaeda is to terror what the Mafia is to crime. But its goal is not making money, its goal is remaking the world and imposing its radical beliefs on people everywhere.

The terrorists practice a fringe form of Islamic extremism that has been rejected by Muslim scholars and the vast majority of Muslim clerics; a fringe movement that perverts the peaceful teachings of Islam. . . .

Our war on terror begins with al Qaeda, but it does not end there. It will not end until every terrorist group of global reach has been found, stopped and defeated.

Americans are asking, "Why do they hate us?"

They hate what they see right here in this chamber: a democratically elected government. Their leaders are self-appointed. They hate our freedoms: our freedom of religion, our freedom of speech, our freedom to vote and assemble and disagree with each other. 15

They want to overthrow existing governments in many Muslim countries such as Egypt, Saudi Arabia and Jordan. They want to drive Israel out of the Middle East. They want to drive Christians and Jews out of vast regions of Asia and Africa.

These terrorists kill not merely to end lives, but to disrupt and end a way of life. With every atrocity, they hope that America grows fearful, retreating from the world and forsaking our friends. They stand against us because we stand in their way.

We're not deceived by their pretenses to piety.

We have seen their kind before. They're the heirs of all the murderous ideologies of the twentieth century. By sacrificing human life to serve their radical visions, by abandoning every value except the will to power, they follow in the path of fascism, Nazism and totalitarianism. And they will follow that path all the way to where it ends in history's unmarked grave of discarded lies.

Americans are asking, "How will we fight 20 and win this war?"

We will direct every resource at our command—every means of diplomacy, every tool of intelligence, every instrument of law enforcement, every financial influence, and every necessary weapon of war—to the destruction and to the defeat of the global terror network.

Now, this war will not be like the war against Iraq a decade ago, with a decisive liberation of territory and a swift conclusion. It will not look like the air war above Kosovo two years ago, where no ground troops were used and not a single American was lost in combat.

Our response involves far more than instant retaliation and isolated strikes. Americans should not expect one battle, but a lengthy campaign unlike any other we have ever seen. It may include dramatic strikes visible on TV and covert operations secret even in success.

We will starve terrorists of funding, turn them one against another, drive them from place to place until there is no refuge or no rest.

And we will pursue nations that provide 25 aid or safe haven to terrorism. Every nation in every region now has a decision to make: Either you are with us or you are with the terrorists.

From this day forward, any nation that continues to harbor or support terrorism will be regarded by the United States as a hostile regime. Our nation has been put on notice, we're not immune from attack. We will take defensive measures against terrorism to protect Americans. . . .

Americans are asking, "What is expected of us?"

I ask you to live your lives and hug your children.

I know many citizens have fears tonight, and I ask you to be calm and resolute, even in the face of a continuing threat.

I ask you to uphold the values of America 30 and remember why so many have come here. We're in a fight for our principles, and our first responsibility is to live by them. No one should be singled out for unfair treatment or unkind words because of their ethnic background or religious faith. . . .

Tonight we face new and sudden national challenges.

We will come together to improve air safety, to dramatically expand the number of air marshals on domestic flights and take new measures to prevent hijacking.

We will come together to promote stability and keep our airlines flying with direct assistance during this emergency.

We will come together to give law enforcement the additional tools it needs to track down terror here at home.

We will come together to strengthen our 35 intelligence capabilities to know the plans of terrorists before they act and to find them before they strike.

We will come together to take active steps that strengthen America's economy and put our people back to work. . . .

After all that has just passed, all the lives taken and all the possibilities and hopes that died with them, it is natural to wonder if America's future is one of fear.

Some speak of an age of terror. I know there are struggles ahead and dangers to face. But this country will define our times, not be defined by them.

As long as the United States of America is determined and strong, this will not be an age of terror. This will be an age of liberty here and across the world.

Great harm has been done to us. We have 40 suffered great loss. And in our grief and anger we have found our mission and our moment.

Freedom and fear are at war. The advance of human freedom, the great achievement of our time and the great hope of every time, now depends on us.

Our nation, this generation, will lift the dark threat of violence from our people and our future. We will rally the world to this cause by our efforts, by our courage. We will not tire, we will not falter, and we will not fail.

It is my hope that in the months and years ahead life will return almost to normal. We'll go back to our lives and routines and that is good. Even grief recedes with time and grace. . . .

The course of this conflict is not known, yet its outcome is certain. Freedom and fear, justice and cruelty, have always been at war, and we know that God is not neutral between them.

Fellow citizens, we'll meet violence with patient justice, assured of the rightness of our cause and confident of the victories to come. 45

In all that lies before us, may God grant us wisdom and may he watch over the United States of America.

LANGUAGE AND STYLE

1. The speech is organized and controlled with many **rhetorical questions**. Identify those questions and discuss how they appeal to the audience. How do these questions directly address exigence and purpose?

2. George W. Bush employs **repetition** throughout the speech. Find some specific examples of repetition and explain how these syntactical choices support his purpose.

3. There are many examples of **juxtaposition** in the speech. List two examples of contrasted ideas and discuss how these contrasts connect to the subject of the speech and the emotional condition of the audience.

4. Bush is seeking the support of the American people. The speech is successful in bringing together a broken nation. Discuss the **rhetorical choices** that connect (the way a writer writes, you may choose **juxtaposition**, **parallel structure**, **rhetorical questions**, or **repetition**) to the content and reinforce the idea of balance.

Don't Understand the Protests? What You're Seeing Is People Pushed to the Edge

Kareem Abdul-Jabbar

THE TEXT IN CONTEXT

Kareem Abdul-Jabbar (b. 1947) is a former National Basketball Association (NBA) player for the Milwaukee Bucks and the Los Angeles Lakers. During his twenty-year basketball career, he was a six-time NBA Most Valuable Player. After retiring from the NBA, he used his talent for writing and community activism. He is a public speaker and has written many articles and published many podcasts. He has authored fifteen *New York Times* best sellers. In the following May 25, 2020, *Los Angeles Times* editorial, Kareem Abdul-Jabbar responded to the death of George Floyd. Floyd, a forty-six-year-old Black man, died in Minneapolis, Minnesota, after a white police officer knelt on his neck for more than nine minutes. Preceded by years of police brutality toward African Americans, the event led to marches and protests affirming that Black lives matter and calling for justice and reform.

Unifying Idea	Don't Understand the Protests? What You're Seeing Is People Pushed to the Edge	Rhetorical Choices	Effects of Choices
racial justice	If you're white, you probably muttered a horrified, "Oh, my God" while shaking your head at the cruel injustice. If you're black, you probably leapt to your feet, cursed, maybe threw something (certainly *wanted* to throw something), while shouting, "Not @#$%! again!" Then you remember the two white vigilantes accused of murdering Ahmaud Arbery as he jogged through their neighborhood in February, and how if it wasn't for that video emerging a few weeks ago, they would have gotten away with it. And how those Minneapolis cops claimed Floyd was resisting arrest but a store's video showed he wasn't. And how the cop on Floyd's neck wasn't an enraged redneck stereotype, but a sworn officer who looked calm and entitled and devoid of pity: the banality of evil incarnate.	audience — evidence — context	second-person "you" makes reader part of audience listing historical facts of racial brutality example: Floyd's death
racial justice	Maybe you also are thinking about the Karen in Central Park who called 911 claiming the black man who asked her to put a leash on her dog was threatening her. Or the black Yale University grad student napping in the common room of her dorm who was reported by a white student. Because you realize it's not just a supposed "black criminal" who is targeted, it's the whole spectrum of black faces from Yonkers to Yale. You start to wonder if it should be all black people who wear body cams, not the cops.	examples as evidence	create a logical appeal
racial justice	What do you see when you see angry black protesters amassing outside police stations with raised fists? If you're white, you may be thinking, "They certainly aren't social distancing." Then you notice the black faces looting Target and you think, "Well, that just hurts their cause." Then you see the police station on fire and you wag a finger saying, "That's putting the cause backward."	rhetorical question	asks reader to reflect

Unifying Idea	Don't Understand the Protests? What You're Seeing Is People Pushed to the Edge	Rhetorical Choices	Effects of Choices
racial justice	You're not wrong—but you're not right, either. ⎤— antithesis The black community is used to the institutional racism inherent in education, the justice system and jobs. And even though we do all the conventional things to raise public and political awareness—write articulate and insightful pieces in the Atlantic, explain the continued devastation ⎫— evidence on CNN, support candidates who promise change —the needle hardly budges. ⎭	antithesis evidence	wrong/right perception to support claim: justice is not served
racial justice	But COVID-19 has been slamming the consequences of all that home as we die at a significantly higher rate than whites, are the first to lose our jobs, and watch helplessly as Republicans try to keep us from voting. Just as the slimy underbelly of institutional racism is being exposed, it feels like hunting season is ⎤— comparison open on blacks. If there was any doubt, President Trump's recent tweets confirm the national zeitgeist as he calls protesters "thugs" and looters fair game to be shot.	comparison	emotional appeal — oppression
racial justice	Yes, protests often are used as an excuse for some to take advantage, just as when fans celebrating a hometown sports team championship burn cars and destroy storefronts. I don't want to see stores looted or even buildings burn. But African Americans have been living in a burning building ⎫ for many years, choking on the smoke as the sensory flames burn closer and closer. Racism in America details is like dust in the air. It seems invisible—even if ⎭ you're choking on it—until you let the sun in. Then you see it's everywhere. As long as we keep shining that light, we have a chance of cleaning it wherever it lands. But we have to stay vigilant, because it's always still in the air.	sensory details	emotional appeal— suffocating/ choking on racism

Unifying Idea	Don't Understand the Protests? What You're Seeing Is People Pushed to the Edge	Rhetorical Choices	Effects of Choices
racial justice	So, maybe the black community's main concern right now isn't whether protesters are standing three or six feet apart or whether a few desperate souls steal some T-shirts or even set a police station on fire, but whether their sons, husbands, brothers and fathers will be murdered by cops or wannabe cops just for going on a walk, a jog, a drive. Or whether being black means sheltering at home for the rest of their lives because the racism virus infecting the country is more deadly than COVID-19. What you should see when you see black protesters in the age of Trump and coronavirus is people pushed to the edge, not because they want bars and nail salons open, but because they want to live. To breathe.	parallel structure/ repetition	creates a contrast between the perceived problems to the real issue: racism
racial justice	Worst of all, is that we are expected to justify our outraged behavior every time the cauldron bubbles over. Almost 70 years ago, Langston Hughes asked in his poem "Harlem": "What happens to a dream deferred? / . . . Maybe it sags / like a heavy load. / Or does it explode?"	allusions	emotional appeal — value of life explains the reaction of the Black community references Black artists to connect with the audience
racial justice	Fifty years ago, Marvin Gaye sang in "Inner City Blues": "Make me wanna holler / The way they do my life." And today, despite the impassioned speeches of well-meaning leaders, white and black, they want to silence our voice, steal our breath.	parallel structure	emphasizes the evidence that Black voices are silenced
	So what you see when you see black protesters depends on whether you're living in that burning building or watching it on TV with a bowl of corn chips in your lap waiting for NCIS to start.	juxtaposition	contrasts those living the problem to those watching the problem
racial justice	What I want to see is not a rush to judgment, but a rush to justice.	thesis	call to action

IDEA BANK

Authority

Conflict

Discrimination

Equality

Fairness

Freedom

Independence

Individualism

Justice

Liberty

Loyalty

Oppression

Persuasion

Pride

Protection

Protest

Reason

Rebellion

Retaliation

Revolution

Rights

The United States began in revolution over two centuries ago, and revolutionary ideas have shaped the country's history ever since. Social and political movements for generations have been rooted in the Enlightenment principles of liberty, individualism, and self-government that inspired the nation's founders. Indeed, the very idea of progress itself originates in Enlightenment thought, which proposed that reason, revolution, freedom, and promotion of democratic and patriotic ideals would lead to a better world.

In many ways, the United States is a product of those European Enlightenment ideas. Known as "the Age of Reason," the Enlightenment era spanned the late seventeenth century to the early nineteenth century. Many philosophers, scientists, and writers during this time challenged traditional authorities, such as priests and kings. These thinkers relied on reason, individual observation, and empirical evidence to understand the world. Their view of authority led to new ideas of individualism, freedom, progress, and self-government. We can hear these ideas in the country's founding documents. For example, in 1775, Patrick Henry delivered his "Speech to the Virginia Convention" (p. 118), which ignited the American Revolution by urging the patriots that the time to fight had come, proclaiming, "Give me liberty, or give me death!"

As the colonies grew and prospered, they became more independent from British rule. In the 1760s, the British Parliament began enacting a series of taxes on the colonies to pay off debts from the French and Indian War. To the British government, the measures were justified: its troops

The Pageant of a Nation, an oil painting by Jean Leon Gerome Ferris (1863–1930), depicts Thomas Jefferson, Benjamin Franklin, and John Adams reviewing a draft of the Declaration of Independence in Philadelphia.

It's been said that the American Revolution was a "war of words." What is the relationship between reason and revolution in this "war of words"?

Library of Congress, Prints & Photographs Division, Reproduction number LC-USZC4-9904

had helped defend the colonies during the conflict. But the colonists viewed these policies as unfair and illegitimate "taxation without representation," as they had no voice in Parliament. After the British enacted a tax on tea in 1773, Bostonians raided three British ships and dumped over 92,000 pounds of British tea into the Boston harbor. In retribution, the harbor was closed, which punished the entire city. Soon, the American Revolution was underway.

America's fight for freedom and justice has continued throughout history — from slavery and the civil rights movement to women's suffrage to LGBT rights. Harvey Milk's "You've Got to Have Hope" (p. 122) appeals to these ideas and envisions a democracy that is both participatory and inclusive for all. Today, most of us have witnessed marches, protests, and uprisings, which often stem from injustice and inequality: the 2017 Women's March, #MeToo movement, Black Lives Matter, protests on different sides of the gun rights debate. Indeed, the United States has not always lived up to the promise of democracy for all. African Americans and women, in particular, faced long struggles just to achieve basic voting rights. But the history of the country has witnessed a steady — if gradual — expansion of democratic participation. The continual quest for freedom, justice, and equality will inspire activists to seek social change in the future as well.

REUTERS/Shannon Stapleton

▲

The Women's March is a foundation committed to breaking down systems of oppression against women through nonviolent resistance. On January 21, 2017, women and men all over the world participated in the largest one-day protest in American history.

What characteristics do the people involved in these marches share with other American revolutionaries?

Speech to the Virginia Convention
Patrick Henry

THE TEXT IN CONTEXT

In 1775, in the midst of political debate about whether to prepare for war or find a peaceful resolution with Britain, the Virginia House of Burgesses held a convention. After listening to other delegates, Patrick Henry (1736–1799), the first governor of Virginia, gave a speech that ultimately persuaded Virginia to prepare for the fight against Britain.

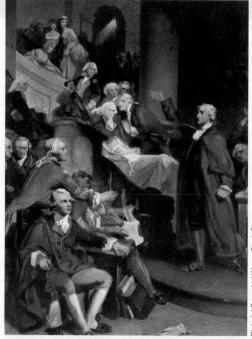

Pictorial Press Ltd/Alamy Stock Photo

No man thinks more highly than I do of the patriotism, as well as abilities, of the very worthy gentlemen who have just addressed the House. But different men often see the same subject in different lights; and, therefore, I hope it will not be thought disrespectful to those gentlemen if, entertaining as I do opinions of a character very opposite to theirs, I shall speak forth my sentiments freely and without reserve. This is no time for ceremony. The question before the House is one of awful moment to this country. For my own part, I consider it as nothing less than a question of freedom or slavery; and in proportion to the magnitude of the subject ought to be the freedom of the debate. It is only in this way that we can hope to arrive at truth, and fulfill the great responsibility which we hold to God and our country. Should I keep back my opinions at such a time, through fear of giving offense, I should consider myself as guilty of treason towards my country, and of an act of disloyalty toward the Majesty of Heaven, which I revere above all earthly kings.

Mr. President, it is natural to man to indulge in the illusions of hope. We are apt to shut our eyes against a painful truth, and listen to the song of that siren till she transforms us into beasts. Is this the part of wise men, engaged in a great and arduous struggle for liberty? Are we disposed to be of the number of those who, having eyes, see not, and, having ears, hear not, the things which so nearly concern their temporal salvation? For my part, whatever anguish of spirit it may cost, I am willing to know the whole truth; to know the worst, and to provide for it.

I have but one lamp by which my feet are guided, and that is the lamp of experience. I know of no way of judging of the future but by the past. And judging by the past, I wish to know what there has been in the conduct of the British ministry for the last ten years to justify those hopes with which gentlemen have been pleased to solace themselves and the House. Is it that insidious smile with which our petition has been lately received? Trust it not, sir; it will prove a snare to your feet. Suffer not yourselves to be betrayed with a kiss. Ask yourselves how this gracious reception of our petition comports with those warlike preparations which cover our waters and darken our land. Are fleets and armies necessary to a work of love and reconciliation? Have we shown ourselves so unwilling to be reconciled that force must be called in to win back our love? Let us not deceive ourselves, sir. These are the implements of war and subjugation; the last arguments to which kings resort. I ask gentlemen, sir, what means this martial array, if its purpose be not to force us to submission? Can gentlemen assign any other possible motive for it? Has Great Britain any enemy, in this quarter of the world, to call for all this accumulation of navies and armies? No, sir, she has none. They are meant for us: they can be meant for no other. They are sent over to bind and rivet upon us those chains which the British ministry have been so long forging. And what have we to oppose to them?

Shall we try argument? Sir, we have been trying that for the last ten years. Have we anything new to offer upon the subject? Nothing. We have held the subject up in every light of which it is capable; but it has been all in vain. Shall we resort to entreaty and humble supplication? What terms shall we find which have not been already exhausted? Let us not, I beseech you, sir, deceive ourselves. Sir, we have done everything that could be done to avert the storm which is now coming on. We have petitioned; we have remonstrated; we have supplicated; we have prostrated ourselves before the throne, and have implored its interposition to arrest the tyrannical hands of the ministry and Parliament. Our petitions have been slighted; our remonstrances have produced additional violence and insult; our supplications have been disregarded; and we have been spurned, with contempt, from the foot of the throne! In vain, after these things, may we indulge the fond hope of peace and reconciliation. There is no longer any room for hope. If we wish to be free—if we mean to preserve inviolate those inestimable privileges for which we have been so long contending—if we mean not basely to abandon the noble struggle in which we have been so long engaged, and which we have pledged ourselves never to abandon until the glorious object of our contest shall be obtained—we must fight! I repeat it, sir, we must fight! An appeal to arms and to the God of hosts is all that is left us!

They tell us, sir, that we are weak; unable to cope with so formidable an adversary. But when shall we be stronger? Will it be the next week, or next year? Will it be when we are totally disarmed, and when a British guard shall be stationed in every house? Shall we gather strength by irresolution and inaction? Shall we acquire the means of effectual resistance by lying supinely on our backs and hugging the delusive phantom of hope, until our enemies shall have bound us hand and foot? Sir, we are not weak if we make a proper use of those means which the God of nature hath placed in our power. The millions of people, armed in the holy cause of liberty, and in such a country as that which we possess, are invincible by any force which our enemy can send against us. Besides, sir, we shall not fight our battles alone. There is a just God who presides over the destinies of nations, and who will raise up friends to fight our battles for us.

The battle, sir, is not to the strong alone; it is to the vigilant, the active, the brave. Besides, sir, we have no election. If we were base enough to desire it, it is now too late to retire from the contest. There is no retreat but in submission and slavery! Our chains are forged! Their clanking may be heard on the plains of Boston! The war is inevitable—and let it come! I repeat it, sir, let it come.

It is in vain, sir, to extenuate the matter. Gentlemen may cry, Peace, Peace—but there is no peace. The war is actually begun! The next gale that sweeps from the north will bring to our ears the clash of resounding arms! Our brethren are already in the field! Why stand we here idle? What is it that gentlemen wish? What would they have? Is life so dear, or peace so sweet, as to be purchased at the price of chains and slavery? Forbid it, Almighty God! I know not what course others may take; but as for me, give me liberty or give me death!

Doug Mills/The New York Times via Associated Press

President Donald Trump stands before a divided nation to give the February 5, 2020, State of the Union address to Congress. The president is the first to campaign for reelection following an impeachment trial. Trump used this speech to exalt his campaign as "the Great America Comeback" while some members of the crowd cheered "four more years." At the end of the speech, Speaker of the House Nancy Pelosi publicly tore up the speech.

How does this image communicate a contrast? Look closely at the audience. What contrasts can you identify? What do they contribute to the photographer's message? In what ways do you think a president's State of the Union address could be like Patrick Henry's Speech to the Virginia Convention?

RHETORICAL SITUATION

1. Henry is **appealing** to his **audience**. Choose an appeal and identify the type of device he is using to achieve that appeal.

2. Considering Henry's **audience** and his **message**, what is Henry's overall **purpose**? Cite particular examples from the text to support your answer.

3. Consider the **audience**. How does Henry **appeal** to the audience, and how do these appeals contribute to the tone of the speech?

CLAIMS AND EVIDENCE

4. In this short speech, Patrick Henry organizes each paragraph beginning with a **claim**. Identify the **line of reasoning** and then discuss the overall effect.

5. **Evidence** and commentary often add the persuasion of a speech. How does the evidence Henry uses add to the effect of his speech?

REASONING AND ORGANIZATION

6. At the end of paragraph 4, Henry states his **call to action**. Identify the call to action. Choose two **reasons** that support and logically affirm this call to action.

7. Patrick Henry begins his speech with contrasting **images** of light and dark. How are these images contrasted, and how does this contrast support his purpose?

8. Describe the **metaphor** that Henry uses in regard to slavery. What ideas are being compared and what message is created?

LANGUAGE AND STYLE

9. Henry sets up several contrasts in this speech. Choose a sentence that contrasts ideas and describe the **syntactical choices** Henry uses to develop the contrast.

10. A famous example of **antithesis** ends the speech. How does that connect to other contrasts throughout the speech?

IDEAS IN AMERICAN CULTURE

11. Henry uses memorable lines that convey his main ideas that resonate even after the speech. Can you think of persuasive slogans or famous sayings that lead movements or revolutions today? Does a line like "give me liberty or give me death" title a movement and give it recognition? Write a slogan or a title that is recognizable today.

PUTTING IT ALL TOGETHER

12. Through the figurative language, the contrasts, the comparisons, and the call to action, Henry insists that the time to fight is now. In a well-written paragraph, analyze how the rhetorical choices contribute to the message.

You've Got to Have Hope

Harvey Milk

THE TEXT IN CONTEXT

Harvey Milk (1930–1978), California's first
openly gay elected official, served on the
San Francisco Board of Supervisors. He
delivered the following speech on June 25,
1978, as part of Gay Freedom Day, otherwise known as San Francisco Pride, a festival and
parade championing the gay community. The following speech was in response to media and
political ads attacking the gay community at the time. Milk was assassinated two days later.

Terry Schmitt/San Francisco Chronicle/Polaris

I'm a person of few surprises so it will come as no surprise to you that what I'm about to say constitutes an announcement of my candidacy for Supervisor of District 5. For all I know, I may be the proverbial straw that broke the camel's back for I'm sure by now that the list of candidates is close to equaling the list of eligible voters. The true test of Democracy is when anybody can run for anything and in this case, almost everybody is. Well, they say Democracy is a participatory process so you can't say we weren't warned. . . .

I've been running for so many things for so long in this city that I wear a pair of sneakers to work . . . after all, you can never tell when another opportunity will present itself. . . .

. . . Let's go back to the beginning. I am announcing my candidacy for Supervisor of a great City. Think about that for a moment. A city isn't a collection of buildings—it isn't downtown with the B of A and a TransAmerica Tower, it isn't the parking lots or the freeways or the theatres or the massage parlors. A city

is people. In this case, some 675,000. Some 60,000 of them live in District 5. They're Latins and Blacks, whites and Chinese, young and old, straight—and gay.

Each of those people has his or her own hopes and aspirations, his or her own viewpoints and problems. Each of them contributes something unique to the life of the city. What they contribute, we call the "quality of life." Friends talking across fences, the baseball players in the playground on Sunday, old ladies tottering down the street hand-in-hand, the smile from a passing stranger.

Buildings have very little to do with the quality of life. They usually go dark at six o'clock at night, concrete hives for the warehousing of workers, monuments to people's greeds and needs. They remain desolate and empty until the people return in the morning to flick the lights back on and fill the corridors with bustle and activity.

There are exceptions, of course, and we happen to be gathered in one of them tonight.

5

It's one of those few buildings that contribute in a very unique way to the hopes and aspirations of a particular group of people. It's not as architecturally beautiful as the B of A or even the TransAmerica. But unlike those buildings, it has a "heart and soul."

Now would you believe this? The city wants to tear it down. For a parking garage. This building—330 Grove—is our Gay Community Center. Our Gay Community Center. Because it has meaning to the Gay people of this city, because for us it has both "heart and soul," we've chosen to pass up the larger hotels, those palaces of marble and ice, and have our dinner here.

Consider this Center. Without it, a few nights ago where would those thousand gays who gather in the aftermath of Dade County gone? Where would they have gathered? Where would the people go who attend the multitude of Gay community meetings here? Where would the people congregate who want to take part in the fight to Save Our Human Rights, in Gay Action, in Lesbians United, in the dozens of other groups who meet here?

In the urban wars, this building has already earned its purple heart. It's played a major part in bringing together a divided people. Without 330 Grove, we would never have been able to get it together, as the saying goes. And right now I would like to give credit to Paul Hardman, without whose foresight and courage this community center would not exist. And why is it in the shape it is in—almost.

Because our Supervisors want to tear this 10 building down. For a parking garage.

For months, this building has served as a focal point for the Gay Community. It's where we meet. It's our own little section of the City's turf. Responsible Gay people have tried for God knows how long to establish a center to which young Gay people can go when they arrive here from the rest of an oppressive America. A place where they can find counseling, friends and most of all, hope. Oh, without this Center, there would still be places they could go. The Tenderloin. Market Street. The St. Francis. They'll find counseling, all right. And they'll find friends. At so much per friend. But they won't find much hope.

Do you blame me if I accuse the present Board of Supervisors of being unresponsive to the needs of the Gay community? Would you deny it if I said the situation is not unique, that the Board is unresponsive to the needs of other groups, both ethnic and social, as well? What about the desire of the Board to move the pornography "Combat Zone" into the lap of Hunter's Point? Were the people of Hunter's Point consulted? When the Black community objected, they were told "it wasn't planned that way, it just happened!"

A few years ago, they closed the Sears store in the Mission district. The store was originally the doorway to the Mission and our city's Latin community. It provided employment, it drew people from other neighborhoods into the Mission so that the economic outlook of the entire area benefitted.

Today, paradoxically enough, it's being turned into an unemployment office. I don't need to tell you what kind of depressing trade-off that is. . . .

And those are only a few examples. . . .   15

There is probably no minority in this city that hasn't been ignored—on the human level—by the present Board of Supervisors. It's no longer the Seniors, the unemployed, the Asian community, the Gay, the Blacks, the Latins and so forth. They're all US. It's US against THEM. If you add up all the USes, you'll find we outnumber the THEMS. And yet the THEMS control.

It's the THEMS who benefit when the Gays and the Blacks and the Latins fight amongst themselves. It's the THEMS who want to tear down the homes and community centers of the USes for their special pet projects. It's the THEMS who divide—and conquer. It's the THEMS who are the real outside agitators in our communities. And they've been here for years.

Who are the THEMS? They're the ones. They pay the taxes and run the corporations and have large investments in the city.

But who buys the soap, the food, the towels, the shoes, the cigarettes, the beer and the cars that make the profits for the corporations? Who buys the insurance which provides the profits for the THEMS? Who puts their money into the banks so the THEMS can invest in their pet projects? Who convinced us all that somehow people removal was the same as urban renewal?

One of the biggest myths spread by the THEMS is that since it's "their" money to begin with, they should say how the taxes are spent. But it's your money. Oh, there's a crumb here and there that's tossed to the different communities. They fund a program, anoint a few "leaders" to run it who then go into the community and shout: "Look what they've done for us!"   20

The THEMS get most of the pie, the anointed leaders get a few crumbs—and therefore sing the praises of their masters— and the community gets a few invisible specks. The anointed leaders are the Uncle Toms—and yes, the Gay community has its fair share. Look at who sings the praises of the government in power and you'll see—for the most part—people who have been granted position or power or income.

Now let's get personal. Okay, Harvey, you say, enough of the rhetoric—what are you

going to do? As a supervisor, I will raise questions in public and demand answers. On how the money is raised. And how the money is spent. I will force the other supervisors to stand up and be counted when it comes to the spending priorities of the city. As one immediate example: Why money for every other parade and none for the Gay Day parade, the second largest in the City? Maybe the largest. And I will question the lack of priority for other groups and communities. It's true that I've run . . . and run . . . and run. . . .

Why?

Because I think there is a tremendous and vital difference between a "friend of the Gay community" and an avowed Gay in public office. Gays have now been slandered nationwide. We have been tarred with the brush of pornography, we have been libelously accused in the Dade County Affair. It is not enough to have a "friend" represent us, no matter how good a friend he or she may be. The Black community made up its mind to that long ago when they realized that the myths about Blacks could only be dispelled by electing black leaders, so that the Black community could be judged by those leaders and not by black criminals and myths.

The Spanish community should not be judged by Latin criminals and myths.   25

The Asian community should not be judged by Asian criminals and myths.

The Italian community should not be judged by the Mafia and myths.

Neither should the Gay community be judged by its minutely few Gay criminals and myths. Like every other group, we should be judged by our leaders. By those who are themselves Gay. By those who are visible. For [the] Invisible, we remain in limbo. A shadowy myth, a person who has no parents, no brothers, no sisters, no friends who are straight,

no important positions of employment.
A tenth of the nation composed solely of
stereotypes and would-be seducers of small
children—and no offense intended to the
stereotypes.

Well, the Black community is not judged
by its "friends" but by its black legislators
and leaders. We must give people outside our
community the chance to judge us by our Gay
legislators and leaders. A gay person in office
can set a tone, can command respect not only
from that larger community but from young
people in our own community who need both
examples and . . . hope.

The first Gay person we elect must be   30
strong, a fighter, one who is not content to
sit in the back of the bus. He must be above
wheeling and dealing. If I had been a wheeler
and dealers, I would be on the Board of Permit
Appeals today. . . . The first Gay person to be
elected must for the good of all of us, be truly
independent. Unbossed and unbought! . . .

I think, perhaps, that too many of our elected
and appointed leaders forget that their first
duty is to lead. And the only way to lead is by
example. I disapprove of almost everything that
Joe Alioto stood for but I would never deny that
he was a leader, that he understood the power
of a public office and how to use it to lead.

And so hid Our appointed Gay leaders. They
did not lead. . . .

. . . It took a group of concerned Gay people
to put out a statement warning of outsiders
starting trouble in the Gay community. It was
a heavy statement—but if you were there you
know it was a necessary one. No other Gay
candidate signed it. I took a strong position
about the tone of the parade this coming Sunday. I made enemies. But I felt it had to be said
and since our gay appointed leaders said nothing, I did. And without the power and office
behind me like others have.

Leadership was called for and where were
the other candidates?

Well, no announcement for candidacy for   35
public office can avoid overuse of the word "I"
and I'm as guilty as anyone. And now it's time
to tell you why I've run so persistently for public office.

I'll never forget what it was like coming out.

I'll never forget the looks on the faces of
those who have lost hope, whether it be young
Gays or seniors of Blacks looking for that
almost-impossible-to-find job or Latins trying
to explain their problems and aspirations in a
tongue that's foreign to them.

I'll never forget that people are more
important than buildings and neighborhoods
more important than freeways.

I've deliberately scheduled this announcement for Gay Pride Week. I've watched a million people close their closet doors behind
them and I know they cannot go back.

I use the word "I" because I'm proud of   40
myself.

I stand here before you tonight because I'm
proud of you.

I've planned for some time to walk in the
march on Sunday because I'm proud of my
sisters and brothers.

And I'm running for public office because
I think it's time we've had a legislator who
was gay and proud of that fact and one who
will not walk away from the responsibilities
that face such a legislator. I walked among
the angry and frustrated after Dade country
[sic]. . . . I walked among the angry and sad
gay sisters and brothers last night at City
Hall and late last night as they lit candles
and stood in silence on Castro Street reaching out for some symbolic thing that would
give them hope. . . .

Hope for a better world.

Hope for a better tomorrow.   45

Hope for a place to go to if the pressures at home are [too] great.

Hope that all will be alright.

Without <u>hope</u>, not only the gays but the blacks, the seniors, the poor, the handicapped the USes give up . . . if you help me get elected that election—no it is not my election it is yours—it will mean that a green light is lit . . . a green light that says to all who feel lost and disenfranchised that you now can go forward—it means <u>hope</u> and we—no, you and you and you and yes, <u>you</u> got to give them hope.

All-gender restrooms have become the most recent civil rights issue for the LGBTQ community. Throughout the country, state and local governments have been considering the need for more inclusive accommodations — and have faced controversy in the process. This issue affects anyone who identifies in a way other than male and female, especially individuals in the nonbinary and transgender communities.

Lucy Nicholson/Reuters

What is the controversy with this image? Why are some schools converting facilities to all-gender bathrooms, while other schools are requiring that all restrooms designate a gender? How does an issue like this connect to Milk's message of hope?

RHETORICAL SITUATION

1. Who is the speaker, and what is his **message**?

2. From Milk's **perspective**, who comprises "US" and "THEM"? How does this contrast contribute to his **message**?

3. How does Milk **appeal** to "US"? How does Milk appeal to "THEM"?

CLAIMS AND EVIDENCE

4. Milk begins supporting his argument by mentioning specific places in the community. Give an example of a specific place and discuss how this place supports his **thesis**.

5. How does Milk's personal experience contribute to the power of his **thesis**? Identify an instance when he uses personal experience as **evidence**. How does this evidence strengthen his argument?

REASONING AND ORGANIZATION

6. Many paragraphs implement **deductive organization**. Give an example from the text of deductive organization and explain how this **line of reasoning** strengthens the paragraph.

LANGUAGE AND STYLE

7. Milk's speech is filled with **repetition**. Focus on the language that is being repeated and consider the effect of the repetition. Why is he choosing to repeat words or phrases, and how does it contribute to the **purpose**?

8. Milk ends his speech with a short, **simple sentence**. What effect does this **syntax** have on the audience?

IDEAS IN AMERICAN CULTURE

9. Milk is speaking to the gay community, but the speech sends a resounding message to other audiences as well. Why is his call to be hopeful a challenge to the community? Does maintaining hope remain a challenge for different communities today?

PUTTING IT ALL TOGETHER

10. Arguments are developed logically through inductive and deductive reasoning. Choose a paragraph that is structured inductively or deductively and then explain how the structure affects the audience.

IDEAS IN AMERICAN CULTURE
Patriotism and Democracy

IDEA BANK

Crisis

Democracy

Exceptionalism

Freedom

Government

Independence

Individualism

Justice

Liberty

Loyalty

Nationalism

Patriotism

Persuasion

Pride

Protection

Resilience

Revolution

Rights

Tradition

Unity

The colonists were not unanimous in their support for American independence. Those who wished to remain loyal to the British crown were called "loyalists." But most of the population supported the "patriots," who sought freedom from British rule. These opposing factions had engaged in a battle of ideas in speeches, pamphlets, newspapers, and even songs before any shots were fired. One such 1776 pamphlet, *The American Crisis* (p. 130), written by the philosopher and patriot Thomas Paine, called for rebellion so that they could establish a democratic and egalitarian form of republican government.

With the Revolutionary War under way in 1775, colonial delegates met at the Second Continental Congress in Philadelphia to declare the colonies free from British rule. They drafted the Declaration of Independence, which drew on Enlightenment ideas, such as natural rights, individual liberties, and the

AP Photo/Evan Vucci

▲

There are 47 million 18- to 29-year-olds who were eligible to vote in the 2020 presidential election. Students for Trump is a student organization founded in 2015. The group brought together an estimated 3,000 young conservative voters in Phoenix, Arizona, on June 23, 2020, to rally for Donald Trump's reelection.

How do political rallies foster hope in the democratic process and encourage political engagement? How important is it for political candidates to involve young voters in campaigns and rallies?

democratic principle that governments derive their legitimacy from the consent of the people. It was adopted on July 4, 1776, when the colonies officially severed ties with Britain. American and British troops fought until 1781, when the last of the British army surrendered to General George Washington at Yorktown. In 1776, the colonies declared their independence; after the war with Britain ended in 1783, a new nation was born.

While the term "patriot" once referred to colonial revolutionaries, "patriotism" also has a more general meaning: national pride and love of country. In this context, it retains a positive connotation. Taken to extremes, however, patriotism can become militant and chauvinistic: the belief that our nation is superior to others — or even that a nation has the right to dominate others. The historian Donald Kagan explores this distinction in "On Patriotism" (p. 134), where he argues that Americans need to be patriotic to face the challenges of the future and to protect our "free, democratic republic."

Individual freedoms are protected by the Constitution which also remains central to a sense of patriotism. Many public and military officials must swear an oath to defend the Constitution before they can take office. Some people even carry a pocket-version around in their daily lives. But, the Constitution also places many limits on democracy to protect state and individual rights. Even so, American patriotism remains resilient. Today, patriotism flourishes through military service, the pledge of allegiance, protest, and youth engagement in democracy.

Artwork by Shepard Fairey for Amplifier.org

▲

We the People (2016), a series of prints created by Shepard Fairey, an American street artist and graphic designer who founded OBEY Clothing. Fairey created the three-image set as part of a Kickstarter campaign that would be used to finance a protest campaign against President Trump.

According to the Kickstarter campaign, the collection is "a series of images that capture the shared humanity of our diverse America." In what ways do these images reflect a spirit of democracy and patriotism?

The American Crisis Number 1

Thomas Paine

THE TEXT IN CONTEXT

A master of persuasion, philosopher and author Thomas Paine (1737–1809) generated support among colonists and motivated Revolutionary soldiers in the camps. In what became the last battle of the Revolutionary War on December 23, 1776, General George Washington ordered that this first in a series of thirteen pamphlets be read aloud in efforts to motivate discouraged, tired, and out-numbered troops.

These are the times that try men's souls. The summer soldier and the sunshine patriot will, in this crisis, shrink from the service of their country; but he that stands it NOW, deserves the love and thanks of man and woman. Tyranny, like hell, is not easily conquered; yet we have this consolation with us, that the harder the conflict, the more glorious the triumph. What we obtain too cheap, we esteem too lightly: it is dearness only that gives everything its value. Heaven knows how to put a proper price upon its goods; and it would be strange indeed if so celestial an article as FREEDOM should not be highly rated. Britain, with an army to enforce her tyranny, has declared that she has a right (*not only to* TAX) but "to BIND *us in* ALL CASES WHATSOEVER," and if being *bound in that manner*, is not slavery, then is there not such a thing as slavery upon earth. Even the expression is impious; for so unlimited a power can belong only to God. . . .

I have as little superstition in me as any man living, but my secret opinion has ever been, and still is, that God Almighty will not give up a people to military destruction, or leave them unsupportedly to perish, who have so earnestly and so repeatedly sought to avoid the calamities of war, by every decent method which wisdom could invent. Neither have I so much of the infidel in me, as to suppose that He has relinquished the government of the world, and given us up to the care of devils; and as I do not, I cannot see on what grounds the king of Britain can look up to heaven for help against us: a common murderer, a highwayman, or a house-breaker, has as good a pretence as he. . . .

But, before the line of irrecoverable separation be drawn between us, let us reason the matter together: Your conduct is an invitation to the enemy, yet not one in a thousand of you has heart enough to join him. Howe is as much deceived by you as the American cause is injured by you. He expects you will all take up arms, and flock to his standard, with muskets on your shoulders. Your opinions are of no use to him, unless you support him personally, for 'tis soldiers, and not Tories, that he wants.

I once felt all that kind of anger, which a man ought to feel, against the mean principles that are held by the Tories: a noted one, who kept a tavern at Amboy, was standing at his door, with as pretty a child in his hand, about eight or nine years old, as I ever saw, and after speaking his mind as freely as he thought was prudent, finished with this unfatherly expression, "Well! give me peace in my day." Not a man lives on the continent but fully believes that a separation must some time or other finally take place, and a generous parent should have said, "If there must be trouble, let it be in my day, that my child may have peace;" and this single reflection, well applied, is sufficient to awaken every man to duty. Not a place upon earth might be so happy as America. Her situation is remote from all the wrangling world, and she has nothing to do but to trade with them. A man can distinguish himself between temper and principle, and I am as confident, as I am that God governs the world, that America will never be happy till she gets clear of foreign dominion. Wars, without ceasing, will break out till that period arrives, and the continent must in the end be conqueror; for though the flame of liberty may sometimes cease to shine, the coal can never expire. . . .

America did not, nor does not want force; but she wanted a proper application of that force. Wisdom is not the purchase of a day, and it is no wonder that we should err at the first setting off. From an excess of tenderness, we were unwilling to raise an army, and trusted our cause to the temporary defence of a well-meaning militia. A summer's experience has now taught us better; yet with those troops, while they were collected, we were able to set bounds to the progress of the enemy, and, thank God! they are again assembling. I always considered militia as the best troops in the world for a sudden exertion, but they will not do for a long campaign. . . . Say not that this is revenge, call it rather the soft resentment of a suffering people, who, having no object in view but the *good of all*, have staked their *own all* upon a seemingly doubtful event. Yet it is folly to argue against determined hardness; eloquence may strike the ear, and the language of sorrow draw forth the tear of compassion, but nothing can reach the heart that is steeled with prejudice. . . .

. . . Let it be told to the future world, that in the depth of winter, when nothing but hope and virtue could survive, that the city and the country, alarmed at one common danger, came forth to meet and to repulse it. Say not that thousands are gone, turn out your tens of thousands; throw not the burden of the day upon Providence, but "show your faith by your works," that God may bless you. It matters not where you live, or what rank of life you hold, the evil or the blessing will reach you all. The far and the near, the home counties and the back, the rich and the poor, will suffer or rejoice alike. The heart that feels not now is dead; the blood of his children will curse his cowardice, who shrinks back at a time when a little might have saved the whole and made *them* happy. I love the man that can smile in trouble, that can gather strength from distress, and grow brave by reflection. 'Tis the business of little minds to shrink; but he whose heart is firm, and whose conscience approves his conduct, will pursue his principles unto death. My own line of reasoning is to myself as straight and clear as a ray of light. Not all the treasures of the world, so far as I believe, could have induced me to support an offensive war, for I think it murder; but if a thief breaks into my house, burns and destroys my property, and kills or threatens to kill me, or those that are in it, and to *"bind me in all cases whatsoever"* to his absolute will, am I to suffer it? What signifies it to me, whether he who does it is a king or a common man; my countryman or not my countryman; whether it be done by an individual villain, or an army of them? If we reason to the root of things we shall find no difference; neither can any just cause be assigned why we should punish in the one case and pardon in the other. Let them call me rebel and welcome, I feel no concern from it; but I should suffer the misery of devils, were I to make a whore of my soul by swearing allegiance to one whose character is that of a sottish, stupid, stubborn, worthless, brutish man. I conceive likewise a horrid idea in receiving mercy from a being, who at the last day shall be shrieking to the rocks and mountains to cover him, and fleeing with terror from the orphan, the widow, and the slain of America.

I thank God, that I fear not. I see no real cause for fear. I know our situation well and can see the way out of it. . . .

This is the first political cartoon published in 1754 in an American newspaper. This illustration is attributed to Benjamin Franklin. The image is a snake segmented in eight pieces and labeled as the original colonies (New England as the head with four colonies; Georgia was not included). The image appeared with an editorial about the "disunited state" of the colonies.

How does this image serve to represent unity? What is the message for a divided nation? Paine and Franklin are communicating to a similar audience. Explain what effect this image would have on their audience.

RHETORICAL SITUATION

1. Identify an ethical, emotional, or logical **appeal** in Paine's argument. What effect does this appeal have on the audience? Why would Paine use such an appeal?

2. How does the organization of the evidence create an **appeal**? How do the evidence and organization work together to persuade the audience?

CLAIMS AND EVIDENCE

3. How does Paine create a shared experience between himself and his **audience**?

4. Paine supports his **claim** with **evidence**. What type of evidence does he choose? Why would this evidence be effective for this audience?

REASONING AND ORGANIZATION

5. How is the pamphlet organized? Choose a paragraph and discuss the development. Is it organized **inductively** or **deductively**? How does the logic contribute to the effect?

LANGUAGE AND STYLE

6. Identify any example of **imagery**. How does the imagery support Paine's message?

7. What contrasts does Paine establish? Which rhetorical choices does Paine use to establish the contrasts? How do the particular contrasts help advance his **perspective**?

IDEAS IN AMERICAN CULTURE

8. Who are the modern-day Thomas Paines? In other words, who is fighting for important causes in our world today? What are some of the similarities in how those individuals are engaging others in their revolutions? What appeals are they using to persuade?

PUTTING IT ALL TOGETHER

9. Explain how Paine uses allusion, analogy, and contrast to advance his message for this particular audience.

On Patriotism
Donald Kagan

THE TEXT IN CONTEXT

Donald Kagan (b. 1932), a historian, classicist, and professor at Yale University, published the following essay in the *Yale Review* in October 2011, ten years after the 9/11 terrorist attacks on Americans. Professor Kagan continues to write about the need for a patriotic education as part of democracy. Professor Kagan won the national humanities medal in 2002.

In October 2001, without dissent, Congress requested that the president designate September 11 "Patriot Day," a national day of remembrance of the attacks by international terrorists on two American cities that killed thousands of innocent civilians. When they had recovered from their shock after the attacks, most Americans reacted in two ways: They clearly and powerfully supported their government's determination to use military force to prevent future attacks by capturing or killing the perpetrators and tearing out their organizations root and branch. And, to this end, they supported the removal of the leaders of states that supported, abetted, or gave refuge to terrorists unless those leaders abandoned such practices. Most Americans also expressed a new sense of unity and an explicit love for their country that had not been seen for a long time.

Not every country deserves the devotion and patriotic support of its citizens. Dictatorships of whatever kind have no right to these commitments, for they rule over unfree, often unwilling, people as if over slaves; they lack moral legitimacy. But citizens of free countries like the United States can vote in elections with real choices for lawmakers and leaders, and those who don't approve of their country's laws and way of life have the right and opportunity to change them by legal process. Failing in such an attempt, they are free to leave the country with all their property. By staying they are tacitly accepting the laws of the country and the principles on which those laws are based. They are free to doubt them and even to denounce them, but they are morally bound to observe them. For Americans, as for citizens of any free country, there really is a social contract like those imagined by the political philosophers, and that contract provides legitimacy. People who tacitly accept that contract have the moral obligation to defend and support the country they have chosen as their own—that is, to be patriotic.

It seems to me, moreover, that Americans have especially good reasons for belief in and devotion to their country. America has been a beacon of liberty to the world since its creation and was especially so in the twentieth century. The September 11 attacks produced a wave of vilification against America from "intellectuals" at home and abroad, but it is worth remembering what Americans did in the twentieth century. They helped save Europe from German domination in two world wars. After World War II they rebuilt the continent from the ashes. They stood against and helped defeat the Soviet Communist government, which along with Nazi Germany and Maoist China, was among the most brutal regimes in history. They stopped the slaughter in the Balkans while Europeans stood by and watched, and they drove Saddam Hussein from Kuwait and ultimately from his seat of power as he prepared to resume his goal of dominating the Middle East.

"People should think," the late David Halberstam said from New York following the attacks, "what the world would be like without the backdrop of American leadership with all its flaws over the past sixty years. Probably, I think, a bit like hell." In my view it doesn't take an American chauvinist to suggest that there is some virtue in a country that has helped save the world from Wilhelmian Germany's right-wing imperialism, Hitler's Nazi regime, Japan's militaristic domination, and Stalin's totalitarianism. Yet voices here and abroad from the world of "intellectual" orthodoxy continue to condemn and blame the United States, as they did throughout the Cold War.

These dissenters' ideas have a wide currency 5 and reflect a serious flaw in American education that should especially concern those of us who take some part in it. The encouragement of patriotism is no longer a part of our public educational system, and the cost of that omission is now making itself felt. In the intellectual climate of our time the very suggestion brings contemptuous sneers or outrage, depending on the mood of the listener. Many have been the attacks on patriotism for its alleged intolerance, arrogance, and bellicosity, but that is to equate it with its bloated distortion, chauvinism. My favorite dictionary defines the latter as "militant and boastful devotion to and glorification of one's country," but a patriot as "one who loves, supports, and defends his country." That does not require us to hate, condemn, denigrate, or attack any other country, nor does it require us to admire our own uncritically. Few countries have been subjected to as much criticism and questioning, even from its patriotic citizens, as our own.

So distant are we from a proper understanding of patriotism that I sometimes hear people say, "It is silly to be patriotic. Why should I love, support, and defend a country just because, quite by chance, I happened to be born there?" In fact, there should be a presupposition in favor of patriotism, for human beings are not solitary creatures but require organized societies if they are to flourish or even survive. Just as individuals must have an appropriate self-love in order to perform well, and an appropriate love of their families if both are to prosper, so, too, must they love their country if it is to survive. Neither family nor nation can flourish without love, support, and defense, and individuals who have benefited from those institutions not only serve their self-interest in defending them but also have a moral responsibility to give them that support.

The assaults on patriotism, therefore, are failures of character. They are made by privileged people who enjoy the full benefits offered by the country they deride and detest—its opportunities, its freedom, its riches—but lack the basic decency to pay the allegiance and respect that honor demands. For the rest of us, our own honor and our devotion to our nation's special virtues require us to respect and defend these privileged people's opportunity to be irresponsible and subversive of our safety—but nothing forbids us from pointing out the despicable nature of their behavior.

Free countries like our own, it seems to me, have an even greater need of patriotic citizens than others. Every country requires a high degree of cooperation and unity among its people if it is to achieve the internal harmony that every good society requires. These must rest on something shared and valued in common. Most countries have relied on the common ancestry and traditions of their people as the basis of their unity, but the United States of America can rely on no such commonality. We are an enormously diverse and varied people, composed almost entirely of immigrants or the descendants of immigrants. We come from almost every continent, our forebears spoke—and many of us still speak—many different languages, and all the races and religions of the world are to be found among us. The great strengths provided by this diversity are matched by great dangers. We are always vulnerable to divisions that can be exploited to set one group against another and destroy the unity and harmony that have allowed us to flourish.

We live in a time when civic devotion has been undermined and national unity is under attack. The individualism that is so crucial a part of our tradition is often used to destroy civic responsibility. The idea of a common American culture, enriched by the diverse elements that compose it but available equally to all, is also under assault, and some are trying to replace it with narrower and politically divisive programs that are certain to set one group of Americans against another. The answer to these problems, and our only hope for the future, must lie in a proper education, which philosophers have long put at the center of the consideration of justice and the good society. We rightly look to education to solve the pressing current problems of our economic and technological competition with other nations, but we must not neglect the inescapable political and ethical effects of education. We in the academic community have too often engaged in miseducation. If we ignore civic education, the forging of a

single people, the building of a legitimate patriotism, we will have selfish individuals, heedless of the needs of others, reluctant to work toward the common good and to defend our country when defense is needed. In telling the story of the American experience we must insist on the honest search for truth; we must permit no comfortable self-deception or evasion. The story of this country's vision of a free, democratic republic and of its struggle to achieve it need not fear the most thorough examination and can proudly stand comparison with that of any other land. It provides the basis for the civic devotion and love of country we so badly need.

Some critics of America's efforts to defend itself against its current enemies, who insist that our wars in Afghanistan and Iraq are too costly and that success is unattainable, who demand that we withdraw from one or both of these battlefronts whatever the cost, claim that they are no less patriotic than others. To be sure, a patriot may disagree with the policy and strategy of the government and legitimately try to argue for change. He or she may not, however, attempt to justify opposition to that policy and gain political advantage from so doing by tendentiously misdescribing the facts, by insisting that the war has been lost when it plainly has not. The war in Iraq was not lost, although opponents of that war, even as the situation improved, rushed to declare America defeated. They offered no plausible alternative to what turned out to be the successful strategy and took no serious notice of the dreadful consequences of swift withdrawal in defeat. They seemed to be panicked by the possibility of success and eager to bring about withdrawal and defeat before success could get in the way. Such are the actions of defeatists and political opportunists; they can never be called patriotic. . . .

In spite of the shock caused by the attacks on New York and Washington and the years of war that have followed, I am not sure that we yet understand how serious is the challenge that now faces us. Early in the Iraq War I noted that "we are only at the beginning of a long and deadly war that will inflict loss and pain, that will require sacrifice and steady commitment and determination even during very dark hours to come. We must be powerfully armed, morally as well as materially, if we are to do what must be done. That will take courage and unity, and these must rest on a justified and informed patriotism to sustain us through the worst times." I think those words are still relevant.

A verse by Edna St. Vincent Millay provides a clear answer to the question of why Americans should love their country and make the sacrifices needed to defend it and its principles:

> Not for the flag
> Of any land because myself was born there
> Will I give up my life.
> But will I love that land where man is free,
> And that will I defend.

Ours is such a land, and it will need the legitimate patriotism of its people in the long, dangerous, and difficult struggle that lies ahead.

15

LLUIS GENE/Getty Images

▲

There is a long tradition of using the flag in public protests. Over the years, people have burned flags, waved flags, or altered them to send a message as this protestor did in 2020.

How does the American flag represent both patriotism and protest? Is the flag a unifying symbol of tradition and revolution? How do these contrasting ideas unite to create an understanding of patriotism? Consider Kagan's perspective on these ideas. How does he reconcile protest in his definition of patriotism?

RHETORICAL SITUATION

1. Who is the **speaker**, and what is his **perspective** on patriotism? Select evidence that supports this perspective.

2. How does the rhetorical situation (**exigence** and **context**) shape the **purpose** of this speech? At the end of the first paragraph, how is Kagan's response to such events a definition of patriotism?

3. Kagan often makes logical appeals in this argument. Give an example of facts, or **analogy**. Explain how Kagan's use of logic also furthers an ethical appeal.

CLAIMS AND EVIDENCE

4. Consider Kagan's evidence. Is the type of **evidence** effective for his argument? Why or why not?

5. Identify Kagan's **thesis** and describe the **line of reasoning** that he uses to support it.

REASONING AND ORGANIZATION

6. How does Kagan build his paragraphs? Are they **inductively** or **deductively** composed? Does this strengthen or weaken his **persuasion**?

7. What is Kagan's **call to action**? How does the evidence connect logically to this challenge?

LANGUAGE AND STYLE

8. Considering the **syntax** and **diction**, what can we gather about the audience? How does this affect this selection?

9. Kagan **juxtaposes** many ideas in this passage. Consider two ideas that are grammatically contrasted, and discuss the relationship of the ideas and the message this opposition creates.

IDEAS IN AMERICAN CULTURE

10. What does patriotism look like in your community? Can you identify and discuss what it means to be a patriot today? More importantly, must we all agree on a definition to be patriotic? Why or why not?

PUTTING IT ALL TOGETHER

11. How does Kagan's definition serve to mitigate the polarized culture of today? Explain how the rhetorical situation affects Kagan's judicious response.

COMPOSITION WORKSHOP
Writing a Persuasive Argument

All around us, we witness things in our lives that we wish to change. This may be something within our homes, our schools, our communities, or our world. When you desire to effect change, you must strategically select reasoning, evidence, and language that will resonate with and influence your intended audience.

In this workshop, you will have the opportunity to develop a persuasive argument that provides logical reasons supported by evidence to convince your audience to take action about an issue or cause of importance to you.

KEY POINT

Persuasive arguments seek to motivate or persuade their audiences through logic, emotion, and credibility.

Phones Create Barriers between Peers
Kalindi Desai

The following student example is an editorial published in the College Station High School newspaper the *Catamount* in 2016. With the help of the marginal notations, discuss the writer's use of evidence, rhetorical strategies, line of reasoning, and call to action to persuade her audience.

The ability to communicate with people through cell phones and social media is a technological discovery that has made it easier than ever to interact with people from many areas of the world. We can talk to our friends that live miles away at any time, see what our favorite celebrities are up to, or keep up with whatever news is going around. But with this advance comes a downfall. People have become too afraid to talk to others about issues in person because confrontation scares them since our generation is so used to confronting others behind their thumbs through a cell phone screen.

writer includes context for the argument

introduces problem: people are afraid of face-to-face conversation

It's the easier option. You don't feel bad calling someone names if you can't see their face or allow them to retaliate in person. We seem to always be taking the easier route. The one that won't make us feel like horrible people for spreading rumors and forming lies about people that are based on assumptions.

reason: (opposing viewpoints) online communication is easier

Friend issues are highly common in high school due to changing personalities. With these friend issues comes confrontation. Our generation has somehow been brainwashed into thinking that it's okay to communicate over text about serious problems that could possibly hurt someone's feelings.

reason: friend issues arise with online communication

*evidence: example
illustrates the
problem*

> But it's not okay. Text messages don't express any emotion whatsoever. You could send something that is meant to be innocently lighthearted, but your words could be interpreted in a completely different way by the receiver of the message.

A large amount of unnecessary conflict results from this.

*reason: online
communication
does not reflect
true feelings*

> Instead of creating new problems by typing words that are sent through phones, we should talk to people in person and discuss our problems through a civilized conversation. 24 years ago, it was

*thesis/claim: writer
links to the idea of
fear once more*

> impossible for people to even communicate through a text, but now here we are in 2016 and we seem to be nearly incapable of talking to our peers without checking our phones every five minutes.

We like people's pictures on Instagram, but we are unable to say

*rhetorical question:
writer invites the
audience to act*

> hello to them in the hallways. If we are so afraid to say one word to someone in person, how are we supposed to talk to people about serious issues that could potentially affect our relationship with them?

 ## YOUR ASSIGNMENT

Imagine that you have been invited to make a presentation at your school or to write an opinion column for your online school or community newspaper. Choose a relevant issue for which you desire change. Write a speech or essay that persuades or calls your audience to action. Support your position with evidence from your experience, observation, and research.

Your persuasive argument should include:

- A thesis statement that makes a claim (perspective + idea) and calls your audience to action
- A line of reasoning to develop your claim
- Evidence to prove your reasoning
- Strategies to appeal to your audience

Look around you and consider what you would like to change. You could be like the revolutionaries in this unit.

Potential Subjects

- Immigration
- Gun control
- Identity
- College costs
- Poverty
- Health care
- Free speech
- Electoral college
- Gender equality

CLAIMS AND EVIDENCE Selecting Relevant Evidence

AP® **Enduring Understanding (CLE-1)**

Writers make claims about subjects, rely on evidence that supports the reasoning that justifies the claim, and often acknowledge or respond to other, possibly opposing, arguments.

You learned in Unit 1 that you combine an idea with your perspective to create a thesis. Persuasion takes the argument one step further, urging readers to take action based on the claims and evidence in the argument. So, in a persuasive argument, you must establish a thesis that calls the reader to action and then support that thesis with relevant evidence.

Writing a Thesis for Persuasion

Subjects or topics are very broad and invite many smaller conversations and debates. In persuasion, you must narrow the topic to have a clear focus and provide a thesis statement that establishes a logical claim and a perspective. Most often, this claim is driven by an overarching idea connected to your perspective. Together, these make your thesis. In the example that follows, the topic is cell phone use in the classroom. An idea associated with the topic is the learning environment. The thesis is connected to the idea of the learning environment.

Your position should be revealed in your perspective. Issues are complex; therefore, the most intriguing arguments are not simply pro or con. Instead, they reveal their position, either in support of or in opposition to the issue at hand, through the perspective they take. Consider the example topic asking you to take a position on smartphones. Rather than simply stating a position, such as smartphones should not be allowed in school, you must offer a thesis with a claim — that smartphones are too distracting and tempting and ultimately harm rather than help the learning environment. By doing so, you reveal your position that they should not be allowed in school through your perspective. The final step will urge your audience to change a behavior or attitude in your call to action.

Supporting the Thesis with Relevant Evidence

Without evidence, the audience may not be convinced to act, so you must generate evidence to support your message. You learned earlier in this unit that evidence can come from a wide range of sources or from your own observations and experiences. Most importantly, it should be carefully chosen with your audience in mind. You can use the STAR acronym to remind you that evidence should be sufficient, typical, accurate, and relevant.

Example Persuasive Thesis with Claim (Call to Action + Perspective + Idea)	
Topic: Smartphones in school classrooms	
Even though smartphones provide instant access to an immeasurable amount of information, **students should refrain from using them** (*call to action*) in the classroom because **they are too distracting and tempting** (*perspective*) to most students and ultimately **harm rather than help the learning environment** (*idea*).	*Rather than simply stating a position such as smartphones should not be allowed in school, you urge the audience to change a behavior and stop using them in class. This call to action is based on your claim — that smartphones are too distracting and tempting and ultimately harm rather than help the learning environment — and your perspective that they harm the learning environment.*

Begin by listing all the evidence that comes to mind or that you can find through your research. In the next step of the process, you will begin to organize that evidence within your persuasive argument. Review the following chart for some examples.

Thesis with a Call to Action	Even though they provide instant access to an immeasurable amount of information, students should refrain from using cell phones in the classroom because they are too distracting and tempting to most students and ultimately harm rather than help the learning environment.	
Possible Evidence		
Facts, Statistics, Expert Opinions, Experiments	**Details, Illustrations, Analogies**	**Personal Experiences or Observations**
Rutgers study links in-class cell phone use with lower test scores. Around 97 percent of college students use their phones during class for noneducational purposes, according to a study published last month in the *Journal of Media Education*. In one survey, 80 percent of students agreed that using a cell phone in class decreases their ability to pay attention.	Trying to pay attention to a class lecture and looking at the phone is like trying to listen to directions from three people at one time. Looking at a text or other content during a lecture essentially works like a delete button, clearing out what the student just read or heard. A passionate lecturer cannot compete with the soothing buzz, warm light, and familiar ding of the phone inviting students to an enticing world of information.	I have seen students cheating with Snapchat during class quizzes. My brother has had to see a counselor because of his addiction to his cell phone. My teachers use smartphone technology in their lessons with polls and discussion boards.

INSIDER AP® TIP

Evidence must connect to the idea. Writers incorporate relevant evidence by connecting it to the idea. If the evidence is not connected to the idea, a writer should leave it out.

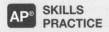

AP® SKILLS PRACTICE | CLAIMS AND EVIDENCE
Selecting Relevant Evidence

1. Develop a thesis with a call to action about your topic.
2. Brainstorm evidence to support your thesis.

Thesis with a Call to Action		
Possible Evidence		
Facts, Statistics, Expert Opinions, Experiments	Details, Illustrations, Analogies	Personal Experiences or Observations

RHETORICAL SITUATION **Appealing to an Audience**

AP® Enduring Understanding (RHS-1)

Individuals write within a particular situation and make strategic writing choices based on that situation.

After writers gather evidence, they choose and arrange that evidence strategically and explain that evidence to appeal to the logic and emotions of their audience and to establish their own expertise, goodwill, and credibility.

As you write your essay, you will do the same. Your thesis and the evidence you choose to support it should resonate with your audience. You should explain your evidence and connect it to your claim. How you explain and incorporate your evidence depends on your audience — what they know and think about your topic.

Examples of Rhetorical Appeals		
Appeal to Logic	Appeal to Emotion	Establishing Credibility
In one survey, 80 percent of students agreed that using a cell phone in class decreases their ability to pay attention. [logos — statistics, research]	Because my brother could not resist checking his social media during class, his grade continued to fall until he ultimately failed the class and had to repeat it in the summer. [pathos — fear of failure]	As a high school student, not only do I enjoy spending time on my phone connecting with friends but I also use many resources to help me with my studies. [ethos — common ground with an audience, experience with the topic]

AP® SKILLS PRACTICE | RHETORICAL SITUATION
Appealing to an Audience

Think about your topic and answer the following questions:

- Who is my audience?
- What do I want my audience to do or stop doing? What is my call to action?
- What do they already know and believe about my topic?
- Will the audience be moved more by logic, emotion, or a combination of both?
- How can I connect to my audience or gain their trust?

Appeal to Logic	Appeal to Emotion	Establishing Credibility

REASONING AND ORGANIZATION   Developing a Line of Reasoning

AP® Enduring Understanding (REO-1)

Writers guide understanding of a text's line of reasoning and claims through that text's organization and integration of evidence.

Now you are ready to establish the reasons to support your claim and to choose relevant evidence from your list. This combination serves as your line of reasoning and is made successful first with careful consideration of your purpose and audience and then with thoughtful commentary connecting claims and evidence.

Evidence is relevant when it supports one of the lines of reasoning that is justifying a writer's claim. It is important to evaluate each piece of information for its usefulness in serving as evidence for your claim and for its effectiveness for your intended audience.

To do this, you must think carefully about how well the evidence supports the line of reasoning. Just because information is presented doesn't mean that it effectively supports the claim. In short, information about the topic that doesn't support a line of reasoning is not relevant — it's just information.

Information becomes evidence when you use it effectively to support your line of reasoning. You may draw on a variety of types of evidence; however, some types of evidence may be more effective depending on the audience or situation. For example, an audience of your peers will think differently about cell phone use than the school administration. That means you must provide evidence to appeal to your audience's logic or emotion or to establish your credibility or authority all in service of your message.

Reasons	Evidence to Support Your Reasons
Students become addicted to their phones and are pulled away with every alert, distracting themselves and others.	• Statistics relating how many times we look at our phones or how long it takes to return to the activity • Study about how phones distract fellow classmates and the instructor
Students compromise academic honesty by looking up answers or texting during exams.	• Personal anecdote of seeing cheating incidents during tests and of AirDrop pictures of exam pages • Easy access to resources has increased the amount of plagiarism

The following is a visual that illustrates how most arguments are organized.

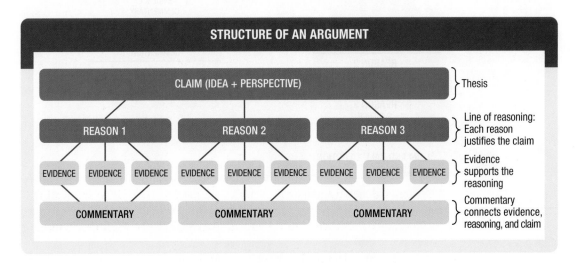

 **SKILLS PRACTICE** | REASONING AND ORGANIZATION
Developing a Line of Reasoning

List your reasons in support of your claim for your topic and brainstorm the type of evidence that would serve to support your argument.

Reasons	Evidence to Support Your Reasons

Engaging an Audience through Induction and Deduction

The next step in the process is to plan the arrangement of claims, evidence, and appeals. Depending on the attitudes of the audience about the topic, you may choose to organize inductively or deductively.

INDUCTION

CONTEXT
QUESTION

REASON 1
EVIDENCE
COMMENTARY

REASON 2
EVIDENCE
COMMENTARY

REASON 3
EVIDENCE
COMMENTARY

CLAIM AND CALL TO ACTION

DEDUCTION

CONTEXT
CLAIM

REASON 1
EVIDENCE
COMMENTARY

REASON 2
EVIDENCE
COMMENTARY

REASON 3
EVIDENCE
COMMENTARY

CALL TO
ACTION

Examples of Organizational Strategies

Induction	Deduction
Inductive arguments begin with the context of the debate and move to supporting evidence and more specific observations. They end with thesis and call to action.	Deductive arguments begin with the writer's claim and move to the specific evidence that supports the claim. Thesis statements are found in the introduction and the call to action in the conclusion.
The audience consists of mostly students who value having access to their phones and may not agree with the claim (or know a great deal about the research), so the essay begins an introduction to the debate followed by reasons and evidence. The thesis and call to action are placed at the end after the audience has heard the full argument.	The audience consists mostly of teachers who will generally agree with the claim and understand the evidence; therefore, the thesis is placed in the introduction and then followed by a combination of reasons and evidence before the final call to action.

 **SKILLS PRACTICE** | REASONING AND ORGANIZATION
Developing a Line of Reasoning

After analyzing your audience, choose either inductive or deductive reasoning to present your claims and evidence. Begin your argument by describing the problem you wish to solve and either stating your claim or posing a question. (Note: You will learn how to write full introductions and conclusions in later units.) Choose one of the following methods.

Induction	Deduction
Describe the problem and then pose a question.	Describe the problem and present your thesis.
In the conclusion, present a thesis that answers the question and your call to action.	In the conclusion, explain the significance of the idea and end with your final call to action.

- Write two or more body paragraphs presenting your reasons and supported with evidence that appeals to your audience.
- Incorporate an explanation and discussion of the evidence.

LANGUAGE AND STYLE   Creating Emphasis through Syntax

AP® Enduring Understanding (STL-1)

The rhetorical situation informs the strategic stylistic choices that writers make.

Even the best claims and evidence will fail to persuade if the writer does not engage the reader. So, writers choose rhetorical strategies carefully, not only to enhance the reading experience but also, more importantly, to create deeper meaning in their own text.

Writers make syntactical choices, which refers to the order of words in sentences and sentences within paragraphs. Earlier in the chapter, you analyzed some effective syntactical moves in the readings and discussed their effects.

Now, review the examples that follow and then try to incorporate some of these moves into your own writing.

Examples of Syntactical Moves	
Syntactical Choice	Example
Fragment	Buzz . . . buzz.
Simple Sentence	Phones distract us.
Repetition	In a busy classroom, smartphones distract the users, distract those around them, and distract the teacher, preventing everyone from full access to learning.
Juxtaposition	Piles of papers and unfinished tasks littered my desk while the small, silver device buzzed on, inviting me to another conversation.
Parallel Structure	Smartphones allow us to access information readily, to organize our lives effortlessly, and to connect to one another constantly.
Rhetorical Question	Why would students pay attention to an instructor when the whole world of news and entertainment is right under their fingertips?
Antithesis	Smartphones offer the wide-open spaces of endless information while creating a prison of distraction.

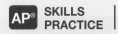 **SKILLS PRACTICE** | LANGUAGE AND STYLE
Creating Emphasis through Syntax

- Finish composing your argument.
- Read through the draft of your argument to begin the revision process.
- Incorporate syntactical moves in ways that engage your audience and emphasize your points.

 **SKILLS PRACTICE** | PUTTING IT ALL TOGETHER
Revising and Editing a Persuasive Argument

Peer-Revision Checklist: Revising and Editing a Persuasive Argument

Questions to Consider	Unit 1 Focus Skills	Comment on the Effectiveness and/or Make a Suggestion
Does the claim in the introduction or conclusion establish the writer's point of view on the topic and conclude with a call to action?	*Persuasion*	
Is the evidence and commentary arranged in an appropriate manner for the audience?	*Inductive or deductive arrangement*	
Has the writer related to, connected with, or appealed to his or her audience? Are these choices effective for the specific audience?	*Logos, ethos, pathos*	
Has the writer crafted the piece of persuasion with effective and appropriate rhetorical strategies?	*Antithesis, rhetorical question, repetition, parallelism, juxtaposition*	
Is the writing free of errors in spelling, punctuation, capitalization, and other writing conventions?	*Punctuating syntactical features*	

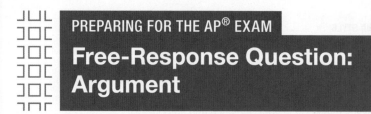

Free-Response Question: Argument

Establishing a Line of Reasoning

One of the free-response questions you will encounter on the AP® English Language and Composition Exam requires that you develop an argument that establishes a defensible position based on a literary or rhetorical concept or idea provided in a prompt. To argue your position effectively, you must establish a line of reasoning and support it with sufficient and relevant evidence.

This workshop will begin to explore the first steps of this process with an example question.

Read the following practice prompt, which is like one you may see on the AP® English Language and Composition Exam.

Prompt:

In considering societal laws that govern nations versus natural laws that guide human behavior, early Christian theologian St. Augustine (354 A.D.–430 A.D.), famously wrote "an unjust law is no law at all." Write an essay that argues your position on St. Augustine's claim that societal laws cannot contradict natural laws.

In your response you should do the following:

- Respond to the prompt with a thesis that presents a defensible position.
- Provide evidence to support your line of reasoning.
- Explain how the evidence supports your line of reasoning.
- Use appropriate grammar and punctuation in communicating your argument.

→ **Step One: Determine Your Unifying Idea and Brainstorm Potential Examples**

Read the prompt carefully so that you understand the question and the writing task. In developing your argument, you will need to convey your position and include your perspective about an idea. Consider the ideas that the quotation in the prompt suggests.

Consider the example prompt. You might connect the abstract ideas of *justice*, *unjust laws*, *society*, *individual*, etc. Next, you will choose one of these abstract concepts to serve as your controlling idea in the argument and convey your perspective. For example, you might determine that *unjust laws are harmful* to others and to oneself. Finally, make a list of examples from your reading, your observation, or your experience that illustrate that unjust laws harm others and oneself.

→ Step Two: Develop a Defensible Claim and Unified Line of Reasoning

Once you have chosen a unifying idea and determined your perspective, you will need to develop your claim which includes your perspective about the unifying idea. Simply restating the original claim or quotation in the prompt is not enough. You must convey your perspective on the topic. Thus the combination of your idea and your perspective about that topic becomes your claim.

Topic:	*Laws*
Idea:	*Unjust Laws*
+	
Perspective:	*Unjust laws harm self and others*
Thesis:	*Citizens should rebel against "unjust laws" because these laws cause harm to others and require citizens to violate their own moral code of behavior.*

This **thesis statement** conveys a position through a claim (idea + perspective) that can now be developed through a line of reasoning. You should now generate two to three reasons to support your claim. These reasons will become your topic sentences for your body paragraphs. Your body paragraph should directly connect to your unifying idea and perspective.

Thesis statements may present a **line of reasoning** to help you structure your argument and help the audience navigate through your reasoning. In other words, claims can be justified by reasons that will serve as the basis for each of your body paragraphs.

Thesis	Effectiveness
I agree with St. Augustine's statement that societal laws should not contradict natural laws.	No original position. It simply restates the prompt. No line of reasoning
Citizens should rebel against "unjust laws" because these laws cause harm to others or require citizens to violate their own moral code of behavior.	Clear position Citizens should rebel against unjust laws. Line of reasoning [because] They cause harm to others. They violate personal moral code.

INSIDER AP® TIP **Your position should be embedded in your perspective.** Issues are complex; therefore, the most intriguing arguments are not simply pro or con. Instead, they reveal their position, either in support of or in opposition to the issue at hand, through the perspective they take.

→ Step Three: Choose Your Evidence

Your thesis requires proof which means you must select and organize relevant evidence in your essay to support each of the reasons that will emerge from your brainstorming. You may have generated many examples related to your topic in Step One, but, ultimately, you should only use evidence that directly relates to your line of reasoning and the idea and perspective you established in your thesis.

During the AP® Exam, you will not be provided sources or permitted to research evidence. You will need to draw evidence from your reading, observation, and experience. The following list will help you consider the types of evidence you might explore:

- History
- Literature
- Science
- Personal experience
- Sports
- Politics
- Current events
- Pop culture

When you explore your list of evidence, you should include examples in your argument that directly relate to your idea, perspective, and purpose. Topics unrelated to the ideas of moral behavior, harm, or laws have been eliminated. For example, in exploring unjust laws, you could include examples of suffragettes or segregation, but not traffic laws which do not relate to the idea of justice.

→ Step Four: Develop Your Commentary

Once you have selected your evidence to support your claim and line of reasoning, you will need to write several sentences that explain the significance and relevance of the evidence in relation to the claim in your thesis. In later units, you will have further practice developing your commentary.

INSIDER AP® TIP

All reasons must connect to a unifying idea. Effective arguments provide a line of reasoning consisting of two or more reasons that justify the claim. A line of reasoning is established when these reasons are connected to the idea, *not* only the topic, in your thesis.

PREPARING FOR THE AP® EXAM

The following is an example of an argument free-response question. Practice the skills you have learned in this workshop to complete the following tasks:

- Write a defensible thesis that includes a claim (idea + perspective).
- List 2–3 reasons to justify your thesis.
- Select relevant evidence for each reason.
- Develop a body paragraph for each reason that explains how the evidence supports your reason and thesis.

Prompt:
Civil rights activist Rosa Parks (1913–2005) once said, "It is better to protest than to accept injustice." Write an essay that argues your position on Parks's claim on the importance of fighting injustice.

In your response, you should do the following:

- Respond to the prompt with a thesis that presents a defensible position.
- Provide evidence to support your line of reasoning.

Explain how the evidence supports your line of reasoning. Use appropriate grammar and punctuation in communicating your argument.

▷ Inaugural Address
John F. Kennedy

1 We observe today not a victory of party but a celebration of freedom — symbolizing an end as well as a beginning — signifying renewal as well as change. For I have sworn before you and Almighty God the same solemn oath our forebears prescribed nearly a century and three-quarters ago.

2 The world is very different now. For man holds in his mortal hands the power to abolish all forms of human poverty and all forms of human life. And yet the same revolutionary beliefs for which our forebears fought are still at issue around the globe — the belief that the rights of man come not from the generosity of the state but from the hand of God.

3 We dare not forget today that we are the heirs of that first revolution. Let the word go forth from this time and place, to friend and foe alike, that the torch has been passed to a new generation of Americans — born in this century, tempered by war, disciplined by a hard and bitter peace, proud of our ancient heritage — and unwilling to witness or permit the slow undoing of those human rights to which this nation has always been committed, and to which we are committed today at home and around the world.

4 Let every nation know, whether it wishes us well or ill, that we shall pay any price, bear any burden, meet any hardship, support any friend, oppose any foe to assure the survival and the success of liberty.

5 This much we pledge — and more.

6 To those old allies whose cultural and spiritual origins we share, we pledge the loyalty of faithful friends. United, there is little we cannot do in a host of cooperative ventures. Divided, there is little we can do — for we dare not meet a powerful challenge at odds and split asunder.

7 To those new states whom we welcome to the ranks of the free, we pledge our word that one form of colonial control shall not have passed away merely to be replaced by a far more iron tyranny. We shall not always expect to find them supporting our view. But we shall always hope to find them strongly supporting their own freedom — and to remember that, in the past, those who foolishly sought power by riding the back of the tiger ended up inside.

8 To those people in the huts and villages of half the globe struggling to break the bonds of mass misery, we pledge our best efforts to help them help themselves, for whatever period is required — not because the communists may be doing it, not because we seek their votes, but because it is right. If a free society cannot help the many who are poor, it cannot save the few who are rich.

9 To our sister republics south of our border, we offer a special pledge — to convert our good words into good deeds — in a new alliance for progress — to assist free men and free governments in casting off the chains of poverty. But this peaceful revolution of hope cannot become the prey of hostile powers. Let all our neighbors

know that we shall join with them to oppose aggression or subversion anywhere in the Americas. And let every other power know that this hemisphere intends to remain the master of its own house.

To that world assembly of sovereign states, the United Nations, our last best hope in an age where the instruments of war have far outpaced the instruments of peace, we renew our pledge of support — to prevent it from becoming merely a forum for invective — to strengthen its shield of the new and the weak — and to enlarge the area in which its writ may run. 10

Finally, to those nations who would make themselves our adversary, we offer not a pledge but a request: that both sides begin anew the quest for peace before the dark powers of destruction unleashed by science engulf all humanity in planned or accidental self-destruction. 11

We dare not tempt them with weakness. For only when our arms are sufficient beyond doubt can we be certain beyond doubt that they will never be employed. 12

But neither can two great and powerful groups of nations take comfort from our present course — both sides overburdened by the cost of modern weapons, both rightly alarmed by the steady spread of the deadly atom, yet both racing to alter that uncertain balance of terror that stays the hand of mankind's final war. 13

So let us begin anew — remembering on both sides that civility is not a sign of weakness, and sincerity is always subject to proof. Let us never negotiate out of fear. But let us never fear to negotiate. 14

1. In the first sentence of the passage, the author states that his inauguration as president is "not a victory of party but a celebration of freedom" primarily to
   (A) assert his control over his party.
   (B) acknowledge and embrace those in the audience who were not of his party or who may not have voted for him.
   (C) characterize his audience as thoughtful people who value freedom over all else.
   (D) argue that too much engagement with party politics is actually harmful to the cause of freedom.
   (E) encourage his audience to reconsider their party alliances and political loyalties.

2. In the first and second paragraphs, the speaker mentions "our forebears" primarily to
   (A) appeal to the authority of history in an attempt to assert his power.
   (B) imply that his election was predicted by history and ultimately unavoidable.
   (C) imply that he has already made history and will be remembered as one of the great forebears of this country.
   (D) appeal to the audience members' combined sense of history and commitment to freedom and the rights of man.
   (E) appeal to the emotional need that many people in his audience feel to reject the expectations of historical figures and pave their own path.

3. In the second paragraph, the speaker states that the "world is very different now" primarily to
   (A) establish the need for his audience to accept change in a world that is always changing.
   (B) distinguish between those who need to change and those who want to change.
   (C) undermine efforts by other countries to resist working together.
   (D) describe the fears that many in America feel toward the changing world and how that changing world sees them.
   (E) create a tone of anxiety and fear in a changed world.

4. In paragraph 13, the author refers to "the steady spread of the deadly atom" as evidence to support his claim that
    (A) the United States would rather destroy itself than be conquered by another country.
    (B) humanity would rather slowly destroy itself than seek peace.
    (C) all countries must seek peace or risk the destruction of mankind.
    (D) some countries would rather destroy all of humanity than to lose a conflict to another country.
    (E) some people must die for the cause of peace.

5. In paragraph 14, what audience(s) is/are the speaker addressing by saying "So let us begin anew"?
    (A) The American people as a whole
    (B) The people of his own political party
    (C) The American people and members of the United Nations
    (D) Adversarial countries and members of the United Nations
    (E) The American people and countries around the world

6. Which of the following statements best represents the thesis of the passage?
    (A) "For man holds in his mortal hands the power to abolish all forms of human poverty and all forms of human life" (paragraph 2).
    (B) "Let every nation know, whether it wishes us well or ill, that we shall pay any price, bear any burden, meet any hardship, support any friend, oppose any foe to assure the survival and the success of liberty" (paragraph 4).
    (C) "This much we pledge — and more" (paragraph 5).
    (D) "If a free society cannot help the many who are poor, it cannot save the few who are rich" (paragraph 8).
    (E) "And let every other power know that this hemisphere intends to remain the master of its own house" (paragraph 9).

7. Which of the following best summarizes the author's purpose?
    (A) To demonstrate the anger and strength with which the United States will react to any countries showing aggression toward it or its citizens
    (B) To affirm the devotion of the United States to the United Nations and its member countries, including commitment to mutual protection
    (C) To reach across party lines in an attempt to unify the people of the United States and prepare the country for the likelihood of nuclear war
    (D) To address our allies around the world and unify them against the adversaries of freedom and human rights while also preparing for the self-destruction of humanity
    (E) To unify those across the United States behind him as the president, comfort allies, show strength to adversaries, and seek peaceful and civil relationships around the world

8. Which of the following best describes the speaker's exigence?
    (A) The threat of nuclear war
    (B) An adversarial election that saw many people angry and threatening to use nuclear weapons on one another
    (C) The failure of the previous president to protect the people and allies of the United States despite the threats of war and destruction
    (D) The beginning of new leadership in the United States and a need to unify people who had been opposed to one another during an election
    (E) Attacks on the leadership and character of the president

9. In the speech, Kennedy makes which of the following claims about the United States under his leadership?
    (A) It will only stand in the way of nuclear war when it means self-destruction of humankind.
    (B) It will only support its allies in the United Nations.
    (C) It will destroy its adversaries regardless of the cost of human life.
    (D) It will do anything to guarantee that freedom survives and succeeds.
    (E) It will never negotiate with those who oppose it.

The passage below is a draft.

(1) Originally, presidential debates took place on an outdoor stage where candidates spoke out to a crowd who rarely got close to them. (2) This meant that the ideas and proposals announced in those debates were most important because people couldn't really see the candidates up close. (3) However, in 1960, Americans witnessed the first-ever televised presidential debate between then-vice president Richard Nixon and the younger and less experienced John F. Kennedy.

(4) This was all painfully obvious even at that debate between Nixon and Kennedy. (5) With years of experience in Congress and around the world, Nixon was favored in the election. (6) Kennedy was well liked, but his lack of experience was expected to keep him from becoming president.

(7) On September 26, the two candidates arrived at CBS studios in Chicago. (8) Kennedy had spent the previous days in a hotel room preparing, while Vice President Nixon had been ill with the flu. (9) To make matters worse for Nixon, he had recently injured his knee and then re-injured it getting out of the car at the debate site.

(10) The debate went on as planned. (11) Nixon answered each question clearly and with a knowledge that showed he needed little or no practice. Kennedy, with his practiced answers, kept up with the ill and hurting Nixon. (12) For his part, Nixon had performed admirably given the circumstances, needing little or no practice to match the well-practiced Kennedy. (13) After the debate, those who had listened on the radio declared it a draw. (14) Obviously, most of the seventy million Americans who watched the live debate declared Kennedy the clear winner. (15) He had appeared much more healthy and energetic than the vice president.

(16) To this day, televised debates give candidates the opportunity to portray themselves as presidential, but looks are not everything. (17) And while the ideas do still matter, voters are often more interested in the appearance and demeanor of the candidates. (18) Even Nixon himself later admitted his mistaken approach to the debate, writing in his memoirs how he "should have remembered that 'a picture is worth a thousand words.'"

1. The writer wants to add a thesis statement after sentence 3. Which of the following choices would be the best thesis statement for this passage?
   (A) From that moment on, the average American voter lost interest in the details of policy and leadership and instead developed an over-reliance on the close-up appearance and live television performance of their candidate.
   (B) Though Kennedy was more prepared, more people should have voted for Nixon because he needed little preparation or practice, clearly showing him to be the stronger candidate.
   (C) Debates that take place without consideration for the health or well-being of the candidates remain unfair and brutal events of political theater.
   (D) Nixon did, indeed, win the debate, though millions who watched on television were swayed toward Kennedy by his healthy appearance and savvy preparation.
   (E) Until that day, debates were respectable events where candidates could showcase what they knew and appeal to an audience of people in the room and not to a faceless audience of millions who knew little about them or their ideas.

2. The writer is considering deleting the underlined portion of sentence 5 (reproduced below), adjusting the punctuation as needed.

   With years of experience in Congress and around the world, Nixon was favored in the election.

   Should the writer keep or delete the underlined text?

   (A) Keep it because it provides a detail that will likely help the audience perceive the shift in the writer's line of reasoning.
   (B) Keep it because it provides a context for the audience to help them better understand the information later in the sentence.
   (C) Keep it because it provides an introduction for the information that is disputed later in the sentence.
   (D) Delete it because it interrupts the reasoning of the paragraph.
   (E) Delete it because it repeats information that was already established in the previous sentence.

3. The writer want s to revise sentence 14 (reproduced below) to better indicate the quality of the information provided.

   Obviously, most of the seventy million Americans who watched the live debate declared Kennedy the clear winner.

   Which version of the underlined portion of sentence 14 best accomplishes this goal?

   (A) (as it is now)
   (B) Some pollsters claimed that
   (C) Though listeners saw Nixon as the winner,
   (D) Nixon's ill health was not a factor and
   (E) According to most nationwide polls,

4. The writer wants to revise sentence 16 (reproduced below) in an attempt to better motivate voters in the audience.

   To this day, televised debates give candidates the opportunity to portray themselves as presidential, but looks are not everything.

   (A) (as it is now)
   (B) and looks are everything.
   (C) and HD TV has made it even more obvious that looks are not everything.
   (D) but voters must remember that looks are not everything.
   (E) but looks are not everything considering the importance of the presidency.

5. Which of the following, if included in the passage, would be the best evidence to strengthen the validity and reasoning of the argument?
   (A) The military records of both candidates
   (B) A comparison of polls of people who listened and people who watched
   (C) A list of Nixon's and Kennedy's accomplishments before running for president
   (D) Quotations from people around the country reacting to the debate
   (E) The actual numbers of who watched and who listened

REUTERS/Ina Fassbender

UNIT

3

Understanding Context

In Unit 1, you learned that a rhetorical situation consists of a writer communicating a message to an audience within a particular context. In this unit, we'll take a deeper look into the meaning and importance of "context."

Context is an unavoidable factor in your own writing. You might be motivated to write about a current event, or you may just take into account the many personal experiences, cultural factors, and other influences that have shaped your perspective. Likewise, context is important for readers too. If you know when a text was written, as well as its rhetorical situation, cultural background, and historical moment, you will gain insight into why a writer created the text.

In the image that opens the unit, it's difficult to understand the message without knowing the context. Why are people in costume? Does someone need information? Where is this scene taking place? What are the circumstances? In short, when we know the answers to questions like these, we can better understand our own perspectives and the perspectives of others.

UNIT GOALS

	Unit Focus	Reading, Analyzing, and Interpreting	Writing
Big Idea: Rhetorical Situation	**Rhetorical Context**	Explain how the context affects the choices a writer makes.	Consider the context when developing an argument for an audience.
Big Idea: Claims and Evidence	**Sources of Evidence**	Explain how the pieces of evidence are used to support the reasons.	Choose pieces of evidence to support the reasons within the rhetorical context.
Big Idea: Reasoning and Organization	**Exposition: Process Argument**	Explain how a writer develops an argument through process analysis.	Write an argument developed through process analysis.
Big Idea: Language and Style	**Transitions**	Explain how a writer uses transitions to illustrate relationships.	Use transitions to illustrate relationships.
Ideas in American Culture	• **The Individual and Nature** • **The Individual and Society**	Analyze the ideas of the individual and nature and the individual and society in classic and contemporary American texts.	
Preparing for the AP® Exam	• **Free Response: Synthesis** • **Multiple Choice**	Analyze rhetorical choices in classic and contemporary nonfiction texts.	Develop a line of reasoning that justifies a claim.

The Rhetorical Context

 Enduring Understanding (RHS-1)

Individuals write within a particular situation and make strategic writing choices based on that situation.

KEY POINT

Writers create texts within a particular context. The context includes the time, place, and occasion.

So far, you've read about the importance of the writer and his or her relationship to the audience. But writing doesn't happen in a vacuum — most texts are prompted by particular circumstances at a particular time.

Think about this: Your team is about to play the championship game in a high-stakes tournament. The pressure has shaken the players' confidence. So your coaches gather the team together before the game. As motivation, they remind you of every lesson you learned, every challenge you overcame, and every victory you celebrated throughout the season.

In this instance, a coach (speaker/writer) and the team (audience) share the same goals, values, and perspectives. This isn't always the case: sometimes the writer and the audience hold opposing values and perspectives. But because your coaches know that you all have the same goal (to win the game), they refer to prior shared experiences to motivate their audience for the occasion at hand.

This particular moment in time is called the **context**. Understanding the context informs your understanding of the entire text.

Context Matters

The **context** includes the following:

- Time
- Place
- Occasion

Each of these factors may inspire, provoke, or motivate a writer to communicate (which you'll recall is the writer's **exigence**).

When you analyze a text, it's not enough to just point out the time, place, and occasion. You've got to see it through the eyes of the writer.

Historical, cultural, and social values are embedded within the context, and they frame the audience's reception of a text. Understanding these values and beliefs is critical to making sense of the relationship between the writer, the audience, and the context.

Within any context, writers have to consider the audience's perspective and position. For example, the audience and the writer share a similar context, but they may not necessarily share the same perspective.

Writers must consider how their audience is affected by the context. As you analyze how a writer relates to his or her audience, ask yourself the following questions:

- What information does the intended audience have?
- Are they likely to see the issue as the writer sees it?
- What does the audience value?

The occasion may provide a clue. While a writer's particular message is likely unique to the specific situation, it may be helpful to consider the general type of situation or event. For example, if a text was written for a graduation or commencement, then the message may be one encouraging the audience to make a difference. If the text is a eulogy, then the writer may be memorializing or paying tribute. Or if the text is a book introduction, the writer may be previewing the major theme or perspective.

Introductions and Conclusions

If writers need to inform their audience of important **context** for their argument, they may provide background in the **introduction**. Writers can do this by using the following techniques:

- Quotations that convey the writer's idea
- Statements about the subject and idea that intrigue or surprise the reader
- Anecdotes that connect the writer or audience to the topic
- Questions about the subject and idea that provoke thought or curiosity
- Data or statistics that suggest the relevance or urgency of the topic
- Contextualized information that provides the background the audience may not be familiar with
- Scenarios or case studies that illustrate the problem, issue, or importance of the subject and idea

Similarly, writers can use the **conclusion** to bring their argument to a close, while also showing how that context connects to an ongoing conversation. The conclusion may do one or more of the following:

- Explain the significance of the argument within a broader context
- Make connections
- Call the audience to act
- Suggest a change in behavior or attitude
- Propose a solution
- Leave the audience with a compelling image
- Explain implications
- Summarize the argument
- Connect to the introduction

Additionally, a writer may be part of the moment as a primary source, or he or she could be writing as a secondary source about a moment in the past. So be aware that an audience may consider how the writer is affected by the context:

- How much distance is there between the writer and the subject?
- Does the writer talk about experiences he or she lived through?
- Is the writer discussing an event in the past?
- Is the writer reflecting on a current event? A historical event?

Analyzing a text involves understanding the relationship between the audience, writer, and context.

INSIDER AP TIP Some contexts resemble ongoing conversations between many different writers with differing perspectives. For example, countless generations, nationalities, and cultures have considered questions such as, "What does it mean to live a good life?" Understanding how to enter the conversation with a new perspective in your new generation includes understanding the context of the perspectives that writers shared before you arrived.

 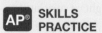

AP SKILLS PRACTICE | RHETORICAL SITUATION
Describing Rhetorical Context

Identify a rhetorical context that you've been part of and then think about how the historical, cultural, and social values of the time, place, and occasion affected the audience and message.

Historical, cultural, and social values of the TIME	Historical, cultural, and social values of the PLACE	Historical, cultural, and social values of the OCCASION

Make Your Bed
William H. McRaven

The University of Texas at Austin, Marsha Miller

THE TEXT IN CONTEXT

This speech was given at the university-wide commencement at the University of Texas at Austin on May 17, 2014, by alum William H. McRaven (b. 1955). At the time, McRaven was a Navy SEAL and four-star admiral. He served as the ninth commander of U.S. Special Operations Command and oversaw the mission that raided Osama bin Laden's compound in 2011. Admiral McRaven was also chancellor of the University of Texas System from 2015 to 2018. This speech inspired his 2017 *New York Times* bestseller titled *Make Your Bed: Little Things That Can Change Your Life . . . and Maybe the World*.

 **SKILLS PRACTICE** | RHETORICAL SITUATION
Analyzing Context

Think about the writer, context, and audience before you read the following speech. Predict what you think this writer would say given his audience and context. As you read the speech, identify the writer's major message or thesis. Then explain why the writer would deliver this message to this particular audience in this particular context.

Analyzing Rhetorical Context		
Writer:	Context (time, place, occasion):	Audience:
Message:		

Explain the significance of the writer's message for this particular audience in this particular context:

Make Your Bed

President Powers, Provost Fenves, Deans, members of the faculty, family and friends and, most importantly, the class of 2014. Congratulations on your achievement.

It's been almost 37 years to the day that I graduated from UT. I remember a lot of things about that day. I remember I had a throbbing headache from a party the night before. I remember I had a serious girlfriend, whom I later married—that's important to remember by the way—and I remember that I was getting commissioned in the Navy that day.

But of all the things I remember, I don't have a clue who the commencement speaker was that evening, and I certainly don't remember anything they said. So, acknowledging that fact, if I can't make this commencement speech memorable, I will at least try to make it short.

The University's slogan is, "What starts here changes the world." I have to admit—I kinda like it. "What starts here changes the world."

Tonight there are almost 8,000 students 5 graduating from UT. That great paragon of analytical rigor, Ask.com, says that the average American will meet 10,000 people in their lifetime. That's a lot of folks. But, if every one of you changed the lives of just 10 people—and each one of those folks changed the lives of another 10 people—just 10—then in five generations—125 years—the class of 2014 will have changed the lives of 800 million people.

800 million people—think of it—over twice the population of the United States. Go one more generation and you can change the entire population of the world—eight billion people.

If you think it's hard to change the lives of 10 people—change their lives forever—you're wrong. I saw it happen every day in Iraq and Afghanistan: A young Army officer makes a decision to go left instead of right down a road in Baghdad and the 10 soldiers in his squad are saved from close-in ambush. In Kandahar province, Afghanistan, a non-commissioned officer from the Female Engagement Team senses something isn't right and directs the infantry platoon away from a 500-pound IED, saving the lives of a dozen soldiers.

But, if you think about it, not only were these soldiers saved by the decisions of one person, but their children yet unborn were also saved. And their children's children were saved. Generations were saved by one decision, by one person.

But changing the world can happen anywhere and anyone can do it. So, what starts here can indeed change the world, but the question is—what will the world look like after you change it?

Well, I am confident that it will look 10 much, much better. But if you will humor this old sailor for just a moment, I have a few suggestions that may help you on your way to a better world. And while these lessons were learned during my time in the military, I can assure you that it matters not whether you ever served a day in uniform. It matters not your gender, your ethnic or religious background, your orientation or your social status.

Our struggles in this world are similar, and the lessons to overcome those struggles and to move forward—changing ourselves and the world around us—will apply equally to all.

I have been a Navy SEAL for 36 years. But it all began when I left UT for Basic SEAL training in Coronado, California. Basic SEAL training is six months of long torturous runs in the soft sand, midnight swims in the cold water off

San Diego, obstacles courses, unending calisthenics, days without sleep and always being cold, wet and miserable. It is six months of being constantly harassed by professionally trained warriors who seek to find the weak of mind and body and eliminate them from ever becoming a Navy SEAL.

But, the training also seeks to find those students who can lead in an environment of constant stress, chaos, failure and hardships. To me basic SEAL training was a lifetime of challenges crammed into six months.

So, here are the 10 lessons I learned from basic SEAL training that hopefully will be of value to you as you move forward in life.

Every morning in basic SEAL training, my [15] instructors, who at the time were all Vietnam veterans, would show up in my barracks room and the first thing they would inspect was your bed. If you did it right, the corners would be square, the covers pulled tight, the pillow centered just under the headboard and the extra blanket folded neatly at the foot of the rack—that's Navy talk for bed.

It was a simple task—mundane at best. But every morning we were required to make our bed to perfection. It seemed a little ridiculous at the time, particularly in light of the fact that we were aspiring to be real warriors, tough battle-hardened SEALs, but the wisdom of this simple act has been proven to me many times over.

If you make your bed every morning you will have accomplished the first task of the day. It will give you a small sense of pride, and it will encourage you to do another task and another and another. By the end of the day, that one task completed will have turned into many tasks completed. Making your bed will also reinforce the fact that little things in life matter. If you can't do the little things right, you will never do the big things right.

And, if by chance you have a miserable day, you will come home to a bed that is made—that you made—and a made bed gives you encouragement that tomorrow will be better.

If you want to change the world, start off by making your bed.

During SEAL training the students are [20] broken down into boat crews. Each crew is seven students—three on each side of a small rubber boat and one coxswain to help guide the dingy. Every day your boat crew forms up on the beach and is instructed to get through the surfzone and paddle several miles down the coast. In the winter, the surf off San Diego can get to be 8 to 10 feet high and it is exceedingly difficult to paddle through the plunging surf unless everyone digs in. Every paddle must be synchronized to the stroke count of the coxswain. Everyone must exert equal effort or the boat will turn against the wave and be unceremoniously tossed back on the beach.

For the boat to make it to its destination, everyone must paddle. You can't change the world alone—you will need some help—and to truly get from your starting point to your destination takes friends, colleagues, the good will of strangers and a strong coxswain to guide them.

If you want to change the world, find someone to help you paddle.

Over a few weeks of difficult training my SEAL class, which started with 150 men, was down to just 35. There were now six boat crews of seven men each. I was in the boat with the tall guys, but the best boat crew we had was made up of the little guys—the munchkin crew we called them—no one was over about five-foot-five.

The munchkin boat crew had one American Indian, one African American, one Polish

American, one Greek American, one Italian American, and two tough kids from the midwest. They out-paddled, out-ran and out-swam all the other boat crews. The big men in the other boat crews would always make good-natured fun of the *tiny little flippers* the munchkins put on their *tiny little feet* prior to every swim. But somehow these little guys, from every corner of the nation and the world, always had the last laugh—swimming faster than everyone and reaching the shore long before the rest of us.

SEAL training was a great equalizer. Nothing mattered but your will to succeed. Not your color, not your ethnic background, not your education and not your social status. [25]

If you want to change the world, measure a person by the size of their heart, not the size of their flippers.

Several times a week, the instructors would line up the class and do a uniform inspection. It was exceptionally thorough. Your hat had to be perfectly starched, your uniform immaculately pressed and your belt buckle shiny and void of any smudges. But it seemed that no matter how much effort you put into starching your hat, or pressing your uniform or polishing your belt buckle—it just wasn't good enough. The instructors would find "something" wrong.

For failing the uniform inspection, the student had to run, fully clothed into the surfzone and then, wet from head to toe, roll around on the beach until every part of your body was covered with sand. The effect was known as a "sugar cookie." You stayed in that uniform the rest of the day—cold, wet and sandy.

There were many a student who just couldn't accept the fact that all their effort was in vain. That no matter how hard they tried to get the uniform right, it was unappreciated.

Those students didn't make it through training. Those students didn't understand the purpose of the drill. You were never going to succeed. You were never going to have a perfect uniform.

Sometimes no matter how well you prepare or how well you perform you still end up as a sugar cookie. It's just the way life is sometimes. [30]

If you want to change the world get over being a sugar cookie and keep moving forward.

Every day during training you were challenged with multiple physical events—long runs, long swims, obstacle courses, hours of calisthenics—something designed to test your mettle. Every event had standards—times you had to meet. If you failed to meet those standards your name was posted on a list, and at the end of the day those on the list were invited to a "circus." A circus was two hours of additional calisthenics designed to wear you down, to break your spirit, to force you to quit.

No one wanted a circus.

A circus meant that for that day you didn't measure up. A circus meant more fatigue—and more fatigue meant that the following day would be more difficult—and more circuses were likely. But at some time during SEAL training, everyone—everyone—made the circus list.

But an interesting thing happened to those who were constantly on the list. Over time those students—who did two hours of extra calisthenics—got stronger and stronger. The pain of the circuses built inner strength, built physical resiliency. [35]

Life is filled with circuses. You will fail. You will likely fail often. It will be painful. It will be discouraging. At times it will test you to your very core.

But if you want to change the world, don't be afraid of the circuses.

At least twice a week, the trainees were required to run the obstacle course. The obstacle course contained 25 obstacles including a 10-foot high wall, a 30-foot cargo net and a barbed wire crawl, to name a few. But the most challenging obstacle was the slide for life. It had a three-level 30-foot tower at one end and a one-level tower at the other. In between was a 200-foot-long rope. You had to climb the three-tiered tower and once at the top, you grabbed the rope, swung underneath the rope and pulled yourself hand over hand until you got to the other end.

The record for the obstacle course had stood for years when my class began training in 1977. The record seemed unbeatable, until one day, a student decided to go down the slide for life head first. Instead of swinging his body underneath the rope and inching his way down, he bravely mounted the TOP of the rope and thrust himself forward.

It was a dangerous move—seemingly fool- 40 ish, and fraught with risk. Failure could mean injury and being dropped from the training. Without hesitation the student slid down the rope perilously fast. Instead of several minutes, it only took him half that time and by the end of the course he had broken the record.

If you want to change the world sometimes you have to slide down the obstacle head first.

During the land warfare phase of training, the students are flown out to San Clemente Island which lies off the coast of San Diego. The waters off San Clemente are a breeding ground for the great white sharks. To pass SEAL training there are a series of long swims that must be completed. One is the night swim.

Before the swim the instructors joyfully brief the trainees on all the species of sharks that inhabit the waters off San Clemente. They assure you, however, that no student has ever been eaten by a shark—at least not recently. But, you are also taught that if a shark begins to circle your position—stand your ground. Do not swim away. Do not act afraid. And if the shark, hungry for a midnight snack, darts towards you—then summon up all your strength and punch him in the snout, and he will turn and swim away.

There are a lot of sharks in the world. If you hope to complete the swim you will have to deal with them.

So, if you want to change the world, don't 45 back down from the sharks.

As Navy SEALs one of our jobs is to conduct underwater attacks against enemy shipping. We practiced this technique extensively during basic training. The ship attack mission is where a pair of SEAL divers is dropped off outside an enemy harbor and then swims well over two miles—underwater—using nothing but a depth gauge and a compass to get to their target.

During the entire swim, even well below the surface, there is some light that comes through. It is comforting to know that there is open water above you. But as you approach the ship, which is tied to a pier, the light begins to fade. The steel structure of the ship blocks the moonlight, it blocks the surrounding street lamps, it blocks all ambient light.

To be successful in your mission, you have to swim under the ship and find the keel—the centerline and the deepest part of the ship. This is your objective. But the keel is also the darkest part of the ship—where you cannot see your hand in front of your face, where the noise from the ship's machinery is deafening and where it is easy to get dis-oriented and fail.

Every SEAL knows that under the keel, at the darkest moment of the mission, is the time when you must be calm, com-posed—when all your tactical skills, your physical power and all your inner strength must be brought to bear.

If you want to change the world, you must 50 be your very best in the darkest moment.

The ninth week of training is referred to as "Hell Week." It is six days of no sleep, constant physical and mental harassment, and one spe-cial day at the Mud Flats. The Mud Flats are an area between San Diego and Tijuana where the water runs off and creates the Tijuana slues, a swampy patch of terrain where the mud will engulf you.

It is on Wednesday of Hell Week that you paddle down to the mud flats and spend the next 15 hours trying to survive the freezing cold mud, the howling wind and the incessant pressure to quit from the instructors. As the sun began to set that Wednesday evening, my training class, having committed some "egre-gious infraction of the rules" was ordered into the mud.

The mud consumed each man till there was nothing visible but our heads. The instruc-tors told us we could leave the mud if only five men would quit—just five men—and we could get out of the oppressive cold. Looking around the mud flat it was apparent that some students were about to give up. It was still over eight hours till the sun came up—eight more hours of bone-chilling cold.

The chattering teeth and shivering moans of the trainees were so loud it was hard to hear anything. And then, one voice began to echo through the night, one voice raised in song. The song was terribly out of tune, but sung with great enthusiasm. One voice became two

and two became three and before long every-one in the class was singing. We knew that if one man could rise above the misery then oth-ers could as well.

The instructors threatened us with more 55 time in the mud if we kept up the singing but the singing persisted. And somehow the mud seemed a little warmer, the wind a little tamer and the dawn not so far away.

If I have learned anything in my time trav-eling the world, it is the power of hope. The power of one person—Washington, Lincoln, King, Mandela and even a young girl from Pakistan, Malala—one person can change the world by giving people hope.

So, if you want to change the world, start singing when you're up to your neck in mud.

Finally, in SEAL training there is a bell. A brass bell that hangs in the center of the com-pound for all the students to see. All you have to do to quit is ring the bell.

Ring the bell and you no longer have to wake up at 5 o'clock. Ring the bell and you no longer have to do the freezing cold swims. Ring the bell and you no longer have to do the runs, the obstacle course, the PT—and you no longer have to endure the hardships of train-ing. Just ring the bell.

If you want to change the world don't ever, 60 ever ring the bell.

To the graduating class of 2014, you are moments away from graduating. Moments away from beginning your journey through life. Moments away from starting to change the world—for the better. It will not be easy.

But, YOU are the class of 2014, the class that can affect the lives of 800 million people in the next century.

Start each day with a task completed. Find someone to help you through life. Respect everyone.

Know that life is not fair and that you will fail often. But if you take some risks, step up when the times are toughest, face down the bullies, lift up the downtrodden and never, ever give up—if you do these things, then the next generation and the generations that follow will live in a world far better than the one we have today.

And what started here will indeed have changed the world—for the better. 65

Thank you very much. Hook 'em horns.

RHETORICAL SITUATION

1. What is the **context** of McRaven's speech? What is his relationship to the context? Who is his intended **audience**?

2. What does McRaven share with his **audience** in the **introduction**? How do these shared values support McRaven's **perspective**?

3. In paragraph five, McRaven provides data that **contextualizes** his speech. What information does he share, and what **purpose** does it serve for this **audience**?

4. Look at the single-sentence paragraphs. How are his examples relevant for this **context** and **audience**?

5. In his **conclusion**, McRaven wants to close with a point that resonates and leaves the audience remembering his message. How does McRaven **conclude** his speech in a way that makes it relevant beyond the audience of graduates?

Sources of Evidence

 Enduring Understanding (CLE-1)

Writers make claims about subjects, rely on evidence that supports their reasoning, and often acknowledge or respond to other, possibly opposing, arguments.

KEY POINT

A source provides information for an argument. Some sources are more reliable or credible than others.

To achieve their purposes, writers must consider context: the time, place, and occasion of their arguments. Depending on that context, a writer might draw upon specific historical allusions, current experts, numerical data, or particular sources of evidence likely to reach and persuade the audience.

Consider this: you pick up your lunch and find where your friends are sitting in the cafeteria. Before you join, they are already engrossed in a discussion about a new video game or music release. After you arrive, you listen for a few minutes to learn what your friends are saying and what they've already discussed. Then when you've understood the context of the discussion, you comment too. Each of your friends is a source, and you are drawing upon the context and arguments of others as you synthesize their ideas into your own argument. Whenever you read a text, you're doing the same thing: understanding what's been said prior to your arrival.

Some Arguments Are Better than Others

When writers make arguments, they often draw upon others' arguments as **evidence**. Drawing upon the ideas of others is a process known as synthesis.

Synthesis requires writers to carefully consider, explain, and integrate other sources into their own arguments. When synthesizing, writers refer to multiple sources and strategically select the most relevant and specific information to combine with their argument.

In other words, synthesis is much more complex than finding the perfect quote.

Unity and Line of Reasoning

From the first sentence of an argument, a writer works to justify his or her claim. As you learned in previous units, a writer justifies claims through **a line of reasoning**. So claims are only valid when a writer logically proves them through the line of reasoning. Because these ideas and perspectives are developed repeatedly, think of them as the through line—the line of reasoning—that ultimately unifies the argument.

Recall that writers often establish a **unifying idea** early in the argument. The unifying idea works like a keystone: a stone archway that uses one stone in the middle to lock in all the rest. Without the keystone, the rest of the arch would fall apart. Similarly, without a unifying idea in the argument to support the writer's reasons, the claim falls apart. Writers also unify arguments by connecting evidence and reasons to their idea. When the reasons logically support the claim through the idea, a writer has established a line of reasoning.

Reliability and Credibility of Sources

Writers rely on different **sources** depending on the rhetorical situation. Academic and professional researchers may focus on peer-reviewed scholarly sources. Journalists might emphasize eyewitness interviews. Just keep in mind, a source is not synonymous with **evidence**. While a source is a person, text, institution, or research organization that produces or archives evidence, evidence is the specific information, such as anecdotes, data, or testimony generated by the source.

In the same way that some arguments are better than others, some sources are better than others — particularly in terms of **reliability** and **credibility**. Sources are reliable when the information they produce can be supported, confirmed, or replicated by others. Credible sources have the relevant background, knowledge, authority, and comprehensiveness to provide insight into a subject.

Selection of Sources and Evidence

As you might recall from the previous unit, writers draw upon different sources to support their claims. After evaluating the ideas and perspectives of sources, writers choose specific, relevant information from them as supporting evidence. Relevant evidence connects to the subject, but, more importantly, it supports a writer's claim (including his or her idea and perspective).

When choosing evidence, writers consider the following questions:

- How do the source and the evidence relate to each other?
- What is the source's perspective in relation to the other sources?
- How does this evidence function within the larger argument?

Evidence isn't one-kind-fits-all. Writers strategically select evidence to achieve a particular purpose for their intended audience. For example, evidence can accomplish the following:

- Clarify through illustration or example
- Connect with the audience by setting a mood or creating an association
- Emphasize claim or reason

Writers synthesize different perspectives and use the evidence to support their own reasoning. When a writer incorporates evidence, he or she will often introduce that evidence in a way that illustrates the relationship between that specific source or evidence and the writer's own claims. Sources and evidence may be used to do the following:

- Establish a source's position
- Support the writer's claim
- Illustrate agreement or disagreement between sources

Writers may indicate their intentions as to how the information relates to other parts of the argument by the verb he or she uses to introduce the evidence.

Sources are created by real people. They represent a person's ideas and perspectives. Therefore, the way a writer introduces sources can reveal the writer's perspective about that source.

VERBS TO INTRODUCE THE WRITER'S INTENDED PURPOSE AND FUNCTION OF EVIDENCE		
Stating the Perspective of Another Source	**Using Another Source to Support the Writer's Claims**	**Introducing Sources That Disagree**
Argues	Acknowledges	Argues
Asserts	Adds	Avoids
Avows	Admits	Cautions
Believes	Affirms	Challenges
Claims	Agrees	Contrasts
Concludes	Compares	Corrects
Declares	Concedes	Denies
Explains	Continues	Denounces
Expresses	Defends	Disagrees
Implies	Emphasizes	Juxtaposes
Indicates	Illustrates	Objects
Insists	Maintains	Protests
Notes	Relates	Qualifies
Observes	Reminds	Rebuts
Offers	Restates	Rejects
Points out		Retorts
Presents		Stipulates
Proclaims		Warns
Proposes		
Reports		
Reveals		
Speculates		
States		
Theorizes		
Thinks		
Volunteers		

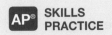

AP® SKILLS PRACTICE | CLAIMS AND EVIDENCE
Identifying Evidence

Imagine you would like to argue that juniors and seniors at your high school should be allowed to leave campus for lunch. In the chart, identify several sources of evidence you would use to convince two distinct audiences of your perspective: school administrators and parents or guardians of students, respectively. What evidence would likely convince the first audience? How might this choice of evidence be different for the second audience?

	Sources of Evidence	Type of Evidence
Parents or guardians		
School administrators		

Mockingbird Players

Bryan Stevenson

Jared Siskin/Getty Images

THE TEXT IN CONTEXT

Bryan Stevenson (b. 1959) is an American lawyer who has been representing capital defendants and death row prisoners in the Deep South since 1985. He is the founder of the Equal Justice Initiative (EJI) in Alabama, a nonprofit law organization focused on criminal justice reform in the United States. This organization works on behalf of individuals who may have been denied justice through racial bias or misconduct. Stevenson is the recipient of numerous awards for his work with human rights including the 2015 Carnegie Medal for Best Nonfiction for his memoir *Just Mercy*, the story of the early days of EJI that centers on Walter McMillian, who was wrongly accused of murder. In 2019, the book was made into a feature film.

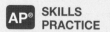 SKILLS PRACTICE | CLAIMS AND EVIDENCE
Analyzing Sources of Evidence

As you read the following article, identify the various sources that Stevenson uses. What type of evidence does each source provide? Note how Stevenson introduces each source. How does the way Stevenson introduces the evidence indicate how that evidence relates to other sources of evidence, as well as to Stevenson's message?

Analyzing Sources and the Function of Evidence

Source of Evidence	Type of Evidence	Function of Evidence • How is this evidence introduced? • How does this evidence relate to other pieces of evidence and the overall argument?

Mockingbird Players

The temporary receptionist was an elegant African American woman wearing a dark, expensive business suit—a well-dressed exception to the usual crowd at the Southern Prisoners Defense Committee (SPDC) in Atlanta, where I had returned after graduation to work full time. On her first day, I'd rambled over to her in my regular uniform of jeans and sneakers and offered to answer any questions she might have to help her get acclimated. She looked at me coolly and waved me away after reminding me that she was, in fact, an experienced legal secretary. The next morning, when I arrived at work in another jeans and sneakers ensemble, she seemed startled, as if some strange vagrant had made a wrong turn into the office. She took a beat to compose herself, then summoned me over to confide that she was leaving in a week to work at a "real law office." I wished her luck. An hour later, she called my office to tell me that "Robert E. Lee" was on the phone. I smiled, pleased that

I'd misjudged her; she clearly had a sense of humor.

"That's really funny."

"I'm not joking. That's what he said," she said, sounding bored, not playful. "Line two."

I picked up the line.

"Hello, this is Bryan Stevenson. May I help   5 you?"

"Bryan, this is Robert E. Lee Key. Why in the hell would you want to represent someone like Walter McMillian? Do you know he's reputed to be one of the biggest drug dealers in all of South Alabama? I got your notice entering an appearance, but you don't want anything to do with this case."

"Sir?"

"This is Judge Key, and you don't want to have anything to do with this McMillian case. No one really understands how depraved this situation truly is, including me, but I know it's ugly. These men might even be Dixie Mafia."

The lecturing tone and bewildering phrases from a judge I'd never met left me completely confused. *"Dixie Mafia"?* I'd met Walter McMillian two weeks earlier, after spending a day on death row to begin work on five capital cases. I hadn't reviewed the trial transcript yet, but I did remember that the judge's last name was Key. No one had told me the Robert E. Lee part. I struggled for an image of "Dixie Mafia" that would fit Walter McMillian.

"'Dixie Mafia'?" 10

"Yes, and there's no telling what else. Now, son, I'm just not going to appoint some out-of-state lawyer who's not a member of the Alabama bar to take on one of these death penalty cases, so you just go ahead and withdraw."

"I'm a member of the Alabama bar."

I lived in Atlanta, Georgia, but I had been admitted to the Alabama bar a year earlier after working on some cases in Alabama concerning jail and prison conditions.

"Well, I'm now sitting in Mobile. I'm not up in Monroeville anymore. If we have a hearing on your motion, you're going to have to come all the way from Atlanta to Mobile. I'm not going to accommodate you no kind of way."

"I understand, sir. I can come to Mobile, if 15 necessary."

"Well, I'm also not going to appoint you because I don't think he's indigent. He's reported to have money buried all over Monroe County."

"Judge, I'm not seeking appointment. I've told Mr. McMillian that we would—"The dial tone interrupted my first affirmative statement of the phone call. I spent several minutes thinking we'd been accidentally disconnected before finally realizing that a judge had just hung up on me.

• • •

I was in my late twenties and about to start my fourth year at the SPDC when I met Walter McMillian. His case was one of the flood of cases I'd found myself frantically working on after learning of a growing crisis in Alabama. The state had nearly a hundred people on death row as well as the fastest-growing condemned population in the country, but it also had no public defender system, which meant that large numbers of death row prisoners had no legal representation of any kind. My friend Eva Ansley ran the Alabama Prison Project, which tracked cases and matched lawyers with the condemned men. In 1988, we discovered an opportunity to get federal funding to create a legal center that could represent people on death row. The plan was to use that funding to start a new nonprofit. We hoped to open it in Tuscaloosa and begin working on cases in the next year. I'd already worked on lots of death penalty cases in several Southern states, sometimes winning a stay of execution just minutes before an electrocution was scheduled. But I didn't think I was ready to take on the responsibilities of running a nonprofit law office. I planned to help get the organization off the ground, find a director, and then return to Atlanta.

When I'd visited death row a few weeks before that call from Robert E. Lee Key, I met with five desperate condemned men: Willie Tabb, Vernon Madison, Jesse Morrison, Harry Nicks, and Walter McMillian. It was an exhausting, emotionally taxing day, and the cases and clients had merged together in my mind on the long drive back to Atlanta. But I remembered Walter. He was at least fifteen years older than me, not particularly well educated, and he hailed from a small rural community. The memorable thing about him was how insistent he was that he'd been wrongly convicted.

"Mr. Bryan, I know it may not matter to 20 you, but it's important to me that you know that I'm innocent and didn't do what they said I did, not no kinda way," he told me in the meeting room. His voice was level but laced with emotion. I nodded to him. I had learned to accept what clients tell me until the facts suggest something else.

"Sure, of course I understand. When I review the record I'll have a better sense of what evidence they have, and we can talk about it."

"But . . . look, I'm sure I'm not the first person on death row to tell you that they're innocent, but I really need you to believe me. My life has been ruined! This lie they put on me is more than I can bear, and if I don't get help from someone who believes me—"

His lip began to quiver, and he clenched his fists to stop himself from crying. I sat quietly while he forced himself back into composure.

"I'm sorry, I know you'll do everything you can to help me," he said, his voice quieter. My instinct was to comfort him; his pain seemed so sincere. But there wasn't much I could do, and after several hours on the row talking to so many people, I could muster only enough energy to reassure him that I would look at everything carefully.

• • •

I had several transcripts piled up in my small Atlanta office ready to move to Tuscaloosa once the office opened. With Judge Robert E. Lee Key's peculiar comments still running through my head, I went through the mound of records until I found the transcripts from Walter McMillian's trial. There were only four volumes of trial proceedings, which meant that the trial had been short. The judge's dramatic warnings now made Mr. McMillian's emotional claim of innocence too intriguing to put off any longer. I started reading.

• • •

Even though he had lived in Monroe County his whole life, Walter McMillian had never heard of Harper Lee or *To Kill a Mockingbird*. Monroeville,

25

Alabama, celebrated its native daughter Lee shamelessly after her award-winning book became a national bestseller in the 1960s. She returned to Monroe County but secluded herself and was rarely seen in public. Her reclusiveness proved no barrier to the county's continued efforts to market her literary classic—or to market itself by using the book's celebrity. Production of the film adaptation brought Gregory Peck to town for the infamous courtroom scenes; his performance won him an Academy Award. Local leaders later turned the old courthouse into a "Mockingbird" museum. A group of locals formed "The Mockingbird Players of Monroeville" to present a stage version of the story. The production was so popular that national and international tours were organized to provide an authentic presentation of the fictional story to audiences everywhere.

Sentimentality about Lee's story grew even as the harder truths of the book took no root. The story of an innocent black man bravely defended by a white lawyer in the 1930s fascinated millions of readers, despite its uncomfortable exploration of false accusations of rape involving a white woman. Lee's endearing characters, Atticus Finch and his precocious daughter Scout, captivated readers while confronting them with some of the realities of race and justice in the South. A generation of future lawyers grew up hoping to become the courageous Atticus, who at one point arms himself to protect the defenseless black suspect from an angry mob of white men looking to lynch him.

Today, dozens of legal organizations hand out awards in the fictional lawyer's name to celebrate the model of advocacy described in Lee's novel. What is often overlooked is that the black man falsely accused in the story was not *successfully* defended by Atticus. Tom Robinson, the wrongly accused black defendant, is found guilty. Later he dies when, full of despair, he makes a desperate attempt to escape from prison. He is shot seventeen times in the back by his captors, dying ingloriously but not unlawfully.

Walter McMillian, like Tom Robinson, grew up in one of several poor black settlements outside of Monroeville, where he worked the fields with his family before he was old enough to attend school. The children of sharecroppers in southern Alabama were introduced to "plowin', plantin', and pickin'" as soon as they were old enough to be useful in the fields. Educational opportunities for black children in the 1950s were limited, but Walter's mother got him to the dilapidated "colored school" for a couple of years when he was young. By the time Walter was eight or nine, he became too valuable for picking cotton to justify the remote advantages of going to school. By the age of eleven, Walter could run a plow as well as any of his older siblings.

Times were changing—for better and for worse. Monroe County had been developed by plantation owners in the nineteenth century for the production of cotton. Situated in the coastal plain of southwest Alabama, the fertile, rich black soil of the area attracted white settlers from the Carolinas who amassed very successful plantations and a huge slave population. For decades after the Civil War, the large African American population toiled in the fields of the "Black Belt" as sharecroppers and tenant farmers, dependent on white landowners for survival. In the 1940s, thousands of African Americans left the region as part of the Great Migration and headed mostly to the Midwest and West Coast for jobs. Those who remained continued to work the land, but the out-migration of African Americans combined with other factors to make traditional agriculture less sustainable as the economic base of the region.

By the 1950s, small cotton farming was becoming increasingly less profitable, even with the low-wage labor provided by black sharecroppers and tenants. The State of Alabama agreed to help white landowners in the region transition to timber farming and forest products by providing extraordinary tax incentives for pulp and paper mills. Thirteen of the state's sixteen pulp and paper mills were opened during this period. Across the Black Belt, more and more acres were converted to growing pine trees for paper mills and industrial uses. African Americans, largely excluded from this new industry, found themselves confronting new economic challenges even as they won basic civil rights. The brutal era of sharecropping and Jim Crow was ending, but what followed was persistent unemployment and worsening poverty. The region's counties remained some of the poorest in America.

Walter was smart enough to see the trend. He started his own pulpwood business that evolved with the timber industry in the 1970s. He astutely—and bravely—borrowed money to buy his own power saw, tractor, and pulpwood truck. By the 1980s, he had developed a solid business that didn't generate a lot of extra money but afforded him a gratifying degree of independence. If he had worked at the mill or the factory or had had some other unskilled job—the kind that most poor black people in South Alabama worked—it would invariably mean working for white business owners and dealing with all the racial stress that that implied in Alabama in the 1970s and 1980s. Walter couldn't escape the reality of racism, but having his own business in a growing sector of the economy gave him a latitude that many African Americans did not enjoy.

That independence won Walter some measure of respect and admiration, but it also cultivated contempt and suspicion, especially outside of Monroeville's black community.

30

Walter's freedom was, for some of the white people in town, well beyond what African Americans with limited education were able to achieve through legitimate means. Still, he was pleasant, respectful, generous, and accommodating, which made him well liked by the people with whom he did business, whether black or white.

Walter was not without his flaws. He had long been known as a ladies' man. Even though he had married young and had three children with his wife, Minnie, it was well known that he was romantically involved with other women. "Tree work" is notoriously demanding and dangerous. With few ordinary comforts in his life, the attention of women was something Walter did not easily resist. There was something about his rough exterior—his bushy long hair and uneven beard—combined with his generous and charming nature that attracted the attention of some women.

Walter grew up understanding how forbidden it was for a black man to be intimate with a white woman, but by the 1980s he had allowed himself to imagine that such matters might be changing. Perhaps if he hadn't been successful enough to live off his own business he would have more consistently kept in mind those racial lines that could never be crossed. As it was, Walter didn't initially think much of the flirtations of Karen Kelly, a young white woman he'd met at the Waffle House where he ate breakfast. She was attractive, but he didn't take her too seriously. When her flirtations became more explicit, Walter hesitated, and then persuaded himself that no one would ever know.

After a few weeks, it became clear that his relationship with Karen was trouble. At twenty-five, Karen was eighteen years younger than Walter, and she was married. As word got around that the two were "friends," she seemed to take a titillating pride in her intimacy with Walter. When her husband found

out, things quickly turned ugly. Karen and her husband, Joe, had long been unhappy and were already planning to divorce, but her scandalous involvement with a black man outraged Karen's husband and his entire family. He initiated legal proceedings to gain custody of their children and became intent on publicly disgracing his wife by exposing her infidelity and revealing her relationship with a black man.

For his part, Walter had always stayed clear of the courts and far away from the law. Years earlier, he had been drawn into a bar fight that resulted in a misdemeanor conviction and a night in jail. It was the first and only time he had ever been in trouble. From that point on, he had no exposure to the criminal justice system.

When Walter received a subpoena from Karen Kelly's husband to testify at a hearing where the Kellys would be fighting over their children's custody, he knew it was going to cause him serious problems. Unable to consult with his wife, Minnie, who had a better head for these kinds of crises, he nervously went to the courthouse. The lawyer for Kelly's husband called Walter to the stand. Walter had decided to acknowledge being a "friend" of Karen. Her lawyer objected to the crude questions posed to Walter by the husband's attorney about the nature of his friendship, sparing him from providing any details, but when he left the courtroom the anger and animosity toward him were palpable. Walter wanted to forget about the whole ordeal, but word spread quickly, and his reputation shifted. No longer the hard-working pulpwood man, known to white people almost exclusively for what he could do with a saw in the pine trees, Walter now represented something more worrisome.

• • •

Fears of interracial sex and marriage have deep roots in the United States. The confluence of race and sex was a powerful force in dismantling

Reconstruction after the Civil War, sustaining Jim Crow laws for a century and fueling divisive racial politics throughout the twentieth century. In the aftermath of slavery, the creation of a system of racial hierarchy and segregation was largely designed to prevent intimate relationships like Walter and Karen's—relationships that were, in fact, legally prohibited by "antimiscegenation statutes" (the word *miscegenation* came into use in the 1860s, when supporters of slavery coined the term to promote the fear of interracial sex and marriage and the race mixing that would result if slavery were abolished). For over a century, law enforcement officials in many Southern communities absolutely saw it as part of their duty to investigate and punish black men who had been intimate with white women.

Although the federal government had prom- 40 ised racial equality for freed former slaves during the short period of Reconstruction, the return of white supremacy and racial subordination came quickly after federal troops left Alabama in the 1870s. Voting rights were taken away from African Americans, and a series of racially restrictive laws enforced the racial hierarchy. "Racial integrity" laws were part of a plan to replicate slavery's racial hierarchy and reestablish the subordination of African Americans. Having criminalized interracial sex and marriage, states throughout the South would use the laws to justify the forced sterilization of poor and minority women. Forbidding sex between white women and black men became an intense preoccupation throughout the South.

In the 1880s, a few years before lynching became the standard response to interracial romance and a century before Walter and Karen Kelly began their affair, Tony Pace, an African American man, and Mary Cox, a white woman, fell in love in Alabama. They were arrested and convicted, and both were sentenced to two years in prison for violating Alabama's racial integrity laws. John Tompkins, a lawyer and part of a small minority of white professionals who considered the racial integrity laws to be unconstitutional, agreed to represent Tony and Mary to appeal their convictions. The Alabama Supreme Court reviewed the case in 1882. With rhetoric that would be quoted frequently over the next several decades, Alabama's highest court affirmed the convictions, using language that dripped with contempt for the idea of interracial romance:

> The evil tendency of the crime [of adultery or fornication] is greater when committed between persons of the two races. . . . Its result may be the amalgamation of the two races, producing a mongrel population and a degraded civilization, the prevention of which is dictated by a sound policy affecting the highest interests of society and government.

CLAIMS AND EVIDENCE

1. What type of **evidence** does Stevenson present? Give an example and discuss the function of the evidence within the argument.

2. The sources offer different perspectives. How does Stevenson **synthesize** different perspectives to support his message? Identify a specific example.

3. Consider how Stevenson use **sources**. Choose two sources and explain their credibility. How do these sources contribute to the larger argument?

4. Choose two pieces of **evidence** from the text. What are the perspectives of this evidence, and how do the two perspectives relate to each other? How do the source and the evidence relate to each other?

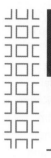

Exposition: Process Argument

AP **Enduring Understanding (REO-1)**

Writers guide understanding of a text's line of reasoning and claims through that text's organization and integration of evidence.

KEY POINT

Process arguments explain and are organized by steps, stages, or phases.

In earlier units, you've learned that writers communicate their messages to specific audiences in different formats. The writer must factor in the context (time, place, and occasion) when choosing a format (or medium) for an argument, as well as the organization, purpose, and message. So context matters. The context may influence not only what and how a writer communicates but also why the writer communicates a specific message.

In Units 1 and 2, you learned that writers can share their messages through narration, or they can move their audience through persuasion. But in an academic context, you will usually analyze subjects by making claims, drawing conclusions, and explaining your reasons. In other words, you will be writing **expository arguments**. You will look at these types of arguments in the next three units. You will also learn about evaluation arguments in Units 7 and 8.

Expository writing allows writers to explain their claims thoroughly. But it helps them accomplish more specific purposes, as well, including the following:

- Defining a term or idea
- Explaining a process
- Analyzing cause and effect

The writer's purpose is the heart of the text. This purpose also determines the mode of development: the organizing structure that allows readers to follow a line of reasoning or argument. Beginning in this unit, and continuing in the subsequent units, you'll discover how writers use different modes to achieve their goals. If you can identify a writer's mode of development in a text, you'll have a good idea of the writer's purpose.

Explaining Processes

One common mode of development is **process analysis**. A process analysis argument explains how something works, how an action occurs, or how a procedure is accomplished. This mode usually focuses on explaining steps, stages, or phases to organize an argument.

A process analysis can explore many procedures and activities:

- How to make a trailer for a romantic comedy
- The stages of human growth and development
- How to unlearn a bad habit
- The process of cell mitosis
- How a bill becomes a law
- How misinformation spreads

But remember that this mode of development does more than list stages in a process. It must also explain the significance of these steps, along with their relationship to the writer's claim. Likewise, keep in mind that a process analysis is not simply an instruction manual. While a set of instructions may offer simple, step-by-step guidance, a process analysis relies on description and explanation.

How detailed does the explanation have to be? That will depend on the audience's background knowledge of the subject. Indeed, a writer can confuse or frustrate an audience by assuming readers have more familiarity with the process than they actually do, so a process analysis should explain why each step or stage is important. Moreover, some process analyses include illustrative examples and visuals to clarify the stages. But regardless of the audience, the writer's claim must connect the stages in the process to some larger outcome, effect, or insight.

Process analyses often arrange steps or phases in chronological order, with each of the stages unified by the writer's claim.

Process Analysis Organization

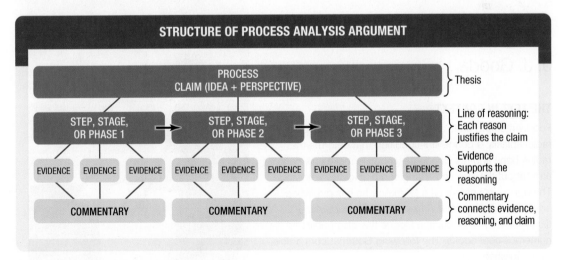

INSIDER **AP® TIP**

Order matters. Writers sequence paragraphs in a logical way to reveal their line of reasoning and to justify their claim.

AP® SKILLS PRACTICE | REASONING AND ORGANIZATION
Describing a Line of Reasoning

Think about a process you've learned about in another class, such as how a bill becomes a law, the stages of mitosis, or the steps in the writing process. Identify the steps, stages, or phases of that process. Then briefly state their importance to the overall outcome of the process.

Step, Stage, or Phase (in Order)	Relationship to Outcome

Single-Handed Cooking

J. J. Goode

THE TEXT IN CONTEXT

Food writer and critic J. J. Goode (b. 1981) was born with radial aplasia, a congenital condition that deforms the radius bone and (as Goode describes it) makes his right arm "about the size and shape of a plucked turkey wing." Throughout his career as a journalist, he has published articles in the *New York Times*, *Wall Street Journal*, *Gourmet*, and other outlets. Goode has also published numerous cookbooks. The following Gourmet.com article was published in 2009.

Max Burkhalter

AP® SKILLS PRACTICE | REASONING AND ORGANIZATION
Analyzing a Line of Reasoning

As you read, identify the steps in this process argument that make up the writer's line of reasoning. Identify two specific details within each step and then explain how those details further Goode's claim (both idea and perspective).

Analyzing Process Arguments

Message/Thesis:

Step	Details	Significance to the Writer's Claim (Idea and Perspective)

Single-Handed Cooking

My back aches. My eyes burn. I've been peeling and chopping for an hour, but I'm still being taunted by a pile of untouched vegetables. My problem is not the quantity. It's that the task of steadying each item falls to an almost useless appendage: the short, goofy arm, inexplicably bent into an L-shape and graced by just three fingers, that dangles from my right shoulder.

No one knows why I was born like this. My mom wasn't exposed to any radiation while she was pregnant, nor did she, say, have one too many sips of wine. Yet I do occasionally wonder whether my dad's Ph.D. dissertation subject—a pre-PETA endeavor for which he plucked the legs from frogs and studied their regeneration—sparked some sort of cosmic payback.

Whatever the reason, I occupy a sort of upper middle class of the handicapped. Sure, there's plenty to complain about, but all in all, things aren't so bad. While the wheelchair-bound struggle to reach their stoves, it feels a bit "Princess and the Pea" of me to grumble that peeling potatoes is as grueling as making *mole*. ("Vegetables are distressingly round," said a commiserating friend.) Or to lament that day last winter when my girlfriend took a trip to Philadelphia, leaving me at home in Brooklyn with a dozen oysters and not enough hands to shuck them with. Disability is relative: I'd rather be incapable of prying open shellfish than allergic to them. Still, I see jimmying an oyster, which otters manage without much difficulty, as an ability that's not too much to ask for.

I happily live without most of the things I can't do. The kitchen, however, is where what I love butts up against what can be so discouragingly difficult. Forget shucking an oyster; even a mundane task such as draining a pot of pasta can be death-defying. After swathing my right arm in towels to prevent it from searing (the last thing I need is for it to be less useful), I lodge it beneath the pot's handle with the same care that I imagine a window washer uses to secure his harness to a skyscraper. Then I inch toward the sink, the whole time bracing for scalding disaster and indulging in an equally scalding torrent of self-pity.

Some people say the kitchen is where they clear their heads; for me, it's where I face my demons.

Every meal is a proving ground, and I suffer mistakes as though they were failures, even when they have nothing to do with my arm. "It's really good," friends insist, as I sulk over hanger steak that doesn't have a perfectly rosy center or a gratin whose top has barely browned, forever fighting the feeling that somehow it all would have gone right had I been born a little more symmetrical. I can even find fault with the faultless because what I'm truly after is unreachable: two normal arms. When I first started to cook, I developed a crush on any ingredient that leveled the playing field. I adored canned anchovies, since the fillets simply melted in hot oil. I loved beets because after I roasted them in foil, their skins would slip right off. But soon my attraction to convenience gave way to a relishing of the arduous. Having previously avoided anything that required peeling, I now dove into recipes that called for celery root and butternut squash. I embraced Thai stir-fries, which had me meticulously slicing raw pork into matching strips so they'd all finish cooking at the same time. I can't count the times friends have watched me tackle an overly complicated prep job—always girding themselves for a bloodbath—and anxiously urged me to try using a food processor. I refuse for the same reason I insist on balancing a pan on my raised right knee when I sauce tableside instead of asking anyone for help. (It's the same reason I refused to sit out in baseball when it came time for me to bat.) I appreciate the thought, I sniff, but I can handle it.

This masochistic streak is why I'm still chopping. I'm having some friends over for dinner and I'm making braised chicken, a dish that's a breeze for most cooks but presents, for me, just the right level of hardship for a dinner party. The only way to get what I casually call my right arm to act like one is to hunch awkwardly over my cutting board, so it can reach the food that needs to be stabilized. For an hour, that was celery, onions, and carrots. A rough chop would surely suffice, but I'm attempting to dice, chasing the satisfaction of seeing perfect cubes conjured by a blur of hand and knife.

My back is bent again. This time, I'm close enough to a chicken to kiss it—unfortunate no matter how comfortable you are with raw poultry. As I try to detach a leg, it slips from my right hand's feeble grasp, spattering my cheek with cold chicken liquid. I seethe but rinse off and continue. I could, of course, have bought chicken parts. But a whole chicken is always cheaper by the pound, and why shouldn't I have access? I like to think of the price discrepancy as a one-arm tax.

Half an hour later, I've successfully dismantled the thing and begun the rewarding task of browning it, savoring the knowledge that any cook would, at this point in the process, be upright at the stove and wielding tongs in exactly the same manner as I am. After setting the chicken aside and spooning some of the golden fat from the pot, I take a seat, sweep the vegetables from my cutting board into a big bowl supported by my knees, and ferry the bowl to the stove. The vegetables sizzle when I dump them in. Now, to add the wine.

The wine! I forgot I'd have to open a bottle, a potential catastrophe. I should turn off the burner, just in case I take as long to open this bottle as I did the last one. Instead, I bet my hard-won diced vegetables that I won't scorch them. Springing into action, I wedge the bottle between my thighs, wrap my right arm around the neck (its effect is almost purely symbolic), and struggle to work the screw through the cork. I already detect a faint acridity wafting from the pot, a whiff of defeat. I quickly adjust my technique, somehow wrenching the cork out in one piece, and rush back to the stove. The vegetables have more color than I wanted, but they're fine. In goes some wine, a few sprigs of thyme, and the chicken. I cover the pot and shove it into the oven.

I know there are more compelling examples of fortitude than me braising chicken. Like a paraplegic racing uphill in a tricked-out wheelchair on marathon day, or my late grandfather, who at 90 walked down and up 20-odd flights in the pitch darkness of New York City's 2003 blackout to get groceries for his wife. But turn a spotlight on any accomplishment, however minor, and it seems like a triumph. Away from that glare, though, there's only the struggle.

My right arm swathed again, my back contorted, I stoop down and heave the pot out of the oven without incident (once I dipped so low to retrieve a casserole dish perched on the bottom rack that I singed my forehead on the top one). I call in my friends, and we sit down to a dinner that, I have to admit, is pretty good. Someone even admires my fastidious touch, the precise little cubes of carrots and celery scattered beneath the burnished chicken. "Thanks," I say. "It was nothing."

10

REASONING AND ORGANIZATION

1. J. J. Goode begins "Single-Handed Cooking" with background information in the introduction. What specific idea does Goode use to **unify** the steps of his **process**?

2. The writer describes each step of the **process**. Identify the steps that Goode describes. Then describe the overall outcome of the steps.

3. Explain how Goode's **line of reasoning** helps achieve his **purpose**.

Transitions

AP Enduring Understanding (STL-1)

The rhetorical situation informs the strategic stylistic choices that writers make.

KEY POINT

Transitions contribute to the coherence of a text by showing relationships among ideas in a text.

A writer's effectiveness in achieving his or her purpose depends on how well an audience understands the message in a given context. As you learned in earlier workshops, writers select and organize their reasons and evidence based on audience and context. A writer must create a coherent message — that is, one that a reader will understand. To achieve coherence, writers must use transitions to show the relationship between their reasons and evidence.

Transitions Explain Relationships

Transitions are words and phrases that move readers through an argument. They may contribute to the writer's style or the readers' interest, but their primary function is to explain the relationship between different parts of the text.

To do this, transitions indicate the logical relationship between ideas in an argument. For example, a writer may use transitions between paragraphs to explain the organization or relationship between the reasons of their argument. Within a paragraph, a writer may show how pieces of evidence or sources are related to the overall argument. So to analyze a text effectively, readers must become sensitive to how a writer uses transitions.

Transitions may indicate

- the sequence and relative importance of ideas or evidence,
- the writer's purpose in using a source or piece of evidence in relation to the overall argument (e.g., to support, to contrast),
- the relationship between pieces of evidence, or
- the arrangement of ideas (chronological, spatial, importance).

The Function of Transitions

As you learned in the previous workshop, writers use evidence deliberately, with a specific purpose in mind. The method of development will likely influence a writer's choice of transitions, revealing purpose. Transitions also may be used to introduce evidence that illustrates, clarifies, emphasizes, or qualifies the writer's argument. If you look closely at the transition a writer uses to introduce evidence, you can determine how that evidence supports the writer's reasoning.

USING TRANSITIONS WITH THE METHODS OF DEVELOPMENT

Method of Development	Purpose	Transitional Words and Phrases
Definition	Explaining and describing what something is *or* Establishing a common ground by explaining what something is	*To use examples in a definition* For example For instance In one category *To describe or explain* In other words That is
Process	Explaining how something works, how to do something, or how something is/was done	*To explain steps, stages, or phases* Before/After During Finally In the end Later/Next Most importantly
Causal	Explaining how a result or effect came about *or* Explaining the short- or long-term effects from causes	*To identify causes* Because Hence Since While *To identify effects* As a result Consequently For this reason Inevitably Resulting in Therefore
Comparison/Contrast	Evaluating two or more things by highlighting significant similarities and/or differences	*To identify similarities and differences* By contrast Conversely Equally However In addition Likewise On the other hand Similarly

It's helpful to pay close attention to how a writer uses transitions because a writer may indicate a shift in tone through the use of contrasting transitions. Shifting tone is usually shown by contrasting transitions, such as the following:

- However
- Although
- But
- Nevertheless

Transitions show tonal shifts. A writer's shift in tone from one part of a text to another may suggest the writer's qualification, refinement, or reconsideration of his or her perspective on a subject.

 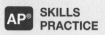

SKILLS PRACTICE

LANGUAGE AND STYLE
Analyzing Transitions

Find the lyrics to one of your favorite songs. Identify the transitions used within the song. Explain how the songwriter uses these transitions to convey important relationships and ideas.

	Transitions Used	Relationship between Ideas, Reasons, or Evidence
Transitions between paragraphs		
Transitions introducing sources		
Transitions between pieces of evidence		

Driving: It's Going Out of Style

Emma Chiu

Courtesy Emma Chiu

THE TEXT IN CONTEXT

Emma Chiu attended Woodside High School and was the coeditor in chief of *The Paw Print*, an online publication. Her work has been published in *Best of SNO*, *The Youth Journal*, and the *New York Times*. The following essay is the runner-up Winning Editorial Essay in 2018.

AP® SKILLS PRACTICE	LANGUAGE AND STYLE **Analyzing Transitions**

Identify the transitions the writer uses. Explain the relationship each transition indicates and how that evidence helps to achieve the writer's purpose.

Analyzing the Effect of Transitions

	Transitions Used	Relationship between Ideas, Reasons, or Evidence
Transitions between paragraphs		
Transitions introducing sources		
Transitions between pieces of evidence		

Driving: It's Going Out of Style

As typical of an American high schooler, I recently underwent a teenage rite of passage: beginning to drive. My friends, who also have their driving permits, frequently joke with me about the woes of lane-changing, parallel parking and three-point turns as we prepare for our looming driver's license tests.

Yet we remain part of a dwindling majority. In 1976, nearly 87 percent of high school seniors held a driver's license. By 2016, this percentage dropped to under 72, a decrease that may correlate with a climbing dependence on parental or public transportation, a lack of car ownership, or simply not needing to drive anywhere.

Then add these declining rates to a rising innovation: autonomous cars. The introduction of effective autonomous cars could drastically reduce vehicular deaths, since 94 percent of traffic fatalities involve human error. Self-driving cars would eliminate the dangers of intoxicated driving, distracted driving or simply incompetent driving—and render learning to drive unnecessary.

But, following the fatal Arizona crash between an autonomous Uber car and a pedestrian, Americans question the true safety of such technology. Company documents reveal that Uber's self-driving cars drove an average of only 13 miles before a human supervisor had to interfere to prevent a crash. In comparison, a study by Virginia Tech found that the average American driver crashes approximately once every 49,505 miles. Juxtaposed with the data of human drivers, Uber's autonomous cars appear laughably incompetent. Nevertheless, autonomous cars collectively travel about 113,636 miles per crash, indicating that they can and will be more reliable than humans.

Autonomous cars remain far from flawlessly navigating the roads, but we often fail to consider that developers designed our traffic regulations with humans—and human error—in mind. An entire network of self-driving cars would optimize traffic congestion and pollution by reducing the number of cars on the road. Consequently, regulations such as speed bumps and parking spaces may become restrictive rather than protective. To take full advantage of autonomous cars, we must prepare to rescind and replace long-standing laws.

As self-driving cars continue to improve, so does public reception of them. The percentage of Americans that distrust driverless cars decreased drastically from 74 percent in 2017 to 47 percent in 2018. If this downward trend continues, autonomous cars will soon be an accepted and integral part of society. Akin to penmanship and opera singing, human driving will soon be a practice of the past. And, given the potential security benefits and efficacy of autonomous cars, this is a future that we must accept—and even embrace.

Works Cited

Bahrampour, Tara. "Not Drinking or Driving, Teens Increasingly Put off Traditional Markers of Adulthood." The *Washington Post*, WP Company, 19 Sept. 2017.

Blanco, Myra. "Automated Vehicle Crash Rate Comparison Using Naturalistic Data." Virginia Tech Transportation Institute, Virginia Polytech Institute and State University, 8 Jan. 2016.

"Critical Reasons for Crashes Investigated in the National Motor Vehicle Crash Causation Survey." National Highway Traffic Safety Administration, Feb. 2015.

Giffi, Craig A. "A Reality Check on Advanced Vehicle Technologies." Deloitte Insights, 5 Jan. 2018.

Wakabayashi, Daisuke. "Uber's Self-Driving Cars Were Struggling Before Arizona Crash." The *New York Times*, 23 March 2018.

LANGUAGE AND STYLE

1. The second paragraph begins with a **transition**. What is the transitional word and what does the transition indicate?

2. The fifth paragraph also begins with a **transition**. What is the function of this transition?

3. Chiu uses **transitions** to introduce evidence. Choose an example and explain how the transition indicates a relationship.

4. Describe how these **transitional** words contribute to the arrangement of ideas and the message of the text.

How the Lawyers Stole Winter
Chris Daly

Dan Bricklin, courtesy of Christopher B. Daly

THE TEXT IN CONTEXT

Chris Daly (b. 1954) is a journalist and freelance writer. He currently teaches journalism at Boston University. He writes for many newspapers and magazines, including the *Washington Post*, *Atlantic Monthly*, and *American Prospect*. He is also the author of the prize-winning history of U.S. journalism, *Covering America: A Narrative History of a Nation's Journalism*.

In the following essay, which appeared in the *Atlantic* in March 1995, Daly shares his childhood experiences skating on an icy pond and his regret that litigation is depriving future generations of this privilege.

Unifying Idea	How the Lawyers Stole Winter	Rhetorical Choices	Effects of Choices
freedom	When I was a boy, my friends and I would come home from school each day, change our clothes (because we were not allowed to wear "play clothes" to school) and go outside until dinnertime. In the early 1960s in Medford, a city on the outskirts of Boston, that was pretty much what everybody did. Sometimes, there might be flute lessons or an organized Little League game, but usually not. Usually, we kids went out and played. In winter, on our way home from the Gleason School, we usually went past Brooks Pond to check the ice. By throwing heavy stones onto it,	context	Daly uses the first two paragraphs as an introduction to describe his childhood free of boundaries

Unifying Idea	How the Lawyers Stole Winter	Rhetorical Choices	Effects of Choices
	hammering it with downed branches and, finally, jumping on it, we could figure out if the ice was ready for skating. If it was, we would hurry home, grab our skates, our sticks, and whatever other gear we had, and then return to play hockey for the rest of the day. When the streetlights came on, we knew it was time to jam our cold, stiff feet back into our green rubber snow boots and get home for dinner.		
freedom	I had all these memories in mind recently when I moved, with my wife and our two young boys, into a house near a lake even closer to Boston, in the city of Newton. As soon as Crystal Lake froze over, I grabbed my skates and headed out. I was not the first one there, though: the lawyers had beaten me to the lake. They had warned the town Recreation Department to put it off limits. So I found a sign that said:	} context	Daly moves from the nostalgic memory of childhood to the current situation — loss of freedom
	<div align="center">**DANGER** **THIN ICE** **NO SKATING**</div>Knowing a thing or two about words myself, I put my own gloss on the sign. I took it to mean, *When the ice is thin, then there is danger, and there should be no skating.* Fair enough, I thought, but I knew that the obverse was also true: *When the ice is thick, then it is safe, and there should be skating.*		
freedom	Finding the ice plenty thick, I laced up my skates and glided out onto the miraculous glassy surface of a frozen lake. My wife, a native of Manhattan, would not let me take our two boys with me. But for as long as I could, I enjoyed the free, open-air delight of skating as it should be. After a few days, others joined me, and we became an outlaw band of skaters.		

Unifying Idea	How the Lawyers Stole Winter	Rhetorical Choices	Effects of Choices
freedom	What we were doing was once the heart of winter in New England—and a lot of other places, too. It was clean, free exercise that needed no Stairmasters, no health clubs, no appointments, and hardly any gear. Sadly, it is in danger of passing away. Nowadays it seems that every city and town and almost all property holders are so worried about liability and lawsuits that they simply throw up a sign or a fence and declare that henceforth there shall be no skating, and that's the end of it.	evidence	amplifies Daly's point that everyone can put up boundaries that limit freedom
freedom	As a result, kids today live in a world of leagues, rinks, rules, uniforms, adults, and rides—rides here, rides there, rides everywhere. It is not clear that they are better off, and in some ways they are clearly *not* better off.	evidence	illustrates and exemplifies that children today experience restrictive boundaries

• • •

Unifying Idea	How the Lawyers Stole Winter	Rhetorical Choices	Effects of Choices
freedom	When I was a boy skating on Brooks Pond, there were no grown-ups around. Once or twice a year, on a weekend day or a holiday, some parents might come by, with a thermos of hot cocoa. Maybe they would build a fire—which we were forbidden to do—and we would gather round.	transition	signifies shift description of how childhood experiences with fewer boundaries contributed to his understanding of risk
freedom	But for the most part the pond was the domain of children. In the absence of adults, we made and enforced our own rules. We had hardly any gear—just some borrowed hockey gloves, some hand-me-down skates, maybe an elbow pad or two—so we played a clean form of hockey, with no high-sticking, no punching, and almost no checking. A single fight could ruin the whole afternoon. Indeed, as I remember it 30 years later, it was the purest form of hockey I ever saw—until I got to see the Russian national team play the game.	process analysis step one	within the freedom, the children created boundaries

Unifying Idea	How the Lawyers Stole Winter	Rhetorical Choices	Effects of Choices
freedom	But before we could play, we had to check the ice. We became serious junior meteorologists, true connoisseurs of cold. We learned that the best weather for pond skating is plain, clear cold, with starry nights and no snow. (Snow not only mucks up the skating surface but also insulates the ice from the colder air above.) And we learned that moving water, even the gently flowing Mystic River, is a lot less likely to freeze than standing water. So we skated only on the pond. We learned all the weird whooping and cracking sounds that ice makes as it expands and contracts, and thus when to leave the ice.	transition process analysis step two	contrasts with current boundaries taking responsibilities for their actions
freedom	Do kids learn these things today? I don't know. How would they? We don't even let them. Instead, we post signs. Ruled by lawyers, cities and towns everywhere try to eliminate their legal liability. But try as they might, they cannot eliminate the underlying risk. Liability is a social construct; risk is a natural fact. When it is cold enough, ponds freeze. No sign or fence or ordinance can change that.	rhetorical question reason	moves from his childhood example to reflection on the current situation lawyers are concerned with liability while children are concerned with risk
freedom	In fact, by focusing on liability and not teaching our kids how to take risks, we are making their world more dangerous. When we were children, we had to learn to evaluate risks and handle them on our own. We had to learn, quite literally, to test the waters. As a result, we grew up to be more savvy about ice and ponds than any kid could be who has skated only under adult supervision on a rink.	thesis process analysis step three	evaluating the risks and setting rules accordingly
freedom	When I was a boy, despite the risks we took on the ice no one I knew ever drowned. The only people I ever heard about who drowned were graduate students at Harvard or MIT who came from the tropics who were living through their first winters. Not knowing about how ice forms	transition	returns to his childhood for the final comparison

Unifying Idea	How the Lawyers Stole Winter	Rhetorical Choices	Effects of Choices
	on moving water (After all, how could they?), they would innocently venture out onto the half-frozen Charles River, fall through, and die. They were literally out of their element.		
freedom	Are we raising a generation of children who will be out of their element? And if so, what can we do about it? We cannot just roll back the calendar. I cannot tell my six-year-old to head down to the lake by himself to play all afternoon—if for no other reason, he will not find twenty or thirty other kids there, full of the collective wisdom about cold and ice that they have inherited from their older brothers and sisters. Somewhere along the line that link got broken.	rhetorical question	*begins the conclusion by asking the audience to reflect*
	The whole setting of childhood has changed. We cannot change it again overnight. I cannot send them out by themselves yet, but at least some of the time, I can go out there with them. Maybe that is a start.		
	• • •		
freedom	As for us, last winter was a very unusual one. We had ferocious cold (near-zero temperatures on many nights) and tremendous snows (about a hundred inches in all). Eventually a strange thing happened. The city gave in—sort of. Sometime in January, the recreation department "opened" a section of the lake, and even dispatched a snowplow truck to clear a good-sized patch of ice. I brought the boys, and we skated the rest of winter. Ever vigilant, the city officials kept the "Thin Ice" signs up, even though their own truck could safely drive on the frozen surface. And they brought in "lifeguards" and all sorts of rules about the hours we could skate and where we had to stay.	conclusion	*Daly includes context—the detail of the community loosening some boundaries and taking safety precautions*
	But at least we were able to skate in the open air, on real ice.		
	And it was still free.		

The Individual and Nature

After winning its independence from Great Britain, the United States faced the future with both hope and uncertainty.

As American exploration moved west, seeking land and natural resources, settlers displaced indigenous peoples. We now view this as conquest and colonization. At the time, however, many viewed it as the fulfillment of "manifest destiny": the idea that expansion was an obligation for Americans.

The spirit of patriotism that helped win the war turned into a spirit of nationalism, setting a path for a new identity and culture.

IDEA BANK

Balance
Beauty
Consolation
Environmentalism
Idealism
Imagination
Individualism
Inspiration
Interdependence
Intuition
Nature
Preservation
Realization
Renewal
Romanticism
Self-reflection
Self-reliance
Simplicity
Sustainability
Truth
Wonder

© Photo JOSSE/Bridgeman Images

Kindred Spirits (1849, oil on canvas) was painted by Asher Durand, a member of the Hudson River School, a mid-nineteenth-century group of artists influenced by the ideas of Romanticism whose paintings captured the American landscape.

———

What is the relationship between individuals and nature that Durand suggests through his painting?

The country's celebratory nationalism influenced writers and artists to create a uniquely American identity in literature and the arts. Early nineteenth-century American writers were drawn to European ideas — particularly Romanticism: a movement that emerged in reaction to the emphasis on reason, tradition, and strict forms of the previous age. Unlike the writers of the Age of Reason, Romantics drew inspiration from nature and celebrated emotion, imagination, and individualism.

For the Romantics, nature was not only a source of truth but also a pathway to self-reliant individualism and authenticity. In his 1836 essay "Nature" (p. 201), Ralph Waldo Emerson explores the individual's connection to nature as a source of wonder, renewal, and self-reflection. This Romantic view of nature, society, and the individual remains powerful today. We can see it in the contemporary focus on sustainability: the idea that humans need to live in a way that preserves — and harmonizes with — the natural world.

Today's global economies and societies rely upon a broader range of national resources. Consequently, our environmental problems are more complex than in the past, including climate change, species extinction, raging wildfires, dying coral reefs, and melting polar ice caps. As one of the most influential environmentalists of the twentieth century, Rachel Carson explores these ideas in "The Obligation to Endure" (p. 204), which argues that humans must find a healthier balance between civilization and the natural world.

Indeed, many people contend that most urgent issues that current — and future — generations face are environmental ones. Whatever their cause, we must continue to adapt and respond to these environmental concerns. The question remains: How do we protect, preserve, and sustain natural resources?

PictureLux/Alamy Stock Photo

▲

The image depicts Carole Baskin, founder of Big Cat Rescue in Tampa, Florida. Big Cat Rescue is one of many private animal sanctuaries in the United States.

How can the many animal sanctuaries around the United States be both beneficial and harmful to the preservation of nature?

from Nature
Ralph Waldo Emerson

THE TEXT IN CONTEXT

Ralph Waldo Emerson (1803–1882) was an essayist, lecturer, philosopher, and poet. Often considered the father of Transcendentalism, he is known for his Romantic beliefs in self-reliance and individualism. In the following excerpt from his 1836 essay "Nature," Emerson provides perhaps the best expression of Transcendentalism. His idea of the Over-Soul — a supreme mind that all individuals share — allowed transcendentalists to disregard external authority and rely on their own intuitions and experiences. Emerson encourages the reader with his motto: "Trust thyself."

To go into solitude, a man needs to retire as much from his chamber [room] as from society. I am not solitary whilst I read and write, though nobody is with me. But if a man would be alone, let him look at the stars. The rays that come from those heavenly worlds, will separate between him and what he touches. One might think the atmosphere was made transparent with this design, to give man, in the heavenly bodies, the perpetual presence of the sublime. Seen in the streets of cities, how great they are! If the stars should appear one night in a thousand years, how would men believe and adore; and preserve for many generations the remembrance of the city of God which had been shown! But every night come out these envoys of beauty, and light the universe with their admonishing smile.

The stars awaken a certain reverence, because though always present, they are inaccessible; but all natural objects make a kindred impression, when the mind is open to their influence. Nature never wears a mean appearance. Neither does the wisest man extort her secret, and lose his curiosity by finding out all her perfection. Nature never became a toy to a wise spirit. The flowers, the animals, the mountains, reflected the wisdom of his best hour, as much as they had delighted the simplicity of his childhood.

When we speak of nature in this manner, we have a distinct but most poetical sense in the mind. We mean the integrity of impression made by manifold natural objects. It is this which distinguishes the stick of timber of the wood-cutter, from the tree of the poet. The charming landscape which I saw this morning, is indubitably made up of some twenty or thirty farms. Miller owns this field, Locke that, and Manning the woodland beyond. But none of them owns the landscape. There is a property in the horizon which no man has but he whose eye can integrate all the parts, that is, the poet. This is the best part of these men's farms, yet to this their warranty-deeds give no title.

To speak truly, few adult persons can see nature. Most persons do not see the sun. At least they have a very superficial seeing. The sun illuminates only the eye of the man, but shines into the eye and the heart of the child. The lover of nature is he whose inward and outward senses are still truly adjusted to each other; who has retained the spirit of infancy even into the era of manhood. His intercourse with heaven and earth, becomes part of his daily food. In the presence of nature, a wild delight runs through the man, in spite of real sorrows. Nature says,—he is my creature, and maugre [despite] all his impertinent griefs, he shall be glad with me. Not the sun or the summer alone, but every hour and season yields its tribute of delight; for every hour and change corresponds to and authorizes a different state of the mind, from breathless noon to grimmest midnight. Nature is a setting that fits equally well a comic or a mourning piece. In good health, the air is a cordial of incredible virtue. Crossing a bare common, in snow puddles, at twilight, under a clouded sky, without having in my thoughts any occurrence of special good fortune, I have enjoyed a perfect exhilaration. I am glad to the brink of fear. In the woods too, a man casts off his years, as the snake his slough, and at what period soever of life, is always a child. In the woods, is perpetual youth. Within these plantations of God, a decorum and sanctity reign, a perennial festival is dressed, and the guest sees not how he should tire of them in a thousand years. In the woods, we return to reason and faith. There I feel that nothing can befall me in life,—no disgrace, no calamity, (leaving me my eyes,) which nature cannot repair. Standing on the bare ground,—my head bathed by the blithe air, and uplifted into infinite space,—all mean egotism vanishes. I become a transparent eye-ball; I am nothing; I see all; the currents of the Universal Being circulate through me; I am part or particle of God. The name of the nearest friend sounds then foreign and accidental: to be brothers, to be acquaintances,—master or servant, is then a trifle and a disturbance. I am the lover of uncontained and immortal beauty. In the wilderness, I find something more dear and connate [inborn] than in streets or villages. In the tranquil landscape, and especially in the distant line of the horizon, man beholds somewhat as beautiful as his own nature.

The greatest delight which the fields and woods minister, is the suggestion of an occult relation between man and the vegetable. I am not alone and unacknowledged. They nod to me, and I to them. The waving of the boughs in the storm, is new to me and old. It takes me by surprise, and yet is not unknown. Its effect is like that of a higher thought or a better emotion coming over me, when I deemed I was thinking justly or doing right.

Yet it is certain that the power to produce this delight, does not reside in nature, but in man, or in a harmony of both. It is necessary to use these pleasures with great temperance. For, nature is not always tricked [dressed] in holiday attire, but the same scene which yesterday breathed perfume and glittered as for the frolic of the nymphs, is overspread with melancholy today. Nature always wears the colors of the spirit. To a man laboring under calamity, the heat of his own fire hath sadness in it. Then, there is a kind of contempt of the landscape felt by him who has just lost by death a dear friend. The sky is less grand as it shuts down over less worth in the population.

Steve Proehl/Getty Images

▲

This image depicts a suburban housing community in California bordering an established farm.

What are some other issues that this image addresses, and how can we reconcile these conflicts as we search to respect and preserve our environment?

RHETORICAL SITUATION

1. How does Emerson **appeal** to the audience's emotions and values in the **introduction**?

2. How do Emerson's rhetorical choices in the **conclusion** not only reflect their **purpose** and **context** but also address the intended audience's needs and perspective on the subject?

REASONING AND ORGANIZATION

3. How does Emerson begin the text? How does this **arrangement** help to communicate his **purpose**?

4. Each paragraph develops an idea. Choose an idea and discuss how Emerson **organizes** and develops that idea within the paragraph.

5. How does Emerson use narrative elements to personify Nature? How does this **personification** communicate his attitude toward Nature?

CLAIMS AND EVIDENCE

6. What is the function of the **evidence** in this text? Discuss whether the evidence is convincing.

7. Emerson offers many **examples** throughout the text to support his **claim**. Choose an example and discuss how the example strengthens his line of reasoning.

8. What is the "transparent eye-ball" (paragraph 5)? Explain the spiritual aspect of this experience and how Emerson uses this as **evidence** to support his line of reasoning.

LANGUAGE AND STYLE

9. Emerson uses contrast throughout the text. Choose a contrast and explain how it creates a shift in **tone**.

10. The final paragraph begins with "yet." How does this **transition** set up the contrast that Emerson reconciles in the conclusion?

IDEAS IN AMERICAN CULTURE

11. Emerson suggests that humans, the natural world, and God are capable of joining in a harmonious union. Discuss this spiritual connection as you consider the perspectives of transcendentalists. Give an example from the text that illustrates the spirituality that Emerson finds in nature.

PUTTING IT ALL TOGETHER

12. How do the ideas in the text connect to our current environmental issues? How can we combine the ideas of Emerson with the issues facing our globalized world? Can we still strive to see nature "with the heart of a child," or are we too immersed in materialism, technology, and other distractions?

The Obligation to Endure

Rachel Carson

THE TEXT IN CONTEXT

Rachel Carson (1907–1964) was a marine biologist and nature writer. She is best known for her 1962 book *Silent Spring*, which helped start the global environmental movement. The book revealed problems with synthetic pesticides and advocated conservation. Although *Silent Spring* (1962) attracted controversy from chemical companies, it ultimately was instrumental in the nationwide ban of DDT and other harmful chemicals. The book also served as a catalyst for the creation of the Environmental Protection Agency. President Carter awarded Carson the Presidential Medal of Freedom posthumously in 1980.

The history of life on earth has been a history of interaction between living things and their surroundings. To a large extent, the physical form and the habits of the earth's vegetation and its animal life have been molded by the environment. Considering the whole span of earthly time, the opposite effect, in which life actually modifies its surroundings, has been relatively slight. Only within the moment of time represented by the present century has one species—man—acquired significant power to alter the nature of his world.

During the past quarter century this power has not only increased to one of disturbing magnitude but it has changed in character. The most alarming of all man's assaults upon the environment is the contamination of air, earth, rivers, and sea with dangerous and even lethal materials. This pollution is for the most part irrecoverable; the chain of evil it initiates not only in the world that must support life but in living tissues is for the most part irreversible. In this now universal contamination of the environment, chemicals are the sinister and little-recognized partners of radiation in changing the very nature of the world, the very nature of its life. Strontium 90, released through nuclear explosions into the air, comes to earth in rain or drifts down as fallout, lodges in soil, enters into the grass or corn or wheat grown there, and in time takes up its abode in the bones of a human being, there to remain until his death. Similarly, chemicals sprayed on croplands or forests or gardens lie long in soil, entering into living organisms, passing from one to another in a chain of poisoning and death. Or they pass mysteriously by underground streams until they emerge and, through the alchemy of air and sunlight, combine into new forms that kill vegetation, sicken cattle, and work unknown harm on those who drink from once pure wells. As Albert Schweitzer has said, "Man can hardly even recognize the devils of his own creation."

It took hundreds of millions of years to produce the life that now inhabits the earth—eons of time in which that developing and evolving and diversifying life reached a state of adjustment and balance with its surroundings. The environment, rigorously shaping and directing the life it supported, contained elements that were hostile as well as supporting. Certain rocks gave out dangerous radiation; even within the light of the sun, from which all life draws its energy, there were short-wave radiations with power to injure. Given time—time not in years but in millennia— life adjusts, and a balance has been reached. For time is the essential ingredient; but in the modern world there is no time.

The rapidity of change and the speed with which new situations are created follow the impetuous and heedless pace of man rather than the deliberate pace of nature. Radiation is no longer merely the background radiation of rocks, the bombardment of cosmic rays, the ultraviolet of the sun that have existed before there was any life on earth; radiation is now the unnatural creation of man's tampering with the atom. The chemicals to which life is asked to make its adjustment are no longer merely the calcium and silica and copper and all the rest of the minerals washed out of the rocks and carried in rivers to the sea; they are the synthetic creations of man's inventive mind, brewed in his laboratories, and having no counterparts in nature.

To adjust to these chemicals would require time on the scale that is nature's; it would require not merely the years of a man's life but the life of generations. And even this, were it by some miracle possible, would be futile, for the new chemicals come from our laboratories in an endless stream; almost five hundred annually find their way into actual use in the United States alone. The figure is staggering and its implications are not easily grasped—500 new chemicals to which the bodies of men and animals are required somehow to adapt each year, chemicals totally outside the limits of biologic experience.

Among them are many that are used in man's war against nature. Since the mid-1940s over 200 basic chemicals have been created for use in killing insects, weeds, rodents, and other organisms described in the modern vernacular as "pests"; and they are sold under several thousand different brand names.

These sprays, dusts, and aerosols are now applied almost universally to farms, gardens, forests, and homes—nonselective chemicals that have the power to kill every insect, the "good" and the "bad," to still the song of birds and the leaping of fish in the streams, to coat the leaves with a deadly film, and to linger on in soil—all this though the intended target may be only a few weeds or insects. Can anyone believe it is possible to lay down such a barrage of poisons on the surface of the earth without making it unfit for all life? They should not be called "insecticides," but "biocides."

The whole process of spraying seems caught up in an endless spiral. Since DDT was released for civilian use, a process of escalation has been going on in which ever more toxic materials must be found. This has happened because insects, in a triumphant vindication of Darwin's principle of the survival of the fittest, have evolved super races immune to the particular insecticide used, hence a deadlier one has always to be developed—and then a deadlier one than that. It has happened also because, for reasons to be described later, destructive insects often undergo a "flareback," or resurgence, after spraying, in numbers greater than before. Thus the chemical war is never won, and all life is caught in its violent crossfire.

Along with the possibility of the extinction of mankind by nuclear war, the central problem of our age has therefore become the contamination of man's total environment with such substances of incredible potential for harm—substances that accumulate in the tissues of plants and animals and even penetrate the germ cells to shatter or alter the very material of heredity upon which the shape of the future depends. . . .

The Other Road

We stand now where two roads diverge. But unlike the roads in Robert Frost's familiar poem, they are not equally fair. The road we have long been traveling is deceptively easy, a smooth superhighway on which we progress with great speed, but at its end lies disaster. The other fork of the road—the one "less traveled by"—offers our last, our only chance to reach a destination that assures the preservation of our earth.

The choice, after all, is ours to make. If, having endured much, we have at last asserted our "right to know," and if, knowing, we have concluded that we are being asked to take senseless and frightening risks, then we should no longer accept the counsel of those who tell us that we must fill our world with poisonous chemicals; we should look about and see what other course is open to us.

A truly extraordinary variety of alternatives to the chemical control of insects is available. Some are already in use and have achieved brilliant success. Others are in the stage of laboratory testing. Still others are little more than ideas in the minds of imaginative scientists, waiting for the opportunity to put them to the test. All have this in common: they are biological solutions, based on understanding of the living organisms they seek to control, and of the whole fabric of life to which these organisms belong. Specialists representing various areas of the vast field of biology are contributing—entomologists, pathologists, geneticists, physiologists, biochemists, ecologists—all pouring their knowledge and their creative inspirations into the formation of a new science of biotic controls. . . .

Through all these new, imaginative, and creative approaches to the problem of sharing our earth with other creatures there runs a constant theme, the awareness that we are dealing with life—with living populations and all their pressures and counter-pressures, their surges and recessions. Only by taking account of such life forces and by cautiously seeking to guide them into channels favorable to ourselves can we hope to achieve a reasonable accommodation between the insect hordes and ourselves.

The current vogue for poisons has failed utterly to take into account these most fundamental considerations. As crude a weapon as the cave man's club, the chemical barrage has been hurled against the fabric of life—a fabric on the one hand delicate and destructible, on the other miraculously tough and resilient, and capable of striking back in unexpected ways. These extraordinary capacities of life have been ignored by the practitioners of chemical control who have brought to their task no "high-minded orientation," no humility before the vast forces with which they tamper. The "control of nature" is a phrase conceived in arrogance, born of the Neanderthal age of biology and philosophy, when it was supposed that nature exists for the convenience of man. The concepts and practices of applied entomology for the most part date from that Stone Age of science. It is our alarming misfortune that so primitive a science has armed itself with the most modern and terrible weapons, and that in turning them against the insects it has also turned them against the earth.

This infographic from the 2018 Earth Day demonstrates ways to reduce the amount of plastic that we consume.

Look closely at the data presented here. Are we only wasting plastic? What other sources of waste could we reduce even as we keep our eye on the reduction of plastics? As you read the infographic, consider what you can do in your community to reduce plastics.

Steelys Drinkware

RHETORICAL SITUATION

1. What is Carson's **claim**?

2. How do the rhetorical choices in the **introduction** reflect Carson's **purpose** and **context**? How do they address the audience's needs on the subject?

3. What **perspectives** on pesticides does Carson convey to convince her **audience** of her **claim**?

4. In the **conclusion**, Carson connects her argument to issues beyond pesticides. Give an example of how this connection strengthens and magnifies Carson's argument.

REASONING AND ORGANIZATION

5. Does Carson use **induction** or **deduction**? How does this **organization** strengthen her argument?

6. How do the **descriptions** advance her purpose? Give an example of a description from the text and discuss the effect.

CLAIMS AND EVIDENCE

7. How do Carson's choices of **evidence** connect to each other in support of Carson's **claim**?

8. What are some of the different perspectives readers can infer from the **evidence**? Choose two pieces of evidence and describe their perspectives.

9. What is the function of the **evidence**, and how does this function help support Carson's argument?

LANGUAGE AND STYLE

10. Give an example of a **transition** and explain how it functions to advance the argument.

11. Identify the pattern of **simple sentences** throughout the text. How does this **syntactic** choice contribute to the effectiveness of Carson's argument?

IDEAS IN AMERICAN CULTURE

12. While Carson's message resonates today and stands as a foundational text for environmentalists, it also speaks to the struggle between humans and nature. Specifically, she asks, How do we share and care for the earth? Discuss this struggle through Carson's text and in your own community. What are some solutions to address this timeless struggle?

PUTTING IT ALL TOGETHER

13. Rachel Carson illustrates a world destroyed by human choices and behavior. Discuss how the illustrations, descriptions, and details further develop her argument.

IDEAS IN AMERICAN CULTURE
The Individual and Society

American writers of the early nineteenth century reflected a strong spirit of individualism. Many became fascinated with the philosophy of transcendentalism in particular. Inspired by the German philosopher Immanuel Kant, Transcendentalists believed that humans could use individual intuition to discover higher truths beyond the power of reason. These insights could often be found by spending time in the natural world. For example, Ralph Waldo Emerson often wrote about the superiority of wisdom acquired from nature over knowledge learned from books and schools.

Many transcendentalists criticized commercialization and materialism while advocating for a more authentic life: one less focused on wealth, materialism, and status. A student of Emerson, Henry David Thoreau, urged people to "simplify, simplify." In "Where I Lived, and What I Lived For" (p. 211) from his book *Walden*, Thoreau recounts his experience living in the woods for two years, two months, and two days with only the barest necessities. The writer E. B. White reflects on Thoreau's lasting legacy in his essay "Walden" (p. 214).

IDEA BANK
Collaboration
Collective
Community
Compromise
Culture
Experience
Harmony
Humanity
Identity
Independence
Materialism
Minimalism
Nationalism
Preservation
Pride
Simplicity
Society
Tradition
Transcendentalism
Utopia
Value

In Walden Pond Revisited (1942, oil on canvas), American artist N. C. Wyeth represents Thoreau set among nature.

What message about individuals and society might Wyeth be offering? What details in the painting support your idea?

Today, this same spirit of anti-materialism often motivates those who choose other values — public service, spirituality, domestic happiness, freedom — over the acquisition of wealth. Indeed, many people prefer to free themselves of material "things" and live simply. Several recent trends, from the tiny house movement and minimalist design to the popularity of celebrity organizing consultant Marie Kondo, attest to the appeal of this "less-is-more" philosophy.

That idea is evident in the world of work, too, as people now understand that community and connection are as vital for human success as plush office buildings. This view, along with an increasing number of freelance workers, has led to the emergence of coworking spaces, which consist of workers from different companies, handling various projects, and sharing in a diverse working community. People who work in a coworking space say that the collective wisdom, collaborative thinking, and shared motivation can foster growth, balance, and meaning in their lives.

These trends toward simplicity, meaningful careers, and work-life balance are likely to continue, as they are generally embraced by younger people in the workforce. For example, members of Generation Z (those born after 1995) are concerned with their own truths and their own voices. While this generation values individualism and independence, it is also mindful of the need for collaboration. While Gen Zs are the first entirely "digital natives," they still rely on their independence and intuition but know that compromise and communication are often the best way to resolve conflicts.

▲

The Subway (1950, tempera on composition board) was painted by George Tooker as a response to social injustices of postwar urban society. It is currently part of the collection at the Whitney Museum of American Art in New York City.

How does materialism of a contemporary society impede our desire for individualism and identity?

from Walden
Henry David Thoreau

Michael Dwyer / Alamy Stock Photo

THE TEXT IN CONTEXT

Henry David Thoreau (1817–1862) was a writer, social reformer, naturalist, philosopher, and transcendentalist. He lived for two years, two months, and two days by Walden Pond in Concord, Massachusetts. His time in Walden Woods became a model of intentional and simplified living. Thoreau published twenty volumes of poems, essays, articles, and journals in his lifetime, but he is best known for his essay "Civil Disobedience" and his book about living in the woods, *Walden* (1854). The following are excerpts from *Walden*.

Where I Lived, and What I Lived For

I went to the woods because I wished to live deliberately, to front only the essential facts of life, and see if I could not learn what it had to teach, and not, when I came to die, discover that I had not lived. I did not wish to live what was not life, living is so dear; nor did I wish to practise resignation, unless it was quite necessary. I wanted to live deep and suck out all the marrow of life, to live so sturdily and Spartan-like as to put to rout all that was not life, to cut a broad swath and shave close, to drive life into a corner, and reduce it to its lowest terms, and, if it proved to be mean, why then to get the whole and genuine meanness of it, and publish its meanness to the world; or if it were sublime, to know it by experience, and be able to give a true account of it in my next excursion. For most men, it appears to me, are in a strange uncertainty about it, whether it is of the devil or of God, and have somewhat hastily concluded that it is the chief end of man here to "glorify God and enjoy him forever." . . .

Conclusion

I left the woods for as good a reason as I went there. Perhaps it seemed to me that I had several more lives to live, and could not spare any more time for that one. It is remarkable how easily and insensibly we fall into a particular route, and make a beaten track for ourselves. I had not lived there a week before my feet wore a path from my door to the pond-side; and though it is five or six years since I trod it, it is still quite distinct. It is true, I fear that others may have fallen into it, and so helped to keep it open. The surface of the earth is soft and impressible by the feet of men; and so with the paths which the mind travels. How worn and dusty, then, must be the highways of the world, how deep the ruts of tradition and conformity! I did not wish to take a cabin passage, but rather to go before the mast and on the deck of the world, for there I could best see the moonlight amid the mountains. I do not wish to go below now.

I learned this, at least, by my experiment; that if one advances confidently in the direction of his dreams, and endeavors to live the life which he has imagined, he will meet with a success unexpected in common hours. He will put some things behind, will pass an invisible boundary; new, universal, and more liberal laws will begin to establish themselves around and within him; or the old laws be expanded, and interpreted in his favor in a more liberal sense, and he will live with the license of a higher order of beings. In proportion as he simplifies his life, the laws of the universe will appear less complex, and solitude will not be solitude, nor poverty poverty, nor weakness weakness. If you have built castles in the air, your work need not be lost; that is where they should be. Now put the foundations under them. . . .

Some are dinning in our ears that we Americans, and moderns generally, are intellectual dwarfs compared with the ancients, or even the Elizabethan men. But what is that to the purpose? A living dog is better than a dead lion. Shall a man go and hang himself because he belongs to the race of pygmies, and not be the biggest pygmy that he can? Let everyone mind his own business, and endeavor to be what he was made.

Why should we be in such desperate haste 5 to succeed, and in such desperate enterprises? If a man does not keep pace with his companions, perhaps it is because he hears a different drummer. Let him step to the music which he hears, however measured or far away. It is not important that he should mature as soon as an apple tree or an oak. Shall he turn his spring into summer? If the condition of things which we were made for is not yet, what were any reality which we can substitute? We will not be shipwrecked on a vain reality. Shall we with pains erect a heaven of blue glass over ourselves, though when it is done we shall be sure to gaze still at the true ethereal heaven far above, as if the former were not? . . .

The life in us is like the water in the river. It may rise this year higher than man has ever known it, and flood the parched uplands; even this may be the eventful year, which will drown out all our muskrats. It was not always dry land where we dwell. I see far inland the banks which the stream anciently washed, before science began to record its freshets. Everyone has heard the story which has gone the rounds of New England, of a strong and beautiful bug which came out of the dry leaf of an old table of apple-tree wood, which had stood in a farmer's kitchen for sixty years, first in Connecticut, and afterward in Massachusetts—from an egg deposited in the living tree many years earlier still, as appeared by counting the annual layers beyond it; which was heard gnawing out for several weeks, hatched perchance by the heat of an urn. Who does not feel his faith in a resurrection and immortality strengthened by hearing of this? Who knows what beautiful and winged life, whose egg has been buried for ages under many concentric layers of woodenness in the dead, dry life of society, deposited at first in the alburnum of the green and living tree, which has been gradually converted into the semblance of its well-seasoned tomb—heard perchance gnawing out now for years by the astonished family of man, as they sat round the festive board—may unexpectedly come forth from amidst society's most trivial and handselled furniture, to enjoy its perfect summer life at last!

I do not say that John or Jonathan will realize all this; but such is the character of that morrow which mere lapse of time can never make to dawn. The light which puts out our eyes is darkness to us. Only that day dawns to which we are awake. There is more day to dawn. The sun is but a morning star.

The image of a tiny house is often associated with a minimalist philosophy — that is, living with less. This tiny house was constructed from a recycled shipping container.

How does living with less align with conservation, preservation, and simplicity? How does this contemporary lifestyle spark the discussion of how we live in the future?

Halfpoint/iStock/Getty Images

RHETORICAL SITUATION

1. In "Where I Lived, and What I Lived For," what is Thoreau's **claim**?

2. How do the writer's rhetorical choices in the **introduction** connect to the beliefs, values, or emotions of the audience?

3. In "Conclusion," the last two paragraphs offer many **perspectives**. Choose one and discuss the implications of this perspective on Thoreau's **message**.

REASONING AND ORGANIZATION

4. How does Thoreau's text reflect a **process analysis method of development**?

5. What **images** and **allusions** does Thoreau use in his text? How do these elements contribute to his message?

6. Does Thoreau's **evidence** — that is, his personal observation and experience — strengthen his argument? Explain.

CLAIMS AND EVIDENCE

7. Describe the **evidence** Thoreau uses to support his line of reasoning.

8. What is the function of his **evidence** (e.g., to illustrate, to provide an example, to associate, or to amplify a point)? Give an example and discuss how the evidence functions.

LANGUAGE AND STYLE

9. Thoreau uses **transitional phrases**. Identify a transitional phrase. Choose an example and explain the relationship it creates: a comparison, a cause-and-effect relationship, or an explanation.

10. Thoreau uses **rhetorical questions** throughout the text. Choose one and explain the effect created from the rhetorical question.

IDEAS IN AMERICAN CULTURE

11. Transcendentalism was a philosophical movement that believed in the inherent goodness of both humans and the natural world. Transcendentalists emphasized individualism, intuition, and imagination. Discuss how these ideas are central to Thoreau's *Walden*. Why would this text be considered a representation of Transcendentalism?

PUTTING IT ALL TOGETHER

12. Discuss how Thoreau's rhetorical choices help connect his ideas and convey his tone. How do all these elements work together to communicate his message?

Walden

E. B. White

Bettmann/Getty Images

THE TEXT IN CONTEXT

E. B. White (1899–1985) was an author most famous for his children's books, such as *Stuart Little* (1945) and *Charlotte's Web* (1952). He was also a writer and contributing editor at the *New Yorker* magazine, as well as the coauthor of the popular guide to good writing, *The Elements of Style*. White won the Presidential Medal of Freedom in 1963 and a special Pulitzer Prize for his lifetime achievement as a writer. In this 1939 essay, White dictates a letter to his assistant, Miss Nims, in which he responds to Thoreau, whose experiment in simplicity left a lasting impact on White.

Miss Nims, take a letter to Henry David Thoreau.

• • •

Dear Henry: I thought of you the other afternoon as I was approaching Concord, doing fifty on Route 62. That is a high speed at which to hold a philosopher in one's mind, but in this century we are a nimble bunch.

On one of the lawns in the outskirts of the village, a woman was cutting the grass with a motorized lawn mower. What made me think of you was that the machine had rather got away from her, although she was game enough, and in the brief glimpse I had of the scene it appeared to me that the lawn was mowing the lady. She kept a tight grip on the handles, which throbbed violently with every explosion of the one-cylinder motor, and as she sheered around bushes and lurched along at a reluctant trot behind her impetuous servant, she looked like a puppy who had grabbed something that was too much for him. Concord hasn't changed much, Henry; the farm implements and the animals still have the upper hand.

I may as well admit that I was journeying to Concord with the deliberate intention of visiting your woods; for although I have never knelt at the grave of a philosopher nor placed wreaths on moldy poets and have often gone a mile out of my way to avoid some place of historical interest, I have always wanted to see Walden Pond. The account which you left of your sojourn there is, you will be amused to learn, a document of increasing pertinence; each year it seems to gain a little headway, as the world loses ground. We may all be transcendental yet, whether we like it or not. As our common complexities increase, any tale of individual simplicity (and yours is the best written and the cockiest) acquires a new fascination; as our goods accumulate, but not our well-being, your report of an existence without material adornment takes on a certain awkward credibility.

My purpose in going to Walden Pond, like yours, was not to live cheaply or to live dearly there, but to transact some private business with the fewest obstacles. Approaching Concord, doing forty, doing forty-five, doing fifty, the steering wheel held snug in my palms, the highway held grimly in my vision, the crown of the road now serving me (on the right-hand curves), now defeating me (on the left-hand curves), I began to rouse myself from the stupefaction a day's motor journey induces. It was a delicious evening, Henry, when the whole body is one sense and imbibes delight through every pore, if I may coin a phrase. Fields were richly brown where the harrow, drawn by the stripped Ford, had lately sunk its teeth; pastures were green; and overhead the sky had that same everlasting great look that you will find on page 144 of the Oxford pocket edition.

I could feel the road entering me, through tire, wheel, spring, and cushion; shall I not have intelligence with earth too? Am I not partly leaves and vegetable mold myself?—a man of infinite horsepower, yet partly leaves.

Stay with me on 62, and it will take you into Concord. As I say, it was a delicious evening. The snake had come forth to die in a bloody S on the highway, the wheel upon its head, its bowels flat now and exposed. The turtle had come up too to cross the road and die in the attempt, its hard shell smashed under the rubber blow, its intestinal yearning (for the other side of the road) forever squashed. There was a sign by the wayside that announced that the road had a "cotton surface." You wouldn't know what that is, but neither, for that matter, did I. There is a cryptic ingredient in many of our modern improvements—we are awed and pleased without knowing quite what we are enjoying. It is something to be traveling on a road with a cotton surface.

The civilization round Concord today is an odd distillation of city, village, farm, and manor. The houses, yards, fields look not quite suburban, not quite rural. Under the bronze beech and the blue spruce of the departed baron grazes the milch goat of the heirs. Under the porte-cochères stands the reconditioned station wagon; under the grape arbor sit the puppies for sale. (But why do men degenerate ever? What makes families run out?)

It was June and everywhere June was publishing her immemorial stanza; in the lilacs, in the syringa, in the freshly edged paths and the sweetness of moist beloved gardens, and the little wire wickets that preserve the tulips' front. Farmers were already moving the fruits of their toil into their yards, arranging the rhubarb, the asparagus, the strictly fresh eggs on the painted stands under the little shed roofs with the patent shingles. And

5

though it was almost a hundred years since you had taken your ax and started cutting out your home on Walden Pond, I was interested to observe that the philosophical spirit was still alive in Massachusetts: in the center of a vacant lot some boys were assembling the framework of the rude shelter, their whole mind and skill concentrated in the rather inauspicious helter-skeleton of studs and rafters. They too were escaping from town, to live naturally, in a rich blend of savagery and philosophy.

That evening, after supper at the inn, I strolled out into the twilight to dream my shapeless transcendental dreams and see that the car was locked up for the night (first open the right front door, then reach over, straining, and pull up the handles of the left rear and the left front till you hear the click, then the handle of the right rear, then shut the right front but open it again, remembering that the key is still in the ignition switch, remove the key, shut the right front again with a bang, push the tiny keyhole cover to one side, insert key, turn, and withdraw). It is what we all do, Henry. It is called locking the car. It is said to confuse thieves and keep them from making off with the lap robe. Four doors to lock behind one robe. The driver himself never uses a lap robe, the free movement of his legs being vital to the operation of the vehicle; so that when he locks the car, it is a pure and unselfish act. I have in my life gained very little essential heat from lap robes, yet I have ever been at pains to lock them up.

The evening was full of sounds, some of which would have stirred your memory. The robins still love the elms of New England villages at sundown. There is enough of the thrush in them to make song inevitable at the end of day, and enough of the tramp to make them hang round the dwellings of men.

10

A robin, like many another American, dearly loves a white house with green blinds. Concord is still full of them.

Your fellow-townsmen were stirring abroad—not many afoot, most of them in their cars; and the sound which they made in Concord at evening was a rustling and a whispering. The sound lacks steadfastness and is wholly unlike that of a train. A train, as you know who lived so near the Fitchburg line, whistles once or twice sadly and is gone, trailing a memory in smoke, soothing to ear and mind. Automobiles, skirting a village green, are like flies that have gained the inner ear—they buzz, cease, pause, start, shift, stop, halt, brake, and the whole effect is a nervous polytone, curiously disturbing.

As I wandered along, the toc-toc of ping-pong balls drifted from an attic window. In front of the Reuben Brown house, a Buick was drawn up. At the wheel, motionless, his hat upon his head, a man sat, listening to Amos and Andy on the radio (it is a drama of many scenes and without an end). The deep voice of Andrew Brown, emerging from the car, although it originated more than two hundred miles away, was unstrained by distance. When you used to sit on the shore of your pond on Sunday morning, listening to the church bells of Acton and Concord, you were aware of the excellent filter of the intervening atmosphere. Science has attended to that, and sound now maintains its intensity without regard for distance. Properly sponsored, it goes on forever.

A fire engine, out for a trial spin, roared past Emerson's house, hot with readiness for public duty. Over the barn roofs the martins dipped and chittered. A swarthy daughter of an asparagus grower, in culottes, shirt, and bandanna, pedaled past on her bicycle. It was indeed a delicious evening, and I returned to the inn (I believe it was your house once) to rock with the old ladies on the concrete veranda.

Next morning early I started afoot for Walden, out Main Street and down Thoreau, past the depot and the Minuteman Chevrolet Company. The morning was fresh, and in a bean field along the way I flushed an agriculturalist, quietly studying his beans. Thoreau Street soon joined Number 126, an artery of the State. We number our highways nowadays, our speed being so great we can remember little of their quality or character and are lucky to remember their number. (Men have an indistinct notion that if they keep up this activity long enough all will at length ride somewhere, in next to no time.) Your pond is on 126.

I knew I must be nearing your woodland retreat when the Golden Pheasant lunchroom came into view—Sealtest ice cream, toasted sandwiches, hot frankfurters, waffles, tonics, and lunches. Were I the proprietor, I should add rice, Indian meal, and molasses—just for old time's sake: The Pheasant, incidentally, is for sale: a chance for some nature lover who wishes to set himself up beside a pond in the Concord atmosphere and live deliberately, fronting only the essential facts of life on Number 126. Beyond the Pheasant was a place called Walden Breezes, an oasis whose porch pillars were made of old green shutters sawed into lengths. On the porch was a distorting mirror, to give the traveler a comical image of himself, who had miraculously learned to gaze in an ordinary glass without smiling. Behind the Breezes, in a sun-parched clearing, dwelt, your philosophical descendants in their trailers, each trailer the size of your hut, but all grouped together for the sake of congeniality. Trailer people leave the city, as you did, to discover solitude and in any weather, at any

hour of the day or night, to improve the nick of time; but they soon collect in villages and get bogged deeper in the mud than ever. The camp behind Walden Breezes was just rousing itself to the morning. The ground was packed hard under the heel, and the sun came through the clearing to bake the soil and enlarge the wry smell of cramped housekeeping. Cushman's bakery truck had stopped to deliver an early basket of rolls. A camp dog, seeing me in the road, barked petulantly. A man emerged from one of the trailers and set forth with a bucket to draw water from some forest tap.

Leaving the highway, I turned off into the woods toward the pond, which was apparent through the foliage. The floor of the forest was strewn with dried old oak leaves and *Transcripts*. From beneath the flattened popcorn wrapper (*granum explosum*) peeped the frail violet. I followed a footpath and descended to the water's edge. The pond lay clear and blue in the morning light, as you have seen it so many times. In the shallows a man's waterlogged shirt undulated gently. A few flies came out to greet me and convoy me to your cove, past the No Bathing signs on which the fellows and the girls had scrawled their names. I felt strangely excited suddenly to be snooping around your premises, tiptoeing along watchfully, as though not to tread by mistake upon the intervening century. Before I got to the cove, I heard something that seemed to me quite wonderful: I heard your frog, a full, clear *troonk*, guiding me, still hoarse and solemn, bridging the years as the robins had bridged them in the sweetness of the village evening. But he soon quit, and I came on a couple of young boys throwing stones at him.

Your front yard is marked by a bronze tablet set in a stone. Four small granite posts, a few feet away, show where the house was. On top of the tablet was a pair of faded blue bathing trunks with a white stripe. Back of it is a pile of stones, a sort of cairn, left by your visitors as a tribute, I suppose. It is a rather ugly little heap of stones, Henry. In fact, the hillside itself seems faded, browbeaten; a few tall skinny pines, bare of lower limbs, a smattering of young maples in suitable green, some birches and oaks, and a number of trees felled by the last big wind. It was from the bole of one of these fallen pines, torn up by the roots, that I extracted the stone which I added to the cairn—a senti-mental act in which I was interrupted by a small terrier from a nearby picnic group, who confronted me and wanted to know about the stone.

I sat down for a while on one of the posts of your house to listen to the bluebottles and the dragonflies. The invaded glade sprawled shabby and mean at my feet, but the flies were tuned to the old vibration. There were the remains of a fire in your ruins, but I doubt that it was yours; also two beer bot-tles trodden into the soil and become part of earth. A young oak had taken root in your house, and two or three ferns, unrolling like the ticklers at a banquet. The only other furnishings were a DuBarry pattern sheet, a page torn from a picture magazine, and some crusts in wax paper.

Before I quit, I walked clear round the pond and found the place where you used to sit on the northeast side to get the sun in the fall, and the beach where you got sand for scrub-bing your floor. On the eastern side of the pond, where the highway borders it, the State has added dressing rooms for swimmers, a float with diving towers, drinking fountains of porcelain, and rowboats for hire. The pond is in fact a State Preserve, and carries a twenty-dollar fine for picking wild flowers, a decree signed in all solemnity by your fellow-citizens Walter C. Wardwell, Erson B. Barlow, and Nathaniel I. Bowditch. There was a smell of creosote where they had been building a wide wooden stairway to the road and the parking area. Swimmers and boaters were arriving; bodies plunged vigorously into the water and emerged wet and beautiful in the bright air. As I left, a boatload of town boys were splashing about in mid-pond, kidding and fooling, the young fellows singing at the tops of their lungs in a wild chorus:

> Amer-ica, Amer-ica, God shed his grace
> on thee,
> And crown they good with brotherhood
> From sea to shi-ning sea!

I walked back to town along the railroad, [20] following your custom. The rails were expand-ing noisily in the hot sun, and on the slope of the roadbed, the wild grape and the blackberry sent up their creepers to the track.

The expense of my brief sojourn in Concord was:

Canvas shoes	$1.95	
Baseball bat	.25	gifts to
Left-handed fielder's glove	1.25	take back to a boy
Hotel and meals	4.25	
In all	$7.70	

As you see, this amount was almost what you spent for food for eight months. I can-not defend the shoes or the expenditure for shelter and food: they reveal a meanness and grossness in my nature that you would find contemptible. The baseball equipment, how-ever, is the kind of impediment with which you were never on even terms. You must remember that the house where you prac-ticed the sort of economy that I respect was haunted only by mice and squirrels. You never had to cope with a shortstop.

▲

This image was taken in 2018 at Walden Pond. According to the *New York Magazine* article "Walden Pond: New England's Daytona Beach," the beach is popular because "it's a rare literary history site."

Explain how the image reinforces the messages of E. B. White or Henry David Thoreau.

RHETORICAL SITUATION

1. What is E. B. White's **purpose** in writing to Thoreau as an imaginary reader?

2. What perspectives on the subject might the **audience** have based on their shared beliefs, values, and needs?

3. How does E. B. White's **perspective** affect the tone of the **message**?

4. Why does E. B. White choose to write a letter? Does it further advance his **purpose**? How?

REASONING AND ORGANIZATION

5. E. B. White describes his surroundings to advance his **message**. Give an example of this **description** and explain how it contributes to the message.

6. How does setting up a posthumous letter to Thoreau function as an **appeal** to his intended **audience**?

CLAIMS AND EVIDENCE

7. What is the **claim** of the letter?

8. What type of **evidence** does White use to support his reasons? Is it effective? Explain.

9. What is the function of the **evidence**? Describe how the evidence works to convince the audience of the writer's claim.

LANGUAGE AND STYLE

10. Choose a **transition** within the essay. Describe the relationship it conveys.

11. White uses personal testimony to describe his visit to Walden Pond. Give an example of a **transitional phrase** that introduces the description of Walden Pond. Explain what this transition illustrates about Walden Pond.

IDEAS IN AMERICAN CULTURE

12. E. B. White's letter is a direct response to the transcendentalist movement. While most of the letter is a description of what he sees, he almost always brings that description back to Thoreau's experiment on Walden Pond. How does White view Transcendentalism? Does this philosophy still provide any insight, wisdom, or value to people living in the contemporary world? Why or why not?

PUTTING IT ALL TOGETHER

13. E. B. White wrote this essay as a response to Henry David Thoreau. Describe how White's attitude toward his subject contributes to the tone of his message.

COMPOSITION WORKSHOP
Writing a Process Argument

When you need to explain how to do something or how something works, you develop your ideas through a process argument. This type of argument depends upon a clear organizational strategy based on a deliberate, often chronological, order. In writing a process argument, you must carefully consider your audience's prior knowledge and your own purpose and message for communicating the process.

In this workshop, you will have the opportunity to develop an argument using process analysis in order to explain the steps, stages, or phases of something you know how to do or understand well. Your purpose is not only to teach your audience but also to convey a message.

> **KEY POINT**
>
> Process arguments explain and are organized by steps, stages, or phases.

It's Time for America to Start Feeling the Love for Ultimate Frisbee

Alex Kucich

The following process argument, written by Alex Kucich, was a runner-up in the 2016 *New York Times* student essay contest.

There is something misleadingly whimsical about the word "frisbee." It brings to mind the flowing hair of golden retrievers and leaping hippies, not serious athletics. However, it is time Americans realized that frisbee has become something far more formidable and new. Yes, Ultimate Frisbee has recently burgeoned into a fiercely competitive, physically demanding and increasingly popular sport. "Disc" has an official governing body, international championships and potential inclusion in future Olympic Games. It's time for Americans to break out the bandanas and start feeling the love for Ultimate Frisbee.

> *writer establishes context connecting frisbee to general audience*
>
> *transitions to a thesis with different perspective*
>
> *thesis states a claim: frisbee is formidable and new*

There was, admittedly, a time when Frisbee was not a legitimate sport. The first Wham-O Frisbees of the 1950s were, at the time, mere toys. Tossed at casual get-togethers and college campuses, Frisbees garnered little serious attention outside the canine community. This image has stuck. Many Americans view Frisbee as nothing more than a laid-back pastime—one primarily reserved for Starbucks baristas.

> *line of reasoning: process phase 1 — the early days of recreational frisbee*

process phase
2 — continues
line of reasoning
by introducing the
beginning of the
movement changing
frisbee from pastime
to organized sport

Behind the scenes, however, a Frisbee Renaissance had begun. In 1968, a group of New Jersey high schoolers invented Ultimate Frisbee, a sport combining the strategy of football, the athleticism of soccer, and the whirlwind pace of basketball with the unique loftiness of the Wham-O Frisbee. Two teams of seven (usually men and women) compete to connect passes for as many "touchdowns" as possible. Layouts, soaring grabs, exotic throws ("the scoober" is my personal favorite), and screaming hipsters only add to the appeal. Indeed,

process phase 3 —
the final phase in line
of reasoning explains
the growth of frisbee
internationally

the game has grown by leaps and bounds. Between 2004 and 2011 alone, USA Ultimate (America's national Ultimate Frisbee organization) memberships grew from 10,000 to 16,000 players. "Disc" has also grown internationally, now played in forty-two countries worldwide. Frisbee is truly the ultimate new sport.

transitions from
phases of the sport
to a discussion of the
misconceptions

Why, then, is Disc dissed? The answer lies in the nature of the game itself. Ultimate — a self-consciously pure sport — has only one piece of equipment, no referees, no advertising agencies, no glittery stadiums, and no commercial interests to distract players from the joy of the game. It is a sport that relies on sportsmanship and integrity instead of jock attitude and fancy gear. This gives Ultimate

transitions signify a
causal relationship

Disc its hippie-anti-capitalist reputation, but also leaves the game unfortunately under-appreciated. No fancy gear means no big-money interest, so no media attention — thus Ultimate Frisbee flies under the radar of most Americans.

writer concludes
with context

The ultimate question facing Disc enthusiasts is how to legitimize the game without corrupting it. Because corporate interest would undermine its counterculture core, Ultimate must rise to eminence through its players. Ultimate Frisbee is already soaring in popularity on college campuses and public parks across the globe. It is high time the American public caught on.

Works Cited

writer incorporates
evidence to support
his claim from general
publications and the
organization's website

Avirgan, Jody. "Ultimate Frisbee at the Olympics?" The New York Times, 11 Aug. 2015. Web. 17 Mar. 2016.

Barta, Jasmine. "Ultimate Frisbee's Popularity Expands on Campuses." USA Today. Gannett, 03 June 2013. Web. 17 Mar. 2016.

Booth, Tina. "End the Marginalization of Ultimate in High Schools First." The New York Times, 12 Aug. 2015. Web. 17 Mar. 2016.

"History of Ultimate." History of Ultimate. World Flying Disc Federation, n.d. Web. 17 Mar. 2016.

YOUR ASSIGNMENT

Imagine you have been asked by a local youth organization to write a blog post that either teaches readers how to do something you can do well or that explains a process you understand well. First, think about your talents, interests, and skills. Next, choose a task or process that you would like to explain. Then draft a multiparagraph process argument that teaches your audience how to complete the task or understand how something works.

Your argument should be organized chronologically and include the following:

- a thesis connecting the process to an idea or desired result,
- relevant and sufficient details,
- an explanation to support the thesis, and
- a conclusion that brings the argument to a unified end by explaining the significance of the argument within a broader context.

Potential Subjects:

- How to gain the advantage while playing *Fortnite*
- How to develop your own engaging podcast
- How to survive a zombie apocalypse
- How to prepare your favorite meal
- How dangerous hurricanes formed
- How to overturn a law that has been vetoed
- How misinformation communicates online
- How social media algorithms manipulate

RHETORICAL SITUATION Establishing Context

AP® Enduring Understanding (RHS-1)

Individuals write within a particular situation and make strategic writing choices based on that situation.

If someone asks you how to get to a room in your school, you will probably reply with a quick list of directions: take the stairs to the third floor, turn right at the second hallway, and go to the fifth room on the left. This is a simple set of technical instructions that requires little else than a set of commands.

However, if someone needs to know how to balance an equation in chemistry or how a smartphone works, your answer will explain the process in greater detail. In writing, when you explain how to do something or how something works, this explanation is called a process analysis.

Types of Process Arguments	Purpose	Sample Subjects
DIRECTIVE: How to do something	To provide directions so that the audience can *complete the task* successfully once they have read the essay	• How to be prepared for bicycle flats • How to gain more Instagram followers • How to make a movie trailer for a horror movie
EXPLANATORY: How something works or something was done	To provide an explanation so that the audience will *understand* the process once they have read the essay	• How to build an effective gaming computer • How social media influences followers • How data can be manipulated

Before you can effectively compose a process analysis, you need to examine the context by considering the following:

- Will you be explaining how to do something or how something works?
- How much does your audience already know about the process?
- What details does the audience need to know to complete the task or understand the process?

Sometimes, a writer will mistakenly assume that readers have more knowledge of the process than they actually do. So it is critical not only to list the steps but also to explain the details and significance of each step. For example, if you are explaining how to balance a chemistry equation but your audience does not already know the periodic table, you will need to explain the naming and classification of elements as well.

You will also need to connect the process to a desired outcome so that your audience will understand the significance of the process or gain valuable insight. For example, if you explain to new drivers how to change a tire, they may not fully understand the value of that skill by itself. But if you also emphasize the potential to save money on repairs or prepare for an emergency, your audience will understand the importance of this knowledge. Essentially, you are connecting the process to a **unifying idea**.

 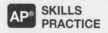 SKILLS PRACTICE | RHETORICAL SITUATION **Establishing Context**

Think about the subject of your process analysis. Then complete a table like the one above as you reflect on both the context and the ideas associated with your process analysis. For this workshop, we will use "how to organize a closet" as a model.

Audience	Potential Unifying Ideas

CLAIMS AND EVIDENCE **Establishing a Purpose**

AP **Enduring Understanding (CLE-1)**

Writers make claims about subjects, rely on evidence that supports the reasoning that justifies the claim, and often acknowledge or respond to other, possibly opposing, arguments.

Considering the context and the ideas related to the process will help you compose the thesis for your process analysis. Introduce the subject with helpful context about the process. After this context, include a thesis that connects the process to the idea you have chosen to establish the significance. For example, a thesis could link how to organize a closet to the idea of efficiency and economy.

Next, with a strong thesis in place, plan the paragraphs of explanation that will follow. In other words, organize the paragraphs according to the steps or phases of the process. Most of the time, the steps, stages, or phases are presented in a chronological order. These steps will become your topic sentences for the paragraphs in your essay. Each topic sentence will be followed by detailed explanations of a particular step or phase. In a process essay, these details serve as your evidence.

Thesis (Subject + Idea)	Steps, Stages, or Phases
Knowing how to organize a closet will ultimately save you both time and money.	Step 1: Only keep items you need or love.
	Step 2: Sort removed items by type or function of item.
	Step 3: Return items back to the closet, arranged with a system to meet your specific needs.

AP **SKILLS PRACTICE** | CLAIMS AND EVIDENCE **Establishing a Purpose**

Write a thesis statement for your subject related to your unifying idea and list the major steps or phases of the process.

Thesis (Subject + Idea)	Steps, Stages, or Phases

REASONING AND ORGANIZATION Explaining Relevance

AP **Enduring Understanding (REO-1)**

Writers guide understanding of a text's line of reasoning and claims through that text's organization and integration of evidence.

When you explain a process, you must lead your audience through the steps or phases of your process. When it is connected to your unifying idea, each step or phase becomes a reason within your line of reasoning and establishes the organization of your essay.

At the center of the process analysis is its chronological organization and meticulous detail. The writer must present the steps or phases of the process in the correct order for the audience to complete the task or understand the process. Then all of the phases can be explained further by additional details, which are also listed in order. The body paragraphs, as well as the details and explanations within these paragraphs, must be presented in the same sequence that they occur in the process. For example, you would not tell your audience how to place items back in the closet (ending step) before you have explained how to discard unwanted items (middle step).

When you develop the body paragraphs, which are guided by the phases of the process, include all important details and omit extraneous details. These explanatory paragraphs should be even more precise, explaining the rationale for each step and making connections to the idea. For example, when you explain how to sort through unwanted items, you may want to add a tip to divide these into boxes for donations and bags for garbage. If you include this step, your audience can save valuable time.

On a final note, you should not distract your audience with unnecessary information. In your essay about closet organization, you should not introduce bargain-hunting tips or other distracting, unrelated details.

Thesis (Subject + Idea)	Steps, Stages, or Phases	Details and Explanation
Knowing how to organize a closet will result in saving both time and money.	Step 1: Only keep items you need or love.	• Take everything out of the closet • Evaluate each item for value
	Step 2: Sort removed items by type or function of item.	• Clothing, shoes, and accessories • Equipment, books, toys, etc. • Items to discard or donate
	Step 3: Return items to the closet, arranged with a system to meet your specific needs.	Further sort by • Color or function • Frequently and infrequently used items • Seasonal items • Memorabilia

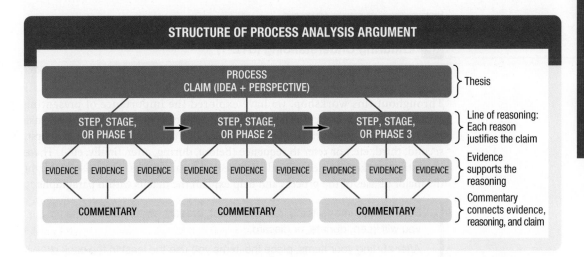

STRUCTURE OF PROCESS ANALYSIS ARGUMENT

PROCESS
CLAIM (IDEA + PERSPECTIVE) } Thesis

STEP, STAGE, OR PHASE 1 → STEP, STAGE, OR PHASE 2 → STEP, STAGE, OR PHASE 3 } Line of reasoning: Each reason justifies the claim

EVIDENCE EVIDENCE EVIDENCE | EVIDENCE EVIDENCE EVIDENCE | EVIDENCE EVIDENCE EVIDENCE } Evidence supports the reasoning

COMMENTARY | COMMENTARY | COMMENTARY } Commentary connects evidence, reasoning, and claim

 **SKILLS PRACTICE** | REASONING AND ORGANIZATION
Explaining Relevance

Generate a list of important details for completing each step of the process. Arrange these details in chronological order to support the subject of the paragraph. If you need to include photographs, images, or other graphics, refer to them in your text. You may continue brainstorming on your graphic organizer.

Use the following graphic organizer to arrange your details.

Thesis (Subject + Idea)	Steps, Stages, or Phases	Details and Explanation

LANGUAGE AND STYLE   Using Transitions

AP **Enduring Understanding (STL-1)**

The rhetorical situation informs the strategic stylistic choices that writers make.

Throughout this workshop, we have explored the importance of presenting evidence in chronological order. To indicate the order of steps effectively, use transitions that relate to time or sequence. You can number the steps (first, second, third, etc.) or refer to sequence (before, during, after, finally, etc.). These important markers guide the reader between the paragraphs. They also highlight the major phases of the process and help explain the details within paragraphs.

> *Before* you remove items from the closet, prepare sorting bins for items you will keep, donate, or discard.
>
> *After* sorting your items, place the items you use the least in the back or on the highest shelves.
>
> *Finally*, arrange your hanging clothes by type (pants, shirts, jackets) and by color.

And while communicating the order of the process is essential, you will also need to signify relationships between the steps of the process and the ideas in the thesis. If you clarify these relationships, you will communicate your line of reasoning. For example, we noted earlier that a helpful time-saving tip in organizing a closet is sorting items as they are removed. In our essay, we would connect that step to the tip with a transition.

> In order to save time and energy, you should sort the items you will keep, donate, or discard into separate bins while you are removing them.

TRANSITIONS TO SIGNIFY TIME OR ORDER		
Beginning	**Middle**	**End**
Before	After	Eventually
First	As soon as	Finally
First of all	During	In the end
Foremost	Following	Lastly
Initially	In the meantime	Most importantly
To begin	Later	To conclude
	Next	Ultimately
	Once	
	Second, Third, etc.	
	Subsequently	
	Then	

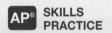

SKILLS PRACTICE | LANGUAGE AND STYLE
Using Transitions

Using the notes you have collected throughout the workshop, begin drafting your essay. Between and within each paragraph, include helpful transitions to indicate the next steps in the process and the relationships between ideas. Consult the Transitions to Signify Time or Order table as a guide.

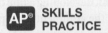

SKILLS PRACTICE | PUTTING IT ALL TOGETHER
Revising and Editing a Process Argument

Peer-Revision Checklist: Revising and Editing a Process Argument		
Revising and Editing Checklist	**Unit 3 Focus Skills**	**Comment on the Effectiveness and/or Make a Suggestion**
Does the claim in the introduction or conclusion connect the process to an idea?	*Process analysis/ how-to essay*	
Are the evidence and commentary divided into phases and arranged in chronological order for the audience?	*Chronological line of reasoning*	
Has the writer accounted for the audience's prior knowledge? Did the writer connect the process to a purpose or benefit?	*Audience/ purpose*	
Has the writer crafted the process essay with clear and specific details connected with transitions that clarify the process?	*Transitions for time or order*	
Is the writing free of errors in spelling, punctuation, capitalization, and other writing conventions?	*Punctuating syntactical features*	

⊐⊔⊏
⊐⊐⊏
⊐⊐⊏
⊐⊐⊏
⊐⊐⊏
⊐⊐⊏

PREPARING FOR THE AP® EXAM

Free-Response Question: Synthesis

Incorporating Evidence from Sources

The first free-response question that you will encounter on the AP® English Language and Composition Exam is called the synthesis question. It requires you to develop a position on a particular subject by arguing a claim, developing a line of reasoning, and supporting your claim with evidence. Unlike the argument prompt that we practiced in Unit 2, the synthesis prompt requires you to incorporate at least three of the six to seven accompanying sources (readings and visual sources). In other words, you will be considering, explaining, and integrating others' perspectives into your own argument.

→ **Step One: Determine a Unifying Idea and Position and Evaluate Sources**

For the synthesis argument, you must incorporate evidence from *at least three* of the sources provided in the question. This will require you to read critically and interact with and incorporate other points of view. To do this, you must preview all source material carefully to determine their perspective and annotate sources that may contribute to your argument.

As you review the sources, determine a unifying idea to guide your evaluation and your argument. In addition, determine your position on the subject. For example, if the subject of the synthesis question is the age requirement for voting, would you favor lowering the required age to sixteen or keeping it the same? Your position will then lead you to choose a unifying idea such as representation, responsibility, equality, engagement, or another of your choosing.

Here are some initial questions to consider when reading the source material:

- Which sources support my position? How can I incorporate evidence from these sources?

- Which sources oppose my position? How might these sources become a part of my conversation?

- What varying perspectives are represented in the sources? How might these perspectives inform my line of reasoning?

- How can I interact with the sources?

- How can the sources interact with each other?

While a complete synthesis on the AP® Exam will have six to seven sources, we will begin by practicing synthesizing sources with four sources. You should annotate directly on the sources.

INSIDER TIP **Titles and publication information of sources give helpful clues.** Because you will need to review the sources quickly, you should review the citation, especially the title and source, that precedes the sources to determine the position and perspective of the source. This may help you evaluate the usefulness of the information.

→ **Step Two: Develop a Defensible Claim and Unified Line of Reasoning**

After evaluating the sources, you will need to write your thesis (idea + perspective) and develop your line of reasoning, both of which may have been influenced by the information in the sources. While you may be tempted to organize your discussion by the sources, a strong synthesis argument will be guided by the reasons you will develop that support your position. Remember that in a synthesis, *your* position should be central (*you* are the lead singer), and the sources serve as evidence to support your reasoning (they are your background singers).

To prepare to write your thesis statement for the synthesis task, you can review the Unit 2 AP® Writing Workshop: Claims and Evidence, which focuses on developing your argument. Both argument and synthesis share these common tasks:

1. Take a perspective on the subject.
2. Write a defensible thesis that includes your position and perspective.
3. Establish a line of reasoning that justifies your position and perspective.
4. Support your thesis with evidence.

Essentially, your body paragraphs will introduce each of your reasons (topic sentences) followed by evidence from sources accompanied by your own discussion and explanation. Clear transitions will allow readers to follow your line of reasoning and distinguish between source information and your perspective. Here are some common transitional or "signal" words and phrases that will help you integrate sources into your synthesis effectively.

Transitions		
To Introduce a Source or Claim or to Establish Credibility	**To Show Agreement or Add a Related Idea**	**To Introduce Evidence**
According to X	Another	As X noted
X acknowledges	Furthermore	For example
X agrees	In addition	For instance
X from Y argues	In addition	In fact
X insists	In the same way	In other words
X proves	Likewise	That is
X suggests	Similarly	

→ **Step Three: Choose Relevant Evidence**

When you do include evidence from sources to support your line of reasoning, you need to introduce this information with transitions to signal that you are presenting someone else's ideas, data, or research. If you do not attribute your source, you are plagiarizing. Remember that synthesis involves your pulling together different perspectives and arguments as evidence to support your own thesis.

It is important to integrate sources in a way that develops a conversation between the sources and your own perspective. Your goal is to find two or more sources that can interact with each of your reasons (or body paragraphs) that support your claim. While this is not a rule, by doing so, you are placing the sources in conversation with each other and yourself. This is what synthesis means.

When you are ready to support your line of reasoning, return to your initial notes and choose the evidence that directly relates to your claim. Consider where this information will be the most useful to support the claim in your argument.

→ **Step Four: Develop Your Commentary**

Once you have selected your evidence to support your claim and line of reasoning, you will need to write several sentences that explain the significance and relevance of the evidence in relation to your idea and perspective. One common problem is that students summarize or paraphrase evidence from the sources and call it synthesis. Commentary actually serves to explain how the sources interact with one another.

In later units, you will learn more about developing effective commentary for the synthesis argument.

PREPARING FOR THE AP® EXAM

The following prompt is an example of a synthesis free-response question. For now, you will practice with four textual sources. Use what you have learned in this workshop to respond to the following synthesis prompt.

Prompt:
During their high school years, students find various ways to prepare for their futures. Some students choose to work part time, some focus their time on academic studies, and some choose to engage in many extracurricular activities. In short, there are many ways for students to prepare for college and/or a career.

Carefully read the following four sources, including the introductory information for each source. Write an essay that synthesizes material from at least three of the sources and develop your position on the best preparation for a future after high school.

Source A (Dickler)

Source B (Thomson)

Source C (Hess)

Source D (Thomson)

In your response, you should do the following:

- Respond to the prompt with a thesis that presents a defensible position.
- Select and use evidence from at least three of the provided sources to support your line of reasoning. Indicate the sources clearly through direct quotation, paraphrase, or summary. Sources may be cited as Source A, Source B, etc., or by using the description in parentheses.
- Explain how the evidence supports your line of reasoning.
- Use appropriate grammar and punctuation in communicating your argument.

Source A

Dickler, Jessica. "Why so Few Teenagers Have Jobs Anymore." CNBC, 7 Oct. 2019, www.cnbc.com/2019/10/06/why-so-few-teenagers-have-jobs -anymore.html.

The following is an article from an online news source.

Most people remember their first summer or after-school job, which provided cash to help pay for college or a car.

Today, vehicles and higher education — among other expenses — cost significantly more. Yet fewer teenagers are working.

The share of teens participating in the labor force peaked 40 years ago and has declined ever since. In 1979, nearly 60% of American teenagers were employed, an all-time high. Today, just over one-third, or 35%, of teens between the ages of 16 and 19 are part of the workforce.

Teens are less likely to work part-time while in school and also less likely to work over the summer, according to a study by the Hamilton Project and Brookings Institution.

"High school has become more intense," said Lauren Bauer, a coauthor of the study.

"We have increasing demands on what it is that high schoolers need to be doing and how much time that takes," she said, including "not only homework and course requirements but other graduation requirements like public service."

"There is less time in the day to hold down a job."

Meanwhile, the advent of summer programs has increased exponentially over the past decade, according to Eric Greenberg, president of Greenberg Educational Group, a New York-based consulting firm with clients throughout the U.S. "The perception out there is that the more things they do, the better."

In fact, the popular conception that kids are spending more time on leisure or screen time is just not the case, Bauer said. "Teenagers are working really hard."

In addition to the time constraints on kids, a reduced demand for low-wage work and increased competition from older workers, among other factors, have also contributed to the sharp drop in labor force participation, the Brookings study found.

Now, more teenagers are enrolled in school and more schools are in session year-round. "The flip side is that graduation rates are way up," Bauer said.

According to the study, teens juggling both work and school spend less time on school than those who are enrolled only, demonstrating the trade-off.

The research also shows that prioritizing education over early work experience can increase the prospects for good job outcomes later in life.

However, kids who don't work also forgo an opportunity to learn valuable lessons about finance when they are young, cautioned Shelly-Ann Eweka, a certified financial planner and wealth management director at financial services firm TIAA.

That's where parents can step in, Eweka said. "Give the child some responsibility in terms of making financial decisions," she said, including the compromises that those decisions often entail.

For example, "give them a budget for back-to-school shopping so they can decide between a fancy pair of sneakers or new clothes," Eweka said.

Further, talk openly about the cost of things, especially college, and open a savings account or Roth individual retirement account to demonstrate the magic of compound interest.

Studies shows that kids who learn to manage money when they're young will be able to better handle their finances as adults.

In fact, young adults who discussed money with their parents are even more likely to have a budget, more likely to have an emergency fund, more likely to put 10% or more of their income toward savings and more likely to have a retirement account, according to one parents, kids & money survey from T. Rowe Price.

Source B

Thomson, Helen. "Why Adolescents Put Themselves First." *New Scientist*, 8 Sept. 2006, www.newscientist.com/article/dn10030-why-adolescents-put-themselves-first/.

The following is an article published on a science and technology website.

Teenagers are more selfish than adults because they use a different part of their brain to make decisions compared to adults, new research suggests.

Previous work has shown that when children reach puberty, there is an increase in connections between nerves in the brain. This occurs particularly in the area involved in decision-making and awareness of other people's feelings, called the "mentalising network."

Now Sarah-Jayne Blakemore, a cognitive neuroscientist from University College London, UK, has used functional magnetic resonance imaging (fMRI) to scan the brains of 19 adolescents (aged 11 to 17) and 11 adults (aged 21 to 37) whilst they were asked questions relating to decision-making. Questions such as: "You're going to the cinema, where do you look for film times?"

Blakemore found that teenagers rely on the rear part of the mentalising network to make their decisions, an area of the brain called the superior temporal sulcus. In contrast, adults use the front part, called the prefrontal cortex.

The superior temporal sulcus is involved in processing very basic behavioural actions, whereas the prefrontal cortex is involved in more complex functions such as processing how decisions affect others. So the research implies that "teenagers are less able to understand the consequences of their actions," says Blakemore.

Taken Care Of

In a separate experiment, Blakemore asked 112 participants (aged from 8 to 37) to make decisions about other people's welfare and timed how long it took them to respond. The questions included: "How would your friend feel if she wasn't invited to your party?"

She found that the response time got shorter as the participants got older, suggesting that the older people found it easier to put themselves in other people's shoes.

Blakemore suggests that both findings might be explained by an evolutionary mechanism in which the development of the brains of adolescents takes precedence over its performance. "You don't need to be on a par with other people because you are looked after until reproductive age. Only then do you need to start to take into account other people's perspectives."

Work in Progress

The work has implications for the types of responsibility given to adolescents, Blakemore says: "Teenager's brains are a work in progress and profoundly different from adults. If you're making decisions about how to treat teenagers in terms of the law, you need to take this new research into account."

Sam Lewis, a specialist in youth crime and justice, from the University of Leeds, says there has in fact been a shift away from welfare-focused approaches to youth punishment in the UK: "Today, responses to youth crime tend to emphasise offender responsibility, accountability and punishment. It seems likely that the concerns of many, including those of Dr Blakemore, may be lost in the tide of punitive policies being pursued by the government."

The research was presented at the British Association for the Advancement of Science Festival in Norwich, UK.

Source C

Hess, Abigail J. "Young People Are Less Likely to Hold Summer Jobs Now—Here's What They're Doing Instead." CNBC, 3 Aug. 2018, www.cnbc.com/2018/08/01/young-people-are-decreasingly-likely-to-hold-a-summer-jobheres-what-.html.

The following article was published on a national news website.

When Warren Buffett was six years old, he spent his summer selling sticks of gum and bottles of Coca-Cola. When Bill Gates was 16, he spent the summer working as a Congressional page. When Jeff Bezos was 16, he spent the summer flipping burgers for McDonalds.

Summer jobs have been a part of the American success story for decades, but according to a recent report from Pew Research Center, the era of the summer job may be coming to an end. In 2016, 35 percent of 16-to-19-year-olds held a summer job, and the teen labor force participation rate in July was 43.2 percent.

Compare that to 1978, when 58 percent of this group held a summer job, and the teen labor force participation during the month of July was 71.8 percent. Wisconsin's state legislature recently passed a bill that lowered the minimum age for lifeguards to 15 so that the state's many indoor and outdoor waterparks could keep their doors open.

There are several reasons for the "death" of the summer job, among them, an overall decline in youth employment as a result of the Great Recession, and an overall decrease in the number of low-skill, entry-level jobs as a result of dramatic changes in the retail industry.

But beyond these economic realities, there are several other factors that are causing younger generations to buck the summer employment tradition.

One cause is the highly-competitive educational landscape that students must navigate today. According to a report from the Bureau of Labor Statistics (BLS), the percentage of young people taking classes over the summer has more than quadrupled, from 10.4 percent in 1985 to 42.1 percent in 2016. Students today need to continue their educations after high school in order to compete in the workforce of tomorrow and for many, that means taking classes over the summer to either get ahead of or keep up with their peers.

Additionally, school years are longer than they were in the 1970s and '80s. "With a shorter summer off from school, students may be less inclined to get a summer job, and employers may be less inclined to hire them," states the BLS report.

Overall, "a focus on education is driving this decline in employment," Martha Ross, a fellow at Brookings, tells USA Today.

When they aren't in class, young people are still getting their hands dirty — even if it's not with a summer job. Teens are increasingly likely to hold unpaid internships (which the BLS does not consider employment) and to volunteer. BLS data shows that a quarter of American 16-to-19-year-olds volunteers regularly, and many high schools require students to volunteer in their local communities in order to graduate.

Like summer jobs, opportunities like these have the capacity to teach important lessons about hard work and responsibility. "You can learn responsibility in any job, if you take it seriously," Jeff Bezos is quoted saying in the book, Golden Opportunity: Remarkable Careers That Began at McDonald's.

Of course, unpaid internships and volunteering don't put money in the bank. But in the 1970s, it was possible to work a low-paying summer job and earn enough to build meaningful savings for college. Today, the cost of college has risen dramatically, making it highly unlikely that a student would be able to make enough cash over the summer to offset the costs of their higher education.

Instead, many students focus on earning a generous scholarship and for many, that means summer classes, unpaid internships and volunteering.

Source D

Chen, Grace. "Should Public Schools Provide Students with Vocational Opportunities?" *Public School Review*, 7 May 2019, publicschoolreview .com/blog/should-public-schools-provide-students-with-vocational -opportunities.

The following article is published on a website dedicated to public school content.

Contrary to popular belief, not all prominent, high-demand careers require a college degree. According to the National Center for Education Statistics, 10 out of the 28 top fastest-growing careers could be pursued with vocational training available through public schools.

Subsequently, many believe that public schools should be providing more extensive vocational programs for interested students. While all high schools are required to provide students with general education courses, only a handful of schools provide students with vocational alternatives.

What Type of Learning Coincides with Vocational Education?

Vocational-technical education programs provide students with practical learning opportunities and hands-on experiences to prepare graduates for a career following high school. As Massachusetts Public Schools explains, vocational programs allow students to develop technical, academic, and professional skills that can be used for either a professional pathway or a continuing education alternative.

While all states have vocational programs at various community colleges, some areas are still struggling to establish or maintain functioning programs at the public high school level. Because the cost of these programs can often add an extra burden to a public school's limited budget, these vocational courses are frequently one of the first venues to be cut during a time of financial struggle.

Despite the balancing, financial planning, and professional accommodations needed to establish these programs, many states have shown tremendous strides in offering vocational opportunities. For example, Massachusetts is one of the leading states offering diverse and extensive vocational venues for students.

According to Massachusetts State Law, public schools that offer vocational programs are required to "Integrate academic and vocational education and shall include competency-based applied learning which contributes to an individual's academic knowledge, higher order reasoning, and problem-solving skills." In fact, according to Massachusetts' vocational course catalog listings, students in various public schools can attend training programs in fields such as:

- Culinary arts
- Horticulture
- Communications (design and visual)

- Cosmetology
- Marketing
- Early education and care
- Carpentry/electricity (including heating, ventilation, air conditioning, etc.)
- Drafting
- Programming and web development
- Automotive repair, technology, and refinishing

Best of all, upon completing the vocational and high school requirements, students are prepared to pursue immediate employment, advanced education opportunities, and added career choices.

What Are the Benefits of Vocational Training?

Upon completing all vocational requirements, not only can students embark upon a professional or academic career, but many high school graduates even continue to immediately pursue apprenticeships, specialized college programs, or other professional routes.

With the diverse skills acquired from their public school vocational programs, students are able to gain unique benefits, such as:

- Hands-on learning experiences
- Training from licensed vocational teachers
- Program-specific experiences and knowledge
- Safety, support, and remedial interventions and training
- Career guidance, placement support, and career explorations for incoming 9th graders
- Academic and vocational assessments
- A high school diploma and proficiency certificate
- Co-ops, internships, job shadows, and/or apprenticeships

In addition to the academic, social, and personal benefits of vocational opportunities, many leaders assert that even non-vocational students can benefit from these programs. Specifically, as vocational programs often cater to the needs of active and kinesthetic learners, students enrolled in a vocational class can engage with more movement, hands-on activities, and unique processes for enhancing their education. When these same students are in a traditional, passive classroom setting, they often struggle to remain quiet and focused, potentially resulting in an overall distraction for all students and the instructor. As a result, students who are provided with the ability to choose their classroom and instructional method with greater freedom may be more able to improve their overall learning experience and behavioral development.

from The Agrarian Standard
Wendell Berry

In my various travels, I have seen a number of small homesteads like that of Virgil's[1] old farmer, situated on "land that no one wanted" and yet abundantly productive of food, pleasure, and other goods. And especially in my younger days, I was used to hearing farmers of a certain kind say "They may run me out, but they won't starve me out" or "I may get shot, but I'm not going to starve." Even now, if they cared, I think agricultural economists could find small farmers who have prospered, not by "getting big," but by practicing the ancient rules of thrift and subsistence, by accepting the limits of their small farms, and by knowing well the value of having a little land.

How do we come at the value of a little land? We do so, following this strand of agrarian[2] thought, by reference to the value of no land. Agrarians value land because somewhere back in the history of their consciousness is the memory of being landless. This memory is implicit, in Virgil's poem, in the old farmer's happy acceptance of "an acre or two of land that no one wanted." If you have no land you have nothing: no food, no shelter, no warmth, no freedom, no life. If we remember this, we know that all economies begin to lie as soon as they assign a fixed value to land. People who have been landless know that the land is invaluable; it is worth everything. Pre-agricultural humans, of course, knew this too. And so, evidently, do the animals. It is a fearful thing to be without a "territory." Whatever the market may say, the worth of the land is what it always was: It is worth what food, clothing, shelter, and freedom are worth; it is worth what life is worth. This perception moved the settlers from the Old World into the New. Most of our American ancestors came here because they knew what it was to be landless; to be landless was to be threatened by want and also by enslavement. Coming here, they bore the ancestral memory of serfdom. Under feudalism, the few who owned the land owned also, by an inescapable political logic, the people who worked the land.

Thomas Jefferson, who knew all these things, obviously was thinking of them when he wrote in 1785 that "it is not too soon to provide by every possible means that as few as possible shall be without a little portion of land. The small landholders are the most precious part of a state. . . ." He was saying, two years before the adoption of our constitution, that a democratic state and democratic liberties depend upon democratic ownership of the land. He was already anticipating and fearing the division of our people into settlers, the people who wanted "a little portion of land" as a home, and, virtually opposite to those, the consolidators and exploiters of the land and the land's wealth, who would not be restrained by what Jefferson called "the natural affection of the human mind." He wrote as he did in 1785 because he feared exactly

---

[1] Roman poet who lived 70–19 B.C. [Ed.].
[2] Relating to, or characteristic of farmers, their way of life, and their values [Ed.].

the political theory that we now have: the idea that government exists to guarantee the right of the most wealthy to own or control the land without limit.

In any consideration of agrarianism, this issue of limitation is critical. Agrarian farmers see, accept, and live within their limits. They understand and agree to the proposition that there is "this much and no more." Everything that happens on an agrarian farm is determined or conditioned by the understanding that there is only so much land, so much water in the cistern, so much hay in the barn, so much corn in the crib, so much firewood in the shed, so much food in the cellar or freezer, so much strength in the back and arms — and no more. This is the understanding that induces thrift, family coherence, neighborliness, local economies. Within accepted limits, these become necessities. The agrarian sense of abundance comes from the experienced possibility of frugality and renewal within limits.

This is exactly opposite to the industrial idea that abundance comes from the violation of limits by personal mobility, extractive machinery, long-distance transport, and scientific or technological breakthroughs. If we use up the good possibilities in this place, we will import goods from some other place, or we will go to some other place. If nature releases her wealth too slowly, we will take it by force. If we make the world too toxic for honeybees, some compound brain, Monsanto[3] perhaps, will invent tiny robots that will fly about pollinating flowers and making honey.

[3]American agrochemical and agricultural biotechnology corporation [Ed.].

1. In paragraphs 1 and 2, the writer both refers to and quotes lines about an "old farmer" from writing by the Roman poet Virgil to
   (A) qualify his own remarks about industrial farming.
   (B) suggest that both poetry and agrarian farming are artforms.
   (C) imply that agrarian values are an ancient part of human societies.
   (D) provide a common foundation for his argument about agrarian farming and landowning as a democratizing force.
   (E) demonstrate the differences between the contexts of ancient Rome and the contemporary United States.

2. In the first sentence of the second paragraph, the author's question serves to introduce the coming line of reasoning by establishing
   (A) that land is only valuable because of the fear of not having it.
   (B) that land is only worth what someone is willing to pay for it.
   (C) the relationship between poverty and land.
   (D) the lack of value that a small piece of land has.
   (E) that something small is indeed valuable.

3. Toward the beginning of the third paragraph, the writer quotes Thomas Jefferson to accomplish which of the following?
   (A) To dismiss the fears of growing industrial farming
   (B) To suggest that those who sought to exploit the land were just as important to the state as small landholders
   (C) To imply that there is a link between the successes of large landholders like Jefferson and small landholders
   (D) To illustrate the early belief that ownership of land was impossible
   (E) To demonstrate the importance of small landholders to the success of a state and country

4. In paragraph 3, the writer's commentary on "democratic state and democratic liberties"
   (A) appeals to his audience's sense of democratic values.
   (B) undermines Jefferson's comments about the values of "small landholders."
   (C) describes the values held by "small landholders."
   (D) contradicts fears about people owning too much land harming American democracy.
   (E) plays to the audience's fears that their values are under attack.

5. In the second sentence of paragraph 4, the writer introduces the idea that "agrarian farmers see, accept, and live within their limits" in order to
   (A) extend the line of reasoning that includes unlimited ownership of land in the previous paragraph.
   (B) contradict the previous points made about the state of small landholders.
   (C) urge control over the resources used by small landowners who do not consider the state of their neighbors.
   (D) express doubt about the line of reasoning some people support regarding industrial abundances and technological breakthroughs.
   (E) suggest that agrarianism cannot be sustained in the world of factory farms and modern political logic.

6. The fifth sentence in paragraph 4 ("This is . . . local economies.") serves to
   (A) illustrate what is lost when people own too much land.
   (B) demonstrate the rapid failure of family farms.
   (C) provide evidence for previous claims about industrial farming.
   (D) explain how agrarianism is the source of certain values.
   (E) suggest that family farms and agrarianism are one and the same.

7. In the context of the passage as a whole, the writer uses the commentary in the final paragraph (5) to
   (A) motivate the reader to activism against agrarianism.
   (B) gesture to the unthinkable consequences of completely abandoning agrarian farming.
   (C) draw attention to historical evidence that has previously been ignored.
   (D) point out a flaw in the line of reasoning of those who disagree with him.
   (E) question the moral integrity of those who do not own their own land.

8. The intended audience of this passage is most likely
   (A) those who wish to rely on industrial farming.
   (B) all the people of the United States.
   (C) agrarian farmers.
   (D) lawmakers.
   (E) those people concerned about where their food comes from.

9. The writer is provoked by which of the following issues?
   (A) Loss of small land ownership and agrarian farming
   (B) Attacks on democratic values made by industrial farming
   (C) Exploitation of resources beyond what nature can provide
   (D) Misunderstanding of American founders' intentions
   (E) Ignorance of ancient poetry and how it relates to our contemporary contexts

10. Which of the following statements best represents the thesis of the passage?

   (A) "Even now, if they cared, I think agricultural economists could find small farmers who have prospered, not by 'getting big,' but by practicing the ancient rules of thrift and subsistence, by accepting the limits of their small farms, and by knowing well the value of having a little land" (paragraph 1).

   (B) "How do we come at the value of a little land? We do so, following this strand of agrarian thought, by reference to the value of no land" (paragraph 2).

   (C) "He was saying, two years before the adoption of our constitution, that a democratic state and democratic liberties depend upon democratic ownership of the land" (paragraph 3).

   (D) "Agrarian farmers see, accept, and live within their limits. They understand and agree to the proposition that there is 'this much and no more'" (paragraph 4).

   (E) "If we make the world too toxic for honeybees, some compound brain, Monsanto perhaps, will invent tiny robots that will fly about pollinating flowers and making honey" (paragraph 5).

PREPARING FOR THE AP® EXAM
Multiple-Choice Questions: Writing

The passage below is a draft.

(1) In 1896, young Swedish scientist and eventual Nobel Prize winner Svante Arrhenius published an article predicting what most scientists today accept: the globe would warm as a result of increased gases that hold heat, like a greenhouse. (2) Few of his fellow scientists disagreed with his theory about global warming, but the causes remained a source of bitter disagreement, with many feeling that the actions of humans were too insignificant to cause such global effects.

(3) Over 100 years later, few of today's serious scientists dispute the reality of global warming, although the causes are still hotly debated. (4) Whether or not humans have caused climate change, most climate scientists agree that humans can help to slow or even halt it. (5) Simple steps that everyday people can do every day can really make a difference. (6) The steps in the process start easy and gradually ask more of people but, if everyone participates, they can be powerful.

(7) Drive less. (8) Even electric cars often get their electricity from those same power plants still running on greenhouse gas-emitting fuels. (9) Walking, biking, riding with others in a carpool: these are all examples of things that everyone could do more. (10) Once people are driving less, they will stop driving altogether and then may be ready for a more difficult but more important change.

(11) Flip switches. (12) The easiest step involves pure common sense: when you leave a room, turn off the light. (13) Many homes get their power from power plants that emit greenhouse gases of some sort, so anytime a light is left on in an empty room, the energy that is wasted is also causing more greenhouse gas emissions. (14) If people begin to think about these kinds of small details, then maybe they can start to make bigger changes.

(15) Eat locally — and less meat. (16) Food that comes from far away requires greenhouse gas-emitting shipping to reach stores. (17) The United Nations says more than half of all food-related greenhouse gases come from farming large animals, so limiting meat in daily diets could also have a significant, positive effect.

(18) None of these suggestions are to say that people should not use lights, drive to work, or eat any meat at all. (19) These only offer suggestions for small ways that people can slow climate change.

1. The writer is considering changing the method of development used in sentences 1 and 2 (reproduced below) to provide a clearer line of reasoning for the audience.

   (1) In 1896, young Swedish scientist and eventual Nobel Prize winner Svante Arrhenius published an article predicting what most scientists today accept: the globe would warm as a result of increased gases that hold heat, like a greenhouse. (2) Few of his fellow scientists disagreed with his theory about global warming, but the causes remained a source of bitter disagreement, with many feeling that the actions of humans were too insignificant to cause such global effects.

   Should the writer use a different method of development in sentences 1 and 2?

   (A) Yes, the writer should detail the scientific process that Arrhenius followed so the audience understands the source of Arrhenius's claims.
   (B) Yes, the writer should provide the process through which those who disagreed with Arrhenius came to disagree with him.
   (C) No, the writer needs to narrate the story of Svante Arrhenius to develop the reader's understanding of who he was as a person.
   (D) No, the writer narrates the story of Svante Arrhenius to illustrate the long-running debates over the causes of global warming.
   (E) No, the writer helps the reader to see why some people would disagree with Svante Arrhenius by narrating the story about some of his work.

2. The writer is considering deleting the underlined portion of sentence 1 (reproduced below).

   In 1896, young Swedish scientist <u>and eventual Nobel Prize winner</u> Svante Arrhenius published an article predicting what most scientists today accept: the globe would warm as a result of increased gases that hold heat, like a greenhouse.

   Should the writer keep or delete the underlined text?

   (A) Keep it. It provides information that helps the reader to question Arrhenius's conclusions.
   (B) Keep it. It helps to create more trust in the work of a scientist the reader has likely never heard of.
   (C) Keep it. It creates a sense of awe for the reader, pushing him or her to want to learn more about Arrhenius.
   (D) Delete it. It distracts from the intention of the sentence to establish Arrhenius as a trustworthy figure.
   (E) Delete it. It brings the focus of the passage to the Nobel Prize and away from global warming.

3. The writer is considering moving sentence 5 (reproduced below) in order to better position the writer's claim in the overall development of the argument.

   Simple steps that everyday people can do every day can really make a difference.

   Where would be the best place for sentence 5?

   (A) (where it is now)
   (B) Before sentence 3
   (C) After sentence 6
   (D) Before sentence 18
   (E) After sentence 19

4. The writer is considering moving the third paragraph (sentences 7–9) so that the sequence of paragraphs best reveals the line of reasoning regarding following the steps in the process the writer is suggesting. Where would the paragraph best be placed?

(A) (where it is now)
(B) Before the first paragraph (sentences 1–2)
(C) Before the second paragraph (sentences 3–6)
(D) After the fourth paragraph (sentences 10–12)
(E) After the fifth paragraph (sentences 13–15)

5. The writer is considering revising sentence 9 (reproduced below), adjusting the punctuation as needed, to avoid a flaw in the line of reasoning.

"Once people are driving less, they will stop driving all together and then may be ready for a more difficult but more important change."

Which of the following revisions would best avoid a flaw in the line of reasoning?

(A) (as it is now)
(B) Once people stop driving altogether, they may be ready for a more difficult but more important change.
(C) Once people drive less, they will not drive at all. Once that has happened, then they may be ready for a more difficult but more important change.
(D) Once they are doing these things, they will stop driving altogether and then may be ready for a more difficult but more important change.
(E) Once people are driving less, they may then be ready for a more difficult but more important change.

6. The writer wants to create coherence. Which of the following can be added to the beginning of sentence 17 (reproduced below), adjusting the capitalization as needed to provide a logical connection between sentence 16 and introduce the supporting information provided in 17.

"The United Nations says more than half of all food-related greenhouse gases come from farming animals."

Which of the following clauses should the writer add?

(A) In addition to the greenhouse gases released during the shipping of food,
(B) People should be concerned with shipping food,
(C) Concerns about food-related emissions continue to grow,
(D) Locally grown food does not matter if it includes meat,
(E) The real concern people should have is about meat,

AP Photo/Rafiq Maqbool

UNIT

4 Analyzing Purpose

n the last unit, you explored the importance of the context when a writer communicates a message. Now, you'll spend some time considering the writer's purpose when communicating his or her message. Purpose is closely related to the writer's exigence — the inspiration, motivation, or prompt for the writer's argument.

The writer's purpose is the goal that he or she hopes to accomplish with the audience and the message. If there are multiple audiences, a writer may have multiple purposes. In this unit, you'll consider how a writer's method of organization helps a writer achieve the purpose. And when you write, you'll want to consider your goals and what you want to accomplish as you develop arguments of your own.

But occasionally, a writer's purpose is less obvious. Consider the image. Why might the individual be serving the soldier tea? Who is this person's audience? Who is the photographer's audience? Could there be multiple purposes and audiences for the person in the image, as well as for the photographer?

UNIT GOALS

	Unit Focus	Reading, Analyzing, and Interpreting	Writing
Big Idea: Rhetorical Situation	**Multiple Purposes**	Identify multiple purposes and the choices a writer makes to achieve each purpose.	Make strategic rhetorical choices to accomplish multiple purposes.
Big Idea: Claims and Evidence	**Function of Evidence**	Explain how a writer uses evidence strategically to achieve a purpose.	Select evidence strategically to achieve a purpose.
Big Idea: Reasoning and Organization	**Exposition: Definition Argument**	Explain how a writer develops an idea through definition.	Write an argument developed through definition.
Big Idea: Language and Style	**Eliminating Ambiguity**	Evaluate the effectiveness of clarity and precision in an argument.	Eliminate ambiguity through effective use of pronoun-antecedent agreement, modifiers, and diction.
Ideas in American Culture	• **Division and Unity** • **Social Discontent and Equality**	Analyze how the ideas of division, unity, social discontent, and equality are reflected in classic and contemporary American texts.	
Preparing for the AP® Exam	• **Free Response: Rhetorical Analysis** • **Multiple Choice**	Analyze rhetorical choices in classic and contemporary nonfiction texts.	Develop commentary that explains relationship between claim and evidence.

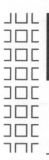

Multiple Purposes

 Enduring Understanding (RHS-1)

Individuals write within a particular situation and make strategic writing choices based on that situation.

KEY POINT

The purpose of a text is what the writer hopes to achieve as a result of writing it. Writers may use the introduction and/or conclusion of a text to convey purpose.

In earlier chapters, we established that purpose refers to what a writer hopes to achieve or accomplish within a text. Generally speaking, writers hope to narrate, persuade, or explain. But they often have more specific purposes, such as to explain a process, define a concept, or link causes and effects.

And depending upon the rhetorical situation, especially the context and audience, a writer may hope to accomplish multiple purposes in one text. This means that some texts are doing double duty.

For example, public service announcements inform their audience *and* persuade them to think and act in specific ways. Commercials often entertain their audience *and* persuade them to buy a service or product. Documentaries narrate authentic stories *and* inform the audience about relevant issues.

Writers Often Have Multiple Purposes

Writers often draw on exposition, narration, and persuasion to accomplish their **purposes**. Therefore, these methods of development often intersect, as you can see in the image that follows. To understand how and why a writer communicates with an intended audience, we must understand the writer's purpose.

Recall that the purpose depends on the writer's audience. Moreover, writers can also address multiple audiences simultaneously.

The relationship between the writer and the audience often determines the purpose or purposes. Writers may have multiple roles, which will affect how their audience perceives them. For example, a writer can be a sibling, *and* an artist, *and* an activist, *and* an athlete. So the writer must choose among different, perhaps overlapping, roles; this choice will inform how he or she will build a relationship with the audience.

To achieve their purpose, writers make strategic choices to connect with an intended audience's values and emotions. The broader context of the rhetorical situation also influences how the writer chooses to relate to the audience's values.

- A *voting parent* emails her state representatives to advocate for more public education funding. She focuses her message on her children's needs and argues that the representatives' action (or inaction) will affect how she votes in the upcoming reelection.

- A *disabled student* gives a TED Talk to fellow students to raise awareness about his disability. He draws upon stories from personal experience and asks the audience to consider how they can be more conscious of their disabled peers.

- An organization of *environmental scientists* writes to condemn a company's ineffective waste management; their statement incorporates their own published research, and asserts that they will take legal action if necessary.

In all of these examples, the writers incorporate each of their purposes and tailor their arguments based on their relationship to the audience. These purposes are directly tied to an idea, which guides the entire argument from the introduction to the conclusion.

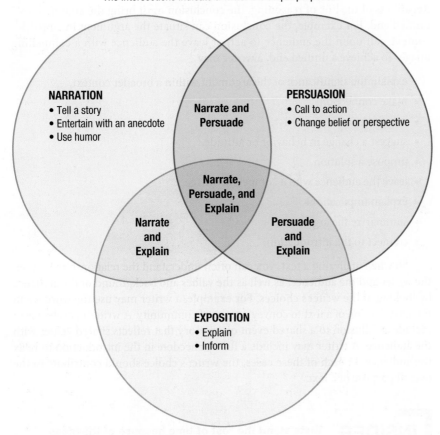

A WRITER'S PURPOSES

The intersections indicate a writer's multiple purposes.

NARRATION
- Tell a story
- Entertain with an anecdote
- Use humor

Narrate and Persuade

PERSUASION
- Call to action
- Change belief or perspective

Narrate, Persuade, and Explain

Narrate and Explain

Persuade and Explain

EXPOSITION
- Explain
- Inform

Introductions and Conclusions

As you learned in Unit 3, writers use the **introduction** of an argument to introduce their purpose and preview the rest of their argument. They may direct the audience's attention to their idea with an anecdote, relevant statistics, rhetorical questions, or other techniques. When choosing the most effective one, they must anticipate the needs and values of their intended audience. Therefore, a writer may choose from many techniques to make an introduction engaging:

- relevant quotations
- intriguing statements
- anecdotes
- questions
- statistics, data, contextualized information
- scenarios

Writers may build their line of reasoning throughout the text to reveal their position on their idea in the **conclusion**. When all the information in the argument revolves around a single idea, the text is unified. This includes the ending. Regardless of the line of reasoning, the conclusion must bring the argument to a unified end. For example, the conclusion can situate the argument in a broader context, call upon the audience to act, or leave the audience with a compelling image. To achieve a unified end, a writer may

- explain the significance of the argument within a broader context,
- make connections,
- call on the audience to act,
- suggest a change in behavior or attitude,
- propose a solution,
- leave the audience with a compelling image,
- explain implications,
- summarize the argument, or
- connect to the introduction.

So when analyzing a text, you can often understand the relationship between the writer and the audience, as well as the values and background of the audience by looking at the writer's choices. For example, a writer may use the word *we* in the introduction of a text to convey a sense of community. A writer may choose to include an allusion to a shared event or memory that reflects shared values with the audience. A writer may include a funny anecdote in the introduction to relax the audience. In each of these cases, the writer's choice should contribute to the overall purpose of a text.

INSIDER AP® TIP Texts stand the test of time because of the ideas that they convey. These ideas resonate across time and remain important to different communities and cultures. Most of the texts that you analyze weren't necessarily written *for you* as an audience. You'll want to consider the situation in which they were created.

 **SKILLS PRACTICE** | RHETORICAL SITUATION
Connecting Purpose and Audience

Identify an issue or subject that is important to you, such as a hobby, interest, or social issue. What do you want to say about the subject or issue? That will be your message. Next, identify an audience that you could address about that subject. Then, identify one or more purposes that you have for your message. What rhetorical choices could best convey your idea and achieve your purpose given that specific audience? Why choose these strategies?

Subject:	
Message/Idea:	
Audience:	
Purpose A	**Purpose B**
Rhetorical Choices to Achieve Purpose with That Audience	**Rhetorical Choices to Achieve Purpose with That Audience**

Why We Should Teach the Truth about American History
Patrick Wang

Patrick Wang

THE TEXT IN CONTEXT

The *New York Times* conducts an annual student editorial contest. In the following editorial, Patrick Wang, who was sixteen at the time of its submission, offers his perspective following a Colorado school board's decision to eliminate AP® U.S. History from its course offerings. This decision followed the release of the College Board's updated AP® U.S. History curriculum, which some groups and organizations viewed as unbalanced. In response to the public criticism, the College Board modified the curriculum the following year.

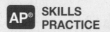 SKILLS PRACTICE | RHETORICAL SITUATION
Describing Purposes

In the following editorial, Wang considers the AP® U.S. History curriculum. As you read, think about his multiple purposes, as well as the different audiences that he is trying to reach. Consider one of the specific audiences. Then, identify at least two purposes that Wang hoped to achieve with that audience. How does he want to change this audience's views or behaviors? What rhetorical choices does Wang draw upon to achieve his overall purpose with different audiences? Use the graphic organizer that follows to record your observations.

Analyzing Multiple Purposes of an Argument	
Subject:	
Message/Idea:	
Audience:	
Purpose A	Purpose B
Rhetorical Choices to Achieve Purpose with Audience	Rhetorical Choices to Achieve Purpose with Audience

Why We Should Teach the Truth about American History

The bell rings, and I barely make it into my AP® U.S. History class. I look up at the board: "Today's Topic: Slavery." I do not think much about it because slavery has been a part of the Georgia curriculum since elementary school. What more could I possibly need to learn about? Yet, as I read through sickening excerpts of *Uncle Tom's Cabin* and watch clips of *Twelve Years a Slave*, I can feel the horror building up inside me. I am confronted by my own ignorance, the cruel reality of history clashing with my own sugar-coated understanding. I realize that I have been fed a filtered version of history all my life. In the end, however, I am thankful for the opportunity to learn the truth in my AP® U.S. history class, because for millions of other students, the truth is a privilege denied in the name of "patriotism."

In 2015, College Board's AP® U.S. History course came under fire for "painting American history in too negative a light." Conservative critics charged that the framework of the course was "biased and unpatriotic," with GOP presidential candidate Ben Carson even calling the course "so anti-American that students who completed it would be ready to sign up for ISIS." Many states such as Texas and Georgia even threatened to pull the course all together. Caving under pressure, the College Board changed the AP® U.S. History framework to include a new emphasis on "American exceptionalism."

This controversy brings to light the U.S.'s inability to own up to its past. Whether we like it or not, the U.S. is a country built upon not just democracy but exploitation and injustice. Events like the My Lai massacre and the slave trade are scary and real. We can not casually sweep the ugly pieces of history under the rug and hope that our rosy facade continues to fool the next generation into being "patriotic." Patriotism is not the pride you feel when you believe that your country has done no wrong. Patriotism is the pride you feel when you know that your country is on the present journey to righting its past wrongs and preventing future wrongs. By indoctrinating students with the idea of "American exceptionalism" rather than teaching them the truth about American history, the only people we end up fooling are ourselves. As the Yale professor of American Studies Jon Butler puts it, "America emerged out of many contentious issues. If we understand those issues, [only then can we] figure out how to move forward in the present." Thus, knowing the truth about American history should not be a privilege. It is a right.

Sources

Ganim, Sara. "Making History: Battles Brew over Alleged Bias in Advanced Placement Standards." CNN, 24 Feb. 2015.

Quinlan, Casey. "College Board Caves to Conservative Pressure, Changes AP® U.S. History Curriculum." Think Progress, 30 July 2015.

Schlanger, Zoe. "Revised AP® U.S. History Standards Will Emphasize American Exceptionalism." Newsweek, 29 July 2015.

Simon, Cecilia Capuzzi. "Taking the Politics Out of American History (and Out of A.P.®)." The New York Times, 8 Apr. 2016.

RHETORICAL SITUATION

1. How do Wang's choices in the **introduction** create interest in the subject for the audience? How do these choices reflect his purpose?

2. In writing this text, Wang achieves multiple purposes. Describe at least two different possible **purposes**.

3. How does Wang conclude the text? Give an example of how the **conclusion** connects and unifies his ideas.

4. How does this text connect to a broader **context**? For example, do his ideas and claims connect to other contemporary issues? Explain.

Function of Evidence

 Enduring Understanding (CLE-1)

Writers make claims about subjects, rely on evidence that supports their reasoning, and often acknowledge or respond to other, possibly opposing, arguments.

KEY POINT

Information becomes evidence when writers use it strategically to achieve their purpose(s) and support their line of reasoning expressed in their thesis.

As you learned in Unit 2, writers use many different types of evidence to support specific reasons within their arguments. And you learned that writers must have evidence that is sufficient, typical, accurate, and relevant. In this unit, we'll consider how and why writers keep their audience in mind when selecting evidence.

Imagine that your local school board is proposing a new policy to require school uniforms. You and your friends oppose this policy. In response, you decide to deliver a speech at the next school board meeting. Before you write your speech, you want to engage others in your school for support, so you develop a social media account. In other words, you will be seeking to persuade two different audiences: online and offline.

Whether you're using social media or giving a speech, your message remains consistent: the school should not require uniforms. But while the message stays the same, you will likely highlight different reasons and evidence to address each audience.

Writers Use Evidence Strategically

Writers use **evidence** to support their **reasons** and to achieve their purpose with a particular audience. So in addition to aligning with the types of reasons necessary for the argument's organization, the evidence must also appeal to the intended audience. For example, a writer may attempt to define a particular term or concept, but he or she will also be supporting a perspective in a way that appeals to that audience.

Certainly, writers choose evidence primarily to support their reasons. But you'll recall from Unit 2 that they also choose the best evidence to achieve their purpose with a *particular audience*. Based on a writer's specific audience, he or she may use evidence to

- illustrate, clarify, or exemplify,
- establish a mood,
- create an association,
- amplify or emphasize a point.

Function of Evidence

Writers cannot include every piece of possible evidence; rather, they select evidence they believe will influence their specific audience. So the evidence that writers exclude from their arguments can be almost as important as the evidence that they include. The following table illustrates the types of information that writers may choose to use as evidence, as well as other considerations that go into making that choice.

TYPES AND FUNCTION OF EVIDENCE		
Type of Information	**Types of Evidence**	**Considerations**
Information from Research or the Library	Facts Details Analogies Examples Quotations	Other sources may affirm, support, or add credibility to the argument. Often, library sources are peer-reviewed, lending additional credibility to the source. Depending on the purpose, library research may not be sufficient or as effective as personal experience.
Personal Experience	Anecdotes Observations	Relevant and interesting experiences may contribute to an ethical appeal. Emotional stories may create a sense of pathos in the reader. Personal stories may not be sufficient to support a line of reasoning or claim.
Information from Cases	Examples Analogies Illustrations	Real examples may provide effective illustrations of a writer's claim. Some "fringe" cases may be outliers and not truly representative of your claim.
Information from Others	Expert Opinion Testimony	Expert sources may lend credibility to your argument. Some may see personal testimony as less effective than facts and data.
Quantitative Data as Information	Facts Statistics Data	Hard numerical data lends truth to your claims. Some skeptics claim that "statistics lie" or that data can be interpreted in multiple ways.
Information from Surveys or Interviews	Experiments Anecdotes	The way a survey was designed or constructed determines the conclusions you can draw from it. Careful interpretation of statistical data is necessary to avoid making claims that aren't true.

INSIDER AP TIP   **Writers generally do not generate their own evidence.** Instead, they draw upon the research, data, and insights of others when developing their own arguments and reasoning. When a writer draws upon the insight and research of others, he or she strengthens and establishes credibility of his or her own argument.

AP® SKILLS PRACTICE	CLAIMS AND EVIDENCE **Selecting Evidence Strategically**

Choose a policy issue that the local school board or education authority might consider, such as school uniforms, year-round school, or the elimination of standardized testing. Next, identify one additional audience, such as students, parents, educators, or lawmakers, with whom you can address the issue. After you've identified your claim (idea and perspective), select *one* of the potential audiences and respond to the following prompts:

- List the reasons that you would use to justify your claim with that specific audience.
- Identify the evidence that you would use to support each reason and appeal to that specific audience.
- Explain why you believe that evidence would be most effective for that specific audience.

Audience:

Claim:

Reasons	Evidence	Function of Evidence

Meet Gen Z Activists

Alyssa Biederman, Melina Walling, and Sarah Siock

THE TEXT IN CONTEXT

In this 2020 article first published by the *Bucks County Courier Times*, a team of journalists reported on the emerging demographic called Generation Z. The label refers to those born between 1997 and 2015. The article looks at Generation Z and the events that have shaped their experiences, including 9/11, the Iraq War, the Great Recession, and the COVID-19 pandemic. As the writers show, Generation Z brings diverse perspectives and connects to the causes that they care about through social media.

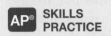

SKILLS PRACTICE | CLAIMS AND EVIDENCE
Explaining the Function of Evidence

In the following article, the writers examine the importance of activism to Generation Z. Identify the intended audience and the writers' claim. Next, identify the reasons used to justify the claim. Then, describe the evidence and explain how it functions to appeal to the intended audience.

Explaining the Function of Evidence		
Audience:		
Claim:		
Reasons	Evidence	Function of Evidence

Meet Gen Z Activists

Lily Mandel has already lived through a national security crisis, two recessions, nationwide civil unrest, a looming concern over climate change and school violence and a pandemic.

She's 17.

"We've had this idea of growing up thinking, what the heck is this? What the heck is going on?" Mandel said. "This whole time we've been growing up thinking this isn't right. This is crazy. We need a whole new system."

Mandel is just one of many young people whose life experience has pushed her to fight for change. She's the organizer at Bucks Students for Climate Action and Protection of the Environment, an activist group she created in her hometown of Warwick. Since its creation in 2019, BSCAPE's members have hosted forums, held climate strikes and raised money to build a greenhouse before 2021.

"It's really just this fresh set of eyes that Gen Z has," Mandel said. "OK, you guys might have been raised to think that this system benefits you, but you've been brainwashed. Let us give it to you straight." 5

Generation Z refers to people ages 13 to 23, beginning with people born in the late 1990s. Although most don't remember 9/11, this generation grew up in its aftermath, felt the effects of the 2008 recession, and are now the first kids to navigate social media, which, as the Black Lives Matter movement and ongoing protests against police brutality have shown, is an activism force of its own.

And now, all of that is against the backdrop of COVID-19, the worst pandemic the world has seen in 100 years.

So perhaps it is no surprise that Gen Z has a unique view of the world, said Jason Del

Gandio, a professor of communications and social influence at Temple University.

"It's like this fluctuation in social expectations of Gen Z," Del Gandio said. "When you live through the first Black president, I think it's going to affect how you perceive race relations. Gen Z's also lived through the legalization of same sex marriage and lived through the first and second iteration of Black Lives Matter. Along with the climate catastrophe, that's a lot to deal with."

About 70% of young people in Gen Z want an activist government, according to a study conducted by the Pew Research Center. Two thirds of this generation say Black people are treated less fairly than white people, as compared to about half of baby boomers and Generation X. Gen Z is also more progressive than previous generations in their views on gay marriage, climate change and gender identity.

Members of Gen Z organized marches nationwide after a gunman killed 17 people at Marjory Stoneman Douglas High School in Parkland, Florida, in February 2018. Seventeen-year-old Greta Thunberg travels the world bringing awareness to climate change, while 23-year-old Malala Yousafzai leads the feminist movement in the Middle East.

"Gen Z is simply being called to action because of the conditions they're living in," Del Gandio said.

Kiley Allgor first stepped into activism in 2018, when 24 school shootings killed or injured 114 people, according to data collected by Education Week. That year, Allgor organized Lenape Middle School's walkout to protest gun violence and helped to organize a protest with Bucks Students Demand Action, a group fighting against gun violence, which was attended by about 3,000 people.

Allgor, 17, works as the social media manager for Bucks Students Demand Action. She's a member of BSCAPE and Doylestown Youth 4 Unity, a new group formed in response to the Black Lives Matter protests in April.

As a social media manager, Allgor understands the impact technology has on her generation.

"Young people have the most access to education through technology," she said. "Our minds are still malleable so we process information and form our own thoughts rather than keeping the same mindset."

From the 1960s to Now

Though the activism of Gen Z is unique in many ways, it does bear some resemblance to the social movements of the '60s and '70s, said Del Gandio, who wrote *Rhetoric for Radicals: A Handbook for 21st Century Activists*.

"When we think about the 1960s, it's often marked by radical activism, radical social change, and often led by the youth. I think that's sort of what's going on now," he said. "In both time periods, there are very polarized politics, and a polarized society is more active and more people want to get involved because of what they're experiencing. Gen Z will parallel this militancy in the demand for social change."

Chris Bursk said he sees the same passion for social change in today's generation as he did when he protested during the Vietnam War and the civil rights movement in the 1960s.

"The beginning of a movement has a belief in possibility and belief that voices will be heard," Bursk said. "That is what I am seeing happening now."

After demonstrating as a young person, Bursk became a professor at Bucks County Community College, where he started the Human Rights Club, in which student members planned on-campus protests and other social justice initiatives from 1975 until 2005.

Still, Del Gandio and Bursk agree that the largest difference is who is orchestrating the change.

"The joy of these protests today is they are organized by students. In most cases high school students," Bursk said. "That has been so inspirational and so liberating to see."

In the 1960s, Del Gandio said, movements often lacked diversity. Most activism was led by white men—another difference taking shape in 21st century activism.

"Nowadays, I see a lot of young activists that are really outspoken about making sure multiple voices are represented," Del Gandio said. "If you come from a place of privilege and take a step back, and those who did not come from privilege stick their heads forward, it leads to concepts like intersectionality and allyship. Those weren't present in the 1960s."

In 2020, young activists are focused on representing all groups of people who are impacted by a certain issue and support people with different racial, ethnic, sexual or gender backgrounds than themselves, Del Gandio said.

This also reflects the growing diversity of America: Nearly 70% of the country's largest cities are more diverse than they were in 2010, according to U.S. News and World Report. In addition, Gen Z, as a group, is more diverse than previous generations. About half of Gen Zers are white, while more than 60 percent of Millennials are white, according to the Pew Research Center.

Betsy Watson is a 20-year-old Black woman who's part of the LGBTQ community. When she was attending Central Bucks West High School, she witnessed several things that shaped her activism.

During her senior year, a member of the football team was rumored to be gay and the team threatened to jump him. Around the same time, students at Central Bucks East hanged a dead deer on the bleachers with a noose. On a day-to-day basis while in high school, white students would regularly use the N-word around her.

"I felt so disheartened. There was this hate for no necessary reason," Watson said. "It felt like people hated me just for existing in the world, and being Black was too much space taken up in the school. I lost a lot of hope at that time, because I didn't see a world where I would be ever considered valuable or intelligent or beautiful. It was hard."

Watson founded the P.E.A.C.E. (People for Equality, Acceptance, Cooperation & Empathy) club at CB West, which brings students together to improve the school and world by focusing on cultural awareness and social justice. Now, as a 20-year-old communications student at Bucks County Community College, she's continuing her activism on social media by posting educational content on Instagram, Snapchat and TikTok, where she has more than 17,000 followers.

"I think the good thing about Gen Z is that they're not being silenced," Watson said. "There's power in numbers and Gen Z is coming together for the greater good. I do think they're going to be the generation of change. They're seeing things from different perspectives and they have social media on their side, which shows you different outlooks on the world."

Social Media Activism

Gen Z grew up with social media—Facebook was founded in 2004, YouTube in 2005 and Twitter in 2006—which gives them a widespread digital platform no generation has had before, Del Gandio said.

"The speed at which social media moves is mind boggling," he said. "You'll be sitting today on Twitter and not heard of an issue and then within 24 hours, there's thousands and thousands of retweets about this one issue. Technology allows us to keep real time and these tweets or TikTok videos or whatever the case may be, can go across the globe within a matter of minutes and allows us to see each other in each other's struggles."

For Watson, her exposure to so many differ- 35 ent causes through social media has led her to get involved with several different causes.

"My biggest passion is justice for Black trans women, but also I'm very passionate about income inequality, helping the poor and the homeless, and I also care a lot about animal justice," said Watson.

What's most important to her, Watson said, is "overall equality and human decency."

For Kashyap Nathan, a 16-year-old student activist at Great Valley High School in Malvern, social media is also a helpful tool for on-the-ground organizing.

"I feel strongly about social media. In terms of activism it's played a major role," he said. "If you look back at the Arab Spring, which was some time ago, that was all on social media. It has major implications. It's done a great job of furthering the activism efforts of a lot of people."

Nathan is a fellow at the Germination Proj- 40 ect, a progressive organization in Philadelphia aimed at giving young people the tools they need to be leaders in their communities. He's passionate about fighting for immigrant rights and ending systemic racism.

Mandel also said social media has played a huge role in her activism and how people in her generation interact.

"We can quickly share ideas which creates new conversations," she said. "If you're not having those conversations and you're not constantly having an influx of new information you're bound to keep with the traditions of the past."

She said social media has made it easy for people to learn about injustices like the murder of George Floyd and keeps her generation educated and engaged in ways that were impossible before the invention of the internet.

"Social media allows things that are happening to be really displayed in ways that it wasn't before," she said. "It's essentially like going to a library and reading every book in there."

What's Next?

Even with new tools like social media, this   45 generation of activists has faced its fair share of obstacles.

Causes led by young people can sometimes cause those in power to write them off, Nathan said.

"People are hesitant to take you seriously," he said. "If I go and make a point, if I bring up a data point or draw a connection in a meeting, people would be more inclined to take that point (if I were older)."

Nathan has met with state lawmakers and proposed amendments to city council. Allgor met with Congressman Brian Fitzpatrick to talk about supporting a bill that would prevent gun violence.

Despite bureaucratic roadblocks, these Gen Z activists are hopeful for the future.

"Something that I've learned is that we   50 need systematic change and not reform to fix these things. One bill has not ended systemic racism, or environmental racism, it's always just a sprinkle on the top of things," Mandel said. "That might help people alleviate some problems, especially in the public eye, but not necessarily solve the problems. In order to change a systemic issue you have to really go for the foundation of the system."

"(We) have this hope and energy and passion for activism," Watson said. "Small change is still major change. I hope people don't lose sight of that."

CLAIMS AND EVIDENCE

1. Identify the different types of **evidence** used to develop the argument. Give two examples. Describe the function of each type of evidence.

2. How is each type of **evidence** used for a particular audience?

3. As you consider all of the **evidence** in the article, explain how this evidence advances the overall argument.

4. Where in this argument do the writers refer to evidence from other **sources**? How do these types of sources contribute to the effectiveness of their argument?

Exposition: Definition Argument

 Enduring Understanding (REO-1)

Writers guide understanding of a text's line of reasoning and claims through that text's organization and integration of evidence.

KEY POINT

Definition arguments explain and are organized by characteristics, traits, features, or attributes.

As you've learned in previous units, a writer's purpose drives the choices he or she makes. As a writer thinks about achieving his or her goal or purpose with an intended audience, he or she must consider how to organize the information. A writer's purpose can determine the organizational method, including the type of reasons necessary for the mode of development and how they are sequenced within an argument.

As you think about definitions, you might remember looking up the meaning of words when you were in elementary school. Yes, you were learning the definitions of different terms. You may have discovered that some words have multiple meanings (*lead*), while others have definitions that changed over time (*decimate*). But perhaps most significantly, you learned that a word's definition might depend on the context: how and when it is used. In such cases, a word or concept might have both a general meaning and a more precise, context-specific meaning.

Defining a Term or Concept

The act of defining is essential to our lives — at home, in school, at work, and beyond. Parents will define house and family rules. Teachers may define their subjects or grading criteria. Attorneys might try to establish the **definition** of words such as *justice*, *authority*, or even *premeditation* in a court case. Activists may take aim at the definition of *democracy*, *freedom*, or *community*. Literary scholars and historians define concepts and movements such as *existentialism*, *Modernism*, or the *American Dream* in their interpretations. Even political candidates usually offer their own definitions of *progress*, *hope*, or fairness in their speeches. Just keep in mind that these — like all definitions — are arguments.

The Line of Reasoning When Defining

Writers define words, terms, or concepts by establishing their

- traits,
- attributes,
- features,
- characteristics, and/or
- qualities.

For example, consider the word *democracy*. While it has a common dictionary definition, individuals may emphasize different traits, characteristics, or attributes when defining it. These attributes, characteristics, qualities, or traits become the defining elements of the term or concept and together they make up the line of reasoning for the concept of democracy. When establishing an extended definition, a writer must provide clear and compelling attributes to justify that definition. But the writer may also have other purposes, such as explaining what something is not, addressing the consequences of accepting that definition, or proposing a new definition of a familiar term.

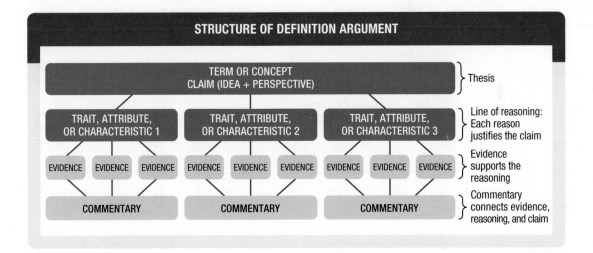

Developing a Definition

Writers often develop their definitions by providing examples or illustrations of a term's elements, characteristics, and attributes. They may also use a comparison, which is usually called an **analogy**. Analogies are comparisons that writers use to illustrate or clarify their point. They can also help writers define new or unfamiliar terms by using concepts that are more familiar to an audience.

Here are some analogies that help define people, objects, and concepts:

- A great movie director is like a great chef.
- We can think of the internet as an enormous city.
- As human bodies function better when healthy, so do societies.

Or, a writer may set up a contrast as an example to show what something is *not*. This technique is called **negation**.

Negation is especially helpful when defining a term or concept that is commonly misunderstood. For example, while many assume it is a synonym for *sympathy*, the word *empathy* denotes a different process: one that, unlike sympathy, suggests individuals can identify and "step into the shoes" of another person's emotions.

AP® | SKILLS PRACTICE | REASONING AND ORGANIZATION
Creating a Definition Argument

Think of a term or concept that could be presented through definition. You might consider a concept such as the following:

- A good education
- A literary or artistic movement, such as Romanticism
- A type of government, such as democracy or autocracy
- A principle such as justice, friendship, or greed

In the following table, note the traits, attributes, characteristics, or qualities of the term that would serve as reasons to justify your definition of it. Then, identify some examples, illustrations, analogies, or contrasts that you might use to support each reason.

Term or Concept to Be Defined:	
Trait, Attribute, Feature, Characteristic, or Quality	Example, Illustration, Analogy, or Contrast

from Letters of an American Farmer: What Is an American?

J. Hector St. John de Crèvecoeur

Sarin Images/GRANGER - Historical Picture Archive

THE TEXT IN CONTEXT

J. Hector St. John de Crèvecoeur (1735–1813) was born in France and served in the French Army in Canada during the French and Indian War (1754–1763). After the war, he remained in America for many years, becoming a naturalized citizen, a farmer, and a surveyor in New York State. He was also a perceptive writer. In 1782, he published *Letters from an American Farmer*, which included many sharp observations of Americans, American society, and even the American Dream.

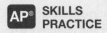

SKILLS PRACTICE | REASONING AN ORGANIZATION
Analyzing Definition Arguments

In this essay, Crèvecoeur asks and answers the question, "What is an American?" Use the following graphic organizer to note how Crèvecoeur defines an "American" by presenting characteristics and traits, as well as examples and illustrations.

Analyzing Definition Arguments

Trait, Attribute, Feature, Characteristic, or Quality	Example, Illustration, Analogy, or Contrast

from Letters of an American Farmer: What Is an American?

In this great American asylum, the poor of Europe have by some means met together, and in consequence of various causes; to what purpose should they ask one another what countrymen they are? Alas, two thirds of them had no country. Can a wretch who wanders about, who works and starves, whose life is a continual scene of sore affliction or pinching penury—can that man call England or any other kingdom his country? A country that had no bread for him, whose fields procured him no harvest, who met with nothing but the frowns of the rich, the severity of the laws, with jails and punishments; who owned not a single foot of the extensive surface of this planet? No! Urged by a variety of motives, here they came. Everything has tended to regenerate them: new laws, a new mode of living, a new social system; here they are become men: in Europe they were as so many useless plants, wanting vegetative mold, and refreshing showers; they withered, and were mowed down by want, hunger, and war; but now, by the power of transplantation, like all other plants they have taken root and flourished! Formerly they were not numbered in any civil lists of their country except in those of the poor; here they rank as citizens. By what invisible power has this surprising metamorphosis been performed? By that of the laws and that of their industry. . . .

What, then, is the American, this new man? He is either a European or the descendant of a European, hence that strange mixture of blood which you will find in no other country. I could point out to you a family whose grandfather was an Englishman, whose wife was Dutch, whose son married a French woman, and whose present four sons have now four wives of different nations. He is an American, who, leaving behind him all his ancient prejudices and manners, receives new ones from the new mode of life he has embraced, the new government he obeys, and the new rank he holds.

He becomes an American by being received in the broad lap of our great *Alma Mater*. Here individuals of all nations are melted into a new race of men, whose labors and posterity will one day cause great changes in the world. Americans are the Western pilgrims, who are carrying along with them that great mass of arts, sciences, vigor, and industry which began long since in the East; they will finish the great circle.

The Americans were once scattered all over Europe; here they are incorporated into one of the finest systems of population which has ever appeared, and which will hereafter become distinct by the power of the different climates they inhabit. The American ought therefore to love this country much better than that wherein either he or his forefathers were born. Here the rewards of his industry follow with equal steps the progress of his labor; his labor is founded on the basis of nature, self-interest; can it want a stronger allurement? Wives and children, who before in vain demanded of him a morsel of bread, now, fat and frolicsome, gladly help their father to clear those fields whence exuberant crops are to arise to feed and clothe them all, without any part being claimed either by a despotic prince, a rich abbot, or a mighty lord. Here religion demands but little of him: a small voluntary salary to the minister, and gratitude to God; can he refuse these? The American is a new man, who acts upon new principles; he must therefore entertain new ideas, and form new opinions. From involuntary idleness, servile dependence, penury, and useless labor, he has passed to toils of a very different nature, rewarded by ample subsistence—This is an American.

REASONING AND ORGANIZATION

1. Does Crèvecoeur's **reasoning** *proceed from* a stated claim, or does the reasoning *advance toward* a claim? Why is this approach important to his argument?

2. Crèvecoeur develops his idea with the method of definition. What **line of reasoning** does he use to organize his argument?

3. How does the argument develop? Specifically, how does Crèvecoeur support each **reason** within his line of reasoning?

4. Select a body paragraph that conveys one of Crèvecoeur's **reasons** in his argument. How does this paragraph contribute to the development and success of the writer's central claim?

LANGUAGE AND STYLE
Eliminating Ambiguity

AP **Enduring Understanding (STL-1)**
The rhetorical situation informs the strategic stylistic choices that writers make.

For a writer to achieve his or her goal with an audience, he or she must be clear and precise. A lack of specificity leads to a lack of clarity, or ambiguity, which means that an audience may not fully understand what a writer is communicating. Therefore, it is important to consider the writer's precise words, images, phrases, and sentences, and determine how those choices contribute to the writer's message.

As you've already learned, a writer develops an argument one sentence at a time. Similarly, writers create each sentence one word at a time. Each word is an opportunity for the writer to define, emphasize, or clarify an argument. As Natalie Goldberg says, "Be specific. Don't say 'fruit.' Tell what kind of fruit — 'It is a pomegranate.' Give things the dignity of their names."

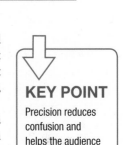

KEY POINT

Precision reduces confusion and helps the audience understand the writer's perspective.

Precision Eliminates Ambiguity

It's easy to write confusing, ambiguous sentences if you're not intentionally writing to be precise. Writers must recall their purpose when communicating (for example, to encourage and achieve a particular feeling, behavior, or point of view). A few careless word choices can disrupt an entire sentence; they can even detract from a writer's credibility and overall purpose.

The audience also determines the writer's **diction** (or **word choice**). When writers know the audience's background, level of education, profession, and familiarity with the subject, they can more effectively choose their words — and avoid unnecessary **ambiguity**.

Writers eliminate ambiguity with careful specificity. When writers are precise in their language, they allow the audience to focus on the argument instead of trying to decode confusing sentences.

Let's look at three common sources of confusion in sentences:

- pronoun references,
- misplaced modifiers, and
- inflated diction.

Pronoun References

Pronouns are used in place of nouns. They help avoid continuous repetition of a noun and establish clear relationships between sentences. A pronoun's **antecedent** is the original noun replaced by the pronoun. Often, a writer will establish an antecedent noun early in a paragraph. Then the sentences that follow will use pronouns that refer to that initial antecedent.

Each pronoun takes the place of one noun at a time. So when a pronoun's antecedent is unclear, the audience may become confused. Consider the following example:

> When Casey dropped her <u>laptop</u> on the glass <u>table</u>, <u>it</u> broke.

What is the antecedent of *it*? Did the laptop break or did the glass table?

Always make sure that your audience can follow the noun antecedents of your pronouns. Make sure that you can too: even the best writers can lose track of antecedents as they write. When you review and revise your texts, also remember that the pronouns *it* and *they* are especially prone to ambiguity.

Sometimes, writers will strategically use the personal pronouns *we, us, them, they*, and *you* to include or exclude themselves or others from a particular claim or perspective. For example, when writers use the pronoun *we*, they identify themselves with their audience:

> <u>The people</u> here today know that all of <u>us</u> must all become more knowledgeable, thoughtful, and engaged citizens.

In contrast, when writers use a pronoun like *them* or *they*, they may be deliberately excluding the antecedent of the pronoun from the audience.

> But many <u>other people</u> remain apathetic, so we must persuade <u>them</u> that citizenship is an action, not simply a condition.

So keep in mind the effect of pronouns as well. They can unite, divide, accuse, alienate, or provoke your audience. They may also support — or work against — your purpose.

***They/Them*: singular or plural?** Both *they* and *them* are now acceptable when they refer to singular, nonbinary individuals or (more generally) when they are used to avoid gender-specific singular pronouns. While this usage has already become common in informal conversations, as of 2019, many major style guides (including the Modern Language Association, Associated Press, *The Chicago Manual of Style*, and APA style guide) accept the singular *they* and *them* in formal writing as well.

Misplaced Modifiers

A **modifier** is any word, phrase, or clause that describes another word, phrase, or clause. In general, writers place modifiers as close to the modified word or phrase as possible. But when these modifiers are misplaced, they can make a sentence confusing. Consider the following example:

> <u>Driving down the road</u>, a bird hit the truck.

The phrase *driving down the road* could modify either the bird or the truck. Was the bird driving down the road when it hit the truck? The sentence is unclear. So make sure that your modifiers accurately describe the words and phrases that you intend them to describe.

Inflated Diction

Finally, writers can create confusion by using flowery, multisyllabic words or complex phrasing. This kind of writing is often clunky, awkward, and unnecessarily confusing. Focus on being a clear, accessible writer, not on sounding like a pseudo-intellectual. Be especially wary of online thesauruses and complicated words that are unfamiliar to you or that you would never use in a conversation.

At times, specialized words (or *jargon*) are necessary when addressing a specific group with its own insider language (for example, lawyers, financial experts, or football fans). But for a general audience, these terms will be hard to understand. Similarly, be careful when using *euphemisms* and *colloquialisms*. A euphemism is a gentle or indirect expression used in place of a word or phrase that might be harsh, embarrassing, or even too "ordinary." Indeed, writers sometimes deploy them to make their subjects sound more "serious" or "important." Colloquialisms include slang terms, regional expressions, and other informal language.

Inflated Diction	Example	Effect
Jargon	Many gamers prefer **LARPing** to playing **MMORPGs**, but both can be fun.	A general audience unfamiliar with these video- and role-playing game abbreviations will become lost and confused.
Euphemism	While there was some **collateral damage**, the **overseas contingency operation** achieved its mission.	These wartime euphemisms are vague; an audience may find them misleading, as well as hard to understand.
Colloquialism	After examining my ninety-year-old great-grandfather, the doctor **reckoned** he was **fit as a fiddle**.	In academic writing, colloquialisms can appear lazy or even jarring if the overall tone is more formal. Some audiences may be unfamiliar with certain slang terms.

INSIDER AP® TIP

Ambiguity can be intentional. While most ambiguous writing is unintentional, some writers intentionally create confusion or uncertainty on purpose. They may be trying to evade responsibility for a problem, cover over unpleasant realities, or avoid taking a strong stand on an issue or controversial topic.

Consider each of the following statements, which illustrate different types of ambiguities. Explain what is ambiguous and how that affects meaning.

Types of Ambiguity	Effect on Meaning
Pronoun References: At lunch, one of your friends says the following: *"They said that all assignments were going to be pass/fail in the future."*	
Misplaced Modifiers: The following announcement was heard on the school intercom: *"Hitting the winning run in the game last night, the coach awarded Johnny most valuable player."*	
Inflated Diction: The following appeared in a student-written article for the online school paper: *"The third-year athlete allowed the team to be victorious by causing his opponent to relinquish the ball in the penultimate quarter of the athletic contest."*	

"They" Is the Word of the Year, Merriam-Webster Says, Noting Its Singular Rise

Amy Harmon

Lars Klove/The New York Times/Redux

THE TEXT IN CONTEXT

Amy Harmon (b. 1968) is a national correspondent for the *New York Times* who covers the intersection of science and society. Harmon has won two Pulitzer Prizes for her work, as well as a Guggenheim Fellowship. She is also author of the book *Asperger Love: Searching for Romance When You're Not Wired to Connect* (2013). In the article, "'They' Is the Word of the Year, Merriam-Webster Says, Noting Its Singular Rise," which was published on December 12, 2019, Harmon explores the evolving connotations of the pronoun "they" and its contemporary usage.

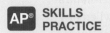

AP® SKILLS PRACTICE | LANGUAGE AND STYLE
Explaining the Effects of Ambiguity

Use the following graphic organizer to identify any examples of ambiguity in Harmon's article. What is the effect of this ambiguity? Keep in mind that writers may intentionally and strategically create ambiguity.

Explaining the Effects of Ambiguity	
Types of Ambiguity and Example	**Effect on Meaning**
Pronoun References:	
Misplaced Modifiers:	
Inflated Diction:	

"They" Is the Word of the Year, Merriam-Webster Says, Noting Its Singular Rise

Merriam-Webster announced the pronoun "they" as its word of the year on Tuesday, marking the rise of the use of the venerable plural pronoun to refer to a single person whose gender identity is nonbinary.

The word of the year, the dictionary publisher said, is based on data: Searches for the definition of "they" on the publisher's website and apps increased by 313 percent in 2019 over the previous year. Last year's word was "justice." In 2017, it was "feminism."

The public's interest in words is often driven by major news events, said Peter Sokolowski, an editor-at-large at Merriam-Webster. Other words that generated high year-over-year comparisons this year—"quid pro quo" and "impeachment"—are tied to political headlines.

But a surge of searches for the meaning of a utilitarian word like "they" is less common. It is likely to reflect both curiosity and confusion about the growing use of the pronoun for non-binary individuals.

"A pronoun like 'they' is one of the building blocks of the language," Mr. Sokolowski said. "But with the nonbinary usage, people are sensing that it means something new or different, and they are going to the dictionary. When you see lookups for it triple, you know that 'they' is a word that is in flux." 5

Many Americans, especially older ones, stumble over the use of "they" as a singular pronoun. "For those who haven't kept up, the complaint is this," Merriam-Webster wrote in an earlier blog post on the topic. "The use of *they* as a gender-neutral pronoun (as in, 'Ask each of the students what *they* want for lunch.') is ungrammatical because *they* is a plural pronoun."

But for nonbinary individuals who identify as a gender other than male or female, being referred to as "he" or "she" is inaccurate. Over a third of Americans in their teens and early 20s know someone who uses gender-neutral pronouns, according to a Pew Research survey conducted last fall. That is double the number of those in their 40s, and triple those in their 50s and 60s.

Efforts to destigmatize other gender identities have sparked the disclosure of pronouns on social media profiles and email signatures. Some state and city governments have recently added an "X" option for nonbinary genders on state identification documents, which used to be limited to the options "M" and "F." And amid efforts this year in at least six states to make the practice law, state legislators have been grappling with the singular "they," the *New York Times* reported.

Merriam-Webster added the singular "they" for a person with a nonbinary gender as a definition of the word in its dictionary, noting that the use of the singular "they" to refer to nonbinary individuals is increasingly common in published, edited text, as well as on social media.

To illustrate, the dictionary cited a passage   10
from a recent *Times* article:

> I knew certain things about . . . the
> person I was interviewing . . . *They*

had adopted their gender-neutral name a few years ago, when *they* began to consciously identify as nonbinary—that is, neither male nor female. *They* were in their late 20s, working as an event planner, applying to graduate school.

On Tuesday, Merriam-Webster cited several 2019 news events to explain the curiosity that appears to have driven searches for "they." During a House Judiciary Committee hearing, Representative Pramila Jayapal noted that "they" is her child's pronoun; the singer Sam Smith announced that their pronouns are "they" and "them"; and the American Psychological Association recommended that singular "they" be used in academic writing to refer to a person whose gender is unknown or who uses it.

"As a word lover, what's interesting in this story is to see that social factors play so directly into language change," Mr. Sokolowski said. "That is something that we sort of know intuitively but we don't often see it as clearly as we see it here."

LANGUAGE AND STYLE

1. How does the writer use precise **word choice** to connect to the beliefs, values, or needs of the audience?

2. This article originally appeared in the *New York Times* and was intended for an educated general audience. Where does Harmon use **inflated diction**? Identify an example. Why might she have made this word choice, considering her intended audience?

3. How does the writer use pronoun references and ambiguous **antecedents** to explain the relationship between the content of the text and her message?

4. Does the precise **word choice** convince you that "social factors play so directly into language change?" Explain.

PUTTING IT ALL TOGETHER
Modeled Text

2008 Election Victory Speech
Barack Obama

Chip Somodevilla/Getty Images

THE TEXT IN CONTEXT

Barack Obama (b. 1961) served as the forty-fourth president of the United States from 2009 to 2017. He was also the first African American to hold the highest position in American government. Obama delivered this speech on November 4, 2008, from his hometown of Chicago, Illinois, to acknowledge his victory over Republican candidate, Senator John McCain.

Unifying Idea	2008 Election Victory Speech	Rhetorical Choices	Effects of Choices
hope for change	If there is anyone out there who still doubts that America is a place where all things are possible; who still wonders if the dream of our founders is alive in our time; who still questions the power of our democracy, tonight is your answer.	poses question	directly addresses audience's desire for change
hope for change	It's the answer told by lines that stretched around schools and churches in numbers this nation has never seen; by people	pronoun reference	"It" refers to night of victory; pronoun is repeated effectively in the next three paragraphs
	who waited three hours and four hours, many for the very first time in their lives, because they believed that this time must be different; that their voice could be that difference.	details as evidence	

Unifying Idea	2008 Election Victory Speech	Rhetorical Choices	Effects of Choices
	It's the answer spoken by young and old, rich and poor, Democrat and Republican, black, white, Latino, Asian, Native American, gay, straight, disabled and not disabled—Americans who sent a message to the world that we have never been a collection of red states and blue states; we are, and always will be, the United States of America.	details as evidence	details of voters suggest a widespread desire for change
	It's the answer that led those who have been told for so long by so many to be cynical, and fearful, and doubtful of what we can achieve to put their hands on the arc of history and bend it once more toward the hope of a better day.		
hope for change	It's been a long time coming, but tonight, because of what we did on this day, in this election, at this defining moment, change has come to America.	narration	signals the beginning of a second purpose: to thank those also fighting for change
hope for change	I just received a very gracious call from Sen. McCain. He fought long and hard in this campaign, and he's fought even longer and harder for the country he loves. He has endured sacrifices for America that most of us cannot begin to imagine, and we are better off for the service rendered by this brave and selfless leader. I congratulate him and Gov. Palin for all they have achieved, and I look forward to working with them to renew this nation's promise in the months ahead.		
	I want to thank my partner in this journey, a man who campaigned from his heart and spoke for the men and women he grew up		

Unifying Idea	2008 Election Victory Speech	Rhetorical Choices	Effects of Choices
	with on the streets of Scranton and rode with on that train home to Delaware, the vice-president-elect of the United States, Joe Biden.		
	I would not be standing here tonight without the unyielding support of my best friend for the last 16 years, the rock of our family and the love of my life, our nation's next first lady, Michelle Obama. Sasha and Malia, I love you both so much, and you have earned the new puppy that's coming with us to the White House. And while she's no longer with us, I know my grandmother is watching, along with the family that made me who I am. I miss them tonight, and know that my debt to them is beyond measure.	reference to personal experiences as evidence	establishes his own personal investment in the desire for change
	To my campaign manager, David Plouffe; my chief strategist, David Axelrod; and the best campaign team ever assembled in the history of politics—you made this happen, and I am forever grateful for what you've sacrificed to get it done.		
hope for change	But above all, I will never forget who this victory truly belongs to—it belongs to you.	transition	shifts from personal thank-yous to the American people who also value change
hope for change	I was never the likeliest candidate for this office. We didn't start with much money or many endorsements. Our campaign was not hatched in the halls of Washington—it began in the backyards of Des Moines and the living rooms of Concord and the front porches of Charleston.		

Unifying Idea	2008 Election Victory Speech	Rhetorical Choices	Effects of Choices
hope for change	It was built by working men and women who dug into what little savings they had to give $5 and $10 and $20 to this cause. It grew strength from the young people who rejected the myth of their generation's apathy; who left their homes and their families for jobs that offered little pay and less sleep; from the not-so-young people who braved the bitter cold and scorching heat to knock on the doors of perfect strangers; from the millions of Americans who volunteered and organized, and proved that more than two centuries later, a government of the people, by the people and for the people has not perished from this earth. This is your victory.	anecdotes as evidence	uses anecdotes to support the idea that change takes sacrifice
		pronoun	includes the audience in the change and the work ahead
hope for change	I know you didn't do this just to win an election, and I know you didn't do it for me. You did it because you understand the enormity of the task that lies ahead. For even as we celebrate tonight, we know the challenges that tomorrow will bring are the greatest of our lifetime—two wars, a planet in peril, the worst financial crisis in a century. Even as we stand here tonight, we know there are brave Americans waking up in the deserts of Iraq and the mountains of Afghanistan to risk their lives for us. There are mothers and fathers who will lie awake after their children fall asleep and wonder how they'll make the mortgage, or pay their doctor's bills, or save enough for college. There is new energy to harness and new jobs to be created; new schools to build and threats to meet and alliances to repair.	examples as evidence	appeals to emotion to compel the audience to plan for future challenges

Unifying Idea	2008 Election Victory Speech	Rhetorical Choices	Effects of Choices
hope for change	The road ahead will be long. Our climb will be steep. We may not get there in one year, or even one term, but America—I have never been more hopeful than I am tonight that we will get there. I promise you: We as a people will get there.	definition: line of reasoning (trait/ characteristic) pronoun reference	defining the challenges ahead through analogy—climbing a hill uses "I" and "you" to establish that his role is different from the audience's role, but both will help achieve change
hope for change	What began 21 months ago in the depths of winter must not end on this autumn night. This victory alone is not the change we seek—it is only the chance for us to make that change. And that cannot happen if we go back to the way things were. It cannot happen without you.		
hope for change	So let us summon a new spirit of patriotism; of service and responsibility where each of us resolves to pitch in and work harder and look after not only ourselves, but each other. Let us remember that if this financial crisis taught us anything, it's that we cannot have a thriving Wall Street while Main Street suffers. In this country, we rise or fall as one nation—as one people.	definition: line of reasoning (trait/ characteristic)	defining a new spirit of patriotism by identifying its traits of service and responsibility
hope for change	Let us resist the temptation to fall back on the same partisanship and pettiness and immaturity that has poisoned our politics for so long. Let us remember that it was a man from this state who first carried the banner of the Republican Party to the White House—a party founded on the values of self-reliance, individual liberty and national unity. Those are values	pronoun reference	uses "us" to show inclusion and unification

Unifying Idea	2008 Election Victory Speech	Rhetorical Choices	Effects of Choices
	we all share, and while the Democratic Party has won a great victory tonight, we do so with a measure of humility and determination to heal the divides that have held back our progress.		
hope for change	As Lincoln said to a nation far more divided than ours, "We are not enemies, but friends. . . . Though passion may have strained, it must not break our bonds of affection." And, to those Americans whose support I have yet to earn, I may not have won your vote, but I hear your voices, I need your help, and I will be your president, too.	allusion as evidence	uses Lincoln to inspire unity in the work for change
hope for change	And to all those watching tonight from beyond our shores, from parliaments and palaces to those who are huddled around radios in the forgotten corners of our world—our stories are singular, but our destiny is shared, and a new dawn of American leadership is at hand. To those who would tear this world down: We will defeat you. To those who seek peace and security: We support you. And to all those who have wondered if America's beacon still burns as bright: Tonight, we proved once more that the true strength of our nation comes not from the might of our arms or the scale of our wealth, but from the enduring power of our ideals: democracy, liberty, opportunity and unyielding hope.	pronoun references	uses "we" to show inclusion and unification
hope for change	For that is the true genius of America— that America can change. Our union can be perfected. And what we have already achieved gives us hope for what we can and must achieve tomorrow.	line of reasoning	establishes a plan for change that contributes to the overall idea in the claim

Unifying Idea	2008 Election Victory Speech	Rhetorical Choices	Effects of Choices
hope for change	This election had many firsts and many stories that will be told for generations. But one that's on my mind tonight is about a woman who cast her ballot in Atlanta. She's a lot like the millions of others who stood in line to make their voice heard in this election, except for one thing: Ann Nixon Cooper is 106 years old.	example as evidence	uses voter Ann Nixon Cooper as an illustration of the need for change
	She was born just a generation past slavery; a time when there were no cars on the road or planes in the sky; when someone like her couldn't vote for two reasons—because she was a woman and because of the color of her skin.		
	And tonight, I think about all that she's seen throughout her century in America— the heartache and the hope; the struggle and the progress; the times we were told that we can't and the people who pressed on with that American creed: Yes, we can.	pronoun reference	begins with "them" and moves to "we" illustrates his message of unity
hope for change	At a time when women's voices were silenced and their hopes dismissed, she lived to see them stand up and speak out and reach for the ballot. Yes, we can.		
	When there was despair in the Dust Bowl and depression across the land, she saw a nation conquer fear itself with a New Deal, new jobs and a new sense of common purpose. Yes, we can.	expert testimony as evidence	evidence of prior struggles
	When the bombs fell on our harbor and tyranny threatened the world, she was there to witness a generation rise to greatness and a democracy was saved. Yes, we can.		

Unifying Idea	2008 Election Victory Speech	Rhetorical Choices	Effects of Choices
	She was there for the buses in Montgomery, the hoses in Birmingham, a bridge in Selma and a preacher from Atlanta who told a people that "We Shall Overcome." Yes, we can.	expert testimony as evidence	evidence and commentary connects to purpose: inspiring the audience
hope for change	A man touched down on the moon, a wall came down in Berlin, a world was connected by our own science and imagination. And this year, in this election, she touched her finger to a screen and cast her vote, because after 106 years in America, through the best of times and the darkest of hours, she knows how America can change. Yes, we can.	third purpose	the shift to the change that America faces
hope for change	America, we have come so far. We have seen so much. But there is so much more to do. So tonight, let us ask ourselves: If our children should live to see the next century; if my daughters should be so lucky to live as long as Ann Nixon Cooper, what change will they see? What progress will we have made?	pronoun references	shifts to "they" to reference future generations
hope for change	This is our chance to answer that call. This is our moment. This is our time—to put our people back to work and open doors of opportunity for our kids; to restore prosperity and promote the cause of peace; to reclaim the American Dream and reaffirm that fundamental truth that out of many, we are one; that while we breathe, we hope, and where we are met with cynicism, and doubt, and those who tell us that we can't, we will respond with that timeless creed that sums up the spirit of a people: Yes, we can.	final purpose and call to action	concludes with a persuasive call to action
	Thank you, God bless you, and may God bless the United States of America.		

IDEAS IN AMERICAN CULTURE
Division and Unity

Since 1782, when it was first included on the Great Seal of the United States, America's motto has been the Latin phrase "E Pluribus Unum": "Out of many, one." It is fitting. Throughout its history, the United States has brought together people from all countries, cultures, religions, and backgrounds. The motto suggests that diversity makes the country stronger and more unified. Of course, that idea remains an aspiration, much like the ideals expressed in the Declaration of Independence and the Constitution.

Principles like unity, equality, and liberty are foundations for a democratic society. But in practice, these ideas have often been at odds with each other. Even the Constitution came about because the Articles of Confederation, the original agreement between the U.S. states, provided little unity for the new country.

In the mid-nineteenth century, manufacturing and big business flourished in the North, especially in cities and towns. In contrast, the South continued to rely on the labor of enslaved people to support an agricultural economy. This division was becoming unsustainable. In 1858, Abraham Lincoln famously proclaimed, "A house divided against itself cannot stand."

Still, what kind of "house" was the United States exactly? Jeffersonian democracy valued the rights of individual states and guarded against overreach by the federal government. But the growing debate about slavery called into question the nature of individual liberty, economic rights, state power, and the authority of national political institutions. For example, did the federal government have the power to abolish slavery in new territories?

The abolitionist movement became stronger. As new states became a part of the Union, they raised the question, Is this a "free" state or "slave" state?

IDEA BANK
Abolition
Animosity
Compromise
Conflict
Courage
Defeat
Division
Expansion
Exploitation
Hostility
Independence
Progress
Prosperity
Realism
Rights
Slavery
Union
Unity
Victory

▲ Mexican painter Diego Rivera's 1940 mural *Pan American Unity* evokes images of American identity, history, and culture that transcend the United States to encompass both the North American and South American continents.

As you view this section of the mural, what imagery and opposition do you notice? Does the painting still have something to say to contemporary viewers? What is the message?

281

Who should decide? Although several compromises were made, the debate over slavery — and the relationship between the North and the South — became increasingly hostile. After the 1860 election of President Abraham Lincoln, who had pledged to stop the spread of slavery, eleven southern states eventually seceded from the Union and formed the Confederate States of America in 1861.

On April 12, 1861, the Civil War began when the Confederate Army attacked Fort Sumter, a U.S. military installation in South Carolina. Young men from both sides were eager to fight, hoping for a chance to become heroes. In some cases, families fought against families, reflecting the larger animosities that tore the country apart. Over the four-year period, southern victories gave way to northern ones until April 1865, when Confederate General Robert E. Lee surrendered to Commanding U.S. Army General Ulysses S. Grant. The Civil War was over.

During the original constitutional debates, the founders sought to balance liberty and equality in a way that would unify the states. We can see the importance of that balance in moments when the union failed during the 1861–1865 U.S. Civil War. We can also hear it in the rhetoric of Abraham Lincoln's "Second Inaugural Address" (p. 283), which seeks to heal the country after the war. But the divisions between the North and the South — as well as the problems that caused the conflict — would remain during postwar Reconstruction and then haunt the twentieth century. Many issues still divide us today, such as immigration, race, gender, and and economic class. In their excerpt from *Free to Choose* (p. 287), economists Milton and Rose Friedman explore the relationship between equality and liberty and their importance in our country. In many ways, the United States remains a nation that is both unified and at odds with itself.

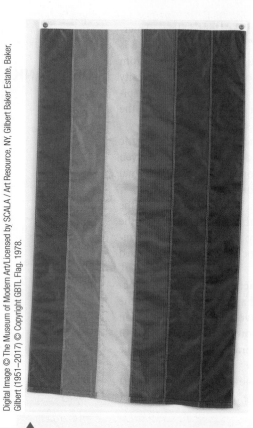

Digital Image © The Museum of Modern Art/Licensed by SCALA / Art Resource, NY, Gilbert Baker Estate, Baker, Gilbert (1951–2017) © Copyright GBTL Flag. 1978.

▲
This rainbow flag, which became a global symbol for LGBTQ Pride, is now part of the permanent collection at the Museum of Modern Art. The flag was designed in 1978 by the San Francisco artist Gilbert Baker.

The flag has been carried in Pride events around the globe. As you consider the universal symbol for the LGBTQ Pride movement, what are some issues of division and unity that the community continues to combat? In what ways does the flag communicate both the diversity and unity that makes up the LGBTQ community?

Second Inaugural Address

Abraham Lincoln

Jon Hicks/Getty Images

THE TEXT IN CONTEXT

Abraham Lincoln (1809–1865) served as the sixteenth president of the United States. First taking office in 1861, he was commander in chief during the entire Civil War: a brutal conflict that left well over half a million dead. After being elected to a second term just before the end of the war, Lincoln delivered the following speech on March 4, 1865. In the speech, Lincoln sought to usher in a season of healing and reconciliation. He was assassinated forty-one days later.

Fellow Countrymen:

At this second appearing to take the oath of the presidential office, there is less occasion for an extended address than there was at the first. Then a statement, somewhat in detail, of a course to be pursued, seemed fitting and proper. Now, at the expiration of four years, during which public declarations have been constantly called forth on every point and phase of the great contest which still absorbs the attention, and engrosses the energies of the nation, little that is new could be presented. The progress of our arms, upon which all else chiefly depends, is as well known to the public as to myself; and it is, I trust, reasonably satisfactory and encouraging to all. With high hope for the future, no prediction in regard to it is ventured.

On the occasion corresponding to this four years ago, all thoughts were anxiously directed to an impending civil-war. All dreaded it—all sought to avert it. While the inaugural address was being delivered from this place, devoted altogether to saving the Union without war, insurgent agents were in the city seeking to destroy it without war—seeking to dissolve the Union, and divide effects, by negotiation. Both parties deprecated war; but one of them would make war rather than let the nation survive; and the other would accept war rather than let it perish. And the war came.

One eighth of the whole population were colored slaves, not distributed generally over the Union, but localized in the Southern part of it. These slaves constituted a peculiar and powerful interest. All knew that this interest was, somehow, the cause of the war. To strengthen, perpetuate, and extend this interest was the object for which the insurgents would rend the Union, even by war; while the government claimed no right to do more than to restrict the territorial enlargement of it. Neither party expected for the war, the magnitude, or the duration, which it has already attained. Neither anticipated that the cause of the conflict might cease with, or even before, the conflict itself should cease. Each looked for an easier triumph, and a result less fundamental and astounding. Both read the same Bible, and pray to the same God; and each invokes His aid against the other. It may seem strange that any men should dare to ask a just God's assistance in wringing their bread from the sweat of other men's faces; but let us judge not that we be not judged. The prayers of both could not be answered; that of neither has been answered fully. The Almighty has His own purposes. "Woe unto the world because of offences! for it must needs be that offences come; but woe to that man by whom the offence cometh!" If we shall suppose that American Slavery is one of those offences which, in the providence of God, must needs come, but which, having continued through His appointed time, He now wills to remove, and that He gives to both North and South, this terrible war, as the woe due to those by whom the offence came, shall we discern therein any departure from those divine attributes which the believers in a Living God always ascribe to Him? Fondly do we hope—fervently do we pray—that this mighty scourge of war may speedily pass away. Yet, if God wills that it continue, until all the wealth piled by the bond-man's two hundred and fifty years of unrequited toil shall be sunk, and until every drop of blood drawn with the lash, shall be paid by another drawn with the sword, as was said three thousand years ago, so still it must be said "the judgments of the Lord, are true and righteous altogether."

With malice toward none; with charity for all; with firmness in the right, as God gives us to see the right, let us strive on to finish the work we are in; to bind up the nation's wounds; to care for him who shall have borne the battle, and for his widow, and his orphan—to do all which may achieve and cherish a just, and a lasting peace, among ourselves, and with all nations.

1864 ELECTORAL COLLEGE ELECTION RESULTS

Lincoln (R) 212

McClellan (D) 21

Did not vote (Confederate States)

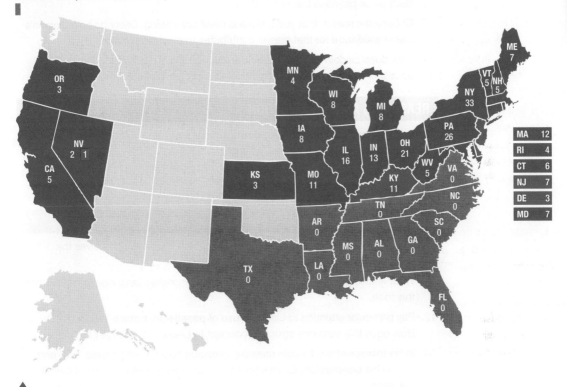

▲

Look closely at this image. It represents the election results for the 1864 election won by Abraham Lincoln.

What does this image say about a divided country? What does it reveal about the context of the "Second Inaugural Address"?

RHETORICAL SITUATION

1. Explain how Lincoln considers the values and needs of the **audience**. Provide at least two examples in your explanation.

2. Describe the **occasion** and **audience** for Lincoln's address. Explain how this audience and occasion affect his overall **message**.

3. How does Lincoln appeal to both the North and the South to achieve his **purpose**?

CLAIMS AND EVIDENCE

4. Lincoln's **claim** in the third paragraph is pivotal to the message of the speech. What is the claim and how does it serve as the foundation for his message?

5. Identify at least two pieces of **evidence** (including facts, data, examples, and details) that Lincoln uses to support each of his reasons. Then describe how each piece provides that support.

6. Choose the reason that you believe is most convincing. Describe how Lincoln's use of **evidence** for that reason contributes to his overall **claim**.

7. How does Lincoln balance his **evidence**, especially given his audience? How does this balance contribute to the logic and organization of the speech?

REASONING AND ORGANIZATION

8. Does Lincoln use **inductive** or **deductive** organization? Explain why his chosen method is appropriate for his audience.

9. The "Second Inaugural Address" is a short speech. Describe the few **reasons** Lincoln provides to justify his thesis.

LANGUAGE AND STYLE

10. How might Lincoln's **word choice** affect how the audience perceives the perspective of the speech?

11. What is Lincoln's **tone**? Give an example of descriptive language that illustrates this tone.

12. Pay particular attention to Lincoln's use of **parallel structure** in the speech. How does this sentence structure connect to Lincoln's message? Explain.

13. In his **introduction**, Lincoln uses the **pronoun** "our." Then he uses "we" and "us" in his **conclusion**. Explain how these pronouns contribute to his overall message.

IDEAS IN AMERICAN CULTURE

14. Lincoln is speaking to a severed nation. How does Lincoln seek to unify the nation? What are some examples of the ideas from this historic speech? Do any of these ideas speak to our nation today? If so, how?

PUTTING IT ALL TOGETHER

15. Lincoln gave this speech on March 4, 1865, within days of the Union victory over the Confederacy. How does this context affect Lincoln's message? How does this message reflect the ideas of the Civil War era?

from Free to Choose: A Personal Statement

Milton Friedman and Rose Friedman

TIM SLOAN/Getty Images

THE TEXT IN CONTEXT

Milton Friedman (1912–2006) and his wife Rose Friedman (1910–2009) were economists whose ideas influenced U.S. government policy. Milton Friedman, an expert in monetary economics, won the Nobel Prize for Economics in 1976. As a conservative who promoted laissez-faire (the notion of less government intervention) policies, Milton Friedman served as an advisor to presidents Richard Nixon and Ronald Reagan. In addition to collaborating with her husband on multiple books about economics, Rose worked at both the National Bureau of Economic Research as well as with the Federal Deposit Insurance Corporation (FDIC). The following excerpt is from their book, *Free to Choose: A Personal Statement*.

"Equality," "liberty"—what precisely do these words from the Declaration of Independence mean? Can the ideals they express be realized in practice? Are equality and liberty consistent one with the other, or are they in conflict?

Since well before the Declaration of Independence, these questions have played a central role in the history of the United States. The attempt to answer them has shaped the intellectual climate of opinion, led to bloody war, and produced major changes in economic and political institutions. This attempt continues to dominate our political debate. It will shape our future as it has our past.

In the early decades of the Republic, equality meant equality before God; liberty meant the liberty to shape one's own life. The obvious conflict between the Declaration of Independence and the institution of slavery occupied the center of the stage. That conflict was finally resolved by the Civil War. The debate then moved to a different level. Equality came more and more to be interpreted as "equality of opportunity" in the sense that no one should be prevented by arbitrary obstacles from using his capacities to pursue his own objectives. That is still its dominant meaning to most citizens of the United States.

Neither equality before God nor equality of opportunity presented any conflict with liberty to shape one's own life. Quite the opposite. Equality and liberty were two faces of the same basic value—that every individual should be regarded as an end in himself.

A very different meaning of equality has emerged in the United States in recent decades—equality of outcome. Everyone should have the same level of living or of income, should finish the race at the same time. Equality of outcome is in clear conflict with liberty. The attempt to promote it has been a major source of bigger and bigger government, and of government-imposed restrictions on our liberty. . . .

Equality of Opportunity

Once the Civil War abolished slavery and the concept of personal equality—equality before God and the law—came closer to realization, emphasis shifted, in intellectual discussion and in government and private policy, to a different concept—equality of opportunity.

Literal equality of opportunity—in the sense of "identity"—is impossible. One child is born blind, another with sight. One child has parents deeply concerned about his welfare who provide a background of culture and understanding; another has dissolute, improvident parents. One child is born in the United States, another in India, or China, or Russia. They clearly do not have identical opportunities open to them at birth, and there is no way that their opportunities can be made identical.

Like personal equality, equality of opportunity is not to be interpreted literally. Its real meaning is perhaps best expressed by the French expression dating from the French Revolution: *Une carriere ouverte aux les talents*—a career open to the talents. No arbitrary obstacles should prevent people from achieving those positions for which their talents fit them and which their values lead them to seek. Not birth, nationality, color, religion, sex, nor any other irrelevant characteristic should determine the opportunities that are open to a person—only his abilities.

On this interpretation, equality of opportunity simply spells out in more detail the meaning of personal equality, of equality before the law. And like personal equality, it has meaning and importance both want to and can pursue different careers.

Equality of opportunity, like personal equality, is not inconsistent with liberty; on the contrary, it is an essential component of liberty. If some people are denied access to particular positions in life for which they are qualified simply because of their ethnic background, color, or religion, that is an interference with their right to "Life, Liberty, and the pursuit of Happiness." It denies equality of opportunity and, by the same token, sacrifices the freedom of some for the advantage of others. . . .

Conclusion

A society that puts equality—in the sense of equality of outcome—ahead of freedom will end up with neither equality nor freedom. The use of force to achieve equality will destroy freedom, and the force, introduced for good purposes, will end up in the hands of people who use it to promote their own interests.

On the other hand, a society that puts freedom first will, as a happy by-product, end up with both greater freedom and greater equality. Though a by-product of freedom, greater equality is not an accident. A free society releases the energies and abilities of people to pursue their own objectives. It prevents some people from arbitrarily suppressing others. It does not prevent some people from achieving positions of privilege, but so long as freedom is maintained, it prevents those positions of privilege from becoming institutionalized; they are subject to continued attack by other able, ambitious people. Freedom means diversity but also mobility. It preserves the opportunity for today's disadvantaged to become tomorrow's privileged and, in the process, enables almost everyone, from top to bottom, to enjoy a fuller and richer life.

Home Language Survey

To make sure that all students receive the education services they need, the law requires us to ask questions about students' language backgrounds. The answers to Section A below will tell us if a student's proficiency in English should be evaluated and help us to ensure that important opportunities to receive programs and services are offered to students who need them. The answers to Section B below will help us communicate with you regarding the student and all school matters in the language you prefer.

Student's Name: _____   Date of Birth: _____

SECTION A: Please answer the questions below.

1. What are the primary languages used in the home regardless of the language spoken by the student? *(Select up to three.)*

☐ English	☐ Cape Verdean	☐ Haitian-Creole	☐ Russian	☐ Other
☐ Arabic	Creole	☐ Italian	☐ Somali	(Please specify)
☐ Burmese	☐ French	☐ Korean	☐ Spanish	
☐ Cambodian	☐ Greek	☐ Mandarin	☐ Toishanese	_____
☐ Cantonese	☐ Hmong	☐ Portuguese	☐ Vietnamese	

2. What is the language most often spoken by the student? *(Select only one.)*

☐ English	☐ Cape Verdean	☐ Haitian-Creole	☐ Russian	☐ Other
☐ Arabic	Creole	☐ Italian	☐ Somali	(Please specify)
☐ Burmese	☐ French	☐ Korean	☐ Spanish	
☐ Cambodian	☐ Greek	☐ Mandarin	☐ Toishanese	_____
☐ Cantonese	☐ Hmong	☐ Portuguese	☐ Vietnamese	

3. What is the language that the student first acquired? *(Select only one.)*

☐ English	☐ Cape Verdean	☐ Haitian-Creole	☐ Russian	☐
☐ Arabic	Creole	☐ Italian	☐ Somali	☐ Other
☐ Burmese	☐ French	☐ Korean	☐ Spanish	(Please specify)
☐ Cambodian	☐ Greek	☐ Mandarin	☐ Toishanese	_____
☐ Cantonese	☐ Hmong	☐ Portuguese	☐ Vietnamese	

Parent/Guardian Signature: _____   Date: _____

SECTION B: Please answer the questions below.

1. In which language do you prefer to receive **written** school communications? (Select only one.)

☐ English	☐ Cape Verdean	☐ Haitian-Creole	☐ Russian	☐ Other
☐ Arabic	Creole	☐ Italian	☐ Somali	(Please specify)
☐ Burmese	☐ French	☐ Korean	☐ Spanish	
☐ Cambodian	☐ Greek	☐ Mandarin	☐ Toishanese	_____
☐ Cantonese	☐ Hmong	☐ Portuguese	☐ Vietnamese	

2. In which language do you prefer to receive **oral** school communications? (Select only one.)

☐ English	☐ Cape Verdean	☐ Haitian-Creole	☐ Russian	☐ Other
☐ Arabic	Creole	☐ Italian	☐ Somali	(Please specify)
☐ Burmese	☐ French	☐ Korean	☐ Spanish	
☐ Cambodian	☐ Greek	☐ Mandarin	☐ Toishanese	_____
☐ Cantonese	☐ Hmong	☐ Portuguese	☐ Vietnamese	

▲

This is an image of the Home Language Survey, a survey given to English language learners by schools to make sure that their needs are met.

Discuss the irony of this survey and its format. What does this survey tell you about the desire for unity and equality in our culture, and the challenges in achieving it?

RHETORICAL SITUATION

1. How do the writers establish **credibility** with their audience?

2. Describe at least two distinct **purposes** that the Friedmans aim to fulfill with this argument.

3. The conclusion emphasizes the authors' **message** in the text. What is the claim expressed in the conclusion?

CLAIMS AND EVIDENCE

4. What kinds of **evidence** do the authors use to support their line of reasoning? Give an example and discuss the effect of this evidence.

5. What is the function of the **evidence** in this argument? Choose two pieces of evidence and then describe how each supports the argument and relates to the authors' purpose.

REASONING AND ORGANIZATION

6. How do the authors' rhetorical choices in the **introduction** and **conclusion** create a relationship between the **writers** and the **audience**?

7. What **method of development** is used by the authors? How do you know?

8. What **reasoning** do the authors use to suggest that their argument is only "ideal"?

LANGUAGE AND STYLE

9. How does the authors' precise **word choice** reduce potential confusion? How might this **diction** affect how the audience receives the argument?

10. How does the authors' use of **pronouns** create a relationship with the audience? Describe how this relationship contributes to their overall message.

11. How do the writers use **transitions** to show the relationship between ideas and create a cohesive argument?

IDEAS IN AMERICAN CULTURE

12. How does this argument speak to the issues of unity and equality in America?

PUTTING IT ALL TOGETHER

13. What is the claim in this argument? How do the authors logically connect the evidence to the established claim? Give an example and explain how the rhetorical situation contributes to their rhetorical choices.

IDEAS IN AMERICAN CULTURE
Equality and Social Discontent

In the American tradition, we have generally viewed equality as fair treatment under the law, especially with regard to legal status, civil liberties, and economic opportunities. In the words of the Declaration of Independence, we all have the equal right to "life, liberty, and the pursuit of happiness." We also understand that this principle should apply to everyone, regardless of race, religion, gender, or other differences unrelated to the worth of an individual. To fulfill this ideal, the United States has often created pathways — educational, economic, social, and legal — to help secure opportunities for all Americans.

Slowly after the Civil War, the divided country began to heal. But that painful process brought about a new unity with a revised national identity. It also brought new problems and struggles.

Despite the Emancipation Proclamation and the ratification of the Thirteenth Amendment to the Constitution, which ended slavery, many former slaves faced new challenges: securing voting rights, becoming landowners, earning fair wages. This difficult period would also be a time for action, progress, and the expansion of rights.

While the United States was founded on lofty ideals, the realities of prejudice and discrimination have always lurked beneath our aspirations. These persistent social and legal biases — against people of a certain race, gender, religion, economic class, or nationality — have meant that certain groups and individuals must still work to secure freedom and equality. Indeed, these people struggle to be a

IDEA BANK

Activism

Advocacy

Authority

Balance

Challenge

Civil Unrest

Democracy

Discontent

Discrimination

Diversity

Equality

Equity

Heroism

Individualism

Inequality

Injustice

Liberty

Opportunity

Power

Prejudice

Protest

Strength

In *War and Peace* (1952), Pablo Picasso uses oil and wood to create a decoration of the chapel of the *château-musée de Vallauris*, "The Temple of Peace." Some protests become "wars" for those who are part of them. Their quest for equality often initiates social discontent.

How does Picasso's message in his painting offer a solution to social discontent? Give an example from your experience.

Picasso, "The Temple of Peace". 1952. © RMN-Grand Palais/Art Resource, NY, ARS, New York, Artwork © 2021 Estate of Pablo Picasso/Artists Rights Society (ARS), New York.

part of a country that has not always welcomed them. Frederick Douglass directly addresses this challenge in "What to a Slave Is the Fourth of July?" (p. 293).

The delicate balance of equality and individual rights remains important in the United States. So do the tensions between unity and diversity. These competing ideas have formed the basis of historic social movements, such as abolition, women's suffrage, and civil rights, in which individuals and groups fought for freedom and equality.

Today, similar social discontent drives movements such as Black Lives Matter, the #MeToo movement, and LGBTQ activism, which spark protest and even civil unrest. It's not uncommon for well-known writers and artists to use their influence for advocacy. For example, novelist and poet Barbara Kingsolver, author of *Animal Dreams*, wrote "#MeToo Isn't Enough" (p. 298) in response to the injustice and the inequality confronting women today.

During these moments of protest, we see the strength, passion, and courage of individuals and groups striving for equality and other ideals. Until these ideals are achieved for all, the United States remains a work in progress.

Amber Lee

▲
Amber Lee, from Valencia High School, was selected as a national finalist in Sister Cities International's 2020 Young Artists and Authors Showcase for her piece titled, "United We Stand." Each entry for the 2020 YAAS focused on the theme, "One World: Out of Many, We Are One." Lee's dynamic artwork shows many different colors and representations on a single face. According to Lee, what inspired her was "the constant division between people and coming to the realization that we are no different from one another."

How does this "constant division between people" lead us to the question of equality in the world today? How does this representation of contrast lead us to a discussion of unity?

What to the Slave Is the Fourth of July?

Frederick Douglass

Buyenlarge/Getty Images

THE TEXT IN CONTEXT

Frederick Douglass (1818–1895) was born a slave in the state of Maryland. When he was a young boy, his master's wife taught him the alphabet and the basics of reading. This experience compelled Douglass to teach himself to read and write, which lead him to the antislavery arguments that inspired him to escape. Once he made his way to the North, Douglass became a pivotal figure in the abolitionist movement, writing his famous *Narrative of the Life of Frederick Douglass, an American Slave*, among other writings. The following is an excerpt from a speech that he delivered on July 5, 1852, to the Rochester Ladies' Anti-Slavery Society of Rochester, New York.

Fellow-citizens, pardon me, allow me to ask, why am I called upon to speak here to-day? What have I, or those I represent, to do with your national independence? Are the great principles of political freedom and of natural justice, embodied in that Declaration of Independence, extended to us? and am I, therefore, called upon to bring our humble offering to the national altar, and to confess the benefits and express devout gratitude for the blessings resulting from your independence to us?

Would to God, both for your sakes and ours, that an affirmative answer could be truthfully returned to these questions! . . .

But such is not the state of the case. I say it with a sad sense of the disparity between us. I am not included within the pale of this glorious anniversary! Your high independence only reveals the immeasurable distance between us. The blessings in which you, this day, rejoice, are not enjoyed in common. The rich inheritance of justice, liberty, prosperity and independence, bequeathed by your fathers, is shared by you, not by me. The sunlight that brought light and healing to you, has brought stripes and death to me. This Fourth [of] July is yours, not mine. You may rejoice, I must mourn. To drag a man in fetters into the grand illuminated temple of liberty, and call upon him to join you in joyous anthems, were inhuman mockery and sacrilegious irony. Do you mean, citizens, to mock me, by asking me to speak to-day? If so, there is a parallel to your conduct. And let me warn you that it is dangerous to copy the example of a nation whose crimes, towering up to heaven, were thrown down by the breath of the Almighty, burying that nation in irrevocable ruin! I can to-day take up the plaintive lament of a peeled and woe-smitten people! . . .

Fellow-citizens; above your national, tumultuous joy, I hear the mournful wail of millions! whose chains, heavy and grievous yesterday, are, to-day, rendered more intolerable by the jubilee shouts that reach them. If I do forget, if I do not faithfully remember those bleeding children of sorrow this day, "may my right hand forget her cunning, and may my tongue cleave to the roof of my mouth!" To forget them, to pass lightly over their wrongs, and to chime in with the popular theme, would be treason most scandalous and shocking, and would make me a reproach before God and the world. My subject, then fellow-citizens, is American slavery. I shall see, this day, and its popular characteristics, from the slave's point of view. Standing there identified with the American bondman, making his wrongs mine, I do not hesitate to declare, with all my soul, that the character and conduct of this nation never looked blacker to me than on this 4th of July! Whether we turn to the declarations of the past, or to the professions of the present, the conduct of the nation seems equally hideous and revolting. America is false to the past, false to the present, and solemnly binds herself to be false to the future. Standing with God and the crushed and bleeding slave on this occasion, I will, in the name of humanity which is outraged, in the name of liberty which is fettered, in the name of the constitution and the Bible which are disregarded and trampled upon, dare to call in question and to denounce, with all the emphasis I can command, everything that serves to perpetuate slavery—the great sin and shame of America! "I will not equivocate; I will not excuse;" I will use the severest language I can command; and yet not one word shall escape me that any man, whose judgment is not blinded by prejudice, or who is not at heart a slaveholder, shall not confess to be right and just.

But I fancy I hear some one of my audi-   5
ence say, "It is just in this circumstance that you and your brother abolitionists fail to make a favorable impression on the public mind. Would you argue more, and denounce less, would you persuade more, and rebuke less, your cause would be much more likely to succeed." But, I submit, where all is plain there is nothing to be argued. What point in the anti-slavery creed would you have me argue? On what branch of the subject do the people of this country need light? Must I undertake to prove that the slave is a man? That point is conceded already. Nobody doubts it. The slaveholders themselves acknowledge it in the enactment of laws for their government. They acknowledge it when they punish disobedience on the part of the slave. There are seventy-two crimes in the State of Virginia which, if committed by a black man (no matter how ignorant he be), subject him to the punishment of death; while only two of the same crimes will subject a white man to the like punishment. What is this but the acknowledgment that the slave is a moral, intellectual and responsible being? The manhood of the slave is conceded. It is admitted in the fact that Southern statute books are covered with enactments forbidding, under severe fines and penalties, the teaching of the slave to read or to write. When you can point to any such laws in reference to the beasts of the field, then I may consent to argue the manhood of the slave. When the dogs in your streets, when the fowls of the air, when the cattle on your hills, when the fish of the sea, and the reptiles that crawl, shall be unable to distinguish the slave

from a brute, then will I argue with you that the slave is a man!

For the present, it is enough to affirm the equal manhood of the Negro race. Is it not astonishing that, while we are ploughing, planting, and reaping, using all kinds of mechanical tools, erecting houses, constructing bridges, building ships, working in metals of brass, iron, copper, silver and gold; that, while we are reading, writing and cyphering, acting as clerks, merchants and secretaries, having among us lawyers, doctors, ministers, poets, authors, editors, orators and teachers; that, while we are engaged in all manner of enterprises common to other men, digging gold in California, capturing the whale in the Pacific, feeding sheep and cattle on the hill-side, living, moving, acting, thinking, planning, living in families as husbands, wives and children, and, above all, confessing and worshipping the Christian's God, and looking hopefully for life and immortality beyond the grave, we are called upon to prove that we are men!

Would you have me argue that man is entitled to liberty? that he is the rightful owner of his own body? You have already declared it. Must I argue the wrongfulness of slavery? Is that a question for Republicans? Is it to be settled by the rules of logic and argumentation, as a matter beset with great difficulty, involving a doubtful application of the principle of justice, hard to be understood? How should I look to-day, in the presence of Americans, dividing, and subdividing a discourse, to show that men have a natural right to freedom? speaking of it relatively, and positively, negatively and affirmatively. To do so, would be to make myself ridiculous, and to offer an insult to your understanding. There is not a man beneath the canopy of heaven that does not know that slavery is wrong for him.

What, am I to argue that it is wrong to make men brutes, to rob them of their liberty, to work them without wages, to keep them ignorant of their relations to their fellow men, to beat them with sticks, to flay their flesh with the lash, to load their limbs with irons, to hunt them with dogs, to sell them at auction, to sunder their families, to knock out their teeth, to burn their flesh, to starve them into obedience and submission to their masters? Must I argue that a system thus marked with blood, and stained with pollution, is wrong? No! I will not. I have better employment for my time and strength than such arguments would imply.

What, then, remains to be argued? Is it that slavery is not divine; that God did not establish it; that our doctors of divinity are mistaken? There is blasphemy in the thought. That which is inhuman, cannot be divine! Who can reason on such a proposition? They that can, may; I cannot. The time for such argument is past.

At a time like this, scorching irony, not convincing argument, is needed. O! had I the ability, and could I reach the nation's ear, I would, to-day, pour out a fiery stream of biting ridicule, blasting reproach, withering sarcasm, and stern rebuke. For it is not light that is needed, but fire; it is not the gentle shower, but thunder. We need the storm, the whirlwind, and the earthquake. The feeling of the nation must be quickened; the conscience of the nation must be roused; the propriety of the nation must be startled; the hypocrisy of the nation must be exposed; and its crimes against God and man must be proclaimed and denounced.

What, to the American slave, is your 4th of July? I answer; a day that reveals to him, more than all other days in the year, the gross injustice and cruelty to which he is the constant victim. To him, your celebration is a sham; your boasted liberty, an unholy license; your national greatness, swelling vanity; your sounds of rejoicing are empty and heartless; your denunciations of tyrants, brass fronted impudence; your shouts of liberty and equality, hollow mockery; your prayers and hymns, your sermons and thanksgivings, with all your religious parade and solemnity, are, to Him, mere bombast, fraud, deception, impiety and hypocrisy—a thin veil to cover up crimes which would disgrace a nation of savages. There is not a nation on the earth guilty of practices more shocking and bloody than are the people of these United States, at this very hour. . . .

. . . Allow me to say, in conclusion, notwithstanding the dark picture I have this day presented, of the state of the nation, I do not despair of this country. There are forces in operation which must inevitably work the downfall of slavery. . . . Nations do not now stand in the same relation to each other that they did ages ago. No nation can now shut itself up from the surrounding world and trot round in the same old path of its fathers without interference. The time was when such could be done. Long established customs of hurtful character could formerly fence themselves in, and do their evil work with social impunity. Knowledge was then confined and enjoyed by the privileged few, and the multitude walked on in mental darkness. But a change has now come over the affairs of mankind. Walled cities and empires have become unfashionable. The arm of commerce has borne away the gates of the strong city. Intelligence is penetrating the darkest corners of the globe. It makes its pathway over and under the sea, as well as on the earth. Wind, steam, and lightning are its chartered agents. Oceans no longer divide, but link nations together. From Boston to London is now a holiday excursion. Space is comparatively annihilated. —Thoughts expressed on one side of the Atlantic are distinctly heard on the other. . . .

This image is of Jefferson County, Colorado, students protesting in 2014. Nearly 700 students walked out of school in protest of the school board's decision to eliminate Advanced Placement® United States History from the course offerings.

How can social discontent bring about change, equity, or unity?

AP Photo/Brennan Linsley

RHETORICAL SITUATION

1. How are the **context** and **exigence** of Douglass's speech related? How do they work together?

2. How does the **writer** try to engage the **audience** in the first paragraph? Give an example of Douglass's rhetorical choices to explain the strategy.

3. How do both the **introduction** and **conclusion** reflect Douglass's consideration of the **audience**? How do they reflect the audience's needs and perspectives? How do they communicate Douglass's **purpose**?

CLAIMS AND EVIDENCE

4. What is the writer's main **claim**?

5. How does Douglass's **evidence** consider the beliefs, values, and needs of the audience and advance the purpose?

6. What type of **evidence** does the writer use to support his line of reasoning? Provide specific examples that illustrate how the supporting evidence is appropriate for the audience.

REASONING AND ORGANIZATION

7. Is this speech organized **inductively** or **deductively**? Why does Douglass choose this approach?

8. What **reasons** does the writer give to justify his main claim? Explain how these reasons logically support the claim.

LANGUAGE AND STYLE

9. What is the **tone** of the text? Where does the tone shift? Identify a shift and explain its effects.

10. Identify the **pronouns** in the text. When do the pronouns shift from singular to plural? Explain the effect of this shift.

11. How does the writer use **repetition** to convey his message? Explain whether this repetition is effective.

12. How does Douglass's **word choice** contribute to his message? Give an example and explain the effect.

IDEAS IN AMERICAN CULTURE

13. Douglass was invited by the female abolitionist group to give this speech. How do you think they responded to Douglass's criticism of the country's founders, the Constitution, and the American way of life? How do you feel today about his criticism? Do we still see "gross injustice and cruelty" with regard to race in the United States? Explain.

PUTTING IT ALL TOGETHER

14. Considering the rhetorical situation, what reasons and evidence might convince the audience of Douglass's claim?

#MeToo Isn't Enough

Barbara Kingsolver

Jessica Tezak/Guardian/eye vine/Redux

THE TEXT IN CONTEXT

Novelist Barbara Kingsolver (b. 1955) grew up in rural Kentucky. She earned her undergraduate degree at DePauw University and a master's degree from the University of Arizona. Since beginning her writing career in the 1980s, she has published many essays, short stories, and novels. Kingsolver often writes about her life experiences as well. In 2018, she published this response after the *New York Times* report on Harvey Weinstein, a Hollywood executive accused of sexually harassing and assaulting women for decades.

In each of my daughters' lives came the day in fifth grade when we had to sit on her bed and practise. I pretended to be the boy in class who was making her sick with dread. She had to look right at me and repeat the words until they felt possible, if not easy: "Don't say that to me. Don't do that to me. I hate it." As much as I wanted to knock heads around, I knew the only real solution was to arm a daughter for self-defence. But why was it so hard to put teeth into that defence? Why does it come more naturally to smile through clenched teeth and say "Oh, stop," in the mollifying tone so regularly, infuriatingly mistaken for flirtation?

Women my age could answer that we were raised that way. We've done better with our daughters but still find ourselves right here, where male puberty opens a lifelong season of sexual aggression, and girls struggle for the voice to call it off. The *Mad Men* cliche of the boss cornering his besotted secretary is the modern cliche of the pop icon with his adulating, naked-ish harem in a story that never changes: attracting male attention is a woman's success. Rejecting it feels rude, like refusing an award. It feels ugly.

Now, all at once, women are refusing to accept sexual aggression as any kind of award, and men are getting fired from their jobs. It feels like an earthquake. Men and women alike find ourselves disoriented, wondering what the rules are. Women know perfectly well that we hate unsolicited sexual attention, but navigate a minefield of male thinking on what "solicit" might mean. We've spent so much life-force on looking good but not too good, being professional but not unapproachable, while the guys just got on with life. And what of the massive costs of permanent vigilance, the tense smiles, declined work assignments and lost chances that are our daily job of trying to avoid assault? Can we get some backpay?

I think we're trying to do that now, as the opening volleys of #MeToo smack us with backlash against backlash. Patriarchy persists because power does not willingly cede its clout; and also, frankly, because women are widely complicit in the assumption that we're separate and not quite equal. If we're woke, we inspect ourselves and others for implicit racial bias, while mostly failing to recognise explicit gender bias, which still runs rampant. Religious faiths that subordinate women flourish on every continent. Nearly every American educational institution pours the lion's share of its athletics budget into the one sport that still excludes women—American football.

Most progressives wouldn't hesitate to attend a football game, or to praise the enlightened new pope—the one who says he's sorry, but women still can't lead his church, or control our reproduction. In heterosexual weddings, religious or secular, the patriarch routinely "gives" his daughter to the groom, after which she's presented to the audience as "Mrs New Patriarch," to joyous applause. We have other options, of course: I kept my name in marriage and gave it to my daughters. But most modern brides still embrace the ritual erasure of their identities, taking the legal name of a new male head of household, as enslaved people used to do when they came to a new plantation owner.

I can already hear the outcry against conflating traditional marriage with slavery. Yes, I know, the marital bargain has changed: women are no longer chattels. Tell me this giving-away and name-changing are just vestiges of a cherished tradition. I'll reply that some of my neighbours here in the south still fly the Confederate flag—not with hate, they insist, but to honour a proud tradition. In either case, a tradition in which people legally control other people doesn't strike me as worth celebrating, even symbolically.

If any contract between men required the non-white one to adopt the legal identity of his

Caucasian companion, would we pop the champagne? If any sport wholly excluded people of colour, would it fill stadiums throughout the land? Would we attend a church whose sacred texts consign Latinos to inferior roles? What about galas where black and Asian participants must wear painful shoes and clothes that reveal lots of titillating, well-toned flesh while white people turn up comfortably covered?

No wonder there is confusion about this volcano of outrage against men who objectify and harass. Marriage is not slavery, but a willingness to subvert our very names in our primary partnership might confound everyone's thinking about where women stand in our other relationships with men. And if our sex lives aren't solely ours to control, but also the purview of men of the cloth, why not employers too? We may ache for gender equality but we're rarely framing or fighting for it in the same ways we fight for racial equality. The #MeToo movement can't bring justice to a culture so habituated to misogyny that we can't even fathom parity, and women still dread losing the power we've been taught to use best: our charm.

Years ago, as a college student, I spent a semester abroad in a beautiful, historic city where the two sentences I heard most in English, usually conjoined, were "You want to go for coffee?" and "You want to have sex with me, baby?" I lived near a huge public garden where I wished I could walk or study, but couldn't, without being followed, threatened and subjected to jarring revelations of some creep's penis among the foliages. My experiment in worldliness had me trapped, fuming, in a tiny apartment.

One day in a fit of weird defiance I tied a sofa cushion to my belly under a loose dress and discovered this was the magic charm: I could walk anywhere, unmolested. I carried my after-class false pregnancy to the end of the

5

10

term, happily ignored by predators. As a lissom 20-year-old I resented my waddly disguise, but came around to a riveting truth: being attractive was less useful to me than being free.

Modern women's magazines promise we don't have to choose, we can be sovereign powers and seductresses both at once. But study the pictures and see an attractiveness imbued with submission and myriad forms of punitive self-alteration. Actually, we have to choose: not one or the other utterly, but some functional point between these poles. It starts with a sober reckoning of how much we really need to be liked by the universe of men. Not all men confuse "liking" with conquest, of course—just the handful of jerks who poison the well, and the larger number who think they are funny. Plus the majority of the US male electorate, who put a boastful assaulter in charge of us all.

This is the point. The universe of men does not merit women's indiscriminate grace. If the #MeToo revolution has proved anything, it's that women live under threat. Not sometimes, but all the time.

We don't have unlimited options about working for male approval, since here in this world that is known as "approval." We also want to be loved, probably we want it too much. But loved. Bear with us while we sort this out, and begin to codify it in the bluntest terms. Enduring some guy's copped feel or a gander at his plumbing is so very much not a Valentine. It is a letter bomb. It can blow up a day, an interview, a job, a home, the very notion of safety inside our bodies.

It shouldn't be this hard to demand safety while we do our work, wear whatever, walk where we need to go. And yet, for countless women enduring harassment on the job, it is this hard, and escape routes are few. The path to freedom is paved with many special words

for "hideously demanding person" that only apply to females.

Chaining the links of our experiences behind [15] a hashtag can help supply the courage to be unlovely while we blast an ugly reality into the open. The chain doesn't negate women's individuality or our capacity to trust men individually, nor does it suggest every assault is the same. Raped is not groped is not catcalled on the street: all these are vile and have to stop, but the damages are different. Women who wish to be more than bodies can use our brains to discern context and the need for cultural education. In lieu of beguiling we can be rational, which means giving the accused a fair hearing and a sentence that fits the crime. (Let it also be said, losing executive power is not the death penalty, even if some people are carrying on as if it were.) Polarisation is as obstructive in gender politics as in any other forum. Sympathetic men are valuable allies.

Let's be clear: no woman asks to live in a rape culture: we all want it over, yesterday. Mixed signals about female autonomy won't help bring it down, and neither will asking nicely. Nothing changes until truly powerful offenders start to fall. Feminine instincts for sweetness and apology have no skin in this game. It's really not possible to overreact to uncountable, consecutive days of being humiliated by men who say our experience isn't real, or that we like it actually, or are cute when we're mad. Anger has to go somewhere—if not out then inward, in a psychic thermodynamics that can turn a nation of women into pressure cookers. Watching the election of a predator-in-chief seems to have popped the lid off the can. We've found a voice, and now is a good time to use it, in a tone that will not be mistaken for flirtation.

Don't say that to me. Don't do that to me. I hate it.

In 1917, these activists for women's voting rights (or *suffragettes*) picketed the White House with signs that read, "Mr. President, how long must women wait for liberty?"

How do these protesters from over a century ago connect to the message of the contemporary #MeToo movement? Explain the relationship between the two movements in context, purpose, and message.

Library of Congress, Prints & Photographs Division, Reproduction number LC-DIG hec-07113 (digital file from original negative)

RHETORICAL SITUATION

1. How do Kingsolver's rhetorical choices in the **introduction** and the **conclusion** reflect the **context** of her argument?

2. How does Kingsolver **appeal** to her audience? How do these appeals fit the **rhetorical situation** and the intended **audience's perspective** on the subject?

3. How do the ideas in the **introduction** and the **conclusion** strengthen her argument?

CLAIMS AND EVIDENCE

4. What is the writer's **claim**? Where does Kingsolver reveal it? How does this contribute to her overall argument?

5. What kind of **evidence** does Kingsolver use (e.g., facts, expert opinions, personal observation) to support her line of reasoning? Choose an example of one type of evidence. Then discuss its likely effect on her intended audience.

6. What is the function of the **evidence** (e.g., to illustrate, clarify, set a mood)? How does the writer communicate that function at different points in the text?

REASONING AND ORGANIZATION

7. What **reasons** does Kingsolver use to justify her argument? How do they help establish her **line of reasoning**?

LANGUAGE AND STYLE

8. How does Kingsolver's precise **word choice** provide clarity and reduce confusion? Choose an example and explain how it might reveal the writer's perspective to the audience.

9. What is the **tone** of the argument? Explain how Kingsolver's particular word choice contributes to that tone.

10. Point out examples of **parallel structure** in the text. What is the rhetorical effect of this syntax? For example, does it help her reinforce her points?

11. How does Kingsolver use **transitions** to connect her ideas? Identify at least three examples of transitional words or phrases. Then describe the relationships that these transitions establish.

IDEAS IN AMERICAN CULTURE

12. The idea of equality resonates throughout this text. Can you think of a time when you recognized inequality in your school, community, neighborhood, or city? How was the inequality addressed? Did this solution change the culture, or do you continue to witness the inequality? Kingsolver suggests ways of stopping injustice and changing a culture. In your response, consider how changing the culture might impact your example of inequality.

PUTTING IT ALL TOGETHER

13. Pay attention to Kingsolver's pronouns. Explain how this word choice is influenced by the rhetorical situation. Does Kingsolver's choice of pronouns amplify her tone and message?

Writing a Definition Argument

One of the most common and effective ways to develop an argument is through definition. This mode of development is especially useful when a writer needs to clarify an abstract idea like democracy, freedom, or justice. The line of reasoning centers on the traits or characteristics of the concept; then the writer includes evidence and explanation to exemplify those qualities. By defining the concept, the writer can share a perspective and ultimately a message with the audience.

In this workshop, you have the opportunity to develop an argument by defining a concept for your audience. You will develop your perspective on the concept by identifying, exemplifying, and explaining its traits or characteristics. In doing so, you will convey your message to your audience.

KEY POINT

Definition arguments explain and are organized by characteristics, traits, features, or attributes.

Redefining Ladylike

Zoie Taylore

The following essay by Zoie Taylore was published in the *New York Times* as a finalist in their student essay contest in 2015.

"I did it five times."

"Well—I did it 12 times."

"I've got all of you beat. I did it 16 times!"

No—this isn't a scene from a raunchy high school movie, but rather a group of young women discussing how many times they've said the naughty word: sorry.

> *introduction establishes purpose of argument—connection between saying "sorry" and femininity*

Saying sorry, especially for women, has become the new norm. <u>As natural nurturers</u> this instinctive space-filler keeps the peace, while simultaneously ensuring our likability and ladylikeness. This instant "belly up" tactic works to defeat women on a daily basis.

> *writer lists first characteristic of saying "sorry"— new norm*
>
> *this dangling modifier needs clarification*

This "sorry" epidemic is detrimental to women, especially for the future of female leadership. According to the *New York Times* article "Speaking While Female," when a woman speaks in a professional setting, she walks a tightrope. This tightrope being the fine line between being barely heard, and being too aggressive. Speaking up puts you into the automatic bitch box. But not speaking up gets you nowhere, creating the ultimate female catch-22. This lexical faux pas

> *second characteristic: "sorry" is detrimental to female leadership*
>
> *evidence: analogy illustrates the dilemma*

evidence: statistics showing consequence — could very well be the reason only 5.2 percent of Fortune 500 CEO's are women, and that women hold a mere 1 percent of the world's wealth.

third characteristic: opposing idea through negation

evidence: expert opinion defining types of "sorry" — Now, sorry in itself is not a bad word, nor is it gender exclusive. In fact, it is a common trait of politeness. And, according to a Salon article called "I'm Not Sorry for Saying Sorry: Women Should Feel Free to Apologize as Much as They Want," sorry is just a "ritual of restoring balance to a conversation." In other words, a form of chitchat to make people more comfortable. But constantly apologizing for speaking your mind, or for things that are not your fault is exhausting, incarcerating and usually exclusive to women.

evidence: expert opinion provides different perspective — Melissa Atkins Wardy, author of "Redefining Girly," recently stated in a CNN article that "Our girls need to learn their voice has every right to take up space in a conversation, in a room, and in an argument." Confidence counts just as much as competence and this generation of girls is lacking in one of the two. With 60 percent of all university graduates being women, it certainly isn't competence. And in addition, saying and feeling sorry for doing day-to-day activities causes a serious confidence gap between men and women. This is why men are more likely to feel over-confident, while women are prone to underestimation.

the writer's purpose is to increase awareness and try to redefine "ladylike" — The recent Dove commercial "Sorry Not Sorry" has brought attention to the sorry sickness. With more women acknowledging the excessive use of this appeaser, the apology apocalypse will hopefully be a thing of the past.

"Women have been trained to speak softly and carry a lipstick. Those days are over."—Bella Abzug

the writer was informed by a variety of sources of evidence

Sources

ABC News. "Pantene Commercial Asks Whether Women Say 'Sorry' Too Much." ABC News, 18 June 2014. Web. 04 Mar. 2015.

Klingle, Kylah. "I'm Not Sorry for Saying Sorry: Women Should Feel Free to Apologize as Much as They Want." Salon, 12 July 2014. Web. 04 Mar. 2015.

Sandberg, Sheryl, and Adam Grant. "Speaking While Female." The New York Times, 10 Jan. 2015. Web. 04 Mar. 2015.

Wallace, Kelly. "Sorry to Ask but . . . Do Women Apologize More than Men?" CNN, 26 June 2014. Web. 04 Mar. 2015.

Warner, Judith. "Fact Sheet: The Women's Leadership Gap." Center for American Progress. 7 March 2014. Web. 11 Feb. 2015.

YOUR ASSIGNMENT

Your school principal is developing a list of exemplary qualities to be displayed on a banner in the school's front office. The banner will be a reminder of the school's values, ideals, and expectations. As an upperclassman, you have been invited to propose one of these characteristics for the display. However, you will then have to explain why the trait is important for students. Choose one admirable quality. Then write a multi-paragraph definition argument in which you explain your choice with a definition of the quality and illustrations of this idea in action.

Your argument should include the following:

- An introduction that provides a basic denotative definition and context for discussing the idea (term, concept, or ideal)
- A thesis statement that connects the unifying idea to your perspective
- A line of reasoning that develops your definition by the concept's key attributes or characteristics
- Evidence that illustrates or exemplifies each attribute
- Commentary that further explains the evidence and connects it to your perspective
- A conclusion that brings the argument to a unified end and leaves the audience with a compelling image

Potential Subjects

- Character
- Leadership
- Generosity
- Empathy
- Inclusivity

RHETORICAL SITUATION Connecting Audience and Purpose

AP® Enduring Understanding (RHS-1)

Individuals write within a particular situation and make strategic writing choices based on that situation.

A definition argument explains an abstract or complicated concept more thoroughly than a brief dictionary entry can. For this assignment, you will write an extended definition of a concept or idea. In the process, you will both identify its traits and offer a perspective so your readers can better understand the concept. Essentially, you are presenting an extended definition of the word from *your* perspective.

In developing your definition, you will

- include the context in which the concept is found,
- identify its attributes and characteristics,
- share examples or illustrations of these characteristics, and
- make comparisons to similar ideas.

These steps will help deepen the audience's understanding of the idea. For example, you might be writing the extended definition of a familiar concept like *integrity*. But depending on the context, your purpose, and your audience, your definition would vary. For example, note the different contexts for the word *integrity* represented in the following example.

	Context	Audience and Purpose
	Interpersonal	Audience: friends and family interested in the dynamics of relationships and behavior among friends and family. Related ideas: honesty, loyalty, and trustworthiness
Integrity	School, Business, or Politics	Audience: classmates and teachers, supervisors and coworkers, candidates and voters, etc., interested in rules of behavior for an organization or community. Related ideas: academic honesty, business ethics, teamwork, confidentiality, credentials
	Technology, Science, or Engineering	Audience: engineers, programmers, builders, and managers. Related ideas: functionality, comprehensiveness, security

When you write a definition argument, you must give readers a comprehensive understanding of the concept or idea. But you may have other purposes as well. In this unit, we have noted that writers often have multiple purposes within a single text or argument. Some writers may focus on definition as the first step in argument because readers must understand a concept generally before a writer can make more specific claims. In other words, writers begin arguments with definition so that they can move the audience beyond the term's basic meaning to a more nuanced, sophisticated understanding.

For example, a school establishing a code of conduct for its students may need to develop a definition of the word *integrity*. Using illustrations, examples, and analogies, this preliminary definition will introduce students to new expectations and policies. Once students know the meaning of integrity and can recognize its attributes, they will better understand the benefits of belonging to an organization whose members behave with integrity. Ultimately, writers may use their introductions and conclusions to achieve their purposes.

Introductions

To begin your definition argument, you will need to write an introduction that orients, engages, and focuses your audience. Introductions begin with an engaging hook that conveys the importance of the subject to both you and your audience. This is also the opportunity to establish the context of the subject and either pose a question (inductive reasoning) or state your thesis (deductive reasoning). Writers use a number of different introduction strategies, or hooks, to orient, engage, or focus their audience, including

- quotations,
- intriguing statements,
- anecdotes,
- questions,
- statistics,
- data,
- contextualized information, or
- a scenario.

So, once you have determined your perspective and message, you need to plan how you will introduce your definition argument.

Conclusions

Writers also establish context for their audience in their conclusions. The conclusion of an argument brings the argument to a unified end. It may present the argument's thesis. It may also engage the audience by doing one or more of the following

- explaining the significance of the argument within a broader context,
- making connections,
- calling the audience to act,
- suggesting a change in behavior or attitude,
- proposing a solution,
- leaving the audience with a compelling image,
- explaining implications,
- summarizing the argument, or
- connecting to the introduction.

As you develop your introduction, it may be helpful to consider how you will bring your argument to a close for your audience.

1. Consider the context for your extended definition.
2. Choose an engaging hook to begin your argument.
3. Write an introduction for your definition argument.

What is the concept that you are defining?	
Who is your audience?	
What is your purpose(s)?	
How will you orient, engage, or focus the audience?	

REASONING AND ORGANIZATION Explaining Significance

AP® Enduring Understanding (REO-1)

Writers guide understanding of a text's line of reasoning and claims through that text's organization and integration of evidence.

As you will likely define a concept that is abstract, complex, or subjective, you will need to focus your discussion on two to four defining characteristics. These become the line of reasoning that guides your body paragraphs. Here is one common organizational strategy: First, identify the key characteristics of your concept. Next, illustrate the characteristics with evidence.

But before you start writing, you may want to review synonyms and antonyms of the concept, along with the origins and history of the word. In your definition argument, you will combine this research with your own impressions and related ideas. Gathering this information might spark ideas and associations that help you with your final list. For example, examine the following brainstorming list, which explores the concept of *integrity* in a school setting.

Integrity in School	Synonyms	Honesty, trustworthiness, uprightness, dependability, fairness, honor, ethics, morals, unity, wholeness, solidarity, rightness, selflessness
	Antonyms	Dishonesty, division, injustice, unfairness, partiality, selfishness
	Word Origin	From the word *integer*, meaning intact or whole

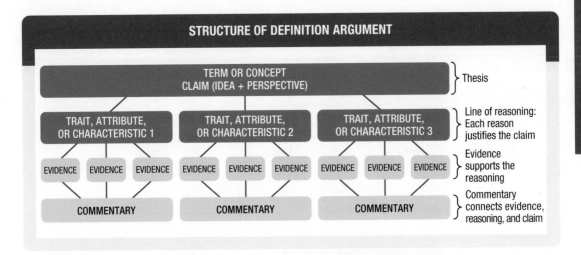

STRUCTURE OF DEFINITION ARGUMENT

After looking at these notes, you might notice certain qualities that stand out, perhaps because of their repetition or their associations. As specific attributes emerge, they should help you narrow your focus and highlight the key elements of the concept in your argument. These characteristics will also be the basis for your line of reasoning and serve as the topic sentences of your body paragraphs. Think of your concept and line of reasoning as a string of lights. The string holds all of the ideas together, and the idea is illuminated throughout.

But merely identifying characteristics is not enough to develop your argument. Your line of reasoning must justify the claim within your thesis. More specifically, you will develop commentary that explains the significance of each reason in relation to your unifying idea and perspective. In other words, how does each reason make the claim true?

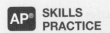 **SKILLS PRACTICE** | REASONING AND ORGANIZATION
Explaining Significance

1. Create a word web with as many attributes and characteristics as you can generate for your concept. You might consider synonyms, antonyms, and word origins to help you brainstorm. Next, sort the list by common ideas.

2. Circle three or four of the best attributes to use as topic sentences for your body paragraphs. Note: You may also organize part of your discussion around what the concept is *not*.

3. Explain the significance of each reason in relation to your unifying idea.

(continued)

Concept to Be Defined:		
Unifying Idea and Perspective:		
Characteristic 1	Characteristic 2	Characteristic 3
Significance to Unifying Idea	Significance to Unifying Idea	Significance to Unifying Idea

CLAIMS AND EVIDENCE Selecting Purposeful Evidence

AP® Enduring Understanding (CLE-1)

Writers make claims about subjects, rely on evidence that supports the reasoning that justifies the claim, and often acknowledge or respond to other, possibly opposing, arguments.

In previous workshops, you have learned to compose a thesis statement by connecting an idea to a claim. In a definition argument, the concept you are defining *is* the idea. So your thesis will connect this idea to your perspective. The thesis may also include the attributes of the concept. To write this sentence, consult the list of strong verbs for a definition thesis.

THESIS VERBS FOR DEFINITION ARGUMENTS

Articulates	Demonstrates	Identifies	Reveals
Categorizes	Depicts	Illustrates	Shows
Characterizes	Distinguishes	Portrays	Specifies
Consists	Elaborates	Presents	States
Defines	Exemplifies	Represents	Unearths

Sample Thesis Statements	Effectiveness
There are many characteristics of a person with integrity.	INEFFECTIVE: *Vague*
The word *integrity* means to be honest and have strong moral principles.	INEFFECTIVE: *Merely a definition*
Leaders with integrity exemplify honesty, trustworthiness, and selflessness.	EFFECTIVE: *Makes a claim and connects the idea to its attributes*

After you have a solid thesis statement, plan your line of reasoning and generate your supporting evidence. Keep in mind, your thesis may preview the line of reasoning of your argument. In other words, the thesis can list the points of the argument, aspects to be analyzed, or specific evidence to be used in an argument.

As you evaluate support for your thesis and line of reasoning, choose evidence that does the following:

- creates an association with ideas that readers will find familiar;
- illustrates, clarifies, or exemplifies your concept; and
- amplifies a point that you are making about your concept.

Writers support each characteristic or attribute in their line of reasoning with evidence. In a definition argument, writers often draw upon the following types of evidence:

TYPES AND FUNCTIONS OF EVIDENCE	
Example	Provides an illustration of the trait or characteristic and explains the significance of that example
Negation	Provides a contrast with important characteristics to describe what something is not. Then explains the importance of the contrast by considering the connections between the two objects or subjects
Analogy	Provides a comparison that illustrates the concept or its attributes and explains the concept in terms of another subject, object, or idea

Review the following examples of evidence to support the line of reasoning.

Thesis with Claim (Idea + Perspective)

Leaders with integrity exemplify honesty, trustworthiness, and selflessness.

	Characteristic 1	Characteristic 2	Characteristic 3
Types of Evidence	Honest (to others and to oneself)	Trustworthy and Dependable	Fair and Selfless
Examples/ Illustrations	Anecdote of academic honesty about the time that an answer key was found online and a student informed the teacher or chose not to use it while classmates did	Anecdote of a collaborative assignment that recounts an occasion when all students completed their portions of the project	Anecdote of a generous student who helped another student by editing a college application essay even though both were trying to get accepted to the same college

(continued)

	Characteristic 1	Characteristic 2	Characteristic 3
Types of Evidence	Honest (to others and to oneself)	Trustworthy and Dependable	Fair and Selfless
Negation	Not cheating, plagiarizing, or accepting an unfair advantage on assignments	Not gossiping or divulging confidentialities Not missing appointments or failing to complete assignments	Not hoarding resources or dominating classroom discussions, not sabotaging or undermining others
Comparison/ Analogy	Like holding water in our hands, if we open our fingers slightly, the whole truth escapes	Like the clocks in Geneva, people of integrity have a consistency against which all others are measured	Like people who donate money rather than spending it, those who put others ahead of themselves will see a kindness returned to them

However, simply listing evidence or synonyms will not fully develop your definition argument. As a final step, you must explain that evidence and connect it to your line of reasoning and your thesis. Each piece of evidence should be accompanied by several sentences that make connections. To think of it another way, your audience should not have to guess why you have included a particular anecdote, analogy, or fact. Rather, it should be clear that the line of reasoning and each piece of evidence directly support the thesis. To achieve this unity and coherence throughout the argument, keep returning to the original concept or idea as the definition develops.

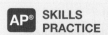 **SKILLS PRACTICE** | CLAIMS AND EVIDENCE
Selecting Purposeful Evidence

1. Write a thesis statement for your definition argument that includes your perspective on the concept. You may also choose to include characteristics of the concept.

2. Plan two to four body paragraphs focused on the characteristics of your concept.

3. Choose evidence to support each of your topic sentences and include evidence in each body paragraph.

4. Begin composing your body paragraphs by developing your evidence with commentary and explanation. Be sure to connect the examples to your perspective and ideas.

LANGUAGE AND STYLE Eliminating Ambiguity

AP® Enduring Understanding (STL-1)

The rhetorical situation informs the strategic stylistic choices that writers make.

Precise Word Choice

Perhaps more than any other type of writing, definition arguments require you to choose the most precise words to clarify meaning and express your perspective. So when you revise the argument, consider the attributes that are guiding your line of reasoning. Are these as precise as they can be? Is there any vague, confusing, or ambiguous language? If so, try to choose a more precise word or phrase.

For example, in our definition argument, the line of reasoning includes the quality of *honesty*. To develop this idea, the writer should choose the word that suggests the most suitable connotations (*authenticity? verity? legitimacy?*). The more precise you can make your language, the clearer your perspective will be to your audience.

Honest			
straightforward	blunt	sincere	truthful

Eliminating Ambiguity

To write with clarity, you should revise for common errors with pronouns, modifiers, and diction that can confuse readers. Here are a few mistakes to avoid.

Source of Confusion	Needs Editing	Problem Solved
Unclear pronoun reference (sentence has more than one noun that could be the antecedent)	Mrs. Rodriquez asked Emily to meet her before school for tutorials, but **she** was thirty minutes late. [Who was late?]	Mrs. Rodriquez and Emily had a tutorial appointment before school, but **Mrs. Rodriquez** forgot and arrived thirty minutes late.
Dangling modifier (modified word is missing from the sentence)	To create a positive school environment, **it** becomes important to think of others before oneself. [Who is part of the school environment?]	To be a part of a positive school environment, **students and teachers** should think of others before themselves.

(continued)

Source of Confusion	Needs Editing	Problem Solved
Misplaced modifier (modified word is too far away from the description)	After being caught cheating, **the teacher** asked the student to retake the exam. [The teacher was not cheating.]	After **the student** was discovered cheating, the teacher asked her to retake the exam. or After being caught cheating, **the student** retook the exam for the teacher.
Inflated diction (word choice is too verbose for effective communication)	The school's premier violinist surrendered his reservation for a designated rehearsal chamber to an inferior musician who was endeavoring to perfect her portion of the concerto.	The first chair violinist canceled his time slot for the practice room so that a struggling student could practice longer.

SKILLS PRACTICE

LANGUAGE AND STYLE
Eliminating Ambiguity

1. Revise your argument to include precise language that develops and clarifies your ideas.
2. Eliminate any unclear pronoun references or misplaced modifiers.
3. Revise any vocabulary or syntax that may be unnecessarily complicated or hard to follow. You may want to read your argument aloud to catch these problems: they often become more obvious when you hear them.

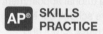

SKILLS PRACTICE

PUTTING IT ALL TOGETHER
Revising and Editing a Definition Argument

Peer-Revision Checklist: Revising and Editing a Definition Argument		
Revising and Editing Checklist	Unit 4 Focus Skills	Comment on the Effectiveness and/or Make a Suggestion
Does the claim in the introduction or conclusion connect the concept to a perspective?	Definition argument	

Is the evidence and commentary organized by attributes or qualities of the concept?	Line of reasoning	
Has the writer developed the definition with effective and appropriate evidence?	Analogies and comparisons	
Has the writer explained the evidence and connected the concept to the perspective? Are these choices effective for the specific audience and purpose?	Developing commentary	
Is the writing clear and specific? Is the diction precise? Is the writing free of error in pronoun references and misplaced and dangling modifiers?	Avoiding ambiguity	
Is the writing free of errors in spelling, usage, punctuation, capitalization, and agreement?	Writing conventions	

```
JUL
JOC
JOC
JOC
JOC
JOL
```
PREPARING FOR THE AP® EXAM

Free-Response Question: Rhetorical Analysis

Writing Commentary

In Unit 1, we examined the two tasks in a rhetorical analysis prompt: (1) describing the writer's message and (2) explaining how the writer conveys that message through his or her rhetorical choices. You also practiced writing thesis statements that connect the message to those choices. Remember that your analysis should focus on a controlling idea that unifies your analysis.

Now, you will prepare to write a full rhetorical analysis. Your rhetorical analysis argument will likely be four to five paragraphs, including

- an introduction that provides rhetorical context and a thesis statement,
- two to three body paragraphs that develop your line of reasoning with evidence and commentary, and
- a conclusion that examines the implications of the text—either by exploring its complexity or situating it within a larger context.

→ **Step One: Annotate the Passage Based on a Unifying Idea**

Remember to read the prompt and passage carefully so that you can situate the passage within a rhetorical context (speaker, audience, occasion). The prompt often includes helpful information about this context. It may also help you identify a unifying idea that will guide the writer's message. As you annotate the passage, you may record ideas and perspectives along the left margin. In the right margin, record the writer's rhetorical choices.

Once you have read a passage and identified its message and rhetorical choices, you will need to present your ideas with a logical line of reasoning. In your analysis, keep big-picture rhetorical choices in mind. Students often mistakenly emphasize the particular devices that a writer uses (e.g., diction, syntax, figurative language, details) over the more overarching strategies (e.g., comparison, contrast, appeals) or purposes for writing.

To avoid focusing strictly on devices, consider the following strategies for annotation.

ANNOTATION STRATEGIES	
Identify a Controlling and Unifying Idea	Highlight the passage in the text where the writer illustrates this controlling or unifying idea.
Look for a Shift or Contrast	Note any shifts. Where in the text is there a shift in tone or perspective?
Look for Comparisons/Contrasts	Note the contrasts that are established.
	Are any elements of the text juxtaposed or placed together to amplify a contrast?
	What comparisons or representations can you find?
Identify Patterns	Identify patterns that relate to the central unifying idea.

Earlier in this unit, you read President Barack Obama's Victory Speech. The examples throughout this workshop use Obama's speech to demonstrate sample responses to the rhetorical analysis prompts.

Once you've annotated the text based on the rhetorical choices, you'll need to identify and describe the writer's claim (unifying idea + perspective). You'll want to answer the following questions:

- What is the unifying or controlling idea of the passage?
- What is the overall purpose of the text?
- What is the writer's message to his or her audience?

For example, in Barack Obama's speech, his unifying idea is *hope for change.* His purpose for the speech is *to address the nation and the world after being elected president.* Finally, his message to his audience is that *Americans have faced challenges in the past, and they are fully capable of meeting new challenges head-on.*

→ **Step Two: Develop a Defensible Claim and a Unified Line of Reasoning**

Once you have annotated the passage and considered the rhetorical situation, you can develop a thesis statement and a line of reasoning to guide your argument. Recall in Unit 1, you examined a few templates to help you develop a defensible thesis statement. Your thesis will connect the text's overall idea and purpose to the writer's choices that convey the message.

Sample Thesis for Barack Obama's Speech:

By juxtaposing historical examples of victory in struggle with an attitude of hope for future victories, Obama asserts that Americans can hope for change when they work together to overcome challenges.

Once your thesis is established, identify the reasons that justify the writer's claim and the strategies the writer employs in the argument. These observations will help you later as you develop your own line of reasoning for your analysis. You'll want to answer the following questions:

- Is there an obvious pattern of organization such as analogy, contrast, juxtaposition, shift, or characterization? What is it?
- What strategies (e.g., appeals, comparison, contrast, irony, organization, emphasis) does the writer use to convey his message?

For example, Barack Obama *contrasts past struggles and challenges with evidence of victories and encouragement for the future.* He also *compares the past struggles Americans faced and overcame to Americans' current struggles to create hope for future victories.*

Think of strategies like different buckets that writers carry: each bucket contains techniques and devices that a writer can use to fulfill the strategy. After you identify the writer's strategies and precisely name these techniques or devices, you must connect these strategies to the writer's purpose. Without this explanation, you are only identifying rhetorical features and not analyzing the passage.

RHETORICAL STRATEGIES	
Strategies	**Techniques and Devices**
Contrast	Irony, juxtaposition, paradox, antithesis, imagery
Comparison	Similes, metaphors, conceits, images, allusion
Logic	Induction, deduction, concession, refutation
Pacing	Sentence structure, flashback, foreshadowing, suspense, pause, variety
Emphasis	Subordination, coordination, cumulative sentence, periodic sentence, rhetorical question, exaggeration, repetition, simple sentence, fragment
Balance	Coordination, parallelism, coordinating conjunctions
Appeal	Evidence, details, allusion, connotation, imagery
Purpose	Narration, cause/effect, comparison/contrast, call to action

Using your annotations of the writer's ideas, message, and **rhetorical strategies**, you can decide how to support your thesis with a line of reasoning. Choose two or more reasons to develop your thesis. These reasons are informed by the writer's unifying idea, message, and rhetorical strategies.

The following reasons support the sample thesis about Barack Obama's speech.

Reason 1: *Obama uses historical references of hardships to inspire hope for victory.*

Reason 2: *Obama connects America's past hardships through comparisons to current struggles that Americans face to create hope for more progress in the future.*

These reasons will become your topic sentences. In this step, remember to keep the writer's unifying idea and big-picture rhetorical strategies in focus. In the previous example, we see the idea of *hope* as a unifying element. Additionally, the line of reasoning follows logically: The first topic sentence highlights the historical references that inspire hope. Then, the second topic sentence builds upon the first to explore how these references lead to a comparison between past and current struggles.

If you keep your focus on these big-picture strategies, you will be able to develop a more effective line of reasoning about them. Make sure to emphasize the overarching "moves" (e.g., comparison, contrast, and logic) over the particular devices that a writer uses (e.g., diction, syntax, figurative language, and details).

→ Step Three: Choose Relevant Evidence

With your thesis and line of reasoning established, you can arrange sufficient and relevant evidence to support each topic sentence. As you support these sentences and develop your commentary, you will want to reflect on the idea in your thesis. Use a graphic organizer (like the following one) to plan your topic sentences, evidence, and commentary.

Thesis (Message + Choices)		
Developing a Body Paragraph	**Reasons**	
IDENTIFY Topic Sentences: Identify the reason (a strategy) and the devices the writer uses to develop that strategy	Strategy: Devices:	Strategy: Devices:
EVIDENCE Textual Evidence: Exemplify the message and identify author choices	Text evidence:	Text evidence:
LINK Provide commentary that connects the choices to the message (idea) by explaining the significance in relation to the claim (idea + perspective)	Commentary:	Commentary:

→ **Step Four: Develop Your Commentary**

Effective **commentary** in rhetorical analysis explains why the writer's choices matter for a particular audience or context. Writers make intentional choices for a specific audience and/or context. When you analyze these choices, you must understand the rhetorical situation (writer, audience, context) and connect it to the writer's choices. Commentary allows you to explain your reasons for connecting evidence to your claim. More importantly, effective writers use commentary to explain the significance of the evidence in relation to their line of reasoning.

Keep in mind: A well-developed paragraph will include more commentary and explanation than direct evidence and quoted material, summary, or paraphrase.

Remember: it is not your job to compliment the writer. Rather, you must explain how the writer makes his or her argument. You will want to avoid writing descriptions like "the writer uses amazing diction," or "the writer incorporates extraordinary syntax." Similarly, avoid overly general or empty comments, such as "this totally gets the reader's attention" or "that really makes the point." Instead, focus specifically on *how* the writer's choice makes an impact. Here is one technique for shifting to commentary: Add the word *because* to the end of your topic sentence followed by an explanation or rationale.

Examine the following examples to see how you can develop commentary from your notes.

Identify: Strategy and Device	Evidence: Textual Support	Link: Evidence and Commentary
Strategy = comparison **Device** = allusion	"despair in the Dust Bowl" "bridge in Selma"	Obama alludes to historical struggles such as the **"despair in the Dust Bowl"** and a **"bridge in Selma"** to show that Americans have faced hardships in the past. He intends to **compare** these historical moments with modern-day struggles. Even though the references are meant to show these past challenges, the president's desired effect is **to provide hope** to his listeners since all of these hardships resulted in improvement and a new sense of purpose for America. Obama reminds citizens that although their current hardships seem overwhelming, Americans can overcome any obstacles by staying **hopeful**.

INSIDER AP® TIP

Strategies and devices are not the same thing. Develop your line of reasoning and paragraphs based on the writer's strategies rather than structuring paragraphs that merely illustrate rhetorical devices. Devices are more concrete techniques (e.g., similes, allusions, diction, repetition, antithesis), while strategies are *how* writers achieve an effect (e.g., comparison, historical references, balance, contrast). Writers use devices to support their strategies.

PREPARING FOR THE AP® EXAM

The following prompt is an example of a rhetorical analysis free-response question. You may recall that in Unit 1, you practiced the first steps of this process by selecting your evidence. Now, you will write a full rhetorical analysis. Use what you have learned in this workshop to respond to the following prompt.

Prompt:

In June 2019, Ta-Nehisi Coates testified at a hearing of a subcommittee of the House Judiciary on reparations for slavery. Read the speech carefully. Write an essay that analyzes the rhetorical choices Coates makes to convey his message: that America owes a debt to African Americans for their contribution to the collective wealth of our country.

In your response, you should do the following:

- Respond to the prompt with a thesis that analyzes the writer's rhetorical choices.
- Select and use evidence to develop and support your line of reasoning.
- Explain how the evidence supports your line of reasoning.
- Demonstrate an understanding of the rhetorical situation.
- Use appropriate grammar and punctuation in your argument.

Testimony before the House Judiciary Committee

Ta-Nehisi Coates

Yesterday, when asked about reparations, Senate Majority Leader Mitch McConnell offered a familiar reply: America should not be held liable for something that happened 150 years ago, since none of us currently alive are responsible.

This rebuttal proffers a strange theory of governance, that American accounts are somehow bound by the lifetime of its generations. But well into this century, the United States was still paying out pensions to the heirs of Civil War soldiers. We honor treaties that date back some 200 years, despite no one being alive who signed those treaties. Many of us would love to be taxed for the things we are solely and individually responsible for. But we are American citizens, and thus bound to a collective enterprise that extends beyond our individual and personal reach. It would seem ridiculous to dispute invocations of the Founders, or the Greatest Generation, on the basis of a lack of membership in either group. We recognize our lineage as a generational trust, as inheritance. And the real dilemma posed by reparations is just that: a dilemma of inheritance.

It is impossible to imagine America without the inheritance of slavery. As historian Ed Baptist has written, enslavement, quote, "shaped every crucial aspect of the economy and politics" of America, so that by 1836 more than $600 million, or almost half of the economic activity in the United States, derived directly or indirectly from the cotton produced by the million-odd slaves. By the time the enslaved were emancipated, they comprised the largest single asset in America — $3 billion in 1860 dollars, more than all the other assets in the country combined.

The method of cultivating this asset was neither gentle cajoling nor persuasion, but torture, rape and child trafficking. Enslavement reigned for 250 years on these shores. When it ended, this country could have extended its hallowed principles — life, liberty and the pursuit of happiness — to all, regardless of color. But America had other principles in mind. And so, for a century after the Civil War, black people were subjected to a relentless campaign of terror, a campaign that extended well into the lifetime of Majority Leader McConnell.

It is tempting to divorce this modern campaign of terror, of plunder, from enslavement. But the logic of enslavement, of white supremacy, respects no such borders, and the god of bondage was lustful and begat many heirs — coup d'états and convict leasing, vagrancy laws and debt peonage, redlining and racist G.I. bills, poll taxes and state-sponsored terrorism.

We grant that Mr. McConnell was not alive for Appomattox. But he was alive for the electrocution of George Stinney. He was alive for the blinding of Isaac Woodard. He was alive to witness kleptocracy in his native Alabama and a regime premised on electoral theft. Majority Leader McConnell cited civil rights legislation yesterday, as well he should, because he was alive to witness the harassment, jailing and betrayal of those responsible for that legislation by a government sworn to protect them. He was alive for the redlining of Chicago and the

5

looting of black homeowners of some $4 billion. Victims of that plunder are very much alive today. I am sure they'd love a word with the majority leader.

What they know, what this committee must know, is that while emancipation dead-bolted the door against the bandits of America, Jim Crow wedged the windows wide open. And that is the thing about Senator McConnell's "something." It was 150 years ago. And it was right now.

The typical black family in this country has one-tenth the wealth of the typical white family. Black women die in childbirth at four times the rate of white women. And there is, of course, the shame of this land of the free boasting the largest prison population on the planet, of which the descendants of the enslaved make up the largest share.

The matter of reparations is one of making amends and direct redress, but it is also a question of citizenship. In H.R. 40, this body has a chance to both make good on its 2009 apology for enslavement and reject fair-weather patriotism, to say that a nation is both its credits and its debits, that if Thomas Jefferson matters, so does Sally Hemings, that if D-Day matters, so does Black Wall Street, that if Valley Forge matters, so does Fort Pillow, because the question really is not whether we will be tied to the somethings of our past, but whether we are courageous enough to be tied to the whole of them. Thank you.

Address at the Groundbreaking Ceremony of the U.S. Diplomacy Center

Colin Powell

1 Thank you, Patrick, and thank you, ladies and gentlemen. It's a great pleasure to be with you this afternoon on this memorable occasion.

2 Another memorable occasion was my first day as Secretary of State. And I was sitting in my office, and one of the senior members of the staff came in and closed the door and said, "Sir, I have to ask you something, and a lot of confusion in the building." I said, "What's wrong?" He said, "Well, what do we call you? Do we call you General[1] or Mr. Secretary?" And I said, "By all means, it's Mr. Secretary. Now drop and give me ten." He almost did. I had to stop him, you know.

3 Another question I've always gotten for many, many years now has to do with the connection between my time as Chairman [of the Joint Chiefs of Staff] and my time as Secretary of State. And they say, "Is the leadership challenge the same? Was it the same?" And the answer is two different organizations, two different cultures, two different histories, two different, but complementary jobs that the military and the Department of State do.

4 But there's one thing they have in common: They are manned by volunteers.[2] They're manned by people in our Foreign Service,[3] in our Civil Service, and our Foreign Service nationals, people who volunteer to serve their nation both in the military and in the Department of State. They want to have a vision; they want to have a purpose: Why are we doing this? How does this serve the interests of the American people? How does this serve the interest of freedom and democracy around the world? How do we help the world?

5 They want to be taken care of. They want to make sure they get all the resources needed to get the job done. And above all, both of these, soldiers and statesmen, want to make sure that they are serving the country to the best of their ability. They're people of courage, people of competence, people who want to make sure the American people are safe and that we're trying to bring safety to as many people in the world as we possibly can.

6 If you walk out the front of this building and go down the hill, the first memorial you'll come

---

[1]Prior to becoming Secretary of State in 2001, Powell served thirty-five years in the military, rising to become a four-star general and chairman of the Joint Chiefs of Staff, the group of high-ranking officers from the different branches of the military who advise the president and other leaders.

[2]This term is used here to refer to someone who is paid for their work but who does that work voluntarily without being forced, as opposed to someone who volunteers their time without pay.

[3]Government organization focused on representing the United States to other countries.

to is the Vietnam Wall. If you continue across the Mall,[4] you'll then see the Korean War Memorial, and then up the Reflecting Pool, at the other end, you'll see the World War II Memorial. And in the distance, you'll see the Marine Memorial. You'll see the Navy Memorial further up the Mall. You'll see all sorts of recognition to those men and women I was privileged to serve with as a soldier and as chairman to the Joint Chiefs of Staff.

7   And you can do this all over this city, but you will never see anything until this moment — until this program — that pays tribute to the men and women of the Department of State: the diplomats, the Foreign Service officers, the political appointees, all of the others — Civil Service included and Foreign Service — nationals who do such a great job for this Department.

8   What do they do? Through diplomacy, we do everything we can to prevent wars. We do everything we can to stop wars or bring conflict to an end. We help after wars to rebuild the societies and economies of our former enemies. We execute treaties. We negotiate treaties and get them ratified, treaties that reduce arms or bring a peaceful level of action to different parts of the world.

9   We spread our values throughout the world — without lecturing — just by showing ourselves as a successful nation and demonstrating our values system. We execute trade negotiations and treaties which benefit us. We focus on human rights, on health, the environment. We talk to friends and adversaries, and we work with adversaries to make sure they do not become enemies.

10   This is vital work. This is work that is the best interest of the nation.

11   We talk about all the ambassadors and other diplomats we have, but my favorite Foreign

Service person is the young, in his first tour, her first tour, consular office — in some consular office somewhere in the world. This is America to the rest of the world, that person at the window. And when somebody comes up and asks for help or says "I want to go to America," it's that young person in their first tour who paves the way and gives a face to the American people to the people wanting to know more about America, wanting to come here.

12   And so we should be so proud of what these men and women have done over the years. It is only fitting, proper, and timely they get this kind of recognition through the U.S. Diplomacy Center, where we can demonstrate all that they have done and let it take its rightful place among all the other monuments and memorials and tributes that exist throughout this city.

1. In the context of the passage as a whole, paragraphs 1–3 serve to
   (A) establish a contrast between the two different organizations so that the speaker can explain why that contrast is so important.
   (B) identify factors that create contrasts between the two organizations so the speaker can then provide a critique of those organizations.
   (C) express the speaker's concerns about the different positions he has held so that he can then focus on the common good that each position allowed him to accomplish.
   (D) orient the audience to a comparison between the two different organizations so that the speaker can then focus on what they have in common.
   (E) define the role of volunteers in the two different organizations so that the speaker can then celebrate those volunteers and their contributions.

[4]The National Mall, the grassy area in Washington, D.C., that is home to a number of monuments and memorials.

2. In the context of the passage as a whole, the last sentence in paragraph 9 ("We talk to friends . . . enemies.") serves as
   (A) an argument for allowing nonelected officials to serve in the Foreign Service and Civil Service.
   (B) a reminder of what can be lost if a Foreign Service and Civil Service volunteer makes a mistake.
   (C) commentary on the relationships between the United States and other adversarial nations.
   (D) an example of how Foreign Service and Civil Service volunteers focus on human rights as a priority.
   (E) evidence that the work done by these Foreign Service and Civil Service volunteers is sometimes difficult and dangerous.

3. Which of the following best describes the function of paragraphs 8 through 11?
   (A) They combine to define the roles of these volunteers.
   (B) They create a contrast between the State Department and the Joint Chiefs of Staff.
   (C) They demonstrate the need for more people to volunteer for the Foreign Service and Civil Service.
   (D) They explain the need for the U.S. Diplomacy Center.
   (E) They describe the personality necessary to be a successful Foreign Service or Civil Service volunteer.

4. In the context of the passage as a whole, the questions, commentary, examples, and explanations provided in paragraphs 8–11 serve to
   (A) engage anyone who would argue about the roles those volunteers play as he tries to support their work.
   (B) assert his knowledge of those people and their work so that the audience will trust him more.
   (C) support the decision to build the U.S. Diplomacy Center in the heart of Washington, D.C.
   (D) generalize about the personalities of those volunteers.
   (E) appeal to the common values and interests of the American people, whom those volunteers represent.

5. Which of the following best describes the function of the second half of the last sentence ("where we can . . . throughout this city") in the context of the passage as a whole?
   (A) It suggests that there are certain limitations to how we can celebrate the work and sacrifice of those who have not given their lives for their country.
   (B) It means to leave the audience with the impression that the U.S. Diplomacy Center has a fitting place among the monuments in Washington, D.C.
   (C) It restates the speaker's celebration of volunteers who commit themselves to the success and safety of the United States.
   (D) It celebrates the successes of the people of Washington, D.C., in maintaining such beautiful and meaningful memorials and monuments.
   (E) It allows the audience to understand why the U.S. Diplomacy Center had to exist.

6. Which of the following does NOT occur as an aspect of the speaker's line of reasoning?
   (A) Establish the grandeur and appropriateness of the setting in Washington, D.C.
   (B) Explain Foreign and Civil Service volunteers' needs and wants.
   (C) Describe who he is and why he has been invited to speak.
   (D) Define the important roles of Foreign and Civil Service volunteers.
   (E) Narrow focus onto volunteers for Foreign and Civil Services.

7. The speaker makes use of narrative when describing
   (A) his greeting and acknowledgment (paragraph 1).
   (B) his first day as Secretary of State (paragraphs 2 and 3).
   (C) the needs and wants of the volunteers (paragraphs 4 and 5).
   (D) the monuments and memorials of Washington, D.C. (paragraph 6).
   (E) the importance of Foreign Service and Civil Service volunteers (paragraph 8).

8. Which of the following quotations best represents the thesis statement of the speech?
   (A) "They want to have a vision; they want to have a purpose: Why are we doing this? How does this serve the interests of the American people? How does this serve the interest of freedom and democracy around the world? How do we help the world?" (paragraph 4, sentence 3).
   (B) "They're people of courage, people of competence, people who want to make sure the American people are safe and that we're trying to bring safety to as many people in the world as we possibly can" (paragraph 5, sentence 4).
   (C) "We focus on human rights, on health, the environment. We talk to friends and adversaries, and we work with adversaries to make sure they do not become enemies" (paragraph 9, sentence 3).
   (D) "This is America to the rest of the world, that person at the window" (paragraph 11, sentence 2).
   (E) "It is only fitting, proper, and timely they get this kind of recognition through the U.S. Diplomacy Center, where we can demonstrate all that they have done and let it take its rightful place among all the other monuments and memorials and tributes that exist throughout this city" (paragraph 12, sentence 2).

9. The speaker is primarily concerned
    with addressing which of the following
    issues?
    (A) The necessity of honoring and
        celebrating volunteers for the Foreign
        Service and Civil Service.
    (B) The importance of placing the U.S.
        Diplomacy Center in Washington, D.C.
    (C) The dangerous yet critical work done by
        the Foreign Service and Civil Service.
    (D) Distinguishing between the Joint Chiefs
        of Staff and the State Department.
    (E) Explaining the role of Foreign Service
        and Civil Service volunteers.

PREPARING FOR THE AP® EXAM
Multiple-Choice Questions: Writing

The passage below is a draft.

(1) For some Americans, one-quarter to one-third of what they make in their paychecks goes directly to local, state, or federal taxes. (2) Interestingly, however, the United States did not officially have "income taxes" until just over one hundred years ago with the ratification of the Sixteenth Amendment in 1913. (3) That means that the country grew and found success for over one hundred years without collecting money from the hard-earned wages of its citizens. (4) Once income taxes were constitutional law, the government immediately began spending working citizens' tax dollars on programs that rewarded those who wouldn't work, and to this day, too many people are allowed to draw money from the government without working. (5) Supporting those who cannot work undermines the values on which America was founded and on which it grew to such prominence.

(6) When people were not able to draw unemployment support from the government, a lot more people were willing and able to find work to do. (7) For example, just a generation ago, there were a number of jobs employing Americans — farm jobs, hard labor, etc. — that today are filled by immigrant labor because many Americans who would have filled those positions began to think they could do just as well financially by drawing unemployment. (8) And it is the tax dollars of working Americans and the tax dollars collected from those immigrant paychecks that pay for Americans not to do the jobs immigrants now do.

(9) This argument is not meant as an indictment of immigrant labor: immigrants work hard at jobs many Americans won't do. (10) Instead, this means to call attention to the failures of a system that supports those who won't work on the backs of those who will. (11) Using taxes paid by working people to support people who won't work is an insult to those workers. (12) Until this system is changed, an entire generation of people will learn to rely on others who work and not themselves.

1. The writer wants to add a sentence after sentence 1 to provide factual support for the claim and focus the audience on the foundation of the argument. Which of the following sentences best accomplishes this purpose?

   (A) Daniel J. Mitchel at the CATO Institute argues that the government doesn't spend as much on welfare as it appears but only because a good chunk of it is lost to fraud and misspending.

   (B) The IRS reports that income tax avoidance plots are nothing but "schemes [that] have evolved into sophisticated arrangements to give the appearance that taxpayers are not in control of their money."

   (C) The Senate budget office reports that welfare programs cost more than $1 trillion yearly.

   (D) The Urban Institute has reported that each year, the government spends nearly as much on public education as on unemployment and other welfare programs.

   (E) According to the Heritage Foundation, for the average household, income taxes amount to giving the government $20,000 every year, on which they see little return.

2. The writer is considering adding the following sentence before sentence 4.

Many people would define income tax as money taken by the government only to support working people and businesses by keeping roads safe and securing other things that help commerce.

Should the writer make this addition?

(A) Yes, because the sentence explains something with which many readers will likely be unfamiliar.
(B) Yes, because in defining income taxes, it also creates a lead-in to the argument of the passage by stating what many believe income taxes are used for.
(C) No, because the writer should assume the readers' knowledge and not appear patronizing to them.
(D) No, because the sentence makes a generalization that is impossible to prove without government statistics or independent survey data.
(E) No, because it assumes too much regarding working people and businesses in the United States.

3. The writer is considering revising the underlined portion of sentence 4 (reproduced below) to better appeal to the intended audience's emotions and values.

Once income taxes were constitutional law, the government immediately began spending working citizens' tax dollars on *programs that rewarded those who wouldn't work, and to this day, too many people are allowed to draw money from the government without working.*

Which of the following would be the best revision of the underlined portion?

(A) (as it is now)
(B) using working citizens' tax dollars on
(C) allocating working citizens' tax dollars for
(D) wasting working citizens' tax dollars on
(E) reserving working citizens' tax dollars on

4. Which version of sentence 5 (reproduced below) provides the most effective thesis statement for the passage?

Supporting those who cannot work undermines the values on which America was founded and on which it grew to such prominence.

(A) (As it is now)
(B) Using the wages of working citizens to support those who refuse to work undermines the values on which America was founded and on which it grew to such prominence.
(C) Taking from tax dollars to support those who cannot work undermines the initial reasons for income taxes.
(D) Tax dollars are meant only to protect those who pay taxes.
(E) Contrary to popular belief, relying on tax dollars to support immigrants, whether they work or not, ignores the initial reasons for collecting those taxes.

5. The writer is considering deleting the underlined portion of sentence 9 (reproduced below), adjusting punctuation as needed to better maintain the line of reasoning.

This argument is not meant as an indictment of immigrant labor: immigrants work hard at jobs many Americans won't do.

Should the writer delete this underlined portion?

(A) Yes, immigrants are not a part of the argument.
(B) Yes, this draws too much attention to an unessential part of the argument and detracts from the line of reasoning.
(C) No, immigrant labor is a different kind of labor that should not be considered here.
(D) No, this helps to strengthen the contrast between those who will work and those who won't in this argument.
(E) No, this helps create a more cohesive connection with the previous paragraph.

6. The writer is considering deleting sentence 11 (reproduced below).

Using taxes paid by working people to support people who won't work is an insult to those workers.

Should the writer delete this sentence?

(A) Yes, because it will bring sentences 10 and 12 closer together to emphasize the conclusive call for a change in the system that supports people who don't work with the taxes of those who do.

(B) Yes, because it develops an argument about immigrants that diverges from the central line of reasoning.

(C) Yes, because the comment about insulting those who do work does not match the tone of the rest of the passage.

(D) No, because it reiterates the dependent relationship between immigrant labor and Americans who will not work.

(E) No, because it connects the idea of the "failures of a system" in sentence 10 with the needed change in the system in sentence 12 to bring the passage to a conclusion and call the reader to act accordingly.

Mike Ehrmann/Getty Images

UNIT

5

Creating Coherence

ime lapse photographs, like the one shown here, take a series of rapid photos so that (in this example) audiences can see — and understand — how a skier's move develops step-by-step. Writers use a similar process when making arguments: they lay out a series of points that proceed logically from one to the next. Along with the writer's other choices, including syntax and effective transitions, these elements of organization and style come together to create coherence. Coherence makes arguments much easier for audiences to follow and comprehend. In other words, it helps writers achieve their purpose. What other processes or creative forms (like music) must progress in a coherent way to work effectively?

UNIT GOALS

	Unit Focus	Reading, Analyzing, and Interpreting	Writing
Big Idea: Rhetorical Situation	The Writer's Exigence	Describe the writer's exigence for an argument.	Respond to an issue that motivates you.
Big Idea: Claims and Evidence	Unity and Coherence	Describe how information and evidence are related to the writer's claim, and explain how the writer unifies the argument.	Use transitions and verbs to convey the relationship between and among reasons and evidence.
Big Idea: Reasoning and Organization	Exposition: Causal Argument	Explain how a writer develops an idea through cause and effect.	Write an argument developed through cause and effect.
Big Idea: Language and Style	Syntax for Emphasis	Explain how a writer uses subordination and coordination to emphasize ideas and information.	Use subordination and coordination to emphasize ideas and information.
Ideas in American Culture	• Place and Values • Opportunity and Oppression	Analyze how the ideas of place, values, opportunity, and oppression are reflected in classic and contemporary American texts.	
Preparing for the AP® Exam	• Free Response: Argument • Multiple Choice	Analyze rhetorical choices in classic and contemporary nonfiction texts.	Develop a line of reasoning that creates coherence and unity.

The Writer's Exigence

 Enduring Understanding (RHS-1)

Individuals write within a particular situation and make strategic writing choices based on that situation.

KEY POINT

Writers are inspired or provoked by events and other external factors.

In the last unit, you learned that writers have purposes for the texts that they create. This purpose is informed by the writer's exigence or motivation. To achieve this purpose, the writer must arrange information in a logical and coherent way so that the reader understands the message. In this unit, we'll focus on understanding what motivates a writer to compose an argument.

Consider the following examples:

- A new school policy restricts your right to free speech.
- A person earns your respect through hard work and dedication.
- You and your community are grieving a tragic injustice.

Each of these scenarios (among countless other possibilities) could motivate you to respond. These events — and your feelings about them — would be your exigence.

Writers Are Compelled to Create

Recall that in the rhetorical situation, the exigence is like the lightning bolt that sparks a writer to create a text. The exigence could be an event, a memory, another text, or any other provocation that spurs a writer to achieve a purpose for an audience within a specific **context**. When writers engage with or respond to an exigence, they make a rhetorical act authentic to both their audience and themselves. Moreover, the exigence can allow the text's meaning to extend beyond the rhetorical situation.

The situation that motivated the writer to take a stand or have an opinion on a subject or issue is the writer's **exigence**. The **message** is the writer's **position** or stance on the subject. But keep in mind that a writer's position and the writer's **perspective** are not the same. The perspective is a lens through which a writer sees and understands the exigence. The writer's perspective is informed by his or her individual background, values, and interests. Two different writers may have the same position on an idea, but their perspectives (that is, how they interpret whatever is inspiring them to write) can differ based on a writer's individual experience.

Connecting Exigence, Purpose, and Audience

As exigence motivates the writer, it is also directly connected to the writer's purpose. But exigence is also linked to the audience. Consider these examples again:

- A new school policy restricts your right to free speech.
- A person earns your respect through hard work and dedication.
- You and your community are grieving a tragic injustice.

For the first example, if the writer was provoked by the school's new speech restrictions, he or she may intend to persuade school administrators to reverse their policy. Alternatively, the writer could be addressing his or her peers with the **purpose** of organizing a protest against the policy. For the second example, a writer trying to honor another person could compose a speech that celebrates the subject's life or work. Alternatively, the speech could be written to motivate others to uphold the values of hard work and dedication embodied by the person. For the final example, a writer might compose a speech that raises awareness of an injustice and calls on the audience to hold the responsible parties accountable.

Understanding Exigence and Context

Because the exigence of a text is situated within the **context**, readers must know the writer's time, place, and occasion to accurately understand the writer's exigence.

But identifying a writer's exigence may be difficult for several reasons:

- You are not part of the intended audience.
- You are unfamiliar with the writer's culture and time period.
- You are unfamiliar with the writer's subject or issue.
- The text is unclear or confusing.

Indeed, unless a writer states their exigence or purpose directly, readers must infer the following from the text:

- The writer's role(s)
- The writer's motivation
- The writer's relationship to the audience
- The writer's relationship to the subject or issue

Readers infer this information by interpreting textual clues provided by the writer. Sometimes, the writer communicates exigence in the introduction, along with the thesis. Remember that a thesis indicates a controlling idea and perspective, which are motivated by the writer's exigence.

But the exigence is much more than the time, place, and occasion for a text. Rather, it is the key to understanding the writer's purpose, audience, and message.

INSIDER AP® TIP

Texts come from authentic contexts. Exigence is determined through an inference about the writer and his or her relationship to the audience and the issue.

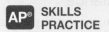

AP® SKILLS PRACTICE | **RHETORICAL SITUATION**
Describing Exigence

Consider the following scenarios and connect your exigence with purpose, audience, and message.

	Scenario A	Scenario B
	An issue or situation that angered or provoked you	A situation or event where you felt gratitude or inspiration
What is the exigence?		
What is the issue?		
What is your position, perspective, and message?		
What is your goal?		
Who will you communicate with to achieve your goal?		
How will you communicate your message?		

MTV Video Music Awards Speech
P!NK

Laura Cavanaugh/Getty Images

THE TEXT IN CONTEXT

After receiving the Michael Jackson Video Vanguard award at the 2017 MTV Video Music Awards, P!NK (b. 1979) delivered the following powerful and memorable speech. The singer was addressing her daughter, but her resounding message about identity, self-acceptance, and beauty resonated with a much wider audience. P!NK continues to advocate for the Human Rights Campaign, the LGBTQ community, UNICEF, Save the Children, and other causes and organizations.

AP® SKILLS PRACTICE | RHETORICAL SITUATION
Describing Exigence

Before you read P!NK's speech, identify her exigence by considering the following questions. As you read, consider how her exigence is related to her overall purpose.

Determining the Writer's Exigence	
What is the context of the speech?	
What is the writer's role in this context?	
What is the writer's relationship to the audience?	
What is the writer's relationship to the issue?	
The Writer's Purpose	

MTV Video Music Awards Speech

"I know I don't have a lot of time, but if I may tell you a quick story. Recently, I was driving my daughter to school and she said to me, out of the blue, 'Mama?' I said, 'Yes, baby?' She said, 'I'm the ugliest girl I know.' And I said, 'Huh?' And she was like, 'Yeah, I look like a boy with long hair.' And my brain went to, 'Oh my god, you're six. Why? Where is this coming from? Who said this? Can I kick a 6-year-old's ass, like what?'

"But I didn't say anything. Instead I went home and I made a PowerPoint presentation for her. And in that presentation were androgynous rockstars and artists that live their truth, are probably made fun of every day of their life, and carry on, wave their flag and inspire the rest of us. And these are artists like Michael Jackson and David Bowie and Freddie Mercury and Annie Lennox and Prince and Janis Joplin and George Michael, Elton John, so many artists—her eyes glazed over. But then I said, 'You know, I really want to know why you feel this way about yourself.' And she said, 'Well I look like a boy,' and I said, 'Well what do you think I look like?' And she said, 'Well you're beautiful.' And I was like, 'Well, thanks. But when people make fun of me, that's what they use. They say I look like a boy or I'm too masculine or I have too many opinions, my body is too strong.'

"And I said to her, 'Do you see me growing my hair?' She said, 'No, Mama.' I said, 'Do you see me changing my body?' 'No, Mama.' 'Do you see me changing the way I present myself to the world?' 'No, Mama.' 'Do you see me selling out arenas all over the world?' 'Yes,

Mama.' 'OK! So, baby girl. We don't change. We take the gravel and the shell and we make a pearl. And we help other people to change so they can see more kinds of beauty.' And to all the artists here, I'm so inspired by all of you. Thank you for being your true selves and for lighting the way for us. I'm so inspired by you guys. There's so much rad s--- happening in music. And keep doing it. Keep shining for the rest of us to see.

"And you, my darling girl, are beautiful, and I love you."

RHETORICAL SITUATION

1. What is P!NK's **exigence**? How does this exigence support her **message** within the **context**?

2. Could P!NK's speech have multiple **audiences**? If so, whom might she be addressing? What is her **message** for each of those audiences?

3. What is P!NK's **position** on the subject? What is her **perspective** on the subject? How are these revealed in her **claim**?

4. Consider that the **context** of this speech was a music awards ceremony. How does the speaker's relationship with the **audience** affect her **message**?

5. How does the inclusion of personal testimony as evidence contribute to the speech's **appeal**?

Unity and Coherence

 Enduring Understanding (CLE-1)
Writers guide understanding of a text's lines of reasoning and claims through that text's organization and integration of evidence.

You've already learned that an argument is unified when each part of the text functions to convey the writer's claim (idea and perspective). That means that the writer

- justifies the claim with reasons and
- supports the reasons with relevant and sufficient evidence.

    But in addition to being unified, an effective argument must be coherent too.

> **KEY POINT**
> Writers reveal their purpose in their arrangement of reasons and evidence, as well as in their choice of transitions.

Writers Lead Readers

To achieve **coherence**, writers need to organize their reasons and evidence logically. But they must also present their argument in a way that shows readers how its various ideas and elements fit together.

Imagine that you come upon a table with hundreds of puzzle pieces on it. You see that the colorful puzzle pieces follow patterns and could compose a picture, but you have one problem: the box is nowhere in sight. So you start looking for the pieces with corners and straight edges to start the framework. After you establish the outline, you develop the inside of the picture by identifying the patterns in the way the pieces connect with each other. After a while, a picture starts to emerge, and after every piece is arranged, the puzzle makes perfect sense. Remember: You had all the elements of the puzzle at the beginning of the process, but it only became meaningful and coherent after it was assembled.

Writers do something similar when creating a text: the exigence prompts them to communicate a message and achieve a purpose. Writers start with their ideas and evidence in a pile. They establish their line of reasoning, which works like a frame or outline for the rest of the text. Then, by stitching together carefully selected evidence, writers develop the argument until, eventually, every word, sentence, and paragraph contributes to the overall message (like the completed puzzle picture).

Arrangement

We call the ordering of reasons and evidence within an argument its **arrangement**. Good writers are mindful about how they arrange the elements of their texts. That is because the arrangement must suit a writer's purpose, claims, and message. For example, a writer explaining how a caterpillar transforms into a butterfly may use chronological order: this arrangement matches the sequence of the transformation.

In contrast, a writer urging people to vote may arrange the argument so that the most important reason appears first. In other words, it is important to present reasons and details strategically.

A writer's audience can influence the arrangement of an argument — especially if it is a targeted audience. For example, if a writer knows that an audience is likely to be skeptical, he or she may arrange reasons and evidence in a way that builds toward a thesis at the conclusion. This arrangement uses **inductive organization**, which you learned about in Unit 2 (along with **deductive organization**). When you read arguments, consider why the writer has chosen a particular method of arrangement or a specific form of logical development. In many cases, the audience will be a key factor.

As you learned in Unit 3, writers use **transitions** to communicate the relationships between sentences and paragraphs. Transitional words and phrases also help guide the audience through the writer's line of reasoning. Strategically chosen transitions clarify the text's arrangement and help establish the text's coherence. Also, keep in mind that writers use transitions between pieces of evidence, as well as between sentences and paragraphs.

INSIDER
AP® TIP

Everything must connect. Good writers know their controlling idea and ensure that every reason and every piece of evidence is logically connected to that controlling idea. Avoid assuming that that your reasoning is obvious to your audience.

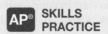 **AP® SKILLS PRACTICE** | **CLAIMS AND EVIDENCE**
Arranging Evidence for Coherence

Consider the following purposes and audiences as a writer. What method would you use to arrange your reasons and evidence? Why?

Purpose and Audience	Method of Arrangement	Rationale
You're telling an entertaining story to your best friend.		
You're writing a proposal to gain permission from the principal to start a new school club.		
You're creating a podcast episode on the effects of climate change for your local community.		
You're explaining the effects of a health issue in an academic paper for your health teacher.		
You're describing a place that you visited on a trip.		

ARRANGING REASONS AND EVIDENCE

Arrangement	Function/ Purpose	Methods of Development	Transitions That Indicate Relationships	
Chronological	Time order Sequence Series of steps	Narrative Process argument Cause-effect	At first Initially Later on Next	Subsequently Last Finally To conclude
Spatial	Position in terms of relative location, space, or geography - nearest to farthest - farthest to nearest	Evaluation Comparison-contrast Cause-effect	In this specific instance On the other hand Further Relative to Above Below Beyond Nearby Inside Outside	
Importance	- least to most - most to least	Persuasion Definition Problem-solution Cause-effect Process	Most notably More importantly Above all Without question Significantly Worst Best of all	
Specificity	- general to specific - specific to general	Definition	To be more specific Generally Specifically For instance Broadly Similarly Correspondingly In order to clarify	
Comparison or Contrast	- subject by subject - characteristic	Evaluation	Similarly Likewise In the same way In contrast On the other hand Conversely However	

He Was Telling a Different Type of Truth
Kendrick Lamar

Kevin Winter/Getty Images

THE TEXT IN CONTEXT

Kendrick Lamar (b. 1987), is one of the most recognized and influential rappers of his generation. Lamar has earned many awards for his music, including thirteen Grammys, six *Billboard* Music Awards, and eleven MTV Video Music Awards, among many others. In 2018, Lamar was awarded a Pulitzer Prize for his hip-hop album, *DAMN*. In the following statement dictated to *Paper* magazine in 2015, Lamar pays tribute to Eazy-E, a rapper from the groundbreaking '80s and '90s group N.W.A. Eazy-E died in 1995.

 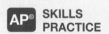

AP® SKILLS PRACTICE | CLAIMS AND EVIDENCE **Analyzing Evidence**

In the following statement, Kendrick Lamar uses transitions to move from point to point. Use the following graphic organizer to identify the transitions Lamar uses and describe the relationships these transitions convey.

Describing Coherence		
Transition and Location	**What Is Revealed about Organization and Arrangement**	**Function and Effect**

He Was Telling a Different Type of Truth

I remember when I was five or six years old, "We Want Eazy" — I think the concept of the video was that he was actually in jail and he had to get to his show and the only way to get to his concert was to film him from jail, and he eventually busted through the jail and came onstage. I remember looking at that video and just feeling like, "Man, this dude feels like an action superhero." Little did I know, Eazy-E came from my same neighborhood in Compton.

My pops would play N.W.A. records all day, every day; my uncles would play it. My older cousins would play it. And I would go outside and see the same imagery in my reality as the things they were talking about on the record. From the way these guys talked to the way they carried themselves to the type of activities that they were involved in, the whole thing was a real-life introspective report from the ghetto. Looking at them and sitting inside my community, it left a big toll on me because it always let me know that no matter how far I go, I gotta stay in reach of the people and what's going on in the neighborhood, whether it's a harsh reality or not.

What made Eazy special was that he was telling a different type of truth, a truth that wasn't heard in music yet. Before them, rap was fun — you had your battles and whatnot, but this time around, when it came to what Eazy wanted to do, being a visionary, he had the idea of speaking the honest truth, and I think it really resonated with a lot of people because it was the shock value of, "Okay, these guys are really standing out and focused on telling their reality, no matter how pissed off you get by it." And it got interest from people. People actually wanted to hear it and wanted to know what was going on.

But as a kid, I really couldn't grasp the idea that the world knew about what we're going through in my neighborhood. I didn't get that idea until my debut album, *good kid, m.A.A.d city*, came out and that's when I truly understood how N.W.A. felt, coming from this small neighborhood but going all the way around the world and seeing these people singing these words lyric-for-lyric and understanding the trials and tribulations that are going on in the community. I understand how they feel now. It's an inspiring thing. Once I got the idea that people are actually listening, it made me want to continue making music more.

Somebody told me this early on: "You're nothing without your own backyard." Period. If my backyard — and my backyard being my city and my county — doesn't believe me, then no one else will. I always remember that. I always kept that in the back of my mind and I think that's exactly what N.W.A. did, and that's why they said they want to make music for the community first, because to have that home love is like nothing else. You can go all the way across the world ten times but when you come back to your city and see the pride and joy in these kids' faces, it's the ultimate feeling. I think that's exactly what they were thinking and it's exactly how I think today.

I wouldn't be here today if it wasn't for Eazy and I wouldn't be able to say the things that I say, talk about my community the way I talk about it, for good or for bad. He's 100% influenced me in terms of really being not only honest with myself, but honest about where I come from and being proud of where I come from.

And it's not just me. Artists today wouldn't be able to talk about the things they talk about if it wasn't for Eazy-E and if it wasn't for gangsta rap. Period. You don't even have to be a gangsta rapper, but the fact that you can be able to talk about your community and some of its harsh realities, that comes from none other than Eazy-E, period. *Period.*

Because before then, everything was pop. People were scared to talk about these kinds of tough situations, but because he and the group took it upon themselves to talk about [these things], every artist is able to and they owe it to him. He's not only the birth of gangsta rap, but he's the birth of a whole legacy of being able to say what you want to say on a record and not being in fear of what others may think and not offending your own art and your own reflection. He'll always live forever, not only fifty years from now but a thousand years from now. His name will always be in people's hearts because he gave people the opportunity and the voice to say what they want and how they feel.

Eazy-E (left) and Dr. Dre (right) from the rap group N.W.A. in 1990. ▶

CLAIMS AND EVIDENCE

1. What is Lamar's **claim**? What reasons does Lamar use to justify his claim?

2. Choose an example of **evidence** that Lamar uses to support one of his reasons. Explain how that evidence functions within Lamar's argument.

3. Find an example where Lamar uses a **transition** to connect his reasons. What transition is used? What does the use of this transition reveal about the relationship between the reasons?

4. Find an example where Lamar connects pieces of **evidence** with a **transition**. What transition is used? What does the use of this transition reveal about the relationship between these pieces of evidence?

5. How does Lamar **arrange** his argument? How do you know?

JUL
JOC
JOC
JOC
JOC
JOC
JOC
JOC
JNC

REASONING AND ORGANIZATION

Exposition: Causal Argument

AP **Enduring Understanding (REO-1)**

Writers make claims about subjects, rely on evidence that supports the reasoning that justifies the claim, and often acknowledge or respond to other possibly opposing arguments.

KEY POINT

Causal arguments are organized by causes, by effects, or by linking cause and effect.

As you've learned in previous units, a writer's purpose drives the organization of an argument. The line of reasoning within an argument helps us understand the writer's purpose as well. For example, the line of reasoning in a process argument is made up of steps or stages. In contrast, a definition argument focuses its line of reasoning on the traits or characteristics of the subject. But in both cases, the line of reasoning and pattern of development unify the essay.

Linking Causes and Effects

Over the past units, you've learned that writers have clear purposes and that these purposes influence the way they organize their arguments. So far, you've learned how to explain a process or define a concept. In this unit, we will consider **causal arguments** or the strategy that writers use to explain **cause-and-effect** relationships.

Statisticians, psychologists, public health experts, political scientists, historians, marketers, and even students like you analyze causal relationships. This type of analysis can explain an event in history, trace the emergence of a cultural trend, or even help predict the spread of a virus. To write cause-and-effect arguments, writers must identify patterns, connections, and relationships in their data and supporting evidence.

Causal arguments are the foundational method of development for nearly every discipline because explaining relationships is the heart of analysis and critical thinking. But we also use cause-and-effect analysis in our everyday conversations, explanations, and debates. For example, a causal argument may analyze the following:

- The implications of a public policy
- The impact of media on politics
- The causes of a historical event
- The benefits of saving or investing money
- The difficulties faced by college athletes

Line of Reasoning in a Causal Argument

In a causal argument, the writer presents an overarching idea as part of the **claim**. In turn, the claim will control the line of reasoning and unify the argument.

When writers explain causal relationships, they have specific goal, such as:

- explain the reasons something came about;
- explain the effects, consequences, or implications of an event or issue;
- link multiple causes with their effects; or
- explain a series of linked events that lead to an event or issue.

As a result, a causal argument's **line of reasoning** or **organization** will likely follow one cause-and-effect relationship, or a series of linked causes and effects.

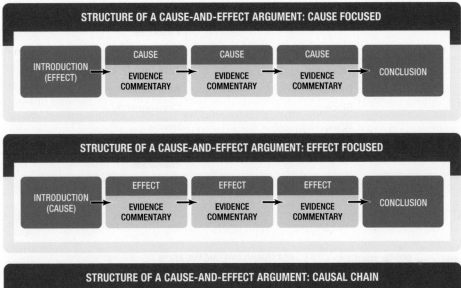

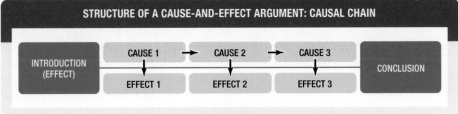

Explaining Cause-and-Effect Relationships

Cause-and-effect relationships can take on many forms. They may be long term or short term. They may be actual or predicted. They may be probable or surprising. But in all cases, writers analyzing these relationships must provide evidence to support their reasoning.

To understand how writers link cause and effect in causal arguments, you'll want to note the verbs and **transitions** that they use to introduce their **commentary** or analysis.

INSIDER AP TIP

Description is not explanation. Analysis must go beyond a summary of contributing factors or preceding events. The writer needs to describe the links and dynamics between causes and effects. Then he or she must explain the larger significance of these causal relationships.

EXPLAINING CAUSE-AND-EFFECT RELATIONSHIPS

	Illustrate Causation	Illustrate Effect
Verbs	Affected	Brings about
	Caused by	Contributes to
	Influenced	Creates
	Initiated	Fosters
	Precipitated	Incites
	Sparked	Leads to
		Produces
		Results in
Transitions	Although	Accordingly
	Because	As a result
	Since	Consequently
	While	Hence
		Inevitably
		Therefore

AP® SKILLS PRACTICE | REASONING AND ORGANIZATION
Organizing by Cause and Effect

1. **Examining Causes.** Think of an event (social, political, natural) that has happened within the last month. What are the likely causes of that event?

Causes		Effect
	Leads to	

2. **Examining Effects.** Now, think of something that is happening right now or within the last two days. What are the likely effects of that event or issue?

Event/Issue		Effects
	Precipitated	

How *Sesame Street* Started a Musical Revolution

Melena Ryzik

THE TEXT IN CONTEXT

Journalist Melena Ryzik reports on cultural and social issues for the *New York Times*. Her reporting has also been featured on CBS News. Along with several *New York Times* colleagues, Ryzik won a 2018 Pulitzer Prize for her reporting on sexual harassment in the workplace. In the following August 22, 2019, *New York Times* article, Ryzik examines the social and cultural relevance of *Sesame Street*, a long-running educational television program for children, in the year of its fiftieth anniversary.

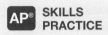 **SKILLS PRACTICE** | REASONING AND ORGANIZATION
Analyzing Causal Arguments

As you read "How *Sesame Street* Started a Musical Revolution," identify the causal factors that Ryzik describes. How do they serve as her line of reasoning?

Analyzing Causal Arguments	
Causes	**Effect**

How *Sesame Street* Started a Musical Revolution

How many ways can you sing about the letter B? On *Sesame Street*, that question has many furry answers.

Since its inception in 1969, the public television show has redefined what it means to teach children through TV, with music as its resounding voice. Before *Sesame Street*, it wasn't even clear that you could do that; once the series began, as a radical experiment that joined educational research and social idealism with the lunacy of puppets and the buoyancy of advertising jingles, it proved that kids are very receptive to a grammar lesson wrapped in a song.

Big-name stars lined up to make guest appearances that have become the stuff of legend (Stevie Wonder and Grover; Loretta Lynn and the Count; Smokey Robinson and a marauding letter U). And long before inclusion was a curriculum goal, *Sesame Street* made a point to showcase Afro-Caribbean rhythms, operatic powerhouses, Latin beats, Broadway showstoppers and bebop alongside its notably diverse cast.

Sesame Street is one of the earliest examples of a musical I experienced," said Lin-Manuel Miranda, who grew up adoring "I Love Trash" and called its singer, Oscar the Grouch, "a character so singular that he changes the way you see the world at large."

"I learned from *Sesame Street* that music is not only incredibly fun, but also an extremely effective narrative and teaching tool," he added in an email. "On top of that, their songs are the closest thing we have to a shared childhood songbook." 5

Miranda began composing for *Sesame* not long after his first Tony win in 2008; his friend Bill Sherman, a fellow Tony winner, became the *Sesame* music director the following year. Today, with online viewership in the hundreds of millions, the series still hosts pop superstars—Janelle Monáe, Romeo Santos, Ed Sheeran, Sia, Katy Perry, Bruno Mars—on the updated streetscape where Nina Simone sang "To Be Young, Gifted and Black" in 1972.

Now, as it marks its 50th anniversary—after 4,526 episodes, not to mention specials, movies, albums and more—the legacy of *Sesame* is clear: It impacted the music world as much as it shaped TV history, inspiring countless fans and generations of artists. And the show is still innovating, finding ever more ways to sing out loud.

Getting to *Sesame Street*

In the late '60s, when Joan Ganz Cooney, a television producer, and Lloyd Morrisett, a psychologist and philanthropy executive, set out to develop *Sesame Street*, their aim was to build school preparedness and narrow the educational gap between lower- and upper-income children. They brought in a Harvard professor for pedagogy advice and borrowed from commercial TV to create memorable characters, including Jim Henson's Muppets.

Research also showed that children were more attuned when they watched with caregivers, so in came the celebrity appearances (on the second episode, James Earl Jones enunciates the alphabet in theatrically sloooow tones) and parodies of songs that mom and dad would know.

The sonic identity of *Sesame Street* had many creators: Jon Stone, the first head writer and a longtime producer and director, helped conceive the theme song, and the writer Jeff Moss (like Stone, an alum of *Captain Kangaroo*) 10 gave us "Rubber Duckie," "The People in Your Neighborhood" and "I Love Trash."

But the person most associated with the show's musical style was its inaugural music director, the classically trained, Harvard-educated composer and jazz pianist Joe Raposo.

In the early years, when *Sesame* did a now unheard-of 130 hourlong episodes a year (it sometimes aired as often as five times a day) Raposo's output was prodigious: He wrote over 3,000 pieces for the show, original compositions that could range from a few seconds to full-blown production numbers.

"He would receive the cans of film from the office, watch them overnight and score them," said his son Nick Raposo.

With a pencil and a legal pad, he wrote "everywhere," his son said, including in taxis, sometimes handing his freshly jotted arrangements off to the music coordinator through the window. The first few seasons were definitely trippy; you could blame the era, or the pace. In those early years, "he was in the studio or on set probably 18 hours a day," Nick Raposo said. "They would just sleep under the mixing board and wake up and start mixing the next day."

(Like many of his early *Sesame* compatriots, 15 including Jim Henson, Joe Raposo died young, in 1989, at 51.)

Music on *Sesame* functioned in three ways: as backing tracks for animation and film clips (a lonely orangutan looking for a zoo playmate, say); as live performances by well-known guest artists; and as songs for the human actors and Muppets to sing. Raposo, who loved Jelly Roll Morton and Chopin, fado and klezmer, wrote "C is for Cookie"—Henson originally developed Cookie Monster for snack commercials—and "Bein' Green," which took on extra poignancy when it was performed by Lena Horne and later Ray Charles, who told puppeteers that he identified with the song's message about getting

comfortable in your own skin, whatever the shade.

Among the *Sesame* breakthroughs was the belief that—in a show that had characters of different ethnicities living in harmonious urban proximity—the music should be multicultural, too. "Joe really pushed for that," said Christopher Cerf, a Harvard classmate who joined him at *Sesame* in 1970 and went on to write hundreds of songs over the next 45 years.

And as the *Sesame* universe expanded, it pulled more and more major musical talent into its orbit. The jazz musician Toots Thielemans, who performed with Benny Goodman, Ella Fitzgerald and Charlie Parker, played harmonica on the theme song. Grace Slick provided vocals for animated counting sequences. The guitarist in the first *Sesame* traveling band was Carlos Alomar, who toured with James Brown and then wrote the riff for David Bowie's "Fame." Alomar's replacement, who was 19 or so and showed up at his audition with a Muppet-esque green-tinged Afro, was Nile Rodgers. It was his first real paying gig as an artist.

Sesame Street was "part of my musical development," said Rodgers, the Chic frontman and Grammy-winning producer.

The harmonies were highly sophisticated.   20 "You got to be a real player to play that stuff," he said. "When we played 'People in Your Neighborhood,' it was almost like we were a fusion band."

Famous Faces in the Neighborhood

The show's first year set the tone for its mission of social and emotional uplift, with folky guests like Pete Seeger and Odetta. But as *Sesame Street* exploded with attention, the pop firmament rolled in. In 1973, Stevie Wonder arrived as an episode-long musical guest, to teach Grover about vocal dynamics. With his full band on set, he performed "Superstition" live to an audience of children—not professional actors—head-banging and playing maracas in their '70s acrylics. It quickly became one of TV's iconic musical moments.

By then, "You really could approach almost anyone and have a shot at getting them to come on," said Cerf, the longtime songwriter. "And people started to call us, especially celebrities who had just had kids."

In his first appearance, in 1973, Johnny Cash brought his young son to the taping—and in the '90s returned with his granddaughter and daughter Rosanne Cash. Throughout the late '70s and '80s, the artists that graced the *Sesame* stoop were a crossover with the Billboard charts: Carly Simon, Linda Ronstadt (doing a mariachi number!), Diana Ross, Paul Simon (upstaged by a little girl), Billy Joel. In the '90s and 2000s, there was Celine Dion, the Dixie Chicks and Destiny's Child.

For generations of children watching at home or at school, the message was that even world-famous stars could be accessible. "No one was too big for *Sesame Street*, which made it so cool," said Patrick Stump, the Fall Out Boy frontman, who credited the show with invigorating his curiosity about music and more. Norah Jones vividly recalled Cab Calloway's 1981 performance, in white tie and tails, of a Muppet call-and-response "Hi-De-Ho" as "definitely the first time I saw any jazz musicians."

The show remained committed to spot-lighting artists who might not be familiar to mainstream audiences. The jazz percussionist Max Roach appeared in 2000; the Latin queen Celia Cruz in 1987.

And there was always room for classical stars, often repeat visitors. The violinist Itzhak Perlman made several appearances in the '80s, and still gets recognized from them. Because the show mixed music so seamlessly with other segments, "it became a classical pill that was very easy to swallow," he said. (Perlman, who has used crutches since he had childhood polio, also took part in an influential 1981 segment that addressed his physical difference.)

Lang, the star pianist from China, began watching the show at 15, when he first came to the U.S.—precisely because he saw people like Perlman on it. He was invited to appear early in his career, and considered it a crossover coup. *Sesame*, he said, connected classical music to kids' everyday lives, in a way that stripped it of its highbrow connotation.

In his appearance, he went a step further: "I was trying to speak like Elmo, to be funnier." (The producers, he recalled, told him to just be himself.)

Being on *Sesame* is simultaneously surreal and deeply comforting. If you grew up with it, it's as familiar as your childhood bedroom—but a fever-dream version, with a cast of adults scooting around the floor on cushioned dollies, staring at monitors while they speak in incongruously high-pitched or gravelly voices that travel out of their perpetually aloft arms.

And yet, guest artists almost instantly forget that there's anyone inside Ernie or Abby Cadabby. "I knew, of course, it was a puppeteer," said Jones, of her 2004 bit, spoofing her Grammy-winning "Don't Know Why" with a song called "Don't Know Y." And yet, "I definitely felt like it was Elmo and the letter Y. I could feel, like, his heart beating; it was really like—whoa, he's real."

Bursting into tears is also common. Tracy Chapman needed a break to compose herself during her 1998 performance; Gloria Estefan, who connected with Sonia, Luis and Maria, the show's trailblazing Latino characters, "cried when she walked in, because she said she was able to see herself and identify with somebody on TV," said Carmen Osbahr, who performed alongside her as the Spanish-speaking Muppet Rosita.

When R.E.M. came on to do "Happy Furry Monsters," a takeoff on their hit "Shiny Happy People," they hung around the set all day, adding jokes to their number and watching other segments being produced, said Cerf. "That happened all the time," the songwriter said. "I was there when Melissa Etheridge came, and she wanted to sit in Big Bird's nest before she left."

Harry Styles, the One Direction star, also "had to meet Big Bird," said Bill Sherman, the show's music director. "And Will.i.am needed to talk to Grover."

Like Lin-Manuel Miranda, Chance the Rapper is an Oscar guy. "I always just felt like he was misunderstood," he said. When he came on to do a theatrical scene with Cookie and Elmo, he also invented a bit for himself and Oscar.

"People are so happy to be on the show that they'll almost do anything," Sherman noted, with some glee. "You're like, 'stand on your head and count to 10!' They're like, 'sure!'"

In 2009, Carrie Underwood appeared, in voice only, as the character Carrie Underworm, an orange crawler with long blonde hair. The lessons *Sesame* taught "have impacted me in ways that I don't even realize," she wrote in an email. "My favorite 'friends' on TV were always singing and having fun, and I felt like I was a part of it. That's a lot of what I try to do as an artist today."

Chance, too, said *Sesame* affects him even now. The Raposo classic "Sing," he said, "felt like it was a song telling me not only to just be confident and keep going in all ways, but specifically as an artist to this day, it makes me feel like I should be creating."

Building a *Sesame* Song

How does a *Sesame* song come to be? It's started the same way for the last half-century: with a curriculum.

Each year, outside experts outline pressing academic and social issues; from that, and the input of Dr. Rosemarie Truglio, the show's senior vice president for curriculum and content, an educational theme for the season is built. Episodes can have individual goals, too, and preschool basics like numbers, letters and reading-readiness are perennials.

Then, the script writers step in (*Sesame* writers generally only pen lyrics). "Little kids have short attention spans," said Christine Ferraro, a *Sesame* writer. "If it's too talky, you're going to lose them."

Ferraro, who started at *Sesame* right out of college as a secretary and has now been a writer and lyricist there for 26 years, is responsible for one of Elmo's most popular numbers, "Brushy Brush," a celeb-filled ode to brushing your teeth. It has nearly half a billion YouTube views, and the gratitude of legions of toddler parents.

Cerf is known for his rock parodies: He was behind the Grammy-nominated "Born to Add," a Bruce Springsteen take-off featuring Bruce Stringbean, with Cookie as Clarence Clemons on the album cover. (Though *Sesame* normally has its choice of stars, there are some that have remained out of reach. Despite entreaties, the Boss has never appeared. Neither has Madonna, Paul McCartney or the Rolling Stones.)

After a song has lyrics, Sherman and his team score it. Brevity and repetition are key; *Sesame* songs are mostly just verse and chorus, but they're tuned for catchiness. "You try to make the verse a hook, and then the chorus even more earwormy, if possible," Sherman said. Demos go to producers and artists for approval and production suggestions, but they must also pass the ultimate litmus test: his two daughters, now 6 and 8.

"They're very honest, and if they aren't humming it or singing it, I will usually throw it away and write it again," he said.

His track record is stellar: "What I Am," the 45 first song he co-wrote, for Will.i.am, became a viral hit, with more than 88 million views, and won an Emmy. A number for Janelle Monáe, "The Power of Yet"—inspired by her hit "Tightrope," and written "in my basement in like 20 minutes"—was so convincing that she told him it could appear on her next album. From musicians, said Sherman, that's "the best compliment I ever get."

If Sherman doesn't compose a song himself, he sends it out to his team of seven or eight musicians, a who's-who of Broadway, movie and pop heavyweights, including Chris Jackson, a star of *Hamilton*, who contributed to something like 100 songs over the last decade; Benj Pasek and Justin Paul, who composed for *La La Land* and *The Greatest Showman*; Jennifer Nettles of the country band Sugarland; and Stump of Fall Out Boy, who will have a recurring, synthy theme song in the 50th season. "Stylistically, it's so far afield from any stuff I do," Stump said.

Even for veterans, the curriculum goals—Season 50: "The Power of Possibilities: Embracing Oops and Aha's"—don't always make for easy assignments. On the other hand, said Cerf, "You know that if you can't figure out an ending, you can just have Cookie Monster eat whatever you're writing about."

Composing for a furry creature is its own head trip. "Nothing is more surreal than

getting an email with an attached .pdf with the 'vocal ranges' of the *Sesame Street* Muppets," Lin-Manuel Miranda shared. "It's like receiving a national security briefing."

The show has endured long enough that children who were reared on its voices are now creating them. When Matt Vogel auditioned to play Big Bird (he took over as the originator, Caroll Spinney, retired), he prepped by listening to a classic Big Bird album—but he also based the vocals on his own memories of the character and the show in the early '80s. "I still hear the sound effects and the instruments in my head," he said.

The music and puppeteering also inform 50 each other. Except for Cookie, the Muppets only have four fingers (three fingers and a thumb—because, essentially, it's cuter, said Jason Weber, creative supervisor at the Jim Henson Company, where all the Muppets are made). When they play instruments, it involves dexterity—Rosita strumming her guitar takes four hands, three of them fur-clad—and imagination.

"Abby plays the guitar lefty, and she can only move her hand in a certain direction, so you have to keep it in this, like, punk vibe," Sherman said. Whereas Hoots the Owl, a saxophonist, can really wail. One person does his hands and another, his mouth, "so you can nail all these really cool saxophone licks."

The multi-instrumental Elmo—he plays the violin, piano, drums and more—occasionally has his arms elongated to fit his repertoire. There are Muppet instruments, too, which present their own conundrums: Does a pair of Muppet bongos, for example, have one face or two? And what is the personality of a bongo drum, anyway? These are the workaday conversations that Henson people have with their *Sesame* colleagues.

"It's a weird job," Sherman said, laughing.

What unites the cast and crew is their fervent dedication to the *Sesame* mission. Carmen Osbahr, who grew up in Mexico, recalled learning English from its songs. Mesmerized since childhood, she worked on *Plaza Sésamo*, the Mexican version of the show, and was recruited by Henson and crew to help create Rosita. "The same happiness, sadness—all the feelings that music brings—and everything that *Sesame Street* has to give, I really wanted to be part of it, so I can pass it along," she said.

Sherman knows the weight of the legacy 55 acutely, and uses it as his spark. "It feels like a relay race, and I've been handed a baton," he said.

"I've written hundreds of songs about the letter A, and I'm always trying to get better," he added. "How can I make a song so that every kid, when they sing this song, all they can think about is the letter A?"

REASONING AND ORGANIZATION

1. What is the **claim** in this argument?

2. Throughout the text, Ryzik describes causes and explains the effects and consequences of *Sesame Street*. Choose one of these **cause-and-effect** relationships. Then explain how that relationship contributes to her **message**.

3. How does Ryzik use **transitions** and causal verbs in this argument? Choose two examples. Then explain the relationships that are described by each example.

4. How does the writer's **line of reasoning** contribute to a **unified message**?

Syntax for Emphasis

AP Enduring Understanding (STL-1)

The rhetorical situation informs the strategic stylistic choices that writers make.

KEY POINT

Writers use coordination to show equality of ideas and subordination to show inequality of ideas.

When crafting sentences in an argument, writers try to communicate information and ideas. But they must also communicate the relationships between ideas and supporting evidence. For example, a writer may emphasize one idea more than another or even create a sense of suspense within a sentence. These stylistic choices contribute to the coherence of an argument. They connect ideas within sentences, and they arrange sentences within paragraphs so that readers understand how the writer prioritizes information.

Sentences Reveal Relationships

The term **syntax** refers to the order of words in a sentence. Along with **tone** and **diction**, it is a key element of style. Note that in this context, style is not merely decorative or superficial: the arrangement of specific words often conveys the relationship between — and the relative importance of — the writer's ideas. Indeed, readers should pay as much attention to *how* writers construct sentences as they do to the substantive meaning of those sentences. Writers can vary syntax in many different ways for many different effects, but two of the most important syntactical strategies are **coordination** and **subordination**.

Coordination

Writers use **coordination** to show that two ideas in a sentence are equally important. They indicate equality by connecting the two ideas with a coordinating conjunction, such as *and* or *but*. Consider the following example:

> Olivia is passionate about creative writing, **and** she wants to become an English teacher.

By connecting these two ideas with the coordinating conjunction *and*, the writer indicates that they are of equal importance. Often, coordination joins two independent clauses that could stand alone equally as complete sentences.

Subordination

In contrast, a writer may want to illustrate that two ideas are not equal: that one idea is less important than — or perhaps dependent upon — another idea.

To highlight this relationship, the writer can use **subordination**. This strategy uses subordinating conjunctions such as *after, although, because, if,* and *while,* which illustrate the relative importance between ideas, as well as their relationship. Consider the following example:

> Although she thought about other majors, Olivia decided to complete a degree in English.

Often, a subordinate clause follows the main clause of a sentence. This syntax creates a "cumulative" or "loose" sentence: the writer states a main clause and then adds less important information, phrases, or clauses. Consider the following example:

> Olivia decided to major in English, although she has other interests and considered other subjects.

However, a writer may highlight the cause over the effect by placing the subordinate clause first. This emphasis can create suspense as the subordinate details lead the reader to a conclusion in the main clause. This type of construction is called a "periodic" sentence.

Consider the following example:

> After he submitted twelve resumes, sat through five interviews, traveled to three different states, and gave two sample presentations, Juan finally got the job that he had always wanted.

In this sentence, the writer emphasizes the work that Juan did to get the position by delaying the main clause until the conclusion.

ACHIEVING COHERENCE			
Transitions to Indicate Equality	**Transitions to Indicate Inequality**		
Coordinating Conjunctions (FANBOYS)	**Subordinating Conjunctions (Frequently Used)**		
for	after	before	supposing
and	although	despite	though
nor	as	even if	when
but	as if	even though	whenever
or	as long as	if	whereas
yet	because	provided that	whether
so		since	while

Simple Sentences

When analyzing a text, readers must also be sensitive to which types of sentences (and patterns of sentence types) the writer uses.

For example, a writer may isolate an idea in a short, simple sentence to emphasize its importance. Or a writer may ask the reader to reflect on an idea by posing a rhetorical question. At times, a writer may even emphasize an idea through an intentional sentence fragment. All of these syntactical choices produce specific effects.

The syntax at both the sentence and paragraph levels contributes to the writer's overall argument. That's why it's important to pay close attention to the writer's syntactical choices.

INSIDER AP® TIP

Main ideas are always in independent clauses. Writers can also use subordinate clauses to transition from emphasizing one idea to showing the relative importance of one idea to another. At times, a writer may draw upon subordination to concede or rebut another argument.

Just keep in mind that the main idea of a paragraph or argument will be presented in a main clause or simple sentence. So pay special attention to simple sentences, as they are most likely to communicate the writer's main idea or message.

SYNTAX FOR EMPHASIS

Questions to Consider for Syntax

- Why has the writer arranged the sentences in this order?
- Does the writer use simple sentences to emphasize the main idea?
- How do the main ideas within individual sentences contribute to the writer's claim?
- Why has the writer presented the main idea first (or last) in a specific sentence?
- What is the relationship between the ideas within a particular sentence?
- How do the relationships presented within sentences reinforce the writer's overall argument?

Syntactical Strategy	Effect/Function	Example
Coordination	Indicates equal ideas Shows balance of ideas	*Video gaming has changed over the last two decades, and the best games now have the complexity of great novels or films.*
Subordination	Indicates inequality of ideas Emphasizes one idea over another Builds suspense Provides causal information/details	*While some critics still dismiss video games as childish, many artists, writers, and academics view them with intellectual interest and admiration.*
Simple Sentence	Emphasizes the main idea	*Video games are now works of art.*
Rhetorical Question	Asks the reader to pause and reflect	*Why do critics reject this characterization?*
Intentional Fragment	Highlights an idea	*Their snobbery and ignorance.*

AP® SKILLS PRACTICE | LANGUAGE AND STYLE
Analyzing Syntax

Consider the following sentence pairs. Each pair presents the same information; however, the writer is evaluating which syntax would be more effective. How do changes in syntax change the meaning of the sentences? Explain the differences in each pair.

Subordination

While I was cooking dinner last night, I found out that I won a full scholarship.

While I found out that I won a full scholarship last night, I was cooking dinner.

Coordination

He is afraid of heights. He enjoyed skydiving with his friends.

He is afraid of heights, but he enjoyed skydiving with his friends.

Breaking the Blue Wall of Silence: Changing the Social Narrative About Policing in America
Narain Dubey

Photo by Mako Barmon

THE TEXT IN CONTEXT

Narain Dubey wrote "Breaking the Blue Wall of Silence: Changing the Social Narrative About Policing in America" as a senior at Grant High School in Portland, Oregon. Dubey was prompted to write about this issue after his cousin Isaiah was shot and killed by a police officer in 2017. His argument was a 2019 winner of the *New York Times* annual editorial contest. Now a student at the University of Chicago, Dubey is the founder of Guy Talk, an online community that encourages conversations among high school boys and their younger peers about masculinity, gender, and social norms.

 | LANGUAGE AND STYLE
Analyzing Syntax

As you read Narain Dubey's article, identify examples of his syntactical choices. For each example, describe its function within the argument.

Analyzing the Effects of Syntax

Questions to Consider for Syntactical Choices

- Why has the writer arranged the sentences in this order?
- Does the writer use simple sentences to present the main idea?
- How do the main ideas within individual sentences contribute to the writer's claim?
- Why has the writer presented the main idea first (or last) in a specific sentence?
- What is the relationship between the ideas within a particular sentence?
- How do the relationships presented within sentences reinforce the writer's overall argument?

Syntactical Strategy	Effect/Function	Example
Coordination	Indicates equal ideas Shows balance of ideas	
Subordination	Indicates inequality of ideas Emphasizes one idea over another Builds suspense Provides causal information/details	
Simple Sentence	Emphasizes the main idea	
Rhetorical Question	Asks the reader to pause and reflect	
Intentional Fragment	Highlights an idea	

Breaking the Blue Wall of Silence: Changing the Social Narrative About Policing in America

As a child, I thought of police officers with veneration—if I saw a cop in the park, I felt safer. I told myself that when I got older, I would be wearing the badge too.

At 12 years old, I learned about police brutality. When I first saw the video of Eric Garner being thrown to the ground by police officers, I thought it was a movie. Despite knowing that the officers were at fault, I refused to change my internal rhetoric; I thought the media was only portraying the bad side of the people I saw as heroes.

Then on July 31, 2017, a police officer shot and killed my cousin, Isaiah Tucker, while he was driving. Isaiah wasn't just my cousin. He was also a young, unarmed, African-American man. I no longer dreamt of becoming a police officer.

But the issue is much larger than what happened to Isaiah. As highlighted in the *New York Times*, the Center for Policing Equity found that African-Americans are 3.6 times more likely to experience force by police officers as compared to whites.

Despite this blatant disproportionality, [5] there is still overwhelming ignorance about it. Just last August, a group of people marched in Philadelphia, countering Black Lives Matter protests with signs and chants of "Blue Lives Matter." People are quick to challenge discussions of police violence with the idea that "not all cops are bad cops."

But when we argue in defense of the morality of individual police officers, we are undermining a protest of the larger issue: the unjust system of policing in the United States.

When I met Wesley Lowery, a journalist from the *Washington Post*, he was adamant that the social narrative regarding police brutality in the United States needs to change. "Conversations about police reform and accountability are about systems and structures, not about individuals," said Lowery.

It is not that some police officers aren't doing admirable things in our communities, but revering police officers for not abusing their power is dangerous—it normalizes police violence and numbs society to these issues. The idea that "not all cops are bad cops" belittles attempts to uproot the system. When we go out of our way to controvert this fight, we are perpetuating the inherent problems with racialized policing.

So as you think about policing in America, think of Eric Garner. Think of Alton Sterling, my cousin Isaiah, and the families that were left behind.

We have a responsibility as citizens of this [10] country to call out corruption in systems of power. Policing in America is rooted in racism, oppression and privilege—it's time that we recognize that.

I learned to change my perspective. So can you.

Works Cited

Williams, Timothy. "Study Supports Suspicion That Police Are More Likely to Use Force on Blacks." *New York Times*. 7th July, 2016.

Lowery, Wesley. (2018, August 2nd). Personal communication at Asian American Journalist Association's JCAMP.

LANGUAGE AND STYLE

1. Give an example of both a cumulative and a periodic sentence. Explain the effect of Dubey's use of **subordination** in each sentence.

2. Dubey includes several simple sentences in his argument. Explain the effect of this **syntactic** choice.

3. Choose two of Dubey's sentences: one that uses **coordination** and one that uses **subordination**. Explain how each choice illustrates a relationship and contributes to the **coherence** of the argument.

Tina Theory: Notes on Fierceness

Madison Moore

THE TEXT IN CONTEXT

A DJ, artist, cultural critic, and assistant professor of queer studies at Virginia Commonwealth University, Madison Moore (b. 1982) was born in Ferguson, Missouri, and earned a PhD from Yale University. His work has appeared in both scholarly and popular publications, such as *Interview*, *VICE*, the *Paris Review*, and *Journal of Popular Music Studies*, where the following article was first published on March 1, 2012.

Taylor Hill/Getty Images

Unifying Idea	Tina Theory: Notes on Fierceness	Rhetorical Choices	Effect
pride in identity	Everything I know about being queer I learned from Tina Turner. More specifically, you might say that Ike and Tina's cover of "Proud Mary"— the soundtrack of my childhood—taught me, through camp performance, how to be a "Mary." During the holiday parties at my great-grandmother Lucille "Big Momma" Jones' house, for as long as I can remember, we kids ended up in the "Children's Room" so the grown folks could curse, drink whiskey, smoke, laugh, and be as loose as they felt. The "Children's	writer's credibility (ethos)	connects with first-hand experiences

Unifying Idea	Tina Theory: Notes on Fierceness	Rhetorical Choices	Effect
	Room" was not that special. It was usually a bedroom with a computer or television and a few board games, located next to the food which was always laid out buffet style. My favorite moments were when we would lip sync for our lives by doing drag karaoke, where my cousins and I would lock ourselves away and perform great popular music hits for an invisible audience. We pulled songs from Christina Aguilera or Britney Spears' latest album to older joints that circulated long before our time, songs like "Stop! (In the Name of Love)" by Diana Ross and The Supremes and Patti LaBelle's "Lady Marmalade." But one song we kept in our catalog and that we seemed to have the most fun with was the Ike and Tina Turner cover of "Proud Mary."	exigence	childhood experiences shaped who the writer is
pride in identity	Whenever we did "Mary" I insisted on being Tina. But what was it that drew me—a black gay boy rooted, like Tina, in Saint Louis, which is either the South or the Midwest depending on who you ask—into her style of performance? And why "Proud Mary" in particular? Was it Tina's way with sequins and fringe that turned me on? Or did it have to do with the way she instinctively knew how to work a stage? Gay men idolize many kinds of divas, as the cultural critic Wayne Koestenbaum has revealed. But perhaps the one commonality they share among them is the virtuosic styling of the body: the use of sequins, fringe, sunglasses, big shoulder pads, and bedazzled hats—accessories that help transform the diva from a mere mortal into a fantastical image, or what Guy Debord might describe as "capital accumulated to the point where it becomes image" even if the pearls are fake (24).	periodic sentence detail purpose evidence	emphasizes his connection to Turner describes the stereotype emphasizes the impact of Turner on gay men supports the claim that style transforms

Unifying Idea	Tina Theory: Notes on Fierceness	Rhetorical Choices	Effect
pride in identity	I did not have a bedazzler when we did "Proud Mary," but I did put a T-shirt on my head since I did not have hair or wigs. There we were, performing Tina's exact choreography, quoting her dance moves and facial expressions. Eyebrows furrowed, I would strut around the room back and forth on the tips of my toes, mouthing the lyrics to the song. I felt like I was wearing a pair of stilettos, swinging my makeshift T-shirt hair extensions in the service of working an invisible crowd. As I now arrive at my own theorizations of black glamour and the political thrust of spectacular sartorial style, I've come to realize that it was through my performances as Tina Turner that I learned what queerness meant for me—it meant a spectacular presence—and this is how, as a Midwestern boy trapped in a basement and quoting a diva five times my age, that I was able to touch queerness.	perspective / cumulative sentence	emphasizes the transformation / conveys the impact of Turner on his identity
pride in identity	I idolized many divas and pop singers during my youth but there was always something extra that drew me to Tina Turner. . . .		
	. . . I've realized that my interest in Tina Turner has to do with her embodiment of "fierceness" as a disruptive strategy of performance. By fierceness, I mean a spectacular way of being in the world—a transgressive over-performance of the self through aesthetics. . . .	evidence	establishes a characteristic of fierceness
pride in identity	. . . In many ways fierceness is It: "a quality that makes certain people interesting all the time" (Roach 9). But even as I front load my remarks on fierceness with a definition of the term, I need to point out that, like It, fierceness embodies several contradictions all at once. As I will show, fierceness is both	coordination	balances the contradictory qualities of fierceness

Unifying Idea	Tina Theory: Notes on Fierceness	Rhetorical Choices	Effect
	ownership and the loss of control, simultaneously deliberateness and spontaneity. If fierceness presents this set of contradictions, it is because, as Joseph Roach describes, "'It' is the power of effortless embodiment of contradictory qualities simultaneously: strength and vulnerability, innocence and experience, and singularity and typicality" (5). This set of contradictions allows the term to be noticeable yet unpredictable which, the way I see it, helps to keep it interesting. . . .	coordination cont'd	
pride in identity	. . . "Proud Mary" stands as the fiercest song in Ike and Tina Turner's catalog. But what was so exciting to audiences about "Proud Mary," and how did the song capture Tina's fierceness? What has always struck me about the song in particular is the drastic separation between the spoken word first half and the speedy second. This might seem obvious, but I'm not thinking in terms of fastness and slowness. Rather, I see it as it relates to what I would call the "diva moment." By "diva moment," I mean the special, unique quality that a performer brings to their version of a cover song that stamps their identity and makes the song their own. What made "Proud Mary" Ike and Tina's was not simply the change in musical form, but the addition of the call-and-response. I have always thought that the one quality that separates divas from the conveyor belt of traditional pop singers is the ability to work a crowd through spoken word. We need the rawness and immediacy of the spoken. Sometimes the most interesting moments during a concert occur not when the singer sings, but when she or he narrates the space between the songs with camp stories and witty dialogue. The diva moment is precisely when fierceness speaks. . . .	writer's credibility (ethos) coordination	reinforces the writer's experience with fierceness emphasizes the most interesting moments

Unifying Idea	Tina Theory: Notes on Fierceness	Rhetorical Choices	Effect
pride in identity	. . . I said that Tina Turner is a nodal point in terms of fierceness as a whole-body aesthetic, and by whole-body I mean fierceness as the use of fashion, style, and movement. Across Tina's performance practice we witness fierceness as a spastic bodily possession—a seemingly uncontrollable, unrestrained energy. For Tina, every handclap, ad lib, stomp, and bead of sweat is a moment of possession; she is taken over by the performance. At several points throughout the performance, Tina's face appears glazed over, her eyes fluttering quickly. She reaches, both physically and emotionally, for the right character of note to sing, and makes heroic attempts to pull the song out. When she does a cover of "Come Together" by The Beatles and sings "got to be a joker he just do what he please," her eyes remain closed, the head tilted back and the neck pulled tight, as if she is trying to pull the song out of her vocal cords, as if not even she can tame the song. The live performance, like an exorcism, possesses her. This is what the cultural critic Francesca Royster has called a "playfully outrageous bodily knowledge" ("Nice and Rough" 4). But even as fierceness evokes the sense of being out of control, the fact is that it also requires a certain level of mastery, of virtuosity and deliberateness. In her performance work, Tina demonstrates a sense of control and expertise. More than simply singing the song, she means it. Meaning it implies ownership. Fierceness demonstrates a mastery and an ownership of the self that gives minoritarian subjects the power to re-create and assert themselves through aesthetics.	effect of the causal argument	fierceness results in the ownership of self

Works Cited

Debord, Guy. *The Society of the Spectacle*. New York: Zone Books, 1995.

Roach, Joseph. *It*. Ann Arbor: University of Michigan Press, 2007.

Royster, Francesca. "Nice and Rough: The Promise of Privacy in Tina Turner's 'What's Love Got to Do with It' and *I, Tina*," *Performance Research: A Journal of the Performing Arts* 12.3 (2007) 103–113.

IDEAS IN AMERICAN CULTURE
Place and Values

Regional differences have long been a source of both celebration and conflict in the United States. A sense of place, as well as local cultural values, can contribute to individual and community identity. For example, we still see this in Americans who strongly identify with a city, a home state, or a particular part of the country (such as the South or the Pacific Northwest). At the same time, these regional elements must be balanced with a sense of national identity. The period after the Civil War (or "Reconstruction") recalibrated this tension as the federal government sought to reintegrate the Confederate States into the Union. Moreover, the country was still industrializing and expanding.

As states and localities formed their governments and American expansion continued westward, regional and cultural identities, or "regionalism," emerged. Just as Northeastern cities such as New York took on specific characteristics, so too did regions in the South, the mid-Atlantic, the Midwest, and the West.

The Romantic sensibility of the early nineteenth century advanced the ideas of individualism, imagination, and inspiration from nature. But as regional identities became stronger and the nation became more diverse, this Romanticism gave way to Realism. In literature, the Realist literary movement tried to capture life as it is really lived, which meant presenting lifelike characters, ordinary situations, realistic dialogue, and other elements rooted in everyday life.

IDEA BANK

Belonging
Community
Culture
Custom
Diversity
Division
Expansion
Home
Identity
Immigration
Local Color
Poverty
Realism
Regionalism
Ritual
Place
Tradition
Value

In the Missouri Capitol ▶
Building, Thomas Hart
Benton painted a mural
titled *A Social History
of the State of Missouri*
(1936, illustration).
This stand-alone
panel features a scene
from Mark Twain's
*The Adventures of
Huckleberry Finn.*

How does this image
communicate a sense
of place and culture?
What values does it
communicate about
that place and culture?

akg-images/Fototeca Gilardi; © 2021 T.H. and R.P. Benton Trusts/Licensed by Artists Rights Society (ARS), New York

369

alike to me; they were monotonously unpicturesque. I hoped Mr. Bixby would change the subject. But no, he would crowd up around a point, hugging the shore with affection, and then say: 'The slack water ends here, abreast this bunch of China trees; now we cross over.' So he crossed over. He gave me the wheel once or twice, but I had no luck. I either came near chipping off the edge of a sugar plantation, or I yawed too far from shore, and so dropped back into disgrace again and got abused.

The watch was ended at last, and we took supper and went to bed. At midnight the glare of a lantern shone in my eyes, and the night watchman said—

'Come! turn out!'

And then he left. I could not understand ⁵ this extraordinary procedure; so I presently gave up trying to and dozed off to sleep. Pretty soon the watchman was back again, and this time he was gruff. I was annoyed. I said—

'What do you want to come bothering around here in the middle of the night for? Now, as like as not, I'll not get to sleep again tonight.'

The watchman said—

'Well, if this ain't good, I'm blessed.'

The 'off-watch' was just turning in and I heard some brutal laughter from them, and such remarks as 'Hello, watchman! ain't the new cub turned out yet? He's delicate, likely. Give him some sugar in a rag and send for the chambermaid to sing rock-a-bye Baby to him.'

About this time Mr. Bixby appeared on the ¹⁰ scene. Something like a minute later I was climbing the pilothouse steps with some of my clothes on and the rest in my arms. Mr. Bixby was close behind, commenting. Here was something fresh—this thing of getting up in the middle of the night to go to work. It was a detail in piloting that had never occurred to

me at all. I knew that boats ran all night but somehow I had never happened to reflect that somebody had to get up out of a warm bed to run them. I began to fear that piloting was not quite so romantic as I had imagined it was; there was something very real and work-like about this new phase of it.

It was a rather dingy night, although a fair number of stars were out. The big mate was at the wheel and he had the old tub pointed at a star and was holding her straight up the middle of the river. The shores on either hand were not much more than half a mile apart, but they seemed wonderfully far away and ever so vague and indistinct. The mate said—

'We've got to land at Jones's plantation, sir.'

The vengeful spirit in me exulted. I said to myself, 'I wish you joy of your job, Mr. Bixby; you'll have a good time finding Mr. Jones's plantation such a night as this, and I hope you never *will* find it as long as you live.'

Mr. Bixby said to the mate—

'Upper end of the plantation, or the lower?' ¹⁵

'Upper.'

'I can't do it. The stumps there are out of water at this stage: It's no great distance to the lower and you'll have to get along with that.'

'All right, sir. If Jones don't like it he'll have to lump it, I reckon.'

And then the mate left. My exultation began to cool and my wonder to come up. Here was a man who not only proposed to find this plantation on such a night but to find either end of it you preferred. I dreadfully wanted to ask a question, but I was carrying about as many short answers as my cargo room would admit of, so I held my peace. All I desired to ask Mr. Bixby was the simple question whether he was ass enough to really imagine he was going to find that plantation on a night when all plantations were exactly alike and all the same color. But I held in. I used to have fine inspirations of prudence in those days.

Mr. Bixby made for the shore and soon was 20 scraping it, just the same as if it had been daylight. And not only that, but singing:

‘Father in heaven, the day is declining,’ etc.

It seemed to me that I had put my life in the keeping of a peculiarly reckless outcast. Presently he turned on me and said—

‘What’s the name of the first point above New Orleans?’

I was gratified to be able to answer promptly, and I did. I said I didn’t know.

‘Don’t *know*?’

This manner jolted me. I was down at the 25 foot again, in a moment. But I had to say just what I had said before.

‘Well, you’re a smart one!’ said Mr. Bixby. ‘What’s the name of the *next* point?’

Once more I didn’t know.

‘Well, this beats anything. Tell me the name of *any* point or place I told you.’

I studied a while and decided that I couldn’t.

‘Look here! What do you start out from, 30 above Twelve-Mile Point, to cross over?’

‘I—I—don’t know.’

‘You—you—don’t know?’ mimicking my drawling manner of speech. ‘What *do* you know?’

‘I—I—nothing, for certain.’

‘By the great Caesar’s ghost, I believe you! You’re the stupidest dunderhead I ever saw or ever heard of, so help me Moses! The idea of you being a pilot—you! Why, you don’t know enough to pilot a cow down a lane.’

Oh, but his wrath was up! He was a nervous 35 man, and he shuffled from one side of his wheel to the other as if the floor was hot.

He would boil a while to himself and then overflow and scald me again.

‘Look here! What do you suppose I told you the names of those points for?’

I tremblingly considered a moment and then the devil of temptation provoked me to say—

‘Well—to—to—be entertaining, I thought.’

This was a red rag to the bull. He raged and stormed so (he was crossing the river at the time) that I judge it made him blind, because he ran over the steering oar of a trading scow. Of course the traders sent up a volley of red-hot profanity. Never was a man so grateful as Mr. Bixby was, because he was brimful and here were subjects who could *talk back*. He threw open a window, thrust his head out, and such an irruption followed as I never had heard before. The fainter and farther away the scowmen’s curses drifted, the higher Mr. Bixby lifted his voice and the weightier his adjectives grew. When he closed the window he was empty. You could have drawn a seine through his system and not caught curses enough to disturb your mother with. Presently he said to me in the gentlest way—

‘My boy, you must get a little memorandum 40 book, and every time I tell you a thing, put it down right away. There’s only one way to be a pilot and that is to get this entire river by heart. You have to know it just like ABC.’

That was a dismal revelation to me; for my memory was never loaded with anything but blank cartridges. However, I did not feel discouraged long. I judged that it was best to make some allowances, for doubtless Mr. Bixby was ‘stretching.’ Presently he pulled a rope and struck a few strokes on the big bell. The stars were all gone now, and the night was as black as ink. I could hear the wheels churn along the bank, but I was not entirely certain that I could see the shore. The voice of the invisible watchman called up from the hurricane deck—

'What's this, sir?'

'Jones's plantation.'

I said to myself, I wish I might venture to offer a small bet that it isn't. But I did not chirp. I only waited to see. Mr. Bixby handled the engine bells, and in due time the boat's nose came to the land, a torch glowed from the forecastle, a man skipped ashore, a darky's voice on the bank said, 'Gimme de k'yarpet-bag, Mars' Jones,' and the next moment we were standing up the river again, all serene. I reflected deeply awhile, and then said—but not aloud—'Well, the finding of that plantation was the luckiest accident that ever happened; but it couldn't happen again in a hundred years.' And I fully believed it was an accident, too.

By the time we had gone seven or eight hundred miles up the river, I had learned to be a tolerably plucky upstream steersman, in daylight, and before we reached St. Louis I had made a trifle of progress in night-work, but only a trifle. I had a notebook that fairly bristled with the names of towns, 'points,' bars, islands, bends, reaches, etc., but the information was to be found only in the notebook—none of it was in my head. It made my heart ache to think I had only got half of the river set down; for as our watch was four hours off and four hours on, day and night, there was a long four-hour gap in my book for every time I had slept since the voyage began.

My chief was presently hired to go on a big New Orleans boat and I packed my satchel and went with him. She was a grand affair. When I stood in her pilothouse I was so far above the water that I seemed perched on a mountain, and her decks stretched so far away, fore and aft, below me, that I wondered how I could ever have considered the little *Paul Jones* a large craft. There were other differences too. The *Paul Jones*'s pilothouse was a cheap, dingy, battered rattletrap, cramped for room, but here was a sumptuous glass temple: room enough to have a dance in, showy red and gold window curtains, an imposing sofa; leather cushions and a back to the high bench where visiting pilots sit to spin yarns and 'look at the river,' bright, fanciful 'cuspidors' instead of a broad wooden box filled with sawdust, nice new oilcloth on the floor, a hospitable big stove for winter, a wheel as high as my head costly with inlaid work, a wire tiller-rope, bright brass knobs for the bells, and a tidy, white-aproned, black 'texas tender,' to bring up tarts and ices and coffee during midwatch, day and night. Now this was 'something like,' and so I began to take heart once more to believe that piloting was a romantic sort of occupation after all. The moment we were under way I began to prowl about the great steamer and fill myself with joy. She was as clean and as dainty as a drawing room; when I looked down her long, gilded saloon, it was like gazing through a splendid tunnel; she had an oil-picture, by some gifted sign painter, on every stateroom door; she glittered with no end of prism-fringed chandeliers; the clerk's office was elegant, the bar was marvelous, and the barkeeper had been barbered and upholstered at incredible cost. The boiler deck (i.e., the second story of the boat, so to speak) was as spacious as a church, it seemed to me, so with the forecastle, and there was no pitiful handful of deckhands, firemen, and roustabouts down there, but a whole battalion of men. The fires were fiercely glaring from a long row of furnaces and over them were eight huge boilers! This was unutterable pomp. The mighty engines—but enough of this. I had never felt so fine before. And when I found that the regiment of natty servants respectfully 'sir'd' me, my satisfaction was complete.

A Daring Deed

When I returned to the pilothouse St. Louis was gone and I was lost. Here was a piece of river which was all down in my book but I could make neither head nor tail of it: you understand, it was turned around. I had seen it when coming upstream, but I had never faced about to see how it looked when it was behind me. My heart broke again, for it was plain that I had got to learn this troublesome river *both ways.*

The pilothouse was full of pilots, going down to 'look at the river.' What is called the 'upper river' (the two hundred miles between St. Louis and Cairo, where the Ohio comes in) was low, and the Mississippi changes its channel so constantly that the pilots used to always find it necessary to run down to Cairo to take a fresh look when their boats were to lie in port a week, that is, when the water was at a low stage. A deal of this 'looking at the river' was done by poor fellows who seldom had a berth and whose only hope of getting one lay in their being always freshly posted and therefore ready to drop into the shoes of some reputable pilot, for a single trip, on account of such pilot's sudden illness or some other necessity. And a good many of them constantly ran up and down inspecting the river, not because they ever really hoped to get a berth but because (they being guests of the boat) it was cheaper to 'look at the river' than stay ashore and pay board. In time these fellows grew dainty in their tastes and only infested boats that had an established reputation for setting good tables. All visiting pilots were useful, for they were always ready and willing, winter or summer, night or day, to go out in the yawl and help buoy the channel or assist the boat's pilots in any way they could. They were likewise welcomed because all pilots are tireless talkers when gathered together, and as they talk only about the river they are always understood and are always interesting. Your true pilot cares nothing about anything on earth but the river, and his pride in his occupation surpasses the pride of kings.

We had a fine company of these river inspectors along this trip. There were eight or ten, and there was abundance of room for them in our great pilothouse. Two or three of them wore polished silk hats, elaborate shirtfronts, diamond breastpins, kid gloves, and patent-leather boots. They were choice in their English, and bore themselves with a dignity proper to men of solid means and prodigious reputation as pilots. The others were more or less loosely clad, and wore upon their heads tall felt cones that were suggestive of the days of the Commonwealth.

I was a cipher in this august company, 50 and felt subdued, not to say torpid. I was not even of sufficient consequence to assist at the wheel when it was necessary to put the tiller hard down in a hurry; the guest that stood nearest did that when occasion required—and this was pretty much all the time, because of the crookedness of the channel and the scant water. I stood in a corner, and the talk I listened to took the hope all out of me. One visitor said to another—

'Jim, how did you run Plum Point, coming up?'

'It was in the night, there, and I ran it the way one of the boys on the *Diana* told me; started out about fifty yards above the woodpile on the false point and held on the cabin under Plum Point till I raised the reef—quarter less twain—then straightened up for the middle bar till I got well abreast the old one-limbed cottonwood in the bend, then got my stern on the cottonwood and head on the low place above the point, and came through a-booming—nine and a half.'

'Pretty square crossing, ain't it?'

'Yes, but the upper bar's working down fast.'

Another pilot spoke up and said—   55

'I had better water than that and ran it lower down; started out from the false point—mark twain—raised the second reef abreast the big snag in the bend and had quarter less twain.'

One of the gorgeous ones remarked—

'I don't want to find fault with your leadsmen, but that's a good deal of water for Plum Point, it seems to me.'

There was an approving nod all around as this quiet snub dropped on the boaster and 'settled' him. And so they went on talk-talk-talking. Meantime, the thing that was running in my mind was, 'Now if my ears hear aright, I have not only to get the names of all the towns and islands and bends, and so on by heart, but I must even get up a warm personal acquaintanceship with every old snag and one-limbed cottonwood and obscure woodpile that ornaments the banks of this river for twelve hundred miles; and more than that, I must actually know where these things are in the dark, unless these guests are gifted with eyes that can pierce through two miles of solid blackness; I wish the piloting business was in Jericho and I had never thought of it.'

At dusk Mr. Bixby tapped the big bell   60
three times (the signal to land) and the captain emerged from his drawing-room in the forward end of the "texas," and looked up inquiringly. Mr. Bixby said—

'We will lay up here all night, captain.'

'Very well, sir.'

That was all. The boat came to shore and was tied up for the night. It seemed to me

a fine thing that the pilot could do as he pleased, without asking so grand a captain's permission. I took my supper and went immediately to bed, discouraged by my day's observations and experiences. My late voyage's notebooking was but a confusion of meaningless names. It had tangled me all up in a knot every time I had looked at it in the daytime. I now hoped for respite in sleep, but no, it reveled all through my head till sunrise again, a frantic and tireless nightmare.

Next morning I felt pretty rusty and low-spirited. We went booming along, taking a good many chances, for we were anxious to 'get out of the river' (as getting out to Cairo was called) before night should overtake us. But Mr. Bixby's partner, the other pilot, presently grounded the boat, and we lost so much time in getting her off that it was plain the darkness would overtake us a good long way above the mouth. This was a great misfortune, especially to certain of our visiting pilots, whose boats would have to wait for their return, no matter how long that might be. It sobered the pilothouse talk a good deal. Coming upstream, pilots did not mind low water or any kind of darkness; nothing stopped them but fog. But downstream work was different; a boat was too nearly helpless, with a stiff current pushing behind her, so it was not customary to run downstream at night in low water.

There seemed to be one small hope, how-   65
ever: if we could get through the intricate and dangerous Hat Island crossing before night, we could venture the rest, for we would have plainer sailing and better water. But it would be insanity to attempt Hat Island at night. So there was a deal of looking at watches all the rest of the day, and a constant ciphering upon the speed we were making; Hat Island

was the eternal subject; sometimes hope was high and sometimes we were delayed in a bad crossing and down it went again. For hours all hands lay under the burden of this suppressed excitement; it was even communicated to me, and I got to feeling so solicitous about Hat Island, and under such an awful pressure of responsibility, that I wished I might have five minutes on shore to draw a good, full, relieving breath and start over again. We were standing no regular watches. Each of our pilots ran such portions of the river as he had run when coming upstream, because of his greater familiarity with it, but both remained in the pilothouse constantly.

An hour before sunset, Mr. Bixby took the wheel and Mr. W. stepped aside. For the next thirty minutes every man held his watch in his hand and was restless, silent, and uneasy. At last somebody said, with a doomful sigh—

'Well, yonder's Hat Island—and we can't make it.'

All the watches closed with a snap, everybody sighed and muttered something about its being 'too bad, too bad—ah, if we could only have got here half an hour sooner!' and the place was thick with the atmosphere of disappointment. Some started to go out, but loitered, hearing no bell tap to land. The sun dipped behind the horizon, the boat went on. Inquiring looks passed from one guest to another, and one who had his hand on the doorknob and had turned it, waited, then presently took away his hand and let the knob turn back again. We bore steadily down the bend. More looks were exchanged and nods of surprised admiration—but no words. Insensibly the men drew together behind Mr. Bixby, as the sky darkened and one or two dim stars came out. The dead silence and sense of waiting became oppressive. Mr. Bixby pulled the cord and two deep, mellow notes

from the big bell floated off on the night. Then a pause, and one more note was struck. The watchman's voice followed from the hurricane deck—

'Labboard lead, there! Stabboard lead!'

The cries of the leadsmen began to rise out 70 of the distance and were gruffly repeated by the word-passers on the hurricane deck.

'M-a-r-k three! M-a-r-k three! Quarter-less three! Half twain! Quarter twain! M-a-r-k twain! Quarter-less—'

Mr. Bixby pulled two bell-ropes and was answered by faint jinglings far below in the engine room, and our speed slackened. The steam began to whistle through the gauge cocks. The cries of the leadsmen went on—and it is a weird sound, always, in the night. Every pilot in the lot was watching now, with fixed eyes, and talking under his breath. Nobody was calm and easy but Mr. Bixby. He would put his wheel down and stand on a spoke, and as the steamer swung into her (to me) utterly invisible marks—for we seemed to be in the midst of a wide and gloomy sea—he would meet and fasten her there. Out of the murmur of half-audible talk, one caught a coherent sentence now and then—such as—

'There; she's over the first reef all right!'

After a pause, another subdued voice—

'Her stern's coming down just *exactly* right, 75 by George! Now she's in the marks; over she goes!'

Somebody else muttered—

'Oh, it was done beautiful—*beautiful!*'

Now the engines were stopped altogether, and we drifted with the current. Not that I could see the boat drift, for I could not, the stars being all gone by this time. This drifting was the dismalest work; it held one's heart still. Presently I discovered a blacker gloom than that which surrounded us. It was the head of the island. We were closing right down upon it. We entered its deeper shadow, and so imminent seemed the peril that I was likely to suffocate; and I had the strongest impulse to do something, anything, to save the vessel. But still Mr. Bixby stood by his wheel, silent, intent as a cat, and all the pilots stood shoulder to shoulder at his back.

'She'll not make it!' somebody whispered.

The water grew shoaler and shoaler, by the leadsman's cries, till it was down to— 80

'Eight-and-a-half! E-i-g-h-t feet! E-i-g-h-t feet! Seven-and—'

Mr. Bixby said warningly through his speaking tube to the engineer—

'Stand by, now!'

'Aye, aye, sir!'

'Seven-and-a-half! Seven feet! Six-and—' 85

We touched bottom! Instantly Mr. Bixby set a lot of bells ringing, shouted through the tube, '*Now*, let her have it—every ounce you've got!' then to his partner, 'Put her hard down! snatch her! snatch her!' The boat rasped and ground her way through the sand, hung upon the apex of disaster a single tremendous instant, and then over she went! And such a shout as went up at Mr. Bixby's

back never loosened the roof of a pilothouse before!

There was no more trouble after that. Mr. Bixby was a hero that night; and it was some little time, too, before his exploit ceased to be talked about by river men.

Fully to realize the marvelous precision required in laying the great steamer in her marks in that murky waste of water, one should know that not only must she pick her intricate way through snags and blind reefs, and then shave the head of the island so closely as to brush the overhanging foliage with her stern, but at one place she must pass almost within arm's reach of a sunken and invisible wreck that would snatch the hull timbers from under her if she should strike it—and destroy a quarter of a million dollars' worth of steamboat and cargo in five minutes, and maybe a hundred and fifty human lives into the bargain.

The last remark I heard that night was a compliment to Mr. Bixby, uttered in soliloquy and with unction by one of our guests. He said—

'By the Shadow of Death, but he's a lightning pilot!' 90

The image depicts school-age students at daily tours at the Statue of Liberty, America's symbol of freedom.

To Mark Twain, the Mississippi River represents a pathway to freedom. For many others, the Statue of Liberty has a similar symbolic meaning. Examine the image, including the children, the statue, and the crowds. What values might the statue represent for people touring this site?

Drew Angerer/Staff Collection: Getty Images News

RHETORICAL SITUATION

1. Describe the **context** for this text. How might the writer's time, place, and occasion affect the **exigence**?

2. What is the **claim** of the text? How does the writer convey his position on the subject?

3. How do Twain's **rhetorical choices** reflect the beliefs, values, and needs of the **audience**?

CLAIMS AND EVIDENCE

4. What kind of **evidence** does Twain use to defend his **claim**? Describe the function and the effect of this evidence.

5. How does Twain contextualize the argument through boundaries or **limitations of evidence**?

REASONING AND ORGANIZATION

6. Look closely at the writer's choice of organization. Does Twain organize the text **inductively** or **deductively**? Explain.

7. How does Twain create **cohesion** in the text? Find an example of sentence-to-sentence cohesion. How does that cohesion contribute to the **purpose** of the text?

8. Give an example of both a **transition** and a **causal verb** in Twain's text. Then explain the relationship that each example communicates.

LANGUAGE AND STYLE

9. Identify both a **periodic** and a **cumulative** sentence. Then try to explain the writer's choice for each type of sentence. How does stylistic choice help develop the writer's position?

10. At times, the writer balances the sentences using **coordination**. Give an example and explain the effect.

IDEAS IN AMERICAN CULTURE

11. Regional writers often focus on the distinctive identities, customs, and behaviors rooted in specific places. How does this text incorporate local color? Give an example of language, dialect, or reference that reflects the Mississippi River. Does your region have any colloquialisms or local figures of speech? If so, how do they reflect distinct cultural identities in your community?

PUTTING IT ALL TOGETHER

12. How does Twain use both hyperbole and understatement to create comic effects? How do these rhetorical choices reflect the audience's beliefs, needs, and values? Explain.

from Harlem Is Nowhere

Sharifa Rhodes-Pitts

Mark Peterson/Redux

THE TEXT IN CONTEXT

A native of Houston, Texas, Sharifa Rhodes-Pitts (b. 1978) is an award-winning American writer and historian. After graduating from Harvard University, she was a Fulbright Scholar at St. Andrews University in Scotland. Her 2011 book *Harlem Is Nowhere* (excerpted here) is the first of a planned trilogy that will focus on African Americans and Utopia. Rhodes-Pitts's work has appeared in many publications, including the *New York Times*, *Boston Globe*, *Nation*, and *Vogue*. The Harlem section of New York City gained much of its fame from the Harlem Renaissance of the 1920s and 1930s: a flowering of African American culture, including painting, poetry, and jazz. But today, this neighborhood is highly commercialized. In her text, Rhodes-Pitts reflects on Harlem as both a literal and metaphorical space.

I had already put the key into the door of my building on Lenox Avenue when the question came at my back. In one movement I withdrew the key and turned to face my inquisitor. He stood waiting for my reply and then asked again: *Do you think you'll ever go home?*

It was one of the neighborhood men who stand outside the front door during the day, sentinels keeping a vigilant watch. When I first moved here they were almost invisible to me; we did not speak and exchanged only the occasional nod. Neither I nor the men were being standoffish. There seemed to be an unspoken rule—perhaps a universal prudence for any strange girl arriving in any strange place—that I should come to know the women first. After I had been accepted by the women, the men began to make themselves

known. By that point, the women had warned me about which men to avoid, I'd learned to discriminate between geezer flirtation and jive, and I could hold my own with the biggest jive talkers. Soon, I was drawn into a form of protection. My new friends declared this adoption at unexpected moments—one or another of the neighbors would introduce me as their daughter. If I was stranded in the midst of an unwanted conversation with a persistent sidewalk suitor, one of the sentinels would swoop in to see him off. But if I came home accompanied by a man of my own choosing, I was later expected to give an account of his intentions, employment, and character.

Home, he said again to my puzzled stare. *Down South. Do you think you'll ever go back home?*

It was a time when I was often in and out of the city. During phone conversations with friends, if I said I was at *home* they'd always ask, *Where?* But on this day, the man's question came out of nowhere. As I'd approached the stoop he'd remarked, *Cold enough for you?* on what was a relatively warm day a few weeks before the start of spring. I'd responded, *Not bad, not bad at all,* noting how easily that banality passed my lips—approximating the tones of a northerner, feigning comprehension of their seasons. Maybe he sensed the falseness of my reply. Maybe that's why he asked that question, presuming a desire I was not in contact with on that particular morning.

I answered cheerfully. *Home to Texas? But I* [5] *go back all the time. . . .* This sent him scattering into an apologetic retreat, as if he suddenly had a sense of invading my privacy. *Oh,* he said, and *Oh,* he repeated, as if the problem of my dislocation had suddenly been made right.

I did not ask him if he ever went home. I did not think of it until I was already in the narrow corridor that leads to the staircase that leads to my apartment, and now, in the act of recording it, this passing forgetfulness that he was also far from home strikes me as a failure of empathy. The yearning may have been more his than my own.

It was odd that he should think of me, even as I crossed my own threshold, as a stranger—someone on the verge of departure, highly susceptible to the mere mention of flight. (I might at that moment have turned around and gone; I might just then have been thinking of it.) But it says much about the impermanent status of my residence here. My neighbors were accustomed to seeing me leave with luggage in the earliest part of the morning. I had maintained an innocence of city

politics and refused certain hallmarks of the committed citizen of New York, like a red or black wire rolling cart for groceries, or a tabloid newspaper selected on the basis of the best horoscopes. I should not have been surprised that some of my neighbors on Lenox Avenue were still trying to understand my presence in their midst. On a different occasion, a different man from outside my door had asked where I was from. He was surprised—pleased, even—to hear I was from Texas. *Oh,* he'd said. *I thought you were a foreigner.*

• • •

One restless, idle hour, I sat at the library on 135th Street and consulted *The Columbia-Lippincott Gazetteer of the World,* copying out the following entry, as if to gain my bearings:

Harlem: A residential and business district of N Manhattan borough of New York City, SE N.Y., bounded approximately by Central Park and 110th St. (S), East R. (E), Harlem R. (NE), 168th St (W). Largest Negro community (pop. More than 400,000) in U.S. grew up here after 1910; one of the most congested districts in U.S., Harlem also has large colonies of Puerto Rican, Italian, and Latin American background. The Du. Settlement of Nieuw Haarlem was est. here 1658 by Peter Stuyvesant; in the Revolution, Continental forces stopped the British advance up Manhattan in battle (Sept., 1776) of Harlem Heights. Area remained virtually rural until improvement in 19th cent. of transportation links with lower Manhattan. Public-housing projects (begun in 1930s) and other attempts to relieve unfavorable conditions there have been made.

At first it seems to give an all-encompassing [10] view—complete with official borders, colonial heroics, and important urban planning highlights. Yet it manages to say nothing at all. In search of further detail I seized upon another definition, from the pages of *The Handbook of Geographical Nicknames*. This volume reveals that a city called Hankow is "The Pittsburgh of China"; that "The Happy Valley" refers to war-torn Kashmir and to the riverine gorge cut by the Tennessee; and that the Harz Mountains of Germany, the location of the silver mines where Leibniz once toiled, is now or once was "The Stronghold of Paganism." Situated near these is Harlem, whose nickname, "The Capital of the Negro Population of the United States," was not nearly as catchy or evocative as I'd expected. Though the phrase lacks poetry, it retains an accidental precision: the outdated term "Negro" (already antique when the book was published, in 1980) fixes our attention on the past.

At the library I found another source of coordinates. *Harlem is blocked in by the high ridges of Morningside Heights and St. Nicholas Terrace, by the East and Harlem rivers, and by Central Park*. Those declared boundaries did not tell me anything new. More important was the action of those physical frontiers: *Harlem is blocked in*. Geography is destiny. The WPA Guide to New York City, first published in 1939, goes on to describe who and what is blocked in by those ridges, those rivers, and that pastoral fiction of a park:

Negro Harlem, into which are crowded more than a quarter of a million Negroes from southern states, the West Indies, and Africa, has many different aspects. To whites seeking amusement, it is an exuberant, original, and unconventional entertainment center; to Negro college graduates it is an opportunity to practice a profession among their own people; to those aspiring to racial leadership it is a domain where they may advocate their theories unmolested; to artists, writers, and sociologists it is a mine of rich material; to the mass of Negro people it is the spiritual capital of Black America . . .

Only two decades had passed when the prophecy was borne out under slightly altered circumstances. A Negro colony spread from the concentrated area around Philip Payton's original buildings on 134th Street, until it became an onslaught no wall could contain. White New Yorkers quit Harlem. Some sold their property at a loss, others abandoned houses and apartment buildings, preferring to board them up rather than rent or sell to black people. Eventually, the move of blacks into Harlem reached the physical limits of the ridges, the rivers, and 110th Street. Alain Locke, writing in the introduction to his 1925 anthology *The New Negro*, found that the concentration of black New Yorkers crowding into that physical space mirrored a metaphysical force then gaining strength.

In Harlem, Negro life is seizing upon its first chances for group expression and self-determination. That is why our comparison is taken with those nascent centers of folk expression and self-determination which are playing a creative part in the world today. Without pretense to their political significance, Harlem has the same role to play for the New Negro as Dublin has had for the New Ireland or Prague for the New Czechoslovakia.

Locke was among the first to define Har- 15 lem as *a race capital*, a physical center that *focuses a people*. It was the *stage of the pageant of contemporary Negro life* on which would unfold *the resurgence of a race*. Locke invokes two young European republics whose people had rejected imperialism through nationalism. But he did not aspire to self-determination by means of actual political sovereignty or a separate nation for blacks. Locke believed that Harlem would be a place of cultural and social uplift. This, in time, would lead to equality for blacks within the wider American scene. In 1925, Locke asserted that *Harlem represents the Negro's latest thrust towards Democracy.*

Others tried to add their own pronouncements to Locke's prophecy. *The New Negro* anthology includes Charles S. Johnson reaching for Locke's gravitas, while waxing nostalgic about events still in progress: *And there was New York City with its polite personal service and its Harlem—the Mecca of the Negroes the country over. Delightful Harlem of the effete East! Old families, brownstone mansions, a step from wonderful Broadway, the end of the rainbow.*

In 1928, Wallace Thurman's *Negro Life in New York's Harlem* noted that the neighborhood—*known as The Mecca of the New Negro, the center of black America's cultural renaissance, Nigger Heaven, Pickaninny Paradise, Capital of Black America,* among other monikers—had been surveyed and interpreted, explored and exploited. But Thurman launches his own survey and interpretation, producing a lively picture of a popular and interesting section that reads like a travel guide, with chapters on social life, night life, amusement, house rent parties, the numbers, the church, and newspapers. The resulting vision of Harlem is a great deal less than the sum of its parts.

Langston Hughes riffs on Harlem in his contribution to a 1963 special Harlem issue of *Freedomways* magazine. Hughes mixes sentimentality with a dose of his typically biting wit, in the following incantation:

Harlem, like a Picasso painting in his cubistic period. Harlem—Southern Harlem—the Carolinas, Georgia, Florida—looking for the Promised Land—dressed in rhythmic words, painted in bright pictures, dancing to jazz—and ending up in the subway at morning rush time—headed downtown. West Indian Harlem—warm rambunctious sassy remembering Marcus Garvey, Haitian Harlem, Cuban Harlem, little pockets of tropical dreams in alien tongues. Magnet Harlem, pulling an Arthur Schomburg from Puerto Rico, pulling an Arna Bontemps all the way from California, a Nora Holt from way out West, an E. Simms Campbell from St. Louis, likewise a Josephine Baker, a Charles S. Johnson from Virginia, an A. Phillip Randolph from Florida, a Roy Wilkins from Minnesota, an Alta Douglas from Kansas. Melting pot Harlem—Harlem of honey and chocolate and caramel and rum and vinegar and lemon and lime and gall. Dusky dream Harlem rumbling into a nightmare tunnel where the subway from the Bronx keeps right on downtown, where the jazz is drained to Broadway whence Josephine [Baker] goes to Paris, Robeson to London, Jean Toomer to a Quaker Meeting House, Garvey to Atlanta Federal Penitentiary, and Wallace Thurman to his grave; but Duke Ellington to fame and fortune, Lena Horne to Broadway, and Buck Clayton to China.

The business of defining Harlem has already been perfected. You have heard them all before: Harlem is a *ruin*, it is *the home of the Negro's Zionism*; it is *a third world country*; an *East Berlin whose Wall is 110th Street*. This is hyperbolic Harlem, the *cultural capital of black America* or its *epicenter* (likening the place to a natural disaster). There is Harlem as Mecca—a city of sanctuary, a place that merges devotion and duty.

In *The New Negro* Alain Locke declared: *Harlem, I grant you, isn't typical—but it is significant, it is prophetic. No sane observer, however sympathetic to the new trend, would contend that the great masses are articulate as yet, but they stir, they move, they are more than physically restless.*

But in another essay included in the 1925 anthology, James Weldon Johnson offered a different kind of prophecy. In the tradition of the best oracles, it comes in the form of a riddle:

The question naturally arises, "Are the Negroes going to be able to hold Harlem?" If they have been steadily driven northward for the past hundred years and out of less desirable sections, can they hold this choice bit of Manhattan Island? It is hardly probable that Negroes will hold Harlem indefinitely, but when they are forced out it will not be for the same reasons that forced them out of former quarters in New York City. The situation is entirely different and without precedent. When colored people do leave Harlem, their homes, their churches, their investments and their businesses, it will be because the land has become so valuable they can no longer afford to live on it. But the date of another move northward is very far in the future.

Johnson suspected that Locke's restless masses would be forced—as before in New York, but compelled by a different propulsion—to move yet again. But he did not dwell much on the possibility, or divulge a spell to stop events from coming to pass.

In the 1920s, New York City's Harlem neighborhood was the epicenter for African American writers, painters, and intellectuals. It was home to legendary jazz artists, such as Duke Ellington, Billie Holiday, and Louis Armstrong, who played in Harlem jazz clubs like the Cotton Club and the Apollo Theater. Over time, the neighborhood has experienced many social and economic changes, as you can see in this photo showing a chain hotel next to the more typical small business. In 2020, Harlem celebrated the one hundredth anniversary of the Harlem Renaissance.

As historical neighborhoods evolve, how do they maintain the culture and values of the community? Does maintaining this continuity require more than preserving history? Explain.

RHETORICAL SITUATION

1. What is the writer's **exigence**? How does the exigence contribute to the writing context?

2. Give an example of an appeal to ethos or credibility. Then explain how the writer's ethos contributes to the **message** of the text.

3. How does the writer address the **audience's** beliefs, values, and needs?

CLAIMS AND EVIDENCE

4. Give an example of evidence from the text. Then explain the effectiveness of the **evidence**. What idea or claim does the evidence support?

5. How does the evidence strengthen the **credibility** of the writer?

6. Rhodes-Pitts frequently uses dashes to indicate a relationship. Choose one example from the text. Then explain how the punctuation creates a relationship — and how that relationship contributes to the writer's **claim**.

REASONING AND ORGANIZATION

7. How does the **purpose** of the speech reflect both the history and the future of African Americans in Harlem?

8. What **reasons** does Rhodes-Pitts give to explain the value of Harlem?

9. The writer's **conclusion** leaves the reader reflecting on the future of Harlem, as well as its current inhabitants. What does Rhodes-Pitts want her readers to consider at the end of her text?

LANGUAGE AND STYLE

10. Rhodes-Pitts writes many long **cumulative sentences**. Choose one example. Then explain the effect of the sentences.

11. What is the tone of the text? Give a specific example of the writer's **diction** that contributes to the **tone**.

12. Consider how Rhodes-Pitts uses **transitions** to make connections in her text. Choose two examples. Then discuss how the transitions create a relationship between ideas.

IDEAS IN AMERICAN CULTURE

13. Rhodes-Pitts evokes a strong sense of place, both past and present. She also argues for the enduring historical and cultural value of Harlem, as well as its centrality to African American culture. What evidence does she use to support her claims? Find specific examples and explain.

PUTTING IT ALL TOGETHER

14. Rhodes-Pitts offers a brief history of Harlem. How does this history (along with the writer's experience) help establish a purpose and message for the audience?

IDEAS IN AMERICAN CULTURE
Opportunity and Oppression

IDEA BANK

Development

Discrimination

Disillusionment

Diversity

Division

Education

Exploitation

Fairness

Fate

Industrialization

Labor

Monopoly

Opportunity

Oppression

Poverty

Progress

Prosperity

Realism

Reform

Risk

Unionization

Urbanization

Wealth

Expansion did not come without problems. Westward migration propelled the exploitation of natural resources, while technological advances and mass production fueled conflicts between workers and business owners. Waves of immigrants arrived during this North American industrial revolution, leading U.S. cities to become overcrowded, polluted, and dangerous for those new residents. At the same time, wealth became more concentrated among the wealthiest Americans. As they became more politically powerful, the country entered what writer Mark Twain called the "Gilded Age." Indeed, if the Gilded Age was a time of materialism and splendor, it was also an era of political corruption and inequity.

After the Civil War, America's industrialization accelerated, including steam engines and train lines. The country also required more labor, especially in urban areas where most factories were located. So the United States became an international source of technological and economic development. It also became a beacon of hope and opportunity for immigrants who arrived in increasing numbers. Between 1892 and 1954, Ellis Island received more than twelve million immigrants. As the country grew more prosperous, it also grew more diverse.

Jacob Lawrence, *This Is Harlem*, 1943 (Gift of Joseph H. Hirshhorn, Hirshhorn Museum and Sculpture Garden) © 2021 The Jacob and Gwendolyn Knight Lawrence Foundation, Seattle/Artists Rights Society (ARS), New York

This 1943 painting, called *This Is Harlem*, was created by the Harlem Renaissance artist Jacob Lawrence.

Describe the images in Lawrence's painting, which tell the story of urban vitality and community. Explain how he uses colors, contrasts, and other elements to convey both opportunity and oppression.

The American writers confronting these cultural, social, economic, and scientific developments rejected the idealism of the preceding Romantic period. In contrast to their predecessors, writers of the Realist movement tried to capture life as it was really lived, with realistic characters, storylines, and language. This desire to capture a true "slice of life" often led to stories that were provocative and shocking. For example, in *The Jungle* (p. 388), Upton Sinclair draws upon real experiences to expose the squalor and savagery of the meatpacking industry. The book led directly to reform and federal regulations.

Toward the end of the nineteenth century, writers who were influenced by science and psychology, as well as by their own observations of American economic realities, became more disillusioned and pessimistic. Often called "naturalists," these writers viewed individuals as largely powerless in the face of biological determinism, social conditions, and economic circumstances. This kind of writing remains relevant today. For example, J.D. Vance examines the challenges of intergenerational poverty specific to the Appalachian region of Kentucky in his best-selling 2016 book *Hillbilly Elegy* (p. 395).

As in the nineteenth and early twentieth centuries, America still struggles with issues of diversity and assimilation, as well as class and poverty. The country has long been considered the land of immigrants, but some would prefer to restrict immigration. While immigration quotas, restrictions, and laws began in the 1800s, recent years have also seen laws restricting immigration from some countries into the United States. The question of how to be a land of opportunity remains a subject of contemporary debate.

Bloomberg/Getty Images

▲

Members of the media and U.S. Border Patrol agents walk along the existing border wall. Construction crews are planning to take down Monument Hill, a sacred burial site to several Native American tribes, to build a new border wall in Lukeville, Arizona.

How does the image portray America's struggle with immigration? How do we remain the land of opportunity while also maintaining borders and national integrity?

from The Jungle
Upton Sinclair

THE TEXT IN CONTEXT

Novelist, journalist, and activist Upton Sinclair (1878–1968) wrote many books in a number of genres. But most of his work focuses on the issues of the Progressive Era, such as political corruption, corporate power, and the conditions of the working poor. In 1906, Sinclair published his best-known work, *The Jungle*: a fact-based fictional account that exposed labor exploitation and unsanitary conditions in the U.S. meatpacking industry. The book caused public outrage — and led to a public demand for the regulation of meatpacking and processing industries. In fact, Sinclair worried that the book's repulsive depictions of sanitation problems distracted readers from his main point: exposing the dehumanizing effects of factory labor and the mistreatment of animals. As he said, "I aimed at the public's heart, and, by accident, I hit it in the stomach."

Jurgis talked lightly about work, because he was young. They told him stories about the breaking down of men, there in the stockyards of Chicago, and of what had happened to them afterward—stories to make your flesh creep, but Jurgis would only laugh. He had only been there four months, and he was young, and a giant besides. There was too much health in him. He could not even imagine how it would feel to be beaten. "That is well enough for men like you," he would say, "*silpnas*, puny fellows—but my back is broad."

Jurgis was like a boy, a boy from the country. He was the sort of man the bosses like to get hold of, the sort they make it a grievance they cannot get hold of. When he was told to go to a certain place, he would go there on the run. When he had nothing to do for the moment, he would stand round fidgeting, dancing, with the overflow of energy that was in him. If he were working in a line of men, the line always moved too slowly for him, and you could pick him out by his impatience and restlessness. That was why he had been picked out on one important occasion; for Jurgis had stood outside of Brown and Company's "Central Time Station" not more than half an hour, the second day of his arrival in Chicago, before he had been beckoned by one of the bosses. Of this he was very proud, and it made him more disposed than ever to laugh at the pessimists. In vain would they all tell him that there were men in that crowd from which he had been chosen who had stood there a month—yes, many months—and not been chosen yet. "Yes," he would say, "but what sort of men? Broken-down tramps and good-for-nothings, fellows who have spent all their money drinking, and want to get more for it. Do you want me to believe that with these arms"—and he would clench his fists and hold them up in the air, so that you might see the rolling muscles—"that with these arms people will ever let me starve?"

"It is plain," they would answer to this, "that you have come from the country, and from very far in the country." And this was the fact, for Jurgis had never seen a city, and scarcely even a fair-sized town, until he had set out to make his fortune in the world and earn his right to Ona. His father, and his father's father before him, and as many ancestors back as legend could go, had lived in that part of Lithuania known as Brelovicz, the Imperial Forest. This is a great tract of a hundred thousand acres, which from time immemorial has been a hunting preserve of the nobility. There are a very few peasants settled in it, holding title from ancient times; and one of these was Antanas Rudkus, who had been reared himself, and had reared his children in turn, upon half a dozen acres of cleared land in the midst of a wilderness. There had been one son besides Jurgis, and one sister. The former had been drafted into the army; that had been over ten years ago, but since that day nothing had ever been heard of him. The sister was married, and her husband had bought the place when old Antanas had decided to go with his son.

It was nearly a year and a half ago that Jurgis had met Ona, at a horse fair a hundred miles from home. Jurgis had never expected to get married—he had laughed at it as a foolish trap for a man to walk into; but here, without ever having spoken a word to her, with no more than the exchange of half a dozen smiles, he found himself, purple in the face with embarrassment and terror, asking her parents to sell her to him for his wife—and offering his father's two horses he had been sent to the fair to sell. But Ona's father proved

as a rock—the girl was yet a child, and he was a rich man, and his daughter was not to be had in that way. So Jurgis went home with a heavy heart, and that spring and summer toiled and tried hard to forget. In the fall, after the harvest was over, he saw that it would not do, and tramped the full fortnight's journey that lay between him and Ona.

He found an unexpected state of affairs— for the girl's father had died, and his estate was tied up with creditors; Jurgis's heart leaped as he realized that now the prize was within his reach. There was Elzbieta Lukoszaite, Teta, or Aunt, as they called her, Ona's stepmother, and there were her six children, of all ages. There was also her brother Jonas, a dried-up little man who had worked upon the farm. They were people of great consequence, as it seemed to Jurgis, fresh out of the woods; Ona knew how to read, and knew many other things that he did not know, and now the farm had been sold, and the whole family was adrift—all they owned in the world being about seven hundred rubles, which is half as many dollars. They would have had three times that, but it had gone to court, and the judge had decided against them, and it had cost the balance to get him to change his decision.

Ona might have married and left them, but she would not, for she loved Teta Elzbieta. It was Jonas who suggested that they all go to America, where a friend of his had gotten rich. He would work, for his part, and the women would work, and some of the children, doubt- less—they would live somehow. Jurgis, too, had heard of America. That was a country where, they said, a man might earn three rubles a day, and Jurgis figured what three rubles a day would mean, with prices as they were where he lived, and decided forthwith that he would go to America and marry, and be a rich man in the bargain. In that country, rich or poor, a man was free, it was said; he did not have to

5

go into the army, he did not have to pay out his money to rascally officials—he might do as he pleased, and count himself as good as any other man. So America was a place of which lovers and young people dreamed. If one could only manage to get the price of a passage, he could count his troubles at an end.

It was arranged that they should leave the following spring, and meantime Jurgis sold himself to a contractor for a certain time, and tramped nearly four hundred miles from home with a gang of men to work upon a railroad in Smolensk. This was a fearful experience, with filth and bad food and cruelty and overwork, but Jurgis stood it and came out in fine trim, and with eighty rubles sewed up in his coat. He did not drink or fight, because he was thinking all the time of Ona, and for the rest, he was a quiet, steady man, who did what he was told to, did not lose his temper often, and when he did lose it made the offender anxious that he should not lose it again. When they paid him off he dodged the company gamblers and dramshops, and so they tried to kill him; but he escaped, and tramped it home, working at odd jobs, and sleeping always with one eye open.

So in the summer time they had all set out for America. At the last moment there joined them Marija Berczynskas, who was a cousin of Ona's. Marija was an orphan, and had worked since childhood for a rich farmer of Vilna, who beat her regularly. It was only at the age of twenty that it had occurred to Marija to try her strength, when she had risen up and nearly murdered the man, and then come away.

There were twelve in all in the party, five adults and six children—and Ona, who was a little of both. They had a hard time on the passage; there was an agent who helped them, but he proved a scoundrel, and got them into a trap with some officials, and cost them a good deal of their precious money, which they clung to with such horrible fear. This happened to them again in New York—for, of course, they knew nothing about the country, and had no one to tell them, and it was easy for a man in a blue uniform to lead them away, and to take them to a hotel and keep them there, and make them pay enormous charges to get away. The law says that the rate card shall be on the door of a hotel, but it does not say that it shall be in Lithuanian.

It was in the stockyards that Jonas' friend had gotten rich, and so to Chicago the party was bound. They knew that one word, Chicago—and that was all they needed to know, at least, until they reached the city. Then, tumbled out of the cars without ceremony, they were no better off than before; they stood staring down the vista of Dearborn Street, with its big black buildings towering in the distance, unable to realize that they had arrived, and why, when they said "Chicago," people no longer pointed in some direction, but instead looked perplexed, or laughed, or went on without paying any attention. They were pitiable in their helplessness; above all things they stood in deadly terror of any sort of person in official uniform, and so whenever they saw a policeman they would cross the street and hurry by. For the whole of the first day they wandered about in the midst of deafening confusion, utterly lost; and it was only at night that, cowering in the doorway of a house, they were finally discovered and taken by a policeman to the station. In the morning an interpreter was found, and they were taken and put upon a car, and taught a new word—"stockyards." Their delight at discovering that they were to get out of this adventure without losing another share of their possessions, it would not be possible to describe.

They sat and stared out of the window. They were on a street which seemed to run on forever, mile after mile—thirty-four of them, if they had known it—and each side of it one uninterrupted row of wretched little two-story frame buildings. Down every side street they could see, it was the same—never a hill and never a hollow, but always the same endless vista of ugly and dirty little wooden buildings. Here and there would be a bridge crossing a filthy creek, with hard-baked mud shores and dingy sheds and docks along it; here and there would be a railroad crossing, with a tangle of switches, and locomotives puffing, and rattling freight cars filing by; here and there would be a great factory, a dingy building with innumerable windows in it, and immense volumes of smoke pouring from the chimneys, darkening the air above and making filthy the earth beneath. But after each of these interruptions, the desolate procession would begin again—the procession of dreary little buildings.

A full hour before the party reached the city they had begun to note the perplexing changes in the atmosphere. It grew darker all the time, and upon the earth the grass seemed to grow less green. Every minute, as the train sped on, the colors of things became dingier; the fields were grown parched and yellow, the landscape hideous and bare. And along with the thickening smoke they began to notice another circumstance, a strange, pungent odor. They were not sure that it was unpleasant, this odor; some might have called it sickening, but their taste in odors was not developed, and they were only sure that it was curious. Now, sitting in the trolley car, they realized that they were on their way to the home of it—that they had traveled all the way from Lithuania to it. It was now no longer something far off and faint, that you caught in whiffs; you could literally taste it, as well as smell it—you could take hold of it, almost, and examine it at your leisure. They were divided in their opinions about it. It was an elemental odor, raw and crude; it was rich, almost rancid, sensual, and strong. There were some who drank it in

as if it were an intoxicant; there were others who put their handkerchiefs to their faces. The new emigrants were still tasting it, lost in wonder, when suddenly the car came to a halt, and the door was flung open, and a voice shouted—"Stockyards!"

They were left standing upon the corner, staring; down a side street there were two rows of brick houses, and between them a vista: half a dozen chimneys, tall as the tallest of buildings, touching the very sky—and leaping from them half a dozen columns of smoke, thick, oily, and black as night. It might have come from the center of the world, this smoke, where the fires of the ages still smolder. It came as if self-impelled, driving all before it, a perpetual explosion. It was inexhaustible; one stared, waiting to see it stop, but still the great streams rolled out. They spread in vast clouds overhead, writhing, curling; then, uniting in one giant river, they streamed away down the sky, stretching a black pall as far as the eye could reach.

Then the party became aware of another strange thing. This, too, like the odor, was a thing elemental; it was a sound, a sound made up of ten thousand little sounds. You scarcely noticed it at first—it sank into your consciousness, a vague disturbance, a trouble. It was like the murmuring of the bees in the spring, the whisperings of the forest; it suggested endless activity, the rumblings of a world in motion. It was only by an effort that one could realize that it was made by animals, that it was the distant lowing of ten thousand cattle, the distant grunting of ten thousand swine.

They would have liked to follow it up, 15 but, alas, they had no time for adventures just then. The policeman on the corner was beginning to watch them, and so, as usual, they started up the street. Scarcely had they gone a block, however, before Jonas was heard to give a cry, and began pointing excitedly across the street. Before they could gather the meaning of his breathless ejaculations he had bounded away, and they saw him enter a shop, over which was a sign: "J. Szedvilas, Delicatessen." When he came out again it was in company with a very stout gentleman in shirt sleeves and an apron, clasping Jonas by both hands and laughing hilariously. Then Teta Elzbieta recollected suddenly that Szedvilas had been the name of the mythical friend who had made his fortune in America. To find that he had been making it in the delicatessen business was an extraordinary piece of good fortune at this juncture; though it was well on in the morning, they had not breakfasted, and the children were beginning to whimper.

Thus was the happy ending to a woeful voyage. The two families literally fell upon each other's necks—for it had been years since Jokubas Szedvilas had met a man from his part of Lithuania. Before half the day they were lifelong friends. Jokubas understood all the pitfalls of this new world, and could explain all of its mysteries; he could tell them the things they ought to have done in the different emergencies—and what was still more to the point, he could tell them what to do now. He would take them to poni Aniele, who kept a boarding house the other side of the yards; old Mrs. Jukniene, he explained, had not what one would call choice accommodations, but they might do for the moment. To this Teta Elzbieta hastened to respond that nothing could be too cheap to suit them just then; for they were quite terrified over the sums they had had to expend. A very few days of practical experience in this land of high wages had been sufficient to make clear to them the cruel fact that it was also a land of high prices, and that in it the poor man was almost as poor as in any other corner of the earth; and so there vanished in a night all the wonderful dreams of wealth that had been haunting Jurgis. What had made the discovery all the more painful was that they were spending, at American prices, money which they had earned at home rates of wages—and so were really being cheated by the world! The last two days they had all but starved themselves—it made them quite sick to pay the prices that the railroad people asked them for food.

Yet, when they saw the home of the Widow Jukniene they could not but recoil, even so. In all their journey they had seen nothing so bad as this. Poni Aniele had a four-room flat in one of that wilderness of two-story frame tenements that lie "back of the yards." There were four such flats in each building, and each of the four was a "boarding house" for the occupancy of foreigners—Lithuanians, Poles, Slovaks, or Bohemians. Some of these places were kept by private persons, some were cooperative. There would be an average of half a dozen boarders to each room—sometimes there were thirteen or fourteen to one room, fifty or sixty to a flat. Each one of the occupants furnished his own accommodations—that is, a mattress and some bedding. The mattresses would be spread upon the floor in rows—and there would be nothing else in the place except a stove. It was by no means unusual for two men to own the same mattress in common, one working by day and using it by night, and the other working at night and using it in the daytime. Very frequently a lodging-house keeper would rent the same beds to double shifts of men. . . .

Later that afternoon [Jurgis] and Ona went out to take a walk and look about them, to see more of this district which was to be their home. In back of the yards the dreary two-story frame houses were scattered farther apart, and there were great spaces bare—that seemingly had been overlooked by the great sore of a city as it spread itself over the surface of the prairie. These bare places were grown up with dingy, yellow weeds, hiding innumerable tomato cans; innumerable children played upon them, chasing one another here and there, screaming and fighting. The most uncanny thing about this neighborhood was the number of the children; you thought there must be a school just out, and it was only after long acquaintance that you were able to realize that there was no school, but that these were the children of the neighborhood—that there were so many children to the block in Packingtown that nowhere on its streets could a horse and buggy move faster than a walk!

It could not move faster anyhow, on account of the state of the streets. Those through which Jurgis and Ona were walking resembled streets less than they did a miniature topographical map. The roadway was commonly several feet lower than the level of the houses, which were sometimes joined by high board walks; there were no pavements—there were mountains and valleys and rivers, gullies and ditches, and great hollows full of stinking green water. In these pools the children played, and rolled about in the mud of the streets; here and there one noticed them digging in it, after trophies which they had stumbled on. One wondered about this, as also about the swarms of flies which hung about the scene, literally blackening the air, and the strange, fetid odor which assailed one's nostrils, a ghastly odor, of all the dead things of the universe. It impelled the visitor to questions—and then the residents would explain, quietly, that all this was "made" land, and that it had been "made" by using it as a dumping ground for the city garbage. After a few years the unpleasant effect of this would pass away, it was said; but meantime, in hot weather—and especially when it rained—the flies were apt to be annoying. Was it not unhealthful? the stranger would ask, and the residents would answer, "Perhaps; but there is no telling."

A little way farther on, and Jurgis and Ona, 20 staring open-eyed and wondering, came to the place where this "made" ground was in process of making. Here was a great hole, perhaps two city blocks square, and with long files of garbage wagons creeping into it. The place had an odor for which there are no polite words; and it was sprinkled over with children, who raked in it from dawn till dark. Sometimes visitors from the packing houses would wander out to see this "dump," and they would stand by and debate as to whether the children were eating the food they got, or merely collecting it for the chickens at home. Apparently none of them ever went down to find out.

Beyond this dump there stood a great brickyard, with smoking chimneys. First they took out the soil to make bricks, and then they filled it up again with garbage, which seemed to Jurgis and Ona a felicitous arrangement, characteristic of an enterprising country like America. A little way beyond was another great hole, which they had emptied and not yet filled up. This held water, and all summer it stood there, with the nearby soil draining into it, festering and stewing in the sun; and then, when winter came, somebody cut the ice on it, and sold it to the people of the city. This, too, seemed to the newcomers an economical arrangement; for they did not read the newspapers, and their heads were not full of troublesome thoughts about "germs."

They stood there while the sun went down upon this scene, and the sky in the west turned blood red, and the tops of the houses shone like fire. Jurgis and Ona were not thinking of the sunset, however—their backs were turned to it, and all their thoughts were of Packingtown, which they could see so plainly in the distance. The line of the buildings stood clear-cut and black against the sky; here and there out of the mass rose the great chimneys, with the river of smoke streaming away to the end of the world. It was a study in colors now, this smoke; in the sunset light it was black and brown and gray and purple. All the sordid suggestions of the place were gone—in the twilight it was a vision of power. To the two who stood watching while the darkness swallowed it up, it seemed a dream of wonder, with its tale of human energy, of things being done, of employment for thousands upon thousands of men, of opportunity and freedom, of life and love and joy. When they came away, arm in arm, Jurgis was saying, "Tomorrow I shall go there and get a job!"

The image depicts a modern meatpacking factory in May 2020, during the outbreak of the COVID-19 pandemic. During the pandemic, the health of workers, especially those in meatpacking plants, was often compromised. As a result, meatpacking plants were again criticized for unsafe working conditions.

As you examine the image, consider the details of the factory, the people, and the production lines. How do production lines continue to illustrate both opportunity and oppression? Specifically, explain the details that support the need for labor laws and regulation.

REUTERS/Dane Rhys

RHETORICAL SITUATION

1. What is the **context** for this text? How does the **exigence** connect to that context?
2. How does the writer appeal to **ethos** or build credibility through the characters?
3. What is the **purpose** of the text?

CLAIMS AND EVIDENCE

4. How does the **evidence** lend to the **credibility** of the writer? Give an example of evidence that strengthens the writer's ethos.
5. Sinclair incorporates specific and graphic **evidence** into the text. Explain how this evidence contributes to his claim.

REASONING AND ORGANIZATION

6. Does the **line of reasoning** proceed from an established claim, or does the reasoning advance toward a claim? Explain how this organizational choice helps achieve Sinclair's purpose.

LANGUAGE AND STYLE

7. **Word choice** and **description** contribute to the perspective of this text. Find an example of descriptive writing. Then explain how the specific word choice reveals and supports the writer's perspective.

8. The writer uses **coordination** and **subordination** throughout the text. Choose one example of each. Then explain the relationship — between ideas, evidence, or claims — that each example creates.

9. Sinclair uses many long **cumulative sentences**. What is the effect of these sentences? For example, do they help emphasize or support his claims? Do you find them difficult to follow? Why or why not?

IDEAS IN AMERICAN CULTURE

10. This text offers insight into the paradox of the American Dream: on one hand, the hope that America offered and, on the other hand, the harsh realities that greeted working immigrants of the early twentieth century. How does this text conclude? Does Sinclair's view still seem relevant to immigration and labor issues today?

PUTTING IT ALL TOGETHER

11. The writer uses both connotative and denotative language to create memorable descriptions. How do word choice and descriptive language contribute to the tone of the text? Choose a specific example and explain.

from Hillbilly Elegy
J.D. Vance

THE TEXT IN CONTEXT

Author and venture capitalist J.D. Vance (b. 1984) grew up in both the Rust Belt town of Middletown, Ohio, and the Appalachian town of Jackson, Kentucky. After high school, he served in Iraq as a marine. Following his military service, Vance went on to graduate from Ohio State University and earn a law degree at Yale. He has written for *National Review*, the *New York Times*, and many other publications. In the following introduction to his best-selling 2016 memoir, *Hillbilly Elegy*, Vance examines how the defining values of Appalachia have also contributed to social and economic problems within the region.

Andrew Spear/Redux

My name is J.D. Vance, and I think I should start with a confession: I find the existence of the book you hold in your hands somewhat absurd. It says right there on the cover that it's a memoir, but I'm thirty-one years old, and I'll be the first to admit that I've accomplished nothing great in my life, certainly nothing that would justify a complete stranger paying money to read about it. The coolest thing I've done, at least on paper, is graduate from Yale Law School, something thirteen-year-old J.D. Vance would have considered ludicrous. But about two hundred people do the same thing every year, and trust me, you don't want to read about most of their lives. I am not a senator, a governor, or a former cabinet secretary. I haven't started a billion-dollar company or a world-changing nonprofit. I have a nice job, a happy marriage, a comfortable home, and two lively dogs.

So I didn't write this book because I've accomplished something extraordinary. I wrote this book because I've achieved something quite ordinary, which doesn't happen to most kids who grow up like me. You see, I grew up poor, in the Rust Belt, in an Ohio steel town that has been hemorrhaging jobs and hope for as long as I can remember. I have, to put it mildly, a complex relationship with my parents, one of whom has struggled with addiction for nearly my entire life. My grandparents, neither of whom graduated from high school, raised me, and few members of even my extended family attended college. The statistics tell you that kids like me face a grim future—that if they're lucky, they'll manage to avoid welfare; and if they're unlucky, they'll die of a heroin overdose, as happened to dozens in my small hometown just last year.

I was one of those kids with a grim future. I almost failed out of high school. I nearly gave in to the deep anger and resentment harbored by everyone around me. Today people look at me, at my job and my Ivy League credentials, and assume that I'm some sort of genius, that only a truly extraordinary person could have made it to where I am today. With all due respect to those people, I think that theory is a load of bullshit. Whatever talents I have, I almost squandered until a handful of loving people rescued me.

That is the real story of my life, and that is why I wrote this book. I want people to know what it feels like to nearly give up on yourself and why you might do it. I want people to understand what happens in the lives of the poor and the psychological impact that spiritual and material poverty has on their children. I want people to understand the American Dream as my family and I encountered it. I want people to understand how upward mobility really feels. And I want people to understand something I learned only recently: that for those of us lucky enough to live the American Dream, the demons of the life we left behind continue to chase us.

There is an ethnic component lurking in the background of my story. In our race-conscious society, our vocabulary often extends no further than the color of someone's skin—"black people," "Asians," "white privilege." Sometimes these broad categories are useful, but to understand my story, you have to delve into the details. I may be white, but I do not identify with the WASPs of the Northeast. Instead, I identify with the millions of working-class white Americans of Scots-Irish descent who have no college degree. To these folks, poverty is the family tradition—their ancestors were day laborers in the Southern slave economy, sharecroppers after that, coal miners after that, and machinists and millworkers during more recent times. Americans call them hillbillies, rednecks, or white trash. I call them neighbors, friends, and family.

The Scots-Irish are one of the most distinctive subgroups in America. As one observer noted, "In traveling across America, the Scots-Irish have consistently blown my mind as far and away the most persistent and unchanging regional subculture in the country. Their family structures, religion and politics, and social lives all remain unchanged compared to the wholesale abandonment of tradition that's occurred nearly everywhere else." This distinctive embrace of cultural tradition comes along with many good traits—an intense sense of loyalty, a fierce dedication to family and country—but also many bad ones. We do not like outsiders or people who are different from us, whether the difference lies in how they look, how they act, or, most important, how they talk. To understand me, you must understand that I am a Scots-Irish hillbilly at heart.

If ethnicity is one side of the coin, then geography is the other. When the first wave of Scots-Irish immigrants landed in the New World in the eighteenth century, they were deeply attracted to the Appalachian Mountains. This region is admittedly huge—stretching from Alabama to Georgia in the South to Ohio to parts of New York in the North—but the culture of Greater Appalachia is remarkably cohesive. My family, from the hills of eastern Kentucky, describe themselves as hillbillies, but Hank Williams, Jr.—born in Louisiana and an Alabama resident—also identified himself as one in his rural white anthem "A Country Boy Can Survive." It was Greater Appalachia's political reorientation from Democrat to Republican that redefined American politics after Nixon. And it is in Greater Appalachia where the fortunes of working-class whites seem dimmest. From low social mobility to poverty to divorce and drug addiction, my home is a hub of misery.

It is unsurprising, then, that we're a pessimistic bunch. What is more surprising is that, as surveys have found, working-class whites are the most pessimistic group in America. More pessimistic than Latino immigrants, many of whom suffer unthinkable poverty. More pessimistic than black Americans, whose material prospects continue to lag behind those of whites. While reality permits some degree of cynicism, the fact that hillbillies like me are more down about the future than many other groups—some of whom are clearly more destitute than we are—suggests that something else is going on.

Indeed it is. We're more socially isolated than ever, and we pass that isolation down to our children. Our religion has changed—built around churches heavy on emotional rhetoric but light on the kind of social support necessary to enable poor kids to do well. Many of us have dropped out of the labor force or have chosen not to relocate for better opportunities. Our men suffer from a peculiar crisis of masculinity in which some of the very traits that our culture inculcates make it difficult to succeed in a changing world.

When I mention the plight of my community, I am often met with an explanation that goes something like this: "Of course the prospects for working-class whites have worsened, J.D., but you're putting the chicken before the egg. They're divorcing more, marrying less, and experiencing less happiness because their economic opportunities have declined. If they only had better access to jobs, other parts of their lives would improve as well." 10

I once held this opinion myself, and I very desperately wanted to believe it during my youth. It makes sense. Not having a job is stressful, and not having enough money to live on is even more so. As the manufacturing center of the industrial Midwest has hollowed out, the white working class has lost both its economic security and the stable home and family life that comes with it.

But experience can be a difficult teacher, and it taught me that this story of economic insecurity is, at best, incomplete. A few years ago, during the summer before I enrolled at Yale Law School, I was looking for full-time work in order to finance my move to New Haven, Connecticut. A family friend suggested that I work for him in a medium-sized floor tile distribution business near my hometown. Floor tile is extraordinarily heavy: Each piece weighs anywhere from three to six pounds, and it's usually packaged in cartons of eight to twelve pieces. My primary duty was to lift the floor tile onto a shipping pallet and prepare that pallet for departure. It wasn't easy, but it paid thirteen dollars an hour and I needed the money, so I took the job and collected as many overtime shifts and extra hours as I could.

The tile business employed about a dozen people, and most employees had worked there for many years. One guy worked two full-time jobs, but not because he had to: His second job at the tile business allowed him to pursue his dream of piloting an airplane. Thirteen dollars an hour was good money for a single guy in our hometown—a decent apartment costs about five hundred dollars a month—and the tile business offered steady raises. Every employee who worked there for a few years earned at least sixteen dollars an hour in a down economy, which provided an annual income of thirty-two thousand—well above the poverty line even for a family. Despite this relatively stable situation, the managers found it impossible to fill my warehouse position with a long-term employee. By the time

I left, three guys worked in the warehouse; at twenty-six, I was by far the oldest.

One guy, I'll call him Bob, joined the tile warehouse just a few months before I did. Bob was nineteen with a pregnant girlfriend. The manager kindly offered the girlfriend a clerical position answering phones. Both of them were terrible workers. The girlfriend missed about every third day of work and never gave advance notice. Though warned to change her habits repeatedly, the girlfriend lasted no more than a few months. Bob missed work about once a week, and he was chronically late. On top of that, he often took three or four daily bathroom breaks, each over half an hour. It became so bad that, by the end of my tenure, another employee and I made a game of it: We'd set a timer when he went to the bathroom and shout the major milestones through the warehouse—"Thirty-five minutes!" "Forty-five minutes!" "One hour!"

Eventually, Bob, too, was fired. When it hap-15 pened, he lashed out at his manager: "How could you do this to me? Don't you know I've got a pregnant girlfriend?" And he was not alone: At least two other people, including Bob's cousin, lost their jobs or quit during my short time at the tile warehouse.

You can't ignore stories like this when you talk about equal opportunity. Nobel-winning economists worry about the decline of the industrial Midwest and the hollowing out of the economic core of working whites. What they mean is that manufacturing jobs have gone overseas and middle-class jobs are harder to come by for people without college degrees. Fair enough—I worry about those things, too. But this book is about something else: what goes on in the lives of real people when the industrial economy goes south. It's about reacting to bad circumstances in the worst way possible. It's about a culture that increasingly encourages social decay instead of counteracting it.

The problems that I saw at the tile warehouse run far deeper than macroeconomic trends and policy. Too many young men immune to hard work. Good jobs impossible to fill for any length of time. And a young man with every reason to work—a wife-to-be to support and a baby on the way—carelessly tossing aside a good job with excellent health insurance. More troublingly, when it was all over, he thought something had been done *to him*. There is a lack of agency here—a feeling that you have little control over your life and a willingness to blame everyone but yourself. This is distinct from the larger economic landscape of modern America.

It's worth noting that although I focus on the group of people I know—working-class whites with ties to Appalachia—I'm not arguing that we deserve more sympathy than other folks. This is not a story about why white people have more to complain about than black people or any other group. That said, I do hope that readers of this book will be able to take from it an appreciation of how class and family affect the poor without filtering their views through a racial prism. To many analysts, terms like "welfare queen" conjure unfair images of the lazy black mom living on the dole. Readers of this book will realize quickly that there is little relationship between that specter and my argument: I have known many welfare queens; some were my neighbors, and all were white.

This book is not an academic study. In the past few years, William Julius Wilson, Charles Murray, Robert Putnam, and Raj Chetty have authored compelling, well-researched tracts demonstrating that upward mobility fell off in the 1970s and never really recovered, that some regions have fared much worse than others (shocker: Appalachia and the Rust Belt score poorly), and that many of the phenomena I saw in my own life exist across society. I may quibble with some of their conclusions, but they have demonstrated convincingly that America has a problem. Though I will use data, and though I do sometimes rely on academic studies to make a point, my primary aim is not to convince you of a documented problem. My primary aim is to tell a true story about what that problem feels like when you were born with it hanging around your neck.

I cannot tell that story without appealing to the cast of characters who made up my life. So this book is not just a personal memoir but a family one—a history of opportunity and upward mobility viewed through the eyes of a group of hillbillies from Appalachia. Two generations ago, my grandparents were dirt-poor and in love. They got married and moved north in the hope of escaping the dreadful poverty around them. Their grandchild (me) graduated from one of the finest educational institutions in the world. That's the short version. The long version exists in the pages that follow.

Though I sometimes change the names of people to protect their privacy, this story is, to the best of my recollection, a fully accurate portrait of the world I've witnessed. There are no composite characters and no narrative shortcuts. Where possible, I corroborated the details with documentation—report cards, handwritten letters, notes on photographs—but I am sure this story is as fallible as any human memory. Indeed, when I asked my sister to read an earlier draft, that draft ignited a thirty-minute conversation about whether I had misplaced an event chronologically. I left my version in, not because I suspect my sister's memory is faulty (in fact, I imagine hers is better than mine), but because I think there is something to learn in how I've organized the events in my own mind.

Nor am I an unbiased observer. Nearly every person you will read about is deeply flawed. Some have tried to murder other people, and a few were successful. Some have abused their children, physically or emotionally. Many abused (and still abuse) drugs.

But I love these people, even those to whom I avoid speaking for my own sanity. And if I leave you with the impression that there are bad people in my life, then I am sorry, both to you and to the people so portrayed. For there are no villains in this story. There's just a ragtag band of hillbillies struggling to find their way—both for their sake and, by the grace of God, for mine.

The infographic titled *Cycle of Poverty* highlights the challenges resulting from both generational and situational poverty.

What challenges do generational and situational poverty create for communities? The image suggests that poverty can become ingrained over time. If this is true, how can a community change a culture? Consider some institutions, programs, or individual actions that may influence or change a culture.

RHETORICAL SITUATION

1. How does the writer appeal to **ethos**? Explain how this **credibility** advances the argument.

2. What is the writer's **exigence**? How does the writer's **context** affect the **exigence**?

3. How does Vance's perception of the **audience** guide his rhetorical choices in the text?

CLAIMS AND EVIDENCE

4. What types of **evidence** does Vance use to develop his argument? How does this evidence contribute to his **purpose**?

5. Explain how the **evidence** strengthens the writer's **credibility**.

6. Explain how Vance's arrangement of ideas helps him achieve his **purpose**.

REASONING AND ORGANIZATION

7. What **causal relationship** does *Hillbilly Elegy* attempt to explain?

8. Identify the **reasons** Vance offers to support his **claim**. Are they persuasive and effective? Why or why not?

9. How does Vance create **unity** in the text through his **line of reasoning**?

LANGUAGE AND STYLE

10. Identify a **simple sentence** in the text. Then, based on your example, explain how the writer uses simple sentences for effect.

11. How does the writer use **transitions** to establish a relationship between the **reasons** in the argument?

IDEAS IN AMERICAN CULTURE

12. Explain how this text speaks to the beliefs, values, and needs of the audience. Are Vance's perceptions and message about opportunity and oppression true beyond places like Appalachia? Can we break the cycle of poverty?

PUTTING IT ALL TOGETHER

13. How do Vance's narrative and his personal experience work to create the causality of the text? Does Vance's personal perspective strengthen the narrative? Explain.

Writing a Causal Argument

KEY POINT

Causal arguments are organized by causes, by effects, or by linking cause and effect.

If you have used scientific processes in biology, chemistry, or physics, you are probably familiar with causal analysis. This method of thinking applies to history, economics, political science, and other fields of study as well. But we also use this form of analysis in our daily lives, as we spend much of our time identifying causes and evaluating effects.

In this workshop, you have the opportunity to develop an argument that explains the relationship between a single cause and its subsequent effects or (alternatively) a single effect and its multiple causes. Using this method of development, you will argue your perspective on the subject of your choice. The causal relationships will serve as your line of reasoning.

Why I, a High School Football Player, Want to See Tackle Football Taken Away

Keegan Lindell

The following causal argument was written by high school student Keegan Lindell. It was named as a finalist in the *New York Times* 6th Annual Student Editorial Contest.

introduction that includes the reader

You feel a cool drop of sweat slide down your spine, sparking chills throughout your body. Your eyes dart back and forth in hopes of spotting the kamikaze player coming in. Shoulder to shoulder, you are a shield for the returner; however, a man disguised as a bomb sails through a gap five yards away and strikes head first into the teammate next to you. With a loud disturbing crack, anger, hatred, fear, and desperation fill your body. Paler than an albino, he rises with a stumble and it's apparent that fear has overtaken his eyes along with a look of confusion. Knowing he isn't alright, you insist he gets off the field; nevertheless, he needs to prove his manhood and forces himself back into the huddle.

detailed description of experiences connects to the purpose

Sadly, this is the reality of tackle football.

Excitement, brotherhood, life lessons are all extraordinary things that the game brings to your life; however, it brings brain diseases, concussions, and lifelong ripple effects as well. With the knowledge

lists the effects of tackle football

that our brain doesn't stop developing until our mid-twenties, the last thing you want to do is injure it. According to the Nida Blog Team article, teens and children are at a higher risk for concussions because the "brain's nerve fibers can be torn apart more easily." Why expose our nation's future to potential brain damage?

evidence that strengthens validity

rhetorical question amplifies the writer's exigence

Human anatomy is not built for football. Humans lack a "safety belt" for the brain and instead have protective fluid that can send the brain flying into your skull wall and severely bruise it. Meanwhile, a woodpecker that slams its beak into a tree can absorb the force through its beak and a muscle that wraps around the brain so it can't collide into the skull. Since humans lack this, we are prone to concussions. According to the *New York Times*, a former NFL player is "three to four times more likely" to develop "brain diseases, including Alzheimer's, Parkinson's, and amyotrophic lateral sclerosis." Instead of being oblivious to these problems, we should be concerned about the symptoms of football and take action.

transition links analogy claim

analogies as evidence

second effect of tackle football

evidence supports the effect

periodic sentence emphasizes message

At such a vital point in my developmental life, I am ripped apart between my love of the game and my growing realization that tackle football is not safe. As an avid football player since the fourth grade, I have reluctantly come to the conclusion that if I have future sons, they will not play tackle football. We need to make the wiser choice and lead ourselves into a safer future by removing one of my greatest passions. It's sad, but it is time for tackle football to go.

connects the idea of safety to the thesis

Sources

Gonchar, Michael. "If Football Is So Dangerous to Players, Should We Be Watching It?" The *New York Times*, 13 Sept. 2012.

The NIDA Blog Team. "Traumatic Brain Injury, Drug Addiction, and the Developing Teen Brain." National Institute on Drug Abuse for Teens, 19 Mar. 2015.

 YOUR ASSIGNMENT

Your community government is organizing a youth forum to discuss local and national issues that affect young people. But the organizers want to do more than hold a discussion: they also want to find ways to address these growing concerns.

Propose a discussion topic for this event by writing a multi-paragraph causal argument. In your text, identify an issue or problem. Then either explain the roots of the issue (a cause-related argument) or explain the consequences of the issue (an effect-related argument).

Your argument should include the following:

- An introduction that identifies the subject, provides context, and represents the writer's exigence
- A thesis statement that connects the unifying idea to your perspective and makes a claim about the causes or effects of the subject
- A line of reasoning that organizes your argument either by causes or effects
- Sufficient and relevant evidence that supports or further explains each cause or effect
- Commentary that explains the evidence and connects the evidence to your perspective
- A conclusion that brings the argument to a unified end by connecting the cause(s) and effect(s) to each other and to the writer's message.

Potential Subjects:

- The rising costs of higher education
- Elective course offerings for high schoolers
- Bullying within the community
- The community curfew for teenagers
- Public health issues

RHETORICAL SITUATION Writing an Introduction

AP® Enduring Understanding (RHS-1)

Individuals write within a particular situation and make strategic writing choices based on that situation.

Causal arguments generally come in two different forms. The first, an **effect-driven argument**, resembles the process that a doctor may go through. That is, when patients have a problem, they provide a list of their symptoms so that doctors can determine the cause of the illness. Knowing the cause, the physician can then inform the patient how the illness will be treated. The second type, **a cause-driven argument**, reverses that process. For example, an online social influencer notices an increase in "likes" and comments on her Instagram page. Then she explores why engagement is up. If she can discover the causes of this increase, that knowledge will inform her future decisions about the content on her page. In the same way, you identify effects and explore causes to make more informed decisions in your daily life.

Earlier in this unit, you learned that exigence is the spark that ignites communication. Your surroundings — including daily experiences, natural occurrences, local and national news events, and government policies — affect your life. These influences, both positive and negative, prompt you to reflect and respond with your own perspective. Like the doctor's patient or the curious influencer, you frequently examine the effects of events and occurrences in your life. As you do this, you are often governed by your perspective: that personal lens through which you view the world. So if you are writing about a specific event, your exigence might include the event itself, the event's impact on your life, and your perspective on that impact. In this way, the motivation for communication is born.

Consider the relationship between a single event (an increase in grade point average) and its possible causes and effects. If you are communicating this to an audience of new high school students, you might choose to write through the lens of causes (tutorials, high-interest courses, time management) so that you could offer advice on how to be successful in school. Focusing on the causes allows you to replicate them. If you have a different audience, you might want to stress the value of striving for improvement by highlighting the effects of your success. Thus, your personal account may persuade others to follow suit.

Cause-Driven: Causes → Effect	
More focused on studying/tutorials	Why do grades generally improve as students become juniors and seniors?
More high-interest, elective courses	
Better time management	

Effect-Driven: Cause ← Effects	
Does earning good grades improve students' lives?	Eligibility for scholarships and financial aid
	Increased trust and privileges at home
	Increased confidence to tackle challenging courses

	Issue One: Focus on Causes or Effects
What has prompted you to write about this subject?	What causes precipitate a single effect? or What effects result from a single cause?
Describe the subject and why it is important to you.	*I struggled my first year of high school, but I am excited to share with others how I improved.*
Describe your perspective and message for your audience.	*Focusing and having a study plan results in an overall improvement in GPA.* *Improving my GPA resulted in surprising personal improvements.*
Explain your goal for sharing your perspective.	*I would like unmotivated students to see the benefits of focusing on improvement.* *I would like new students to see practical ways to achieve success.*
List details related to your subject.	• *time management* • *intentional studying* • *carefully choosing courses* • *eliminating distractions* • *self-advocating*

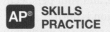

AP® SKILLS PRACTICE | **RHETORICAL SITUATION**
Writing an Introduction

1. Make a list of possible subjects for your causal argument. Consider both cause-driven subjects and effect-driven subjects.

2. Choose either a cause-driven or effect-driven subject. Then record details related to your exigence in a chart. Consider how you might use some of these details in your argument.

Exigence	Issue One: Focus on Causes
	What causes result from a single effect?
Describe the subject and why it is important to you.	
Describe your perspective and message for your audience.	
Explain your goal for sharing your perspective.	
List details and possible evidence related to your subject.	

REASONING AND ORGANIZATION **Unifying an Argument**

AP® Enduring Understanding (REO-1)

Writers guide understanding of a text's line of reasoning and claims through that text's organization and integration of evidence.

Writing a Thesis

Once you have explored your subject and identified either its causes or its effects, you will need to write a thesis statement. You will also need to organize your argument logically so that you can establish the cause-effect relationship and convey your message. You should choose either the cause-driven or effect-driven model to develop your argument. Your audience, your purpose, and your preliminary list of evidence will determine your line of reasoning.

Planning a Line of Reasoning

In a causal argument, the causes or effects will determine the topic sentences for your body paragraphs.

Cause-Driven		Effect-Driven	
Why do students' grades generally improve as students get older?		Does earning good grades improve students' lives?	
Thesis (idea + perspective)	*Because older students have developed focus and time management skills, along with the opportunity to choose more high-interest courses, juniors and seniors generally earn higher grades than ninth and tenth graders.*	**Thesis (idea + perspective)**	*Earning good grades improves students' lives inside and outside of school.*
Cause 1 Topic sentence + details	*They are managing their time better.*	**Effect 1 Topic sentence + details**	*Students have increased confidence to tackle challenging courses.*
Cause 2 Topic sentence + details	*They are focusing more on studying and attending tutorials.*	**Effect 2 Topic sentence + details**	*Students have increased trust and privileges at home.*
Cause 3 Topic sentence + details	*They are taking high-interest courses.*	**Effect 3 Topic sentence + details**	*Students become eligible for scholarships and financial aid.*

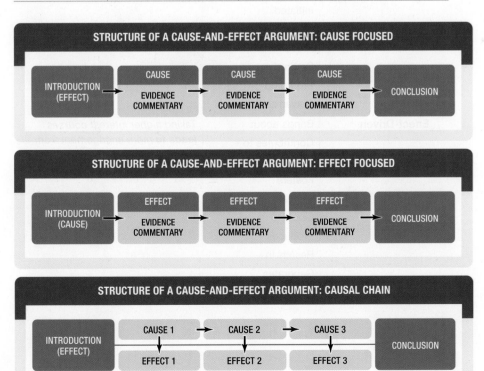

STRUCTURE OF A CAUSE-AND-EFFECT ARGUMENT: CAUSE FOCUSED

INTRODUCTION (EFFECT) → CAUSE EVIDENCE COMMENTARY → CAUSE EVIDENCE COMMENTARY → CAUSE EVIDENCE COMMENTARY → CONCLUSION

STRUCTURE OF A CAUSE-AND-EFFECT ARGUMENT: EFFECT FOCUSED

INTRODUCTION (CAUSE) → EFFECT EVIDENCE COMMENTARY → EFFECT EVIDENCE COMMENTARY → EFFECT EVIDENCE COMMENTARY → CONCLUSION

STRUCTURE OF A CAUSE-AND-EFFECT ARGUMENT: CAUSAL CHAIN

INTRODUCTION (EFFECT) → CAUSE 1 → CAUSE 2 → CAUSE 3 → CONCLUSION
EFFECT 1   EFFECT 2   EFFECT 3

INSIDER AP TIP **Writers may organize with a causal chain.** A causal chain is a series of interrelated causes and effects that build upon one another. In an argument, this organization can help represent a complex series of relationships.

Once you have established your thesis, you must consider the order of your cause- or effect-driven body paragraphs. You also need to decide the order of the evidence within the paragraphs. Notice that the order of your paragraphs corresponds to your line of reasoning. The order of your evidence and commentary within these body paragraphs corresponds to your arrangement. Choose your line of reasoning and arrangement based on your evidence and the relationship between your audience and your message.

Communicating causes and effects can be complicated at times. To present your argument in a logical and unified manner, choose precise verbs to establish the relationship between the subject and its causes or effects.

	Verbs	Examples
Cause-Driven	Affected Caused by Influenced Initiated Sparked Precipitated Spurred Prompted Galvanized	*My responsible and effective study habits **influenced** my mom to allow me to have more responsibility at home.*
Effect-Driven	Brings about Contributes to Creates Fosters Incites Leads to Produces Results in Generates Negates	*Taking higher interest courses **leads to** more engagement from the student.*

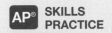 **SKILLS PRACTICE** | **REASONING AND ORGANIZATION**
Unifying an Argument

1. Review your brainstorming notes on subject and exigence.
2. Develop your thesis statement by combining the unifying idea and your perspective.
3. Review the details and possible evidence for your subject.
4. Compose topic sentences communicating the causes or effects of your subject. Carefully consider the order in which you will present these topic sentences.
5. Plan a conclusion that unifies your message and relates back to the central cause or effect in your thesis.

Thesis with claim (idea + perspective)	
Cause or effect 1 Topic sentence	
Cause or effect 2 Topic sentence	
Cause or effect 3 Topic sentence	
Effect or cause Conclusion	

CLAIMS AND EVIDENCE **Connecting Relevant Evidence**

AP® Enduring Understanding (CLE-1)

Writers make claims about subjects, rely on evidence that supports the reasoning that justifies the claim, and often acknowledge or respond to other, possibly opposing, arguments.

Your causal argument depends on your presenting sufficient and relevant evidence. You cannot simply make a claim without supporting it. Recall that evidence can come in a variety of forms, including definitions, facts, statistics, studies, historical accounts, and other research. It can come from many sources, whether encyclopedias, dictionaries, television documentaries, or peer-reviewed scholarly journals. Evidence may also come from your own observation and experience, as in the case of personal anecdotes, descriptions, brief narratives, and references to current events or pop culture. The purpose of evidence is usually to accomplish the following goals:

- Strengthen the validity of the argument (logos)
- Appeal to the audience's emotions (pathos)
- Increase the writer's credibility (ethos)

Creating Coherence

In Unit 4, you learned how using modifiers and eliminating ambiguity can strengthen your argument. When you focus on clarity and guide your audience with effective transitions, you will also make your argument more coherent.

In the body paragraphs of your causal argument, you must explain the significance of the evidence that you include. You must also make connections between the evidence and your thesis statement. Since cause-effect relationships depend so strictly upon one another, you should be deliberate and strategic in choosing transitions that establish relationships.

	Transitions	Examples
Cause-Driven	Although Because Since While	***Because*** *I learned how to manage my time, I actually discovered I had more free time than I thought.*
Effect-Driven	Accordingly As a result Consequently Hence Inevitably Therefore	***As a result*** *of managing my time wisely, I was able to enjoy engaging classes and also time out with my friends.*

ACHIEVING COHERENCE

Transitions to Indicate Equality	Transitions to Indicate Inequality		
Coordinating Conjunctions (FANBOYS)	**Subordinating Conjunctions (Frequently Used)**		
for	after	before	supposing
and	although	despite	though
nor	as	even if	when
but	as if	even though	whenever
or	as long as	if	whereas
yet	because	provided that	whether
so		since	while

 SKILLS PRACTICE | CLAIMS AND EVIDENCE
Connecting Relevant Evidence

1. Revisit your thesis statement and your topic sentences. Make any necessary changes to ensure that you are developing a unified argument.

2. Review the order of your topic sentences and explain the order of your line of reasoning.

3. Generate specific evidence to exemplify your topic sentences and convey your message.

4. Carefully arrange your evidence within the body paragraphs. More generally, arrange your evidence in a logical order within each paragraph to demonstrate the connections and emerging relationships between causes and effects.

Thesis with Claim (Idea + Perspective)		
Topic Sentence Reason 1 (Cause or Effect)	Topic Sentence Reason 2 (Cause or Effect)	Topic Sentence Reason 3 (Cause or Effect)
Supporting Evidence	Supporting Evidence	Supporting Evidence
Supporting Evidence	Supporting Evidence	Supporting Evidence

 LANGUAGE AND STYLE ## Using Subordination and Coordination

AP **Enduring Understanding (STL-1)**

The rhetorical situation informs the strategic stylistic choices that writers make.

As in all arguments, your specific stylistic choices strongly influence how your audience receives your message. Your syntactical choices convey your message by creating connections and reinforcing relationships between ideas. They help the audience understand your perspective as well. In this workshop, we will explore ways to convey the relationships between ideas in causal arguments. Specifically, we will be incorporating coordination and subordination into your sentence structure.

Coordination links up two things of equal importance. We use coordination for two purposes within a sentence:

- to demonstrate equal importance between ideas and
- to represent a balance of ideas.

In sentences, we achieve coordination in two ways:

- using coordinating conjunctions (FANBOYS: for, and, nor, but, or, yet, so) or
- using conjunctive adverbs (however, therefore, for example, in fact, etc.).

Subordination, in contrast to coordination, highlights the importance of one idea over another. We use a **subordinate clause** (a clause that is incomplete without an independent clause to modify) in thesis statements, topic sentences, or commentary when we are

- addressing the complexity of the issue,
- presenting a line of reasoning for the argument,
- offering a concession or rebuttal,
- emphasizing one idea over another,
- clarifying or explaining a noun, or
- establishing causal relationships.

Subordination connects one or more independent clauses with one or more dependent clauses. We achieve it in two ways:

- using subordinating conjunctions (e.g., after, because, whether, while)
- using relative pronouns (i.e., who, whose, whom, which, that)

Therefore, when you are developing commentary for your argument, you might employ a complex sentence structure — for example, a sentence with at least one independent clause and one subordinate clause. Consider the following independent clauses that can stand alone as sentences on their own. Each clause contains an idea:

> Studying for two hours a day after school improves student performance.

> Students need to schedule some time for themselves each day.

As independent clauses, each of these ideas has equal importance, and, if you choose, you can join them together with a coordinating conjunction.

> Studying for two hours a day after school improves student performance, **and** students need to schedule some time for themselves each day.

However, if you want to emphasize one idea over another, you can make one of the sentences subordinate by adding a subordinating conjunction, such as *although*, *while*, *since*, or *because*. Your syntactical decision depends upon your purpose.

For example, to emphasize the importance of free time, you can make the first sentence subordinate. This choice suggests that you favor making free time a priority.

Additionally, the order of this sentence (subordinate clause to independent clause) is called a periodic sentence. This arrangement describes a sentence whose main idea is placed at the end, which gives that idea an even stronger emphasis. Periodic sentences are especially effective for thesis statements because the writer's main claim gets final emphasis.

> **Even though** studying for two hours a day after school improves their performance, <u>students need to schedule some time for themselves each day</u>.

If you reverse the order of these clauses (independent clause to subordinate clause), your sentence would be arranged in a cumulative order, and the final thought would have less emphasis.

> <u>Students need to schedule some time for themselves each day</u> **even though** studying for two hours a day after school improves their performance.

Conversely, if you wanted to emphasize studying over free time, you would reverse the process as follows.

> **While** students need to schedule some time for themselves each day, <u>studying for two hours a day after school improves their performance</u>.

> <u>Studying for two hours a day after school improves their performance</u> **even if** students need to schedule some time for themselves each day.

SYNTACTICAL SUBORDINATION

	Description	Function	Examples
Independent Clause	Contains a subject and a verb and can stand alone	Functions to emphasize both points by isolating them in their own sentence	*Studying for two hours a day after school improves student performance.* *Students need to schedule some time for themselves each day.*
Subordinate Clause in a Periodic Sentence	Begins with a subordinating conjunction, making the clause that follows dependent on another part of the sentence for relevance Clause appears before the main clause and is followed by a comma	Functions to emphasize the information in the independent clause Especially effective for thesis statements when the writer's claim ends the sentence	***Even though*** *studying for two hours a day after school improves their performance, students need to schedule some time for themselves each day.* ***While*** *students need to schedule some time for themselves each day, studying for two hours a day after school improves their performance.*
Subordinate Clause in a Cumulative Sentence	Begins with a subordinating conjunction establishing a relationship with the independent clause that precedes it Clause appears after the main clause and does not require a comma	Functions to emphasize the main clause but may use the dependent clause as a transitional element	*Students need to schedule some time for themselves each day* ***even though*** *studying for two hours a day after school improves their performance.* *Studying for two hours a day after school improves their performance* ***even if*** *students need to schedule some time for themselves each day.*

AP® SKILLS PRACTICE | **LANGUAGE AND STYLE**
Using Subordination and Coordination

- Prepare to draft your essay based on your thesis, line of reasoning, and evidence.
- Compose an introduction, body paragraphs, and conclusion.
- Include at least three sentences that demonstrate subordination in your essay.

AP® SKILLS PRACTICE | PUTTING IT ALL TOGETHER
Revising and Editing a Causal Argument

Peer-Revision Checklist: Revising and Editing a Causal Argument

Revising and Editing Checklist	Unit 5 Focus Skills	Comment on the Effectiveness and/or Make a Suggestion
Does the claim in the introduction or conclusion connect the subject to an idea and perspective?	*Causal argument*	
Are the evidence and commentary organized by causes, effects, or the cause-effect relationship of the concept?	*Line of reasoning*	
Has the writer developed the argument with relevant and sufficient evidence that logically links to the line of reasoning?	*Unity and coherence*	
Has the writer explained the evidence and connected the causes or effects to the perspective? Are these choices effective for the specific audience and purpose?	*Developing commentary*	
Is the writing clear and specific? Does the writer use syntax (subordination and coordination) to link ideas logically and amplify the relationship between causes, effects, and the issue?	*Syntax for emphasis*	
Is the writing free of errors in spelling, usage, punctuation, capitalization, and agreement?	*Writing conventions*	

Free-Response Question: Argument

Creating Unity and Coherence

In Unit 2, you practiced making a claim and developing a line of reasoning for an argument essay, a free-response question on the AP® English Language and Composition Exam. Now, you will build on those skills to review the process for writing an argument. This workshop will focus on how making connections can create unity and coherence in your argument.

Read the following practice prompt, which is like one you may see on the AP® English Language and Composition Exam.

Prompt:

In his letter to the American people written shortly before his death in 2020, the congressman and civil rights activist John Lewis reminded his readers of one of his most ardent messages: "Ordinary people with extraordinary vision can redeem the soul of America by getting in what I call good trouble, necessary trouble."

Write an essay that argues your position on Lewis's claim that "good trouble, necessary trouble" can redeem the "soul of America."

In your response, you should do the following:

- Respond to the prompt with a thesis that presents a defensible position.

- Provide evidence to support your line of reasoning.

- Explain how the evidence supports your line of reasoning.

- Use appropriate grammar and punctuation in communicating your argument.

→ **Step One: Determine Your Unifying Idea and Perspective, and Then Brainstorm Potential Examples**

Read the prompt carefully and determine exactly what you are being asked to do. In this case, you are directed to argue a position on the claim that getting into "good" and "necessary" trouble can redeem America. Take a moment to identify the ideas stated or implied in the prompt. Then record your thoughts and details about Lewis's claim as they come to mind. Evaluate your list of ideas and choose the strongest one as a controlling or unifying idea for your argument. This idea, along with your perspective, will form the claim in your thesis and guide your line of reasoning in the next step.

Next, based on these ideas and your initial perspective, think of potential evidence that you might use to develop your argument. As you learned in Unit 2, you can draw from a variety of sources such as historical examples, media accounts of current events, and your own observations and experiences. Keep in mind that the evidence you choose to support your argument will need to connect directly to your idea and perspective. And it will be up to you to make those connections as you develop a unified and coherent argument.

→ Step Two: Develop a Defensible Claim and Unified Line of Reasoning

As you learned in Unit 2, you need to make a defensible claim that will also unify your argument. Using your notes from the first step, develop a thesis statement. The thesis should include a claim that conveys both a unifying idea and your perspective on the question in the prompt. Consider this example:

Topic:	Good trouble
Idea: + Perspective:	Justice Changing attitudes and behaviors
Thesis:	When ordinary people are willing to get into "good trouble," their selfless sacrifice can influence a nation to change its attitudes and behaviors regarding justice for its people.

As you have learned in this unit, writers achieve unity through their line of reasoning, which serves as a framework for their arguments. Once you have considered the potential evidence to support your thesis, you can begin to develop your reasons based on this evidence.

In the practice prompt, you may have considered historical or contemporary examples of "good trouble," such as the Founding Fathers in the American Revolution, suffragettes of the early twentieth century, fellow civil rights activists and contemporaries of John Lewis, or even modern-day whistleblowers or student protestors. From this list, you then explore the details of these examples: common ideas, historical parallels, traits, implications, and other similarities. These will determine the line of reasoning that supports your thesis. Consider this example:

Thesis with Claim (Idea + Perspective)

When ordinary people are willing to get into "good trouble," their selfless sacrifice can influence a nation to change its attitudes and behaviors regarding justice for its people.

Reason 1	Reason 2
Ordinary people performing extraordinary sacrifices shed light on injustices present in our country.	When citizens begin to recognize the flaws in their views and behavior, they are more willing to change.

A unified line of reasoning connects directly to the idea and perspective as it justifies your thesis. When you have decided on your reasons, you then need to consider the best order for presenting them. The line of reasoning in this argument — and most that you will encounter on the exam — follow the cause-effect organization. For example in this sample question, the first paragraph begins with changing attitudes and leads to changing behaviors. These reasons are unified under the idea of justice and the perspective of change.

→ Step Three: Choose Relevant Evidence

You will need to evaluate the specific question in the prompt to decide which evidence will be most useful and appropriate for the context. While you are allowed to generate evidence from more than one discipline or source, you should consider the coherence of your argument carefully. That means choosing and connecting reasons and evidence that suit the context of the argument, your idea, and your perspective. As you learned in Unit 2, you can draw evidence from common areas and sources for the argument response:

- History
- Literature
- Science

- Personal experience
- Sports
- Politics

- Current events
- Pop culture

Think of the argument task as an invitation to a party and the evidence that supports your claim as the clothes you will wear to the party. Whether you are invited to a formal occasion or to a picnic, you want to dress appropriately. Argument prompts require a similar type of consideration. Some topics may be more suited for examples from history, sociology, psychology, even literature. Other topics may be more personal or relate to more informal elements of culture, so personal anecdotes, or references to pop culture, entertainment, and sports, would fit well. As always, you make choices based on the rhetorical situation: the topic, your experience with the topic, your audience, and your message.

For example, after carefully reading the John Lewis sample, you observe from the information in the prompt that the idea of "necessary trouble" is set within the context of the civil rights movement and the American government (Lewis was a congressman). Additionally, the context suggests the necessity and ramifications of "redeem[ing] the soul of America," which are serious considerations. With that in mind, you will need to generate appropriate evidence based on this context.

Relevant Evidence for "Good Trouble" Prompt	
Area	**Evidence**
History	American revolutionaries
	Suffragettes
	Civil rights activists
Current Events	Whistleblowers
	"Sick Out" in airline industry
Personal Experience	Student protest
	Picket lines at a local factory

Once you have brainstormed relevant evidence, you will want to choose the most relevant and compelling examples to support each reason in your line of reasoning.

Reason 1:

Ordinary people performing extraordinary sacrifices shed light on injustices present in our country and change attitudes.

Evidence:

For example, in the nineteenth and twentieth centuries, suffragettes lobbied and protested, risking bodily harm and imprisonment to petition for a woman's right to vote in the United States.

→ **Step Four: Develop Your Commentary**

To develop your argument, you must do more than provide evidence to support your reasons. You must also explain how and why your evidence supports your reasons, how your reasons support your claim, and how the evidence is significant to the unifying idea in your claim. This explanation is also called *commentary*. Therefore, along with the evidence you provide, you should use your commentary to address one or more of the following questions:

- Why is this evidence significant in supporting the line of reasoning?
- How does this evidence corroborate my claim?
- How is this evidence relevant to the unifying idea and the claim?
- How can I connect the details in the evidence to my unifying idea and perspective?
- How does the evidence qualify or modify the argument by considering alternative perspectives?
- What insight can I offer to address the complexity of the argument?

Consider this example:

Reason 1:

Ordinary people performing extraordinary sacrifices shed light on injustices present in our country and change attitudes.

Evidence:

For example, in the nineteenth and early twentieth centuries, suffragettes not only lobbied and protested, but also risked bodily harm and imprisonment in their fight for the right to vote in the United States.

Commentary:

By making good trouble, these women gained increasing attention and support from citizens who backed their cause: winning the right for women to vote and make decisions that affected their lives. Because of the suffragettes' activism, everyday people began to hear their arguments and understand the value of their message about equality. The extraordinary efforts of ordinary citizens inspired Americans to change their attitude about the issue and ultimately led to the ratification of the Nineteenth Amendment.

Commentary connects evidence and reasoning with the claim. Remember: your readers cannot read your mind. Relevant evidence is a good beginning, but it's never enough on its own. You must explain how the evidence supports your reasons and then explain how each reason justifies the claim. Readers want to understand your reasoning, not merely a list of facts, details, or descriptions. Therefore, effective writers spend as much time and space explaining the relevance of their evidence as they do providing it. As a good rule of thumb, the word length of your commentary should be equal to or greater than that of the evidence.

 **Arguments acknowledge other arguments.** The best arguments consider the perspectives of others and respond to them. That means writers may acknowledge others' perspectives that are relevant to their argument.

PREPARING FOR THE AP® EXAM

The following is an example of an argument free response question. Use what you have learned in this workshop to write a complete argument in response to the prompt.

Prompt:
In her book *My Own Words*, the late Supreme Court Justice Ruth Bader Ginsburg wrote, "When a thoughtless or unkind word is spoken, best tune out. Reacting in anger or annoyance will not advance one's ability to persuade."

In an essay, argue your position on Ginsburg's claim that reacting in anger or annoyance blocks your ability to persuade.

In your response, you should do the following:

- Respond to the prompt with a thesis that presents a defensible position.

- Provide evidence to support your line of reasoning.

- Explain how the evidence supports your line of reasoning.

- Use appropriate grammar and punctuation in communicating your argument.

from The Hiding Place
Corrie ten Boom

The following is an excerpt from a true narrative set during World War II in the Nazi-occupied Netherlands.

1   Mr. Smit examined and approved the hiding place for ration cards beneath the bottom step. He also pronounced acceptable the warning system we had worked out. This was a triangle-shaped wooden sign advertising that Alpina Watches I had placed in the dining room window. As long as the sign was in place, it was safe to enter.

2   But when I showed him a cubby hole behind the corner cupboard in the dining room, he shook his head. Some ancient redesigning of the house had left a crawl space in that corner, and we had been secreting jewelry, silver coins, and other valuables there. Not only had the rabbi brought us his library, but other Jewish families had brought their treasures to the Beje[1] for safekeeping. The space was large enough that we believed a person could crawl in there if necessary, but Mr. Smit dismissed it without a second glance.

3   "First place they'd look. Don't bother to change it, though. It's only silver. We're interested in saving people, not things."

4   He started up the narrow corkscrew stairs, and as he mounted so did his spirits. He paused in delight at the odd-placed landings, pounded on the crooked walls, and laughed aloud as the floor levels of the two old houses continued out of phase.

5   "What an impossibility!" he said in an awe-struck voice. "What an unbelievable, unpredictable impossibility! Miss ten Boom, if all houses were constructed like this one, you would see before you a less worried man."

6   At the top of the stairs, he entered my bedroom. "This is it!" he exclaimed. "You want your hiding place as high as possible. Gives you the best chance to reach it while the search is on below."

7   Mr. Smit began measuring. He moved the wobbly old wardrobe away from the wall and pulled my bed into the center of the room. "This is where the false wall will go!" Excitedly he penciled a line along the floor thirty inches from the back wall. He stood up and gazed at it.

8   "That's as big as I dare," he said. "It will easily take a cot mattress, though."

9   Over the next few days, Mr. Smit and his workmen were in and out of our house. They never knocked. At each visit each man carried in something. Tools in a folded newspaper. A few bricks in a briefcase.

10   I ventured to wonder if a wooden wall would not be easier to build.

11   "Wood sounds hollow," he said. "No. Brick's the only thing for false walls."

12   After the wall was up, the plasterer came, then the carpenter, finally the painter. Six days after he had begun, Mr. Smit called Father, Betsie, and me to see.

13   We stood in the doorway and gaped. The smell of fresh paint was everywhere. But surely nothing in this room was newly painted! All four walls had that streaked and grimy look that old rooms got in coal-burning Haarlem.[2]

[1] A particular kind of tall and narrow home in the Netherlands.

[2] A city in the Netherlands, a European country that was neutral during World War II but invaded by Nazi Germany in May of 1940.

The ancient molding ran unbroken around the ceiling, chipped and peeling here and there, obviously undisturbed for 150 years. Old water stains streaked the back wall—a wall that even I, who had lived half a century in this room, could scarcely believe was not the original, but set back a precious two-and-a-half feet from the true wall of the building.

Built-in bookshelves, old, sagging shelves with 14 the same water stains as the wall behind them, ran along this false wall.

Down in the far left hand corner, beneath the 15 bottom shelf, a sliding panel, two feet high and two wide, opened into the secret room.

Mr. Smit stooped and pulled this panel up. 16 On hands and knees, Betsie and I crawled into the narrow room behind it. Inside we could stand up, sit, or even stretch out one at a time on the single mattress. A concealed vent allowed air to enter from outside.

"Keep a water jug there," said Mr. Smit, crawl- 17 ing in behind us. "Change the water once a week. Hardtack³ and vitamins keep indefinitely. Any-time there is anyone in the house whose presence is unofficial, all possessions except the clothes on his back must be stored in here."

Dropping to our knees again, we crawled out, 18 single-file. "Move back into your bedroom," he told me. "Everything exactly as before."

With his fist he struck the wall above the 19 bookshelves. "The Gestapo could search for a year," he said. "They'll never find this one."

1. In context, the clause "but when I showed him a cubby hole behind the corner cupboard in the dining room" (paragraph 2, sentence 1) serves to
   (A) focus on the argument that Mr. Smit is trying to make in his interactions with the narrator.
   (B) transition to the problem about which the rest of the passage will concern itself.
   (C) shift between different problems about which the passage concerns itself.
   (D) indicate Mr. Smit's concern about hiding belongings instead of people.
   (E) indicate concerns about the architecture of the house.

2. The first sentence of paragraph 3 ("First place they'd look."), refers to which place mentioned elsewhere in the passage?
   (A) "the hiding place for ration cards beneath the bottom step" (paragraph 1)
   (B) "a cubby hole behind the corner cupboard in the dining room" (paragraph 2)
   (C) "the narrow corkscrew stairs" (paragraph 4)
   (D) "odd-placed landings" (paragraph 4)
   (E) "the wobbly old wardrobe" (paragraph 7)

3. The details provided in paragraph 9 advance the reasoning of the narrative by
   (A) describing how the space was built.
   (B) explaining why a brick wall was necessary.
   (C) supporting the need for built-in bookshelves.
   (D) illustrating the secretive nature of the work being done to protect people.
   (E) making the narrator question the decision to hide people in the house.

³Hard, dry bread or biscuit, especially as rations for sailors, soldiers, or others.

4. In the third sentence of paragraph 13, the writer's choice of the descriptive words "streaked and grimy" serves to
    (A) illustrate what the builders did in an attempt to disguise their work and the new room.
    (B) describe the air quality problems in Haarlem.
    (C) explain the terrible condition of the house, even after the builders did their work.
    (D) describe the consequences of leaving a house unrepaired for 150 years.
    (E) illustrate the water problems shown by the stains on the wall.

5. Which of the following best describes the purpose for development in paragraphs 13–15?
    (A) To describe the state of homes in Haarlem and why it was difficult for Mr. Smit and his workmen to build the new wall and disguise the new room
    (B) To illustrate the close attention to detail used by Mr. Smit and his workmen in building the new wall and disguising the new room
    (C) To provide the reader with a better understanding of what Mr. Smit and his workmen were up against as they did their work
    (D) To explain the process that Mr. Smit and his workmen undertook as they were building the new wall and disguising the new room
    (E) To provide ideas to the reader about how to plan and execute similar plans of their own

6. In the context of the passage and paragraph 14, the detail that the bookshelves were "[b]uilt-in" serves to
    (A) show that the wall had to be reinforced with bookshelves because the house was so old.
    (B) illustrate how considerate the workmen were for those who actually had to live in the house.
    (C) describe how things were attached to the wall even though it was brick.
    (D) disguise how people were to get in and out of the hidden room.
    (E) illustrate the care and attention to detail taken to make everything appear older to match the house and show that they had not simply been moved to that wall.

7. Which of the following best describes the main idea reflected on in this narrative?
    (A) Helping people may not be worth the time if those you oppose are too powerful.
    (B) No matter what you do, it may not be possible to help some people if they aren't willing to help themselves.
    (C) Doing the right thing may take more planning and attention to detail than one may be prepared for.
    (D) Our own experiences and abilities are enough when we have good intentions.
    (E) Failure to accept the fears of those we try to help prevents us from helping them at all.

8. Which of the following statements from the passage is most likely to appeal to the emotions and values of the audience?
   (A) "We're interested in saving people, not things" (paragraph 3).
   (B) "What an unbelievable, unpredictable impossibility!" (paragraph 5).
   (C) "Excitedly he penciled a line along the floor thirty inches from the back wall" (paragraph 7).
   (D) "I ventured to wonder if a wooden wall would not be easier to build" (paragraph 10).
   (E) "We stood in the doorway and gaped" (paragraph 13).

9. Which of the following best summarizes the writer's likely purpose with this narrative?
   (A) To show what it takes to resist evil and ensure that those with the best intentions for a society survive
   (B) To display the faith that people have in others to protect and care for them at times of need
   (C) To argue that architects and homeowners should consider these types of things in their homes in preparation for events such as those that occurred in the context during which this narrative is set
   (D) To demonstrate the significant measures that people had — and were willing — to take in order to hide and protect people from the Nazi threat and illustrate what good people do in the face of fear and hatred
   (E) To display the terror that filled people's lives daily during the Nazi occupation and illustrate what people are willing to do to survive

The passage below is a draft.

(1) Since the creation of the first .com website in 1985, the internet has become the greatest ever medium for the exchange of information and the greatest ever source of misinformation. (2) A 1996 article by Tim Berners-Lee, director of the World Wide Web Consortium and a principal research scientist at the Massachusetts Institute of Technology, explained the young internet as an open "shared information space through which people (and machines) could communicate." (3) That open exchange of ideas promised by the internet was expected to be a panacea of democratic and humanitarian ideals around the world.

(4) As with anything ideal, however, reality eventually sets in.

(5) Today, it is easy to find ideas that would never have spread through the popular media, which had been the only source of information before the internet. (6) And it seems there is always an audience of internet users ready and waiting for something new or controversial. (7) Some of these fringe ideas are inert and almost comical; some of them should be heard and considered, while others are harmful or even dangerous.

(8) The truth is that there aren't many truths on the internet. (9) But truth has never really been the goal of the internet; indeed, as Berners-Lee explained in 1996, "shared information" is the goal. (10) Instead, truth comes from closely reading that information. (11) People must be taught how to search for, harvest, and digest all of the different pieces of information coming at them. (12) A skill that has now become known as "information literacy."

(13) The most important thing about information literacy in recent years may also be the most difficult — that is, how to independently verify something. (14) In fact, the related phrase "trust but verify" has seen a 600 percent increase in use across all types of media since Berners-Lee wrote that article in 1996. (15) Reading some surprising or interesting piece of information should be followed by seeking original sources of that information in an attempt to verify it. (16) Learning to consume information like this takes time and practice, but it is essential as more and more people have access to more and more information.

1. The writer is considering adding the following sentence before sentence 2.

   While the internet had existed for a few decades, it wasn't until the early mid-1990s that it became easily accessible to regular people.

   Should the writer make this addition?

   (A) Yes, because the writer needs to create more context for the commentary in the discussion.
   (B) Yes, because the reader may not understand the history of the development of and access to the internet.
   (C) No, because the writer has already established a time line for the conversation in sentence 1 and sentence 2 and then reasonably comments on that.
   (D) No, because the commentary provided is neither necessary for the context of the passage nor to establish the time line of the discussion.
   (E) No, because the proposed sentence offers nothing useful to the conversation.

2. The writer wants to add a sentence immediately following sentence 7 (and in the same paragraph) to better guide the reader through the line of reasoning. Which of the following choices most effectively accomplishes this goal?

   (A) And the most dangerous of all is the lack of truth.
   (B) With all of these ideas flying around different websites and social media, it has become more and more difficult to suss out the truth.
   (C) Recently, the most comical ones to have actually found some believers include those claiming that the earth is flat or that Finland doesn't exist.
   (D) Dangerous ideas may actually hurt people.
   (E) Attention paid to absurd theories pulls attention away from things that actually matter and harms real progress.

3. The writer wants to replace the underlined phrase in sentence 10 (reproduced below) with a more precise phrase, taking into account the context of the paragraph.

   Instead, truth comes from closely reading that information.

   Which of the following choices best accomplishes this goal?

   (A) (as it is now)
   (B) simply paying attention to
   (C) thoughtful and reasonable consideration of
   (D) accepting as true
   (E) doubting and critical skepticism of

4. The writer is considering deleting sentence 4 (reproduced below)

   As with anything ideal, however, reality eventually sets in.

   Should the writer delete this sentence?

   (A) Yes, because deleting it will better connect the reasoning across the two paragraphs that it now splits.
   (B) Yes, because it creates an unnecessary contrast between the ideal and the real.
   (C) Yes, because it fails to take into account the full context of "democratic and humanitarian ideals" as they relate to the reasoning of the passage.
   (D) No, because the reader needs that sentence to better understand the degrees of separation between the ideal and the real.
   (E) No, because it furthers the contrast between the idealism of the early internet and the realities faced by societies with access to so much information.

5. The writer wants to replace the underlined phrase in sentence 13 (reproduced below) with a more precise phrase, taking into account the context of the passage.

   The most important thing about information literacy in recent years may also be the most difficult — that is, how to independently verify something.

   Which of the following choices best accomplishes this goal?

   (A) (as it is now)
   (B) realization
   (C) thought
   (D) consideration
   (E) idea

6. The writer wants to clearly illustrate
   the importance of learning to consume
   information as mentioned in sentence 16
   (reproduced below).

   *Learning to consume information like this
   takes time and practice, but it is essential
   as more and more people have access to
   more and more information.*

   Which of the following revisions
   accomplishes this goal?

   (A) (as it is now)
   (B) Too many people have access to too
       much information.
   (C) Foolish consumer habits will continue
       to shape the way that information is
       accessed and used by those who have no
       business making such decisions in the
       first place.
   (D) Learning about consumer information
       can only be done through those
       programs that study information literacy.
   (E) Learning to consume information like
       this takes time and practice, but it is
       essential as people have access to more
       information.

ZUMA Press, Inc./Alamy Stock Photo

6

Establishing and Evaluating Credibility

Credibility is built throughout a text: it's part of the reason why audiences can trust the writer's perspective. This trust is essential. In fact, you could have the most compelling argument and still not achieve your purpose if you (or your sources) lack credibility. But how do you determine credibility?

For example, you may have been told to use only "unbiased sources" in your writing. But if every writer has a perspective, do unbiased sources even exist? Can biased sources still be credible? Even the best sources are limited in their scope. But a bias is a limitation that functions like a blind spot to other perspectives and positions on an issue. Indeed, every choice a writer makes — from the selection of evidence and the organization of the argument to word choice, syntax, and tone — affects how credible the audience thinks the writer is.

UNIT GOALS

	Unit Focus	Reading, Analyzing, and Interpreting	Writing
Big Idea: Rhetorical Situation	The Writer's Credibility	Explain how the writer establishes credibility with his or her audience.	Employ strategies that establish credibility with your audience.
Big Idea: Claims and Evidence	Strategic Evidence	Explain how a writer strategically selects sources to establish credibility and arranges evidence for emphasis.	Strategically select evidence to establish credibility and arrange reasoning and evidence for emphasis.
Big Idea: Reasoning and Organization	Classification and Division	Explain how a writer develops an idea through classification and division.	Write an argument developed through classification and division.
Big Idea: Language and Style	Precision of Language	Explain how a writer's diction conveys a tone, establishes credibility, and relates to an audience.	Choose words to convey a tone and achieve a purpose.
Ideas in American Culture	• Endurance and Expression • Wealth and Poverty	Explain how the ideas of endurance, expression, wealth, and poverty are reflected in classic and contemporary American texts.	
Preparing for the AP® Exam	• Free Response: Synthesis • Multiple Choice	Analyze rhetorical choices in classic and contemporary nonfiction texts.	Select sources to establish credibility and synthesize evidence to support a line of reasoning.

The Writer's Credibility

 Enduring Understanding (RHS-1)

Individuals write within a particular situation and make strategic writing choices based on that situation.

KEY POINT

A writer's credibility affects the way an audience receives an argument.

Given the complexity of our lives, we must often rely on the experience and judgment of others to help guide our own decisions. For example, before buying a new laptop computer, we may read reviews of different brands and models.

But why should we trust these reviewers? Why are they credible? What factors make one person's judgment better than another's? How might a reviewer's credibility be affected if the review is sponsored by the company that made the product? Why would a company pay for such evaluations in the first place?

Each of these questions speaks to the focus of this unit: the writer's credibility.

Evaluating a Writer's Credibility

Recall that in Unit 2, you learned that writers connect to their audience through three rhetorical appeals: **logos**, **pathos**, and **ethos**. The term *ethos* refers to the writer's credibility. To earn an audience's trust, writers must present themselves in a way that makes them credible authorities.

This appeal will likely be rooted in the writer's background, as well as his or her specific relationship to a subject. Many factors can influence a person's perspective on a subject. But for writers, the most important one is how they connect their own background to the subject, situation, and audience. Here are some key factors that can influence a person's perspective and **credibility**:

- Age
- Gender
- Location
- Religious or cultural values
- Position or title
- Work experience
- Racial or ethnic background
- Personal experience
- Socioeconomic class
- Level of education
- Occupation or skill

You probably consider these factors every day — especially in an academic context. When you take a class in particular subject, for example, your instructor likely has training in that field, as well as experience in teaching it. Moreover, he or she has usually been hired to teach a specific discipline: this professional status confers credibility. You make these judgments in less formal contexts too. Think about a friend who has musical tastes similar to your own: you will probably trust this person's music recommendations because you two have a relationship and share a perspective.

But what if you know little or nothing about a writer? How do you evaluate the writer's credibility? If biographical information about the person is available, it may provide helpful context. You can also look for clues in the way the writer attempts to establish authority and trustworthiness, including personal details, credible evidence, citations to reputable sources, and fair accounts of other perspectives. Moreover, stylistic choices, including diction, syntax, and tone, can reflect ethos too. For example, writers who use needlessly complicated words and unusual jargon may, ironically, undercut their own credibility by appearing pretentious, condescending, or superficial.

ESTABLISHING ETHOS		
Ways a Writer Can Establish Ethos	**Relevant Aspects of the Writer's Identity**	**Details in the Text**
• Credibility • Authority • Trustworthiness • Relationship to audience	• Age • Gender • Location • Religious or cultural values • Position or title • Work experience • Racial or ethnic background • Personal experience • Socioeconomic class • Level of education • Occupation or skill	• Information about the writer • Consideration of other perspectives • Evidence and sources • Word choice, diction • Syntax

Some Sources Are Better Than Others

When considering the validity and effectiveness of an argument, not all perspectives are equal. For example, a medical argument from a licensed physician is likely to carry more weight than a medical argument from a software designer. That is, the doctor is likely more qualified to provide a credible perspective.

But credibility depends on the context and the subject. In other words, writers are not automatically credible on every subject. A professional environmental scientist may be a credible source in a discussion of biodiversity and resource extraction; but that scientist is not automatically credible to discuss the global economic impact of a radical change in harvesting natural resources. They could, however, establish their own credibility by using evidence from reliable and trustworthy sources.

INSIDER AP® TIP

Writers always keep their audience in mind. Different contexts and situations require different strategies. The writer's relationship with the audience can help determine which approach to use and what background information to include.

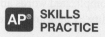

AP® SKILLS PRACTICE | **RHETORICAL SITUATION Establishing Ethos**

Consider something that you know or understand well (e.g., a hobby, an interest, a personal experience) and identify an unknown audience that you'd share that knowledge with. Briefly explain how you could establish your ethos.

Subject:		
Audience:		
Ways You Can Establish Ethos	**Relevant Aspects of Your Identity**	**How would you establish your ethos?** **What details would you present to establish credibility?**
• Credibility • Authority • Trustworthiness • Relationship to audience	• Age • Gender • Location • Religious or cultural values • Position or title • Work experience • Racial or ethnic background • Socioeconomic class • Personal experience • Level of education • Occupation or skill	

Black Superheroes Matter
Tre Johnson

THE TEXT IN CONTEXT

Philadelphia-based writer Tre Johnson (b.1979) is a former teacher who (as he describes his work) focuses "on the connective tissue of who we are, how we live, what we consume, and what it means through examining race, culture and politics." He has written for Vox, the *New York Times*, the *Washington Post*, Slate, *Vanity Fair*, and other publications. This 2017 *Rolling Stone* article appeared shortly after the release of Marvel Comics' *Black Panther* film.

AP® SKILLS PRACTICE | RHETORICAL SITUATION
Analyzing a Writer's Ethos

As you read the following article, identify details from the argument that contribute to the writer's credibility.

<table>
<tr><th colspan="3">Analyzing a Writer's Ethos</th></tr>
<tr><th>Ways a Writer Can Establish Ethos</th><th>Relevant Aspects of the Writer's Identity</th><th>Details in the Text</th></tr>
<tr><td>

- Credibility
- Authority
- Trustworthiness
- Relationship to audience

</td><td>

- Age
- Gender
- Location
- Religious or cultural values
- Position or title
- Work experience
- Racial or ethnic background
- Socioeconomic class
- Personal experience
- Level of education
- Occupation or skill

</td><td></td></tr>
</table>

Black Superheroes Matter

Standing in the bay of a speeding Wakandan jet, a member of the African nation's special forces unit—the Dora Milaje—advises their king, T'Challa: "Don't freeze." Calmly, the leader replies "I never freeze." He's assured, regal, radiating a near subzero-temperature sense of cool. And then, donning the mask of the legendary superhero known as the Black Panther, he torpedo-drops from the sky. A car explodes beneath him. He effortlessly somersaults through the air, lands sideways on a building in a neon-lit metropolis, races along the building's wall, and sails right onto the speeding car. Then the Avenger skewers the driver's side tire and tosses it away like a bottle cap. Screen time: 10 seconds. How long have we been waiting to watch that moment become a reality? A lifetime.

Literally from the jump, director Ryan Coogler and Co. make it clear that we will be watching a Black superhero fully in control and completely occupying the center-stage spotlight. Watch Chadwick Boseman's Black Panther in *Captain America: Civil War*, and you'll see a charismatic character who fills a void in the conflicted do-gooder group. Watch the new trailer, however—the one that dropped months ago for his stand-alone film—and you'll see someone with the arrogance of Shaft, the coolness of Obama, and the hot-headed impulsiveness of Kanye West. This T'Challa is accessible, awe-inspiring, and perhaps most importantly, human. "I think the question that I'm trying to ask and answer in *Black Panther* is, 'What does it truly mean to be African?'" the filmmaker recently told *Rolling Stone*. "The MCU has set itself in the real world as much as possible—so what does it mean for T'Challa to move around as this Black man in a movie reality that tries to be a real world?"

All of which means that, after decades of trying to nail the modern Black superhero, we may *finally* be getting what we've asked for—and getting it right. This journey hasn't been without effort. The Blaxploitation films in the 1970s gave Black audiences their own heroes: *Shaft*, *Cleopatra Jones*, *Coffy*, *Slaughter*, *Foxy Brown*. They were inner-city vigilantes, detectives, nurses, and ex-cons that waged anti-establishment wars against authority, drugs, gangs, and corruption—one-man (or woman) hit-squads operating against the real-world political backdrop of Nixon's "law and order" campaign. Occasionally, movies like *Shaft Goes to Africa*, where Richard Roundtree wears an African dashiki and is equipped with a large unassuming staff that's a piece of advanced tech, and *Dolemite* (that broad hat, that flashy suit pimp-style outfit) had their protagonists don something like costumes and adopt something close to alter-egos to mete out justice.

These Black men and women didn't cower in the face of danger, white power, or guns; their combination of sex appeal and swagger made many audiences fall in love with them. To say that mileage may vary among these portraits of sticking it to the Man would be putting it mildly. But in hindsight, you can see how the Blaxploitation movies influenced a generation of Black musicians and artists by selling a profoundly Afrocentric image, as well as spawning a legacy that can be seen in everything from hip-hop to stand-up comedy. And though the Black Panther first appeared during the Civil Rights era, the main wave of Black superheroes that followed—think Luke Cage, Black Lightning, the Falcon, Storm of the X-Men—were children of the Blaxploitation age. They just weren't getting screen time. At all.

In the Nineties and the early 2000s, attempts to make Black superhero movies tended to play like Blaxploitation-lite, running the gamut from intentionally hilarious (1993's *Meteor Man* and 1994's *Blankman*) or hilariously bad (*Steel* and *Spawn*, both 1997). They were usually analogues of white superheroes like Superman and Batman at best, and a one-note joke at worst. The one exception, the Great Black Hope, was 1998's *Blade*, the first in a series about a leather-clad, mixed breed vampire hunter played by Wesley Snipes. It was critically embraced, commercially successful ($333 million in box-office receipts), and a high-water mark for an obscure superhero character from an obscure comic book horror series. The franchise ended on a sour note—but it also provided a blueprint for what would become Marvel Studios' eventual MCU pop-culture takeover.

Still, even *Blade*'s success wasn't enough to get more top-tier Black superheroes films on the big screen. Audiences had to be content with Halle Berry's African-born mutant superhero Storm, Don Cheadle's War Machine, Anthony Mackie's Falcon—strong performances that still had the whiff of consolation prizes. Hollywood grapevine chatter pondered if Will Smith could play Captain America and Donald Glover campaigned to be cast as Spider-Man; cue widespread backlash from a largely white mainstream fan-base. The less said about poor Michael B. Jordan in that ill-conceived *Fantastic Four* reboot, the better.

Yet *Black Panther* already feels different from all of this. Coogler has set out to do something with the modern Black superhero that all previous iterations have fallen short of doing: making it respectable, imaginative, and powerful. The Afro-punk and Afrofuturism aesthetics, the unapologetic

5 Black swagger, the miniscule appearances from non-Black characters—it's an important resetting of a standard of what's possible around creating a mythology for a Black superhero. The trailers point to a new direction for depicting not only Black superheroes, but also how we imagine *our* heroes. He's not being played for laughs. He's not a sidekick or born out of dire circumstances. His story, one of an ingrained birthright, legacy, and royalty, is a stark difference for how we tend to treat most Black superheroes—and Black superhero movies.

The novelist Chimamanda Ngozi Adichie talks about "the danger of a single story"—about Africa, about Black brilliance, our humanity and the Black experience for too long. There would never be a time when this movie's creation *wouldn't* mean something to Black people in particular, and the inevitable backlash that this movie will receive for its celebration, existence, and confidence in Blackness will be a reminder that there are no new conversations, merely new opportunities to remind us of who we collectively are. Yet that won't matter because the people this movie will speak most deeply to—a rainbow-coalition cross-section of Black comic book readers, African-American movie audiences, Boseman/Jordan/Bassett/Nyong'o fans, Black-culture connoisseurs, and pop-culture nerds—will see something of themselves in this movie. They will also likely be both familiar and resistant to the disdain it will receive for merely existing. Like anything Black in America, *Black Panther* will be politicized for being Black, which is to say for *being* and for announcing itself as having a right to be here and to be heard.

Since the dawn of the modern Golden-Age superhero, we've been treated to over 30 iterations and appearances of Superman, Batman, and Spider-Man (multiply that threefold if you count cartoons, cartoon movies, and video games). We've had a stand-alone *Howard the Duck* movie, and a supergroup with a talking raccoon and a sentient tree as central characters. Wonder Woman, one of DC's most iconic characters created in the 1940s, got a TV show in the 1970s . . . and didn't get a movie until last June.

Fast-forward to 2016, however, and you can stream Netflix's unapologetically Afrocentric *Luke Cage* series, while shows like *Cloak and Dagger*, *Black Lightning*, and the recently-announced series *Raising Dion* (co-produced and starring Michael B. Jordan about a single mother who discovers her young son has magical powers) in various stage of production. And now, finally, we have a *Black Panther* movie, one set to open on thousands of screens and get the full Marvel marketing-blitz treatment.

As a child in school, I rarely reached for the black or brown Crayola crayons in my superhero coloring books; I have a lifetime's worth of Halloweens where I weighed how often I could or should dress as the white superheroes. I couldn't find ones that looked like me both outside of and underneath the mask. An entire generation of children will now know that a Black superhero, society, imagination, and power can exist right alongside Peter Parker, Steve Rogers, and Bruce Wayne. An entire generation of children will not know what it feels like to not see themselves reflected back on costume racks, coloring books, or movie screens. We're at a pivotal time where these characters and stories are coming not out of permission or obligation, but necessity.

It has been someone's time before again and again and again. But 2018's late winter will belong to Wakanda much like 2017's early summer belonged to *Wonder Woman*. We've been waiting to see ourselves on screen, flying through the air and running across buildings and dodging laser blasts from bearded colonialists our entire lives. The future is Ryan Coogler, Chadwick Boseman, T'Challa, *Black Panther*. The future begins on February 16th.

RHETORICAL SITUATION

1. Who is the **writer**? What is the relationship between the writer and the **audience**? What values do the writer and his audience share? How do you know?

2. How does the background and experience of the **writer** contribute to his **credibility** or ethos?

3. How does the writer build trust with his **audience**?

CLAIMS AND EVIDENCE

Strategic Evidence

AP **Enduring Understanding (CLE-1)**

Writers guide understanding of a text's lines of reasoning and claims through that text's organization and integration of evidence.

To establish their credibility with a specific audience, writers choose, arrange, and incorporate strategic evidence into their texts.

Consider the following example: The most successful restaurants employ chefs who know how to make delicious meals. These chefs know they must choose their ingredients carefully — fresh vegetables, premium cuts of meat, and bold, aromatic spices. But it's not enough to have a pantry of ingredients. In addition, chefs must then make specific choices to prepare and incorporate the ingredients so that their flavors and textures work in harmony for each dish. If chefs miscalculate the proportions of any ingredients, or fail to follow the sequence of their recipes, they will ruin dinner — and create disgruntled customers.

Like chefs, writers make strategic choices about what they include in their texts, how they include it, and why they include it.

KEY POINT

Writers strategically select evidence based upon their audience to establish credibility and achieve their specific purpose.

Not All Information Is Evidence

As you'll recall from earlier units, **evidence** always serves a purpose for a writer: they use it to illustrate, clarify, set a mood, exemplify, associate, or amplify a point they're trying to communicate. When a writer strategically uses information in this way, it becomes evidence.

While all of the evidence below could be used for any of these strategic purposes, the table on page 438 presents some typical types of evidence, as well as their common purposes and functions.

Readers often evaluate credibility by assessing the writer's strategically selected evidence and sources. In any given text, writers work to achieve a purpose through

- the perspectives of the sources they incorporate,
- the types of evidence they include from these sources,
- the functions of their evidence within the text,
- the arrangement of the evidence within the text.

Balancing Perspectives

The writer's sources and evidence play a major role in establishing **credibility**. Depending on the context and the audience, some sources are more reliable than others.

EVIDENCE: TYPES, PURPOSES, AND FUNCTIONS

Type of Evidence	Purpose	Function
Data and information from research (e.g., library, databases)	Credibility (ethos) Reason (logos)	Clarify Exemplify Associate Amplify
Personal experience	Credibility (ethos) Emotion (pathos)	Illustrate Set a mood Exemplify
Cases and specific examples	Reason (ethos) Credibility (ethos) Emotion (pathos)	Illustrate Set a mood Associate
Anecdotes and information from others	Logic (logos) Credibility (ethos)	Clarify Associate Amplify
Quantitative data, including interviews and surveys	Logic (logos)	Illustrate Exemplify

The audience's values and background contribute to whether they will be persuaded by the writer's evidence. If an audience considers a text's evidence suspicious, the writer then becomes guilty by association. Therefore, evidence that coincides with the audience's values reflects positively on the writer's credibility.

For example, a doctor who writes a personal narrative about living with arthritis for an audience unfamiliar with the condition might focus on personal experiences, observations, and anecdotes. This evidence would add to the writer's credibility; it would also be accessible to a general audience. However, if that physician was writing about new arthritis treatments for an audience of doctors and specialists, he or she would likely use evidence from research studies and specialized medical journals.

The audience will likely evaluate the writer's biases, as well. Writers may exhibit a bias if they intentionally exclude, ignore, or misrepresent other perspectives on their subject. Depending on the degree to which they address the existence of other perspectives, writers may lose credibility with the audience. The strongest arguments recognize the inherent limitations of their perspective and intentionally include other perspectives to account for this.

Synthesizing and Evaluating Perspectives

Writers bring together sources in a text and **synthesize** them to create their own arguments. Evidence and sources will either support, complement, or challenge a writer's thesis.

It might seem strange for a writer to include evidence that contradicts his or her own thesis. But that the strongest writers can anticipate other perspectives on the subject throughout the text. They often do this by incorporating evidence directly from a source with an alternative perspective and then addressing that opposing view fairly.

As you learned in Unit 3, evidence comes from **sources**, and not all sources are equal. Some are more credible or reliable than others. Recall that sources are reliable when their information can be supported, confirmed, or replicated by others. Credible sources have the relevant knowledge, background, and authority to provide insight into a subject.

Credible sources may also acknowledge their own limitations and biases. But a source's perspective often reveals its bias, deliberately or not. For example, we view political ideology on a continuum from liberal (left-leaning) to conservative (right-leaning).

So readers of the conservative *National Review* magazine or the liberal *Nation* magazine need to be aware of the publication's perspective, which will influence the framing, emphasis, and tone of the articles. Note that "biased" does not mean "false": writers with strong political biases may also be scrupulous in their research and use of evidence. Likewise, some publications provide strong fact-checking and editorial supervision, while others give little editorial oversight.

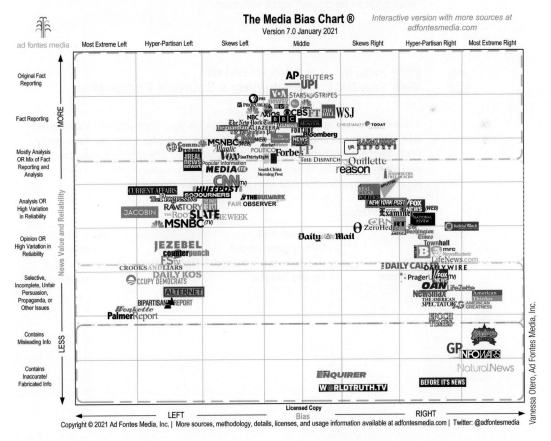

The Media Bias Chart ® Version 7.0 January 2021

Copyright © 2021 Ad Fontes Media, Inc. | More sources, methodology, details, licenses, and usage information available at adfontesmedia.com | Twitter: @adfontesmedia

Vanessa Otero, Ad Fontes Media, Inc.

It's important for readers to consider the source's perspective — and that perspective's effect on an audience. In short, when analyzing an argument, you should ask yourself: why did the writer select this evidence for this particular audience?

Bias is contextual. Bias exists on a spectrum, meaning that some sources are more credible (or more biased) than others. Indeed, a writer may not even know that he or she is exhibiting a bias. But if writers understand the complexity of an issue, including various claims and perspectives that they do not necessarily hold themselves, they will be less biased and more credible.

The Ad Fontes Media Corporation analyzes media sources to rate the reliability and bias of their news coverage. They produce a chart similar to the one on page 439 each year that illustrates both the political ideology and the reliability of these sources on a continuum.

INSIDER **Effective writers address limitations.** By identifying the limitations of their sources and actively addressing those limitations throughout the text, writers demonstrate that they understand the complexity of an issue. Moreover, effective arguments anticipate, recognize, and evaluate other perspectives — even if the writer doesn't agree with them.

 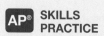

AP® SKILLS PRACTICE	CLAIMS AND EVIDENCE

Evaluating a Source's Perspective

Think of a current issue or subject that interests you. Then, identify four sources that might provide information about this issue. Consider what you know about each source, identifying potential biases that would affect the source's credibility and reliability. Finally, reflect on how receiving information from only those sources would influence your own perspective on the subject.

Subject/Issue:

Source	Position and Information about the Subject Provided by the Source	Potential Biases	How That Source Affects Your Perspective

What Farm-to-Table Got Wrong

Dan Barber

Shutterstock

THE TEXT IN CONTEXT

Dan Barber (b. 1969) is a chef and owner of Blue Hill Restaurant in New York City and Blue Hill at Stone Barns in Pocantico Hills, NY. He is a graduate of Tufts University and the French Culinary Institute. In 2014, he published *The Third Plate: Field Notes on the Future of Food*, a critique of the farm-to-table food culture, as well as a proposal for more sustainable agriculture and consumption. The farm-to-table movement encourages restaurants and cafeterias to purchase regionally sourced ingredients directly from local farmers and producers. While he advocates for the farm-to-table movement, Chef Barber questions the sustainability of its current form in this 2014 *New York Times* article.

 **SKILLS PRACTICE** | **CLAIMS AND EVIDENCE**
Explaining the Function of Evidence

As you read Barber's argument, identify his supporting evidence for each line of reasoning. Next, consider how the evidence may function in appealing to his audience. Then, explain how the inclusion and arrangement of this evidence within the argument further the claim in his thesis.

Analyzing the Function of Evidence		
Writer's Thesis (Identify Perspective and Unifying Idea):		
Evidence	Function of Evidence	How does the writer's strategic inclusion and arrangement of this evidence affect the message?

What Farm-to-Table Got Wrong

POCANTICO HILLS, N.Y.—It's spring again. Hip deep in asparagus—and, soon enough, tomatoes and zucchini—farm-to-table advocates finally have something from the farm to put on the table.

The crowds clamoring for just-dug produce at the farmers' market and the local food co-op suggest that this movement is no longer just a foodie fad. Today, almost 80 percent of Americans say sustainability is a priority when purchasing food. The promise of this kind of majority is that eating local can reshape landscapes and drive lasting change.

Except it hasn't. More than a decade into the movement, the promise has fallen short. For all its successes, farm-to-table has not, in any fundamental way, reworked the economic and political forces that dictate how our food is grown and raised. Big Food is getting bigger, not smaller. In the last five years, we've lost nearly 100,000 farms (mostly mid-size ones). Today, 1.1 percent of farms in the United States account for nearly 45 percent of farm revenues. Despite being farm-to-table's favorite targets, corn and soy account for more than 50 percent of our harvested acres for the first time ever. Between 2006 and 2011, over a million acres of native prairie were plowed up in the so-called Western Corn Belt to make way for these two crops, the most rapid loss of grasslands since we started using tractors to bust sod on the Great Plains in the 1920s.

How do we make sense of this odd duality: a food revolution on one hand, an entrenched status quo on the other?

I got a hint of the answer a few years ago, while standing in a field in upstate New York. I was there because, many years before, I'd decided I wanted local flour for my restaurants. I chose Lakeview Organic, a grain farm operated by Klaas and Mary-Howell Martens. Klaas was growing a rare variety of emmer wheat (also known as farro), nearly extinct but for the efforts of a few farmers.

Milled and baked into whole wheat bread, the emmer was a revelation—intensely sweet and nutty. I spoke routinely about the importance of local grain and the resurrection of lost flavors. I was waving the farm-to-table flag and feeling pretty good about it, too.

Visiting Klaas those years later, hoping to learn what made the emmer so delicious, I realized I was missing the point entirely. The secret to great-tasting wheat, Klaas told me, is that it's not about the wheat. It's about the soil.

In fact, on a tour of his farm, there was surprisingly little wheat to see. Instead, Klaas showed me fields of less-coveted grains and legumes like millet, barley, and kidney beans, as well as cover crops like mustard and clover, all of which he plants in meticulously planned rotations. The rotations dictate the quality of the soil, which means they dictate the flavor of the harvests as well. They are the recipe for his delicious emmer.

Each planting in the sequence has a specific function. Klaas likes his field rotations to begin with a cover crop like the mustard plant. Cover crops are often grown to restore nutrients depleted from a previous harvest. Plowed into the soil after maturity, mustard offers the added benefit of reducing pest and disease problems for subsequent crops.

Next Klaas will plant a legume, which does 10 the neat trick of fixing nitrogen: grabbing it from the atmosphere and storing it in the plant's roots. Soybeans are a good choice; or kidney beans, if the local processor is paying enough to make it worth his while; or cowpeas, which he harvests for animal feed.

If there's a dry spell, he'll forgo beans altogether and pop in some hardy millet. Oats or rye is next; rye builds soil structure and suppresses weeds. Only then is Klaas's soil locked and loaded with the requisite fertility needed for his wheat.

As much as I cling to tried and true recipes, Klaas doesn't. Depending on what the soil is telling him, he may roll out an entirely different rotation. If there's a buildup of fungal disease in the field, the next season he'll plant a brassica like cabbage or broccoli, followed by buckwheat, and then barley. Barley is among Klaas's favorite crops. In addition to cleansing the soil of pathogens, it can be planted along with a nitrogen fixer like clover, further benefiting the soil. Once again, the soil is ready for wheat.

Standing in Klaas's fields, I saw how single-minded I had been. Yes, I was creating a market for local emmer wheat, but I wasn't doing anything to support the recipe behind it. Championing Klaas's wheat and only his wheat was tantamount to treating his farm like a grocery store. I was cherry-picking what I most wanted for my menu without supporting the whole farm.

I am not the only one. In celebrating the All-Stars of the farmers' market—asparagus, heirloom tomatoes, emmer wheat—farm-to-table advocates are often guilty of ignoring a whole class of humbler crops that are required to produce the most delicious food.

With limited American demand for local millet, rye, and barley, 70 percent of Klaas's harvest was going into livestock feed for chickens, pigs, and dairy cattle. In general, Klaas earned pennies on the dollar compared with what he'd make selling his crops for human consumption. And we were missing out as well, on nutritious foods that are staples of the best cuisines in the world.

Diversifying our diet to include more local grains and legumes is a delicious first step to improving our food system. Millet and rye are an easy substitute for rice or pasta. But that addresses only the low-hanging fruit of Klaas's farm. More challenging is to think about how to honor the other underutilized parts of his rotations—classic cover crops like cowpeas and mustard, which fertilize the soil to ensure healthy harvests in the future.

Today, the best farmers are tying up valuable real estate for long periods of time (in an agonizingly short growing season) simply to benefit their soil. Imagine if Macy's reserved half of its shelf space at Christmas for charitable donations. A noble idea. But profitable? Not so much. By creating a market for these crops, we can provide more value for the farmer and for our own diets, while supporting the long-term health of the land.

In Klaas's field, I bent down and ripped off a green shoot of Austrian winter peas. I took a bite. Inedible? No, delicious! Thirty acres of the most tender and sweet pea shoots I'd ever tasted. (Harvesting the leaves would somewhat reduce the amount plowed back into the soil, but the plant's soil benefits would remain.) In the distance I could make out a field of mustards. Klaas plants Tilney mustard, similar to the spicy green you find in a mesclun mix. I realized I wasn't just looking at a cover crop. I was looking at a salad bowl.

Back at the restaurant, I created a new dish called "Rotation Risotto," a collection of all of Klaas's lowly, soil-supporting grains and legumes, cooked and presented in the manner of a classic risotto. I used a purée of cowpea shoots and mustard greens to thicken the grains and replace the starchiness of rice. As one waiter described the idea, it was a "nose-to-tail approach to the farm"—an edible version of Klaas's farming strategy.

It's one thing for chefs to advocate cooking with the whole farm; it's another thing to make these uncelebrated crops staples in ordinary kitchens. Bridging that divide will require a new network of regional processors and distributors.

Take beer, for example. The explosion in local microbreweries has meant a demand for local barley malt. A new malting facility near Klaas's farm recently opened in response. He now earns 30 percent more selling barley for malt than he did selling it for animal feed. For other farmers, it's a convincing incentive to diversify their grain crops.

Investing in the right infrastructure means the difference between a farmer's growing crops for cows or for cafeterias. It will take the shape of more local mills (for grains), canneries (for beans), and processors (for greens). As heretical as this may sound, farm-to-table needs to embrace a few more middlemen.

Perhaps the problem with the farm-to-table movement is implicit in its name. Imagining the food chain as a field on one end and a plate of food at the other is not only reductive, it also puts us in the position of end users. It's a passive system—a grocery-aisle mentality—when really, as cooks and eaters, we need to engage in the nuts and bolts of true agricultural sustainability. Flavor can be our guide to reshaping our diets, and our landscapes, from the ground up.

CLAIMS AND EVIDENCE

1. What type of **evidence** is presented in the text? How does this evidence support the line of reasoning?

2. What is the context of the argument? How does Barber strengthen his **evidence** in that context?

3. How does the **evidence** illustrate two distinct **perspectives**? Explain each perspective and how the evidence works to support each.

4. What **sources** does Barber use in his argument? Would his audience consider those sources credible? Why or why not?

5. How do these sources contribute to Barber's **credibility** in the text? Do you consider the writer a credible **source**? Why or why not?

Exposition: Classification/Division Argument

AP® **Enduring Understanding (REO-1)**

Writers make claims about subjects, rely on evidence that supports the reasoning that justifies the claim, and often acknowledge or respond to other, possibly opposing, arguments.

In this unit, you'll continue to examine a writer's specific **purpose** by looking at different types of expository argument. But regardless of their purpose, writers must find ways to convey authority on their subjects. This is true of narration, illustration, process, compare and contrast, definition, and — as you will see — classification and division.

KEY POINT

Classification arguments explain and are organized by categories or parts.

Considering Qualities and Traits

In Unit 4, you learned about the purpose of definition arguments: they aim to explain the meaning of a term or idea, such as "sandwich," "friendship," or "democracy." Often, the writer will use deductive logic by introducing the concept and its characteristics in the argument's introduction. The line of reasoning will be an explanation of its key attributes.

Classification relies on similar strategies. Instead of providing a definition, however, the writer of a classification argument will use them to place objects or concepts into categories.

For example, imagine that a museum curator receives an old, unknown work of art from a donor who inherited it. To identify the painting, the curator will have to examine its specific attributes so that it can be classified according to its time-period, medium, genre, and other identifying categories. In the process, he or she will be making an argument about the work's origin and context.

The writers of classification arguments engage in a similar process: they present an inductive line of reasoning that identifies and explains their subject's attributes. Then, they argue that their subject should be placed in a specific category because of these specific qualities.

Like a classification argument, a **division** argument often uses categories. But while classification moves from specific examples to larger groupings, division breaks down a large or complex subject by dividing it into its component parts and sub-parts. For example, a writer who makes an argument about video games might divide this subject into several categories, such as puzzle games, role-playing games (RPGs), and adventure games.

When you analyze arguments of classification or division, it is important to understand the writer's categories or classifications. You might ask:

- What is the classification scheme or categories based on?
- How do these categories support the writer's message?

In both classification and division, the writer makes a claim either explicitly or implicitly based on the significance of the classification scheme or categories.

Developing Arguments of Classification or Division

To justify a claim, writers use the classification of traits and characteristics to establish a line of reasoning. They support this reasoning with relevant and sufficient evidence, such as data, examples, and description. As you analyze these arguments, pay attention to the categories of classification or division. They will likely help you understand the values and perspectives behind the main claim.

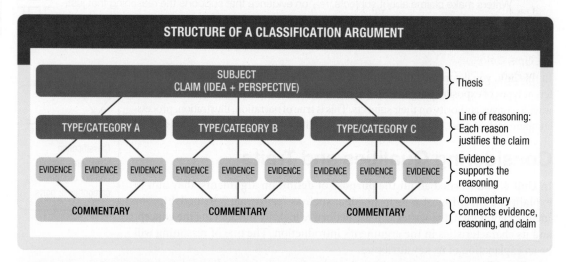

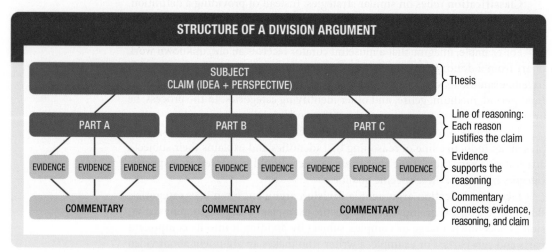

 **INSIDER** **AP® TIP**   **The writer's classification scheme reveals values.** You must do more than merely describe the characteristics of classification. You must also analyze the classification scheme by explaining why the writer uses these particular traits, attributes, or characteristics as the method of classification. In the process, try to determine what values or ideas are associated with the writer's chosen categories.

AP® SKILLS PRACTICE	REASONING AND ORGANIZATION **Organizing by Classification or Division**

Choose a concept (e.g., high school classes, musical artists, phone apps, teachers) that you can break down into two or more categories. Next, identify the types or kinds and explain their significance. Then, describe the attributes of each type and give specific examples.

Concept:			
Type, Category, or Part	Significance	Traits/Attributes	Examples

Types of Women in Romantic Comedies Who Are Not Real

Mindy Kaling

FOX/Getty Images

THE TEXT IN CONTEXT

Born in Cambridge, Massachusetts, Mindy Kaling (b. 1979) is an actress, writer, and producer in film and television. She is best known for her role of Kelly Kapoor on NBC TV's *The Office* (2004–2012) and Fox/Netflix's *The Mindy Project* (2012–2017). Kaling has also written many articles about the role of women in American culture and the resurgence of the romantic comedy genre. In the following excerpt from her 2011 book, *Is Everyone Hanging Out Without Me? (And Other Concerns),* she classifies female character types in romantic comedies.

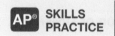 **SKILLS PRACTICE** | REASONING AND ORGANIZATION
Analyzing Arguments of Classification/ Division

As you read Kaling's argument, identify her categories of classification, as well as the traits or attributes of each category. Cite specific textual evidence to illustrate each of the attributes and give examples. What is the significance of each category of classification (or division) for her overall message? What values does her classification method suggest?

Analyzing Classification and Division Arguments

Concept or Value of Classification Method:

Thesis:

Type, Category, or Part	Significance of the Type of Classification or Division	Traits/ Attributes	Examples

Types of Women in Romantic Comedies Who Are Not Real

When I was a kid, Christmas vacation meant renting VHS copies of romantic comedies from Blockbuster and watching them with my parents at home. *Sleepless in Seattle* was big, and so was *When Harry Met Sally*. I laughed along with everyone else at the scene where Meg Ryan fakes an orgasm at the restaurant without even knowing what an orgasm was. In my mind, she was just being kind of loud and silly at a diner, and that was hilarious enough for me.

I love romantic comedies. I feel almost sheepish writing that, because the genre has been so degraded in the past twenty years or so that admitting you like these movies is essentially an admission of mild stupidity. But that has not stopped me from watching them.

I enjoy watching people fall in love on-screen so much that I can suspend my disbelief for the contrived situations that only happen in the heightened world of romantic comedies. I have come to enjoy the moment when the normal lead guy, say, slips and falls right on top of the hideously expensive wedding cake. I actually feel robbed when the female lead's dress doesn't get torn open at a baseball game while the JumboTron is on her. I simply regard romantic comedies as a subgenre of sci-fi, in which the world created therein has different rules than my regular human world. Then I just lap it up. There is no difference between Ripley from *Alien* and any Katherine Heigl character. They're all participating in the same level of made-up awesomeness, and I enjoy every second of it.

So it makes sense that in this world there are many specimens of women who I do not think exist in real life, like Vulcans or UFO people or whatever. They are:

The Klutz

When a beautiful actress is in a movie, executives wrack their brains to find some kind of flaw in her that still allows her to be palatable. She can't be overweight or not perfect-looking, because who would want to see that? A not 100-percent-perfect-looking-in-every-way female? You might as well film a dead squid decaying on a beach somewhere for two hours.

So they make her a Klutz.

The 100-percent-perfect-looking female is perfect in every way, except that she constantly falls down. She bonks her head on things. She trips and falls and spills soup on her affable date. (Josh Lucas. Is that his name? I know it's two first names. Josh George? Brad Mike? Fred Tom? Yes, it's Fred Tom.) Our Klutz clangs into Stop signs while

5

riding a bike, and knocks over giant displays of expensive fine china. Despite being five foot nine and weighing 110 pounds, she is basically like a drunk buffalo who has never been a part of human society. But Fred Tom loves her anyway.

The Ethereal Weirdo

The smart and funny writer Nathan Rabin coined the term Manic Pixie Dream Girl to describe a version of this archetype after seeing Kirsten Dunst in the movie *Elizabethtown*. This girl can't be pinned down and may or may not show up when you make concrete plans. She wears gauzy blouses and braids. She decides to dance in the rain and weeps uncontrollably if she sees a sign for a missing dog or cat. She spins a globe, places her finger on a random spot, and decides to move there. This ethereal weirdo abounds in movies, but nowhere else. If she were from real life, people would think she was a homeless woman and would cross the street to avoid her, but she is essential to the male fantasy that even if a guy is boring, he deserves a woman who will find him fascinating and pull him out of himself by forcing him to go skinny-dipping in a stranger's pool.

The Woman Who Is Obsessed with Her Career and Is No Fun at All

I, Mindy Kaling, basically have two full-time jobs. I regularly work sixteen hours a day. But like most of the other people I know who are similarly busy, I think I'm a pleasant, pretty normal person. I am slightly offended by the way busy working women my age are presented in film. I'm not, like, always barking orders into my hands-free phone device and telling people constantly, "I have no time for this!" I didn't completely forget how to be nice or feminine because I have a career. Also, since when does having a job necessitate women having their hair pulled back in a severe, tight bun? Often this uptight woman has to "re-learn" how to seduce a man because her estrogen leaked out of her from leading so many board meetings, and she has to do all sorts of crazy, unnecessary crap, like eat a hot dog in a libidinous way or something. Having a challenging job in movies means the compassionate, warm, or sexy side of your brain has fallen out.

The Forty-Two-Year-Old Mother of the Thirty-Year-Old Male Lead

I am so accustomed to the young mom phenomenon, that when I saw the poster for *The Proposal* I wondered for a second if the proposal in the movie was Ryan Reynolds suggesting he send his mother, Sandra Bullock, to an old-age home.   10

However, given the popularity of teen moms right now, this could actually be the wave of the future.

The Sassy Best Friend

You know that really horny and hilarious best friend who is always asking about your relationship and has nothing really going on in her own life? She always wants to meet you in coffee shops or wants to go to Bloomingdale's to sample perfumes? She runs a chic dildo store in the West Village? Nope? Okay, that's this person.

The Skinny Woman Who Is Beautiful and Toned but Also Gluttonous and Disgusting

Again, I am more than willing to suspend my disbelief during a romantic comedy for good set decoration alone. One pristine kitchen from a Nancy Meyers movie like in

It's Complicated is worth five Diane Keatons being caught half-clad in a topiary or whatever situation her character has found herself in.

But sometimes even my suspended disbelief isn't enough. I am speaking of the gorgeous and skinny heroine who is also a disgusting pig when it comes to food. And everyone in the movie—her parents, her friends, her boss—are all complicit in this huge lie. They are constantly telling her to stop eating and being such a glutton. And this actress, this poor skinny actress who so clearly lost weight to play the likable lead, has to say things like "Shut up you guys! I love cheesecake! If I want to eat an entire cheesecake, I will!" If you look closely, you can see this woman's ribs through the dress she's wearing—that's how skinny she is, this cheesecake-loving cow.

You wonder, as you sit and watch this movie,   15 what the characters would do if they were confronted by an actual average American woman. They would all kill themselves, which would actually be kind of an interesting movie.

The Woman Who Works in an Art Gallery

How many freakin' art galleries are out there? Are people constantly buying visual art or something? This posh-smart-classy job is a favorite in movies. It's in the same realm as kindergarten teacher in terms of accessibility: guys don't really get it, but the trappings of it are likable and nonthreatening.

ART GALLERY WOMAN: Dust off the Rothko. We have an important buyer coming into town and this is a really big deal for my career. I have no time for this!

This is one of the rare clichés that actually has a male counterpart. Whenever you meet a handsome, charming, successful man in a romantic comedy, the heroine's friend always says the same thing. "He's really success-ful—he's an . . .

   (say it with me)

   . . . architect!"

There are like nine people in the entire world who are architects, and one of them is my dad. None of them looks like Patrick 20 Dempsey.

REASONING AND ORGANIZATION

1. Kaling **classifies** characters based on a concept. What is the concept and how does she define it?

2. How does Kaling use categories to classify characters?

3. What type of **evidence** does Kaling use in her **classification**?

4. How would you describe the diction Kaling uses to **classify** the different types of women? What is Kaling saying about the values that these types of women represent?

Precision of Language

AP Enduring Understanding (STL-1)

The rhetorical situation informs the strategic stylistic choices that writers make.

KEY POINT

A writer's word choice often reveals his or her perspective on a subject.

As you learned in Unit 1, **tone** is the writer's attitude toward the subject or topic. Writers convey their tone through the words, sentences, pacing, evidence, descriptions, images, comparisons — that is, *all* the choices — that they make. These choices not only further the writer's purpose: they also help the writer establish credibility with an audience.

Word Choice Conveys Attitude

A writer's diction often reveals his or her perspective on a subject. In other words, it conveys **tone**. Remember that tone is an effect, not a device: it emerges from a writer's choices within the context of his or her attitude, purpose, and audience. Likewise, tone is not "mood" or "atmosphere," which refers to the feeling that the writer wants to evoke in the audience.

When analyzing a writer's tone, you should use accurate and precise language in your explanation. But keep in mind that tone can be subtle: a writer who understands the complexities of an issue may communicate that complexity in a tone that is neither entirely "positive," nor entirely "negative." Moreover, the words that you choose to describe another writer's tone reveal your understanding of that writer's argument and attitude.

Here are some examples of words used to describe a writer's tone.

Shifts in Tone Reveal Insights

Over the course of an argument, a writer's tone may **shift**. These shifts reveal a change in the writer's initial perspective: they suggest new understanding, insight, or clarity on a subject. For example, a writer may convey a grim tone in the narrative account of a personal disappointment or sad experience. But that may shift to reflect a change in attitude, as the tone becomes hopeful and resilient in the face of a challenge. For example, a writer may come to a new understanding, realization, refinement, or reconsideration of a perspective on a subject. To indicate this to the audience, the writer's tone will noticeably shift.

Word Choice Contributes to Credibility

Diction communicates a writer's position and attitude toward a topic. But it also reflects on a writer's audience. For example, a renowned physicist delivering a

WORDS TO DESCRIBE TONE

absurd	curious	informative	restrained
accusatory	defensive	intimate	reverent
acrimonious	detached	irreverent	sarcastic
aggressive	didactic	jaded	sardonic
alarming	diplomatic	jealous	satirical
angry	disapproving	judgmental	scholarly
apathetic	disdainful	melancholic	scornful
apologetic	disgusted	mocking	sensational
arrogant	disparaging	naive	sentimental
assertive	elegiac	noncommittal	shocking
benevolent	empathetic	nostalgic	sincere
bitter	encouraging	objective	skeptical
buoyant	enthusiastic	outraged	stoic
candid	exasperated	patriotic	subjective
cautionary	facetious	patronizing	submissive
celebratory	flippant	petulant	sympathetic
compassionate	formal	playful	urgent
complacent	frank	pragmatic	vehement
condemning	frustrated	provocative	vengeful
condescending	grim	reflective	vexed
confident	humble	regretful	vindictive
contemptuous	humorous	remorseful	virtuous
contentious	impartial	resentful	whimsical
critical	incredulous	resigned	wrathful
cruel	indignant	resilient	

college commencement address would offer a message suitable to that general audience, rather to specialized experts at a physics conference. The diction would be chosen for this broader audience, as well. The speaker would likely avoid technical jargon, unexplained concepts, and unfamiliar acronyms. If an unusual concept had to be explained, the physicist would use familiar words, allusions, and analogies in the explanation. At the same time, the speaker would avoid language that sounded condescending or patronizing. If you do not match your diction to your audience, you risk confusing them, frustrating them, or losing your credibility with them.

You might think of the audience in the context of *discourse communities*: groups of people who communicate about a specific issue, subject, or professional field. Discourse communities also exist outside of formal, academic, and professional contexts. For example, the news aggregation and discussion website Reddit hosts forums known as "subreddits" on thousands of topics. These online discussion groups are discourse communities where people communicate about shared interests and, as a result, group members are likely to understand the field.

Whether professional, academic, or social, these communities often have conventions, guidelines, and specialized terms that writers are expected to follow. As a writer, make sure you have a clear sense of the discourse communities that you share with your audience: your knowledge of — and adherence to — the conventions will affect your credibility with the audience.

INSIDER
AP® TIP

Simply noticing a shift in tone is not enough. To be effective in your analysis, you must identify the shift and articulate the change it reflects in the writer's attitude and perspective.

AP® SKILLS PRACTICE | LANGUAGE AND STYLE
Choosing Precise Diction

Tone can be tricky to detect, even in our daily text-message conversations. Think about your own experience sending and receiving emojis. What tones do they convey? For each of the following examples, provide words that could accurately describe the tone of that emoji depending on the context.

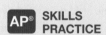

Emoji	Context	Potential Tones
You choose another emoji		

flower travelin man/Shutterstock

A Hunger for Books
Richard Wright

Hulton Archive/Getty Images

THE TEXT IN CONTEXT

The son of a sharecropper, Richard Wright (1908–1960) was born in Natchez, Mississippi. His first novel, *Native Son* (1940), shed light on Black urban life and broke artistic ground as the first African American protest novel. He became a prolific author and social critic, frequently addressing race issues in books such as *The Outsider* (1953) and *The Color Curtain* (1956). In 1951, Wright wrote *I Choose Exile*, which explores his reasons for leaving the United States in 1947 to spend the rest of his life in France. His memoir, *Black Boy* (1945), tells the story of his early years in the Mississippi Delta. In the following excerpt from chapter 14, Wright reflects upon the power of the written word.

AP® SKILLS PRACTICE	LANGUAGE AND STYLE **Describing Tone**	

As you read "A Hunger for Books," use the following organizer to identify a shift in the writer's tone. Next, record the diction used before the shift and the diction used after the shift. Examine each group of words. Then, choose one adjective that describes the tone before the shift and one adjective that describes the tone after the shift.

Identifying Shifts in Tone	
Cite text that indicates a shift in tone:	
Diction before the shift:	Diction after the shift:
Shifts from:	Shifts to:

A Hunger for Books

That night in my rented room, while letting the hot water run over my can of pork and beans in the sink, I opened *A Book of Prefaces* and began to read. I was jarred and shocked by the style, the clear, clean, sweeping sentences. Why did he write like that? And how did one write like that? I pictured the man as a raging demon, slashing with his pen, consumed with hate, denouncing everything American, extolling everything European or German, laughing at the weaknesses of people, mocking God, authority. What was this? I stood up, trying to realize what reality lay behind the meaning of the words . . . Yes, this man was fighting, fighting with words. He was using words as a weapon, using them as one would use a club. Could words be weapons? Well, yes, for here they were. Then, maybe, perhaps, I could use them as a weapon? No. It frightened me. I read on and what amazed me was not what he said, but how on earth anybody had the courage to say it . . .

I ran across many words whose meanings I did not know, and either looked them up in a dictionary or, before I had a chance to do that, encountered the word in a context that made its meaning clear. But what strange world was this? I concluded the book with the conviction that I had somehow overlooked something terribly important in life. I had once tried to write, had once revealed a feeling, had let my crude imagination roam, but the impulse to dream had been slowly beaten out of me by experience. Now it surged up again and I hungered for books, new ways of looking and seeing. It was not a matter of believing or disbelieving what I read, but of feeling something new, of being affected by something that made the look of the world different.

As dawn broke I ate my pork and beans, feeling dopey, sleepy. I went to work, but the mood of the book would not die; it lingered, coloring everything I saw, heard, did. I now felt that I knew what the white men were feeling. Merely because I had read a book that had spoken of how they lived and thought, I identified myself with that book, I felt vaguely guilty. Would I, filled with bookish notions, act in a manner that would make the whites dislike me? . . .

Steeped in new moods and ideas, I bought a ream of paper and tried to write; but nothing would come, or what did come was flat beyond telling. I discovered that more than desire and feeling were necessary to write and I dropped the idea. Yet I still wondered how it was possible to know people sufficiently to write about them. Could I ever learn about life and people? To me, with my vast ignorance, my Jim Crow station in life, it seemed a task impossible of achievement. I now knew what being a Negro meant. I could endure the hunger. I had learned to live with hate. But to feel that there were feelings denied me, that the very breath of life itself was beyond my reach, that more than anything else hurt, wounded me. I had a new hunger.

LANGUAGE AND STYLE

1. What is the **tone** of Wright's introduction? How does he develop that tone? Identify three or four words in the text that contribute to his tone.

2. Reflect on both the **denotative** and the **connotative** meanings of *hunger*: a word that Wright uses repeatedly. How does this choice of words contribute to the message of the text?

3. What does Wright's **diction** reveal about his relationship to his audience?

4. Wright's **tone** shifts within the text. Describe his tone both before and after the shift. How does this shift in tone contribute to his message or perspective?

PUTTING IT ALL TOGETHER
Modeled Text

Speech at the UN Climate Action Summit
Greta Thunberg

Roy Rochlin/Getty Images

THE TEXT IN CONTEXT

Climate-change activist Greta Thunberg was born in Stockholm, Sweden, in 2003. She began speaking out about the issue in 2018. Since then, she has become well-known throughout Europe and the rest of the world as an environmentalist and spokesperson for action on climate change. In the following speech, given on September 23, 2019, Thunberg addresses the UN Climate Action Summit in New York City. That day, the United Nations Children's Fund (UNICEF) hosted a press conference to address carbon-emission reductions around the world.

Unifying Idea	Speech at the UN Climate Action Summit	Rhetorical Strategies	Effect
action	"My message is that we'll be watching you.	directly addressing the audience	motivate through fear
action	"This is all wrong. I shouldn't be up here. I should be back in school on the other side of the ocean. Yet you all come to us young people for hope. How dare you!	writer's credibility	young person engaged in action
action	"You have stolen my dreams and my childhood with your empty words. And yet I'm one of the lucky ones. People are suffering. People are dying. Entire ecosystems are collapsing. We are in the beginning of a mass extinction, and all you can talk about is money and fairy tales of eternal economic growth. How dare you!	line of reasoning	classifying the human effects of global warming

Unifying Idea	Speech at the UN Climate Action Summit	Rhetorical Strategies	Effect
action	"For more than 30 years, the science has been crystal clear. How dare you continue to look away and come here saying that you're doing enough, when the politics and solutions needed are still nowhere in sight.		
action	"You say you hear us and that you understand the urgency. But no matter how sad and angry I am, I do not want to believe that. Because if you really understood the situation and still kept on failing to act, then you would be evil. And that I refuse to believe.	ethos	*inaction has consequences*
action	"The popular idea of cutting our emissions in half in 10 years only gives us a 50% chance of staying below 1.5 degrees [Celsius], and the risk of setting off irreversible chain reactions beyond human control.	strategic evidence	*quantitative evidence supports reason*
action	"Fifty percent may be acceptable to you. But those numbers do not include tipping points, most feedback loops, additional warming hidden by toxic air pollution or the aspects of equity and climate justice. They also rely on my generation sucking hundreds of billions of tons of your CO2 out of the air with technologies that barely exist.	tone	*word choice continues accusatory tone*
action	"So a 50% risk is simply not acceptable to us—we who have to live with the consequences.	tone	*demanding tone conveyed through word choice*
action	"To have a 67% chance of staying below a 1.5 degrees global temperature rise—the best odds given by the [Intergovernmental Panel on Climate Change]—the world had 420 gigatons of CO2 left to emit back on Jan. 1st, 2018. Today that figure is already down to less than 350 gigatons.	strategic evidence	*offers real-life examples to support reason for action*

Unifying Idea	Speech at the UN Climate Action Summit	Rhetorical Strategies	Effect
responsibility	"How dare you pretend that this can be solved with just 'business as usual' and some technical solutions? With today's emissions levels, that remaining CO2 budget will be entirely gone within less than 8 1/2 years.	strategic evidence	quantitative evidence supports reason for action
	"There will not be any solutions or plans presented in line with these figures here today, because these numbers are too uncomfortable. And you are still not mature enough to tell it like it is.		
responsibility	"You are failing us. But the young people are starting to understand your betrayal. The eyes of all future generations are upon you. And if you choose to fail us, I say: We will never forgive you.	directly addresses audience	offers implication of inaction
responsibility	"We will not let you get away with this. Right here, right now is where we draw the line. The world is waking up. And change is coming, whether you like it or not.		
	"Thank you."		

IDEAS IN AMERICAN CULTURE
Endurance and Expression

IDEA BANK

Action

Aesthetic

Alienation

Authority

Convention

Disillusionment

Endurance

Experimentation

Expression

Fragmentation

Freedom

Futility

Hedonism

Isolation

Modernism

Perseverance

Progress

Transcendence

Uncertainty

Work

While the United States was emerging as an industrialized world power, it also faced many challenges at home and abroad. America's industrial revolution and mass production brought a rapid economic boom, at least for some. But the complex hostilities of European imperialism led to World War I, also known as the Great War: a global conflict involving 32 nations, including the United States.

Now a global economic power, the United States began playing a larger role in the world. The inward-looking United States had long avoided involvement in European conflicts, but World War I changed that: for the first time American soldiers fought on European soil. Many soldiers who returned from the war suffered from post-traumatic stress disorder, which was then called "shell shock." The war had other effects, as well. For example, many people in Europe and America had viewed the late nineteenth and early twentieth centuries as an era of improvement and civilization. But the horrors of the first modern war — with its submarines, air attacks, tanks, chemical weapons, and civilian casualties — severely tested the world's faith in "progress."

The war also demolished conventional ideas about the glory of war, along with other lofty ideals such as honor and heroism. As a result, artists and writers

The following painting *Titian* from 1549 depicts a character from Greek mythology, Sisyphus. Zeus punished Sisyphus for his deceitful behavior, and his sentence was to roll a large boulder up a hill only for it to roll down each time it reached the top.

How does this image reflect the ceaseless endurance and perseverance of Sisyphus? How might this myth serve as a metaphor for the plight of modern humanity?

affected by the war rejected traditional forms of expression, instead vowing to "make it new." These writers and artists were coming of age at a time of chaos, alienation, and disillusionment. To capture the complex spirit of modernity, they experimented with new techniques: nonlinear, stream of consciousness narratives, imagistic poetry, and fragmented stories.

Novelist William Faulkner sought to create art that would endure in a precarious and broken modern world: he emphasizes these themes in his 1950 Nobel Prize Acceptance Speech (p. 462).

The modern artists rejected conventional forms of — and ideas about — art. For example, once an artistic form was established and accepted, the modernist would seek to rebel or dispel the stereotype creating a fragmented collection of artistic expression. As a result, modernist art and literature can be shocking, ironic, and demanding.

Today, graffiti and slam poetry express a similar rebellious spirit. Graffiti may include symbols, phrases, or figures spray painted on walls, usually in outdoor spaces. Such images and texts have long been an oppositional form of political discourse: a medium that remains illegal in many cities. Similarly, slam poetry, spoken-word poetry, and performance poetry often use elements of performance, writing, and audience participation to confront social injustices. These forms remain common in coffee houses, bookstores, and bars throughout America.

At the same time, the modernist desire to connect, persevere, and "make it new," continues today, as reflected in contemporary artists. For example, Lin-Manuel Miranda's 2015 Tony Award–winning musical *Hamilton*, an updated and radically re-imagined retelling of the United States' "origin story" in a contemporary form. In his article from the *Atlantic* (p. 465), Miranda writes about the role of artists in bringing about social change. In many ways, writers face the same problems today as the modernists did 100 years ago: How can we make meaningful art that speaks to — and for — the uncertainty, ambiguity, and instability of contemporary life?

Amanda Gorman was the first National Youth Poet Laureate to recite a poem at an inauguration. She delivered her poem "The Hill We Climb" at the 2021 Presidential Inauguration of President Joe Biden and Vice President Kamala Harris.

How does the image of the first National Youth Poet Laureate performing her poem communicate the value of expression in our lives? Why have a poet speak at such events? Do you believe that artistic expression like this brings people together?

Pool/Getty Images

Nobel Prize Acceptance Speech

William Faulkner

Mario De Biasi/Mondadori Portfolio/Bridgeman Images

THE TEXT IN CONTEXT

William Faulkner (1897–1962) was a famous American novelist most known for his depictions of everyday characters, including farmers, slaves, the descendants of slaves, and the aristocracy of the South. His more famous works include *The Sound and the Fury* (1929), *As I Lay Dying* (1930), *Light in August* (1932), and *Absalom, Absalom!* (1936). Faulkner received the 1949 Nobel Prize for Literature. According to Alfred Nobel, the prize's namesake, the award is given to the writer who has "the most outstanding work in an ideal direction." The Nobel Committee for Literature recognized Faulkner "for his powerful and artistically unique contribution to the modern American novel." The following speech was delivered on December 10, 1950, at the awards banquet.

I feel that this award was not made to me as a man, but to my work—a life's work in the agony and sweat of the human spirit, not for glory and least of all for profit, but to create out of the materials of the human spirit something which did not exist before. So this award is only mine in trust. It will not be difficult to find a dedication for the money part of it commensurate with the purpose and significance of its origin. But I would like to do the same with the acclaim too, by using this moment as a pinnacle from which I might be listened to by the young men and women already dedicated to the same anguish and travail, among whom is already that one who will some day stand here where I am standing.

Our tragedy today is a general and universal physical fear so long sustained by now that we can even bear it. There are no longer problems of the spirit. There is only the question: When will I be blown up? Because of this, the young man and woman writing today has forgotten the problems of the human heart in conflict with itself which alone can make good writing because only that is worth writing about, worth the agony and the sweat.

He must learn them again. He must teach himself that the basest of all things is to be afraid; and, teaching himself that, forget it forever, leaving no room in his workshop for anything but the old verities and truths of the heart, the old universal truths lacking which any story is ephemeral and doomed—love and honor and pity and pride and compassion and sacrifice. Until he does so, he labors under a curse. He writes not of love but of lust, of defeats in which nobody loses anything of value, of victories without hope and, worst of all, without pity or compassion. His griefs grieve on no universal bones, leaving no scars. He writes not of the heart but of the glands.

Until he relearns these things, he will write as though he stood among and watched the end of man. I decline to accept the end of man. It is easy enough to say that man is immortal simply because he will endure: that when the last ding-dong of doom has clanged and faded from the last worthless rock hanging tideless in the last red and dying evening, that even then there will still be one more sound: that of his puny inexhaustible voice, still talking.

I refuse to accept this. I believe that man will not merely endure: he will prevail. He is immortal, not because he alone among creatures has an inexhaustible voice, but because he has a soul, a spirit capable of compassion and sacrifice and endurance. The poet's, the writer's, duty is to write about these things. It is his privilege to help man endure by lifting his heart, by reminding him of the courage and honor and hope and pride and compassion and pity and sacrifice which have been the glory of his past. The poet's voice need not merely be the record of man, it can be one of the props, the pillars to help him endure and prevail.

Many students give up on academics and activities. The infographic considers the possible causes for why.

Consider the role of perseverance in your own life. Why might we choose endurance over quitting? What are some specific reasons people quit? Consider successful individuals in your community: In what way did these people choose perseverance and "grit" over giving up?

Abby Weinstein/MindPrint Learning

RHETORICAL SITUATION

1. Who is the **writer**? What does he share with the audience that adds to his **credibility**?

2. What is the **context** for this text? How does that contribute to his **purpose**?

3. What is the writer's **perspective** on the subject? Give an example that reveals this perspective, and explain how this perspective strengthens the message.

CLAIMS AND EVIDENCE

4. What is the **evidence** in the text? How does this evidence function to convince the audience?

5. How does Faulkner arrange his **evidence**? How does this arrangement contribute to his **purpose**?

6. How does each paragraph establish a relationship to the **claim** and advance the argument?

REASONING AND ORGANIZATION

7. How does Faulkner use **classification** to develop his argument?

8. Faulkner uses the **metaphor** of time to advance his message. Explain the comparison and the effect on his message.

9. Does Faulkner use inductive or deductive **reasoning**? How does this choice reinforce his **message**?

LANGUAGE AND STYLE

10. What is the **tone** of the text? Give specific examples of language that supports this tone.

11. Identify another rhetorical choice that creates the **tone**. Then, explain how this choice contributes to the tone.

12. Choose an idea from the text. Identify specific words that Faulkner uses to describe that idea. What are the **connotations** of these words in the text? How does this word choice contribute to his **message**?

13. Faulkner makes **syntactical** choices throughout his text. Explain the effect of the inclusion and placement of **simple sentences**. Give two examples.

IDEAS IN AMERICAN CULTURE

14. During the turbulent time period of modernist literature (1914–1945), the words *prevail* and *endure* had vital and urgent meaning in the United States when Faulkner used them. How is his message still relevant in your community — and our country — today? You might consider his words in the context of economics, politics, education, or even the environment.

PUTTING IT ALL TOGETHER

15. As an artist, Faulkner draws upon his own experience to create a message that could resonate with a wider audience. What was his message, and how did he develop it? You should consider how his word choice, syntax, organization, and evidence help establish a relationship with that audience.

What Artists Can Do

Lin-Manuel Miranda

THE TEXT IN CONTEXT

The son of Puerto Rican immigrants, Lin-Manuel Miranda (b. 1980) is an award-winning writer, composer, and actor. He began writing his Tony- and Grammy-winning musical *In the Heights* while he was still a student at Wesleyan University. But in 2015, Miranda's work became a global phenomenon when he starred in his Pulitzer Prize–winning musical *Hamilton: An American Musical*. This groundbreaking production tells the story of Founding Father Alexander Hamilton, who served as the first U.S. Treasury Secretary and helped create our country's banking system. The show's use of hip-hop music, along with a diverse cast of actors, invites all Americans to share in the history of our nation. In the following 2019 article published in the *Atlantic*, a magazine devoted to cultural and literary topics, Miranda discusses the power of artists in our culture.

All art is political. In tense, fractious times—like our current moment—all art is political. But even during those times when politics and the future of our country itself are not the source of constant worry and anxiety, art is still political. Art lives in the world, and we exist in the world, and we cannot create honest work about the world in which we live without reflecting it. If the work tells the truth, it will live on.

Public Enemy's "911 Is a Joke," George Orwell's *1984*, Rodgers and Hammerstein's whole damn catalog—all are political works that tell the truth.

Yes, Rodgers and Hammerstein. Consider *The Sound of Music*. It isn't just about climbing mountains and fording streams. Look beyond the adorable von Trapp children: It's about the looming existential threat of Nazism. No longer relevant? A GIF of Captain von Trapp tearing up a Nazi flag is something we see 10 times a day on Twitter, because all sorts of Nazis are out there again in 2019. As last spring's searing Broadway revival of *Oklahoma!* revealed, lying underneath Hammerstein's elephant-eye-high corn and chirping birds is a lawless society becoming itself, bending its rules and procedures based on who is considered part of the community (Curly) and who is marginalized (poor Jud . . . seriously, poor Jud). Or consider your parents' favorite, *South Pacific*. At its center, our hero, Nellie Forbush, must confront her own internalized racism when she learns that the new love of her life has biracial children from a previous marriage. Let your parents know if they forgot: Rodgers and Hammerstein musicals form the spine of Broadway's "golden age," and they also deeply engage with the politics of their era.

My first Broadway musical, *In the Heights*, is an example of how time can reveal the politics inherent within a piece of art. When I began writing this musical, as a college project at Wesleyan University, it was an 80-minute collegiate love story with a promising mix of Latin music and hip-hop, but it was pretty sophomoric (which is appropriate; I was a sophomore). After college, I started from scratch with the director Thomas Kail and the playwright Quiara Alegría Hudes, and we shifted the show's focus from the love story to Washington Heights, a neighborhood in Upper Manhattan where everyone is from everywhere. In the 20th century, Washington Heights was often home to the latest wave of immigrants. It was an Irish neighborhood; it was a Russian Jewish neighborhood (Yeshiva University is up there). If you take the Dominican store sign down you'll see a sign for an Irish pub underneath it, and if you take that down you'll find Hebrew. Washington Heights was heavily Dominican when I was growing up, and it remains so, with a vibrant Mexican and Latin American immigrant community as well.

As we wrote about this Upper Manhattan community on the verge of change, we looked to our musical-theater forebears. In *Cabaret*, the upheaval facing the characters in Berlin is the rise of the Nazi Party. In *Fiddler on the Roof*, the town of Anatevka struggles to hold on to its traditions as the world changes around it, and the threat of pogroms looms. For our musical world, upheaval comes in the form of gentrification. This is obviously different from fascism and pogroms; it's not even in the same moral universe. How you begin to dramatize something as subtle and multifaceted as gentrification poses some tricky questions. We threw our characters into the same dilemma faced by their real-life working-class counterparts: What do we do when we can't afford to live in the place we've lived all our lives, especially when we are the ones who make the neighborhood special and attractive to others? Each of the characters confronts this question differently: One sacrifices the family business to ensure his child's educational future. Another relocates to the less expensive Bronx. Our narrator decides to stay, despite the odds, taking on the responsibility of telling this neighborhood's stories and carrying on its traditions.

We received great reviews. If critics had a common criticism, it was that the show, its contemporary music aside, was somehow old-fashioned or "sentimental." Gentrification, the businesses closing, the literal powerlessness as the characters face a blackout that affects only their neighborhood—these issues, always there in the material, didn't register with most theater critics in 2008. *In the Heights* was considered a hit by Broadway standards. It didn't leap off the Arts page and into the national conversation like *Hamilton* would, but we won some Tonys, recouped our investment, and had a wonderful three-year run at the Richard Rodgers Theatre, where *Hamilton* now lives. We posted our Broadway closing notice at the end of 2010.

What a difference 10 years makes.

Right now, Jon M. Chu is editing his feature-film adaptation of *In the Heights*, which is scheduled to be released in June. We spent a joyous summer shooting the film—on location, in our neighborhood—and issues that were always inherent in the text now stand out in bold-faced type. Gentrification

5

has rendered Lower Manhattan, Harlem, and much of Brooklyn unrecognizable to the previous generations that called those neighborhoods home. The East Village of Jonathan Larson's *Rent* is nonexistent, lettered avenues notwithstanding. And the narrative of immigrants coming to this country and making a better life for themselves—the backdrop of everything that happens in *In the Heights*, across three generations of stories—is somehow a radical narrative now. . . .

What artists can do is bring stories to the table that are unshakably true—the sort of stories that, once you've heard them, won't let you return to what you thought before. I think about the crisis on the border constantly. I think about the famous photograph of a little girl crying beside a Border Patrol truck. That picture went viral because it seemed to capture the horror of family separations. But it turned out that the girl wasn't being separated from her mother—her mother had simply been ordered to put her daughter down while she was searched by agents. The family was in distress, and the border crisis was real, but people used the details of this particular incident to close

themselves off from empathy. "Fake news," they said. A child is crying for her mother, but that's not enough to keep people from pushing empathy away. I believe great art is like bypass surgery. It allows us to go around all of the psychological distancing mechanisms that turn people cold to the most vulnerable among us.

At the end of the day, our job as artists is to tell the truth as we see it. If telling the truth is an inherently political act, so be it. Times may change and politics may change, but if we do our best to tell the truth as specifically as possible, time will reveal those truths and reverberate beyond the era in which we created them. We keep revisiting Shakespeare's *Macbeth* because ruthless political ambition does not belong to any particular era. We keep listening to Public Enemy because systemic racism continues to rain tragedy on communities of color. We read Orwell's *1984* and shiver at its diagnosis of doublethink, which we see coming out of the White House at this moment. And we listen to Rodgers and Hammerstein's *South Pacific*, as Lieutenant Cable sings about racism, "You've got to be carefully taught." It's all art. It's all political.

10

The image is of Lin-Manuel Miranda and co-stars playing in *Hamilton: An American Musical*. This musical is one of the most popular Broadway shows of this century. In 2016, it won the Pulitzer Prize for Drama.

How does this image exemplify the human qualities necessary to endure?

Theo Wargo/Getty Images

After Hurricane Maria devastated Puerto Rico in 2017, Lin-Manuel Miranda led efforts to raise funds to provide necessary relief and support to rebuild the island where his family immigrated from. Initiatives to generate donations included partnering with celebrities like Stephen Colbert and Jennifer Lopez, working with the Hispanic Federation (an organization that Miranda's father founded), and putting on a special production of *Hamilton*. All together, Miranda's efforts generated nearly $15 million to help Puerto Ricans rebuild.

Gladys Vega/Getty Images

RHETORICAL SITUATION

1. Explain how the **writer** creates a relationship between himself and the **audience**. What are some beliefs and values shared between the writer and the audience?

2. Explain how Lin-Manuel Miranda creates **credibility**.

3. How does Miranda reveal his **position** and perspective? What is the **purpose** of the text?

4. How does the **introduction** and **conclusion** of his essay contribute to the success of Miranda's **message**?

CLAIMS AND EVIDENCE

5. How do the writer's experiences function as **evidence**? Consider how he references other sources through this evidence.

6. What are the **perspectives** presented in the text? How do these perspectives contribute to the complexity of the text?

REASONING AND ORGANIZATION

7. How does the writer **organize** his argument? Is the text arranged **inductively** or **deductively**? Why does the writer choose this approach?

8. The writer shares several personal experiences. How do each of these experiences establish a **line of reasoning** and justify his **claim**?

9. Consider the sequencing of the paragraphs in this text. How does this **arrangement** contribute to his argument?

LANGUAGE AND STYLE

10. Identify a **rhetorical choice** in the text and explain how the choice contributes to the **tone**.

11. What is the **tone** of the text? Consider when the tone shifts. What change does this shift in tone reveal about the writer's perspective? Support your explanation with textual evidence.

IDEAS IN AMERICAN CULTURE

12. Lin-Manuel Miranda discusses truth and art. Explain what the writer means when he refers to these two ideas. How do these ideas function in the contemporary world? Explain what the writer means when he says, "If telling the truth is inherently a political act, so be it." How does this change the way you view art? Discuss your experience with art and how this affects the response from the audience. Give an example of telling the truth through the expression of art.

PUTTING IT ALL TOGETHER

13. What is Miranda's message? How does his text combine both a narrative structure and persuasive appeals to create a convincing argument?

⅃⊔⅃
⊐⊐⊏
⊐⊐⊏
⊐⊐⊏

IDEAS IN AMERICAN CULTURE
Wealth and Poverty

IDEA BANK

Change

Class

Constraint

Darwinism

Depression

Economy

Economic Progress

Extravagance

Influence

Labor

Leisure

Lifestyle

Luxury

Materialism

Poverty

Reform

Stimulus

Wealth

Work

While World War I ended in 1918, the peace remained unresolved and unstable. This instability set the stage for World War II. At home, wealth inequality (and a politically influential ruling class) led to monopolies, corruption, and the oppression of laborers. The resulting class divisions would reverberate throughout the country for decades to come. Moreover, a progressive political movement arose to address these problems.

The United States homeland was spared from the devastation of World War I. In fact, the U.S. economy boomed in the decade after the war, as the nation's wealth doubled between 1920 and 1929. As a result, a consumer culture emerged that we can recognize as our own. Encouraged by the modern advertising industry, Americans bought cars, washing machines, radios, clothing, jazz records, beauty products, and other goods. They also pursued the images of fashion and wealth that they saw in movies and magazines, just as people follow celebrities and influencers today.

Writers of the early twentieth century often examined the corruption and dissolution that lurked beneath the glamorous surfaces of wealth. The consumer

▲

This image, Thomas Hart Benton's *Departure of the Joads* (1939), depicts John Steinbeck's fictional Joad family from *The Grapes of Wrath* as they flee the plains of Oklahoma. The Great Depression and the devastating drought of the Dust Bowl forced millions of people to migrate west with the hope of opportunity.

How does the image represent the desperation of poverty and the desire for wealth during the Great Depression?

binge of the 1920s was enabled by a boom in credit, which allowed people to buy products that they could not afford. This mirrored the underlying weaknesses of the U.S. economy. On October 29, 1929, the U.S. stock market crashed and the country fell into the Great Depression. Thousands of companies went bankrupt, as did thousands of American farmers many of whom became migrant workers.

The era's social problems and technological advances spawned new interests in the natural and social sciences. New ideas in biology, sociology, and psychology influenced society, including literature and the arts. Charles Darwin had published *The Origin of the Species*, which advanced the idea of evolution in 1859. During the following decades, social scientists latched onto Darwin's concept of natural selection.

In 1932, new President Franklin Roosevelt began implementing a series of economic recovery policies known as the New Deal, which greatly increased federal spending and focused on job creation. Several New Deal programs remain today, including Social Security, the Federal Deposit Insurance Corporation (FDIC), and the Securities and Exchange Commission (SEC). The New Deal was polarizing in its time: critics opposed the expansion of the federal government.

Indeed, the legacy of the New Deal remains controversial today, as the country continues to balance individual liberty with the need for collective action. For example, should the government even have a role in addressing poverty or the country's wealth disparities? In "The Gospel of Wealth" (p. 472), Andrew Carnegie contends that the rich have an obligation to use their wealth to create a more equitable society. In "Why Poverty Is Like a Disease" (p. 481), Christian H. Cooper argues that poverty places unhealthy stressors on people, and that scientific evidence suggests that the government can do more to alleviate poverty.

Today, many argue that the federal government can do more to create public work projects, offer incentives for economic development, and provide additional financial support for Americans. Others maintain that a competitive economic marketplace creates a thriving economy and lifts up the poor, along with the rest of society. In other words, the principles of our economy are often at odds with federal aid and support programs.

The image shows construction workers on a highway improvement project. ▶

As Roosevelt did with the "New Deal," the U.S. government still deploys stimulus packages as a way to affect the economy. These policies often focus on infrastructure projects, like rebuilding highways, bridges, and airports. Why might some view such stimulus as a positive measure for growing the economy, while others view it as needless spending?

Yellow Dog Productions/Getty Images

The Gospel of Wealth
Andrew Carnegie

THE TEXT IN CONTEXT

Andrew Carnegie (1835–1919) emigrated from Scotland to the United States with his parents at the age of twelve. From humble origins, he became what many would call a self-made man. As a teenager, he worked as a telegraph operator; then, he worked for the railroads, where he met business leaders who ended up serving as his mentors. He used his earnings to invest in oil and steel, emerging as a major American industrialist and millionaire. A shrewd businessman, Carnegie turned his attention to finding practical, effective ways to use his fortune for the public good. He is widely known for his financial contributions to museums, libraries, scientific research, and arts venues — Carnegie Hall in New York City being one of the most famous. In the following excerpt from his 1889 essay "The Gospel of Wealth," Carnegie argues that the rich should use their wealth to benefit society; he also hopes that his book will inspire other philanthropists. Carnegie's philanthropic spirit lives on through institutes, foundations, museums, and libraries.

The problem of our age is the proper administration of wealth, so that the ties of brotherhood may still bind together the rich and poor in harmonious relationship. The conditions of human life have not only been changed, but revolutionized, within the past few hundred years. In former days there was little difference between the dwelling, dress, food, and environment of the chief and those of his retainers. The Indians are today where civilized man then was. When visiting the Sioux, I was led to the wigwam of the chief. It was just like the others in external appearance, and even within the difference was trifling between it and those of the poorest of his braves. The contrast between the palace of the millionaire and the cottage of the laborer with us today measures the change which has come with civilization. This change, however, is not to be deplored, but welcomed as highly beneficial. It is well, nay, essential for the progress of the race, that the houses of some should be homes for all that is highest and best in literature and the arts, and for all the refinements of civilization, rather than that none should be so. Much better this great irregularity than universal squalor. Without wealth there can be no Mæcenas. The "good old times" were not good old times. Neither master nor servant was as well situated then as today. A relapse to old conditions would be disastrous to both—not the least so to him who serves—and would sweep away civilization with it. But whether the change be for good or ill, it is upon us, beyond our power to alter, and therefore to be accepted and made the best of. It is a waste of time to criticize the inevitable.

It is easy to see how the change has come. One illustration will serve for almost every phase of the cause. In the manufacture of products we have the whole story. It applies to all combinations of human industry, as stimulated and enlarged by the inventions of this scientific age. Formerly articles were manufactured at the domestic hearth or in small shops which formed part of the household. The master and his apprentices worked side by side, the latter living with the master, and therefore subject to the same conditions. When these apprentices rose to be masters, there was little or no change in their mode of life, and they, in turn, educated in the same routine succeeding apprentices. There was, substantially social equality, and even political equality, for those engaged in industrial pursuits had then little or no political voice in the State.

"The poor enjoy what the rich could not before afford. What were the luxuries have become the necessaries of life. The laborer has now more comforts than the landlord had a few generations ago."

But the inevitable result of such a mode of manufacture was crude articles at high prices. Today the world obtains commodities of excellent quality at prices which even the generation preceding this would have deemed incredible. In the commercial world similar causes have produced similar results, and the race is benefited thereby. The poor enjoy what the rich could not before afford. What were the luxuries have become the necessaries of life. The laborer has now more comforts than the landlord had a few generations ago. The farmer has more luxuries than the landlord had, and is more richly clad and better housed. The landlord has books and pictures rarer,

and appointments more artistic, than the King could then obtain.

The price we pay for this salutary change is, no doubt, great. We assemble thousands of operatives in the factory, in the mine, and in the counting-house, of whom the employer can know little or nothing, and to whom the employer is little better than a myth. All intercourse between them is at an end. Rigid castes are formed, and, as usual, mutual ignorance breeds mutual distrust. Each caste is without sympathy for the other, and ready to credit anything disparaging in regard to it. Under the law of competition, the employer of thousands is forced into the strictest economies, among which the rates paid to labor figure prominently, and often there is friction between the employer and the employed, between capital and labor, between rich and poor. Human society loses homogeneity.

The price which society pays for the law of competition, like the price it pays for cheap comforts and luxuries, is also great; but the advantages of this law are also greater still, for it is to this law that we owe our wonderful material development, which brings improved conditions in its train. But, whether the law be benign or not, we must say of it, as we say of the change in the conditions of men to which we have referred: It is here; we cannot evade it; no substitutes for it have been found; and while the law may be sometimes hard for the individual, it is best for the race, because it insures the survival of the fittest in every department. We accept and welcome therefore, as conditions to which we must accommodate ourselves, great inequality of environment, the concentration of business, industrial and commercial, in the hands of a few, and the law of competition between these, as being not only beneficial, but essential for the future progress of the race. Having accepted these, it follows that there must be great scope for the exercise of special ability in the merchant and in the manufacturer who has to conduct affairs upon a great scale. That this talent for organization and management is rare among men is proved by the fact that it invariably secures for its possessor enormous rewards, no matter where or under what laws or conditions. The experienced in affairs always rate the MAN whose services can be obtained as a partner as not only the first consideration, but such as to render the question of his capital scarcely worth considering, for such men soon create capital; while, without the special talent required, capital soon takes wings. Such men become interested in firms or corporations using millions; and estimating only simple interest to be made upon the capital invested, it is inevitable that their income must exceed their expenditures, and that they must accumulate wealth. Nor is there any middle ground which such men can occupy, because the great manufacturing or commercial concern which does not earn at least interest upon its capital soon becomes bankrupt. It must either go forward or fall behind: to stand still is impossible. It is a condition essential for its successful operation that it should be thus far profitable, and even that, in addition to interest on capital, it should make profit. It is a law, as certain as any of the others named, that men possessed of this peculiar talent for affair, under the free play of economic forces, must, of necessity, soon be in receipt of more revenue than can be judiciously expended upon themselves; and this law is as beneficial for the race as the others.

Objections to the foundations upon which society is based are not in order, because the condition of the race is better with these than it has been with any others which have been tried. Of the effect of any new substitutes proposed we cannot be sure. The Socialist or Anarchist who seeks to overturn present conditions is to be regarded as attacking the foundation upon which civilization itself rests, for civilization took its start from the day that the capable, industrious workman said to his incompetent and lazy fellow, "If thou dost not sow, thou shalt not reap," and thus ended primitive Communism by separating the drones from the bees. One who studies this subject will soon be brought face to face with the conclusion that upon the sacredness of property civilization itself depends—the right of the laborer to his hundred dollars in the savings bank, and equally the legal right of the millionaire to his millions. To these who propose to substitute Communism for this intense Individualism the answer, therefore, is: The race has tried that. All progress from that barbarous day to the present time has resulted from its displacement. Not evil, but good, has come to the race from the accumulation of wealth by those who have the ability and energy that produce it. But even if we admit for a moment that it might be better for the race to discard its present foundation, Individualism,—that it is a nobler ideal that man should labor, not for himself alone, but in and for a brotherhood of his fellows, and share with them all in common, realizing Swedenborg's idea of Heaven, where, as he says, the angels derive their happiness, not from laboring for self, but for each other,—even admit all this, and a sufficient answer is, This is not evolution, but revolution. It necessitates the changing of human nature itself a work of eons, even if it were good to change it, which we cannot know.

It is not practicable in our day or in our age. Even if desirable theoretically, it belongs to another and long-succeeding sociological stratum. Our duty is with what is practicable now;

with the next step possible in our day and generation. It is criminal to waste our energies in endeavoring to uproot, when all we can profitably or possibly accomplish is to bend the universal tree of humanity a little in the direction most favorable to the production of good fruit under existing circumstances. We might as well urge the destruction of the highest existing type of man because he failed to reach our ideal as favor the destruction of Individualism, Private Property, the Law of Accumulation of Wealth, and the Law of Competition; for these are the highest results of human experience, the soil in which society so far has produced the best fruit. Unequally or unjustly, perhaps, as these laws sometimes operate, and imperfect as they appear to the Idealist, they are, nevertheless, like the highest type of man, the best and most valuable of all that humanity has yet accomplished.

We start, then, with a condition of affairs under which the best interests of the race are promoted, but which inevitably gives wealth to the few. Thus far, accepting conditions as they exist, the situation can be surveyed and pronounced good. The question then arises,—and, if the foregoing be correct, it is the only question with which we have to deal,—What is the proper mode of administering wealth after the laws upon which civilization is founded have thrown it into the hands of the few? And it is of this great question that I believe I offer the true solution. It will be understood that fortunes are here spoken of, not moderate sums saved by many years of effort, the returns on which are required for the comfortable maintenance and education of families. This is not wealth, but only competence which it should be the aim of all to acquire.

There are but three modes in which surplus wealth can be disposed of. It can be left to the families of the decedents; or it can be

10

bequeathed for public purposes; or, finally, it can be administered during their lives by its possessors. Under the first and second modes most of the wealth of the world that has reached the few has hitherto been applied. Let us in turn consider each of these modes. The first is the most injudicious. In monarchical countries, the estates and the greatest portion of the wealth are left to the first son, that the vanity of the parent may be gratified by the thought that his name and title are to descend to succeeding generations unimpaired. The condition of this class in Europe to-day teaches the futility of such hopes or ambitions. The successors have become impoverished through their follies or from the fall in the value of land. Even in Great Britain the strict law of entail has been found inadequate to maintain the status of an hereditary class. Its soil is rapidly passing into the hands of the stranger. Under republican institutions the division of property among the children is much fairer, but the question which forces itself upon thoughtful men in all lands is: Why should men leave great fortunes to their children? If this is done from affection, is it not misguided affection? Observation teaches that, generally speaking, it is not well for the children that they should be so burdened. Neither is it well for the state. Beyond providing for the wife and daughters moderate sources of income, and very moderate allowances indeed, if any, for the sons, men may well hesitate, for it is no longer questionable that great sums bequeathed oftener work more for the injury than for the good of the recipients. Wise men will soon conclude that, for the best interests of the members of their families and of the state, such bequests are an improper use of their means.

It is not suggested that men who have failed to educate their sons to earn a livelihood shall cast them adrift in poverty. If any man has seen fit to rear his sons with a view to their living idle lives, or, what is highly commendable, has instilled in them the sentiment that they are in a position to labor for public ends without reference to pecuniary considerations, then, of course, the duty of the parent is to see that such are provided for in moderation. There are instances of millionaires' sons unspoiled by wealth, who, being rich, still perform great services in the community. Such are the very salt of the earth, as valuable as, unfortunately, they are rare; still it is not the exception, but the rule, that men must regard, and, looking at the usual result of enormous sums conferred upon legatees, the thoughtful man must shortly say, "I would as soon leave to my son a curse as the almighty dollar," and admit to himself that it is not the welfare of the children, but family pride, which inspires these enormous legacies.

As to the second mode, that of leaving wealth at death for public uses, it may be said that this is only a means for the disposal of wealth, provided a man is content to wait until he is dead before it becomes of much good in the world. Knowledge of the results of legacies bequeathed is not calculated to inspire the brightest hopes of much posthumous good being accomplished. The cases are not few in which the real object sought by the testator is not attained, nor are they few in which his real wishes are thwarted. In many cases the bequests are so used as to become only monuments of his folly. It is well to remember that it requires the exercise of not less ability than that which acquired the wealth to use it so as to be really beneficial to the community. Besides this, it may fairly be said that no man is to be extolled for doing what he cannot help doing, nor is he to be thanked by the community to which he only leaves wealth at death.

Men who leave vast sums in this way may fairly be thought men who would not have left it at all, had they been able to take it with them. The memories of such cannot be held in grateful remembrance, for there is no grace in their gifts. It is not to be wondered at that such bequests seem so generally to lack the blessing.

The growing disposition to tax more and more heavily large estates left at death is a cheering indication of the growth of a salutary change in public opinion. The State of Pennsylvania now takes—subject to some exceptions—one-tenth of the property left by its citizens. The budget presented in the British Parliament the other day proposes to increase the death-duties; and, most significant of all, the new tax is to be a graduated one. Of all forms of taxation, this seems the wisest. Men who continue hoarding great sums all their lives, the proper use of which for public ends would work good to the community, should be made to feel that the community, in the form of the state, cannot thus be deprived of its proper share. By taxing estates heavily at death the state marks its condemnation of the selfish millionaire's unworthy life.

It is desirable that nations should go much further in this direction. Indeed, it is difficult to set bounds to the share of a rich man's estate which should go at his death to the public through the agency of the state, and by all means such taxes should be graduated, beginning at nothing upon moderate sums to dependents, and increasing rapidly as the amounts swell, until of the millionaire's hoard, as of Shylock's, at least

> "The other half   15
> Comes to the privy coffer of the state."

This policy would work powerfully to induce the rich man to attend to the administration of wealth during his life, which is the end that society should always have in view, as being that by far most fruitful for the people. Nor need it be feared that this policy would sap the root of enterprise and render men less anxious to accumulate, for to the class whose ambition it is to leave great fortunes and be talked about after their death, it will attract even more attention, and, indeed, be a some-what nobler ambition to have enormous sums paid over to the state from their fortunes.

There remains, then, only one mode of using great fortunes; but in this we have the true antidote for the temporary unequal distri-bution of wealth, the reconciliation of the rich and the poor—a reign of harmony—another ideal, differing, indeed, from that of the Com-munist in requiring only the further evolution of existing conditions, not the total overthrow of our civilization. It is founded upon the pres-ent most intense individualism, and the race is projected to put it in practice by degree when-ever it pleases. Under its sway we shall have an ideal state, in which the surplus wealth of the few will become, in the best sense the property of the many, because administered for the common good, and this wealth, passing through the hands of the few, can be made a much more potent force for the elevation of our race than if it had been distributed in small sums to the people themselves. Even the poorest can be made to see this, and to agree that great sums gathered by some of their fellow-citizens and spent for public purposes, from which the masses reap the principal benefit, are more valuable to them than if scat-tered among them through the course of many years in trifling amounts through the course of many years.

If we consider what results flow from the Cooper Institute, for instance, to the best por-tion of the race in New York not possessed of means, and compare these with those

which would have arisen for the good of the masses from an equal sum distributed by Mr. Cooper in his lifetime in the form of wages, which is the highest form of distribution, being for work done and not for charity, we can form some estimate of the possibilities for the improvement of the race which lie embedded in the present law of the accumu-lation of wealth. Much of this sum if distrib-uted in small quantities among the people, would have been wasted in the indulgence of appetite, some of it in excess, and it may be doubted whether even the part put to the best use, that of adding to the comforts of the home, would have yielded results for the race, as a race, at all comparable to those which are flowing and are to flow from the Cooper Insti-tute from generation to generation. Let the advocate of violent or radical change ponder well this thought.

We might even go so far as to take another instance, that of Mr. Tilden's bequest of five millions of dollars for a free library in the city of New York, but in referring to this one cannot help saying involuntarily, how much better if Mr. Tilden had devoted the last years of his own life to the proper administration of this immense sum; in which case neither legal contest nor any other cause of delay could have interfered with his aims. But let us assume that Mr. Tilden's millions finally become the means of giving to this city a noble public library, where the treasures of the world contained in books will be open to all forever, without money and without price. Considering the good of that part of the race which congre-gates in and around Manhattan Island, would its permanent benefit have been better pro-moted had these millions been allowed to cir-culate in small sums through the hands of the masses? Even the most strenuous advocate of Communism must entertain a doubt upon this subject. Most of those who think will probably entertain no doubt whatever.

Poor and restricted are our opportunities in this life; narrow our horizon; our best work most imperfect; but rich men should be thankful for one inestimable boon. They have it in their power during their lives to busy themselves in organizing benefactions from which the masses of their fellows will derive lasting advantage, and thus dignify their own lives. The highest life is probably to be reached, not by such imitation of the life of Christ as Count Tolstoi gives us, but, while animated by Christ's spirit, by recognizing the changed conditions of this age, and adopting modes of expressing this spirit suitable to the changed conditions under which we live; still laboring for the good of our fellows, which was the essence of his life and teaching, but laboring in a different manner.

This, then, is held to be the duty of the man of Wealth: First, to set an example of modest, unostentatious living, shunning display or extravagance; to provide moderately for the legitimate wants of those dependent upon him; and after doing so to consider all surplus revenues which come to him simply as trust funds, which he is called upon to administer, and strictly bound as a matter of duty to administer in the manner which, in his judgment, is best calculated to produce the most beneficial results for the community—the man of wealth thus becoming the mere agent and trustee for his poorer brethren, bringing to their service his superior wisdom, experience and ability to administer, doing for them better than they would or could do for themselves.

We are met here with the difficulty of determining what are moderate sums to leave to members of the family; what is modest, unostentatious living; what is the test of extravagance. There must be different standards for different conditions. The answer is that it is as impossible to name exact amounts or actions as it is to define good manners, good taste, or the rules of propriety; but, nevertheless, these are verities, well known although indefinable. Public sentiment is quick to know and to feel what offends these. So in the case of wealth. The rule in regard to good taste in the dress of men or women applies here. Whatever makes one conspicuous offends the canon. If any family be chiefly known for display, for extravagance in home, table, equipage, for enormous sums ostentatiously spent in any form upon itself, if these be its chief distinctions, we have no difficulty in estimating its nature or culture. So likewise in regard to the use or abuse of its surplus wealth, or to generous, freehanded cooperation in good public uses, or to unabated efforts to accumulate and hoard to the last, whether they administer or bequeath.

The verdict rests with the best and most enlightened public sentiment. The community will surely judge and its judgments will not often be wrong.

The best uses to which surplus wealth can [25] be put have already been indicated. These who, would administer wisely must, indeed, be wise, for one of the serious obstacles to the improvement of our race is indiscriminate charity. It were better for mankind that the millions of the rich were thrown in to the sea than so spent as to encourage the slothful, the drunken, the unworthy. Of every thousand dollars spent in so called charity to-day, it is probable that $950 is unwisely spent; so spent, indeed as to produce the very evils which it proposes to mitigate or cure. A well-known writer of philosophic books admitted the other day that he had given a quarter of a dollar to a man who approached him as he was coming to visit the house of his friend. He knew nothing of the habits of this beggar; knew not the use that would be made of this money, although he had every reason to suspect that it would be spent improperly. This man professed to be a disciple of Herbert Spencer; yet the quarter-dollar given that night will probably work more injury than all the money which its thoughtless donor will ever be able to give in true charity will do good. He only gratified his own feelings, saved himself from annoyance,—and this was probably one of the most selfish and very worst actions of his life, for in all respects he is most worthy.

In bestowing charity, the main consideration should be to help those who will help themselves; to provide part of the means by which those who desire to improve may do so; to give those who desire to use the aids by which they may rise; to assist, but rarely or never to do all. Neither the individual nor the race is improved by almsgiving. Those worthy of assistance, except in rare cases, seldom require assistance. The really valuable men of the race never do, except in cases of accident or sudden change. Every one has, of course, cases of individuals brought to his own knowledge where temporary assistance can do genuine good, and these he will not overlook. But the amount which can be wisely given by the individual for individuals is necessarily limited by his lack of knowledge of the circumstances connected with each. He is the only true reformer who is as careful and as anxious not to aid the unworthy as he is to aid the worthy, and, perhaps, even more so, for in alms-giving more injury is probably done by rewarding vice than by relieving virtue.

The rich man is thus almost restricted to following the examples of Peter Cooper, Enoch Pratt of Baltimore, Mr. Pratt of Brooklyn, Senator Stanford, and others, who know that the best means of benefiting the community is to place within its reach the ladders upon which the aspiring can rise—parks, and means of recreation, by which men are helped in body and mind; works of art, certain to give pleasure and improve the public taste, and public institutions of various kinds, which will improve the general condition of the people; in this manner returning their surplus wealth to the mass of their fellows in the forms best calculated to do them lasting good.

Thus is the problem of Rich and Poor to be solved. The laws of accumulation will be left free; the laws of distribution free. Individualism will continue, but the millionaire will be but a trustee for the poor; intrusted for a season with a great part of the increased wealth of the community, but administering it for the community far better than it could or would have done for itself. The best minds will thus have reached a stage in the development of the race which it is clearly seen that there is no mode of disposing of surplus wealth creditable to thoughtful and earnest men into whose hands it flows save by using it year by year for the general good. This day already dawns. But a little while, and although, without incurring the pity of their fellows, men may die sharers in great business enterprises from which their capital cannot be or has not been withdrawn, and is left chiefly at death for public uses, yet the man who dies leaving behind many millions of available wealth, which was his to administer during life, will pass away "unwept, unhonored, and unsung," no matter to what uses he leaves the dross which he cannot take with him. Of such as these the public verdict will then be: "The man who dies thus rich dies disgraced."

Such, in my opinion, is the true Gospel concerning Wealth, obedience to which is destined some day to solve the problem of the Rich and the Poor, and to bring "Peace on earth, among men good will."

The political cartoon, "The Protectors of Our Industries," from an 1883 issue of *Puck* magazine, depicts the distribution of wealth in a capitalist society and suggests that the majority of the wealth is generated from the laborers.

———

What problem does this cartoon address? Is the message relevant today? Give contemporary examples that either highlight how the cartoon remains relevant or, if you find it irrelevant, give examples of why it no longer applies.

GRANGER - Historical Picture Archive

RHETORICAL SITUATION

1. Who is the **writer**? How does he establish his **credibility**?

2. What is the **context** of "The Gospel of Wealth"? What is the writer's **exigence**?

3. How is the writer's exigence linked to his **purpose**?

4. What does the title of the essay reveal about the **writer**?

CLAIMS AND EVIDENCE

5. What is Carnegie's **claim**?

6. What type of **evidence** does Carnegie use to convince his readers? What is the function of this evidence within the text?

7. How does Carnegie's choice of **evidence** affect his credibility?

REASONING AND ORGANIZATION

8. What is Carnegie's **method of development**? What reasons does Carnegie provide within this method of development?

9. How does Carnegie arrange his **reasoning**? How does this **arrangement** contribute to his message?

10. Does Carnegie's **reasoning** proceed from an established **claim**, or does the reasoning advance toward a claim? Why might this choice be important for his audience?

LANGUAGE AND STYLE

11. How does Carnegie connect evidence within his argument? Choose two or three **transitions**. Then, describe the relationship these transitions reveal.

12. Carnegie varies his **syntactical choices**. Choose two structures (**subordinating** or **coordinating**) and then explain how these structures function.

13. What is the **tone** of the text? How does this tone contribute to the purpose?

IDEAS IN AMERICAN CULTURE

14. Carnegie states, "The contrast between the palace of the millionaire and the cottage of the laborer . . . today measures the change which has come with civilization." Does his claim still apply today?

PUTTING IT ALL TOGETHER

15. Carnegie called this essay "The Gospel of Wealth." What is the denotation of the word *gospel*? What are its connotations? Why do you think he chose the word *gospel*, rather than *philosophy*, *obligations*, or some other term? In what way does the word contribute to Carnegie's message and purpose?

Why Poverty Is Like a Disease

Christian H. Cooper

THE TEXT IN CONTEXT

Christian H. Cooper (b. 1976) was born in Tennessee and grew up (in his words) "poor and hungry." Today, he is a New York City–based writer, trader, banker, and expert in quantitative finance. In the following article, published in 2017, Cooper explores the damaging mental and physiological effects of being poor. He also reflects upon the "American myth of meritocracy." His work has been published in the *Washington Post*, Business Insider, and *New York Daily News*, along with other publications. Cooper also directs Banking for a New Beginning, which focuses on helping countries such as Turkey, Libya, and Pakistan manage their central banks.

Christian H. Cooper

On paper alone you would never guess that I grew up poor and hungry.

My most recent annual salary was over $700,000. I am a Truman National Security Fellow and a term member at the Council on Foreign Relations. My publisher has just released my latest book series on quantitative finance in worldwide distribution.

None of it feels like enough. I feel as though I am wired for a permanent state of fight or flight, waiting for the other shoe to drop, or the metaphorical week when I don't eat. . . . If you knew me personally, you might get glimpses of stress, self-doubt, anxiety, and depression. And you might hear about Tennessee.

. . . My early life was in East Tennessee, in an Appalachian town called Rockwood. I was the eldest of four children with a household income that couldn't support one. Every Pentecostal church in the surrounding hillbilly heroin country smelled the same: a sweaty mix of cheap cleaner and even cheaper anointing oil, with just a hint of forsaken hope. One of those forsaken churches was effectively my childhood home, and my school.

Class was a single room of 20 people running from kindergarten through twelfth grade, part of an unaccredited school practicing what's called Accelerated Christian Education. We were given booklets to read to ourselves, by ourselves. We scored our own homework. There were no lectures, and I did not have a teacher. Once in a while the preacher's wife would hand out a test . . .

On top of it all, I spent a lot of my time pondering basic questions. Where will my next meal come from? Will I have electricity tomorrow? I became intimately acquainted with the embarrassment of my mom trying to hide our food stamps at the grocery store checkout . . . Something was wrong with the tiny microcosm I was born into. I just wasn't sure what it was.

As an adult I thought I'd figured that out. I'd always thought my upbringing had made me wary and cautious, in a "lessons learned" kind of way. Over the past decades, though, that narrative has evolved. We've learned that the stresses associated with poverty have the potential to change our biology in ways we hadn't imagined. It can reduce the surface area of your brain, shorten your telomeres and lifespan, increase your chances of obesity, and make you more likely to take outsized risks.

Now, new evidence is emerging suggesting the changes can go even deeper—to how our bodies assemble themselves, shifting the types of cells that they are made from, and maybe even how our genetic code is expressed, playing with it like a Rubik's cube thrown into a running washing machine. If this science holds up, it means that poverty is more than just a socioeconomic condition. It is a collection of related symptoms that are preventable, treatable—and even inheritable. In other words, the effects of poverty begin to look very much like the symptoms of a disease.

That word—disease—carries a stigma with it. By using it here, I don't mean that the poor are (that I am) inferior or compromised. I mean that the poor are afflicted, and told by the rest of the world that their condition is a necessary, temporary, and even positive part of modern capitalism. We tell the poor that they have the chance to escape if they just work hard enough; that we are all equally invested in a system that doles out rewards and punishments in equal measure. We point at the rare rags-to-riches stories like my own, which seem to play into the standard meritocracy template.

But merit has little to do with how I got out . . .

In the fall of 1991, Aharon Razin and How-ard Cedar published the extraordinary paper "DNA Methylation and Gene Expression," which showed that gene expression works much like a snake tightly coiled around the Rod of Asclepius.[1] Perched atop the indis-soluble warp and weft of our genetic code are methyl groups that control how tightly our genetic code wraps around special pro-teins, called histone proteins. The tighter a portion of code is wrapped, the less likely it is to have any effect (or in the jargon, the less likely it "gets expressed"). This, we now know, is one pillar of the mechanism of the epigenome: Who you are as a person is not just defined by your DNA, but by which parts of it your epigenome permits to be expressed . . .

In human children, epigenetic changes in stress receptor gene expression that lead to heightened stress responses and mood dis-orders have been measured in response to childhood abuse.[2] And last year, researchers at Duke University found that "lower socioeco-nomic status during adolescence is associated with an increase in methylation of the prox-imal promoter of the serotonin transporter gene," which primes the amygdala—the brain's center for emotion and fear—for "threat-related amygdala reactivity"[3] . . . [The] basic message of these studies is consistent: Chronic stress and uncertainty during child-hood makes stress more difficult to deal with as an adult . . .

Even at this stage, then, we can take a few things away from the science. First, that the stresses of being poor have a biological effect that can last a lifetime. Second, that there is evidence suggesting that these effects may be inheritable, whether it is through impact on the fetus, epigenetic effects, cell subtype effects, or something else.

This science challenges us to re-evaluate a cornerstone of American mythology, and of our social policies for the poor: the boot-strap. The story of the self-made, inspirational individual transcending his or her circum-stances by sweat and hard work. A pillar of the framework of meritocracy, where rewards are supposedly justly distributed to those who deserve them most.

What kind of a bootstrap or merit-based   15
game can we be left with if poverty cripples the contestants? Especially if it has intergen-erational effects? The uglier converse of the bootstrap hypothesis—that those who fail to transcend their circumstances deserve them—makes even less sense in the face of the grim biology of poverty. When the firing gun goes off, the poor are well behind the start line. Despite my success, I certainly was . . .

It's easy to attach a post-facto narrative of talent and hard work to my story, because that's what we're fed by everything from Hol-lywood to political stump speeches. But it's the wrong story. My escape was made up of a series of incredibly unlikely events, none of which I had real control over . . .

Why do so few make it out of poverty? I can tell you from experience it is not because some have more merit than others. It is because being poor is a high-risk gamble. The asymmetry of outcomes for the poor is so enormous because it is so expensive to be poor. Imagine losing a job because your phone was cut off, or blowing off an exam because you spent the day in the ER dealing with something that preventative care would have avoided completely . . . The reality is that when you're poor, if you make one mistake, you're done . . .

Now imagine that, on top of that, your brain is wired to multiply the subjective experience of stress by 10. The result is a profound focus on short-term thinking. To those outsiders who, by fortune of birth, have never known the calculus of poverty, the poor seem to make suboptimal decisions time and time again. But the choices made by the poor are supremely rational choices under the circumstances . . .

The standard American myth of meritocracy misinterprets personal narratives like mine. The accumulated social capital of American institutions—stable transfer of power, rule of law, and entrepreneurship— certainly create economic miracles every day. But these institutions are far more suited to exponentially growing capital where it already exists, rather than creating new capital where society needs it. Stories such as mine are treated as the archetype, and we falsely believe they are the path to escape velocity for an entire segment of the population. In doing so, they leave that population behind. I am the face of the self-made rags-to-riches success story, and I'm here to say that story is a myth. The term "meritocracy" was coined in 1958 as a mockery of the very idea of evaluation by merit alone. We've forgotten to laugh, and the joke is on us . . .

We should leverage the lessons of the science of poverty rather than ignore them. Poverty alleviation programs like conditional cash transfers, for example, reward parents or caregivers with direct payment for taking actions, like ensuring school attendance or arranging for preventative care. They encourage stress alleviation and long-term planning that is far upstream of doing well on an exam—they provide exactly the kind of certainty that the poverty-stricken brain needs. In a paper released in June of 2009, Lia Fernald and Megan Gunnar showed that such programs lowered salivary cortisol levels and reduced lifetime risk for a range of mental and physical disorders.[4] There should be more programs like these: For example so-called whole-child policies, which focus on the long-term development of children starting from birth while reducing uncertainty during the first three years of childhood development.

We stand at the precipice if we don't re-evaluate our understanding of poverty and inequality. The narrative in the neo-liberal west is that if you work hard, things work out. If things don't work out, we have the tendency to blame the victim, leaving them without any choices. Brexit, Le Pen, and the defeat of Hillary Clinton are examples of the cracks that result from inequality and poverty, symptoms of my childhood experience writ large. The Piketty pitchforks are out, and the march to global disorder can only be arrested by adopting measures that begin to price in the stacked deck that I and anyone else born into deep poverty sees, and resents . . .

References

1. Razin, A. & Cedar, H. DNA methylation and gene expression. *Microbiological Reviews* 55, 451–458 (1991).

2. McGowan, P.O., et al. Epigenetic regulation of the glucocorticoid receptor in human brain associates with childhood abuse. *Nature Neuroscience* 12, 342–348 (2009).

3. Swartz, J.R., Hariri, A.R., & Williamson, D.E. An epigenetic mechanism links socioeconomic status to changes in depression-related brain function in high-risk adolescents. *Molecular Psychiatry* 22, 209–214 (2017).

4. Fernald, L.C.H. & Gunnar, M.R. Poverty-alleviation program participation and salivary cortisol in very low-income children. *Social Science & Medicine* 68, 2180–2189 (2009).

A homeless person sleeps under an American flag blanket on a park bench in New York City. According to Coalition for Homeless, in 2020 there was a record of 57,341 homeless people in the city including 18,653 homeless children.

Spencer Platt/Getty Images

What does this image suggest about the American Dream? How is the image ironic? What does it imply about hope for impoverished Americans? As the number of homeless people grows across the United States, what solutions might address the causes and lasting effects of poverty?

RHETORICAL SITUATION

1. Consider Cooper's **credibility**. Is he trustworthy? Explain. Do you consider Cooper an authority on this subject? Why or why not?

2. How does Cooper establish a relationship with his **audience**? What are some shared beliefs, values, or experiences that help create this relationship?

3. Cooper has different **purposes** for his **audience**. Identify two purposes.

4. What is the **exigence** for this text? How does the exigence contribute to both the **purpose** and the **audience**?

CLAIMS AND EVIDENCE

5. The article concludes with a wide variety of **sources**. Give an example and describe its credibility.

6. Cooper's article is filled with **evidence**. How is the evidence **arranged**? Explain the significance of this arrangement.

7. How does Cooper use transitions to introduce his **evidence**? Find a specific example. Then, explain how the transition creates the relationship between evidence and audience.

REASONING AND ORGANIZATION

8. What **reasons** support Cooper's **claim**? Explain how these **reasons** are relevant to the argument.

9. How does he **organize** his argument? How does this organization connect to the audience and convey his message?

LANGUAGE AND STYLE

10. How does Cooper employ **diction** to address different audiences? Give an example of a change in diction. Then, explain how he changes his word choice to address each audience.

11. How does Cooper's **diction** convey his perspective on the subject? Give an example and explain.

IDEAS IN AMERICAN CULTURE

12. Cooper suggests that the "American Dream" is a myth, and argues that hard work does not always lead to opportunities. How do you respond to his claims and perspective? Do you agree? Do you believe that hard work can create opportunities for most people, regardless of their socioeconomic class? Explain.

PUTTING IT ALL TOGETHER

13. How does Cooper convince different audiences that poverty is a "disease"? How does he use multiple perspectives, different sources, and a variety of evidence to develop his message?

COMPOSITION WORKSHOP
Writing a Classification/Division Argument

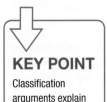

KEY POINT

Classification arguments explain and are organized by categories or parts.

We often use classification in our everyday lives, even when we're unaware of it. For example, most of us are familiar with recycling bins that ask us to sort our garbage into different categories: paper, plastic, aluminum, glass, and trash. So the collection of odds and ends in our hands gets broken down into five categories. Then, based on those categories, these separate elements are sent to different locations, undergo different processes for repurposing, and arrive at a different location once the process is complete. In other words, a jumbled pile can be processed much easier if we can identify and classify its different components.

Similarly, when writers want to explain a difficult or complex concept, they may choose to identify its various types or break it into smaller parts. By using these types or parts as a line of reasoning, writers not only explain the concept, but also convey their perspective and message. We call this type of argument classification or division. When you write arguments of classification, you identify your subject's categories (or types), or you divide your subject into its component parts. When you develop a principle classification or division with specific examples, you will reveal your perspective and support your claim.

In this workshop, you will develop a classification argument about a subject that you know well. You will develop your claim by identifying and organizing the parts or types of your subject. Keep your audience in mind: you want to make your argument as clear and comprehensible as possible.

A Massacre of Art
Josh C.

The following 2015 essay is a classification argument written by Josh C. and published in the *New York Times*. The text was later reprinted in *Student Voice: 100 Argument Essays by Teens on Issues That Matter to Them* (2020).

From Bob Marley to The Black Keys, Bon Iver to Flume, and all the well known to underground artists in between, there's a simple requisite for admission into my musical palette: a song's ability to communicate, provoke thought, and capture emotion. As a music lover, I've spent many hours expanding my iTunes library, and have been able to find obvious talent throughout almost the entire spectrum of genre.

Except pop.

writer's experience (credibility)

claim: pop music does not communicate, provoke thought, or capture emotion

487

Whether it's Ryan Seacrest's Top-40 or a hit-music station's playlist, it's hard to extract even a basic appreciation for this artless genre. "Blah Blah Blah" by Ke$ha, Miley Cyrus's "FU," and JuicyJ's "Bandz a Make Her Dance," are just a few tunes that make pop espe-

1st classification: only focused on emotion

cially hard to respect. . . . Not only is it bad music, it is bad for music, as it degrades the uniquely expressive art form that has left entire audiences intoxicated with emotion (and not because Justin Bieber just took his shirt off while singing in falsetto).

2nd classification: lack of musical merit in pop

It's easy to pinpoint lacking musical elements of pop: lyrically it is shallow, vocally it's mediocre, and instrumentally it's bland. Pit-

word choice conveys critical tone

bull's lyric, "mami got an a** like a donkey with a monkey/Look like King Kong" pretty much sums up the theme of lyrical senselessness.

evidence from music critic

Vocal incompetence is exposed in pitchy live performances, which critic Jon Caramanica says, "reflect . . . the utter dearth of viable contemporary . . . pop stars." And finally, its repetition of overused rhythms and cheesy melodies account for the dreary instrumentals.

However, Lady Gaga doesn't have 44.7 million Twitter followers for nothing, and there's a reason Taylor Swift has 4 number-one albums . . . but what is it? Surprisingly, there's a simple answer:

3rd classification: depends on exposure

evidence from research

the exposure effect. Explained in research out of Gettysburg College, one's likelihood of enjoyment greatly increases when exposure to the stimulus increases. Upon discussing this reality in the music industry, Tom Barnes explains that, "repeated exposure is a much more surefire way of getting the general public to like a song than writing one that suits their taste." He says that this, combined with the reality of payola (a record label's illegal bribing for broadcasting

precise diction highlights frustration

of their song), create almost a perfect pedestal for the acceptance of pop music, however bad it is.

repeated word choice amplifies the writer's attitude

It is disappointing that future generations will be raised on metaphors comparing a donkey/monkey hybrid to a woman's rear end, rather than a properly poetic one in, say, John Mayer's intro to "Bold As Love." It is even more disappointing that inspiration for popularized music has become profit (as Drake says, "as long as the outcome is income"), rather than expression. But this doesn't have to

connects to audience

continue—all it takes is a conscious listener.

You can be that listener.

Sources

Barnes, Tom. "How The Music Industry Is Brainwashing You to Like Bad Pop Songs." Mic. N.p., 04 Aug. 2014. Web. 05 Mar. 2015.

Bornstein, Robert F., and Paul R. D'Agastino. "Stimulus Recognition and the Mere Exposure Effect." *Journal of Personality and Social Psychology* 63 (1992): n. pag. Print.

Caramanica, Jon. "Not Exactly Brilliant, but at Least the Colors Are." The *New York Times*. The *New York Times*, 01 Feb. 2015. Web. 05 Mar. 2015.

Caufield, Keith. "Taylor Swift Collects Fourth No. 1 Album, 'Now 52' Debuts at No. 2." *Billboard*. N.p., 5 Nov. 2014. Web. 05 Mar. 2015.

"I Know You Want Me (Calle Ocho) Lyrics." PITBULL LYRICS. N.p., n.d. Web. 05 Mar. 2015. http://www.azlyrics.com/lyrics/pitbull /iknowyouwantmecalleocho.html

YOUR ASSIGNMENT

You and your friends have decided to start a new podcast called "Tell Me About It" aimed at high school students. What would your subject be for the upcoming episode? Choose a subject that you are well-informed or passionate about. Next, narrow your focus to a subject that you can explain by identifying its different categories or types describing its subsequent parts. Then, write an argument that makes a claim that will lead your audience to a deeper understanding of your perspective.

Your classification argument should include the following:

- A thesis statement that makes a claim (perspective + unifying idea) about your subject
- A line of reasoning to develop your claim by explaining the types or parts of your subject
- Evidence from a variety of sources to support your reasoning
- Attribution of your sources to establish your credibility (Be sure to demonstrate how the sources interact with each other.)
- Strategies that appeal to your audience, especially specific word choices that convey your attitude toward your subject

Potential Subjects

	Method of Development	
Subject	**Classification into Categories or Types**	**Division into Parts**
Football	Types of quarterbacks	Key elements of the game
Music	Subgenres of hip-hop	Essential parts of a symphony
Government	Types of governments	Three branches of U.S. government
Social Media	Categories of social networking apps	Essential components of viral media

CLAIMS AND EVIDENCE **Synthesizing Evidence**

AP® **Enduring Understanding (CLE-1)**

> Writers make claims about subjects, rely on evidence that supports the reasoning that justifies the claim, and often acknowledge or respond to other, possibly opposing, arguments.

As you begin working on your classification argument, you must first generate a comprehensive list of evidence and details about your subject. Ideally, this will become the "pile" that you will sort for your reader so that you can develop your argument effectively and achieve your purpose. When generating your list, you should consider a wide range of details and evidence about your subject. You learned earlier in this unit that you strengthen your argument when you choose a variety of sources of evidence from several credible sources, and when the information you present is balanced and unbiased.

For this workshop, we will take a look at a sample subject related to school. Our claim is that school organizations serve the diverse interests of the student body. So we would begin by making a list of the organizations available to students. Then, we would gather evidence and details that connect these organizations to diverse groups and individuals. This evidence will come from a variety of sources.

Strategic evidence appeals to the audience. But you should include a variety of evidence in your argument to support different appeals. For example, if you only make logical appeals, your audience may understand the idea of the argument, but not the value of it. In other words, you might inform them without giving them any reason to care about your perspective. Likewise, if you focus on personal experiences, anecdotal evidence, and emotional appeals, your readers may not see the logic of your argument. Even though they may care, they will not find your line of reasoning convincing.

As you complete this step, consider how each source of evidence will affect your audience and your message.

Concept: Student Organizations Serve Diverse Interests			
Type of Evidence from Sources	**Example**	**Function of Evidence**	**Purpose**
Personal experience	*Anecdote about your own involvement in choir and film society*	Illustrates firsthand experience	Credibility (ethos)
Anecdotes and information from others	*Anecdotes from students who are involved in school organizations*	Amplifies illustrations from students to support the idea Sets a mood	Logic (logos) Emotion (pathos)
Statistics and data	*List of all organizations in the school and their membership*	Exemplifies the number of options and amount of student involvement	Logic (logos)

Type of Evidence from Sources	Example	Function of Evidence	Purpose
	Percentage of students involved in one or more school activity		
Research	Examine the history behind the school's organizations to determine the purpose for each one	Exemplifies the types of organizations available to students	Logic (logos) Credibility (ethos)
Case studies	Examples of different schools: fewer than 10 organizations, 10–20 organizations, more than 20 choices	Associates the number of options with the diversity of offerings	Logic (logos)
Interviews, surveys, and real-life examples	Interviews with coaches and sponsors of organizations Schoolwide student-poll results about membership in clubs and organizations and questionnaire about the kinds of activities	Exemplifies the real-world significance of participation Illustrates the current involvement and options	Logic (logos)

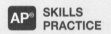

SKILLS PRACTICE | CLAIMS AND EVIDENCE
Synthesizing Evidence

1. List as many details as you can generate about your subject or concept.

2. Consider different sources of evidence and determine the function and purpose of each.

Type of Evidence from Sources	Evidence	Function and Purpose
Personal experience		
Information from others		
Statistics and data		
Research		
Case studies		
Interviews, surveys, and real-life examples		

REASONING AND ORGANIZATION Arranging Reasons and Evidence

AP® Enduring Understanding (REO-1)

Writers guide understanding of a text's line of reasoning and claims through that text's organization and integration of evidence.

When writing a classification or division argument, you will first examine your evidence. Then you will focus on creating categories for (or identifying parts of) your subject that will comprise your line of reasoning. Your choice of categories or essential parts affects the strength of your argument. For example, in the previous discussion of recycling, we know it would make little sense to sort garbage by age, size, or original value because these categories serve no purpose in the recycling process. Similarly, keep your purpose in mind when developing your principle of classification or division.

Additionally, in a classification argument, the categories must be parallel. In the recycling example, the categories on the bin are based on the material composition of the garbage. You would not have a recycling bin that sorts garbage by, say, color, visual style, and country of origin. These categories — which can overlap with each other — have little or no logical relationship in the context of classifying recyclables. This example may seem obvious, but when you are writing about a complex concept, your principle of classification can become blurry or even illogical.

As you develop your principle of classification or division, keep the following questions in mind:

- What is my classification/division scheme based on?

- How does using this principle of classification/division support my overall message?

For the school organizations example, our claim is that these clubs serve the diverse interests of students. Before we settle on an effective principle of classification, let's look at some schemes that are ineffective. For example, organizing the clubs by their meeting times (morning, afternoons, or weekends) provides no logical support for the claim. Similarly, we would not use a scheme that categorizes the clubs based on whether they require tryouts, whether they meet on Thursdays, and whether they expect members to pay dues. These categories are unrelated to the claim; moreover, as they are not parallel, one club could fall into multiple categories, which will confuse your audience.

In contrast, consider the following classification scheme:

Subject: *Clubs and Organizations*

Unifying Idea: *Diverse interests*

　Category A: *Performance-related organizations*
　Category B: *Interest-related organizations*
　Category C: *Service-related organizations*

Claim: *Schools that support a large number and variety of student organizations serve the diverse interests of their student body.*

These categories focus on what students actually do in their organizations. That parallel principle of classification allows the reader to follow and understand the line of reasoning. The arrangement of the categories and evidence is important, as well. Common ordering principles include arranging by chronology, space or placement, relative importance, and level of specificity. The specific arrangement, however, will depend on the specific evidence.

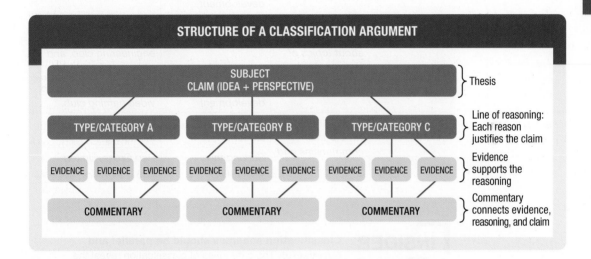

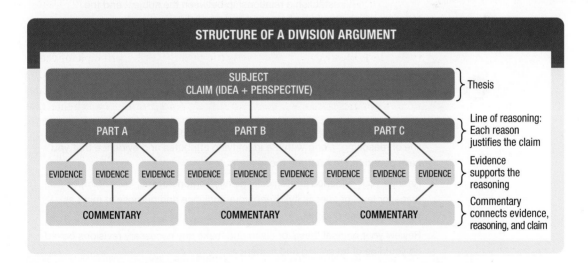

Concept: School Organizations			
Types	Significance	Traits/Attributes	Examples
Performance-related	*Allows students to develop their talents*	*Teamwork, physical skill development, competition*	*Sports and dance*
		Teamwork, fine motor skill development	*Music, theater, and art*
Interest-related	*Allows students to learn more about topics of interest*	*Future career exploration*	*French club, investment club, engineering club, and other academic clubs*
		Future hobby development	*Chess club, yo-yo club, video gaming club*
Service-related	*Allows students to help their communities and develop skills*	*Serving other students*	*Student council, peer mentoring*
		Serving the community	*Red Cross, United Way, Interact*

 **INSIDER AP TIP**

Classification schemes should be parallel and purposeful. The categories of classification reveal the writer's perspective on the subject. The writer must establish a relationship between the subject and the categories, which should be balanced and parallel.

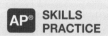 **AP SKILLS PRACTICE** | REASONING AND ORGANIZATION
Arranging Reasons and Evidence

1. Review the categories or component parts that you have identified in your line of reasoning, along with the identifying attributes and evidence that you have generated to illustrate those attributes.

2. Arrange your evidence strategically (spatial, chronological, level of importance, or level of specificity). Keep your audience and purpose in mind as you make these choices.

3. Review your original thesis or claim and make any necessary revisions based on your line of reasoning and evidence.

4. Begin writing by introducing your subject, providing context, and identifying the categories or principle of division that you will use to develop your argument.

(continued on next page)

Concept			
Types/Parts	Significance	Traits/Attributes	Examples

RHETORICAL SITUATION Establishing Credibility

AP® **Enduring Understanding (RHS-1)**

> Individuals write within a particular situation and make strategic writing choices based on that situation.

How can we establish credibility with the audience? First, the introduction provides an opportunity to demonstrate knowledge and familiarity with the subject. For example, if you are writing about school organizations and share that you are a high school student who participates in a school activity, you will demonstrate firsthand knowledge of the subject.

But the process of gathering preliminary evidence and developing a line of reasoning contributes to credibility, as well. That is especially true if the writer draws from a variety of credible sources and considers the audience's knowledge and values as well. Even the arrangement of evidence can build trust in the audience, as they realize that they can follow the line of reasoning clearly.

Writers also build credibility when they address, refute, or concede to opposing arguments. This shows familiarity with other points of view and presents you as a trustworthy and reasonable authority.

These — and other — writing choices may differ depending on the audience and the purpose. For example, if you are trying to convey the importance of funding student organizations to school administrators, you will choose evidence that appeals to their values and experiences. But you might use different evidence when you address incoming ninth graders seeking more information about these clubs.

Word choice can help writers establish credibility, too, which we will explore in the next workshop.

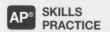 **SKILLS PRACTICE** | RHETORICAL SITUATION
Establishing Credibility

1. Review your chart of evidence and identify at least three different types of evidence in your outline.

2. For each type of evidence, identify the effect of that evidence on the audience. Does it appeal to emotions and values? Does it amplify the logic of your argument? Does it help you refute an opposing claim?

3. Examine the categories in your line of reasoning. Are they clear, precise, and accurate?

LANGUAGE AND STYLE Using Precise Diction

 Enduring Understanding (STL-1)

The rhetorical situation informs the strategic stylistic choices that writers make.

As with any other pattern of development, classification and division arguments will communicate your attitude toward the subject, or tone. Choose words that deliberately and consistently express your tone. This is especially important when choosing categories for the line of reasoning. Depending on your purpose, your diction may suggest seriousness, irony, or positive and negative connotations. While tone reflects your attitude, make sure that it also aligns with the values of your audience.

In our school organizations example, the labels of the categories are largely neutral in tone (skill-oriented, interest-oriented, service-oriented). But the examples and explanations include language with more positive connotations (teamwork, development, serving). These positive words encourage the audience to share your favorable attitude toward clubs and organizations.

 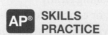 **SKILLS PRACTICE** | LANGUAGE AND STYLE
Using Precise Diction

In the space below, identify the attitude you wish to convey about your subject. In the middle column, write a few sentences about your subject. Then, in the right-hand column, rewrite the sentences using precise diction and syntax that communicate that attitude through tone.

Attitude Toward Subject	Initial Sentences	Revised Sentences

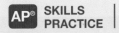 PUTTING IT ALL TOGETHER
**Revising and Editing a Classification/
Division Argument**

COMPOSITION WORKSHOP

Peer-Revision Checklist: Revising and Editing a Classification/Division Argument

Revising and Editing Checklist	Unit 6 Focus Skills	Comment on the Effectiveness and/or Make a Suggestion
Does the claim in the introduction or conclusion connect the subject to a perspective?	*Classification/ division argument*	
Is the evidence and commentary organized by the different types or parts of the subject? Does the writer organize the argument inductively? Deductively?	*Line of reasoning*	
Has the writer developed the argument with a variety of effective and appropriate evidence?	*Multiple sources*	
Has the writer explained the evidence and connected the subject to his or her perspective? Are these choices effective for the specific audience and purpose?	*Developing commentary*	
Is the writing clear and specific? Does the word choice convey the writer's attitude toward the subject?	*Conveying a tone*	
Is the writing free of errors in spelling, usage, punctuation, capitalization, and agreement?	*Writing conventions*	

Free-Response Question: Synthesis

Incorporating Evidence from Sources

In Unit 3, you learned how to prepare for the free-response synthesis question, along with how to incorporate evidence from sources. In this workshop, you will discover how sources appeal to your audience, build your credibility, and strengthen your argument.

→ **Step One: Determine Your Unifying Idea and Brainstorm Potential Sources**

To prepare to write your synthesis argument, read and annotate the introductory material in the prompt and the accompanying sources. Then, begin developing your initial position on the subject. To do this, identify the unifying idea and determine your perspective on it.

In addition to the written sources, you will also be provided with at least two **visual sources** for the synthesis question. Visual sources can include photographs, cartoons, illustrations, artwork, diagrams, advertisements, infographics, and other visual representations of information. At least one of the visual sources will be quantitative. **Quantitative sources**, as the name suggests, provide numerical or statistical data: information that can be measured in numbers and presented in tables, charts, maps, and graphs.

Following are some general guidelines for evaluating visual sources. You will learn more about quantitative sources in Unit 9.

- Read any text associated with the image carefully to determine the purpose of the information.
- Consider all of the visual details of the image, including recognizable symbols, colors, and contrasts.
- Note the context, origin, and date of the image to determine its relevance and timeliness.
- Identify a unifying idea emerging from the image or collection of images and consider how this relates to your argument.

In this step, you are not only gathering information but also considering how the sources might interact with each other and how they may be useful for your own argument.

→ **Step Two: Develop a Defensible Claim and Unified Line of Reasoning**

Examine your annotations and your preliminary evidence for your thesis statement that includes a claim (unifying idea + perspective). Remember that your thesis must take a defensible position. It must also have a claim that can be justified with reasons. Consider these examples:

Not defensible:	*Halloween is a time-honored tradition that occurs annually in October.*
No position established:	*There are advantages and disadvantages to moving the time-honored tradition of Halloween to the final Saturday in October.*
Thesis with position, but no claim:	*Halloween, a time-honored tradition, should be moved to the last Saturday in October.*

After you establish your claim, you will develop your reasons to support that claim. Choose an organizational strategy that will best develop the relationship between your claim and the supporting reasons. Decide whether you will organize deductively or inductively. Next, determine the best way to arrange your reasons, as well as how and where you will address opposing arguments.

Thesis with position, claim and line of reasoning:	*Moving Halloween to the final Saturday in October does not disrespect a time-honored tradition* [**position**]; *rather, it provides more opportunities for celebration* [**claim (unifying idea + perspective)**)] *by making the holiday safer and more practical* [**line of reasoning**].

→ **Step Three: Choose Relevant Evidence**

When you have determined the line of reasoning, review your notes from your sources and select evidence that will support your thesis. Next, arrange your evidence to support each of the reasons in the line of reasoning. Make sure to explain how the evidence supports these reasons and your main claim. You might also include sources that challenge your thesis to give the audience a sense of the broader discussion around your subject. Strong writers include alternative perspectives to demonstrate their understanding of the complexity of an issue.

Remember to choose evidence strategically to achieve your purpose. Statistics, data, and case studies contribute to the logic of your argument and improve your **credibility**. Real-life examples, personal stories, and subjective observations can help the audience understand the larger meaning and value of your subject.

Here is a checklist for choosing evidence:

- Incorporate evidence from at least three sources.
- Include a variety of sources and types of evidence.
- Evaluate the quality of the source by identifying its perspectives and biases.
- Incorporate evidence that supports, complements, and challenges your thesis.
- Use more than one source to support a reason, when appropriate.
- Incorporate personal anecdotes, observations (your own and those of others), and stories, if applicable.
- Arrange evidence to develop your reasons.

 INSIDER AP® TIP

Synthesis is a conversation. Synthesis requires students to show how the sources relate and "speak" to each other. Simply presenting evidence sequentially, one separate source at a time, results in summary, not synthesis. You can avoid this by developing your reasons with more than one source per paragraph. Using and connecting multiple sources and information within the same paragraph is the first step in putting the sources in conversation.

→ **Step Four: Develop Your Commentary**

After you have selected, incorporated, and arranged the evidence to support your line of reasoning, you must explain *how* the evidence contributes to your main claim and connects to your unifying idea. Of course, you must include specific evidence to support all the reasons in your line of reasoning. But you must also explain *how* the evidence supports your line of reasoning.

When you incorporate evidence, present it as it was intended in its original context. That is: do not misrepresent the information, or give a false sense of its meaning. If you fail to explain the context or misrepresent the source's original claim, you may be inaccurate and vague. You may also harm your credibility if the audience thinks you are misleading them. As a general rule, each time you incorporate supporting evidence, you will be writing multiple sentences, not just dropping in a single quotation.

Consider using the following guidelines when introducing evidence and developing commentary for your synthesis argument:

- Introduce your evidence with a signal phrase or transition that illustrates how the sources relate to your argument or another source's argument:
    - "According to . . . ,"
    - "In his article . . ."
    - "Unlike x . . ."
    - "X makes a similar claim . . ."

- Present the evidence with accurate and helpful context from the source.
- Explain the implications of the evidence:
  - relate it to your reason
  - connect it to your unifying idea
  - connect it to another source

Remember, it is not enough to quote from the sources. You must be able to explain the evidence, as well as connect it to your reasons and your thesis. If you cannot explain the connection, then the evidence may not be relevant to your argument.

PREPARING FOR THE AP® EXAM

The following prompt is an example of a synthesis free-response question. You may recall in Unit 3, you practiced with four textual sources. In this unit, you will be given a complete prompt that includes six sources, two of which are visual. Use what you have learned in this workshop to respond to the following prompt.

Prompt:
For many years people relied on professional journalists for the most accurate and current information. But with the influx of social media, everyday citizens can now capture videos and share information immediately on social platforms. This is known as citizen journalism. Some people believe that citizen journalists provide a valuable service by sharing information that may otherwise go unreported. In contrast, others question their accuracy and objectivity.

Carefully read the following six sources, including the introductory information for each source. Write an essay that synthesizes material from at least three of the sources and develops your position on what role, if any, citizens should play in the communication of news and information.

Source A (Tanz)
Source B (Rogers)
Source C (Hogg)
Source D (Olmstead)
Source E (Richter)
Source F (Varvel)

In your response, you should do the following:

- Respond to the prompt with a thesis that presents a defensible position.
- Select and use evidence from at least three of the provided sources to support your line of reasoning. Indicate clearly the sources used through direct quotation, paraphrase, or summary. Sources may be cited as Source A, Source B, etc., or by using the description in parentheses.
- Explain how the evidence supports your line of reasoning.
- Use appropriate grammar and punctuation in communicating your argument.

Source A

Tanz, Jason. "Journalism Fights for Survival in the Post-Truth Era." Gale Opposing Viewpoints Online Collection, Gale, 2020. Gale In Context: Opposing Viewpoints, https://link.gale.com/apps/doc/PMRFRO802551609 /OVIC?u=j021901003&sid=OVIC&xid=eaba01a3. Originally published as "Journalism Fights for Survival in the Post-Truth Era," Wired, 14 Feb. 2017.

The following excerpt was published in a magazine focused on technology and culture.

The news media is in trouble. The advertising-driven business model is on the brink of collapse. Trust in the press is at an all-time low. And now those two long-brewing concerns have been joined by an even larger existential crisis. In a post-fact era of fake news and filter bubbles, in which audiences cherry-pick the information and sources that match their own biases and dismiss the rest, the news media seems to have lost its power to shape public opinion . . .

. . . National-brand advertising has given way to automated exchanges that place ads across thousands of sites, regardless of their content. Politicians no longer need to rely on journalists to reach their audiences but instead can speak to voters directly on Twitter. In fact, the ability to reach a national audience now belongs to everyone. There is nothing to prevent fringe ideas and arguments from entering the informational bloodstream — and nothing to stop them from spreading.

These developments have upended the business logic that once pushed journalists toward middle-of-the-road consensus. When there were only three national news broadcasts, each competed to attract the broadest audience and alienate as few potential viewers as possible. But with infinite news sources, audiences follow the outlets that speak most uniquely to their interests, beliefs, and emotions. Instead of appealing to the broad center of American political opinion, more news outlets are chasing passionate niches. As media theorist Clay Shirky says, they can't rely on captive viewers but always have to hunt down new ones, "recruiting audiences rather than inheriting them."

These trends have been in place since the dawn of the internet, but they were supercharged over the past couple of years as social media — and especially Facebook — emerged as a major news source. Media professionals' already-eroding power to steer the national conversation has largely vanished. Before social media, a newspaper editor had the final say as to which stories were published and where they appeared. Today, readers have usurped that role. An editor can publish a story, but if nobody shares it, it might as well never have been written.

The Decline in News Jobs

The number of Americans whose job it is to "inform the public about news and events . . . for newspapers, magazines, websites, television, and radio" has decreased by nearly 10 percent over the past decade, according to the Bureau of Labor Statistics. The next 10 years aren't looking any better.

If readers are the new publishers, the best way to get them to share a story is by appealing to their feelings — usually not the good ones. A recent paper in *Human Communication Research* found that anger was the "key mediating mechanism" determining whether someone shared information on Facebook; the more partisan and enraged someone was, the more likely they were to share political news online. And the stories they shared tended to make the people who read them even more furious. "You need to be radical in order to gain market share," says Sam Lessin, a former vice president of product management at Facebook. "Reasonableness gets you no points."

In other words, we have gone from a business model that manufactures *consent* to one that manufactures *dissent* — a system that pumps up conflict and outrage rather than watering it down.

This sounds dire. Heck, it is dire. But the answer is not to pine for the days when a handful of publications defined the limits of public discourse. That's never coming back, and we shouldn't want it to. Instead, smart news operations, like the ones profiled in these pages, are finding new ways to listen and respond to their audiences — rather than just telling people what to think. They're using technology to create a fuller portrait of the world and figuring out how to get people to pay for good work. And the best of them are indeed creating really, really good work. As the past 30 years of press history shows, everything changes. Great journalism helps us understand how and why things change, and we need that now more than ever.

Source B

Rogers, Tony. "Understanding Citizen Journalism." ThoughtCo, Aug. 26, 2020, thoughtco.com/what-is-citizen-journalism-2073663.

The following article is from a reference site focused on expert-created education content.

Citizen journalism involves private individuals, who are normally the consumers of journalism, generating their own news content. Citizens collect, report, analyze, and disseminate news and information, just as professional journalists would, creating what is known as user-generated content.

These amateur journalists produce news in many forms, ranging from a podcast editorial to a report about a city council meeting on a blog, and is usually digital in nature. It can also include text, pictures, audio, and video. Social media plays a major role in disseminating news and promoting citizen journalism content.

Since the general public has 24/7 access to technology, citizens are often the first on-scene for breaking news, getting these stories out more quickly than traditional media reporters. However, unlike professional journalists, citizen journalists may not have conducted the same background research and source verification, which can make these leads less reliable.

Collaborations vs. Independent Reporting

Citizens are able to contribute content, in one form or another, to existing professional news sites. This collaboration can be seen through readers posting their comments alongside stories written by professional reporters, like a 21st-century version of a letter to the editor. To prevent obscene or objectionable messages, many websites require readers to register in order to post.

Readers are also adding their information to articles written by professional journalists. For instance, a reporter may do an article about disparities in gas prices around town. When the story appears online, readers can post information about gas prices in areas not covered in the original story and even offer tips on where to buy cheaper gas.

This collaboration allows both citizen and professional journalists to craft a story together. Reporters might even ask readers with expertise in particular areas to send them information on that topic or even do some of their own reporting. That information is then incorporated into the final story.

Some amateur journalists operate fully independent of traditional, professional news outlets. This can include blogs in which individuals can report on events in their communities or offer commentary on the issues of the day, YouTube channels where citizens give their own news reports and commentaries, and even unofficial print publications.

Revolutionizing News

Citizen journalism was once hailed as a revolution that would make news-gathering a more democratic process — one that would no longer solely be the province of professional reporters. It has had a significant impact on today's news, with many believing that citizen journalism is a threat to professional and traditional journalism.

Social media has played a vital role in revolutionizing news. Many citizens are the first to report on breaking stories, with eye-witness videos, first-hand accounts, and real-time information, all using social media. Even news outlets will share breaking stories on social media before traditional means, but they have to still follow up with larger stories quickly or risk being outdated with their material in this fast-paced news environment.

Social media doesn't just play a role in disseminating citizen-generated news; it also stands as a source for professional journalists to identify the stories they need to cover. A 2016 study by Cision indicated that more than 50% of professional journalists used social media to find and build stories.

Despite its vast impact on our daily news, citizen journalism is not without its flaws. The biggest concern is the reliability of news, including fact-checking and the risk of incorrect information being disseminated.

Source C

Hogg, Chris. "Is There Credibility in Citizen Journalism?" *Digital Journal*, 13 May 2009, www.digitaljournal.com/article/271657.

The following article is from a digital media network.

Citizen media is changing the face of journalism, but to what extent? Outlets like CNN, Fox and Canada's CTV have embraced user-generated news, and YouTube hopped onboard awhile ago. The *Washington Times* even devoted an entire section to articles by its citizen reporters.

The *Times'* executive editor John Solomon said, "We know there are many issues and communities we have not been able to fully cover within the confines of a newsroom budget, and we are excited to empower citizens within those communities to provide us news that will interest all our readers."

For all the benefits of citizen media, its critics point out the downsides of this rising trend. It's been called untrustworthy, shoddy and inarticulate. So how can citizen media gain the trust of both reporters and an ever-skeptical news audience? And how can it complement the mainstream media?

Citizen Journalists Are Amateurs

"I worry that many citizen journalists are basically amateurs who are simply mimicking what they see on TV or in the press, to varying degrees of success," says Jack Kapica, a former reporter for Canada's *Globe and Mail* and current writer and editorial advisor for DigitalJournal.com. "Much of the writing I've read, on most citizen journalism sites, shows little understanding of the process of gathering the news and writing it in a conventional form. Conventionality of presentation is important because it can give readers a recognizable framework to assess and understand what's being written."

Kapica believes citizen journalism, when done correctly, can be very powerful because of its speed and the ability of the fledgling industry to be anywhere at any time. That said, he also believes the world of citizen journalism needs to be encouraged to hold high standards of itself and practice sound journalistic principles . . .

. . . Kapica believes it's only a matter of time until citizen journalism starts to field attacks for biased reporting. "If citizen journalism becomes mainstream, then it too will be criticized for not being trustworthy," he notes. "At the moment it's getting a free ride. It's axiomatic in journalism that the more influential you are, the more insults and the bigger lawsuits you attract. Since citizen journalism sites do not yet have a perceptible clout, they are spared criticism, leaving the impression they're 'better' if only because they're not attracting vitriol [bitter criticism]."

When it comes to trust of user-generated media, Kapica believes editing and supervision is necessary. "I know much of what I have written would have killed me had not a sharp-eyed editor spotted me saying something I didn't mean."

The Future of Journalism

The future of journalism, and its business model, remains uncertain. Most people interviewed by DigitalJournal.com agree it will morph into some sort of hybrid journalism, blending the immediacy of social news sites like Twitter and Facebook with the accuracy and dependability of traditional journalism.

Kapica says newspapers that have created citizen journalism websites separate from their newspapers are on the right track, "as long as they nurture their writers and exercise oversight." He adds, "But they have to do it right; you can't create a newsroom from scratch and expect readers to flock to it overnight. You need reputation, and building a reputation takes a lot of time, something the Twittering speed-freaks of online journalism have too little of . . ."

Source D

Olmstead, Gracy. "Verifying Content on Facebook Is the User's Responsibility." Gale Opposing Viewpoints Online Collection, Gale, 2020. Gale In Context: Opposing Viewpoints, https://link.gale.com/apps/doc /NUBNJH254717886/OVIC?u=j021901003&sid=OVIC&xid=6cf5dbb3. Accessed 29 Sept. 2020. Originally published as "Facebook is broken. Let's all fix it together," The Week, 26 July 2018.

The following article is excerpted from a weekly general news magazine.

Age and Fake News

In 2016, a Stanford study found that middle school, high school, and college students struggled to determine the credibility of online sources, and were often fooled by fake news, sponsored content, and biased stories. As a result, many professors and teachers have begun advocating for "media literacy courses," which would help students navigate the internet with greater skill.

"As a university professor, when I frequently ask my students whether they've received any training or education in media literacy, all I get in response is a bunch of shrugs," professor and author Larry Atkins wrote for *HuffPost* last year. "My freshman students often cite obscure websites as sources in their papers and articles instead of authoritative government documents or respected news sources. I need to tell them to cite authoritative sources like MayoClinic .org and CDC.gov when discussing the legalization of medical marijuana, not 'Joe's Weed page.'"

This isn't just about teaching students how to write credible papers, however. Knowing which sources to cite is important, but it doesn't teach students how to sift through their news feeds and read judiciously. Young people need to know how to cross-check questionable material with solid sources, so that they're able to pinpoint a scam or hoax when they see one. Just because we're presented with something phony doesn't mean we have to believe and share it. Let's teach ourselves to be better.

It would also be laudatory (if potentially controversial) to teach students how to read "real" news (aka, political stories that are not fake, but still often volatile) with both eyes open. In our highly partisan era, too few readers can determine the difference between editorializing and hard news — and too few are willing to wrestle with political opinions on the other side of the aisle. To bolster our civic discourse, such skills are increasingly necessary. Helping students read and digest various political opinions could foster a healthy political literacy and deeper sense of empathy — both of which we need in our online and offline interactions.

Of course, young people are not the only social media users who need an education in smart news consumption. Often, those propagating fake news are older Americans, part of a generation that did not grow up with the internet and is less versed in navigating its truths and falsehoods. According to a study conducted by Team LEWIS last September, 42 percent of millennials will validate the accuracy of a news story they read online — whereas only 25 percent of baby boomers and 19 percent of Gen Xers will do the same. How do we teach these people to identify fake news?

Potential Solutions

Facebook's determination to prioritize friends' content and local news on its news feeds will likely have a positive impact. But it (and other social media sites like it) could also help organize ad campaigns that encourage users to cross-check their sources and alert their friends to false news stories. Not only would these efforts ease the burden on Facebook's moderators, they could also foster a salutary sense of responsibility and ownership among site users. Facebook could create a digital version of the "if you see something, say something" slogan that's been used throughout many U.S. airports and metro systems post-9/11. Often, grassroots efforts at rooting out falsehood are more palatable than top-down regulations or censorship — and they may even result in more lasting attitude changes amongst consumers.

The internet has gotten increasingly complex — and perhaps as a result, we've become increasingly lazy in dealing with its chaotic glut of information. But laziness and apathy are a dangerous business when it comes to online news. Sure, Facebook can help keep us safe from misinformation. But ultimately, finding out the truth is our responsibility.

Source E

Pew Research Center. *One-Sided and Inaccurate News Seen as the Biggest Problems with News on Social Media.* Washington, D.C., 2019.

The following chart is from a website that provides information about public opinion.

One-sided and inaccurate news seen as the biggest problems with news on social media

% of U.S. adults who say each is a _____ when it comes to news on social media

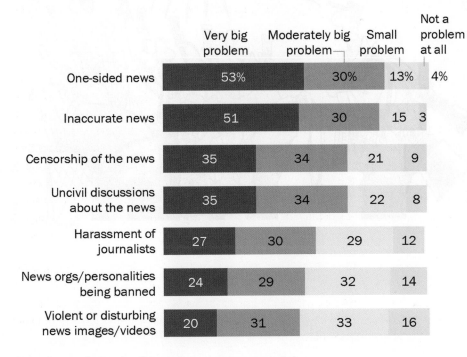

Note: Respondents who did not give an answer are not shown.
Source: Survey conducted July 8-21, 2019.
"Americans Are Wary of the Role Social Media Sites Play in Delivering the News"

PEW RESEARCH CENTER

"One-sided and inaccurate news seen as the biggest problems with news on social media," Pew Research Center, Washington, D.C., September 16, 2019, https://www.journalism.org/2019/10/02/americans-arewary-of-the-role-social-media-sites-play-in-delivering-the-news/pj_2019-09-25_social-media-and-news_0-05/

Source F

Varvel, Gary. "Excuse Me." Cartoon. "Citizen Journalism," 5 August 2013.
    Web. https://maichimai2611.wordpress.com/.

The following cartoon was featured in an online post about citizen journalism.

The New Deal

Franklin D. Roosevelt

Wild radicalism has made few converts, and the greatest tribute that I can pay to my countrymen is that — in these days of crushing want — there persists an orderly and hopeful spirit on the part of the millions of our people who have suffered so much. To fail to offer them a new chance is not only to betray their hopes but to misunderstand their patience.

To meet by reaction that danger of radicalism is to invite disaster. Reaction is no barrier to the radical. It is a challenge, a provocation. The way to meet that danger is to offer a workable program of reconstruction, and the party to offer it is the party with clean hands.

This, and this only, is a proper protection against blind reaction on the one hand and an improvised, hit-or-miss, irresponsible opportunism on the other.

There are two ways of viewing the Government's duty in matters affecting economic and social life. The first sees to it that a favored few are helped and hopes that some of their prosperity will leak through, sift through, to labor, to the farmer, to the small business man. That theory belongs to the party of Toryism,[1] and I had hoped that most of the Tories left this country in 1776.

But it is not and never will be the theory of the Democratic Party. This is no time for fear, for reaction or for timidity. Here and now I invite those nominal[2] Republicans who find that their conscience cannot be squared with the groping and the failure of their party leaders to join hands with us; here and now, in equal measure, I warn those nominal Democrats who squint at the future with their faces turned toward the past, and who feel no responsibility to the demands of the new time, that they are out of step with their Party.

Yes, the people of this country want a genuine choice this year, not a choice between two names for the same reactionary doctrine. Ours must be a party of liberal thought, of planned action, of enlightened international outlook, and of the greatest good to the greatest number of our citizens.

Now it is inevitable — and the choice is that of the times — it is inevitable that the main issue of this campaign should revolve about the clear fact of our economic condition, a depression so deep that it is without precedent in modern history. It will not do merely to state, as do Republican leaders to explain their broken promises of continued inaction, that the depression is worldwide. That was not their explanation of the apparent prosperity of 1928. The people will not forget the claim made by them then that prosperity was only a domestic product manufactured by a Republican President and a Republican Congress. If they claim paternity

[1]Toryism — of or related to a British political party, the Tories, based on a British version of traditionalism and conservatism, which upholds the supremacy of social order as it has evolved in the English culture throughout history.
[2]Nominal — literally, "in name only"

for the one they cannot deny paternity for the other.

I cannot take up all the problems today. I want to touch on a few that are vital. Let us look a little at the recent history and the simple economics, the kind of economics that you and I and the average man and woman talk.

In the years before 1929 we know that this country had completed a vast cycle of building and inflation; for ten years we expanded on the theory of repairing the wastes of the War, but actually expanding far beyond that, and also beyond our natural and normal growth. Now it is worth remembering, and the cold figures of finance prove it, that during that time there was little or no drop in the prices that the consumer had to pay, although those same figures proved that the cost of production fell very greatly; corporate profit resulting from this period was enormous; at the same time little of that profit was devoted to the reduction of prices. The consumer was forgotten. Very little of it went into increased wages; the worker was forgotten, and by no means an adequate proportion was even paid out in dividends — the stockholder was forgotten.

And, incidentally, very little of it was taken by taxation to the beneficent Government of those years.

What was the result? Enormous corporate surpluses piled up — the most stupendous in history. Where, under the spell of delirious speculation,[3] did those surpluses go? Let us talk economics that the figures prove and that we can understand. Why, they went chiefly in two directions: first, into new and unnecessary plants which now stand stark and idle; and second, into the call-money[4] market of Wall Street, either directly by the corporations, or indirectly through the banks. Those are the facts. Why blink at them?

Then came the crash. You know the story. Surpluses invested in unnecessary plants

became idle. Men lost their jobs; purchasing power dried up; banks became frightened and started calling loans. Those who had money were afraid to part with it. Credit contracted. Industry stopped. Commerce declined, and unemployment mounted.

And there we are today.

1. In the context of the passage as a whole, the speaker's direct appeal to "nominal Republicans" and "nominal Democrats" in paragraph 5 serves to
   (A) encourage collaboration and partnership while warning against uncertainty and reluctance.
   (B) criticize loyalties on both sides of the party divide.
   (C) attack the misplaced concerns of his Democratic colleagues while supporting the concerns of those reluctant Republicans.
   (D) examine the ideological distance between the two parties.
   (E) explain the intense work necessary for collaboration between the two parties whether or not he wins the election.

2. In the first sentence of the seventh paragraph, repetition of the word "inevitable" serves primarily to
   (A) acknowledge that he cannot affect the results of the election.
   (B) imply that the audience only has one clear choice and that his party's victory is unavoidable.
   (C) foreshadow loss of the opposition party.
   (D) indicate that the circumstances of the time period demand that the campaign focus on the "economic conditions."
   (E) admit that he could not avoid running for president given the dire "economic conditions" of the country.

[3]speculation — investment in stocks, property, or other ventures with the hope of gain but with the risk of loss.
[4]call-money — money lent by a bank or other institution that must be repaid on demand.

3. The seventh paragraph ("Now it is inevitable . . . paternity for the other.") demonstrates a shift in the speech between
   (A) "blind reaction" with "irresponsible opportunism" mentioned in paragraph 3.
   (B) criticism of the conservative party with comparisons to colonial Britain.
   (C) idealism of party and future hopes with the realities of the world as a political context.
   (D) theories of prominent Democrats with those who are Republicans in name only.
   (E) the overwhelming number of problems faced by the country and the realities of what can actually be addressed.

4. Across the first 7 paragraphs, the speaker compares the policies and reactions of the Republican party to those of his Democratic party to divide and classify each according to how they
   (A) recognize the problems affecting the country.
   (B) accept the protected status of stock brokers.
   (C) share more ideas than they disagree with.
   (D) have collaborated already to improve circumstances.
   (E) have reacted to the hardships of the economic circumstances.

5. In the first sentence of the eighth paragraph ("I cannot . . . today."), the speaker succeeds in
   (A) describing the problem in a new, more practical way for his audience.
   (B) explaining his own failures as a leader.
   (C) appealing to the sense of tradition in his audience.
   (D) admitting the limitations of his argument.
   (E) conceding the opposing viewpoint of his detractors.

6. In the context of the excerpt as a whole, the speaker uses paragraph 8 to
   (A) motivate the audience to resist reactionary thinking.
   (B) transition from an explanation of the opposing party's failures to an examination of the economics realities faced by average people.
   (C) draw attention to evidence of economic hardship that has been ignored and denied by the opposing party.
   (D) point out a flaw in the line of reasoning of those who disagree with him.
   (E) deny that his own party has any responsibility for the worsening economic conditions and focus the blame solely on the opposing party.

7. In context, the speaker's use of the phrase "spell of delirious speculation" (paragraph 11, sentence 3) conveys a tone of
   (A) pity for those drawn into the dangers of the stock market.
   (B) disenchantment with the almost magical effect that making money on the stock market can have over some people.
   (C) disgust with those who feel that the stock market will magically solve the country's economic problems.
   (D) optimism regarding concerns about unemployment and factory work.
   (E) frustration with Republicans who think they can ignore the stock market and allow the rich to get richer and money will make its way to those without it.

8. In context, the tone of the speaker's last remark in the excerpt "And there we are today." (paragraph 13) is best described as
   (A) matter-of-fact.
   (B) uncaring.
   (C) condescending.
   (D) contemptuous.
   (E) critical.

9. Given the excerpt, which of the following best describes the speaker's exigence?
   (A) The economic conditions of the depression era United States
   (B) The desire to be the President of the United States
   (C) The opposing party's reactionary policies and failure to address problematic economic conditions
   (D) The alignment between the opposing party's ideas and those of the British Tory party
   (E) The inability for the average man and woman — those most affected by the depression — to understand the causes of the depression

The passage below is a draft.

(1) In just over thirty years, Americans have moved from laughing at TV's *The Simpsons* to actually wanting to be them. (2) This is a result of how this country has too long abused and ignored the working and middle classes.

(3) In December 1989, *The Simpsons* premiered as a stand alone television show after two years as an animated short of the *Tracy Ullman Show*. (4) In a 2020 interview with *Biography*, show creator Matt Groening explained that he had initially based the family on his own, even naming the yellow, cartoon parents after his parents: Homer and Marge. (5) For years, the Simpson were seen as a solidly working-class family where the husband worked so that the mother could stay home and care for the house and children. (6) In many ways this reflected the lives of millions of Americans, but it also represented something that many Americans — at least at the time of *The Simpsons* premier and the decade following — hated and feared. (7) The Simpsons were often seen as dysfunctional and emblematic of what family should seek not to be.

(8) Fast-forward more than thirty years and much has changed in America while the Simpsons have not. (9) They remain the five member household with a father who works and a mother who stays at home. (10) While these circumstances may have changed on occasion over the years to accommodate different plots and stories, the general idea of the family has remained the same. (11) Initially, many parents and family organizations attacked the show for its portrayal of lax family values and Bart Simpson's lethargic approach to school. (12) While others may have claimed that there was some truth to these representations of the American family, no one actually wanted to be the Simpsons. (13) However, as freelance writer Dani Alexis Ryskamp recently explained in the *Atlantic*, the state of the family seen in *The Simpsons* is one that many Americans actually long for today.

(14) Finding the kind of job that Homer has, one with a union guaranteed contract to ensure wages, healthcare, vacation, and likely other perks is nearly impossible today, not to mention that he worked at a factory, in the United States, in a small town. (15) All things which seem impossible for many working and middle class families today. (16) Those working such jobs today are barely able to happily and easily support a family of five on one income while also owning two cars, paying for a house, and buying the saxophone that Lisa Simpson plays at the beginning of every episode.

1. In sentence 6 (reproduced below), which version of the underlined text best maintains the tone of the passage?

   In many ways this reflected the lives of millions of Americans, but it also represented something that many Americans — at least at the time of The Simpsons *premier and the decade following — hated and feared.*

   (A) (as it is now)
   (B) just could not stand.
   (C) were ashamed of.
   (D) sought to rise above.
   (E) were disgusted by.

2. The writer is considering adding the following sentence after sentence 13.

   Though the difference between working and middle class used to be about the type of job you had — think white collar versus blue collar — today a working class family lives paycheck-to-paycheck with more uncertainty while a middle class family has more savings and more disposable income.

   Should the writer add this sentence to the end of the second paragraph?

   (A) Yes, because it effectively provides more details related to the divide between the middle and working classes.

   (B) Yes, because it provides necessary context about the discussion about class.

   (C) Yes, because it defines the divisions between the two classifications of middle and working class.

   (D) No, because to define these divisions distracts from the actual argument of the passage.

   (E) No, because the information does not relate to the argument being made.

3. The writer would like to incorporate new information from the Pew Research Center Information (reproduced below) into the passage.

   In more than half of 2-parent families, both parents work full time. While those families have more money than other families, most of them report that they cannot find an adequate balance between work and family time — and family often suffers.

   Which of the following changes would the writer need to make in order for this new information to work in the context of the overall argument the writer is making?

   (A) Further develop the reasoning around Marge as a stay-at-home parent and what that says about why people today would like to be the Simpsons.

   (B) Remove the reference to the *Atlantic* article and instead rely on this information to make the statement that people today want to be like the Simpsons.

   (C) Incorporate more information about the role of unions in securing better wages so the reader can better understand how the family can afford for Marge to stay at home.

   (D) Changing the thesis statement to argue that family values are under attack, not the middle and working classes.

   (E) Expanding on the details related to Marge's role as a stay-at-home parent.

4. The writer has found several pieces of new information relating to topics mentioned in the passage.

   Which of the following would most likely prompt the writer to revise the line of reasoning in the passage?

   (A) A study of union memberships and family incomes finding that the strength of the middle class seems directly tied to the strength of American labor unions; as union membership rates have fallen over the past 50 years so, too, has the share of income that goes to the middle 60 percent of American households.

   (B) An article claiming that the family in *The Simpsons* is meant to represent a typical, blue collar, working-class family living in America.

   (C) A study of incomes and prices finding that, despite gains in national income over the past half-century, American households in the middle of the distribution have experienced very little income growth in recent decades.

   (D) A survey saying stay-at-home moms are almost twice as likely to report symptoms of depression than employed moms.

   (E) Government data indicating that the United States has suffered a loss of more than 91,000 factories and nearly 5 million factory jobs since 1997.

5. The writer wants to do research to find additional sources that support the main argument. All of the following are likely to be reliable research sources EXCEPT

   (A) A government report on the relationship between income and union membership.

   (B) An entry on *The Simpsons* on a well-known research website.

   (C) A comment section following an interview with *Simpsons* creator and executive producer, Matt Groening.

   (D) A book on income inequality and family values written by a respected economist.

   (E) An article from an academic journal discussing how representations of family in media affect real families.

6. The writer is considering moving the first paragraph (sentences 1 and 2) to the end of the passage. Should the writer make this change?

   (A) Yes, because an argument should always end with the claims after establishing the reasoning.

   (B) Yes, because it is more reasonable to end the passage with the information and claim provided in these sentences as the reader has more context for understanding at the end.

   (C) Yes, because the comments about the middle and working classes should be close to one another in the passage.

   (D) No, because an argument should always begin with the claim and then proceed into the reasoning for that claim and support for that reasoning.

   (E) No, because that will create a disconnect between the claim and the reasoning which will prevent the argument from developing effectively.

REUTERS/Tyrone Siu

UNIT

7

Comparing Perspectives

So far, in all the previous units, you've been learning how writers convey and defend their ideas through arguments. But they know the wider conversation around their subjects, as well, including alternative arguments and perspectives. Effective writers understand that others may make competing claims or take opposing positions. In short, most issues are complex; good arguments will take that complexity into account.

Consider the image that opens this unit. The photographer captured the people from his own perspective. Yet the people in the photograph have a different perspective. And, of course, the viewer of the photo has another perspective too. Issues can be similar to complex images: if you can see the perspectives of others, you will better understand your own.

Indeed, the most effective writers often qualify, or limit, the scope of their own arguments based on others' perspectives. That includes the viewpoint of the audience — one of the most important elements in any rhetorical situation. You might ask, "How is the audience likely to respond to my claims and evidence? How can I anticipate and address those responses?"

UNIT GOALS

	Unit Focus	Reading, Analyzing, and Interpreting	Writing
Big Idea: Rhetorical Situation	**Nuance, Complexity, and Contradictions**	Explain how multiple components within a rhetorical situation interact.	Write introductions and conclusions that establish context and purpose for an intended audience.
Big Idea: Claims and Evidence	**Qualifying an Argument**	Explain how writers qualify arguments.	Employ strategies to qualify an argument.
Big Idea: Reasoning and Organization	**Evaluation Argument: Comparison/Contrast**	Explain how writers develop ideas through comparison/contrast.	Write an evaluation argument developed through comparison/contrast.
Big Idea: Language and Style	**Syntax for Precision**	Explain how writers use syntactical structures to achieve a purpose.	Use syntactical structures to achieve a purpose.
Ideas in American Culture	• **Identity and Identities** • **Justice and Civil Disobedience**	Explain how the ideas of identity, identities, justice, and civil disobedience are reflected in classic and contemporary American texts.	
Preparing for the AP® Exam	• **Free Response: Rhetorical Analysis** • **Multiple Choice**	Analyze rhetorical choices in classic and contemporary nonfiction texts.	Explain how multiple rhetorical choices work together to contribute to a writer's purpose and message.

Nuance, Complexity, and Contradictions

AP **Enduring Understanding (RHS-1)**

Individuals write within a particular situation and make strategic writing choices based on that situation.

KEY POINT

A writer's perspective about an event, issue, or subject is influenced by his or her relationship, time, and distance from that event, issue, or subject.

Maybe you've written an essay about an important experience in your life — perhaps, learning to ride a bike when you were little. You described all the details, including your fear when you lost balance, the help you got from others when your training wheels came off, and the pride that you felt when you finally rode off on your own. If you had written that essay at the time you learned to ride, you could have described the vivid, immediate details of your experience. But if you wrote this essay in high school, you would provide a different, more reflective account. With time and distance from the experience, you might understand it more deeply and connect it to larger ideas, such as failure, persistence, or developmental milestones. This deeper understanding allows a writer to go beyond a simple "pro" or "con" position.

As you can see, a writer may be writing about an experience from years ago — or an experience from just this morning. The subject may even be the experiences of others, which will require interviews and research. Regardless, when you analyze a text, you should take this narrative distance into account as part of the rhetorical situation.

While the details of an experience or subject may be clearer the closer in time and physical location you are to it, deeper understanding about the significance of an event or subject may increase with chronological time and distance.

Issues Are Complex

When writers have a deeper understanding of a subject, issue, or experience, they can move beyond simple pro/con positions and articulate the complexity of the subject. This understanding also makes them better able to qualify their claims and perspectives.

Narrative Distance

Primary sources are firsthand contemporary accounts of an event or experience: eyewitness testimony, autobiographical writing (including journals and letters), and other direct reporting at the time. When later writers interpret, synthesize, or challenge these firsthand accounts, we refer to their texts as secondary sources.

Both primary and secondary sources are important. If you are using them to write an argument, they will offer different perspectives. But neither source will automatically be more credible based solely on the classification "primary" or "secondary."

A writer's life experiences both before an event *and* after it affect their understanding of that event. In some cases, the meaning of an experience will change as the writer's perspective, values, and beliefs shift and develop over time. With this narrative distance, a writer may discover a deeper understanding, even if the specific sensory details get blurrier.

But **narrative distance** is only one factor that shapes a writer's interpretation of an event. Recall that biases can also play an important role. They function much like cognitive blind spots: by themselves, these biases are not indicators of dishonesty or incompetence. *All* writers have biases. Just because a writer reveals a **bias** does not automatically discredit him or her. Part of your job as a reader is to seek out and consider those biases when analyzing and evaluating a writer's argument.

Events and experiences happen at definable moments (or a series of moments) along the space-time continuum. So make sure to review the time and geographic location of an event when you are analyzing a text about it. As chronological and spatial distance develop in a writer's life after the experience, that distance will shape how he or she interprets the event. For example, a writer who reflects on a memory earlier in his or her life may see the experience through "fresh eyes." In other words, reflection allows us to have new understandings and insights about events in our lives.

Connections within the Rhetorical Situation

As you've learned, the **writer**, **context**, and **audience** are all part of the rhetorical situation. Now, we will learn the relationships between

- the writer and context,
- the audience and context, and
- the writer, audience, and context.

Each of these relationships is part of the narrative distance. Narrative distance is the respective immediacy of the context to both the writer and the audience.

Writers make choices to achieve a purpose with their intended audience. But not all readers fall under the category of "intended audience." You may have already experienced this while analyzing a decades-old journal entry, old newspaper article, or ancient speech. Though you're reading the text, the writer probably didn't have *you* in mind when they were making their writing choices.

You can still discover the rhetorical situation and analyze an older text effectively — much the way an archaeologist can "read" artifacts from the past. That is, you must look for clues within the text. But you can also infer components of the rhetorical situation based on what you know about the writer, audience, and the context, as well as the relationship between these three elements. If you can understand these relationships, you will have more insight into the rhetorical situation. You will also be better able to analyze the writer's specific rhetorical choices.

Contextualizing a Perspective

Some clues can be found in the **introduction**, where the writer contextualizes the event, as well as his or her purpose for writing. An introduction may orient, engage, or focus the audience by presenting the following:

- quotations
- intriguing statements
- anecdotes
- questions
- statistics
- data
- contextualized information
- a scenario

You may also look to the **conclusion** to find the writer's ultimate perspective or realization and understanding of the event. Conclusions may engage or focus the audience by

- explaining the significance of the argument within a broader context,
- making connections,
- calling on the audience to act,
- suggesting a change in behavior or attitude,
- proposing a solution,
- leaving the audience with a compelling image,
- explaining implications,
- summarizing the argument, or
- connecting to the introduction.

INSIDER
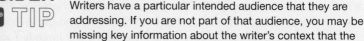
AP® TIP

You are not always the intended audience.
Writers have a particular intended audience that they are addressing. If you are not part of that audience, you may be missing key information about the writer's context that the intended audience would know. You should consider the rhetorical choices a writer makes for the intended audience and context.

 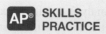

AP® SKILLS PRACTICE	RHETORICAL SITUATION **Analyzing the Rhetorical Situation**

Think of a familiar rhetorical situation that you've been a part of, such as writing a letter, making a phone call, persuading friends, or delivering a speech. Use the following organizer to illustrate the relationships among context, writer, and audience.

Rhetorical Situation:

Context

1. What is the time, place, occasion?

2. What is going on culturally or socially that affects the writer and audience?

Writer	Audience
• What is your relationship to this audience? • What is your perspective on the subject? • What is your purpose? • What is your relationship to the subject?	• Who is the intended audience? • What are their beliefs and values? • What attitudes and biases might they have toward the subject?

This Is Us, It Has Always Been

Ryan Kim

THE TEXT IN CONTEXT

The following student essay by Ryan Kim was published in *The Best Teen Writing of 2018*, an annual anthology of work by teen writers who earn a National Medal in the Scholastic Art & Writing Awards. In this essay, Kim reacts to a 2017 protest held in Charlottesville, Virginia, where a group of white nationalists opposed removing a statue of Confederate General Robert E. Lee.

 **SKILLS PRACTICE** | **RHETORICAL SITUATION**
Analyzing Relationships within a Rhetorical Situation

As you read Kim's argument, consider when it was written and by whom. Find textual evidence within Kim's introduction and conclusion that provides clues about the context, writer, and audience. Then draw inferences about the relationships between (and among) the writer, audience, and context that influence the writer's rhetorical choices.

(continued)

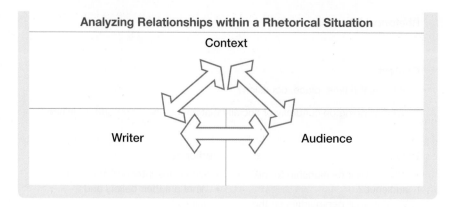

This Is Us, It Has Always Been

On the morning of August 12, 2017, a large crowd of white nationalists and other right-wing groups assembled at Emancipation Park in Charlottesville, Virginia. Many were carrying signs, and some, improvised handmade weapons. The aim of the rally was to oppose the removal of a statue of Robert E. Lee, a Confederate general, from the park. Waiting for them was an equally defiant group of counterprotesters, there to vehemently push back against the racist rhetoric of the former. The surrounding area quickly became a disastrous cluster of punches, swinging bats, and pepper spray. Police officers in riot gear worked futilely to mitigate the violence. Then, in the early afternoon, the violence escalated to the point that one individual rammed his car into a crowd, killing one counterprotester. In all, three people died and more than thirty people were injured because of the chaotic events of the rally. Government leaders, the media, and social pundits were quick to condemn the events at Charlottesville. The general sentiment, even across party lines, was that this was a time for unity, not partisan rhetoric. After all—conservative or liberal, Democrat or Republican—what happened was not representative of the United States of America. Larry Hogan, the Republican governor of Maryland, stated that acts like what transpired in Charlottesville had no place in society and that "American values [had] nothing to do with white supremacy and hate." Mark Warner, the Democratic senator from Virginia, echoed this sentiment, demanding that white nationalists "go back to where [they] came from." Over and again, the nation adopted the mantra "this is not us." What happened was deemed a rogue, abhorrent act by a far-right minority, a growing but insular group that stood for values that America did not condone.

But the "this is not us" narrative is a fiction. To say that white supremacy, xenophobia, bigotry, and violence are foreign to America is plain untrue. At best, this view stems from shortsightedness and a superficial understanding of our history. At its worst, it is a blatant attempt to revise, sanitize and falsify our past. Whether accidental or deliberate, the idea that events like Charlottesville are foreign to our American identity perpetuates a longstanding tradition of American Exceptionalism.

While the idea of American Exceptionalism has no formal definition, its first use within the American vernacular can be traced to the Puritan settlers. Upon landing in New England, John Winthrop, future governor of the Massachusetts Bay Colony, urged his fellow settlers to be a "city upon a hill," a model example for the world (Beeley). Years later, the designers of the Statue of Liberty made sure to utilize Emma Lazarus's poem, which reads in part "Give me your tired, your poor . . ." as if America's welcoming arms were a messianic reprieve to incoming immigrants from the hardships abroad. Even in today's political climate, it is generally believed that America is an "indispensable nation" (Clinton) and the greatest country in the world (Jones). American Exceptionalism is an ideology that doesn't just invoke the term "special" when one thinks of America, but rather invokes something deeper: a belief that America follows a historically different route in terms of governance and morals.

To be sure, there is nothing inherently wrong with the belief that one's country should serve as a model example for other nations. But American Exceptionalism uses the idea as a pretense to gloss over unsavory events and/or people in our nation. When we see images of white nationalists marching defiantly in support of Confederate heroes or read about high school and college students uploading videos with racist rants to social media, we cannot merely brush these individuals off as the "other." To say they do not represent us is to forget our complicated past and dishonor its victims. We are a country that was built on the backs of slaves, a country responsible for Jim Crow, lynchings, and Japanese internment. We are a nation guilty of racially profiling Muslims and forced assimilation of Native Americans. Charlottesville is no different, it is also a part of who we are.

To say otherwise and deny it is not only disingenuous, but it stunts our ability to address the root of the problem. We cannot point fingers at a few wrongdoers without acknowledging our own complicity. Otherwise our denial of racism and our racist past is its own form of racism, a more dangerous kind since it is cloaked in a false sense of rightness. We need to abandon this rhetoric of constantly working to disassociate ourselves from the white supremacists, the radical nationalists, the racists. We must abandon our psychological naiveté and accept that these "bad things" have been and always will be part of America's history. 5

RHETORICAL SITUATION

1. How does the **context** of the text contribute to the **perspective** of the writer?

2. How does the **introduction** orient, engage, or focus the audience within the argument?

3. Who is the **writer**, and what is his relationship to the **subject**?

4. The **conclusion** offers a realization. What is the realization? How does it differ from the writer's perspective in the **introduction**?

Qualification and Concession

 Enduring Understanding (CLE-1)

Writers guide understanding of a text's lines of reasoning and claims through that text's organization and integration of evidence.

KEY POINT

Most arguments are not absolute, so qualification and concession allow a writer to acknowledge other perspectives.

You may have noticed that as you grow older, your ideas and experiences become more complex. For example, when you were young, you might have said, "I always love going to the park." Then, one day, you scraped your knee while playing. Subconsciously, your perspective probably shifted to "I always love going to the park, except when I don't love going to the park."

But as you grew, your perspective might have become more precise and more reflective of your other experiences: "I love going to the park when it's a sunny day, and I don't have to worry about doing work or chores." Note how the qualification is now clear and explicit.

This process of qualification happens subconsciously. But you can also consciously change your perspective to communicate the more complex factors that qualify how you experience things. In fact, writers must frequently qualify their arguments to make them more effective.

Arguments Are Part of Ongoing Conversations

You might ask, "Why offer concessions and qualifications? Shouldn't a writer focus on convincing his or her audience of a particular point of view rather than presenting alternatives?" Indeed, this can seem counterintuitive. But recall that most arguments are written in the context of an ongoing discussion of (or "discourse" about) a particular issue or subject. Part of the writer's job, then, is proving that he or she has a thorough, balanced understanding of both the subject and the wider conversation about the subject. To enter that conversation, writers must spend time listening, researching, and understanding the conversation before they ever set pen to paper.

Effective qualification requires that writers understand their own arguments and the arguments of others. This contributes to a writer's credibility. In contrast, expressing claims, reasoning, and evidence in absolute terms may damage a writer's credibility.

Defending, Challenging, and Qualifying Arguments

When expressing both a position on a subject and a perspective on a unifying idea, a writer often either defends, challenges, or qualifies the argument. Up to this point, you've studied writers who primarily defend their arguments. In later units, you'll consider how writers challenge other arguments. But in this unit, you'll examine how writers qualify their own arguments.

So far, you've been reading and analyzing arguments in absolute terms, without considering alternate perspectives.

However, very few issues and ideas are unequivocally clear-cut. We live in a world filled to the brim with complexities, which exist because of often subtle, yet important, differences in perspectives about ideas and issues.

Effective writers recognize these inherent complexities that affect the issues and ideas within an argument. Writers who don't consider the different aspects of their issue or their unifying idea risk oversimplifying within their argument, which would likely render it ineffective. Instead, as they understand issues from multiple perspectives and acknowledge the perspectives of others, they offer qualifications of their own arguments.

Qualifying with Words, Phrases, and Clauses

Writers can strategically **qualify** their arguments by using words, phrases, and clauses as modifiers. Modifiers help finely tune the meaning of a sentence by specifying key details, limiting the scope of the information, and anticipating potential objections. As a reader, pay particular attention to words, phrases, and clauses that indicate the limitations of a writer's argument.

Qualifying with words.   Some words clearly indicate a qualification.

Other words depend on the context. For example, read the following sentence:

> A new grading scale will be detrimental to students' college competitiveness.

The writer then revises the sentence to qualify the claim and include more precise language. But note that the claim remains strong, despite the qualifications.

> [The long-term effects of introducing] a new grading scale [could be] [potentially] detrimental to students' college competitiveness.

Qualifying with phrases.   Certain phrases can also signal or introduce a qualification, such as the following:

> The long-term effects of introducing a new grading scale could be potentially detrimental to students' college competitiveness [depending on their circumstances].

Qualifying with clauses.   Finally, writers can also embed a qualification within a subordinate clause. When possible, put the qualification first so that the audience's main attention falls on the main idea in the independent clause.

> [Although a majority of students prefer a change to the school policy,] the long-term effects of introducing a new grading scale could be potentially detrimental to students' college competitiveness depending on their circumstances.

SIGNALING QUALIFICATION			
Words		Phrases	Clauses Introduced by Subordinating Conjunctions
almost	often	Depending on	Although
at times	otherwise	More or less	Because
barely	possibly	To some extent	Even though
certainly	potentially	Up to a point	Since
conversely	precisely		When
could	probably		While
frequently	seldom		
hints at	some		
if	sometimes		
majority	somewhat		
may be	supposedly		
might	usually		
nevertheless	very		

Qualification by Concession

At times, writers may strategically choose to recognize a valid claim or compelling reason in an opposing viewpoint: this technique is called a **concession**. Think of a chess player who chooses to sacrifice a piece to gain a larger advantage over an opponent. Similarly, writers can concede certain opposing points. Not all writers qualify their arguments with a concession, but when done purposefully, writers can boost their credibility, pivot to another reason in their argument, or reveal a critical mistake in their opponents' perspective. We'll discuss concessions more in the next unit.

Acknowledging and responding to others' perspectives demonstrates understanding. Writers understand the complexity of an issue or subject when they go beyond their own knowledge and perspectives to realize the implications in a broader context.

 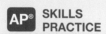

SKILLS PRACTICE | CLAIMS AND EVIDENCE
Qualifying an Argument

Pick a subject or issue of current interest in your school or community. Then develop a claim and select evidence to defend it. Next, develop a claim that challenges your initial claim. Finally, use strategies you learned in this workshop to qualify your first claim with a concession to the second one.

(continued)

Subject:		
Defense of Claim	**Challenge of Claim**	**Qualification of Claim**

Do Robots Deserve Legal Rights?

Tim Sprinkle

Tim Sprinkle

THE TEXT IN CONTEXT

Denver-based journalist Tim Sprinkle has written for *Wired*, the *Washington Post*, the *Atlantic*, and other publications. In this January 19, 2018, article, Sprinkle explores the evolving role of technology in our lives and society. Machine learning and artificial intelligence, in particular, are bringing new opportunities and challenges. For example, robots have taken on many human roles, jobs, and traits. In some countries, people can legally marry robots. Are robots "human" in any meaningful sense? What are their rights and responsibilities, if any? In the following article, Sprinkle explores these questions.

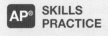 **SKILLS PRACTICE** | CLAIMS AND EVIDENCE
Analyzing Qualification and Concession

Analyzing Qualification and Concession		
Claim and Defense	**Qualification**	**Concession**
Identify the writer's primary claim and defense (reasons that justify that claim).	Identify statements and evidence that qualify the writer's claim.	Identify statements and evidence that offer the writer's concession to other perspectives.

Do Robots Deserve Legal Rights?

Saudi Arabia made waves in late 2017 when it granted citizenship to a humanoid robot named Sophia, developed by the Hong Kong-based Hanson Robotics. What those rights technically include, and what the move might mean for other robots worldwide, remains unclear. But the robot itself wasted no time in taking advantage of her new, high profile to campaign for women's rights in her adopted country.

This would be the same Sophia that, in a CNBC interview with her creator, Dr. David Hanson, said that she would "destroy all humans."

So, granting legal rights to robots clearly remains a complicated subject, even if it is done primarily as a PR stunt to promote an IT conference, as was the case in Saudi Arabia.

But that hasn't stopped a long list of voices in this country and abroad from arguing both for and against the creation of a set of "rights" for robots, based on a variety of concerns. Is robotics beginning to outpace our existing system of ethics and regulations that require a new system to deal with these issues before they surpass what we can control? Or does creating a set of machine-specific rights for these inventions place too much emphasis on robots as a sort of life form?

So far the idea has generated a lot of discussion, but few researchers are throwing their support behind robots as a legally protected class on par with humans. 5

"Let's take autonomous cars," says Avani Desai, principal and executive vice president of independent security and privacy compliance assessor Schellman & Company. "We have allowed computers to drive and make decisions for us, such as if there is a semi coming to the right and a guard rail on the left the algorithm in the autonomous car makes the decision what to do. But if you look back, is it the car that is making the decision or a group of people in a room that discuss the ethics and cost, and then provided to developers and engineers to make that technology work?"

Robots might use machine learning to refine their algorithms over time, he argues, but there is always an engineer who originally coded that information into their databanks. So, the morals, ideals, and thoughts of that engineer could be coded into a robot that is going to potentially make decisions that could affect the population at large.

From a legal perspective, then, who would face trouble in the case of litigation related to a decision that a robot made? Would it be the engineer, the manufacturer, or the retailer who sold and serviced that robot? Or would it be the robot itself?

"We see this issue with autonomous cars and the legal cases we have seen and it has come back to the automobile manufacturer due to a flaw in the algorithm," Desai says. "Until we as a society fully understand the implications of robots, the technology and the decision-making process, we should not apply the same rights we apply to humans to robots."

Whose Rights?

The analogy of the car is a good one, says Chris Roberts, the head of industrial robotics at Cambridge Consultants, in part because both are expensive, complex and valuable machines. They both need to be insured and protected in roughly the same way. 10

And neither deserve their own set of legal rights.

"I work with cutting-edge robotics and neural networks every day, and while the technology is really exciting and we can routinely do things that were science fiction only a few years ago, we're a long, long way from creating sentience and having to worry about the moral rights of the machine, he says. "Sophia may look like a person, and respond in ways that mimic human responses, but it is just a machine. Facial recognition, neural networks, speech synthesis and so on can look convincing, but they're not intelligent, just good at doing a particular task, in this case responding to questions."

Despite those arguments, there are still moral questions around robotics, including the ethics of using machines to make decisions about determining whether or not to program them to save only humans instead of other animals. With robots, a lot of the moral questions revolve around the work they are doing and the jobs they are replacing. If a robot comes in and replaces an entire class of workers overnight, what moral duty do we as a society have to help the people who are directly affected by this change? What sort of retraining and support should we offer them?

"It's the rights of the people that are much more important than the rights of the machine," Roberts says.

Beyond the Machines

At its core, the question of robot rights is less 15 about what those potential rights should look like and more about why we would want to protect them as a group at all. Is it in their interest or ours?

A lot of it comes down to fear, according to Dr. Glenn McGee, an expert in bioethics and a professor at the University of New Haven. Fear that the robots won't need us anymore. Fear that they will get smarter than we are. Fear that these new creations will rise up and come get us.

And we've seen this before.

"It's like when the Europeans first came to the Americas and the colonies began to rebel," he says. "We've historically always begun with the assertion that if you give rights to something, something that didn't have rights before, you're doing so because that will enable them to function without coming to get you. I think a lot of the discussion around rights for robots or entitlements that robots have come less from our sense as a society than the idea that we better get this right or else."

For example, if we encountered an alien race we wouldn't expect them to follow the set of laws and standards that we as humans do. We'd look at them through an anthropological lens first to see what it means for these other creatures to interact with our world and what we need to do to protect ourselves.

"We're not talking about whether or not 20 creatures who otherwise would have a soul will have more of one if we give them rights," Dr. McGee says. "We're really describing whether or not the designed creature, the robots that sort of become animal, whether or not the design will afford them the ability to interact with us in ways that make us feel better."

CLAIMS AND EVIDENCE

1. How does Sprinkle qualify his argument? Explain how this **qualification** recognizes the **limitations** of his argument.

2. Choose a word, phrase, or clause in the text that is used to **modify** or **qualify**. Then describe how it shows a shift in **perspective** on the subject.

3. Identify a **concession** in the argument. How does this concession advance the argument?

4. Explain how Sprinkle conveys the **complexity** of the issue to the **audience**.

Evaluation: Comparison/Contrast Argument

AP® Enduring Understanding (REO-1)

Writers make claims about subjects, rely on evidence that supports the reasoning that justifies the claim, and often acknowledge or respond to other possibly opposing arguments.

KEY POINT

When used in evaluation arguments, comparison and contrast is organized subject by subject or category by category.

As you've learned in previous units, a writer's purpose shapes the organization and reasoning of an argument. You've looked at narrative, persuasive, and expository arguments. In the next two units, you'll look at evaluation arguments. With this pattern of development, the writer makes a judgment, offers a recommendation, or proposes a solution to a problem. More often than not, these evaluations require comparison and contrast as a writer considers, refines, and qualifies his or her argument.

Evaluation arguments often incorporate comparison and contrast. For example, a writer may be reviewing a new video game for the purpose of recommending it to readers. The reviewer will provide a summary and description of the game. But his or her primary purpose is to judge its merits. To accomplish this, the writer will likely compare the game to other similar games or different games from the same publisher. He or she might point out similarities and differences in graphics, game mechanics, character development, plot, or other standard criteria. These standards of comparison will form the basis of the writer's evaluation and recommendation.

Evaluation Requires Comparison

Writers use **comparison and contrast** to analyze two or more similar subjects, people, places, events, or ideas. This pattern of development usually highlights the benefits and drawbacks of each subject, allowing the writer to make a comparative judgment.

But remember, comparison and contrast must reveal insight, information, or a new perspective. In other words, writers need a reason to compare and contrast. The writer must compare the same categories for each subject; categories of comparison must be relevant to a claim or thesis. In an evaluation argument, this pattern of development should lead to a larger judgment, conclusion, or recommendation. Without this larger claim, the writer is merely listing similarities and differences, not making an argument.

Organizing through Comparison and Contrast

Writers typically organize comparison and contrast arguments in one of two ways: subject by subject or category by category. In a subject-by-subject organization, a writer examines all the categories of comparison for one subject and then does the same for the next subject. These comparisons will either support a claim stated in the introduction or lead to a claim in the conclusion of the argument. In the category-by-category (or point-by-point) organization, a writer compares each subject within each category sequentially. As with subject-by-subject comparisons, this analysis can either support a claim in the introduction or lead to a claim in the conclusion.

While both approaches can be logical and effective, a writer may strategically choose one approach over another, depending on his or her purpose within a rhetorical situation.

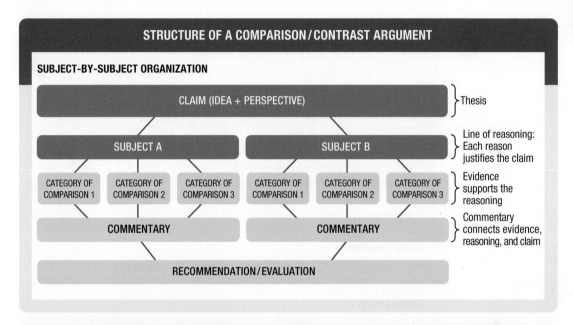

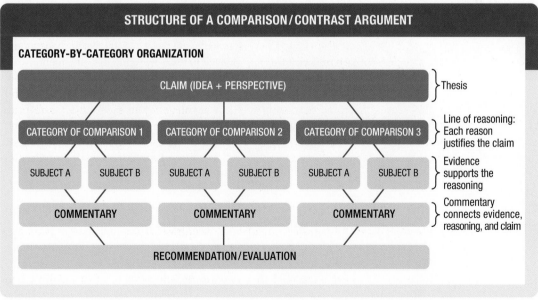

Categories of comparison are critical. The best evaluations come from comparing and contrasting important and often abstract (rather than literal) categories. Further, the categories of comparison should be parallel and consistent for each subject.

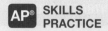 | REASONING AND ORGANIZATION
Identifying Categories of Comparison

Choose one of the following activities (or develop a similar one of your own). Then use comparison and contrast to evaluate the two options. To make an effective evaluation, develop the categories of comparison.

- Purchasing a pet
- Choosing a vacation location
- Deciding what to do over spring break
- Selecting a sport to play or activity to join

Subject:

Goal/Purpose:

	Option 1	Option 2
Category of Comparison A		
Category of Comparison B		
Category of Comparison C		

Suzanne Britt ■ Neat People vs. Sloppy People   535

REASONING AND ORGANIZATION

Neat People vs. Sloppy People

Suzanne Britt

Courtesy of Suzanne Britt

THE TEXT IN CONTEXT

Suzanne Britt (b. 1946) is an essayist, poet, and teacher from North Carolina. She has published in regional literary magazines, as well as national publications, including *Newsweek* and the *Boston Globe*. Britt's books include *Show and Tell* (1982), *Skinny People Are Dull and Crunchy Like Carrots* (1982), and *A Writer's Rhetoric* (1988). In the following well-known 1983 essay, she contrasts the literal qualities of neat and sloppy people to reveal her perspective.

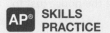 **SKILLS PRACTICE** | REASONING AND ORGANIZATION
Evaluating through Comparison and Contrast

Britt organizes her argument by comparing each of her subjects. As you read the text, use the following organizer to track Britt's reasons and evidence. Pay particular attention to Britt's categories of comparison. How does she use these categories to make a final evaluation part of her claim?

Evaluating through Comparison and Contrast: Subject by Subject

	Categories of Comparison	Details and Evidence
Subject A	First Category of Comparison: Second Category of Comparison: Third Category of Comparison:	
Subject B	First Category of Comparison: Second Category of Comparison: Third Category of Comparison:	
Conclusion	Recommendation/Evaluation:	

Neat People vs. Sloppy People

I've finally figured out the difference between neat people and sloppy people. The distinction is, as always, moral. Neat people are lazier and meaner than sloppy people.

Sloppy people, you see, are not really sloppy. Their sloppiness is merely the unfortunate consequence of their extreme moral rectitude. Sloppy people carry in their mind's eye a heavenly vision, a precise plan, that is so stupendous, so perfect, it can't be achieved in this world or the next.

Sloppy people live in Never-Never land. Someday is their métier. Someday they are planning to alphabetize all their books and set up home catalogs. Someday they will go through their wardrobes and mark certain items for tentative mending and certain items for passing on to relatives of similar shape and size. Someday sloppy people will make family scrapbooks into which they will put newspaper clippings, postcards, locks of hair, and the dried corsage from their senior prom. Someday they will file everything on the surface of their desks, including the cash receipt from coffee purchases at the snack shop. Someday they will sit down and read all the back issues of *The New Yorker*.

For all these noble reasons and more, sloppy people never get neat. They aim too high and wide. They save everything, planning someday to file, order, and straighten out the world. But while these ambitious plans take clearer and clearer shape in their heads, the books spill from the shelves onto the floor, the clothes pile up in the hamper and closet, the family mementos accumulate in every drawer, the surface of the desk is buried under mounds of paper, and the unread magazines threaten to reach the ceiling.

Sloppy people can't bear to part with anything. They give loving attention to every detail. When sloppy people say they're going to tackle the surface of the desk, they really mean it. Not a paper will go unturned; not a rubber band will go unboxed. Four hours or two weeks into the excavation, the desk looks exactly the same, primarily because the sloppy person is meticulously creating new piles of paper with new headings and scrupulously stopping to read all the old book catalogs before he throws them away. A neat person would just bulldoze the desk.

Neat people are bums and clods at heart. They have cavalier attitudes toward possession, including the family heirlooms. Everything is just another dust-catcher to them. If anything collects dust, it's got to go and that's that. Neat people will toy with the idea of throwing the children out of the house just to cut down on the clutter.

Neat people don't care about the process. They like results. What they want to do is get the whole thing over with so they can sit down and watch the rasslin' on TV. Neat people operate on two unvarying principles: Never handle any items twice, and throw everything away.

The only thing messy in a neat person's house is the trash can. The minute something comes to a neat person's hand, he will look at it, try to decide if it has immediate use and, finding none, throw it in the trash.

Neat people are especially vicious with mail. They never go through their mail unless they are standing directly over a trash can. If the trash can is beside the mailbox, even better. All ads, catalogs, pleas for charitable contributions, church bulletins, and money-saving coupons go straight into the trash can without being opened. All letters from home, postcards from Europe, bills, and paychecks are opened, immediately responded to, then dropped into

5

Suzanne Britt ■ Neat People vs. Sloppy People **537**

REASONING AND ORGANIZATION

the trash can. Neat people keep their receipts only for tax purposes. That's it. No sentimental salvaging of birthday cards or the last letter a dying relative ever wrote. Into the trash it goes.

Neat people place neatness above every-thing, even economics. They are incredibly wasteful. Neat people throw away several toys every time they walk through a den. I knew a neat person once who threw away a perfectly good dish drainer because it had mold on it. The drainer was too much trouble to wash. And neat people sell their furniture when they move. They will sell a La-Z-Boy recliner while you are reclining in it.

Neat people are no good to borrow from. Neat people buy everything in expensive little proportions. They get their flour and sugar in two-pound bags. They wouldn't consider clipping coupons, saving a leftover, reusing plastic nondairy whipped cream containers, or rinsing off tin foil and draping it over the unmoldy dish drainer. You can never borrow a neat person's newspaper to see what's playing at the movies. Neat people have the paper all wadded up and in the trash by 7:05 A.M.

Neat people cut a clean swath through the organic as well as the inorganic world. People, animals, and things are all one to them. They are so insensitive. After they've finished with the pantry, the medicine cabinet, and the attic, they will throw out the red geranium (too many leaves), sell the dog (too many fleas), and send the children off to boarding school (too many scuff-marks on the hard-wood floor).

REASONING AND ORGANIZATION

1. What are the categories of **comparison**? Choose one category and explain how it contributes to Britt's evaluation.

2. Britt organizes her argument subject by subject. Why does she choose this **organization** instead of category by category? What are the advantages of this organization?

3. How are the paragraphs arranged? What is the sequence of ideas? Explain the effect of this **arrangement**.

4. What is Britt's **conclusion** or relative evaluation of each subject?

Syntax for Purpose

AP **Enduring Understanding (STL-1)**
The rhetorical situation informs the strategic stylistic choices that writers make.

KEY POINT

Writers purposefully craft and punctuate sentences to convey and emphasize ideas.

In this unit, you've been learning that understanding the perspectives of others and qualifying arguments accordingly contribute to a writer's credibility. But how does a writer make this understanding and complexity evident in their writing? You can often find them reflected in the writer's syntactical choices and punctuation.

As you read arguments, pay close attention to the writer's choice of language. While design features such as boldface lettering may help emphasize terms and concepts, a writer's specific words and punctuation choices will reveal more insight.

In school, you've probably learned conventional punctuation rules, especially in the context of sentences. These rules are called *prescriptive grammar*. However, sentences are more than words, phrases, and clauses with correct punctuation. Rather, writers craft sentences in strategic ways that reveal relationships, emphasize ideas, and provide details — all of which help convey their message. These choices are called *rhetorical grammar*.

Rhetorical Choices May Break the "Rules"

However, there may be multiple ways to communicate ideas, each with its own prescriptive rules of correctness. So a writer must deliberately choose a specific type of sentence and accompanying punctuation that best communicate his or her intended meaning to the audience. To be most effective, the writer will consider all aspects of the rhetorical situation when composing. In short, writers must carefully craft and arrange sentences to best communicate their controlling idea and advance their argument to an intended audience for a specific situation.

Through their syntactical choices, writers may advance their purpose by clarifying, organizing, emphasizing, indicating purpose, supplementing information, or contributing to tone. Writers may use punctuation marks (commas, colons, semicolons, dashes, parentheses, quotation marks, or end marks) to accomplish the following:

- Emphasize an idea
- Balance ideas
- Indicate relationships
- Clarify
- Add detail or description

- Provide an example or instance
- Connect with the reader
- Omit information
- Provoke a thought
- Offer a qualification

ANALYZING SYNTACTICAL CHOICES

Rhetorical Function	Rhetorical Effect	Syntactical and Grammatical Structure
Emphasis	Bringing a sense of finality or emphasis of the idea	Short, simple sentence ending with a period .
	Restating an idea to emphasize a trait, quality, or idea	Two sentences that express the same idea differently connected with a colon :
	Providing an example, insight, or point of emphasis about the idea	Sentence that sets off information with a dash —
Balance	Setting up parallel constructions to indicate equality or balance	Sentence with two independent clauses connected with a comma (,) and a coordinating conjunction
		Sentence with a list of words and phrases in a series separated with commas; a coordinating conjunction is used before the final word or phrase in the series to indicate equality
Relationship	Illustrating a causal or adverbial relationship (how, when, where, why, to what extent)	Sentence with a subordinate clause set off with a comma ,
Clarification	Further describing, modifying, or clarifying a noun	Sentence with an adjective clause introduced by a relative pronoun (e.g., who, whose, whom, which, that) to indicate specificity
Detail or Description	Providing helpful, but nonessential, information or detail	Sentence with an appositive phrase set off with commas ,
Exemplification	Illustrating with either some examples or a clarification	Sentence with examples (e.g.,) or a clarification (i.e.,) in parentheses.
Connection	Creating intimacy or connection between reader and writer with a parenthetical aside	Sentence with information or detail placed within parentheses ( )
Omission	Excerpting relevant consecutive information that has been omitted from another source	Sentence with ellipses (. . .) that indicate omitted information or omitted words in direct quotation
Provocation or Reflection	Posing a reflective or intriguing question without providing an answer to provoke thought	Sentence with a rhetorical question using a question mark ?
Qualification	Qualifying an argument or claim by indicating circumstances where an argument would not apply	Sentence with subordinate clauses followed by a comma ,

Rhetorical Function of Punctuation

For most writers, **syntax** also contributes to the **unity** of an argument. At the sentence level, a writer's choice of **diction**, punctuation, and syntax combine to produce a specific effect on the audience. Some sentences are organized for emphasis, others for contrast, and still others for showing how two pieces of evidence connect. No matter what the sentence is doing, sentences must also connect directly to those that come before and after.

As an advanced reader and writer, you're moving beyond prescriptive grammar to a rhetorical grammar where the sentences and punctuation are used strategically to help convey the writer's unifying ideas and argument. Just remember that phrases or syntactical elements that are used to modify, clarify, or describe must be placed next to the noun or subject they are related to.

EFFECTS OF PUNCTUATION		
Punctuation Mark	**Symbol**	**Rhetorical Function or Effect**
Period	.	• Creates a sense of finality • Signifies the end of a thought
Question Mark	?	• Provokes thought, response, or reflection
Exclamation	!	• Emphasizes a strong emotion • Creates excitement
Comma	,	• Illustrates equality of ideas or information when used for coordination • Indicates inequality or qualification when used for subordination • Clarifies or describes by setting off parenthetical or nonessential information or details • Signifies a pause in thought
Semicolon	;	• Indicates that the connected clauses are closely related or equal
Colon	:	• Clarifies or restates information from the prior clause • Introduces examples or information
Dash	—	• Emphasizes an example or detail • Creates anticipation • Clarifies through exemplification • Signifies a shift or interruption
Ellipses	. . .	• Indicates an omission of information • Signifies the passage of time
Parenthesis	( )	• Provides extra information, clarifies • Indicates an aside to connect with the audience

INSIDER **Commas most often set off clarifying information.**
Any time information in a sentence is set off with a comma
(e.g., appositives, dependent or subordinate clauses),
the writer is alerting the reader that this information
is supplemental and not essential. But these details may help clarify or
exemplify the writer's idea.

SKILLS
PRACTICE │ LANGUAGE AND STYLE
Crafting Syntax for a Purpose

1. Write ten short, simple sentences that tell a story in chronological order, such
   as a narrative account of your summer vacation. The sentences should convey your story and include a beginning, a middle, and an end.

2. Then combine the sentences in ways that illustrate different meanings. For
   example:
   - Identify your main idea and leave it as a stand-alone simple sentence.
   - Combine two of your simple sentences that illustrate equal ideas by using a
     coordinating conjunction.
   - Identify one sentence that shows a cause-and-effect relationship or that
     is dependent on another sentence; combine those two sentences using a
     subordinating conjunction.
   - Examine the remaining sentences and then combine them using coordina-
     tion or subordination, as you did with the previous sentences.
   - Combine two of the sentences (or add a sentence, if necessary) so that
     you're using an adjective clause or appositive to further clarify or describe
     a noun.
   - Include another example of strategic punctuation (e.g., dash, parenthetical
     expressions, rhetorical question) in a purposeful way.

3. Compare your revision with your original. How did your syntactical choices
   help create a desired rhetorical effect?

The "Loser Edit" That Awaits Us All
Colson Whitehead

THE TEXT IN CONTEXT

Novelist and essayist Colson Whitehead (b. 1969) was born and raised in New York City. He has written nine novels, including *The Nickel Boys* (2019) and *Harlem Shuffle* (2021). His 2016 novel *The Underground Railroad* won the 2016 National Book Award for Fiction. In the following 2015 *New York Times Magazine* article, Whitehead writes in the context of reality television shows like *Survivor*, *The Amazing Race*, and *The Bachelor*. He focuses on the "loser edit": a term used when producers of reality shows edit footage to characterize a contestant as incompetent, phony, or inept.

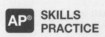 **SKILLS PRACTICE** | LANGUAGE AND STYLE
Analyzing Syntactical Choices

As you read "The 'Loser Edit' That Awaits Us All," pay close attention to Whitehead's syntactical choices, especially his use of punctuation. Use the following table to identify examples of his intentional syntax. Note: Whitehead may not attempt all of the purposes identified in the chart.

Analyzing Syntactical Choices		
Rhetorical Function	Syntactical and Grammatical Structure	Example and Rhetorical Effect
Emphasis	Short, simple sentence ending with a period .	
	Two sentences that express the same idea differently connected with a colon :	
	Sentence that sets off information with a dash —	

Balance	Sentence with two independent clauses connected with a comma , and a coordinating conjunction	
	Sentence with a list of words and phrases in a series separated with commas; a coordinating conjunction is used before the final word or phrase in the series to indicate equality	
Relationships	Sentence with a subordinate clause set off with a comma ,	
Clarification	Sentence with an adjective clause introduced by a relative pronoun (e.g., who, whose, whom, which, that) to indicate specificity	
Detail or Description	Sentence with an appositive phrase set off with commas ,	
Exemplification	Sentence with examples (e.g.,) or a clarification (i.e.,) in parentheses	
Connection	Sentence with information or detail placed within parentheses ( )	
Omission	Sentence with ellipses . . . that indicate omitted information or omitted words in direct quotation	

The "Loser Edit" That Awaits Us All

If you have ever watched a reality TV show and said, "He's going home tonight," you know what the "loser edit" is. I imagine it started as a matter of practicality. If you have 20 contestants, they can't all receive equal airtime. When an obscure character gets the heave-ho, the producers have to cobble together a coherent story line. Intersperse the snippets across the hour, and we can identify sins and recognizable human frailty that need to be punished. Anyone tuning in for the first time catches up quickly. The loser edit is not just the narrative arc of a contestant about to be chopped, or voted off the island, whatever

the catchphrase. It is the plausible argument of failure.

The concept first bubbled up out of the pop-cultural ether when competitive reality shows hit upon their formula, in the form of *Survivor* and *The Amazing Race*. TV enthusiasts—part fan, part Roland Barthes with a TiVo—congregated on online message boards like Television Without Pity, creating a new slang with which to dis and deconstruct their favorites.

Fifteen years later, the critical language used to carve up the phonies, saints and sad-sack wannabes of reality shows has migrated, and the loser edit has become a limber metaphor for exploring our own real-world failures. Fate doles out ideas for subplots—fire her, dump him, all species of mortification—and we eagerly run with them, cutting loser narratives for friends and enemies, the people we have demoted to the status of mere character. Everybody's setbacks or degradations have been foreshadowed if we look hard enough at the old tape. We arrange the sequences, borrowing from cultural narratives of disgrace, sifting through the available footage with a bit of hindsight—and in turn, we endure our own loser edits when we stumble.

With so many media bloggers staggering under daily content quotas, rooting through the digital-content vaults, we can now assemble the montage of public shame more quickly than ever. A few weeks ago, NBC told Brian Williams to pack his knives and go. Cue the supercut of Williams spinning different accounts of dangerous helicopter rides in Iraq, the gradual embellishments creeping in over the years. Cue Williams in a Hurricane Katrina documentary telling us how he heard that a man committed suicide in the Superdome, juxtaposed with an interview years later in which he says he "watched" that suicide actually happen. *How could we have missed it?*

It was inevitable that Bill Cosby would receive a thorough loser edit after his army of accusers began stepping forward. There were too many sleuths nosing around for clues, downloading ancient standup routines, tapping search words into digital scans of out-of-print books: "cocktail hour," "consent," "things America's favorite dad said that are creepy in retrospect." Is he really joking about dosing women with Spanish fly on a 1969 comedy album? On a talk show in 1991? *It was right in front of us all along.* Embed the clip, tweet it out. This Cosby edit is on VHS, recorded over the videotape of your childhood illusions, and it cannot be undone. If that can be erased, what else?

How stupid of them to leave all that incriminating evidence out there.

The footage of *your* loser edit is out there as well, waiting. Taken from the surveillance camera of the gas station where you bought a lottery ticket like a chump. From the A.T.M. that recorded you taking out money for the romantic evening that went bust. From inside the black domes on the ceiling of the train station, the lenses that captured your slow walk up the platform stairs after the doomed excursion. From all the cameras on all the street corners, entryways and strangers' cellphones, building the digital dossier of your days. Maybe we can't clearly make out your face in every shot, but everyone knows it's you. We know you like to slump. Our entire lives as B-roll, shot and stored away to be recut and reviewed at a moment's notice when the plot changes: the divorce, the layoff, the lawsuit. Any time the producers decide to raise the stakes.

Occasionally, on a *Top Chef* or a *Project Runway*, a contestant suffers a monstrous loser edit, one that lasts a whole season. The unlucky contestant isn't sent home at the end of the night, but is instead doomed to perform personality deficits episode after episode. The supporting player trapped first by an aspect of himself or herself, and then by editors who won't let him or her escape the casting. We need a goat.

Perhaps you have a personal acquaintance with this phenomenon, slogging through months and months of your own terrible editing. The audience takes in the spectacle, pressing pause for a quick trip to the kitchen so

5

they won't miss a second of your humiliation: This is destination television. Your co-workers rewind your loser's reel, speculating over why you didn't get that promotion, where it all started to go wrong. *If you ask me, it goes back to the Peterson account.* Your ex's buddies pass the potato chips and barely pay attention, texting pals, making jokes on Twitter—they knew before the first commercial break that you were being voted off the island. Your friends and family, who of course love you very much, are tuning in, even though they know all of your story lines by heart. They've seen this episode before. *There he goes again.*

When life gets the drop on us, we have to submit to the framing. We leave too many traces of our failures, too much material for a ruthless editor to work with. As if we didn't already have one in our heads—cutting and splicing a lifetime of bad decisions and bonehead moves into an existential montage of boobery:

"Why did I say that?"

"What's wrong with me?"

"Why do I keep falling for that?"

Memory is the most malicious cutter of all, preserving, recasting, panning in slow motion across the awful bits so that we retain every detail.

Can we escape our editing? In their wisdom, the philosopher-consumers of Television Without Pity also identified the loser edit's opposite number and antiparticle: the winner edit. If there's a loser edit, there has to be a winner edit. Makes sense. Over the course of a season, the inevitable winner thrives. He or she will suffer some setbacks for drama and suspense, sure, but the groundwork for victory is established challenge by challenge, week by week. It has been written, by fate or the producers, pick your deity. It cannot be reversed.

10

15

You know the golden boys and girls who sail through life without care, recipients of an enviable winner edit that lasts season after season. Untouchable. Everyone else has to do it by himself or herself, assembling our edits through a thousand compulsive Facebook tweaks, endless calibrations of Twitter personas, Instagram posts filtered of all disturbance. *Should I wear glasses in my profile pic? How do I express solidarity with the freedom fighters?* The exaggerations and elisions on your dating profile, and the ridiculous yet oddly calming amount of time you spent choosing the proper font for your résumé. *I hear employers associate Calibri with diligence and follow-through.* Marshal the flattering anecdotes, string them together into a leitmotif of confidence and sophistication. Cut when this scene establishes the perfect pitch of self-deprecation, cut before everyone can see your humility for the false modesty it is.

Do you think it's working? Did you get away with it today?

We give ourselves loser edits and winner edits all the time, to clasp meaning onto experience. Sometimes you render both kinds of edits in the same day, maybe even the same afternoon, deleting certain scenes from your memory, fooling with the contrast, as reality presses on you and directs your perceptions. Pull it off, and maybe you'll make it to bedtime. Why do you think they call it "Survivor"?

Splice and snip. The contradictory evidence falls to the cutting-room floor, and we assert order, shape a narrative, any narrative, out of the chaos. Whether you tend to give yourself a loser edit to feed that goblin part of your psyche or you fancy the winner's edit for the camouflage and safety it provides, it's better than having no arc at all. If we're going down, let us at least be a protagonist, have a story line, not be just one of those miserable players in the background. A cameo's stand-in. The loser edit, with all its savage cuts, is confirmation that you exist. The winner edit, even in its artifice, is a gesture toward optimism, the expectation of rewards waiting for that better self. Whenever he or she shows up.

Take the footage you need. Burn the rest. 20

LANGUAGE AND STYLE

1. Whitehead uses **syntax** strategically. Find one sentence in the text that supplements or adds to the previous sentence. Then find one sentence that contrasts with the previous sentence. Explain the different effects of these two relationships. How do they contribute to Whitehead's argument?

2. Find a **transition** in the text and explain how it creates a relationship between different ideas. How does that relationship contribute to the message of the text?

3. Whitehead uses **rhetorical questions** throughout the text. Identify two questions. Then explain the function and effect of the questions. How do they contribute to the overall argument?

4. Whitehead's **style** features dashes throughout the text. Find one example and then explain the function and the effect of the dash.

How Native American Is Native American Enough?

Tommy Orange

THE TEXT IN CONTEXT

Born and raised in Oakland, California, novelist Tommy Orange (b. 1982) held various jobs before publishing his first novel *There, There* in 2018. The book, which explores the lives of Native Americans living in Oakland, became a finalist for the 2019 Pulitzer Prize. Orange's background as a member of the Cheyenne and Arapaho tribes shaped his perspective, as did his time working at a Native American health center. In this 2018 article, Orange considers ethnicity and its effect on the individual, the family, and the future.

Unifying Idea	How Native American Is Native American Enough?	Rhetorical Strategies	Effect
identity	I'm not trying to be more Native than I am. Less white than I am. I'm trying to be honest about what I have to include. More often than not I've introduced myself as half Native. I know what people want to know as soon as I say that I'm Native: How much? I watch them wait to see what I'll say about it. They don't want to have to ask, and they know I don't want to have to say it. They're testing me that way, so when the quiet between us becomes too much for me, I mumble out the side of my mouth: *From my dad's side.* The other half of me is apparent. My skin is light and I have freckles. I'm brown around the summer months and whiter in the winter. But I look like my dad if you saw me next to him. We	introduction comparison/contrast	contextualizes the argument by personalizing the issue organized by physical characteristics

Unifying Idea	How Native American Is Native American Enough?	Rhetorical Strategies	Effect
	have the same head and body. Same barrel chest, same nose. I reference my dad when I bring up being Native because I'm always doing it, qualifying my quantity. My amount. Where it comes from. And it's never enough. Too many claim great-grandparents. People are tired of hearing about great-grandparents, and great-great-grandparents even more so. It's too much math. Do I think we shouldn't include smaller fractions in the definition of what it means to be Native? I don't know. What I do know is that if I don't include the amount that I am, people assume less. So if asked whether or not I'm Native, I say yeah, and then, maybe sadly, maybe with assertion, maybe both, I say: half.	qualification	answering his own question to acknowledge limitation
identity	Those with less than half lose more than half the battle at the outset. One Native grandparent equals one-quarter blood quantum. Should someone with this amount not be allowed to identify as Native, if their grandmother raised them? If they didn't even know that grandparent? What about great-great-grandparents? That's an eighth—if there's only one. What equations make sense to keep doing? How come math isn't taught with stakes? There are Natives enrolled in tribes with less than a 30 second's worth of Native blood in them—as in, less than 30 seconds after hearing about that kind of low-percentage ancestry, you'll probably have dismissed them as faking. You. Everyone.		
identity	There are full-blooded Native people raised by white families in white communities who don't know a thing about what it means to be Native or how to live in such a way as to be identified as such.		

Unifying Idea	How Native American Is Native American Enough?	Rhetorical Strategies	Effect
identity	Walking between worlds is an old Native half-breed trope. I've never felt that I've walked in two worlds. The half-world feels more like being pulled apart and told to speak in singular terms—to pick a side. Actively identifying as a Native person if you have a valid claim is important work—an act against systematically designed erasure.		
identity	A half is not a number. Mathematically speaking, it doesn't count as a number. I never did well in math, but I understand fractions better now. When I was talking to my dad recently he said, "The way I got it worked out, it's like this, you're 3/64 short of being half Cheyenne."	quotation	father's words, clarify the complexity of defining one's ethnicity
identity	That's about 4% less than half. According to a poll conducted by the *Atlantic*, 4% of Americans believe lizard people control politics. So I'm that amount of crazy Americans short of being half Native American.		
identity	But I'm not half, technically. I can't, for example, technically call myself biracial. I'd have to include 1/32 Sioux* blood and 1/64 German blood. I know this because my dad knows this. Growing up they called him *Vehoe*. It means white man. It also means spider, and references a mythological trickster figure. He told me I'm less than half. He didn't mean it in any way. My dad's an engineer. Exact math matters to him. As it does to all of us who have to figure out the kind of math involved in the equation: Enough Blood times Not Enough Blood equals eligibility or ineligibility for tribal enrollment and therefore citizenship in a sovereign nation.	qualification	"technically" is precise and builds credibility

Unifying Idea	How Native American Is Native American Enough?	Rhetorical Strategies	Effect
	But I am half Native—Cheyenne—from my dad. This half of me is a cutting fraction, which cuts if I rub up against it too firmly, if I slide my finger along its edge. Halving is the beginning of erasure. I'm doing it here again. Qualifying myself. Worried about what you will think of me.	dash	signifies appositive which clarifies his heritage
identity	I had a son in 2011. He'd be a quarter. The last in my line to be able to call himself Cheyenne, officially. He would have been. But he is an eighth Cheyenne. An eighth nothing.	short, simple sentences	isolate each detail for emphasis
identity	We are very clear with our son at home. He knows he's Native. But what that will mean for him in 20 years, I don't know. And what it will mean for his children?		
identity	There is something you'd never know about if you weren't Native or had a close Native relation or friend. It's called the CDIB. Certificate of Degree of Indian Blood. This is a real, actual, official piece of paper with a record writ in fraction how much "Indian blood" I have. An official document about an amount of blood in my body. Which is a metaphor. But it isn't. It's real. We don't have enough blood to keep going for our people. It stops. Ends. My son won't have a CDIB.		
identity	As it is, I am an enrolled member of the Cheyenne and Arapaho Tribes of Oklahoma. On my Certificate of Degree of Indian Blood it says I am one-quarter Cheyenne. One-fourth. The one indicates a person who did not die. Who was not killed. Whose blood has since thinned, and is more than probably on the way down that sloping line. To the stopping point.	fragment	emphasizes the legitimacy of his heritage

Unifying Idea	How Native American Is Native American Enough?	Rhetorical Strategies	Effect
identity	My blood is not enough because my dad's dad never accepted him as a son. So he is half nothing, resulting in my quarter nothingness. This is how I became biracial and bi-nihilist. My son cannot be enrolled in our tribe as a result of being an eighth nothing, as a result of not having the proper documents to prove he has the required amount of blood in his body. It has to be funny that after spilling all that blood, our blood, our government, which first imposed this blood law—that we keep such close track of it—make sure we don't lose its quantity, or quality, or, what are we talking about again? If my skin is white, that's because that's what my mom is. And if it isn't brown, it isn't because of what my dad isn't. I'm not half of two things or made up of fractions. I am made up of whole things, things that are things unto themselves.	subordinate clause	*cause-effect relationship indicates his feeling inauthentic*
		narrative distance	*reflecting on the implications of his ethnicity*
		qualification	*uses conditional clauses to show that he is whole*

* Most Lakota people I've met don't like to be called Sioux because it's the given white name, but when I asked my dad if we're Lakota or Dakota or Nakota, he just said, "The way my grandma told it to me, we're Sioux." There was an *And that's that* feel to the way he said it.

Identity and Identities

IDEA BANK

Assimilation

Collective

Community

Culture

Diversity

Ethnocentrism

Exclusion

Homogeneity

Identity

Inclusion

Individual

Mainstream

Multicultural

Nationalism

Perspective

Pluralism

Privilege

Representation

Voice

As the United States became more industrialized and modern, it also became more urban. By 1920, more people lived in cities than in rural areas. That trend continued throughout the century: by 1970, over 73 percent of Americans lived — and found their identities — in a city. Of course, places like Chicago and New York City had their share of poverty and racism. But in many cases, African Americans built their own communities, neighborhoods, and identities within them. The Harlem Renaissance was the earliest and most culturally significant example. In the 1920s and 1930s, Harlem became a capital of African American culture, which included the jazz of Louis Armstrong, the poetry of Countee Cullen, the paintings of Jacob Lawrence, and the work of many others. Harlem figures like the actor Paul Robeson and the poet Langston Hughes provided distinctly African American voices and perspectives on the American experience. The novelist Ralph Ellison, a literary protégé of Langston Hughes, explores individual and collective identity in "Hidden Name and Complex Fate" (p. 554). In many ways,

Bronzeville at Night, 1949 (oil on canvas)/Motley Jr., Archibald J. (1891-1981)/ Private Collection/Bridgeman Images

▲

Artist Archibald Motley Jr. painted this iconic depiction of Chicago's South Side, called *Bronzeville at Night*, in 1949.

Look closely at the details of the painting. How does the painter use details to represent both individual and community identity? What values and ideas does the painting reinforce?

the Harlem Renaissance became a foundation for the civil rights movement that followed over the next decades.

The cultural significance of the Harlem Renaissance, along with similar communities in other cities, was enormous. This racial urbanization moved African American culture away from the margins and more toward the center of American life, much the way that Delta Blues music migrated from Mississippi to Chicago. But the influential work of African American artists also raised questions about what, exactly, is "American culture." For example, jazz is a distinctively American genre, but it's also a distinctively African American musical form, even if it was appropriated and developed by white musicians. So does jazz "belong" to America as a whole, or does the genre have a separate and essentially African American identity? If a form like jazz becomes part of mainstream American culture, does it lose part of its identity in the process?

These questions mirror similar ones about immigration and identity. For example, the most common metaphor for American assimilation has been the "melting pot." According to this perspective, individuals come to the United States from all over the world; they shed their national, ethnic, or cultural differences and blend in with a homogeneous American culture. This analogy privileges unity over diversity. It also oversimplifies the process of assimilation, as some differences cannot easily be erased. Writer Durga Chew-Bose, the daughter of Indian immigrants, writes about how her dark skin — an inheritance from her family lineage — remains integral to her identity in "Tan Lines" (p. 559).

Today, some have changed the metaphor of assimilation to emphasize multiculturalism and inclusiveness: America as a salad bowl or a mosaic, where individual elements come together but keep their distinct identities. We can see this shift toward diversity elsewhere, as well, from debates about what books belong in the canon of "great literature," to our greater emphasis on racial, ethnic, and gender representation in popular culture.

This installation is called *Make Me a Mask*, by the artist Ruben Torres Llorca. The signs say: MAKE ME A MASK, to fight, to love, to conquer, to cure, to dream, to listen, to speak.

How do people wear masks in a figurative sense? Explain how individuals wear masks to play the roles they serve as both individuals and members of a community.

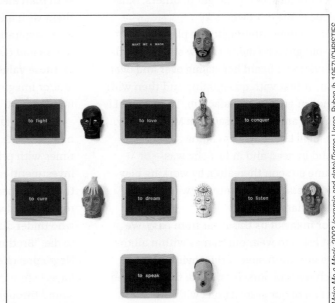

Make Me a Mask, 2003 (ceramic and slate)/Torres Llorca, Ruben (b. 1957)/CHRISTIES IMAGES/Private Collection/Bridgeman Images

from Hidden Name and Complex Fate

Ralph Ellison

James Whitmore/The LIFE Picture Collection/Getty Images

THE TEXT IN CONTEXT

Novelist, critic, and scholar Ralph Ellison (1914–1994) was born and raised in Oklahoma City, Oklahoma. He attended the Tuskegee Institute, an all-Black university in Alabama, but dropped out before graduating. Like many ambitious artists at the time, he moved to New York City in 1936, immersing himself in the African American cultural and political scene during the final years of the Harlem Renaissance. Ellison's literary reputation rests largely on his powerful 1952 novel *Invisible Man*, which explores the unnamed African American narrator's quest for identity — and survival — in a racist society that denies him his humanity. Among other collected works, Ellison also published *Shadow and Act* (1964), a collection of literary and cultural criticism. His long-awaited second novel *Juneteenth* was published posthumously in 1996. In the following autobiographical narrative published in 1964 — the height of the civil rights movement — Ellison explores the importance of naming and identity.

Our names, being the gift of others, must be made our own.

Once while listening to the play of a two-year-old girl who did not know she was under observation, I heard her saying over and over again, at first with questioning and then with sounds of growing satisfaction, "I am Mimi Livisay? . . . I am Mimi Livisay. I *am* Mimi Livisay. . . . I am *Mimi* Li-vi-say! I am Mimi. . . ."

And in deed and in fact she was—or became so soon thereafter, by working playfully to establish the unity between herself and her name.

For many of us this is far from easy. We must learn to wear our names within all the noise and confusion of the environment in which we find ourselves; make them the center of all of our associations with the world, with man and with nature. We must charge them with all our emotions, our hopes, hates, loves, aspirations. They must become our masks and our shields and the containers of all those values and traditions which we learn and/or imagine as being the meaning of our familial past. . . .

Perhaps, taken in aggregate, these European 5 names which (sometimes with irony, sometimes with pride, but always with personal investment) represent a certain triumph of the spirit, speaking to us of those who rallied, reassembled and transformed themselves and who under dismembering pressures refused to die. "Brothers and sisters," I once heard a Negro preacher exhort, "let us make up our faces before the world, and our names shall sound throughout the land with honor! For we ourselves are our *true* names, not their epithets! So let us, I say, Make Up Our Faces and Our Minds!"

Perhaps my preacher had read T. S. Eliot, although I doubt it. And in actuality, it was unnecessary that he do so, for a concern with names and naming was very much a part of that special area of American culture from which I come, and it is precisely for this reason that this example should come to mind in a discussion of my own experience as a writer.

Undoubtedly, writers begin their *conditioning* as manipulators of words long before they become aware of literature—certain Freudians would say at the breast. Perhaps. But if so, that is far too early to be of use at this moment. Of this, though, I am certain: that despite the misconceptions of those educators who trace the reading difficulties experienced by large numbers of Negro children in Northern schools to their Southern background, these children are, in *their* familiar South, facile manipulators of words. I know, too, that the Negro community is deadly in its ability to create nicknames and to spot all that is ludicrous in an unlikely name or that which is incongruous in conduct. Names are not qualities; nor are words, in this particular sense, actions. To assume that they could cost one his life many times a day. Language skills depend to a large extent upon a knowledge of the details, the manners, the objects, the folkways, the psychological patterns, of a given environment. Humor and wit depend upon much the same awareness, and so does the suggestive power of names.

"A small brown bowlegged Negro with the name 'Franklin D. Roosevelt Jones' might sound like a clown to someone who looks at him from the outside," said my friend Albert Murray, "but on the other hand he just might turn out to be a fireside operator. He might just lie back in all of that comic juxtaposition of names and manipulate you deaf, dumb and blind—and you not even suspecting it, because you're thrown out of stance by his name! There you are, so dazzled by the F. D. R. image—which you *know* you can't see—and so delighted with your own superior position that you don't realize that its *Jones* who must be confronted."

Well, as you must suspect, all of this speculation on the matter of names has a purpose, and now, because it is tied up so ironically with my own experience as a writer, I must turn to my own name.

For in the dim beginnings, before I ever   10
thought consciously of writing, there was my own name, and there was, doubtless, a certain magic in it. From the start I was uncomfortable with it, and in my earliest years it caused me much puzzlement. Neither could I understand what a poet was, nor why, exactly, my father had chosen to name me after one. Perhaps I could have understood it perfectly well had he named me after his own father, but that name had been given to an older brother who died and thus was out of the question. But why hadn't he named me after a hero, such as Jack Johnson, or a soldier like Colonel Charles Young, or a great seaman like Admiral Dewey, or an educator like Booker T. Washington, or a great orator and abolitionist like Frederick Douglass? Or again, why hadn't he named me (as so many Negro parents had done) after President Teddy Roosevelt?

Instead, he named me after someone called Ralph Waldo Emerson, and then, when I was three, he died. It was too early for me to have understood his choice, although I'm sure he must have explained it many times, and it was also too soon for me to have made the connection between my name and my father's love for reading. Much later, after I began to write and work with words, I came to suspect that he was aware of the suggestive powers of names and of the magic involved in naming.

I recall an odd conversation with my mother during my early teens in which she mentioned their interest in, of all things, pre-natal culture! But for a long time I actually knew only that my father read a lot, and that he admired this remote Mr. Emerson, who was something called a "poet and philoso-pher"—so much so that he named his second son after him.

I knew, also, that whatever his motives, the combination of names he'd given me caused me no end of trouble from the moment when I could talk well enough to respond to the rit-ualized question which grownups put to very young children. Emerson's name was quite familiar to Negroes in Oklahoma during those days when World War I was brewing, and adults, eager to show off their knowledge of literary figures, and obviously amused by the joke implicit in such a small brown nubbin of a boy carrying around such a heavy moniker, would invariably repeat my first two names and then to my great annoyance, they'd add "Emerson."

And I, in my confusion, would reply, "No, *no, I'm* not Emerson; he's the little boy who lives next door." Which only made them laugh all the louder. "Oh no," they'd say, "*you're* Ralph Waldo Emerson," while I had fantasies of blue murder.

For a while the presence next door of my little friend, Emerson, made it unnecessary for me to puzzle too often over this peculiar adult confusion. And since there were other Negro boys named Ralph in the city, I came to suspect that there was something about the combination of names which produced their laughter. Even today I know of only one other Ralph who had as much comedy made out of his name, a campus politician and deep-voiced orator whom I knew at Tuskegee, who was called in friendly ribbing, *Ralph Waldo Emerson Edgar Allan Poe*, spelled Powe. This must have been quite a trial for him, but I had been initi-ated much earlier.

During my early school years the name continued to puzzle me, for it constantly evoked in the faces of others some secret. It was as though I possessed some treasure or some defect, which was invisible to my own eyes and ears; something which I had but did not *possess*, like a piece of property in South Carolina, which was mine but which I could not have until some future time. I recall find-ing, about this time, while seeking adventure in back alleys—which possess for boys a superiority over playgrounds like that which kitchen utensils possess over toys designed for infants—a large photographic lens. I remem-ber nothing of its optical qualities, of its speed or color correction, but it gleamed with crystal mystery and it was beautiful.

Mounted handsomely in a tube of shiny brass, it spoke to me of distant worlds of possibility. I played with it, looking through it with squinted eyes, holding it in shafts of sunlight, and tried to use it for a magic lan-tern. But most of this was as unrewarding as my attempts to make the music come from a phonograph record by holding the needle in my fingers.

I could burn holes through newspapers with it, or I could pretend that it was a tele-scope, the barrel of a cannon, or the third eye of a monster—*I* being the monster—but I could do nothing at all about its proper func-tion of making images; nothing to make it yield its secret. But I could not discard it.

Older boys sought to get it away from me by offering knives or tops, agate marbles or whole zoos of grass snakes and horned toads in trade, but I held on to it. No one, not even

15

the white boys I knew, had such a lens, and it was my own good luck to have found it. Thus I would hold on to it until such time as I could acquire the parts needed to make it function. Finally I put it aside and it remained buried in my box of treasures, dusty and dull, to be lost and forgotten as I grew older and became interested in music.

I had reached by now the grades where it [20] was necessary to learn something about Mr. Emerson and what he had written, such as the "Concord Hymn" and the essay "Self-Reliance," and in following his advice, I reduced the "Waldo" to a simple and, I hoped, mysterious "W," and in my own reading I avoided his works like the plague. I could no more deal with my name—I shall never really master it than I could find a creative use for my lens. . . .

I could suppress the name of my namesake out of respect for the achievements of its original bearer but I cannot escape the obligation of attempting to achieve some of the things which he asked of the American writer. As Henry James suggested, being an American is an arduous task, and for most of us, I suspect, the difficulty begins with the name.

In the 1990s and 2000s, Harlem experienced gentrification that displaced many residents, changing its culture and identity. Sculptor Elizabeth Catlett was one of many artists who created sculptures and other artwork and placed them throughout Harlem to memorialize and celebrate the Harlem Renaissance. This installation in Harlem's Riverside Park commemorates *Invisible Man: A Memorial to Ralph Ellison* (2003).

What message does the sculpture communicate about identity?

Joseph Michael Lopez/The New York Times/Redux

RHETORICAL SITUATION

1. Ellison begins the text with a scenario. How does this scenario create the relationship between **writer**, **audience**, and **context**?

2. What is the writer's **exigence**? How does the exigence contribute to the **purpose** of the text?

3. Identify a shift. Explain how the shift reveals a change in Ellison's **perspective** on the subject.

4. How do Ellison's **introduction** and the **conclusion** work together to support his text's **message**?

5. What does the **writer** share with the **audience** in his introduction? What does he implicitly leave out?

CLAIMS AND EVIDENCE

6. Explain how Ellison's **evidence** helps establish his credibility.

7. The writer offers many **perspectives** on the subject. Choose one example and explain how the **evidence** offers another perspective.

8. How does Ellison acknowledge the limitations of his argument? Give an example of this **qualification** and explain that limitation.

REASONING AND ORGANIZATION

9. What **method of development** does Ellison use to organize his argument? Explain how the writer's **reasons** help create unity in the text.

10. How does the writer use **transitional** sentences to create **coherence** in the **narrative**?

11. How do the **figurative** elements in Ellison's **narrative** contribute to the overall **message**?

LANGUAGE AND STYLE

12. How do the quotations within the text strengthen the writer's message? Choose an example and then show how this **syntactical** choice connects to the message.

13. Look closely at Ellison's use of **syntax**. Choose a rhetorical question, the use of dashes, or another syntactic choice. Then explain how it achieves a rhetorical **purpose**.

14. Choose one example of **coordination** and one example of **subordination**. Explain the rhetorical effect of each.

IDEAS IN AMERICAN CULTURE

15. How might the title be a metaphor for Ellison's overall message? What do Ellison's struggles reveal about the potential of an individual? How do you see these ideas in your own life and experience? Do you know any examples of individuals who are living up to expectations or filling the shoes of a predecessor? Explain.

PUTTING IT ALL TOGETHER

16. The photographic lens is a symbol in the text that serves as a **motif** for identity. What does this motif suggest about individual growth and self-awareness?

Tan Lines
Durga Chew-Bose

THE TEXT IN CONTEXT

The daughter of Indian immigrants, writer Durga Chew-Bose (b. 1986) was born in Montreal, Canada, and moved to the United States when she was seventeen. Her work has appeared in *GQ*, the *Guardian*, *The New Inquiry*, and many other publications. In the following essay from her first book, the autobiographical *Too Much and Not the Mood* (2017), Chew-Bose reflects on growing up as a brown-skinned girl in a predominantly white culture. The book made Bustle's list (a website focusing on news and politics, alongside celebrities, beauty, and fashion trends) of "15 Most Anticipated Feminist Book Releases of 2017."

Come summer my reluctance kicks in. It's as if the sheer persistence of a July day—the sun's glare, its flecked appraisal of pavement and trees, those bonus evening hours—solicits from me an essential need to withdraw. Thankfully, writing is an indoor sport. Sometimes I go stretches of days without much sun, and even in the swell of midsummer I maintain what could be characterized as my winter pallor. But is pallor a true assessment? Probably not. How might I describe my brownness, my fair brownness that following winter's gloom appears more fair? What's the opposite of *glowing*? Dull? Drab? Rundown? Blah?

These questions are not as good-humored as they seem but fixed instead to my tendency for self-scrutiny, activated long ago when I came to understand my sense of belonging—my *who-ness*—as two-pronged. The beautiful dilemma of being first-generation and all that it means: a reflection of theirs and mine, of source and story. A running start toward blending in among mostly white childhood friends who were rarely curious about my olive-brown skin, the dark shine of my hair, my chestnut eyes. We were kids, after all. We were each other's chorus, encountering parents—and the *elsewhere* that entailed for me—only in consonant environments: a birthday party, ballet recitals, rides to the movies in my parents' burgundy Toyota Previa.

In terms of family, this elsewhere—my parents' *who-ness*—was both abundant yet imperceptible. It was my home, after all. Like the divan and mismatched bolsters on which I would toss my jacket after school, for which my mother would scold me: *Hang it up!* The bitter taste of cardamom, too, those seemingly inescapable pods that I detested yet never managed to avoid, biting into them by accident at dinner. My friends didn't know what a divan was or why we didn't call it a couch. And cardamom, well, cardamom was a flavor they'd never encountered.

These accumulations from life growing up in our house, passed down not merely through memory's piping but in actions, are re-experienced most in the summer. Despite New York City's stifling weather, how the air warps itself into a muggy mass, I drink hot tea and eat hot soup. It cools me down. Because in that sly way science naturally alloys with what we inherit, I've been told since childhood that hot liquids provide remedial chill. This slight reprieve on especially sticky days, I like to imagine, is a discreet reminder that my parents are not always but sometimes right. That the knowledge they've imparted to my brother and me is not purely an expression of love but firm testimony, too—of their own provenance and how what keeps us close does not always reveal itself in facsimile, but over time, in what kindly amounts in kernels. An everyday tip, a turn of phrase and its unusual construction, reminders to not sit on my bed with "outside clothes," for instance, or how in the summer my body yields to the season's balm with what I've come to regard as heritable agency.

Those beads of sweat that collect on my nose are entirely my Mama's. The annual, deep-healing effects of humidity on my dry skin; that's hers as well. If friends come over to my apartment and I offer them "some tea," those two words conjure my father's anticipant inflection on scorching weekend afternoons where he sits on our porch having proudly just fixed something without needing to replace it, like the broken nozzle of our gardening hose or the loose legs of a chair.

In my case, inheritance has never simply been what trickles down through traditions but the work required to disallow how quickly those traditions fade. To recover the various

genetic dispatches like those from my grandfather Felix, who I met once, long ago, in Kolkata, in a kitchen I think, of which I remember little except for the color green. A tablecloth, maybe. A moss stain on concrete wall. Perhaps the whole memory is enameled green because for no discernible reason some colors naturally coat nostalgia with geography. India, for me, has always been protected in a layer of green.

There is also my paternal grandfather, who I never met, and his wife, my grandmother Thama, who I did. And there is also my other grandmother, who died when my mother was a teenager. Her skin was far darker than mine, a trait I noted as I studied one photo album in particular, confusing the musty scent of protective parchment sheets with what I imagined she herself might have smelled like. I remember foolishly wondering as a child if my much lighter skin was an outcome of brown girls growing up in cold climates. A discordance that epitomized how split I felt between life at home and life outside, overcome and enamored by my white friends and every so often experiencing waves of assimilation met by lulls of wanting nothing more than to seek lineage, move backward, claim the brownness of my skin as I only knew how, through family.

• • •

I became more aware of my skin, as most of us do with our bodies, in adolescence, and especially when summer arrived. Halter tops. Collar bones. Shoulder blades. Crop tops. Denim skirts and how their frayed hems trimmed the flop of my thighs. Shorts. A growth spurt marked by how my knees now knocked my bike's handlebars as I pedaled to the park. Bathing suits. Boys. The convention of boys in the summer; how, suddenly, they memorialized the season. Still, I became heedful of the sun's currency on my body. The sun's signature on my skin and how the contrast of tan lines carried merit. That I was expected to feel virtuous was strange to me. I tanned fast. Brown to dark umber in a matter of hours. But what struck me was this: It was as if my white friends were wearing their tanned skin—bathing in it—as opposed to living in it.

The level of excitement among my New York friends has now hit fever-pitch and results in one thing: plans. So many plans. An incessancy of plans. An ambush of them, really. Unspent from winter's reserve, these nascent leisure hours develop into a vague inertia where we sip slushy tequila or inestimable glasses of rosé, or where I park myself on a roof in Brooklyn and characterize the faraway hedge of buildings as "a view," and where I squint at my phone or the same paragraph in my book and feel indebted to the car passing below blasting *that song*.

And let's not forget the beach. Here, among 10 families and unaccustomed sounds like splashing water and seagulls squawking, we zone out, obscure the sun with shades and funny hats, nap in quick spells, signal over friends and scoot over to make room on our towels and blankets. Summer is many things, sure, but it is certainly the season for scooting over. Plans and scooting over.

As new-to-New York adults, living here without history but with the audacity to claim space, these mini migrations from rooftops to small stretches of sand, to the fire escape at sunset where we climb out and gawk and attempt the impossible—to acquire the sky's display in a few inches of touch screen—somehow constitute *spending time*.

Now picture what happens when my skin tans. *When it doesn't*. When over the years my white friends have lathered themselves with

Hawaiian Tropic and announced with a sense of crusading enterprise their plans to "sit out and bake." When they've spent long weekends at a wedding in Palm Springs or a house in Fire Island, coming back to the city with burns they bemoan only too quickly and quite airily re-evaluate: *Well, at least now I have my base layer.*

Tracing back to high school and then college, when my white friends would return from spring break, from all-inclusive resort vacations or a week at their cottage. Without fail, the most common occurrence—one that has persisted through adulthood—is this: My friend will place her arm next to mine, grow visibly thrilled, and exclaim that her skin is now darker than mine.

The things I've heard: I'm *almost* as brown as you. I'm darker than you now. I'm working real hard on this tan. We match. I'm lucky I tan easily. You *look* like you tan easily. You don't even have to work for your tan!

I'll stop after these: I'm basically black. I 15 wish I had your color. Your skin is so nice. I envy your natural glow. We could be related! I'm just trying to get as dark as possible this summer.

Since the average white person's spectrum of darkness is limited, the language of tanning is appropriative at best. An incapacity of words that disguises witlessness as admiration and co-option as obtusely worded praise. Compliments, in some cases, can so quickly feel like audits.

● ● ●

Growing up brown in mostly white circles means learning from a very young age that language is inured to prejudicial glitches. Time and again, I have concealed my amazement because the very semantics of ignorance are oddly extensive and impossible to foresee.

Close friends of mine goof. There is after all, no script. As Wesley Morris recently wrote, "For people of color, some aspect of friendship with white people involves an awareness that you could be dropped through a trapdoor of racism at any moment." Zero notice met with my own, long-harvested ability to recoup, ignore, smile, move on.

Beauty ideals, too, together with health, or at least the jargon of purported health, perpetuate the valuation of skin color—only as long as they pertain to or flatter white norms. Looking "rested," for instance, "skinnier" even, or enjoying a "healthy" glow.

What leaves me uneasy is the covetous near-pricing of quick-tanning skin, so long as the experience is short-lived or euphemistic—a certificate of travel, a token of escape, vacation, R&R, time off. Proof of having *been away*. Like the watch you forgot to leave by your hotel bedside, that you wore to the beach as you dozed off at noon and then again at 3—even that goofy tan becomes, for what it's worth, a holiday trophy. A mark, in some cases, of status.

As a kid, I accepted the compliments my 20 skin would receive from, for instance, the mother offering me orange wedges after a soccer practice or as I reapplied sunscreen at the local pool. I was, as most children are, innocent to the syntax of difference. To how some adulation obscures the act of othering because the luxury of privilege is so vast that praise conceals bias.

I have two bathing suits. Well, two that I wear. A one-piece, navy. A two-piece, black. A couple of summers ago I was gchatting with a friend as we both shopped online for new suits. Bathers, I call them. It must have been late winter or spring because, from what I remember, we were typing in errant ALL CAPS, singular to anticipating a summer that threatens to never come. *Gonna FINALLY buy a bike; can't WAIT to not wear socks; I wish we knew someone with a POOL.* At one point she linked me to an all-white one-piece bather that scooped low in the back. *I could NEVER wear this,* she typed. *But it'll look SO good on you, especially when you're tanned.*

I've come to interpret comments like my friend's consideration of my skin, how it darkens in these summer months (always first inside my elbows, as a boyfriend once pointed out to me), as plain enough. Depending on my mood, I regard or disregard them because I am aware, with both pain and considerable grit, that the world is narrowly accepting, rarely seeking significance in my many enthusiasms and instead pancaking them into platitudes. She is *this*. Looks great in *that*.

That my skin "goes well" with paler shades has never discouraged me from wearing black, which I ordinarily do. That the contrast of my skin against pastels elicits attention has perhaps made me resist those shades entirely. My brown skin, it turns out, means growing accustomed to uninvited sartorial *shoulds*: You should wear yellow. More red, coral. Mauve.

In the summer, my skin might bronze or redden and even freckle. It silhouettes my scars and turns sweat at sunset into liquid gold. But it might also, as if in defiance, preserve its paleness. It's okay, I tell myself, because it's only after a day outside, when my eyes readjust to an interior space, that I'll catch glimpses of not just myself, but my hands, my ring tan, and the length of my fingers: my Mama's. Or how my cheeks, now ruddy pink, have rounded my long face, and briefly, there he is in my reflection. My father's smile. His father's jawline. My brother's, too. It's in these moments that my skin is nobody else's and belongs to nobody's compliments. It just glows, completely on its own.

Crayola introduced Colors of the World crayons as a way of representing skin tones of people around the world.

Can you think of other instances where manufacturers have responded in order to accurately represent identities? How do these approaches connect with ideas in Durga Chew-Bose's argument?

RHETORICAL SITUATION

1. What values and beliefs do Chew-Bose and the **audience** share? How do these shared beliefs contribute to the argument?

2. How does the writer establish **credibility**? Cite specific details.

3. Explain how the **narrative distance** impacts the message.

CLAIMS AND EVIDENCE

4. What is Chew-Bose's **claim**?

5. Chew-Bose offers personal experience as **evidence**. Give an example and explain how that evidence supports her argument.

6. What other perspective does the writer offer, and how do these different **perspectives** affect her argument?

REASONING AND ORGANIZATION

7. How does the sequencing of paragraphs create a **line of reasoning** and contribute to the **unity** of the argument?

8. How does Chew-Bose **arrange** her argument? What are the **implications** of this arrangement?

LANGUAGE AND STYLE

9. How does Chew-Bose craft her **syntax** to emphasize ideas? Give an example that illustrates this syntax.

10. How does the writer choose her **diction** to achieve a **tone**? Consider the **connotations** and **denotations** of her word choice.

11. Identify where the writer uses dashes. Explain how this **syntactical** choice contributes to the relationship of ideas.

IDEAS IN AMERICAN CULTURE

12. How do individuals maintain their identity in multiple communities? What are some barriers and biases that exist in our culture that affect individuals' sense of belonging and their identity? Give an example in your community that embraces diversity and strengthens an individual's sense of belonging.

PUTTING IT ALL TOGETHER

13. How do the multiple perspectives in the text address the complexity of the issue? Consider the evidence presented and explain the implications and limitations of the argument.

IDEAS IN AMERICAN CULTURE
Justice and Civil Disobedience

How can the United States live up to its national motto, E Pluribus Unum: "Out of many, one"? Just what is an "American" anyway? These questions became increasingly complex as waves of European immigrants arrived in the late nineteenth and early twentieth centuries. The answers had evolved since J. Hector St. John Crevecoeur addressed them in 1782. Certainly, African Americans — originally brought to America as slaves — had been denied their rightful place as part of the "one." Even into the modern era, the United States failed to secure the "liberty and justice for all" promised by the Pledge of Allegiance. The struggle to achieve national ideals was difficult and even violent at times. In some cases, it required sustained civil disobedience from those who opposed unjust laws and customs.

But the central source of domestic struggle and protest remained racial injustice and inequality. In *Brown vs. Board of Education* (1954), the Supreme Court struck down state laws establishing segregated public schools. Many cite that decision as the beginning of the modern civil rights era. From 1954 to 1968, the federal government expanded voting rights, prohibited employment discrimination, and set guidelines for fair housing, among other far-reaching legislation. Equally, the most important work for justice and equal rights occurred outside the

IDEA BANK

Activism
Advocacy
Allegiance
Civil Disobedience
Demonstration
Discrimination
Dissent
Equality
Injustice
Justice
Liberty
Morality
Opposition
Patriotism
Protest
Respect
Responsibility
Right
Tolerance
Unity
Violence

hundreddays/Getty Images

▲
The image depicts the front entrance to the United States Supreme Court in Washington, D.C.

A reference to the Fourteenth Amendment to the United States Constitution, the phrase "equal justice under the law" expresses the ultimate responsibility of the Supreme Court. How does the Supreme Court fulfill this responsibility?

565

halls of government, as citizens participated in marches, boycotts, and acts of civil disobedience. For example, in 1955, civil rights icon Rosa Parks refused to obey a Montgomery, Alabama, city ordinance requiring her to give up her bus seat to a white person. Her defiance led to a year-long bus boycott that ended when the Supreme Court ordered the buses integrated in 1956.

Rosa Parks's act of defiance became iconic, but she was not alone in her protest. In 1963, Martin Luther King Jr. was arrested for disobeying an Alabama court injunction that essentially prohibited public demonstrations. He spent over a week imprisoned, using the time to write "Letter from Birmingham Jail" (p. 567), which eloquently captured the spirit of civil disobedience. The civil rights movement would reach its height in 1963 when 250,000 people attended the March on Washington for Jobs and Freedom.

In time, the United States made progress, from expanded voting rights and racial integration to the feminist movement. That increasing commitment to tolerance, justice, and pluralism (and sometimes the backlash against it) is reflected throughout the art, music, and literature of the twentieth century.

In our time, the tradition of protest and slow progress toward equality, justice, and a more perfect union continues. For example, the Black Lives Matter movement protests against racially motivated police brutality. Young activists — reacting to mass shootings and gun violence — formed March for Our Lives to lobby for stricter gun regulations. Likewise, we still see acts of civil disobedience by figures such as Edward Snowden: a CIA worker who deliberately leaked classified information from the National Security Agency. He provides his rationale in "The System" (p. 582), a chapter from his book *Permanent Record*. Others advocate for Second Amendment rights, promote religious freedoms, or participate in pro-life activism, such as the March for Life movement. Despite occupying different places on the political spectrum, most individual activists and groups are striving for equality, justice, and a more perfect union.

The twentieth- and twentieth-first-century artist Banksy makes his art a modern act of civil disobedience. His illegal street art seeks to provoke public opinion and elicit change. In this painting, he seems to both endorse anarchism and comment on it ironically while using the symbols, images, and language associated with the anarchist movement.

———

How do artists use their work as acts of justice and civil disobedience?

Bruce McGowan/Alamy Stock Photo

Letter from Birmingham Jail

Martin Luther King Jr.

Hulton-Deutsch Collection/CORBIS/Getty Images

THE TEXT IN CONTEXT

Martin Luther King Jr. (1929–1968) was born in Atlanta, Georgia. He graduated from Morehouse College and later earned a PhD from Boston University. As a Baptist minister and leader of the Southern Christian Leadership Conference, King became a driving force in the civil rights movement of the 1950s and 1960s: organizing, marching, speaking, writing, and engaging in acts of nonviolent civil disobedience. After being arrested on April 12, 1963, for defying a court order stating he could not hold protests in Birmingham, Alabama, King responded to a letter written by eight clergymen in the *Birmingham Post Herald* criticizing his activities in the Birmingham campaign.

This text includes the n-word, which we have chosen to reprint in this textbook to accurately reflect Martin Luther King Jr.'s original intent as well as the time period, culture, and racism discussed in the text. We recognize that this word has a long history as a disrespectful and deeply hurtful expression when used by white people toward Black people. Be mindful of context, both King's and yours, as you read and discuss this text.

The following is a public statement directed to Martin Luther King Jr. by eight Alabama clergymen. King's letter was a response to this statement.

We the undersigned clergymen are among those who, in January, issued "an appeal for law and order and common sense," in dealing with racial problems in Alabama. We expressed understanding that honest convictions in racial matters could properly be pursued in the courts, but urged that decisions of those courts should in the meantime be peacefully obeyed.

Since that time there has been some evidence of increased forbearance and a willingness to face facts. Responsible citizens have undertaken to work on various problems which cause racial friction and unrest. In Birmingham, recent public events have given indication that we all have opportunity for a new constructive and realistic approach to racial problems.

However, we are now confronted by a series of demonstrations by some of our Negro citizens, directed and led in part by outsiders. We recognize the natural impatience of people who feel that their hopes are slow in being realized. But we are convinced that these demonstrations are unwise and untimely.

We agree rather with certain local Negro leadership which has called for honest and open negotiation of racial issues in our area. And we believe this kind of facing of issues can best be accomplished by citizens of our own metropolitan area, white and Negro, meeting with their knowledge and experience of the local situation. All of us need to face that responsibility and find proper channels for its accomplishment.

Just as we formerly pointed out that "hatred and violence have no sanction in our religious and political traditions," we also point out that such actions as incite to hatred and violence, however technically peaceful those actions may be, have not contributed to the resolution of our local problems. We do not believe that these days of new hope are days when extreme measures are justified in Birmingham.

We commend the community as a whole, and the local news media and law enforcement officials in particular, on the calm manner in which these demonstrations have been handled. We urge the public to continue to show restraint should the demonstrations continue, and the law enforcement officials

to remain calm and continue to protect our city from violence.

We further strongly urge our own Negro community to withdraw support from these demonstrations, and to unite locally in working peacefully for a better Birmingham. When rights are consistently denied, a cause should be pressed in the courts and in negotiations among local leaders, and not in the streets. We appeal to both our white and Negro citizenry to observe the principles of law and order and common sense.

Bishop C. C. J. Carpenter, D.D., LL.D., Episcopalian Bishop of Alabama

5 Bishop Joseph A. Durick, D.D., Auxiliary Bishop, Roman Catholic Diocese of Mobile, Birmingham

Rabbi Milton L. Grafman, Temple Emanu-El, Birmingham, Alabama

Bishop Paul Hardin, Methodist Bishop of the Alabama–West Florida Conference

Bishop Nolan B. Harmon, Bishop of the North Alabama Conference of the Methodist Church

Rev. George M. Murray, D.D., LL.D., Bishop Coadjutor, Episcopal Diocese of Alabama

Rev. Edward V. Ramage, Moderator, Synod of the Alabama Presbyterian Church in the United States

Rev. Earl Stallings, Pastor, First Baptist Church, Birmingham, Alabama April 12, 1963

Letter from Birmingham Jail

16 April 1963

My Dear Fellow Clergymen:

While confined here in the Birmingham city jail, I came across your recent statement calling my present activities "unwise and untimely." Seldom do I pause to answer criticism of my work and ideas. If I sought to answer all the criticisms that cross my desk, my secretaries would have little time for anything other than such correspondence in the course of the day, and I would have no time for constructive work. But since I feel that you are men of genuine good will and that your criticisms are sincerely set forth, I want to try to answer your statement in what I hope will be patient and reasonable terms.

I think I should indicate why I am here in Birmingham, since you have been influenced by the view which argues against "outsiders coming in." I have the honor of serving as president of the Southern Christian Leadership Conference, an organization operating in every southern state, with headquarters in Atlanta, Georgia. We have some eighty five affiliated organizations across the South, and one of them is the Alabama Christian Movement for Human Rights. Frequently we share staff, educational and financial resources with our affiliates. Several months ago the affiliate here in Birmingham asked us to be on call to engage in a nonviolent direct action program if such were deemed necessary. We readily consented, and when the hour came we lived up to our promise. So I, along with several members of my staff, am here because I was invited here. I am here because I have organizational ties here.

But more basically, I am in Birmingham because injustice is here. Just as the prophets of the eighth century B.C. left their villages and carried their "thus saith the Lord" far beyond the boundaries of their home towns, and just as the Apostle Paul left his village of Tarsus and carried the gospel of Jesus Christ to the far corners of the Greco Roman world, so am I compelled to carry the gospel of freedom beyond my own home town. Like Paul, I must constantly respond to the Macedonian call for aid.

Moreover, I am cognizant of the interrelatedness of all communities and states. I cannot sit idly by in Atlanta and not be concerned about what happens in Birmingham. Injustice anywhere is a threat to justice everywhere. We are caught in an inescapable network of mutuality, tied in a single garment of destiny. Whatever affects one directly, affects all indirectly. Never again can we afford to live with the narrow, provincial "outside agitator" idea.

Anyone who lives inside the United States can never be considered an outsider anywhere within its bounds.

You deplore the demonstrations taking place in Birmingham. But your statement, I am sorry to say, fails to express a similar concern for the conditions that brought about the demonstrations. I am sure that none of you would want to rest content with the superficial kind of social analysis that deals merely with effects and does not grapple with underlying causes. It is unfortunate that demonstrations are taking place in Birmingham, but it is even more unfortunate that the city's white power structure left the Negro community with no alternative.

In any nonviolent campaign there are four basic steps: collection of the facts to determine whether injustices exist; negotiation; self purification; and direct action. We have gone through all these steps in Birmingham. There can be no gainsaying the fact that racial injustice engulfs this community. Birmingham is probably the most thoroughly segregated city in the United States. Its ugly record of brutality is widely known. Negroes have experienced grossly unjust treatment in the courts. There have been more unsolved bombings of Negro homes and churches in Birmingham than in any other city in the nation. These are the hard, brutal facts of the case. On the basis of these conditions, Negro leaders sought to negotiate with the city fathers. But the latter consistently refused to engage in good faith negotiation.

Then, last September, came the opportunity to talk with leaders of Birmingham's economic community. In the course of the negotiations, certain promises were made by the merchants—for example, to remove the stores' humiliating racial signs. On the basis of these promises, the Reverend Fred Shuttlesworth and the leaders of the Alabama Christian Movement for Human Rights agreed to a moratorium on all demonstrations. As the weeks and months went by, we realized that we were the victims of a broken promise. A few signs, briefly removed, returned; the others remained. As in so many past experiences, our hopes had been blasted, and the shadow of deep disappointment settled upon us. We had no alternative except to prepare for direct action, whereby we would present our very bodies as a means of laying our case before the conscience of the local and the national community. Mindful of the difficulties involved, we decided to undertake a process of self purification. We began a series of workshops on nonviolence, and we repeatedly asked ourselves: "Are you able to accept blows without retaliating?" "Are you able to endure the ordeal of jail?" We decided to schedule our direct action program for the Easter season, realizing that except for Christmas, this is the main shopping period of the year. Knowing that a strong economic-withdrawal program would be the by product of direct action, we felt that this would be the best time to bring pressure to bear on the merchants for the needed change.

Then it occurred to us that Birmingham's mayoral election was coming up in March, and we speedily decided to postpone action until after election day. When we discovered that the Commissioner of Public Safety, Eugene "Bull" Connor, had piled up enough votes to be in the run off, we decided again to postpone action until the day after the run off so that the demonstrations could not be used to cloud the issues. Like many others, we waited to see Mr. Connor defeated, and to this end we endured postponement after postponement. Having aided in this community need, we felt that our direct action program could be delayed no longer.

You may well ask: "Why direct action? Why sit ins, marches and so forth? Isn't

negotiation a better path?" You are quite right in calling for negotiation. Indeed, this is the very purpose of direct action. Nonviolent direct action seeks to create such a crisis and foster such a tension that a community which has constantly refused to negotiate is forced to confront the issue. It seeks so to dramatize the issue that it can no longer be ignored. My citing the creation of tension as part of the work of the nonviolent resister may sound rather shocking. But I must confess that I am not afraid of the word "tension." I have earnestly opposed violent tension, but there is a type of constructive, nonviolent tension which is necessary for growth. Just as Socrates felt that it was necessary to create a tension in the mind so that individuals could rise from the bondage of myths and half truths to the unfettered realm of creative analysis and objective appraisal, so must we see the need for nonviolent gadflies to create the kind of tension in society that will help men rise from the dark depths of prejudice and racism to the majestic heights of understanding and brotherhood. The purpose of our direct action program is to create a situation so crisis packed that it will inevitably open the door to negotiation. I therefore concur with you in your call for negotiation. Too long has our beloved Southland been bogged down in a tragic effort to live in monologue rather than dialogue.

One of the basic points in your statement is that the action that I and my associates have taken in Birmingham is untimely. Some have asked: "Why didn't you give the new city administration time to act?" The only answer that I can give to this query is that the new Birmingham administration must be prodded about as much as the outgoing one, before it will act. We are sadly mistaken if we feel that the election of Albert Boutwell as mayor will

10

bring the millennium to Birmingham. While Mr. Boutwell is a much more gentle person than Mr. Connor, they are both segregationists, dedicated to maintenance of the status quo. I have hope that Mr. Boutwell will be reasonable enough to see the futility of massive resistance to desegregation. But he will not see this without pressure from devotees of civil rights. My friends, I must say to you that we have not made a single gain in civil rights without determined legal and nonviolent pressure. Lamentably, it is an historical fact that privileged groups seldom give up their privileges voluntarily. Individuals may see the moral light and voluntarily give up their unjust posture; but, as Reinhold Niebuhr has reminded us, groups tend to be more immoral than individuals.

We know through painful experience that freedom is never voluntarily given by the oppressor; it must be demanded by the oppressed. Frankly, I have yet to engage in a direct action campaign that was "well timed" in the view of those who have not suffered unduly from the disease of segregation. For years now I have heard the word "Wait!" It rings in the ear of every Negro with piercing familiarity. This "Wait" has almost always meant "Never." We must come to see, with one of our distinguished jurists, that "justice too long delayed is justice denied."

We have waited for more than 340 years for our constitutional and God given rights. The nations of Asia and Africa are moving with jetlike speed toward gaining political independence, but we still creep at horse and buggy pace toward gaining a cup of coffee at a lunch counter. Perhaps it is easy for those who have never felt the stinging darts of segregation to say, "Wait." But when you have seen vicious mobs lynch your mothers and

fathers at will and drown your sisters and brothers at whim; when you have seen hate filled policemen curse, kick and even kill your black brothers and sisters; when you see the vast majority of your twenty million Negro brothers smothering in an airtight cage of poverty in the midst of an affluent society; when you suddenly find your tongue twisted and your speech stammering as you seek to explain to your six year old daughter why she can't go to the public amusement park that has just been advertised on television, and see tears welling up in her eyes when she is told that Funtown is closed to colored children, and see ominous clouds of inferiority beginning to form in her little mental sky, and see her beginning to distort her personality by developing an unconscious bitterness toward white people; when you have to concoct an answer for a five year old son who is asking: "Daddy, why do white people treat colored people so mean?"; when you take a cross county drive and find it necessary to sleep night after night in the uncomfortable corners of your automobile because no motel will accept you; when you are humiliated day in and day out by nagging signs reading "white" and "colored"; when your first name becomes "nigger," your middle name becomes "boy" (however old you are) and your last name becomes "John," and your wife and mother are never given the respected title "Mrs."; when you are harried by day and haunted by night by the fact that you are a Negro, living constantly at tiptoe stance, never quite knowing what to expect next, and are plagued with inner fears and outer resentments; when you are forever fighting a degenerating sense of "nobodiness"—then you will understand why we find it difficult to wait. There comes a time when the cup of endurance runs over, and men are no longer willing to be plunged into the abyss of despair. I hope, sirs, you can understand our legitimate and unavoidable impatience. You express a great deal of anxiety over our willingness to break laws. This is certainly a legitimate concern. Since we so diligently urge people to obey the Supreme Court's decision of 1954 outlawing segregation in the public schools, at first glance it may seem rather paradoxical for us consciously to break laws. One may well ask: "How can you advocate breaking some laws and obeying others?" The answer lies in the fact that there are two types of laws: just and unjust. I would be the first to advocate obeying just laws. One has not only a legal but a moral responsibility to obey just laws. Conversely, one has a moral responsibility to disobey unjust laws. I would agree with St. Augustine that "an unjust law is no law at all."

Now, what is the difference between the two? How does one determine whether a law is just or unjust? A just law is a man made code that squares with the moral law or the law of God. An unjust law is a code that is out of harmony with the moral law. To put it in the terms of St. Thomas Aquinas: An unjust law is a human law that is not rooted in eternal law and natural law. Any law that uplifts human personality is just. Any law that degrades human personality is unjust. All segregation statutes are unjust because segregation distorts the soul and damages the personality. It gives the segregator a false sense of superiority and the segregated a false sense of inferiority. Segregation, to use the terminology of the Jewish philosopher Martin Buber, substitutes an "I it" relationship for an "I thou" relationship and ends up relegating persons to the status of things. Hence segregation is not only politically, economically and sociologically unsound, it is morally wrong and sinful. Paul Tillich has said that sin is separation. Is not segregation an existential expression of man's tragic separation, his awful estrangement, his terrible sinfulness? Thus it is that I can urge men to obey the 1954 decision of the Supreme Court, for it is morally right; and I can urge them to disobey segregation ordinances, for they are morally wrong.

Let us consider a more concrete example of just and unjust laws. An unjust law is a code that a numerical or power majority group compels a minority group to obey but does not make binding on itself. This is difference made legal. By the same token, a just law is a code that a majority compels a minority to follow and that it is willing to follow itself. This is sameness made legal. Let me give another explanation. A law is unjust if it is inflicted on a minority that, as a result of being denied the right to vote, had no part in enacting or devising the law. Who can say that the legislature of Alabama which set up that state's segregation laws was democratically elected? Throughout Alabama all sorts of devious methods are used to prevent Negroes from becoming registered voters, and there are some counties in which, even though Negroes constitute a majority of the population, not a single Negro is registered. Can any law enacted under such circumstances be considered democratically structured?

Sometimes a law is just on its face and unjust in its application. For instance, I have been arrested on a charge of parading without a permit. Now, there is nothing wrong in having an ordinance which requires a permit for a parade. But such an ordinance becomes unjust when it is used to maintain segregation and to deny citizens the First-Amendment privilege of peaceful assembly and protest.

I hope you are able to see the distinction I am trying to point out. In no sense do I advocate evading or defying the law, as would the rabid segregationist. That would lead to anarchy. One who breaks an unjust law must do so openly, lovingly, and with a willingness to accept the penalty. I submit that an individual who breaks a law that conscience tells him is unjust, and who willingly accepts the penalty of imprisonment in order to arouse the conscience of the community over its injustice, is in reality expressing the highest respect for law.

Of course, there is nothing new about this kind of civil disobedience. It was evidenced sublimely in the refusal of Shadrach, Meshach and Abednego to obey the laws of Nebuchadnezzar, on the ground that a higher moral law was at stake. It was practiced superbly by the early Christians, who were willing to face hungry lions and the excruciating pain of chopping blocks rather than submit to certain unjust laws of the Roman Empire. To a degree, academic freedom is a reality today because Socrates practiced civil disobedience. In our own nation, the Boston Tea Party represented a massive act of civil disobedience.

We should never forget that everything Adolf Hitler did in Germany was "legal" and everything the Hungarian freedom fighters did in Hungary was "illegal." It was "illegal" to aid and comfort a Jew in Hitler's Germany. Even so, I am sure that, had I lived in Germany at the time, I would have aided and comforted my Jewish brothers. If today I lived in a Communist country where certain principles dear to the Christian faith are suppressed, I would openly advocate disobeying that country's antireligious laws.

I must make two honest confessions to you, my Christian and Jewish brothers. First, I must confess that over the past few years I have been gravely disappointed with the white moderate. I have almost reached the regrettable conclusion that the Negro's great stumbling block in his stride toward freedom is not the White Citizen's Counciler or the Ku Klux Klanner, but the white moderate, who is more devoted to "order" than to justice; who prefers a negative peace which is the absence of tension to a positive peace which is the presence of justice; who constantly says: "I agree with you in the goal you seek, but I cannot agree with your methods of direct action"; who paternalistically believes he can set the timetable for another man's freedom; who lives by a mythical concept of time and who constantly advises the Negro to wait for a "more convenient season." Shallow understanding from people of good will is more frustrating than absolute misunderstanding from people of ill will. Lukewarm acceptance is much more bewildering than outright rejection.

I had hoped that the white moderate would understand that law and order exist for the purpose of establishing justice and that when they fail in this purpose they become the dangerously structured dams that block the flow of social progress. I had hoped that the white moderate would understand that the present tension in the South is a necessary phase of the transition from an obnoxious negative peace, in which the Negro passively accepted his unjust plight, to a substantive and positive peace, in which all men will respect the dignity and worth of human personality. Actually, we who engage in nonviolent direct action are not the creators of tension. We merely bring to the surface the hidden tension that is already alive. We bring it out in the open, where it can be seen and dealt with. Like a boil that can never be cured so long as it is covered up but must be opened with all its ugliness to the natural medicines of air and light, injustice must be exposed, with all the tension its exposure creates, to the light of human conscience and the air of national opinion before it can be cured.

In your statement you assert that our actions, even though peaceful, must be condemned because they precipitate violence. But is this a logical assertion? Isn't this like condemning a robbed man because his possession of money precipitated the evil act of robbery? Isn't this like condemning Socrates because his unswerving commitment to truth and his philosophical inquiries precipitated the act by the misguided populace in which they made him drink hemlock? Isn't this like condemning Jesus because his unique God consciousness and never ceasing devotion to God's will precipitated the evil act of crucifixion? We must come to see that, as the federal courts have consistently affirmed, it is wrong to urge an individual to cease his efforts to gain his basic constitutional rights because the quest may precipitate violence. Society must protect the robbed and punish the robber. I had also hoped that the white moderate would reject the myth concerning time in relation to the struggle for freedom. I have just received a letter from a white brother in Texas. He writes: "All Christians know that the colored people will receive equal rights eventually, but it is possible that you are in too great a religious hurry. It has taken Christianity almost two thousand years to accomplish what it has. The teachings of Christ take time to come to earth." Such an attitude stems from a tragic misconception of time, from the strangely irrational notion that there is something in the very flow of time that will inevitably cure all ills. Actually, time itself is neutral; it can be used

either destructively or constructively. More and more I feel that the people of ill will have used time much more effectively than have the people of good will. We will have to repent in this generation not merely for the hateful words and actions of the bad people but for the appalling silence of the good people. Human progress never rolls in on wheels of inevitability; it comes through the tireless efforts of men willing to be coworkers with God, and without this hard work, time itself becomes an ally of the forces of social stagnation. We must use time creatively, in the knowledge that the time is always ripe to do right. Now is the time to make real the promise of democracy and transform our pending national elegy into a creative psalm of brotherhood. Now is the time to lift our national policy from the quicksand of racial injustice to the solid rock of human dignity.

You speak of our activity in Birmingham as extreme. At first I was rather disappointed that fellow clergymen would see my nonviolent efforts as those of an extremist. I began thinking about the fact that I stand in the middle of two opposing forces in the Negro community. One is a force of complacency, made up in part of Negroes who, as a result of long years of oppression, are so drained of self respect and a sense of "somebodiness" that they have adjusted to segregation; and in part of a few middle-class Negroes who, because of a degree of academic and economic security and because in some ways they profit by segregation, have become insensitive to the problems of the masses. The other force is one of bitterness and hatred, and it comes perilously close to advocating violence. It is expressed in the various black nationalist groups that are springing up across the nation, the largest and best known being Elijah

Muhammad's Muslim movement. Nourished by the Negro's frustration over the continued existence of racial discrimination, this movement is made up of people who have lost faith in America, who have absolutely repudiated Christianity, and who have concluded that the white man is an incorrigible "devil."

I have tried to stand between these two forces, saying that we need emulate neither the "do nothingism" of the complacent nor the hatred and despair of the black nationalist. For there is the more excellent way of love and nonviolent protest. I am grateful to God that, through the influence of the Negro church, the way of nonviolence became an integral part of our struggle. If this philosophy had not emerged, by now many streets of the South would, I am convinced, be flowing with blood. And I am further convinced that if our white brothers dismiss as "rabble rousers" and "outside agitators" those of us who employ nonviolent direct action, and if they refuse to support our nonviolent efforts, millions of Negroes will, out of frustration and despair, seek solace and security in black nationalist ideologies—a development that would inevitably lead to a frightening racial nightmare.

Oppressed people cannot remain oppressed forever. The yearning for freedom eventually manifests itself, and that is what has happened to the American Negro. Something within has reminded him of his birthright of freedom, and something without has reminded him that it can be gained. Consciously or unconsciously, he has been caught up by the Zeitgeist, and with his black brothers of Africa and his brown and yellow brothers of Asia, South America and the Caribbean, the United States Negro is moving with a sense of great urgency toward the promised land of racial justice. If one recognizes this vital urge that has engulfed the Negro community, one should readily understand why public demonstrations are taking place. The Negro has many pent up resentments and latent frustrations, and he must release them. So let him march; let him make prayer pilgrimages to the city hall; let him go on freedom rides—and try to understand why he must do so. If his repressed emotions are not released in nonviolent ways, they will seek expression through violence; this is not a threat but a fact of history. So I have not said to my people: "Get rid of your discontent." Rather, I have tried to say that this normal and healthy discontent can be channeled into the creative outlet of nonviolent direct action. And now this approach is being termed extremist. But though I was initially disappointed at being categorized as an extremist, as I continued to think about the matter I gradually gained a measure of satisfaction from the label. Was not Jesus an extremist for love: "Love your enemies, bless them that curse you, do good to them that hate you, and pray for them which despitefully use you, and persecute you." Was not Amos an extremist for justice: "Let justice roll down like waters and righteousness like an ever flowing stream." Was not Paul an extremist for the Christian gospel: "I bear in my body the marks of the Lord Jesus." Was not Martin Luther an extremist: "Here I stand; I cannot do otherwise, so help me God." And John Bunyan: "I will stay in jail to the end of my days before I make a butchery of my conscience." And Abraham Lincoln: "This nation cannot survive half slave and half free." And Thomas Jefferson: "We hold these truths to be self evident, that all men are created equal. . . ." So the question is not whether we will be extremists, but what kind

25

of extremists we will be. Will we be extremists for hate or for love? Will we be extremists for the preservation of injustice or for the extension of justice? In that dramatic scene on Calvary's hill three men were crucified. We must never forget that all three were crucified for the same crime—the crime of extremism. Two were extremists for immorality, and thus fell below their environment. The other, Jesus Christ, was an extremist for love, truth and goodness, and thereby rose above his environment. Perhaps the South, the nation and the world are in dire need of creative extremists.

I had hoped that the white moderate would see this need. Perhaps I was too optimistic; perhaps I expected too much. I suppose I should have realized that few members of the oppressor race can understand the deep groans and passionate yearnings of the oppressed race, and still fewer have the vision to see that injustice must be rooted out by strong, persistent and determined action. I am thankful, however, that some of our white brothers in the South have grasped the meaning of this social revolution and committed themselves to it. They are still all too few in quantity, but they are big in quality. Some—such as Ralph McGill, Lillian Smith, Harry Golden, James McBride Dabbs, Ann Braden and Sarah Patton Boyle—have written about our struggle in eloquent and prophetic terms. Others have marched with us down nameless streets of the South. They have languished in filthy, roach infested jails, suffering the abuse and brutality of policemen who view them as "dirty nigger-lovers." Unlike so many of their moderate brothers and sisters, they have recognized the urgency of the moment and sensed the need for powerful "action" antidotes to combat the disease of segregation. Let me take note of my other major disappointment. I have been so greatly disappointed with the white church and its leadership. Of course, there are some notable exceptions. I am not unmindful of the fact that each of you has taken some significant stands on this issue. I commend you, Reverend Stallings, for your Christian stand on this past Sunday, in welcoming Negroes to your worship service on a nonsegregated basis. I commend the Catholic leaders of this state for integrating Spring Hill College several years ago.

But despite these notable exceptions, I must honestly reiterate that I have been disappointed with the church. I do not say this as one of those negative critics who can always find something wrong with the church. I say this as a minister of the gospel, who loves the church; who was nurtured in its bosom; who has been sustained by its spiritual blessings and who will remain true to it as long as the cord of life shall lengthen.

When I was suddenly catapulted into the leadership of the bus protest in Montgomery, Alabama, a few years ago, I felt we would be supported by the white church. I felt that the white ministers, priests and rabbis of the South would be among our strongest allies. Instead, some have been outright opponents, refusing to understand the freedom movement and misrepresenting its leaders; all too many others have been more cautious than courageous and have remained silent behind the anesthetizing security of stained glass windows.

In spite of my shattered dreams, I came to Birmingham with the hope that the white religious leadership of this community would see the justice of our cause and, with deep moral concern, would serve as the channel through which our just grievances could reach the power structure. I had hoped that each of you would understand. But again I have been disappointed.

I have heard numerous southern religious leaders admonish their worshipers to comply with a desegregation decision because it is the law, but I have longed to hear white ministers declare: "Follow this decree because integration is morally right and because the Negro is your brother." In the midst of blatant injustices inflicted upon the Negro, I have watched white churchmen stand on the sideline and mouth pious irrelevancies and sanctimonious trivialities. In the midst of a mighty struggle to rid our nation of racial and economic injustice, I have heard many ministers say: "Those are social issues, with which the gospel has no real concern." And I have watched many churches commit themselves to a completely other worldly religion which makes a strange, un-Biblical distinction between body and soul, between the sacred and the secular.

I have traveled the length and breadth of Alabama, Mississippi and all the other southern states. On sweltering summer days and crisp autumn mornings I have looked at the South's beautiful churches with their lofty spires pointing heavenward. I have beheld the impressive outlines of her massive religious education buildings. Over and over I have found myself asking: "What kind of people worship here? Who is their God? Where were their voices when the lips of Governor Barnett dripped with words of interposition and nullification? Where were they when Governor Wallace gave a clarion call for defiance and hatred? Where were their voices of support when bruised and weary Negro men and women decided to rise from the dark dungeons of complacency to the bright hills of creative protest?"

Yes, these questions are still in my mind. In deep disappointment I have wept over the laxity of the church. But be assured that my tears have been tears of love. There can be no deep disappointment where there is not deep love. Yes, I love the church. How could I do otherwise? I am in the rather unique position of being the son, the grandson and the great grandson of preachers. Yes, I see the church as the body of Christ. But, oh! How we have blemished and scarred that body through social neglect and through fear of being nonconformists.

There was a time when the church was very powerful—in the time when the early Christians rejoiced at being deemed worthy to suffer for what they believed. In those days the church was not merely a thermometer that recorded the ideas and principles of popular opinion; it was a thermostat that transformed the mores of society. Whenever the early Christians entered a town, the people in power became disturbed and immediately sought to convict the Christians for being "disturbers of the peace" and "outside agitators." But the Christians pressed on, in the conviction that they were "a colony of heaven," called to obey God rather than man. Small in number, they were big in commitment. They were too God-intoxicated to be "astronomically intimidated." By their effort and example they brought an end to such ancient evils as infanticide and gladiatorial contests. Things are different now. So often the contemporary church is a weak, ineffectual voice with an uncertain sound. So often it is an archdefender of the status quo. Far from being disturbed by the presence of the church, the power structure of the average community is consoled by the church's silent—and often even vocal—sanction of things as they are.

But the judgment of God is upon the church as never before. If today's church does not recapture the sacrificial spirit of the early church, it will lose its authenticity, forfeit the loyalty of millions, and be dismissed as an irrelevant social club with no meaning for the twentieth century. Every day I meet young people whose disappointment with the church has turned into outright disgust.

Perhaps I have once again been too optimistic. Is organized religion too inextricably bound to the status quo to save our nation and the world? Perhaps I must turn my faith to the inner spiritual church, the church within the church, as the true ekklesia and the hope of the world. But again I am thankful to God that some noble souls from the ranks of organized religion have broken loose from the paralyzing chains of conformity and joined us as active partners in the struggle for freedom. They have left their secure congregations and walked the streets of Albany, Georgia, with us. They have gone down the highways of the South on tortuous rides for freedom. Yes, they have gone to jail with us. Some have been dismissed from their churches, have lost the support of their bishops and fellow ministers. But they have acted in the faith that right defeated is stronger than evil triumphant. Their witness has been the spiritual salt that has preserved the true meaning of the gospel in these troubled times. They have carved a tunnel of hope through the dark mountain of disappointment. I hope the church as a whole will meet the challenge of this decisive hour. But even if the church does not come to the aid of justice, I have no despair about the future. I have no fear about the outcome of our struggle in Birmingham, even if our motives are at present misunderstood. We will reach the goal of freedom in Birmingham and all

35

over the nation, because the goal of America is freedom. Abused and scorned though we may be, our destiny is tied up with America's destiny. Before the pilgrims landed at Plymouth, we were here. Before the pen of Jefferson etched the majestic words of the Declaration of Independence across the pages of history, we were here. For more than two centuries our forebears labored in this country without wages; they made cotton king; they built the homes of their masters while suffering gross injustice and shameful humiliation—and yet out of a bottomless vitality they continued to thrive and develop. If the inexpressible cruelties of slavery could not stop us, the opposition we now face will surely fail. We will win our freedom because the sacred heritage of our nation and the eternal will of God are embodied in our echoing demands. Before closing I feel impelled to mention one other point in your statement that has troubled me profoundly. You warmly commended the Birmingham police force for keeping "order" and "preventing violence." I doubt that you would have so warmly commended the police force if you had seen its dogs sinking their teeth into unarmed, nonviolent Negroes. I doubt that you would so quickly commend the policemen if you were to observe their ugly and inhumane treatment of Negroes here in the city jail; if you were to watch them push and curse old Negro women and young Negro girls; if you were to see them slap and kick old Negro men and young boys; if you were to observe them, as they did on two occasions, refuse to give us food because we wanted to sing our grace together. I cannot join you in your praise of the Birmingham police department.

It is true that the police have exercised a degree of discipline in handling the demonstrators. In this sense they have conducted themselves rather "nonviolently" in public. But for what purpose? To preserve the evil system of segregation. Over the past few years I have consistently preached that nonviolence demands that the means we use must be as pure as the ends we seek. I have tried to make clear that it is wrong to use immoral means to attain moral ends. But now I must affirm that it is just as wrong, or perhaps even more so, to use moral means to preserve immoral ends. Perhaps Mr. Connor and his policemen have been rather nonviolent in public, as was Chief Pritchett in Albany, Georgia, but they have used the moral means of nonviolence to maintain the immoral end of racial injustice. As T. S. Eliot has said: "The last temptation is the greatest treason: To do the right deed for the wrong reason."

I wish you had commended the Negro sit inners and demonstrators of Birmingham for their sublime courage, their willingness to suffer and their amazing discipline in the midst of great provocation. One day the South will recognize its real heroes. They will be the James Merediths, with the noble sense of purpose that enables them to face jeering and hostile mobs, and with the agonizing loneliness that characterizes the life of the pioneer. They will be old, oppressed, battered Negro women, symbolized in a seventy two year old woman in Montgomery, Alabama, who rose up with a sense of dignity and with her people decided not to ride segregated buses, and who responded with ungrammatical profundity to one who inquired about her weariness: "My feets is tired, but my soul is at rest." They will be the young high school and college students, the young ministers of the gospel and a host of their elders, courageously and nonviolently sitting

in at lunch counters and willingly going to jail for conscience' sake. One day the South will know that when these disinherited children of God sat down at lunch counters, they were in reality standing up for what is best in the American dream and for the most sacred values in our Judaeo Christian heritage, thereby bringing our nation back to those great wells of democracy which were dug deep by the founding fathers in their formulation of the Constitution and the Declaration of Independence.

Never before have I written so long a letter. I'm afraid it is much too long to take your precious time. I can assure you that it would have been much shorter if I had been writing from a comfortable desk, but what else can one do when he is alone in a narrow jail cell, other than write long letters, think long thoughts and pray long prayers?

If I have said anything in this letter that overstates the truth and indicates an unreasonable impatience, I beg you to forgive me. If I have said anything that understates the truth and indicates my having a patience that allows me to settle for anything less than brotherhood, I beg God to forgive me.

I hope this letter finds you strong in the faith. I also hope that circumstances will soon make it possible for me to meet each of you, not as an integrationist or a civil-rights leader but as a fellow clergyman and a Christian brother. Let us all hope that the dark clouds of racial prejudice will soon pass away and the deep fog of misunderstanding will be lifted from our fear drenched communities, and in some not too distant tomorrow the radiant stars of love and brotherhood will shine over our great nation with all their scintillating beauty.

Yours for the cause of Peace and Brotherhood, Martin Luther King Jr.

A protestor against police brutality in Portland, Oregon, in 2020 waves a flag. While the overwhelming number of protests in the United States are peaceful, some are not.

Is violence or destruction ever justified when engaging in civil disobedience? In your view, is violence and destruction more effective in bringing about change than nonviolent resistance or less effective? Why?

ANKUR DHOLAKIA/Getty Images

RHETORICAL SITUATION

1. What is the **context** of King's argument? How does the immediacy of the context contribute to King's position?

2. How does King attempt to relate to his **audience's** emotions and values? Find one example in the introduction and one in the conclusion. How does each of these **appeals** strengthen his argument?

3. King has multiple **purposes** in writing this argument, as well as multiple **audiences**. What are two or three different purposes? How does he address different audiences? Find a specific example and explain.

CLAIMS AND EVIDENCE

4. What is King's primary **claim**?

5. How does King's **evidence** both establish his credibility and appeal to his audience's emotions?

6. What **sources of evidence** does King include? Choose two sources and explain how they contribute to his argument.

7. King **qualifies** his claims throughout the letter. He also makes **concessions**. Find one qualification and one concession. How does each strengthen his argument?

8. King uses **analogies** to explain difficult concepts. Choose one or two examples. Then explain how they support his message.

REASONING AND ORGANIZATION

9. What specific **reasons** make up King's **line of reasoning**? How do they help **unify** his argument?

10. How is King's argument an example of **persuasion**? What is his **call to action**?

11. How does King **arrange** the ideas within his argument? How does his choice of arrangement contribute to his purpose?

LANGUAGE AND STYLE

12. How does the writer's precise **diction** affect the **tone** of the text? Give an example of both **connotative** and **denotative** diction that contribute to King's tone.

13. How do King's **transitional** words and phrases connect — and establish relationships between — the ideas in his argument? Give an example and explain.

14. Give an example of balanced **syntax** within the text. What syntactical structure does King use to achieve that balance? How does that syntactical choice affect the argument?

IDEAS IN AMERICAN CULTURE

15. Some of King's more moderate allies ask him to be more patient and wait for justice. How does he reframe the idea of "waiting" to justify civil disobedience to unjust laws? Does King's argument still apply to contemporary problems? Give a current example of civil disobedience and discuss the reasons for the protest.

PUTTING IT ALL TOGETHER

16. Discuss how the multiple purposes in the text work to present multiple perspectives. How do these different purposes unite to create a compelling message?

The System

Edward Snowden

Gary Miller/Getty Images

THE TEXT IN CONTEXT

Originally from Elizabeth City, North Carolina, Edward Snowden (b. 1983) enlisted in the U.S. Army in 2004 to fight in the Iraq War but received a medical discharge after a training injury later that year. In 2006, he accepted a position with the Global Communications Division of the CIA, where he was responsible for computer networking security. He later became a subcontractor for companies such as Dell and Booz Allen Hamilton. While assigned as a system administrator at the National Security Agency over the next several years, Snowden became increasingly alarmed by the vast surveillance system built by the intelligence services of the United States and its allies. Snowden claims that he pursued official channels with his concerns. But when his concerns were dismissed, he leaked hundreds of thousands of highly classified documents. Charged with espionage by the U.S. Justice Department, Snowden traveled to Russia, which has granted him permanent residency. In this chapter from his autobiography *Permanent Record* (2019), Snowden explains how his career taught him the intricacies of intelligence work — and why he became a self-described "whistleblower."

At the age of 22, when I entered the American intelligence community, I didn't have any politics. Instead, like most young people, I had solid convictions that I refused to accept weren't truly mine but rather a contradictory cluster of inherited principles. My mind was a mash-up of the values I was raised with and the ideals I encountered online.

It took me until my late twenties to finally understand that so much of what I believed, or of what I thought I believed, was just youthful imprinting. We learn to speak by imitating the speech of the adults around us, and in the process of that learning we wind up also imitating their opinions, until we've deluded ourselves into thinking that the words we're using are our own.

My parents were, if not dismissive of politics in general, then certainly dismissive of politicians. To be sure, this dismissal had little in common with the disaffection of nonvoters or partisan disdain. Rather, it was a certain bemused detachment particular to their class, which nobler ages have called the federal civil service or the public sector, but which our own time tends to refer to as the deep state or the shadow government.

None of those epithets, however, really captures what it is: a class of career officials (incidentally, perhaps one of the last functional middle classes in American life) who—nonelected and nonappointed—serve or work in government, either at one of the independent agencies (from the CIA and NSA to the IRS, the FCC, and so on) or at one of the executive departments (State, Treasury, Defense, Justice, and the like).

These were my parents, these were my people: a nearly 3-million-strong professional government workforce dedicated to assisting the amateurs chosen by the electorate, and appointed by the elected, in fulfilling their political duties—or, in the words of the oath, in faithfully executing their offices. These civil servants, who stay in their positions even as administrations come and go, work as diligently under Republicans as under Democrats because they ultimately work for the government itself, providing core continuity and stability of rule.

These were also the people who, when their country went to war, answered the call. That's what I had done after 9/11, and I found that the patriotism my parents had taught me was easily converted into nationalist fervor. For a time, especially in my run-up to joining the Army, my sense of the world came to resemble the duality of the least sophisticated videogames, where good and evil are clearly defined and unquestionable.

However, once I returned from the Army and rededicated myself to computing, I gradually came to regret my martial fantasies. The more I developed my abilities, the more I matured and realized that the technology of communications had a chance of succeeding where the technology of violence had failed. Democracy could never be imposed at the point of a gun, but perhaps it could be sown by the spread of silicon and fiber.

In the early 2000s the internet was still just barely out of its formative period, and, to my mind at least, it offered a more authentic and complete incarnation of American ideals than even America itself. A place where everyone was equal? Check. A place dedicated to life, liberty, and the pursuit of happiness? Check, check, check.

It helped that nearly all of the major founding documents of internet culture framed it in terms reminiscent of American history: Here was this wild, open new frontier that belonged to anyone bold enough to settle it, swiftly becoming colonized by governments and corporate interests that were seeking to regulate it for power and profit. The large companies that were charging large fees—for hardware, for software, for the long-distance phone calls that you needed back then to get online, and for knowledge itself, which was humanity's common inheritance and so, by all rights, should have been available for free—were irresistible contemporary avatars of the British, whose harsh taxation ignited the fervor for independence.

This revolution wasn't happening in history 10 textbooks but now, in my generation, and any of us could be part of it solely by dint of our abilities. This was thrilling—to participate in the founding of a new society, one based not on where we were born or how we grew up or our popularity at school but on our knowledge and technological ability.

In school, I'd had to memorize the preamble to the US Constitution: Now its words were lodged in my memory alongside John Perry Barlow's "A Declaration of the Independence of Cyberspace," which employed the same self-evident, self-elect plural pronoun: "We are creating a world that all may enter without privilege or prejudice accorded by race, economic power, military force, or station of birth. We are creating a world where anyone, anywhere may express his or her beliefs, no matter how singular, without fear of being coerced into silence or conformity."

This technological meritocracy was certainly empowering, but it could also be humbling, as I came to understand when I first went to work in the intelligence community. The decentralization of the internet merely emphasized the decentralization of computing expertise. I might have been the top computer person in my family, or in my Beltway neighborhood, but to work for the IC meant testing my skills against everyone in the country and the world. The internet showed me the sheer quantity and variety of talent that existed, and made clear that to flourish I had to specialize.

There were a few different careers available to me as a technologist. I could have become a software developer, or, as the job is more commonly called, a programmer, writing the code that makes computers work. Alternatively, I could have become a hardware or network specialist, setting up the servers in their racks and running the wires, weaving the massive fabric that connects every computer, every device, and every file.

Computers and computer programs were interesting to me, and so were the networks that linked them together. But I was most intrigued by their total functioning at a deeper level of abstraction, not as individual components but as an overarching system.

I thought about this a lot while I was driving, to and from Lindsay's house and to and from community college. Car time has always been thinking time for me, and commutes are long on the crowded Beltway. To be a software developer or programmer was to run the rest stops off the exits and to make sure that all the fast food and gas station franchises accorded with each other and with user expectations; to be a hardware specialist was to

lay the infrastructure, to grade and pave the roads themselves; while to be a network specialist was to be responsible for traffic control, manipulating signs and lights to safely route the time-crunched hordes to their proper destinations.

To get into systems, however, was to be an urban planner, to take all of the components available and ensure their interaction to maximum effect. It was, pure and simple, like getting paid to play God, or at least a tinpot dictator.

There are two main ways to be a systems guy. One is that you take possession of the whole of an existing system and maintain it, gradually making it more efficient and fixing it when it breaks. That position is called a systems administrator, or sysadmin. The second is that you analyze a problem, such as how to store data or how to search across databases, and solve it by engineering a solution from a combination of existing components or by inventing entirely new ones.

This position, the most prestigious, is called a systems engineer. I eventually would do both of these, working my way into administration and from there into engineering, oblivious throughout about how this intense engagement with the deepest levels of integration of computing technology was exerting an influence on my political convictions.

I'll try not to be too abstract here, but I want you to imagine a system. It doesn't matter what system: It can be a computer system, a legal system, or even a system of government. Remember, a system is just a bunch of parts that function together as a whole, which most people are only reminded of when something breaks. It's one of the great chastening facts of working with systems that the part of a system that malfunctions is almost never the part in which you notice the malfunction.

15

To find what caused the system to collapse, you have to start from the point where you spotted the problem and trace it logically through all of the system's components.

Because systems work according to instructions, or rules, such an analysis is ultimately a search for which rules failed, how, and why—an attempt to identify the specific points where the intention of a rule was not adequately expressed by its formulation or application. Did the system fail because something was not communicated or because someone abused the system by accessing a resource they weren't allowed to or by accessing a resource they were allowed to but using it exploitatively? Was the job of one component stopped or impeded by another? Did one program or computer or group of people take over more than their fair share of the system?

Over the course of my career, it became increasingly difficult for me to ask these questions about the technologies I was responsible for and not about my country. And it became increasingly frustrating to me that I was able to repair the former but not the latter. I ended my time in intelligence convinced that my country's operating system—its government—had decided that it functioned best when broken.

AP Photo/Timothy D. Easley

▲

In 2015, elected Kentucky court clerk Kim Davis was jailed for refusing to issue same-sex marriage licenses, a decision she made because of her religious beliefs.

How does the image depict the conviction of an individual who chooses to follow her conscience rather than obey the law? What can we infer from the reactions of the other people in the picture? What is being contrasted, and what does the image imply about the outcome of the action?

RHETORICAL SITUATION

1. How does Snowden begin this argument? Explain how the **introduction** establishes the relationship between the writer and the **audience**.

2. How does Snowden's narrative distance build his **credibility**? Find an example in the text that illustrates this.

3. How does Snowden's **context** place boundaries or limitations on his claim? Explain those boundaries.

CLAIMS AND EVIDENCE

4. What kind of **evidence** does Snowden use? Does he provide sufficient evidence for his **claim**? Why or why not?

5. How does Snowden **arrange** the **evidence** in his argument? What effect does this arrangement have on his **message**?

6. Give an example of Snowden **qualifying** his argument in the text. What **perspective** does the qualification suggest?

REASONING AND ORGANIZATION

7. Snowden uses many **comparisons** throughout the text. Give two examples of comparison. Then explain how the comparison contributes to the overall argument.

8. Does Snowden use **induction** or **deduction**? How might this choice affect the audience's reception of the argument?

LANGUAGE AND STYLE

9. How does Snowden's precise **diction** affect how the audience understands the writer's position?

10. Find two **syntactical** choices (e.g., a sentence that balances an idea, indicates a relationship, or provides more details). Then explain how the sentence functions to develop Snowden's argument.

11. Find a parenthesis or a dash in the text. Then explain how the punctuation contributes to the writer's **message**.

IDEAS IN AMERICAN CULTURE

12. Snowden is probably the most famous whistleblower in recent history. How does his account offer insight into his choices? Have you ever been in a position to tell the truth in the name of justice but feared the consequences? Can you think of other examples in history?

PUTTING IT ALL TOGETHER

13. When this chapter ran as an article in *Wired* magazine it was given the title "Why I Became a Whistleblower." Does Snowden's text answer that title in a satisfying way? Look closely at Snowden's organization, as well as his carefully arranged evidence. Is his conclusion effective and convincing? Do his reasons justify his claim? Explain.

COMPOSITION WORKSHOP

Writing an Evaluation Argument Using Comparison/Contrast

In previous units, you have written a personal narrative, a persuasive argument, and four types of expository arguments: process, definition, cause-effect, and classification. We will now focus on evaluation arguments. These arguments require you to make a recommendation, propose a solution, or draw a conclusion.

You are already familiar with evaluation arguments, as we all use them in our daily lives to make choices. Now, as you near the end of high school, you will face many key decisions about your future. For example, you may need to decide on a place to live, a job to pursue, a college to attend, a course of study to follow for your chosen career path, or any number of decisions. You will evaluate these options based on your goals and preferences. But to make an informed choice, you must establish meaningful categories of comparison. You must also state a thesis and develop your argument with a line of reasoning.

In this workshop, you will draft an evaluation argument using compare and contrast, which is the most common pattern of organization for evaluation arguments. You will establish your line of reasoning through meaningful categories of comparison. After analyzing your two subjects, you will come to a conclusion or make a recommendation.

KEY POINT

When used in evaluation arguments, comparison and contrast are organized subject by subject or category by category.

Climate Activists Must Fight for System Change and Individual Change

Riley Stevenson

The following argument was written by high school student Riley Stevenson. Stevenson's essay appears on the website *Students 4 Social Change*, an online platform for students to express their opinions on current issues.

Often, when one first considers making a change and joining the growing environmental movement, one's first instinct is to consider their own carbon footprint, choices, and lifestyle. This train of thought can lead to a decrease in plastic usage, eating less meat, or choosing to travel differently. Although this kind of lifestyle change is important, it is more important to fight for system change, which

comparison between individual and systematic action

qualifying language acknowledges the benefits of individual action thesis: importance of systematic change

accommodates everyone and makes the world a better place. Activists must work against oppressive systems in our society, such as capitalism and other ideas that prioritize the few over the many and disenfranchise marginalized communities.

1st category: individual <u>food choices</u> versus industry changes

Your Diet Won't Save the Planet

One of the first areas often considered in lessening one's carbon footprint is on the topic of food. Eating less meat, shortening the distance between production and consumption of food, and supporting sustainable growers are all important steps to take, but they do not address the underlying issues of the climate crisis and have only a minimal effect on the issue as a whole. Underlying systems such as capitalism, which value wealth and resources over human lives and the environment, harms both marginalized communities and the planet. Choosing not to eat red meat, while it may affect local supply chains, does not help solve this intersectional issue.

qualifying language emphasizes the claim

In addition, research shows that new sustainable methods for raising cattle will solve many of the emissions-related issues with red meat consumption, and other solutions similarly seek to solve these issues as demand for food grows with our population. Instead, individuals should work to join movements and call for systematic change on a larger level, simultaneously creating more positive change and including more communities in the fight for justice.

2nd category of comparison: costly <u>lifestyle choices</u> versus true accountability

Mentality versus Habits

Another reason that individual lifestyle change is not the best way to solve the climate crisis is because one's habits do not always reflect their mentality or motivations. While it is important for people of privilege to do everything possible to lessen their own impact, if the motivations for these actions are non-inclusive, they are not meaningful. For example, buying expensive, sustainable products in order to lower one's plastic waste can be helpful in achieving this goal, but also plays into harmful capitalism. For example, not everyone can afford fancy new solutions, and by propping these up as the answer to all problems, many people who cannot afford these luxuries are excluded from the movement and doing meaningful work.

subordinate clause offers a small concession, and then a rebuttal

evidence illustrates the writer's claim

pronoun "we" connects the writer to the audience and the issue

Instead, we must work to dismantle these systems and instead rethink our consumption in a way that includes the perspectives of marginalized communities most affected by the action of the privileged, not just the opinions of those already in power. By playing into schemes or incentives created by polluting companies, people can similarly be sucked into the facade of greenwashing, in which companies try to appear more sustainable and thoughtful than they actually are. These companies, despite claims of change and cooperation, are far more responsible for the climate crisis than individuals, and need to be held accountable for their actions.

More Powerful Together

Instead of dividing ourselves into isolated pods of individuals practicing sustainable methods—a phenomenon some say is caused by neoliberalism, such as Canadian journalist Martin Lukacs, it is important to see ourselves as a community working for change together. Individuals should look for organizations to join and work with other people on this issue, such as the Sunrise movement, local 350.org chapters, and other groups dedicated to dismantling our current systems and working for a better future for all. It is important to connect with these groups that are dedicated to connecting activists nationwide and globally, in turn allowing for the sharing of stories and struggles, creating a more inclusive movement.

3rd category of comparison: isolation versus association

evidence provides further details of organizations

How to Fight Oppressive Systems

On an individual and group level, there are many ways to approach the overwhelming climate crisis from a system-dismantling lens. Engaging in mass protests, boycotting harmful brands, and voting for climate-forward candidates are all important ways to work to reverse current standards. Individuals should be banding together in their communities to stop harmful local projects by polluting companies, like this example from 2014 in which residents of South Portland, Maine successfully blocked a tar sands operation from their city. Wins on a local, statewide, and nationwide are all important, so long as they are done with the intention of helping the many, not just the few.

4th category of comparison: solutions

evidence: concrete example of a successful campaign

In dismantling systems, it is also important to look inwardly and see what things one can give up and work against in their own lives. Buying less, for example, or purchasing secondhand items, not because you believe that you alone can stop the climate crisis but as a way to refute capitalism, is a worthwhile step in considering one's lifestyle and how it affects others.

qualification emphasizes the importance of individual efforts as well

All Actions Are Important

At the end of the day, any actions someone takes to address the climate crisis are important and worthwhile. Wealthy individuals have even more work to do than others to actively lessen their impact, as they are more likely to have higher carbon footprints

conclusion: proposes solutions and emphasizes benefits of systematic change

than lower-income individuals. These individuals should also join movements centering marginalized voices, and become involved in these system-dismantling actions, especially as they are most likely to benefit from those systems. These six actions, which include reducing personal emissions *and* demanding sustainable practices from elected officials, are all worthwhile in their own right. However, it is important that activists don't quit after making one of these changes, and consider whether their actions are inclusive and helpful for all. To create an inclusive movement, it is important to include these different approaches and make sure that all can engage in the important work of dismantling unjust and polluting systems in order to create a more just world.

 ## YOUR ASSIGNMENT

Your school's career and college counselor is assembling a handbook for next year's junior class. You have been asked to write a feature that evaluates two possible options for high school graduates. Narrow your focus to two choices (your subjects) and then determine important categories of comparison that will contribute to your purpose for making the evaluation. Keep in mind that the categories of comparison should be the same for both subjects. Write an evaluation argument in which you compare and contrast the subjects based on these meaningful categories of comparison. In your argument, convey your perspective on the subjects and either discuss the implications of a choice or make a recommendation to your audience.

Your comparison-contrast argument should include:

- A thesis statement that makes a claim (unifying idea + perspective)
- A line of reasoning organized by categories of comparison to justify your claim
- Evidence to support your reasoning, qualify your argument, and illustrate the complexity of the subject
- Strategies — especially syntactical choices — that achieve a desired effect

Potential Subjects:

- College choices (private/public, in state/out of state, technical/liberal arts, university/community)
- Living arrangements (alone/roommates, dorm/apartment/home)
- Military branches (army/navy/air force/marines/coast guard)
- Full-time or part-time work or study
- Online or in-person school

RHETORICAL SITUATION **Introducing and Concluding an Argument**

AP **Enduring Understanding (RHS-1)**

Individuals write within a particular situation and make strategic writing choices based on that situation.

You make hundreds of decisions and judgments each day of your life. Most of the time, you are unaware of your mental processes as you decide which way to walk to class, where to sit when you arrive, what to eat for lunch, what to do after school. But some choices require a more conscious, deliberative process: what classes to take next year, what activities to participate in, or whether to get a part-time job.

Similarly, much of our casual, political, philosophical, and scholarly conversations revolve around the relative assessment of different ideas, policies, and people.

- Who is the greatest college football coach of all time?
- Which economic policies are best for our country?
- Is civil disobedience more effective than lawful protests?
- Which playwright made the biggest impact on twentieth-century American theater?

For all of these questions, you would analyze each subject using categories of comparison and then make a final evaluation based on your purpose. Your criteria and your conclusion would depend on context: your purpose, your situation, your values. In other words, other writers exploring the same question might analyze the subjects using different criteria for comparison based on their own perspectives.

Your goal is to convince the audience of your perspective. Therefore, when you develop your comparison-and-contrast argument, you must first establish context for the comparison. That context allows the audience to understand the reasons for your comparison. Remember: you should avoid simply listing similarities and differences. Instead, try to convey the complexity of each subject and acknowledge perspectives that may be different from your own. By presenting the complexities of the argument, you not only convey your perspective on the subjects but also establish yourself as knowledgeable, trustworthy, and fair to your audience. Look closely at the following example of a debatable subject:

- **Subject:** *Where is the best place to view a blockbuster film?*
- **Subjects of comparison:** *Home theater/movie theater*
- **Purpose of the comparison:** *To examine the future of the movie theater experience for viewers*
- **Context for the comparison:** *Movie theaters shut down for a time; decline in theater attendance in recent years*
- **Audience:** *General movie audiences*
- **Unifying idea:** *Aesthetic experience*
- **Perspective:** *Movie theaters offer not only a superior audiovisual experience but also, more importantly, create a sense of community for audience members*

Introductions

In Unit 5, we looked at different types of hooks that you can use in introductions. For a comparison-contrast argument, you can engage the audience with any of these techniques (e.g., quotations, anecdotes, questions, statistics, and surprising or paradoxical statements). Your hook must engage your reader, but it also must be clearly related to your purpose. After beginning the introduction with your hook, you must introduce your subjects and establish the purpose for the comparison.

Because this is an argument, you are conveying a perspective, not just information or a list of traits. Your purpose is larger; therefore, if you are organizing deductively, you should establish your claim (perspective + unifying idea) to determine your final evaluation. In most cases, you will decide that one subject is better than another. Your claim should explain why this is so and prepare your audience to follow your line of reasoning and evidence in the body of your argument. You may also pose the question in the introduction and wait until your conclusion to reveal which of the subjects you favor in your evaluation.

Conclusions

The final paragraph of your argument should bring your readers to a satisfying and logical conclusion. If the evidence and commentary in your argument are specific, relevant, and thorough, then you will effectively reveal your perspective and prove your claim. But the reader still needs a sense of finality. Many evaluation arguments are organized inductively so that the writer poses the question in the introduction, presents the evidence in the body, and makes the evaluation in the conclusion. In this case, the thesis statement will be placed in the conclusion.

You can achieve a unified ending in your conclusions by using some of the following methods:

- Finalize your evaluation or recommendation.
- Explain the significance of the argument within a broader context.
- Explain the implications of your argument.
- Connect back to a claim or element in your introduction.
- Leave the audience with a compelling image or thought.

The most engaging arguments amplify their message with a final clever statement or insight in the conclusion. These statements, also known as clinchers, create that welcome sense of finality for the reader.

INSIDER AP TIP   **Effective conclusions often "bookend" the introduction.** A "bookend conclusion" makes a direct reference to the hook in the argument's introduction. Connecting back to the introduction achieves unity, which brings the reader full circle and creates a satisfying ending.

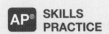 **SKILLS PRACTICE** | RHETORICAL SITUATION
Introducing and Concluding an Argument

Begin planning your comparison-contrast argument by considering the following:

- What is my main **subject**?
- What are the **categories of comparison**?
- What is the **purpose of the comparison**?
- What is the **context for the comparison**?
- Who is the **audience**?
- What is my **unifying idea**?
- What is my **perspective**?

REASONING AND ORGANIZATION   ## Connecting Reasons and Evidence

 Enduring Understanding (REO-1)

Writers guide understanding of a text's line of reasoning and claims through that text's organization and integration of evidence.

Once you have established the context of your comparison-contrast argument, you can begin to organize your argument. In this step, you need to examine the details of your comparison subjects and then narrow your focus to a few meaningful categories of comparison. These categories must be relevant to the context and your purpose. Once you have these finalized, they will guide your line of reasoning and potentially become the subjects for your body paragraphs. Comparison-contrast arguments are typically organized in one of two ways: subject by subject or category by category. Both are valid methods, but one may be more effective than the other depending on the rhetorical situation. Whichever method you choose, use clear transitions to establish the relationships between ideas so your readers can follow your organizational strategy.

One way to organize comparison-contrast arguments is subject by subject. In this organizational structure, you write about one of your subjects fully within a single body paragraph. Using details about the subject, you develop your two or three categories of comparison. When you complete your discussion of the first subject, you then move to the next body paragraph and develop the second subject fully. Make sure to include helpful transitions between each comparison and each body paragraph. For clarity and unity, you should also present the categories of comparison in the same order for each paragraph. In your final paragraph, conclude by evaluating the information that you have presented and, if appropriate, making a recommendation. Note the following sample outline for our evaluation of movie-viewing choices:

Introduction	
Hook: *Detailed description of watching a blockbuster in a full theater with surround sound*	
Context: *Temporary closures and decades-long declining attendance at movie theaters*	
Question: *Which movie-watching experience, home viewing or movie theater, offers the best aesthetic experience?*	
Home Theaters	Movie Theaters
First Category of Comparison *Audiovisual quality*	**First Category of Comparison** *Audiovisual quality*
Second Category of Comparison *Sense of community*	**Second Category of Comparison** *Sense of community*
Conclusion	
Evaluation: *While it may be convenient and comfortable to view movies at home, movie theaters provide a superior experience not only in their audiovisual quality but also in the **sense of community** they create.*	
Thesis: *Movie theaters offer an optimal viewing environment and the excitement of the crowd's reaction, especially for "event movies," because theaters provide an intense high-fidelity experience that cannot be exactly replicated with home audiovisual equipment.*	
Recommendation: *At least for the big blockbusters, movie lovers should get out of the house and see a movie.*	

The second way to organize a comparison-contrast argument is category by category. In this organizational structure, you write about both of your subjects within a paragraph. That is, each body paragraph focuses on a category of comparison and develops details from each subject. For clarity and unity, you should present your comparison subjects in the same order. This category-by-category strategy is, in many cases, more effective than the subject-by-subject approach because the subjects are directly juxtaposed. As the details of each choice are in close proximity, you can develop your evaluation more clearly and more directly. To help your readers follow your line of reasoning, use transitions that guide them within — and between — paragraphs.

Transitions of comparison also contribute to the line of reasoning and increase the coherence of the text. Readers can more easily follow your line of reasoning if you connect your paragraphs and sentences with helpful transitions to show similarities (e.g., *similarly, like, in the same way*) or differences (e.g., *conversely, unlike, on the other hand*).

Introduction

Hook: *Detailed description of a surround-sound blockbuster in a crowded theater*

Context: *Temporary closures and declining attendance at movie theaters*

Question: *Which movie-watching experience, home viewing or movie theater, offers the best aesthetic experience?*

First Category of Comparison	Second Category of Comparison
Audiovisual Quality	*Community Experience*
Home Theaters	*Home Theaters*
Movie Theaters	*Movie Theaters*

Conclusion

Evaluation: *Movie theaters offer an optimal viewing environment. The crowd's excitement — especially for "event movies" — provides a unique communal experience that cannot be replicated with home theater equipment.*

Thesis: *While it may be convenient and comfortable to view movies at home, movie theaters provide a superior experience not only in audiovisual quality but also in the **sense of community** they create.*

Recommendation: *At least for the big blockbusters, movie lovers should get out of the house and see a movie.*

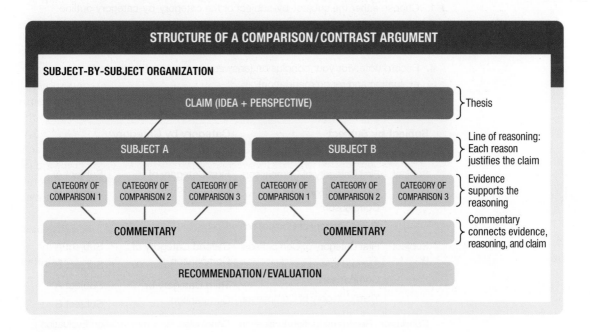

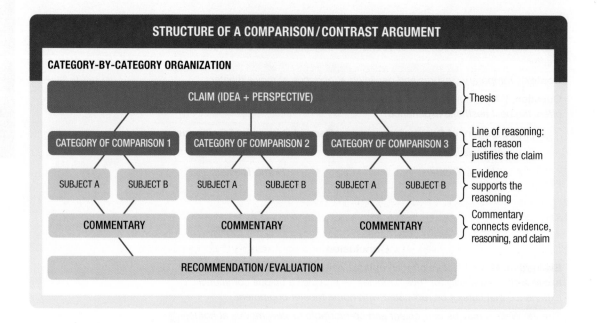

STRUCTURE OF A COMPARISON/CONTRAST ARGUMENT

CATEGORY-BY-CATEGORY ORGANIZATION

CLAIM (IDEA + PERSPECTIVE) — } Thesis

CATEGORY OF COMPARISON 1 | CATEGORY OF COMPARISON 2 | CATEGORY OF COMPARISON 3 — } Line of reasoning: Each reason justifies the claim

SUBJECT A | SUBJECT B | SUBJECT A | SUBJECT B | SUBJECT A | SUBJECT B — } Evidence supports the reasoning

COMMENTARY | COMMENTARY | COMMENTARY — } Commentary connects evidence, reasoning, and claim

RECOMMENDATION/EVALUATION

 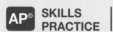

AP® SKILLS PRACTICE | REASONING AND ORGANIZATION
Unifying an Argument

Plan your comparison-contrast argument using the following chart:

1. Choose either the subject-by-subject or the category-by-category outline.
2. Record notes for your introduction (including hook, context, and question).
3. Compose topic sentences that convey a perspective (either by subject or category).
4. Record notes for your conclusion (answering your question through evaluation and recommendation).

Organizing Evaluation Arguments: Comparison and Contrast

Subject by Subject		Category by Category	
Introduction		Introduction	
Subject A	First Category of Comparison Second Category of Comparison Third Category of Comparison	First Category of Comparison	Subject A Subject B
Subject B	First Category of Comparison Second Category of Comparison Third Category of Comparison	Second Category of Comparison	Subject A Subject B
		Third Category of Comparison	Subject A Subject B
Conclusion: Recommendation/Evaluation		Conclusion: Recommendation/Evaluation	

CLAIMS AND EVIDENCE Qualifying an Argument

AP® Enduring Understanding (CLE-1)

Writers make claims about subjects, rely on evidence that supports the reasoning that justifies the claim, and often acknowledge or respond to other, possibly opposing, arguments.

In previous workshops, you worked to incorporate relevant and sufficient evidence into your arguments. Now, we will practice qualifying your arguments. When you qualify your evidence and commentary, you reveal the complexities of your subjects and account for multiple perspectives. In a comparison-contrast argument, you can use qualifying language to acknowledge that both subjects likely have merit, even though one may be the better choice in a particular context. You are also taking the audience into account: when you inform them about other perspectives, you may help them understand *your* perspective. Review the following examples of qualifying language, which includes signal words, phrases, and clauses.

Qualifying an Argument		
Words		**Examples**
almost	often	*Certainly, some home-viewing experiences create fond and lasting memories for the audience.*
at times	otherwise	
barely	possibly	
certainly	precisely	
could	probably	
conversely	seldom	
frequently	some	
hints at	sometimes	
if	somewhat	
majority	supposedly	
maybe	usually	
might	very	
nevertheless		
Phrases		**Examples**
depending on the circumstance		*The visual and sound quality provided in a movie theater can have a significant impact on the viewing experience, depending on the amount of action and special effects offered in the film.*
more or less		
to some extent		
up to a point		

(*continued*)

Clauses	Examples
although because even though since when while	*Since many homes are now equipped with large-screen televisions and high-quality soundbars, more and more people are viewing movies in the comfort of their own living rooms.*

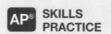 **SKILLS PRACTICE** | CLAIMS AND EVIDENCE
Qualifying an Argument

Begin composing your argument using the outline that you created for the subjects and the categories of comparison.

1. Write a complete introduction (hook, context, and question).

2. Develop each body paragraph so that it includes the following:

   a. topic sentence,

   b. evidence, and

   c. commentary that links evidence to your claim.

3. Incorporate examples of qualifying language in each body paragraph (underline the words, phrases, or clauses that indicate qualifications).

4. Write a conclusion that

   a. presents a thesis that conveys your perspective and

   b. brings your argument to a unified end.

LANGUAGE AND STYLE Crafting Purposeful Syntax

 Enduring Understanding (STL-1)

   The rhetorical situation informs the strategic stylistic choices that writers make.

As you write your comparison-contrast argument, you should use strategic syntax and punctuation to achieve a specific rhetorical purpose. Your language and style contribute to your purpose when you craft your argument deliberately at the sentence level. More specifically, different syntactical structures yield different effects because they balance ideas, create emphasis, control the pace of the information, and connect clarifying details.

In short, through your syntactical choices, you can achieve the following effects:

- Emphasize or clarify an idea
- Balance ideas
- Indicate relationships
- Add detail or description
- Provide examples or instances
- Omit unnecessary information
- Connect with the reader
- Offer qualifications
- Provoke thought

Review the following examples of deliberate syntactical structures that achieve a rhetorical effect.

Punctuation Mark	Effect	Example
period	• Creates a sense of finality • Signifies the end of a thought	Pass the popcorn.
question	• Provokes thought, response, or reflection	What will movie viewing look like in ten years? Twenty years? Fifty years?
exclamation	• Emphasizes a strong emotion • Creates excitement	Nothing beats experiencing our heroes in Dolby sound and 3D!
comma	• Illustrates equality of ideas or information when used for coordination • Indicates inequality or qualification when used for subordination • Clarifies or describes by setting off parenthetical or nonessential information or details • Signifies a pause in thought	The parking lot of the Premiere Cinema, a movie venue once crowded with eager moviegoers, now remains virtually empty.
semicolon	• Indicates that the connected clauses are closely related or equal	A moviegoer pays for tickets and concessions; a home viewer pays for equipment and streaming services.

(continued)

Punctuation Mark	Effect	Example
colon	• Clarifies and restates information from the prior clause • Introduces examples or information	*More and more modern movie viewers are opting for the comforts of home: a cozy couch, the anytime bathroom break, and the freedom to wear pajamas.*
dash	• Emphasizes an example or detail • Creates anticipation • Clarifies through exemplification • Signifies a shift or interruption	*No home viewing can recreate the shared experience — the collective excitement, the communal sense of suspense, the sigh of relief when the hero triumphs — provided by a movie theater.*
ellipses	• Indicates an omission of information • Signifies the passage of time	*The conversion to digital projectors has put some smaller theaters out of business . . . they need expensive equipment to show newer films.* *What happens when our favorite theaters begin to close? . . . We will have to wait and see.*
parentheses	• Provides extra information, clarify • Indicates an aside to connect with the audience	*Blockbuster films (also known as "event movies") comprise a small percentage of releases but a large percentage of revenue for the film industry.*

 **SKILLS PRACTICE** | LANGUAGE AND STYLE
Crafting Purposeful Syntax

Revise your comparison-contrast argument to incorporate strategic punctuation where appropriate.

1. Identify places in your argument where you want to achieve a specific rhetorical purpose (e.g., balance, emphasis, clarification). Then craft sentences with appropriate syntax and punctuation to achieve that purpose.

2. Circle these choices and make a note of your desired effect.

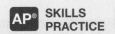 **SKILLS PRACTICE** | PUTTING IT ALL TOGETHER
Revising and Editing a Comparison/ Contrast Argument

Peer-Revision Checklist: Revising and Editing a Comparison/Contrast Argument		
Revising and Editing Checklist	**Unit 7 Focus Skills**	**Comment on the Effectiveness and/or Make a Suggestion**
Does the claim in the introduction or conclusion connect the audience to the writer's unifying idea and perspective?	*Narrative distance*	
Are the comparisons, evidence, and commentary organized subject by subject or category by category? Is each subject evaluated using the same categories of comparison?	*Line of reasoning (comparison-contrast)*	
Has the writer developed the argument with a variety of relevant and sufficient evidence? Does the writer recognize the inherent complexities of the argument by using qualifying language?	*Qualifying an argument*	
Has the writer explained the evidence and connected the subjects and categories of comparison? Are these choices effective for the specific audience and purpose?	*Comparison/ contrast argument*	
Is the writing clear and specific? Do the syntactical choices contribute to the purpose?	*Strategic syntax and punctuation*	
Is the writing free of errors in spelling, usage, punctuation, capitalization, and agreement?	*Writing conventions*	

⊐⊐⊏
⊐⊐⊏
⊐⊐⊏
⊐⊐⊏

PREPARING FOR THE AP® EXAM
Free-Response Question: Rhetorical Analysis

Explaining Significance

In this final workshop for rhetorical analysis, you will practice the skills we learned in Units 1 and 4. Here, you will put everything together to create a sophisticated analysis. At this point, you should also be practicing within a time limit. The College Board suggests that you spend forty minutes writing the rhetorical analysis free-response essay. Because of this time limitation, you may feel the pressure to begin writing immediately. However, you should first spend a few minutes preparing to write before you start writing.

In this workshop, we will review the process of writing an analysis and focus specifically on developing commentary that explains the significance of the writer's choices to convey the message.

→ **Step One: Annotate the Passage Based on the Unifying Idea**

The prompt instructs you to write an essay analyzing how the writer's rhetorical choices convey the writer's message. But before you begin writing your analysis, you need to read and annotate both the prompt and the passage carefully. As you recall, the prompt also offers you valuable context to help you understand the rhetorical situation in the passage. In most cases, the prompt will include information to help you arrive at the writer's message as well. This will guide your reading and annotating as you focus on a unifying idea.

With the unifying idea in mind, identify the writer's strategies in the text. Rather than haphazardly marking devices, analyze the relationship between these strategies and the writer's idea and central message. Examine how these elements work together for this unified purpose. You learned to distinguish between devices and strategies in Unit 4. You might recall that some strategies include representation, appeals, comparisons, contrasts (see p. 255).

Additionally, consider the medium and genre. In other words, what would you anticipate or expect the writer to say to this audience through this form? Consider the following examples:

- If the text is a commencement speech, what is the message to the graduates likely to be?
- If the text is a eulogy, how might the writer feel about the subject being eulogized?
- If the text is a letter, what is the likely relationship between the writer and the recipient?
- If the text is a presidential State of the Union address, what message is the leader likely to convey to the nation?

Consider the text's organization as part of the writer's strategy too. In your annotations, it is helpful to look at how the text is organized. You can start by dividing the passage by rhetorical shifts (e.g., beginning, middle, end). Note how the writer uses transitions to signify these shifts to achieve his or her purpose. Also, pay attention to meaningful comparisons or patterns in the text. Once you determine how the writer organizes the passage, you can build on that organizational strategy to determine the topics for your own body paragraphs. If you clearly understand the passage's organization, you will also be able to answer the "So what?" question about the features of the passage. Now, you must prepare to explain *how* the writer's choices play a part in a larger picture.

→ Step Two: Develop a Defensible Claim and Unified Line of Reasoning

After reading and annotating the passage, review the writer's overall purpose and message. Carefully review the rhetorical situation, and be careful not to oversimplify the writer's message or the rhetorical situation. As you gain experience with analysis, you need to consider that writers often have multiple purposes and communicate within complex situations to diverse audiences. Because of these complex situations, writers also qualify their arguments to communicate effectively.

Because your analysis will explore the complexities and tensions within the argument, your thesis must do two things:

- convey the writer's message and/or purpose and
- state the choices and/or strategies the writer uses to craft the message in the text.

An effective thesis establishes your line of reasoning. A thesis is defensible when it makes a claim (unifying idea + perspective) about how a writer achieves his or her purpose in a text. This idea in your claim should unify your reasoning; therefore, if your claim does not establish a unifying idea, you will be unable to develop a line of reasoning.

Students sometimes mistakenly organize their analysis using the writer's devices instead of the writer's purpose to guide the line of reasoning. For example, students may develop one paragraph about a writer's diction, another about syntax, and perhaps another about comparisons. This method is ineffective because it fails to explain how these choices work *together* to achieve a purpose. In any given text, a writer typically incorporates many strategies that combine to present the writer's unified argument. But the writer's purpose determines all the rhetorical choices. When you plan your line of reasoning around the purpose, you can develop a more unified and sophisticated analysis in response.

→ Step Three: Choose Relevant Evidence

With your claim and line of reasoning established, you can review your annotations and choose the best supporting evidence for your claim. You must support all claims in your line of reasoning with evidence that is both specific and relevant. Even though a passage contains a number of strategies and details, you should only incorporate text that directly supports your interpretation of the purpose and message. For example, you might notice a strong word choice, a syntactical feature, a compelling detail, or another rhetorical choice. But if the example does not connect to your unifying idea and relate to your analysis of the writer's message, you should not include it in your analysis. The key question to ask is "So what?"

If you cannot answer this question about the importance of a detail or device, that feature is likely irrelevant to your analysis.

Refer back to your line of reasoning (organized by the writer's purpose) and identify two or more of the writer's strategies that work to achieve that purpose. Choose textual evidence that demonstrates these choices and include them in the corresponding body paragraph of the analysis.

Evidence should be specific and sufficient to support all reasons in the argument. You should provide textual evidence for each reason within your line of reasoning. Keep in mind that you should provide enough evidence to support each reason and exemplify multiple rhetorical choices in the passage that support the writer's purpose. Rarely is one example from the text sufficient.

→ **Step Four: Develop Your Commentary**

As you develop your body paragraphs, you will need to demonstrate that you understand (not just know) the rhetorical situation — the writer, the audience, and the purpose — and keep that rhetorical situation in mind as you analyze the writer's argument. In most cases, you will not be the intended audience, so you should avoid explaining the effects that these choices have on you, the current reader. Instead, focus on how these choices might affect the intended audience for the writer's immediate purpose. Effective commentary, then, explains *how* the writer's choices are meaningful within the rhetorical context and *why* they are appropriate for the intended audience at that time.

Essentially, all evidence that you choose to support your line of reasoning should be accompanied by meaningful commentary. In addition to your specific evidence in support of all claims, the strongest writers *consistently* explain how *multiple* rhetorical choices contribute to an interpretation of the passage. When writers explain how the rhetorical choices work together to support a writer's message, they are creating a unified analysis.

To explain the significance of a writer's rhetorical choices, you must do more than summarize his or her message, or paraphrase the textual evidence you have chosen for support. Your commentary must reveal *how you know* that message. This requires you to explain why the writer made those choices for that rhetorical situation. In other words, you must explain how those rhetorical choices affect the audience in that context.

As we learned in Unit 4, commentary is insufficient if it merely paraphrases the text or makes general statements of purpose such as "to add emphasis" or "to further the writer's purpose." Instead, explain what the choices *suggest* or *convey*, or why the choices are *appropriate*, *significant*, or *effective*. Most importantly, leave nothing for your reader to infer or puzzle over: directly state the writer's purpose in all of your commentary.

For instance, if you provide a specific example of precise word choice, you must consider how and why the writer chose this word for the particular audience and for that specific rhetorical context. You must explain the word's connotations, connect the choice to the writer's purpose, and explain why that word is the best word for that audience. The same principle applies if you provide examples of appeals, comparisons, syntactical structures, or other choices.

Review the following chart, which shows a thesis and one supporting body paragraph analyzing Tommy Orange's essay "How Native American Is Native American Enough?" from (p. 547). Note that without the commentary, the paragraph would simply read as a summary.

Developing Your Commentary

Thesis	Topic Sentence for Body Paragraph One		
By contrasting references to the arbitrary calculations of Native American bloodlines with personal details of his authentic cultural connections, Tommy Orange argues that identity cannot be measured in fractions but is a whole experience that should not be reduced.	*Orange first questions and then mocks the outdated and inappropriate system of calculating Native bloodlines to authenticate or even erase identity.*		
	Rhetorical Choice	**Evidence →**	**Commentary →**
	syntax (question/ answer) and anecdote	*To introduce his frustration with the system of calculating and reducing Native American identity, Orange asks whether "smaller fractions" should be included in the definition of Native [American] and then answers with the assertion, "I don't know." He then adds that if he doesn't include the amount, "people assume less."*	*This question invites his audience to consider the issue of authenticating bloodlines along with him, especially if they have not considered the prevalence of labeling Native American identity in proportions before now. Orange's admission that he does not know the answer seems to offer a concession to those who may also be grappling with the practice and demonstrates his understanding that the issue is complex. However, he immediately follows this concession with a personal anecdote to reveal that some people mistakenly believe this kind of identity labeling is necessary to prove authenticity.*
Notes: **unifying idea** *identity* **perspective** *authentic identity is whole* **strategy =** *contrast*	*motif (pattern of diction related to mathematics)*	*In reference to these calculations, Orange repeatedly incorporates mathematical language, such as "fractions . . . amount . . . equals . . . quantity . . . equation" and direct references to actual calculations, such as "3/64 . . . one-quarter . . .*	*Orange repeats literal numbers and calculations along with the motif of mathematical references in almost every paragraph of the argument. Because the repetition is so prevalent, it conveys the heightened frustration and burden that Orange and his fellow Native Americans feel. Additionally, these pervasive mathematical references begin to mock the system as they sound more and more ridiculous as Orange speculates formulas such as "Enough Blood times*

(continued)

	Rhetorical Choice	Evidence →	Commentary →
		one-half . . ." *to explore the constant burden of authenticating identity in the Native American community.*	*Not Enough Blood equals eligibility or ineligibility for tribal enrollment." The audience understands Orange's message that identity cannot be reduced to a formula.*

INSIDER **AP TIP**

Sophisticated arguments demonstrate a complex understanding. Strong rhetorical analyses do the following. They (1) explain the significance or relevance of the writer's rhetorical choices, (2) explain a passage's complexities or tensions, and (3) use a style that is consistently vivid and persuasive. When these features are consistent within an entire argument, and not merely in a single reference, the analysis overall is considered "sophisticated."

PREPARING FOR THE AP® EXAM

The following prompt is an example of a rhetorical analysis free-response question. Practice the skills you have learned in this workshop to write an analysis essay in response to the prompt.

Prompt:
The following excerpt is from *Quiet Strength* (1994), the autobiographical account of Rosa Parks, an African American woman from Montgomery, Alabama. In December 1955, while on her way home from work, Parks defied local segregation ordinances and refused to give up her seat on a bus to a white passenger. Her subsequent arrest sparked a bus boycott that eventually led to a Supreme Court ruling desegregating public transportation.

Read the passage carefully. Write an essay that analyzes the rhetorical choices Parks makes to develop her message about the fight for civil rights.

In your response, you should do the following:

- Respond to the prompt with a thesis that analyzes the writer's rhetorical choices.
- Select and use evidence to support your line of reasoning.
- Explain how the evidence supports your line of reasoning.
- Demonstrate an understanding of the rhetorical situation.
- Use appropriate grammar and punctuation in communicating your argument.

Quiet Strength
Rosa Parks and Gregory J. Reed

I did not get on the bus to get arrested; I got on the bus to go home. Getting arrested was one of the worst days in my life. It was not a happy experience. Since I have always been a strong believer in God, I knew that He was with me, and only He could get me through the next step.

I had no idea that history was being made. I was just tired of giving in. Somehow, I felt that what I did was right by standing up to that bus driver. I did not think about the consequences. I knew that I could have been lynched, manhandled, or beaten when the police came. I chose not to move. When I made that decision, I knew that I had the strength of my ancestors with me.

There were other people on the bus whom I knew. But when I was arrested, not one of them came to my defense. I felt very much alone. One man who knew me did not even go by my house to tell my husband I had been arrested. Everyone just went on their way.

In jail I felt even more alone. For a moment, as I sat in that little room with bars, before I was moved to a cell with two other women, I felt that I had been deserted. But I did not cry. I said a silent prayer and waited.

Later that evening, to my great relief, I was released. It is strange: after the arrest, I never did reach the breaking point of shedding tears. The next day, I returned to work. It was pouring down rain, so I called a cab. The young man at work was so surprised to see me. He thought I would be too nervous and shaken to go back to work.

Three days later I was found guilty and ordered to pay a ten-dollar fine plus four dollars in court costs. The case was later appealed with the help of one of my attorneys, Fred Gray, and I did not have to pay anything.

It is funny to me how people came to believe that the reason that I did not move from my seat was that my feet were tired. I did not hear this until I moved to Detroit in 1957. My feet were not tired, but I was tired — tired of unfair treatment. I also heard later that Mother Pollard, one of the marchers in Montgomery, said that my feet were tired but my soul was rested. She was right about my soul.

On Monday, December 5, the day I went to court, the Montgomery Improvement Association (MIA) was formed to start the bus boycott. It is sad, in a way, to think about what we had to go through to get to that point. We, as a people, all felt discouraged with our situation, but we had not been united enough to conquer it. Now, the fearfulness and bitterness was turning into power.

So the people started organizing, protesting, and walking. Many thousands were willing to sacrifice the comfort and convenience of riding the bus. This was the modern mass movement we needed. I suppose they were showing sympathy for a person who had been mistreated. It was not just my arrest that year. Many African-Americans, including Emmet Till, had been killed or beaten for racist reasons. I was the third woman in Montgomery to be arrested on a bus. We reached the point where we simply had to take action.

Nearly a year later the segregated-bus ordinance was declared unconstitutional by the U.S. Supreme Court. One day after the boycott ended, I rode a nonsegregated bus for the first time.

A month after the boycott began, I lost my twenty-five-dollar-a-week job when the now defunct Montgomery Fair department store closed its tailor shop. I was given no indication from the store that my boycott activities were the reason I lost my job. People always wanted to say it was because of my involvement in the boycott.

5

10

I cannot say this is true. I do not like to form in my mind something I do not have any proof of.

Four decades later I am still uncomfortable with the credit given to me for starting the bus boycott. Many people do not know the whole truth; I would like them to know I was not the only person involved. I was just one of many who fought for freedom. And many others around me began to want to fight for their rights as well.

At that time, the Reverend Martin Luther King Jr. was emerging on the scene. He once said, "If you will protest courageously and yet with dignity and Christian love, when the history books are written in future generations, the historians will have to pause and say: there lived a great people — a black people — who injected new meaning and dignity into the veins of civilization." It was these words that guided many of us as we faced the trials and tribulations of fighting for our rights.

PREPARING FOR THE AP® EXAM
Multiple-Choice Questions: Reading

Be Specific
Natalie Goldberg

Be specific. Don't say "fruit." Tell what kind of fruit — "It is a pomegranate." Give things the dignity of their names. Just as with human beings, it is rude to say, "Hey, girl, get in line." That "girl" has a name. (As a matter of fact, if she's at least twenty years old, she's a woman, not a "girl" at all.) Things, too, have names. It is much better to say "the geranium in the window" than the "flower in the window." "Geranium" — that one word gives us a much more specific picture. It penetrates more deeply into the beingness of that flower. It immediately gives us the scene by the window — red petals, green circular leaves, all straining toward sunlight.

About ten years ago I decided I had to learn the names of plants and flowers in my environment. I bought a book on them and walked down the tree-lined streets of Boulder [Colorado], examining leaf, bark, and seed, trying to match them up with their descriptions and names in the book. Maple, elm, oak, locust. I usually tried to cheat by asking people working in their yards the names of the flowers and trees growing there. I was amazed how few people had any idea of the names of the live beings inhabiting their little plot of land.

When we know the name of something, it brings us closer to the ground. It takes the blur out of our mind;[1] it connects us to the earth. If I walk down the street and see "dogwood," "forsythia," I feel more friendly toward the environment. I am noticing what is around me and can name it. It makes me more awake.

If you read the poems of William Carlos Williams, you will see how specific he is about plants, trees, flowers — chicory, daisy, locust, poplar, quince, primrose, black-eyed Susan, lilacs — each has its own integrity. Williams says, "Write what's in front of your nose." It's good for us to know what is in front of our nose. Not just "daisy," but how the flower is in the season we are looking at it. . . . Continue to hone your awareness: to the name, to the month, to the day, and finally to the moment.

Williams also says: "No idea, but in things." Study what is "in front of your nose." By saying "geranium" instead of "flower," you are penetrating more deeply into the present and being there. The closer we can get to what's in front of our nose, the more it can teach us everything. "To see the World in a Grain of Sand, and a heaven in a Wild Flower. . . ."

In writing groups and classes, too, it is good to quickly learn the names of all the other group members. It helps to ground you in the group and make you more attentive to each other's word.

Learn the names of everything: birds, cheese, tractors, cars, buildings. A writer is all at once everything — an architect, French cook, farmer — and at the same time, a writer is none of these things.

[1] "It takes the blue out of your mind" means to bring down from lofty — blue sky — thinking.

1. Which of the following best describes the function of the passage's first paragraph in the context of the passage as a whole?
   (A) It names and introduces the writer as a person in whom the reader should place their trust.
   (B) It establishes, engages, and connects to the audience as a specific type of reader and writer.
   (C) It creates a connection between the author's experiences and those of the reader.
   (D) It explains and provides examples of the importance of flowers to the craft of writing.
   (E) It orients, engages, and focuses the reader on both the purpose and the message.

2. In the third paragraph, the author introduces the sentence "When we . . . the ground." with a subordinate clause primarily to
   (A) contrast the need to name things with the need for a writer to have broad, unspecific knowledge.
   (B) refute those who would argue against the claims made here.
   (C) indicate that there is a further purpose for knowing the names of things.
   (D) create a conflict between opposing perspectives about a writer's role in society.
   (E) suggest that writers are too focused on themselves and often ignore the world surrounding them.

3. In the third paragraph, the semicolon in the second sentence ("It takes . . . the earth.") serves which of the following purposes?
   (A) It connects a figurative statement to a more literal statement to better clarify the intent of the full idea captured in the complete sentence.
   (B) It creates a distinction between the idea of having clarity about something new and connecting that new knowledge beyond that experience.
   (C) It separates related but slightly different objections that the writer anticipates and to which they are proactively responding.
   (D) It sets off two clauses that are not closely related but that clarify an idea introduced in the previous sentence.
   (E) It connects the author's ideas to those of an imagined audience.

4. In the fourth paragraph, the last two sentences ("Not just . . . the moment.") do which of the following?
   (A) They qualify the statement made in the previous sentence by narrowing the scope of the passage to a particular time period.
   (B) They refute a claim made in the previous sentence by suggesting that it is not about the flower itself but the condition and context of the flower.
   (C) They elaborate upon the idea that Williams's poetry is the standard for writers hoping to develop their writing with more detail.
   (D) They illustrate the awareness a writer should have and the detail to which writers should be able to go, as has previously been stated in the passage.
   (E) It counters claims about too much detail distracting from the purpose that a writer has.

5. The example provided in the fourth paragraph works as effective evidence for the writer's argument because
   (A) it refutes any reasoning that might be brought against the argument of the passage.
   (B) it strengthens the validity and reasoning of the argument by showing how the suggestions being made by this writer have been used by another writer.
   (C) it demonstrates the restraint with which a writer chooses details for their writing so that those choices are the most appropriate for the writing.
   (D) it explains why poets are better at specific details than are other writers.
   (E) it provides information that cannot be refuted.

6. In the seventh paragraph, the writer provides examples of what a writer should and should not be "— an architect, French cook, farmer —" to emphasize
   (A) the types of professions that make for good writers.
   (B) the range of knowledge into which a writer should show interest.
   (C) the people who are interested in poetry.
   (D) the many roles the audience members play in society.
   (E) the many different interests that one person can have.

7. The multiple uses of the word "ground" in paragraphs 3 and 6 do which of the following?
   (A) Illustrate the reasoning behind using William Carlos Williams as an example
   (B) Qualify the fears of a writer not being familiar with his or her surroundings
   (C) Emphasize the ultimate effect of a writer being able to name things
   (D) Explain how a writer can better understand his or her surroundings
   (E) Counter the argument that too much detail in a text can be distracting

8. Which of the following describes the types of evidence used throughout this passage?
   (A) Examples, anecdotes, personal observation, and expert opinions
   (B) Examples, statistics, illustrations, and expert opinions
   (C) Anecdotes, illustrations, experiments, and analogies
   (D) Facts, analogies, personal experiences, and statistics
   (E) Details, expert opinions, personal observations, and testimonies

9. The writer uses the word "you" throughout the passage to
   (A) divide the audience from the writer and portray the expertise of the writer.
   (B) appeal to the audience's need to trust the writer.
   (C) divide the roles of the reader and writer so that the readers see themselves as students who need to learn from the writer.
   (D) appeal to the need for the audience members to see themselves as writers who can benefit from the suggestions being made.
   (E) create confusion to demonstrate how anyone could be the audience for this.

The passage below is a draft.

(1) Child safety seats are a scam. (2) Car seats only provide a sense of security because they are required by law and not legally allowed to be resold to others, does little more than guarantee that manufacturers get paid for their products that must be constantly bought new.

(3) In the 1950s, car manufacturers began making seat belts additional paid options on many of their vehicles. (4) For example, Ford Motor Company offered seat belts as an option in 1955. (5) These were not popular, with only 2 percent of Ford buyers choosing to pay for seat belts. (6) Nearly a decade passed before Congress got involved, passing the 1966 National Traffic and Motor Vehicle Safety Act requiring that U.S. car-makers meet certain safety standards, including adding seat belts to all cars without additional charges.

(7) Over the next few decades, seat belts became standard equipment and eventually required by law to be worn in many states. (8) Seat belts soon became common. (9) Concerns started to emerge about children being strapped into adult-sized seat belts. (10) While some car manufacturers did experiment with pull-down or even adjustable seats and seat belts for children prebuilt into their models, most were too scared to take on the responsibility — and liability — for children's safety. (11) At the same time, independent researchers were doing research and experiments on the effect of car accidents on infants and children and finding that children were often likely to be thrown from a vehicle or harmed in some other way even if they were strapped into a seat belt.

(12) Eventually, third-party companies began creating and selling special "child safety seats" that eventually came to be colloquially referred to as "car seats." (13) The first law requiring a child seat was passed in 1985, and by the early 1990s, all states had laws requiring children under a certain age or weight or height (or some combination of those) to be in a car seat.

(14) However, some research has shown that the safety provided by car seats is only a little better than — or just as good as — regular seat belts. (15) Economists and researchers Steven Levitt and Stephen Dubner have found that "for children older than 2, there is no significant difference in the fatality rate between car seats and seat belts, 18.2 percent versus 18.1 percent respectively." (16) The result is a piece of expensive equipment that all families with young children must have, that cannot be bought or sold "used," and that is barely — if at all — safer than a regular seat belt.

(17) What a rip-off.

1. The writer wants to combine sentences 8 and 9 (reproduced below) in a way that expresses the parallel development of the ideas expressed in them.

   Seat belts soon became common. Concerns started to emerge about children being strapped into adult-sized seat belts.

   In the context of the passage as a whole, which of the following choices best achieves this goal?

   (A) Concerns about children in seat belts grew faster than the common use of the seat belt by adults.
   (B) While seat belts grew in popularity, so did concerns about children sitting with adult seat belts around them.
   (C) Seat belts became common; however, so did concerns about children being strapped into adult-sized seat belts.
   (D) Seat belts found common use among children and adults, though there were concerns about children using them.
   (E) Seat belts soon became common; concerns started to emerge about children being strapped into adult-sized seat belts.

2. The writer is considering flipping the placement of sentences 10 and 11 (reproduced below).

   While some car manufacturers did experiment with pull-down or even adjustable seats and seat belts for children prebuilt into their models, most were too scared to take on the responsibility — and liability — for children's safety. At the same time, independent researchers were doing research and experiments on the effect of car accidents on infants and children and finding that children were often likely to be thrown from a vehicle or harmed in some other way even if they were strapped into a seat belt.

   Should the writer make this revision?

   (A) Yes, the information provided about the researchers' experiments leads to the reluctance of carmakers to address child safety.
   (B) Yes, to emphasize the cause-effect relationship of carmakers' reluctance and the researchers' experiments.
   (C) No, because the relationship between the carmakers and the researchers is not the subject of the passage.
   (D) No, because stating what is said about the carmakers first contextualizes the experiments being done by those researchers.
   (E) No, because such a change would imply a conspiracy between the carmakers and the researchers.

3. The writer wants to add a sentence immediately following sentence 13 (and in the same paragraph) to better guide the reader through the line of reasoning. Which of the following choices most effectively accomplishes this goal?

   (A) All of these new requirements soon met the skeptical eye of economists.
   (B) In some states, the laws could only be enforced if a person were first stopped in the car for doing something else illegal.
   (C) People who had to drive across multiple states often ran into legal issues with different laws for different sizes and ages of children.
   (D) These laws proved controversial, especially among libertarians and civil liberties purists.
   (E) With all of these new requirements, the experiences of children as passengers in cars should be safer than ever before.

4. In sentence 16 (reproduced below), the writer wants to set up a conclusion that reinforces the reasoning and evidence used in the passage.

   The result is a piece of expensive equipment that all families with young children must have, that cannot be bought or sold "used," and that is barely — if at all — safer than a regular seat belt.

   Which of the following versions of the underlined portion of the sentence best accomplishes this purpose?

   (A) (as it is now)
   (B) safe
   (C) worth the cost to families who can't afford it
   (D) helping families
   (E) worn out by the time families are done with it

5. The writer is considering revising the passage to focus on first engaging the audience and then presenting the research and commentary.

   Which of the following revisions would be the most likely to accomplish this?

   (A) Deleting sentence 7
   (B) Moving sentence 2 to immediately before sentence 17 and in the same paragraph
   (C) Deleting sentences 1 and 2 and starting with sentence 3
   (D) Moving sentence 15 to immediately before sentence 2
   (E) Moving sentence 13 to immediately before sentence 3 and in the same paragraph

6. The writer would like to incorporate new information from other economists (reproduced below) into the passage.

Also, recent research by economists Jordan Nickerson and David Solomon seems to indicate that requiring car seats leads many families to choose to have fewer children because of the added expense of both more car seats and larger cars to carry them.

Which of the following changes would the writer need to make for this new information to work in the context of the overall argument the writer is making?

(A) Provide an explanation for why economists are the best professionals for studying these topics.

(B) Explain that there are too few studies on the effectiveness of safety seats.

(C) Develop more commentary about how requirements for child safety seats are affecting families.

(D) Change the focus to be on the unintended consequences of driving with children in the car.

(E) Expand on the historical details related to car seat requirements.

Carolyn Eaton/Alamy Stock Photo

UNIT

8

Explaining Complexities

By now, you've had the opportunity to explore and analyze important civic and social issues. You've discovered that people from different backgrounds view the same subject from different perspectives and that they express unique ideas about issues they care about. But we truly see how complex many issues are when different perspectives and ideas about them come together. In other words, they are complex because there are so many different, often competing, perspectives about them.

Consider how the situation in the image can be viewed from several perspectives. You may see the Ferris wheel and think how fun it would be to go to the county fair with your friends. Or you may be someone working at the fair who has to remain there long hours to ensure the safety of visitors. Or you may be an organizer of the fair who had hoped to make a profit but didn't when very few showed up. What perspectives are reflected in the image? In this unit, you'll discover how writers demonstrate their understanding of complexity by exploring and responding to the perspectives of others.

UNIT GOALS

	Unit Focus	Reading, Analyzing, and Interpreting	Writing
Big Idea: Rhetorical Situation	**The Dynamic Rhetorical Situation**	Explain how a text can resonate within various contexts for intended and unintended audiences.	Employ rhetorical strategies that convey the complexity of an argument.
Big Idea: Claims and Evidence	**Counterarguments: Refutation and Rebuttal**	Explain how writers respond to others' arguments.	Develop a claim by employing concession, rebuttal, and refutation.
Big Idea: Reasoning and Organization	**Evaluation: Problem-Solution Arguments**	Explain how writers develop ideas through problem-solution.	Write an evaluation argument that proposes a solution.
Big Idea: Language and Style	**Contrasts and Incongruity**	Explain how writers use contrast and incongruity to convey a message.	Employ contrast and incongruity to convey a message.
Ideas in American Culture	• **Mind and Matter** • **Criticism and Critique**	Explain how the ideas of mind, matter, criticism, and critique are reflected in classic, as well as contemporary, texts.	
Preparing for the AP® Exam	• **Free Response: Argument** • **Multiple Choice**	Analyze rhetorical choices in classic and contemporary nonfiction texts.	Acknowledge and respond to others' arguments.

The Dynamic Rhetorical Situation

AP® **Enduring Understanding (RHS-1)**

Individuals write within a particular situation and make strategic writing choices based on that situation.

KEY POINT

Writers continually attempt to connect with their intended audience through comparisons and other strategies from the introduction of their arguments through the conclusion.

Have you ever rewatched a beloved movie from childhood and noticed different details or jokes that you didn't see before? That is because many children's movies are carefully designed to appeal to two different audiences: younger children and the older teenagers or adults watching along with the children.

When you recognize aspects in a movie that didn't make sense when you were younger, you're experiencing a real-life example of how rhetorical situations change and adapt throughout time.

The same thing happens with written texts too. When you reread a novel, a story, or even an essay later in life, you will have had different experiences that affect your perspective and bring new meaning to the text. As a result, your understanding of the text will change and develop.

It's All about the Audience

So far, you've learned about the importance of identifying and understanding a rhetorical situation when analyzing a text. Whether you're working with DreamWorks' *Shrek* or Thoreau's *Civil Disobedience*, rhetorical situations are dynamic. Texts are written during a particular time and for an intended audience, but they may be read at a completely different time by a completely different audience.

Not all texts are intended for the audience that eventually reads them. Nonfiction texts often have a very targeted intended audience. When you're reading an eighteenth-century essay, the writer probably wasn't thinking of you as an audience member. Likewise, if you're reading a letter addressed to a particular person, the writer was probably not considering you as an audience member either. But these texts are still relevant and important to analyze today.

Writers have a particular audience in mind when they make references or **allusions**. By using this technique, the writer assumes that the intended audience will understand. On one hand, a writer may use similes, metaphors, analogies, and anecdotes that are familiar to a particular audience. On the other hand, a member of the writer's "unintended" audience may or may not understand the references and allusions. In some cases, he or she might even miss the overall point of the argument.

Because writers are writing for particular audiences, they often make rhetorical choices about evidence and organization based on their audience's perspective.

These choices affect both how well an argument will be accepted by an audience and how credible the writer may be for that audience.

How Texts Stand the Test of Time

The **conclusion** of an argument isn't just a perfunctory bookend. Rather, the conclusion brings a sense of finality and unity. In fact, powerful conclusions can serve as the culmination of the writer's ideas. In a conclusion, writers may

- make relevant connections to illustrate the universality, relevance, or timelessness of their unifying or controlling idea,
- connect back to the introduction,
- propose a solution,
- call on the audience to act,
- explain implications of an argument, or
- predict a future outcome.

Comparison as a Way of Connecting with the Audience

A writer will strategically select objects of **comparison** that relate to the audience. For the comparison to have the intended effect, the audience must understand it, as well as the writer's reason for choosing it. For example, a writer may draw upon relevant historical, cultural, or religious references while making an argument. If the audience shares the same frame of reference, the writer will likely achieve his or her goal. Rhetorical choices that rely on the strategic use of comparisons include **allusions**, **extended metaphors**, and **arguments by analogy**.

RHETORICAL COMPARISONS		
Organizational Choice	Description	Example
Analogy	Presents two things as similar based on common attributes and then draws an inference, hypothesis, or conclusion about a similarity that has yet to occur or been observed	No one knows who first said it, but the saying remains true: writing about music is like dancing about architecture.
Extended Metaphor	Establishes a comparison between two unlike things throughout the text, which draws attention to the shared characteristics and emphasizes an idea critical to the writer's claim	If President John F. Kennedy was King Arthur in the glamorous and doomed Camelot of his administration, then the prestigious experts and intellectuals in Kennedy's cabinet were the noble but tragically flawed Knights of the Roundtable.
Allusion	Refers to history, pop culture, literature, or art that's familiar to the audience as a way of illustrating a similarity	"I laugh in my head 'cause I bet my ex looking back like a pillar of salt": Chance the Rapper and Kanye West referring to an Old Testament story in the song "Ultralight Beam."

INSIDER AP® TIP

Consider the intended audience. The key to effective rhetorical analysis is to consider the perspectives, values, and identities of the writer's intended audience. In other words, try to understand the text as the intended audience may have.

AP® SKILLS PRACTICE | **RHETORICAL SITUATION**
Understanding the Dynamic Rhetorical Situation

Think of a speech that you have seen or heard recently. What was the context? Who was the intended audience? Were there also unintended audiences? In other words, who else read or heard that speech outside its immediate context? Now, fast-forward twenty years. Who might read or listen to this speech two decades from now? How would that unintended audience respond to the speech? What factors would influence that audience's understanding of the speech?

Banksy and the Tradition of Destroying Art
Preminda Jacob

Photo by Marlayna Demond for UMBC

THE TEXT IN CONTEXT

Preminda Jacob (b. 1958) is an associate dean of fine arts and assistant professor of art history and theory in the Department of Visual Arts at the University of Maryland, Baltimore. Her research focuses on urbanism, public art, modern and contemporary art, and the history of the art museum. Jacob is the author of *Celluloid Deities: The Visual Culture of Cinema and Politics in South India* (2008). In this article from the online nonprofit news and commentary publication *The Conversation*, Jacob writes about the controversial anonymous artist and activist Banksy, whose work continues to satirize, shock, and provoke.

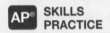

AP® SKILLS PRACTICE | **RHETORICAL SITUATION**
Analyzing Rhetorical Comparisons

As you read Jacob's article, use the following graphic organizer to record any rhetorical comparisons that she uses. Briefly describe how these examples help Jacob communicate her message to her audience.

Analyzing Rhetorical Comparisons for an Audience

Organizational Choice	Description	Example and Intended Effect on Audience
Analogy	Presents two things as similar based on common attributes and then draws an inference, hypothesis, or conclusion about a similarity that has yet to occur or be observed	
Extended Metaphor	• Establishes a comparison that extends throughout the argument between two unlike things • Draws attention to the shared characteristics that emphasize a value or idea critical to the writer's claim	
Allusion	Refers to history, pop culture, literature, or art that the audience knows as a way of illustrating a similarity	

Banksy and the Tradition of Destroying Art

When the British street artist Banksy shredded his "Girl With Balloon" after it was purchased for US$1.4 million at Sotheby's, did he know how the art world would react?

Did he anticipate that the critics would claim that the work, in its partially shredded state, would climb in value to at least $2 million? That the purchaser would not object and would instead rejoice?

We have no way of really knowing, though the famously anonymous artist did suggest that the shredder malfunctioned: The painting was supposed to be fully shredded, not partially destroyed.

As an art historian, I view his act in a larger context—as the latest example of artists deploying guerrilla tactics to expose their disdain for the critics, dealers, gallery owners and museum curators whom they depend on for their livelihood.

In shredding "Girl With Balloon," Banksy seems to be pointing to a central absurdity of his graffiti art being treated as fine art. When it appears on city streets, anyone can vandalize 5 it; now that the same images are in galleries and auction houses, they must be handled with white gloves.

But, as he may well know, the art market is far too wealthy and adaptable to be undone by a shredder.

In fact, we've seen the same pattern play out, time and again: An artist will launch a withering critique and instead of taking offense, the market simply tightens its embrace.

The Many Versions of Subversion

Some of the most well-known of Banksy's subversive artistic predecessors were part of the early-20th century Dada movement. One of their principal strategies involved denying the market of objects that could be commodified.

French-American artist Marcel Duchamp is perhaps the most well-known Dadaist. In 1917, his "Fountain," a urinal laid on its back and remounted on a pedestal, was his first volley against the art market's intellectual pretenses about art.

Duchamp wanted to force the art world to acknowledge that its judgments about quality were based on media hype and money rather than artistic innovation. [10]

However, years later Duchamp admitted to the futility of his gesture.

"I threw . . . the urinal into their faces as a challenge," he lamented, "and now they admire [it] for [its] aesthetic beauty."

In 1920, Francis Picabia, a Cuban-French Dadaist would follow Duchamp's lead and participate in a performance purposefully designed to provoke the French art world.

Before a Parisian audience gathered at the Palais des Fêtes, Picabia unveiled a chalk drawing entitled "Riz au Nez" ("Rice on the Nose"). The artist's friend, André Breton, one of the hosts of the event, then erased the drawing. The artwork lasted for just a couple of hours and is now lost to history. The work's title, it's been noted, sounds too similar to "rire au nez" ("to laugh in one's face") to be coincidental.

In 1953, Robert Rauschenberg, who was then an up-and-coming American artist, plucked up the courage to ask Willem de Kooning, an established abstract expressionist, for one of his drawings. Rauschenberg didn't tell de Kooning much—just that he intended to use it for an unusual project. Although de Kooning was disapproving, he acquiesced. [15]

After securing his gift, Rauschenberg proceeded, over the period of a month, to carefully erase all traces of the expressive pencil, charcoal and crayon drawing that de Kooning had put to paper.

Rauschenberg then re-titled the work, now preserved in the collection of the San Francisco Museum of Art, "Erased de Kooning Drawing."

Jean Tinguely's auto-destructing work, "Homage to New York" (1960), is probably the closest parallel to Banksy's stunt. Made of scrap found in New Jersey junkyards, the massive work—27 feet high and 23 feet in length—was supposed to be a mechanical display, sort of like a Rube Goldberg device.

The piece was set up in the sculpture garden of New York's Museum of Modern Art, and those attending the show included collectors Walter Arensberg and John D. Rockefeller III, and artists John Cage, Mark Rothko and Robert Rauschenberg.

Tinguely briefly set the piece in motion— and then it burst into flames. [20]

The Museum of Modern Art described the scene: ". . . a meteorological trial balloon inflated and burst, colored smoke was discharged, paintings were made and destroyed, and bottles crashed to the ground. A player piano, metal drums, a radio broadcast, a recording of the artist explaining his work, and a competing shrill voice correcting him provided the cacophonic sound track to the machine's self-destruction—until it was stopped short by the fire department."

Apart from a fragment from Tinguely's "Homage" preserved in the MoMA collection, all that remains of the work is some choppy film footage.

It's difficult to imagine anyone surpassing Tinguely's sound-and-light spectacle. But in 2001, Michael Landy of the Young British Artists group orchestrated the most comprehensive "art as destruction" work to date.

Titled "Break Down," Landy placed objects on a conveyor belt running into a machine that pulverized them. In the process, he destroyed all of his belongings—7,227 pieces in all—including his own paintings and the art of his Young British Artist peers.

Guerrillas in the Midst

These acts of destruction are motivated by the same impulse. 25

In the late 19th century, art production largely became untethered from patronage offered by the church or the state, and artists turned to powerful art dealers for their livelihood.

But many found that the radical, critical aspect of the artistic act was severely compromised—or erased altogether—when the most well-known feature of a work became the dollar sign attached to it.

To many, the market symbolized nothing more than a void.

With the urban street as his studio and insurgency as part of his artistic mission, Banksy's graffiti often critiques institutions, such as the art museum, and authority figures like the police) and the Queen of England.

Though the market value of his work has soared in recent years, Banksy continues to paint images in public spaces that make preservation near impossible—and even invite theft or defacement. 30

Still, as guerrilla theater, Banksy's recent act will be tough to beat. It's certainly his most subversive and penetrating public foray into the elite art marketplace.

But even with all his critique, the question continues to nag: Is Banksy complicit with the art market? The very society he undermines, one that feeds on spectacle, has made him famous and his art immensely profitable.

In the wake of World War I, Dadaist artists made a practice of shocking their public audiences by wantonly destroying their own artistic creations. The public soon learned to cheer them on, and to detach themselves from the attack artists [who] were actively waging on their sensibilities.

A century later, at Sotheby's, the initial shock of a shredded "Girl With Balloon" dissipated quickly. The hype only grew. The market adapted.

Sotheby's has since released a statement declaring that the piece—renamed "Love is in the Bin"—is "the first artwork in history to have been created live during an auction." 35

RHETORICAL SITUATION

1. How do Jacob's various references to other works of art help build her argument? What is she comparing? How do those **comparisons** support her **purpose**?

2. What **audience** is she writing for? How would you describe it? How do the writer's organizational and rhetorical choices connect to the audience's **perspective**, **context**, and needs?

3. Give an example of **evidence** that compares two similar things and then suggests that the reader make an inference. How does this evidence strengthen the text's **message**?

4. How does the writer use her **conclusion** to reinforce the **perspective**, values, and identities of the **audience**? How does she communicate the implications of fragmented art for the artistic community and the art market?

CLAIMS AND EVIDENCE

Counterarguments: Refutation and Rebuttal

AP® **Enduring Understanding (CLE-1)**

Writers guide understanding of a text's lines of reasoning and claims through that text's organization and integration of evidence.

The complexity of an issue emerges because of divergent, competing, and opposing perspectives and arguments about the subject or issue.

When writers address opposing views, they build their own arguments while contributing to their credibility. Additionally, writers often find valuable new evidence and information when researching the work of others. At these times, they might need to revise their theses. These revisions and adjustments are a natural part of the writing process; they show that writers are considering subjects rationally and are willing to adjust their claims based on the available evidence. If writers choose not to adapt their claims or reasoning in light of new evidence, they run the risk of invalidating their arguments.

Not all arguments explicitly address counterarguments. Some may do so implicitly by incorporating different sources of evidence or addressing reasons that reveal weaknesses in another argument.

If you have a nuanced understanding of other arguments, you are in a better position to concede points within your own argument. These concessions indicate that you are thinking critically about a subject; they allow you to acknowledge why another perspective is valid.

KEY POINT

A writer demonstrates understanding of the subject's complexity by responding to counterarguments through refutation, concession, and rebuttal.

Qualification Addresses Absolutes

Recall from the last unit that writers may defend their own claims, challenge another writer's argument, or qualify their own arguments. When writers strategically **qualify** their arguments, they acknowledge the **limitations** of their claims, reasons, or evidence. To do so, writers use words, phrases, and clauses as modifiers. These modifiers finely tune the meaning of a sentence by specifying key details, limiting the scope of the information, and anticipating potential objections. These qualifications demonstrate to the audience that the writer understands the issue from multiple perspectives.

One-sided arguments are effective only if an audience largely agrees with the writer at the outset. In such cases, the writer may choose to organize his or her argument inductively, where the claim is found at the beginning. This approach is more likely to work if readers or listeners already tend to agree with the writer's position and evidence. In contrast, a deductive argument presents examples or evidence before guiding the audience to the claim at the end. In other words, a more skeptical audience might need the writer to show his or her evidence and logic before accepting the writer's claims.

Responding to Others' Arguments

When writers address another argument, they do so through refutation, concession, and rebuttal.

The placement of a **refutation**, **concession**, or **rebuttal** influences the audience's understanding of the text. Recall that the arrangement of sentences within a paragraph or extended argument may emphasize a unifying idea. With that in mind, writers often use transitions to introduce qualifications or counterarguments. Additionally, many writers express qualifying statements by subordinating them within a dependent clause; with this syntactical choice, they keep the sentence's focus on their main point rather than on its limitations.

INSIDER AP TIP   **Understanding creates credibility.** When writers truly understand an issue, they know other perspectives and anticipate opposing arguments. Writers build credibility with carefully structured reasoning as they address these perspectives and arguments.

RESPONDING TO OTHERS' ARGUMENTS: REFUTATION, CONCESSION, AND REBUTTAL		
Rhetorical Move	**Definition**	**Example**
Refutation	Demonstrates with evidence that all (or a portion) of a competing claim is invalid	"There are those who are asking the devotees of civil rights, 'When will you be satisfied?' We can never be satisfied as long as [African Americans are] the victim[s] of the unspeakable horrors of police brutality." — Martin Luther King Jr., "I Have a Dream" speech
Concession	Accepts all or a portion of a competing claim as correct, or correct under different circumstances, or acknowledges the limitations of the writer's own argument	While advocates of paying college athletes rightly point out that these athletes should receive compensation, they also tend to downplay the ways that college players already receive financial benefits — in tuition remission, in coverage for food costs, in clothing, and more.
Rebuttal	Offers a contrasting perspective on an argument and its evidence, or provides alternative evidence to propose that all (or a portion) of a competing claim is invalid	The media has long stoked fears of sharks with data about the frequency of shark attacks in shallow water, but these fears are largely unfounded: statistically, you are five times more likely to be killed by a cow than by a shark.

| **AP®** SKILLS PRACTICE | CLAIMS AND EVIDENCE **Identifying Counterarguments** |

Take a position on a complex or controversial issue in your school or community. Write a claim that includes your position, a controlling or unifying idea, and your perspective. Then consider other perspectives that might support, complement, question, or contradict your claim. Describe how you would offer refutation, concession, or rebuttal to address those competing positions.

Issue:		
Claim: (position, idea, and perspective)		
Refutation	Concession	Rebuttal

Guns: Ban the Things. Ban Them All.

Molly Ivins

THE TEXT IN CONTEXT

Pulitzer Prize–winning journalist Molly Ivins (1944–2007) was born in Monterey, California, and raised in Houston, Texas. After earning degrees at Smith College and Columbia University's School of Journalism, she worked as a reporter for several newspapers, including the *Minneapolis Tribune* and the *New York Times*. But Ivins is best known for her sharp, witty syndicated columns in the *Dallas Times Herald* and later the *Fort Worth Star-Telegram*. She once remarked, "Satire is traditionally the weapon of the powerless against the powerful. I only aim at the powerful. When satire is aimed at the powerless, it is not only cruel — it's vulgar." In the following editorial published on March 16, 1993, Ivins provides her perspective on gun legislation.

Mark Perlstein/Getty Images

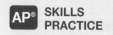 SKILLS PRACTICE | CLAIMS AND EVIDENCE
Identifying Refutation, Concession, and Rebuttal

As you read Ivins's editorial, describe how she responds to differing or opposing views through refutation, concession, and rebuttal.

Identifying Refutation, Concession, and Rebuttal		
Rhetorical Move	**Definition**	**Example and Effect**
Refutation	Demonstrates with evidence that all (or a portion) of a claim is invalid	
Concession	Accepts all (or a portion) of a competing claim as correct, or correct under different circumstances, or acknowledges the limitations of the writer's own argument	
Rebuttal	Offers a contrasting perspective on an argument and its evidence or provides alternative evidence to propose that all (or a portion) of a competing claim is invalid	

Guns: Ban the Things. Ban Them All.

Guns. Everywhere guns.

Let me start this discussion by pointing out that I am not anti-gun. I'm pro-knife. Consider the merits of the knife.

In the first place, you have to catch up with someone in order to stab him. A general substitution of knives for guns would promote physical fitness. We'd turn into a whole nation of great runners. Plus, knives don't ricochet. And people are seldom killed while cleaning their knives.

As a civil libertarian, I of course support the Second Amendment. And I believe it means exactly what it says: "A well-regulated militia being necessary to the security of a free state, the right of the people to keep and bear arms

shall not be infringed." Fourteen-year-old boys are not part of a well-regulated militia. Members of wacky religious cults are not part of a well-regulated militia. Permitting unregulated citizens to have guns is destroying the security of this free state.

I am intrigued by the arguments of those who claim to follow the judicial doctrine of original intent. How do they know it was the dearest wish of Thomas Jefferson's heart that teenage drug dealers should cruise the cities of this nation perforating their fellow citizens with assault rifles? Channeling?

There is more hooey spread about the Second Amendment. It says quite clearly that guns are for those who form part of a

Molly Ivins ■ Guns: Ban the Things. Ban Them All. **629**

CLAIMS AND EVIDENCE

well-regulated militia, i.e., the armed forces including the National Guard. The reasons for keeping them away from everyone else get clearer by the day.

The comparison most often used is that of the automobile, another lethal object that is regularly used to wreak great carnage. Obviously, this society is full of people who haven't got enough common sense to use an automobile properly. But we haven't outlawed cars yet.

We do, however, license them and their owners, restrict their use to presumably sane and sober adults and keep track of who sells them to whom. At a minimum, we should do the same with guns.

In truth, there is no rational argument for guns in this society. This is no longer a frontier nation in which people hunt their own food. It is a crowded, overwhelmingly urban country in which letting people have access to guns is a continuing disaster. Those who want guns—whether for target shooting, hunting or potting rattlesnakes (get a hoe)—should be subject to the same restrictions placed on gun owners in England—a nation in which liberty has survived nicely without an armed populace.

The argument that "guns don't kill people" is patent nonsense. Anyone who has ever worked in a cop shop knows how many family arguments end in murder because there was a gun in the house. Did the gun kill someone? No. But if there had been no gun, no one would have died. At least not without a good footrace first. Guns do kill. Unlike cars, that is all they do. Michael Crichton makes an interesting argument about technology in his thriller *Jurassic Park*. He points out that power without discipline is making this society into a wreckage. By the time someone who studies the martial arts becomes a master—literally able to kill with bare hands—that person has also undergone years of training and discipline. But any fool can pick up a gun and kill with it.

"A well-regulated militia" surely implies both long training and long discipline. That is the least, the very least, that should be required of those who are permitted to have guns, because a gun is literally the power to kill.

For years, I used to enjoy taunting my gun-nut friends about their psycho-sexual hang-ups—always in a spirit of good cheer, you understand. But letting the noisy minority in the National Rifle Association force us to allow this carnage to continue is just plain insane.

I do think gun nuts have a power hangup. I don't know what is missing in their psyches that they need to feel they have the power to kill. But no sane society would allow this to continue.

Ban the damn things. Ban them all.

You want protection? Get a dog. 15

---

1. What is Ivins's **thesis** in this argument? What is her **claim**?

2. Ivins addresses other **perspectives** as she makes her argument. Give an example of **evidence** that is drawn from another perspective and explain the function of this evidence.

3. Ivins uses both **refutation** and **rebuttal** in the argument. Choose one of each and then explain how her responses to **counterarguments** contribute to her overall message.

4. Do you find the writer's conclusion effective? Why or why not? Would you describe the conclusion as a **concession**? Explain.

Evaluation: Problem-Solution Argument

AP® Enduring Understanding (REO-1)

Writers make claims about subjects, rely on evidence that supports the reasoning that justifies the claim, and often acknowledge or respond to other, possibly opposing, arguments.

KEY POINT

Writers organize proposal arguments by first explaining the problem or issue and then establishing a goal. Then they evaluate the pros and cons of different options. Finally, they propose a solution with the best chance of achieving their goal.

In the last unit, you learned that writers use comparison and contrast to evaluate two or more subjects. When they ultimately come to a conclusion about their subjects based on established criteria, that conclusion becomes their main claim. In this unit, you'll extend your understanding of comparison-contrast as you read arguments that propose a solution. These proposal arguments require the writers to understand the complexities of a subject. In other words, they need to consider multiple alternatives before making a recommendation.

Maybe a community is considering how to address homelessness in their neighborhood. Perhaps your school administration wants to solve the problem of grade inflation. Maybe a local business is trying to attract more customers. All of these issues can be addressed in a problem-solution argument.

A Proposal Argument Offers a Solution

To propose an effective solution, writers must have a deep understanding of the issue or problem. This understanding allows the person proposing the solution to address the root problem instead of a secondary or superficial one. Often, writers will consider the problem through multiple lenses or perspectives. This requires them to understand the context of the problem: its background, its history, its effects on specific individuals and groups. For example, a writer proposing a solution to the student debt crisis would likely talk about the total amount of debt, the debt's effects on borrowers, and the factors that have contributed to the problem.

To that end, writers making proposal arguments typically explain the problem and its complexities in the introduction. Moreover, they usually provide enough evidence to convince the audience that they are addressing a "real" problem. But keep in mind the larger goal: to propose an effective solution, not merely explain the problem.

Identifying the Goal

In a proposal argument, the writer's claim must establish the criteria and goal for solving the problem. For example, the community hoping to address homelessness may be looking for a solution that encourages the construction of low-income housing. The school administration responding to grade inflation may want to provide fair and consistent grading standards. The business looking for more customers may hope to attract a loyal teenage market. But regardless of the specific circumstances, writers must understand the problem before they can articulate their goal. Once they identify the goal, the argument's line of reasoning will focus on evaluating options that can achieve it.

Considering the Pros and Cons

Next, a proposal argument will present several alternatives and evaluate each one in light of the overall goal and criteria for success established in the introduction. In other words, the writer must use the overall goal when explaining both the pros and the cons of each option.

When identifying and analyzing options, writers often consider the following questions:

- Has this problem (or a similar one) occurred elsewhere?
- How has the problem or issue been addressed previously?
- What solutions were effective and why?
- How are the writer's context, criteria, and overall goal similar to these prior examples?

Proposing a Solution

The proposed solution is the writer's main claim. At times, a writer's proposal may ultimately be one of the options evaluated in the text. But more often, writers propose solutions of their own. A solution may be new and innovative or even a synthesis of two or more of the possibilities discussed in the argument. Regardless, the bulk of any proposal argument will be an explanation and justification of the proposed solution.

Here is a common organization of a proposal argument:

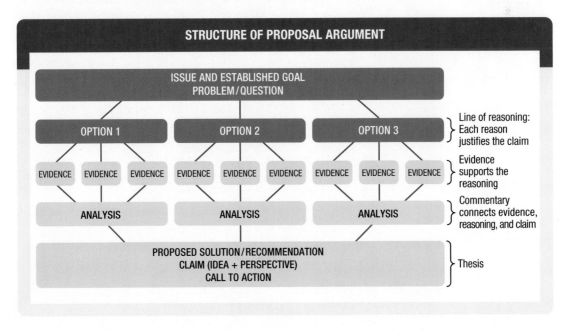

INSIDER
AP TIP

Proposal arguments require describing, evaluating, and persuading. Writers describe the problem or issue, evaluate the potential alternatives with compare and contrast, and then persuade the audience by calling on them to act.

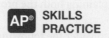

SKILLS PRACTICE | REASONING AND ORGANIZATION
Proposing a Solution

Imagine that a local community is concerned about record low voter turnout among eighteen-year-olds in the most recent election. You have been asked to propose a solution to this problem. Before you consider possible solutions, you must identify the goal or criteria for success. Identify three or four potential goals or criteria. Then identify one that you will use when evaluating possible alternatives and solutions.

Issue: Record low voter turnout of eighteen-year-olds	
Potential Success Criterion	
Potential Success Criterion	
Potential Success Criterion	
Potential Success Criterion	
Final Selection for Success Criterion:	

Are We So Connected That We're Disconnected? Three Ways to Break through the Clutter

Paul Jankowski

New Heartland Group

THE TEXT IN CONTEXT

Paul Jankowski (b. 1950) is the founder and CEO of New Heartland Group, a marketing, brand strategy, and customer engagement agency in Nashville, Tennessee. The agency's clients include Pepsi, Pizza Hut, and Lipton. Jankowski is also the author of several books, including *How to Speak American: Building Brands in the New Heartland* (2011) and *The New Heartland Speaks: The Marketer's Guide to Reaching America's Most Powerful Cultural Segment* (2020). In this 2018 article from the business magazine *Forbes*, Jankowski explores the problem of technological isolation, as well as strategies that companies and brands can use to reconnect with consumers.

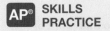 **SKILLS PRACTICE** | REASONING AND ORGANIZATION
Analyzing Evaluation Arguments That Propose a Solution

As you read the text, consider how Jankowski draws on description, compare and contrast, and persuasion to develop his argument. Use the organizer to record details from the text included in each method of development. Then explain how each method of development and its supporting details contribute to the overall argument.

Understanding a Problem-Solution Argument			
	Method of Development		
	Description	**Evaluation through Comparison-Contrast**	**Persuasion**
Details from Text			
Purpose or Function in Argument			

Are We So Connected That We're Disconnected? Three Ways to Break through the Clutter

Brands aren't the only ones fighting for their audiences' attention in today's society. Everyone, from musicians to school administrators, must get clever at connecting with distracted audiences. And with U.S. adults now consuming 11 hours of media daily, the challenge gets harder as technology and social norms morph.

Americans aren't in the moment anymore, and it's a struggle for brands to reach us. On top of being distracted, we're exposed to 4,000 to 10,000 ads daily, creating layers upon layers of clutter for brands to break through.

That brings us to the question: Have we become so over-connected that we've become disconnected? Watch a group of teenagers. Maybe they're your own kids. It's mind-numbing their need to be digitally connected with people outside of the group they're sitting with physically.

A friend of mine is a highly influential sports agent. He represents the who's who in professional sports and is always on his phone. He thought taking his two young boys to school was his way of connecting with them since he travels most of the time. His boys, however, weren't feeling connected at all. As a matter of fact, they asked him to stop using his phone on their ride to school because he didn't talk to them. He told me it was like he got hit in the head with a 2 × 4. He was there, but he wasn't *there* for his boys. We are all guilty of this.

The launch of cell phone-bagging service Yondr has helped various individuals and organizations better connect with audiences. 5

Yondr locks cell phones in individual pouches, eliminating cell phone use during events. But did we ever think "cell phone-bagging" would be needed to make us *connect*? After all, don't cell phones *help* us connect with each other?

Colorado school principal, Garrett Rosa told the *Denver Post* why cell phone-bagging is necessary for her school.

"People are not experiencing things anymore, whether it's deep learning or live comedy, because we're too focused on taking selfies and not being in the moment," Rosa said.

How Brands Can Break through the Clutter

To successfully build a connection with consumers, brands must break through the clutter. And to truly connect, the brand must create a one-on-one, fully engaged, non-distracted conversation between itself and the consumer. The value of that conversation is creating an emotional connection; the holy grail of branding.

So, how can brands get to that point of real connection? Some musicians and comedians are setting great examples.

Physically leaving the clutter. Physically leaving the clutter behind can drastically decrease distractions for consumers. Kanye West escaped the clutter of the city to launch his latest album in the Heartland. The album, "Ye," was launched at a 200-person listening party around a bonfire in Wyoming. 10

West served the crowd booze and barbecue, then enjoyed the album with his guests. Escaping the clutter allowed attendees to embrace the environment and have a (nearly) one-on-one listening experience with the rapper.

Does this mean the New Heartland—the 26 states that make up the Midwest, Southwest and Southeast—is less connected than the coasts? Of course not. New Heartlanders are just as digitally connected as their coastal counterparts. But, folks in the New Heartland are less focused on societal distractions and more focused on *each other*—it's the lifestyle. So, it makes sense that West would host his release party in a location where both the environment and lifestyle encourage honest connections.

Removing the clutter. A little more than a quarter of Americans say they are online "almost constantly." So, removing digital clutter removes virtually all distractions for consumers—which is why Yondr has become so popular.

At Yondr-present events, every attendee is required to slip his phone into a Yondr bag that locks the phone inside. The attendee maintains possession of the phone the entire show, but can only access the phone by stepping outside and unlocking the bag at an unlocking station.

Dave Chappelle started using Yondr at his   15 comedy shows a few years back, and others have followed suit, including musician Jack White, country duo Dan + Shay, and comedian Chris Rock. During their album listening party at CMA Fest this year, Dan + Shay told fans in attendance that they wanted everyone to *be* in the moment. More than 600 U.S. schools also have Yondr bags.

But, you don't have to lock away someone's phone to remove clutter. At recent concerts, pop artist Harry Styles asked fans to put away phones to enjoy the moment, listen, and connect with those around them.

Removing clutter in any way helps the consumer be in the moment, so that a *true* connection can be formed.

Cutting through the clutter with a real connection. While social shares, likes and engagements increase brand exposure, human connection builds loyalty and trust. Why would musicians and comedians—people who thrive on social media shares and mentions—discourage phones that allow those social interactions? Because the real value is in the connection. Creating a moment and being in it together is powerful stuff.

Connecting isn't a follow or a mention. Connecting is understanding your audience and tapping into what each individual cares about. When your message revolves around your audience's values, and it's delivered in the right place at the right time, your brand message will hit home. You'll cut through clutter and grab your consumer's attention.

The New Heartland consumers care about   20 their values, culture and how they live their lives. Their lifestyle revolves around a love of music, great food, fashion, technology, hunting, fishing, camping and sports (youth, college). It's connecting at the lifestyle level that brands can build a real relationship that can last for generations.

Marketers once thought the number of likes or shares determined the success of branded content. Then, the focus changed to measuring engagement and conversion. But real digital branding success stems from creating a two-way conversation with your audience.

By understanding the culture, values and lifestyle nuances of your audience, you'll talk with them, not *at* them, like so many other brands. You'll form a real connection with consumers. And, you'll break through all that clutter.

REASONING AND ORGANIZATION

1. Where does the writer draw upon **description**, **evaluation**, and **persuasion**?

2. Is the text organized by **induction** or **deduction**? How does this organization impact the **audience**?

3. How does the goal or success criterion reveal the writer's **perspective** on the subject?

4. How do the options connect with the beliefs, values, and needs of the **audience**?

Contrast and Incongruity

AP® **Enduring Understanding (STL-1)**

The rhetorical situation informs the strategic stylistic choices that writers make.

If you have seen Disney's *Monsters, Inc.*, you might recall the surprising premise of the movie: monsters are afraid of children rather than the reverse. If you saw the *Star Wars* movie, *Episode I: The Phantom Menace*, maybe you remember the scene in which a young Anakin Skywalker (the future Darth Vader) exclaims, "No one can kill a Jedi!" Or perhaps you have read Ray Bradbury's classic dystopian novel *Fahrenheit 451*: a 1953 book about a futuristic society that outlaws all books, which — in real life — has itself been banned from classrooms on many occasions.

As audience members watching the two films, we get an appealing jolt from the incongruities. In the case of *Fahrenheit 451*, we may be startled by the insight that our society is closer to the one in the novel than we would like to believe.

All these examples illustrate the idea of irony: situations in which our expectations are thwarted in surprising ways, situations in which surface meaning clashes with a deeper significance or situations in which words (or images) have multiple meanings that collide with each other. In other words, we perceive an incongruity: something that is jarring or counter to expectations but also revealing in a significant way.

KEY POINT

Writers create irony and other incongruities by contrasting words, images, and ideas.

Incongruities Create Interest

Earlier in this unit, you examined how writers make comparisons (such as similes, metaphors, and analogies) so that they can convey their message and connect to their audience. Similarly, **irony**, **incongruity**, and other **ambiguities** add another layer of complexity to the text and engage active interpretation from the audience.

Most obviously, writers create irony when they deliberately choose words or make stylistic decisions that mean the opposite of what they are normally intended to mean. This could be in the form of simple sarcasm: a friend observing a raging storm and saying, "Nice weather." Or the irony could be more complex: a teacher writing a deliberately awkward, wordy sentence about why writers should avoid awkwardness and wordiness. In such cases, the difference between the audience's expectation and reality produces a comic or dramatic effect.

Along with screenwriters, novelists, and poets, writers of arguments use irony — including puns, exaggerations, sarcasm, satire, and other incongruities — to advance the purpose of their arguments. The table on the next page describes some rhetorical choices that contribute to an ironic perspective.

Satire

A common form of comic writing, satire draws upon an extended use of irony and sarcasm throughout a text. **Satire** usually criticizes or ridicules a subject familiar to the audience. At times, that ridicule might be obvious or it might be covert, depending on the context. We see satire throughout popular culture: television shows such as *South Park*, *The Office*, *The Daily Show*, and *Saturday Night Live*; websites like The Onion and The Hard Times; and satirical movie comedies such as the *Scary Movie* series. But more serious novels and films can be satirical, as well, such as *Animal Farm*, *Fight Club*, and *Get Out*. Of course, the tradition of satirical writing goes all the way back to ancient Greece and Rome. As it does now, satire has always targeted religion, political institutions, and prominent cultural figures for criticism. Likewise, satirical writers still use hyperbole, understatement, sarcasm, and irony in their texts.

CONTRAST AND INCONGRUITY		
	Definition	**Example**
Irony	Difference between an argument's claim or conclusion and the readers' expectations or values	In recent years, many sincere environmentalists have argued that recycling may do more harm than good — a surprising claim that counters our expectations.
Sarcasm	Stating the opposite of what is really meant in order to criticize or ridicule	In *Harry Potter and the Order of the Phoenix*, Harry dismisses a friend's warning that his life could become difficult: "Wow, I wonder what it'd be like to have a difficult life."
Juxtaposition	Presents evidence or examples side by side to emphasize similarities or differences, often about ideas or values	In Mary Shelley's novel *Frankenstein*, the monster is physically repulsive and terrifying but also sensitive, articulate, and cultured: the juxtaposition highlights the tragedy of the story.
Pun	A play on words that sound alike or have multiple meanings	A newspaper headline about unpopular soft-drink regulations puns on the word "flat": "NYC Soda Ban Goes Flat."
Hyperbole	An exaggeration that is not meant to be taken literally	Advertisers often use this form of overstatement, as in slogans such as Adidas's "Impossible Is Nothing" and Gillette's "The best a man can get."
Understatement	Presenting information or an idea as less important than it really is to emphasize its obvious importance	In *The Avengers* (2012), Tony Stark uses understatement when he first meets Bruce Banner (the Incredible Hulk): "It's good to meet you, Dr. Banner. Your work on antielectron collisions is unparalleled. And I'm a huge fan of the way you lose control and turn into an enormous green rage-monster."

Punctuation marks may reveal an aside. Writers sometimes use quotation marks or parenthetical elements (e.g., parentheses, dashes) to indicate irony. These marks may reveal a shared intimacy between writer and reader.

SKILLS PRACTICE | LANGUAGE AND STYLE
Identifying Contrast and Incongruity

Choose a contemporary social media meme or an example of satire (e.g., a post on Instagram or Twitter, a sketch from *Saturday Night Live*, or an article from The Onion). First, describe the literal or surface meaning of the text or images. Then explain how your chosen example draws on irony, incongruity, understatement, or other satirical elements to mock its subject and entertain its audience.

Subject:

Literal Description:

	Example	Purpose and Commentary
Irony		
Sarcasm		
Juxtaposition		
Pun		
Hyperbole		
Understatement		

Trendy Restaurant Menu
Lydia Wei

Hayley Madden for The Poetry Society

THE TEXT IN CONTEXT

As an eleventh grader at Richard Montgomery School in Rockville, Maryland, Lydia Wei won a Scholastic Art and Writing Award for the following satire. Wei is also a prolific poet whose work has appeared in *Sine Theta*, *Polyphony Lit*, *harana poetry*, and other publications. Her writing has been recognized by the National Young Arts Foundation, the U.S. Presidential Scholars in the Arts Programs, and other organizations. In "Trendy Restaurant Menu," she turns a sharp eye on affluent patrons of high-end restaurants, as well as on consumerism more generally.

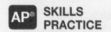 SKILLS PRACTICE | LANGUAGE AND STYLE
Analyzing Contrast and Incongruity

As you read "Trendy Restaurant Menu," notice how Wei uses contrasts and incongruities to convey her message. Use the following organizer to identify specific examples and then explain their purpose within her argument.

Analyzing Contrast and Incongruity		
Subject:		
Literal Description:		
	Example	Purpose and Commentary
Irony		
Sarcasm		
Juxtaposition		
Pun		
Hyperbole		
Understatement		

Trendy Restaurant Menu

Frittata with Chorizo and Fresh Spring Greens

Our creamy, custardy frittata is filled with smoky chorizo bits and tender spring greens to power you throughout your day. As a socially conscious restaurant, we pledge to use free-range eggs, which allow chickens to go outdoors for brief periods while still living in otherwise enclosed factory farms because the USDA's definition for the label is so loose!

Buttermilk Blueberry Pancakes with Lemon-Ricotta Whipped Cream

Start your morning off right with a stack of our buttermilk pancakes, studded with blueberries harvested by vulnerable and impoverished immigrant workers! These light, fluffy pancakes are garnished with a bright lemon-ricotta whipped cream that perfectly disguises the bitter taste of wage theft, poverty, hostile working conditions, and intimidation from large corporations controlling immigrant work visas!

Avocado Toast with Smoked Chile Flakes and Lime

A signature brunch dish! Our farm-to-table partners (or, large corporations) harvest avocados in water-deficient valleys in Chile, drilling deep wells to provide nutrients for the plant and lowering the regional water table so that impoverished locals lack safe drinking water. These exquisite green malnutrition bombs are then smeared onto toasted sourdough bread and confetti-covered with chili and lime for an extra zing!

Sesame-Soy Ahi Tuna Poke Bowl

A bright and colorful bowl with a delightful sesame crunch and savory soy sauce, our poke is made with yellowfin tuna, a near-threatened species with a strong mercury content from industrial emissions! Our seafood is always fresh because we only use quality-sourced ingredients (and because our distributor only uses carbon monoxide to preserve tuna's pink color)!

New Orleans-Style Shrimp Jambalaya

Authentic New Orleans-style jambalaya gets a kick of heat with jalapeños and a   5 generous dose of hot sauce. This dish is also bursting with tender Asian factory farm shrimp most likely uninspected by the FDA, which inspects only 2% of seafood imports. And if your shrimp from Thailand contains klebsiella, a bacteria resistant to numerous antibiotics, consider it a real taste of the Big Easy!

Burgers with Caramelized Onions and Chipotle Ketchup

Soft, toasted potato buns, caramelized onions, tangy chipotle ketchup, ruffles of lettuce, and succulent patties all come together to form our perfect burgers. With a sizzling griddle and the perfect fat ratios, our patties are crunchy and compact, oozing out rivers of juice much like the cattle manure that accumulates on factory farms and flows into waterways and drinking water. Careful—you'll need a paper towel for that!

Pork Meatball Banh Mi with Pickled Vegetables and Secret Hot Sauce

A modern twist on the traditional Vietnamese sandwich, this banh mi is fully loaded with crisp, pickled vegetables and pork meatballs, all tucked into a crackly baguette. Our pork comes from farms whose operations are as secret as our hot sauce due to Ag-Gag bills making it illegal to take farm jobs undercover or as a journalist. The meatballs add the perfect hearty bite to this towering sandwich full of underhanded policies and contrasting flavors!

Four-Layer Chocolate Cake with Dark Chocolate Ganache

Treat yourself to a decadent slice of silky-smooth chocolate cake, prepared in-house by our expert pastry chef. It's the perfect guilty pleasure: moist, indulgent, and the force behind deforestation in the Ivory Coast as farmers clear tropical forests to plant cacao trees and meet the global demand for chocolate. But shh—your hips and African deforestation will be our little secret!

LANGUAGE AND STYLE

1. Each menu item describes the dish and then uses **contrasts** to create an **ironic** or **incongruous** effect. Choose one example and explain its effect as a rhetorical choice.

2. Choose another menu item. How do the writer's rhetorical choices create the **incongruity**? How might it affect the audience's response to the item?

3. Choose a menu item that has a mocking or a sarcastic **tone**. What is being ridiculed? How might the tone affect the audience's response?

Don't Scoff at Influencers

Kevin Roose

DEMETRIUS FREEMAN/The New York Times/Redux

THE TEXT IN CONTEXT

A native of Oberlin, Ohio, Kevin Roose wrote his first book while he was a student at Brown University: after meeting a group of students from Liberty University, an evangelical college, he transferred to Liberty and then wrote about his experience in *The Unlikely Disciple: A Sinner's Semester at America's Holiest University* (2009). Roose is now a technology columnist for the *New York Times* and a writer at large for the *New York Times Magazine*. He is also the author of *Young Money: Inside the Hidden World of Wall Street's Post-Crash Recruits* (2015). His writing has appeared in *GQ*, *Esquire*, *Vanity Fair*, and other publications. In the following *New York Times* article, he discusses a prominent figure in contemporary culture: the "influencer."

Unifying Idea	Don't Scoff at Influencers	Rhetorical Strategies	Effect
innovation	ANAHEIM, Calif.—When the first TikTok star is elected president, I hope she will save some room in her cabinet for older and more conventional bureaucrats, even if they don't have millions of followers, great hair or amazing dance moves.	irony	gently mocking tone
innovation	I say "when," not "if," because I just spent three days at VidCon, the annual social media convention in Anaheim, hanging out with a few thousand current and future internet celebrities. And it's increasingly obvious to		

Unifying Idea	Don't Scoff at Influencers	Rhetorical Strategies	Effect
	me that the teenagers and 20-somethings who have mastered these platforms—and who are often dismissed as shallow, preening narcissists by adults who don't know any better—are going to dominate not just internet culture or the entertainment industry but society as a whole.	problem	people dismiss influencers as mere entertainment
innovation	On the surface, this can be a terrifying proposition. One day at VidCon, I hung out with a crew of teenage Instagram stars, who seemed to spend most of their time filming "collabs" with other creators and complimenting one another on their "drip," influencer-speak for clothes and accessories. (In their case, head-to-toe Gucci and Balenciaga outfits with diamond necklaces and designer sneakers.) Another day, I witnessed an awkward dance battle between two budding TikTok influencers, neither of whom could have been older than 10. (Adults who are just catching up: TikTok is a short-form video app owned by the Chinese internet company Bytedance.)	concession	they appear to be caught up in image
innovation	But if you can look past the silliness and status-seeking, many people at VidCon are hard at work. Being an influencer can be an exhausting, burnout-inducing job, and the people who are good at it have typically spent years working their way up the ladder. Many social media influencers are essentially one-person start-ups, and the best ones can spot trends, experiment relentlessly with new formats and platforms, build an authentic connection with an audience, pay close attention to their channel analytics, and figure out how to distinguish themselves in a crowded media environment—all while churning out a constant stream of new content.	solution line of reasoning	begins proposing solution by qualifying influencers' work is innovative

Unifying Idea	Don't Scoff at Influencers	Rhetorical Strategies	Effect
innovation	Not all influencers are brilliant polymaths, of course. Some of them have succeeded by virtue of being conventionally attractive, or good at video games, or in possession of some other surface-level attribute. Others have made their names with dubious stunts and extreme political commentary.	concession	writer acknowledges limitation of the argument
innovation	But as social media expands its cultural dominance, the people who can steer the online conversation will have an upper hand in whatever niche they occupy—whether that's media, politics, business or some other field.	line of reasoning	asserts that influencers manage the online conversation
innovation	"The way to think of influencers or creators is as entrepreneurs," said Chris Stokel-Walker, the author of "YouTubers." "These people are setting up businesses, hiring staff, managing budgets. These are massively transferable skills."	evidence/ option	influencers create businesses
innovation	Just look at Representative Alexandria Ocasio-Cortez, the New York Democrat who has become a powerful force in Congress by pairing her policy agenda with an intuitive understanding of what works online. Or look at what's happening in Brazil, where YouTubers are winning political elections by mobilizing their online fan bases.	evidence/ option	influencers know their audience
innovation	In the business world, influencer culture is already an established force. A generation of direct-to-consumer brands that were built using the tools and tactics of social media has skyrocketed to success—like Glossier, the influencer-beloved beauty company that recently raised $100 million at a valuation of more than $1 billion, or Away, the luggage start-up whose ubiquitous Instagram ads	juxtaposition	contrasts new "direct-to-consumer brands" with "sleepy old-line industries"

Unifying Idea	Don't Scoff at Influencers	Rhetorical Strategies	Effect
	helped it reach a valuation of $1.4 billion. Many social media stars strike endorsement deals with major brands, in addition to earning money through advertising and merchandise sales. And even executives in sleepy, old-line industries now hire "personal branding consultants" to help increase their online followings.		
innovation	Natalie Alzate, a YouTuber with more than 10 million subscribers who goes by Natalies Outlet, is an example of the wave of influencers who treated their online brand-building as a business rather than a fun hobby. Four years ago, when Ms. Alzate first came to VidCon, she was a marketing student with fewer than 7,000 subscribers. She decided to study her favorite YouTubers, watch how they made their videos and then test videos in multiple genres, seeing which ones performed best on her channel.	]—evidence	provide example of innovation
	"I grew up watching people, like Michelle Phan, that were building legacies out of, honestly, just being really relatable online," Ms. Alzate said. "It was always an aspiration."		
	Eventually, she hit on formats—like beauty tips and lifehacks—that reliably performed well, and she was off to the races. Today, she is a full-time YouTuber with a small staff, a production studio and the kind of fame she once coveted.		

Unifying Idea	Don't Scoff at Influencers	Rhetorical Strategies	Effect
innovation	In truth, influencers have been running the world for years. We just haven't called them that. Instead, we called them "movie stars" or "talk-radio hosts" or "Davos attendees." The ability to stay relevant and attract attention to your work has always been critical. And who, aside from perhaps President Trump, is better at getting attention than a YouTube star?	rhetorical situation/ occasion and audience	we have always had influencers
	VidCon, which started 10 years ago as a meet-and-greet event for popular YouTubers, is a perfect place to observe influencers in their natural habitat. And many of them were here to promote their channels, to network with other creators and to make strides toward the dream of internet fame.		
	Sometimes, that meant appearing in photos and videos with more popular influencers in an attempt to increase their own following, a practice known in influencer circles as "clout chasing." Other times, it meant going to panels with titles like "Curating Your Personal Brand" and "How to Go Viral and Build an Audience." For VidCon's featured creators, the super-famous ones with millions of followers, it can mean spending the day at a meet-and-greet with fans before going out to V.I.P. parties at night.		
	Not all of the young people I met at VidCon will spend their whole lives pursuing internet fame. Some of them will grow up, go off to college and wind up becoming doctors, lawyers or accountants. Some will fizzle out and be replaced by a younger generation of internet stars.		

Unifying Idea	Don't Scoff at Influencers	Rhetorical Strategies	Effect
innovation	But the lessons they learned from performing on YouTube, Instagram, and TikTok will stick with them, regardless of where they end up.	line of reasoning	the online experience is valuable
	Just as the 20th century groomed a generation of children steeped in the ethos of TV culture, the 21st century will produce a generation of business moguls, politicians and media figures who grew up chasing clout online and understand how to operate the levers of the attention economy.	analogy	represents the timelessness of influencers
	"In the early days, it felt like this was a sub-niche of youth culture," Beau Bryant, the general manager of talent at Fullscreen, a management agency for digital creators, told me at VidCon. He gestured around at a room filled with influencers sitting on velvet couches. Some were taking selfies and editing their Instagram stories. Others were holding business meetings about partnerships and sponsored content deals.		
innovation	"Now, it just feels like this is what youth culture is," Mr. Bryant said.		
	In other words, influencers are the future. Dismiss them at your peril.	recommendation	asserts that influencers need to be taken seriously

IDEAS IN AMERICAN CULTURE
Mind and Matter

IDEA BANK

Alienation

Anxiety

Belief

Conflict

Contradiction

Counterculture

Discovery

Eternity

Evolution

Existence

Fear

Impulse

Innovation

Inquiry

Memory

Mortality

Motivation

Philosophy

Spirituality

Survival

Wonder

The decades after World War II were filled with enormous promise and triumph — and enormous fear and anxiety. Scientific innovation progressed rapidly as jets carried passengers safely between continents; the polio vaccine ended a devastating disease; doctors performed kidney transplants and heart bypass surgeries; birth control became widely available; and psychiatrists dispensed mood-regulating medications. Indeed, the Space Race between the United States and the Soviet Union inspired America to put human beings on the moon in 1969. But that rivalry between the United States and Soviet Union cast a dark shadow over this period, as Americans, Soviets, and everyone else on Earth considered the possibility of nuclear annihilation during what was called the Cold War.

As science and technology began to explain more about the universe, it began to offer possible answers to questions that were once only in the realm of religion. Where did we come from? How was the universe created? Perhaps no one exemplifies the search to answer big questions like these more than the late

Leonardo da Vinci's drawing ▶ of the *Vitruvian Man* (c. 1490) depicts the ideal body proportions of a man. But the artist also created the sketch to illustrate the relationship between human beings and the larger universe.

What might this image suggest about the relationship between the natural world and humans?

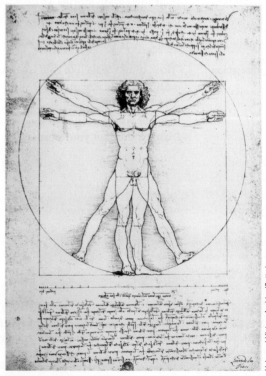

Universal History Archive/Getty Images

theoretical physicist Stephen Hawking, as in his piece "Questioning the Universe" (p. 650).

Despite the ascendency of science as a way of understanding the world, the United States remains the most religious of all the developed nations. In the postwar decades, many Americans also sought meaning outside conventional Western religions: in subcultures such as the Beats and the hippies, in non-Western religions like Buddhism in their careers, and in self-help programs, social activism, and many other pursuits. Likewise, psychology and psychiatry suggested that we are bundles of barely understood drives, impulses, and chemical reactions that take place in the brain. And if we place these ideas in the context of modern evolutionary science and our growing knowledge of the universe, human existence itself can start to seem accidental, precarious, and even meaningless.

Our sense of mortality drives much of this search for a larger purpose and meaning. In the nineteenth century, most people died at home, with their families. Today, most people die in hospitals, surrounded by technology. In "How to Know If You're Dead" from her book *Stiff* (p. 654), Mary Roach looks at dying in the practical context of working physicians and the organ donation process.

Today, we still place great hope in scientific discoveries, such as the rapid development of the COVID-19 vaccines in 2020. In space, NASA's *Perseverance* rover, which landed on Mars in 2021, beams back information on astrobiology — that is, life on other planets — to astronomers. The space agency has plans for a human mission to Mars by 2033. But scientific progress creates ethical challenges — about the side effects of medications, the moral implications of gene editing, and the unintended consequences of artificial intelligence, among other quandaries. America remains a culture fascinated by death, from the recent popularity of TV shows, books, and podcasts devoted to the forensics of true-crime murders. But Americans still seek — and find — meaning in their families, careers, friends, and spirituality.

After landing on Mars in 2021, NASA's ▶ rover *Perseverance* is expected to return to Earth in the 2030s. The geologic samples it's bringing home will allow researchers to examine the climate and geology of the planet, as well as search for evidence of ancient life. Virginia middle schooler Alexander Mather won a NASA contest to name the craft. He chose *Perseverance*: a name that, like those of past Mars rovers, reflects humanity's spirit, curiosity, and determination.

How are these qualities reflected in our everyday life?

GREGG NEWTON/Getty Images

Questioning the Universe

Stephen Hawking

Tom Pilston/Panos Pictures/Redux

THE TEXT IN CONTEXT

English theoretical physicist Stephen Hawking (1942–2018) was arguably the most famous scientist of the last sixty years. His research on black holes and string theory explores important questions about our universe. Despite his fifty-five-year battle with Lou Gehrig's disease, Hawking made groundbreaking scientific discoveries, wrote several books about the universe, and taught at Cambridge University from 1977 until his death in 2018. But his popularity reached beyond the scientific community into American popular culture: Hawking made featured appearances in *Star Trek: The Next Generation*, *The Big Bang Theory*, and *The Simpsons*. He also taught and lectured all over the world during his career. His life and work became the focus of the 2014 feature film *The Theory of Everything*. In the following 2008 TED Talk, Hawking tackles some of the most profound questions about the universe — and our place within it.

There is nothing bigger or older than the universe. The questions I would like to talk about are: one, where did we come from? How did the universe come into being? Are we alone in the universe? Is there alien life out there? What is the future of the human race?

Up until the 1920s, everyone thought the universe was essentially static and unchanging in time. Then it was discovered that the universe was expanding. Distant galaxies were moving away from us. This meant they must have been closer together in the past. If we extrapolate back, we find we must have all been on top of each other about 15 billion years ago. This was the Big Bang, the beginning of the universe.

But was there anything before the Big Bang? If not, what created the universe? Why did the universe emerge from the Big Bang the way it did? We used to think that the theory of the universe could be divided into two parts. First, there were the laws like Maxwell's equations and general relativity that determined the evolution of the universe, given its state over all of space at one time. And second, there was no question of the initial state of the universe.

We have made good progress on the first part, and now have the knowledge of the laws of evolution in all but the most extreme conditions. But until recently, we have had little idea about the initial conditions for the universe. However, this division into laws of evolution and initial conditions depends on time and space being separate and distinct. Under extreme conditions, general relativity and quantum theory allow time to behave like another dimension of space. This removes the distinction between time and space, and means the laws of evolution can also determine the initial state. The universe can spontaneously create itself out of nothing.

Moreover, we can calculate a probability that the universe was created in different states. These predictions are in excellent agreement with observations by the WMAP satellite of the cosmic microwave background, which is an imprint of the very early universe. We think we have solved the mystery of creation. Maybe we should patent the universe and charge everyone royalties for their existence.

I now turn to the second big question: are we alone, or is there other life in the universe? We believe that life arose spontaneously on the Earth, so it must be possible for life to appear on other suitable planets, of which there seem to be a large number in the galaxy.

But we don't know how life first appeared. We have two pieces of observational evidence on the probability of life appearing. The first is that we have fossils of algae from 3.5 billion years ago. The Earth was formed 4.6 billion years ago and was probably too hot for about the first half billion years. So life appeared on Earth within half a billion years of it being possible, which is short compared to the 10-billion-year lifetime of a planet of Earth type. This suggests that the probability of life appearing is reasonably high. If it was very low, one would have expected it to take most of the ten billion years available.

On the other hand, we don't seem to have been visited by aliens. I am discounting the reports of UFOs. Why would they appear only to cranks and weirdos? If there is a government conspiracy to suppress the reports and keep for itself the scientific knowledge the aliens bring, it seems to have been a singularly ineffective policy so far. Furthermore, despite an extensive search by the SETI project, we haven't heard any alien television quiz shows. This probably indicates that there are no alien civilizations at our stage of development within a radius of a few hundred light years. Issuing an insurance policy against abduction by aliens seems a pretty safe bet.

This brings me to the last of the big questions: the future of the human race. If we are the only intelligent beings in the galaxy, we should make sure we survive and continue. But we are entering an increasingly dangerous period of our history. Our population and our use of the finite resources of planet Earth are growing exponentially, along with our technical ability to change the environment for good or ill. But our genetic code still carries the selfish and aggressive instincts that were of survival advantage in the past. It will be difficult enough to avoid disaster in the next hundred years, let alone the next thousand or million.

Our only chance of long-term survival is not to remain inward-looking on planet Earth, but to spread out into space. The answers to these big questions show that we have made remarkable progress in the last hundred years. But if we want to continue beyond the next hundred years, our future is in space. That is why I am in favor of manned—or should I say, personned—space flight.

All of my life I have sought to understand the universe and find answers to these questions. I have been very lucky that my disability has not been a serious handicap. Indeed, it has probably given me more time than most people to pursue the quest for knowledge. The ultimate goal is a complete theory of the universe, and we are making good progress.

Founded in 2002 by engineer, designer, and entrepreneur Elon Musk, SpaceX is an American aerospace manufacturer and space transportation services company. SpaceX seeks to reduce space transportation costs, create reusable launch systems, and, ultimately, colonize Mars.

Do you believe that SpaceX (and NASA, which has similar aims) can reach these goals? Are these goals worth pursuing? What obstacles might prevent SpaceX from achieving its goals?

REUTERS/Thom Baur

RHETORICAL SITUATION

1. Why does Hawking choose to begin with rhetorical questions? What is the effect of this choice on his **audience**?

2. Who is Hawking's **audience**? How does the evidence, organization, and language of the argument address the audience's **perspective** and **context**?

3. How does the **conclusion** of the text explain an implication or predict a future outcome? Explain these implications or predictions. Does Hawking suggest alternatives to his conclusion throughout the text?

CLAIMS AND EVIDENCE

4. What type of **evidence** does Hawking present in the text? How does it contribute to his **thesis**?

5. Hawking makes **concessions** throughout his argument. Choose one example and then explain how the concession strengthens his argument.

6. Hawking **qualifies** his argument throughout the text. How do these qualifications reinforce the relationship between the writer and the **audience**?

REASONING AND ORGANIZATION

7. How is the text **arranged**? How does this arrangement contribute to the message of the argument?

8. How does the **line of reasoning** contribute to the writer's **perspective** on the subject?

LANGUAGE AND STYLE

9. How does the **diction** in the text reinforce the relationship between the writer and the audience? Give an example of Hawking's diction. Then explain how the specific word choices help him connect to his audience.

10. Note the pronouns that Hawking chooses as part of the **diction** in his speech. Do they indicate the writer's assumptions about his audience?

IDEAS IN AMERICAN CULTURE

11. Hawking states, "Our only chance of long-term survival is not to remain inward-looking on planet Earth, but to spread out into space." Do you agree that we are too "inward-looking"? Do you think that "our future is in space"? What are the implications of this idea? For example, is it necessary that we support a space program for our survival?

PUTTING IT ALL TOGETHER

12. Analyze how Hawking creates unity and coherence throughout his speech. How does his argument use evidence to develop a line of reasoning in order to answer these big questions about the universe?

from Stiff

Mary Roach

San Francisco Chronicle/Hearst Newspapers via Getty Images/Getty Images

THE TEXT IN CONTEXT

Writer Mary Roach (b. 1959) specializes in making complex scientific concepts accessible (and often funny) for general audiences. Her books include *Spook: Science Tackles the Afterlife* (2005), *Bonk: The Curious Coupling of Science and Sex* (2008), *Gulp: Adventures on the Alimentary Canal* (2013), and *Grunt: The Curious Science of Humans at War* (2016). Roach has also written for publications such as *Vogue*, *GQ*, *National Geographic*, and *Wired*. On choosing her subjects, Roach once remarked, "Well, it's got to have a little science, it's got to have a little history, a little humor — and something gross." In the following excerpt from *Stiff: The Curious Lives of Human Cadavers* (2003), Roach explores the distinction between life and death as she examines what happens to human bodies after they die.

A patient on the way to surgery travels at twice the speed of a patient on the way to the morgue. Gurneys that ferry the living through hospital corridors move forward in an aura of purpose and push, flanked by caregivers with long strides and set faces, steadying IVs, pumping ambu bags, barreling into double doors. A gurney with a cadaver commands no urgency. It is wheeled by a single person, calmly and with little notice, like a shopping cart.

For this reason, I thought I would be able to tell when the dead woman was wheeled past. I have been standing around at the nurses' station on one of the surgery floors of the University of California at San Francisco Medical Center, watching gurneys go by and waiting for Von Peterson, public affairs manager of the California Transplant Donor Network, and a cadaver I will call H. "There's your patient," says the charge nurse. A commotion of turquoise legs passes with unexpected forward-leaning urgency.

H is unique in that she is both a dead person *and* a patient on the way to surgery. She is what's known as a "beating-heart cadaver," alive and well everywhere but her brain. Up until artificial respiration was developed, there was no such entity; without a functioning brain, a body will not breathe on its own. But hook it up to a respirator and its heart will beat, and the rest of its organs will, for a matter of days, continue to thrive.

H doesn't look or smell or feel dead. If you leaned in close over the gurney, you could see her pulse beating in the arteries of her neck. If you touched her arm, you would find it warm and resilient, like your own. This is perhaps why the nurses and doctors refer to H as a patient, and why she makes her entrance to the OR at the customary presurgery clip.

Since brain death is the legal definition of death in this country, H the person is certifiably dead. But H the organs and tissues is very much alive. These two seemingly contradictory facts afford her an opportunity most corpses do not have: that of extending the lives of two or three dying strangers. Over the next four hours, H will surrender her liver, kidneys, and heart. One at a time, surgeons will come and go, taking an organ and returning in haste to their stricken patients. Until recently, the process was known among transplant professionals as an "organ harvest," which had a joyous, celebratory ring to it, perhaps a little too joyous, as it has been of late replaced by the more businesslike "organ recovery."

In H's case, one surgeon will be traveling from Utah to recover her heart, and another, the one recovering both the liver and the kidneys, will be taking them two floors down. UCSF is a major transplant center, and organs removed here often remain in house. More typically, a transplant patient's surgeon will travel from UCSF to a small town somewhere to retrieve the organ—often from an accident victim, someone young with strong, healthy organs, whose brain took an unexpected hit. The doctor does this because typically there is no doctor in that small town with experience in organ recovery. Contrary to rumors about surgically trained thugs cutting people open in hotel rooms and stealing their kidneys, organ recovery is tricky work. If you want to be sure it's done right, you get on a plane and go do it yourself.

Today's abdominal recovery surgeon is named Andy Posselt. He is holding an electric cauterizing wand, which looks like a cheap bank pen on a cord but functions like a scalpel. The wand both cuts and burns, so that as the incision is made, any vessels that are severed are simultaneously melted shut. The result is

that there is a good deal less bleeding and a good deal more smoke and smell. It's not a bad smell, but simply a seared-meat sort of smell. I want to ask Dr. Posselt whether he likes it, but I can't bring myself to, so instead I ask whether he thinks it's bad that I like the smell, which I don't really, or maybe just a little. He replies that it is neither bad nor good, just morbid.

I have never before seen major surgery, only its scars. From the length of them, I had imagined surgeons doing their business, taking things out and putting them in, through an opening maybe eight or nine inches long, like a woman poking around for her glasses at the bottom of her purse. Dr. Posselt begins just above H's pubic hair and proceeds a good two feet north, to the base of her neck. He's unzipping her like a parka. Her sternum is sawed lengthwise so that her rib cage can be parted, and a large retractor is installed to pull the two sides of the incision apart so that it is now as wide as it is long. To see her this way, held open like a Gladstone bag, forces a view of the human torso for what it basically is: a large, sturdy container for guts.

On the inside, H looks very much alive. You can see the pulse of her heartbeat in her liver and all the way down her aorta. She bleeds where she is cut and her organs are plump and slippery-looking. The electronic beat of the heart monitor reinforces the impression that this is a living, breathing, thriving person. It is strange, almost impossible, really, to think of her as a corpse. When I tried to explain beating-heart cadavers to my stepdaughter Phoebe yesterday, it didn't make sense to her. But if their heart is beating, aren't they still a person? she wanted to know. In the end she decided they were "a kind of person you could play tricks on but they wouldn't know." Which, I think, is a pretty good way of summing up most donated cadavers. The things that happen to the dead in labs and ORs are like gossip passed behind one's back. They are not felt or known and so they cause no pain.

The contradictions and counterintuitions ¹⁰ of the beating-heart cadaver can exact an emotional toll on the intensive care unit (ICU) staff, who must, in the days preceding the harvest, not only think of patients like H as living beings, but treat and care for them that way as well. The cadaver must be monitored around the clock and "life-saving" interventions undertaken on its behalf. Since the brain can no longer regulate blood pressure or the levels of hormones and their release into the bloodstream, these things must be done by ICU staff, in order to keep the organs from degrading. Observed a group of Case Western Reserve University School of Medicine physicians in a *New England Journal of Medicine* article entitled "Psychosocial and Ethical Implications of Organ Retrieval": "Intensive care unit personnel may feel confused about having to perform cardiopulmonary resuscitation on a patient who has been declared dead, whereas a 'do not resuscitate' order has been written for a living patient in the next bed." . . .

• • •

The modern medical community is on the whole quite unequivocal about the brain being the seat of the soul, the chief commander of life and death. It is similarly unequivocal about the fact that people like H are, despite the hoochy-koochy going on behind their sternums, dead. We now know that the heart keeps beating on its own not because the soul is in there, but because it contains its own bioelectric power source, independent of the brain. As soon as H's heart is installed in someone else's chest and that person's blood begins to run through it, it will start beating

anew—with no signals from the recipient's brain.

The legal community took a little longer than the physicians to come around to the concept of brain death. It was 1968 when the *Journal of the American Medical Association* published a paper by the Ad Hoc Committee of the Harvard Medical School to Examine the Definition of Brain Death advocating that irreversible coma be the new criterion for death, and clearing the ethical footpath for organ transplantation. It wasn't until 1974 that the law began to catch up. What forced the issue was a bizarre murder trial in Oakland, California.

The killer, Andrew Lyons, shot a man in the head in September 1973 and left him brain-dead. When Lyons's attorneys found out that the victim's family had donated his heart for transplantation, they tried to use this in Lyons's defense: If the heart was still beating at the time of surgery, they maintained, then how could it be that Lyons had killed him the day before? They tried to convince the jury that, technically speaking, Andrew Lyons hadn't murdered the man, the organ recovery surgeon had. According to Stanford University heart transplant pioneer Norman Shumway, who testified in the case, the judge would have none of it. He informed the jury that the accepted criteria for death were those set forth by the Harvard committee, and that that should inform their decision. (Photographs of the victim's brains "oozing from his skull," to quote the *San Francisco Chronicle*, probably didn't help Lyons's case.) In the end, Lyons was convicted of murder. Based on the outcome of the case, California passed legislation making brain death the legal definition of death. Other states quickly followed suit.

Andrew Lyons's defense attorney wasn't the first person to cry murder when a transplant surgeon removed a heart from a brain-dead patient. In the earliest days of heart transplants, Shumway, the first U.S. surgeon to carry out the procedure, was continually harangued by the coroner in Santa Clara County, where he practiced. The coroner didn't accept the brain-death concept of death and threatened that if Shumway went ahead with his plans to remove a beating heart from a brain-dead person and use it to save another person's life, he would initiate murder charges. Though the coroner had no legal ground to stand on and Shumway went ahead anyway, the press gave it a vigorous chew. New York heart transplant surgeon Mehmet Oz recalls the Brooklyn district attorney around that time making the same threat. "He said he'd indict and arrest any heart transplant surgeon who went into his borough and harvested an organ."

The worry, explained Oz, was that someday 15 someone who wasn't actually brain-dead was going to have his heart cut out. There exist certain rare medical conditions that can look, to the untrained or negligent eye, a lot like brain death, and the legal types didn't trust the medical types to get it right. To a very, very small degree, they had reason to worry. Take, for example, the condition known as "locked-in state." In one form of the disease, the nerves, from eyeballs to toes, suddenly and rather swiftly drop out of commission, with the result that the body is completely paralyzed, while the mind remains normal. The patient can hear what's being said but has no way of communicating that he's still in there, and that no, it's definitely not okay to give his organs away for transplant. In severe cases, even the muscles that contract to change the size of the pupils no longer function. This is bad news, for a common test of brain death is to shine a light in the patient's eyes to check for the reflexive contraction of the pupils.

Typically, victims of locked-in state recover fully, provided no one has mistakenly wheeled them off to the OR to take out their heart.

Like the specter of live burial that plagued the French and German citizenry in the 1800s, the fear of live organ harvesting is almost completely without foundation. A simple EEG will prevent misdiagnosis of the locked-in state and conditions like it.

On a rational level, most people are comfortable with the concept of brain death and organ donation. But on an emotional level, they may have a harder time accepting it, particularly when they are being asked to accept it by a transplant counselor who would like them to okay the removal of a family member's beating heart. Fifty-four percent of families asked refuse consent. "They can't deal with the fear, however irrational, that the true end of their loved one will come when the heart is removed," says Oz. That they, in effect, will have killed him.

Even heart transplant surgeons sometimes have trouble accepting the notion that the heart is nothing more than a pump. When I asked Oz where he thought the soul resided, he said, "I'll confide in you that I don't think it's all in the brain. I have to believe that in many ways the core of our existence is in our heart." Does that mean he thinks the brain-dead patient isn't dead? "There's no question that the heart without a brain is of no value. But life and death is not a binary system." It's a continuum. It makes sense, for many reasons, to draw the legal line at brain death, but that doesn't mean it's really a line. "In between life and death is a state of near-death, or pseudo-life. And most people don't want what's in between." . . .

• • •

The harvesting of H is winding down. The last organs to be taken, the kidneys, are being brought up and separated from the depths of her open torso. Her thorax and abdomen are filled with crushed ice, turned red from blood. "Cherry Sno-Kone," I write in my notepad. It's been almost four hours now, and H has begun to look more like a conventional cadaver, her skin dried and dulled at the edges of the incision.

The kidneys are placed in a blue plastic bowl with ice and perfusion fluid. A relief surgeon arrives for the final step of the recovery, cutting off pieces of veins and arteries to be included, like spare sweater buttons, along with the organs, in case the ones attached to them are too short to work with. A half hour later, the relief surgeon steps aside and the resident comes over to sew H up. 20

As he talks to Dr. Posselt about the stitching, the resident strokes the bank of fat along H's incision with his gloved hand, then pats it twice, as though comforting her. When he turns back to his work, I ask him if it feels different to be working on a dead patient.

"Oh, yes," he answers. "I mean, I would never use this kind of stitch." He has begun stitching more widely spaced, comparatively crude loops, rather than the tight, hidden stitches used on the living.

I rephrase the question: Does it feel odd to perform surgery on someone who isn't alive?

His answer is surprising. "The patient *was* alive." I suppose surgeons are used to thinking about patients—particularly ones they've never met—as no more than what they see of them: open plots of organs. And as far as that goes, I guess you could say H *was* alive. Because of the cloths covering all but her opened torso, the young man never saw her face, didn't know if she was male or female.

While the resident sews, a nurse picks stray danglies of skin and fat off the operating table with a pair of tongs and drops them inside 25

the body cavity, as though H were a handy wastebasket. The nurse explains that this is done intentionally: "Anything not donated stays with her." The jigsaw puzzle put back in its box.

The incision is complete, and a nurse washes H off and covers her with a blanket for the trip to the morgue. Out of habit or respect, he chooses a fresh one. The transplant coordinator, Von, and the nurse lift H onto a gurney. Von wheels H into an elevator and down a hallway to the morgue. The workers are behind a set of swinging doors, in a back room. "Can we leave this here?" Von shouts. H has become a "this." We are instructed to wheel the gurney into the cooler, where it joins five others. H appears no different from the corpses already here.*

But H is different. She has made three sick people well. She has brought them extra time on earth. To be able, as a dead person, to make a gift of this magnitude is phenomenal. Most people don't manage this sort of thing while they're alive. Cadavers like H are the dead's heroes.

It is astounding to me, and achingly sad, that with eighty thousand people on the waiting list for donated hearts and livers and kidneys, with sixteen a day dying there on that list, that more than half of the people in the position H's family was in will say no, will choose to burn those organs or let them rot. We abide the surgeon's scalpel to save our own lives, our loved ones' lives, but not to save a stranger s life. H has no heart, but heartless is the last thing you'd call her.

---

*Unless H's family is planning a naked open-casket service, no one at her funeral will be able to tell she's had organs removed. Only with tissue harvesting, which often includes leg and arm bones, does the body take on a slightly altered profile, and in this case PVC piping or dowels are inserted to normalize the form and make life easier for mortuary staff and others who need to move the otherwise somewhat noodle-ized body.

The infographic represents the history of forensic science, which refers to the application of science to criminal and civil law. We may be most familiar with it from movie and television crime programs. But the practice of forensic science began all the way back in 44 B.C.

As you look at its long history, consider how the study and practice of forensic science enrich our understanding of physical evidence generally.

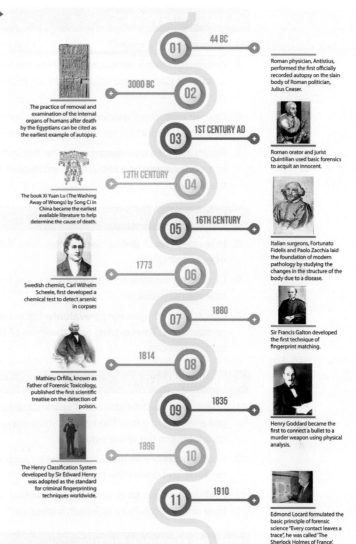

Incognito Forensic Foundation (IFF Lab)

01 44 BC
Roman physician, Antistius, performed the first officially recorded autopsy on the slain body of Roman politician, Julius Ceaser.

3000 BC 02
The practice of removal and examination of the internal organs of humans after death by the Egyptians can be cited as the earliest example of autopsy.

03 1ST CENTURY AD
Roman orator and jurist Quintilian used basic forensics to acquit an innocent.

13TH CENTURY 04
The book Xi Yuan Lu (The Washing Away of Wrongs) by Song Ci in China became the earliest available literature to help determine the cause of death.

05 16TH CENTURY
Italian surgeons, Fortunato Fidelis and Paolo Zacchia laid the foundation of modern pathology by studying the changes in the structure of the body due to a disease.

1773 06
Swedish chemist, Carl Wilhelm Scheele, first developed a chemical test to detect arsenic in corpses

07 1880
Sir Francis Galton developed the first technique of fingerprint matching.

1814 08
Mathieu Orfilla, known as Father of Forensic Toxicology, published the first scientific treatise on the detection of poison.

09 1835
Henry Goddard became the first to connect a bullet to a murder weapon using physical analysis.

1896 10
The Henry Classification System developed by Sir Edward Henry was adopted as the standard for criminal fingerprinting techniques worldwide.

11 1910
Edmond Locard formulated the basic principle of forensic science "Every contact leaves a trace", he was called 'The Sherlock Holmes of France'.

RHETORICAL SITUATION

1. How does the introduction establish the writer's **context**? How does Roach engage the **audience** and prepare it for her subject?

2. Explain the multiple **purposes** and multiple **audiences** of the text. How does this multiplicity contribute to Roach's purpose in a broader **context**?

3. Roach compares and contrasts throughout the text. Choose one of her juxtapositions. Then discuss the relationship of the two ideas. For example, what is the **message** created by this choice? What does the contrast reveal about the two ideas?

CLAIMS AND EVIDENCE

4. What is Roach's **claim**?

5. Roach uses many **sources** throughout the text. Do you find them **reliable** and **credible**? Choose one source and then explain how it contributes to the writer's purpose.

6. Give an example of **evidence** that offers another **perspective** in the text. How does this perspective contribute to the writer's **purpose**?

7. Roach includes **counterarguments** throughout the text. Choose one example of a **concession** or a **rebuttal**. Then explain how it offers further explanation of the subject.

REASONING AND ORGANIZATION

8. How does Roach define *death*? How does this **definition** contribute to her **line of reasoning**?

9. Choose an illustration or an **analogy** in the text. Then explain how it contributes to Roach's message.

10. Roach uses comparison to **evaluate** her subject. Choose one of her comparisons. Then explain how the ideas of the comparison contribute to the writer's purpose.

LANGUAGE AND STYLE

11. Roach uses **coordination** and **subordination** throughout the text. Choose one example of each. Then explain how each of these **syntactical** choices contributes to the writer's purpose.

12. Roach incorporates quotation marks throughout the text. How does this affect her **tone** and contribute to the relationship between the writer and the audience?

13. Find the pronoun **shift** at the end of the text. What is the implication of this shift? How does it contribute to Roach's message?

IDEAS IN AMERICAN CULTURE

14. In part, this text explores the tension between the scientific perspective that (on one hand) "the brain is the seat of the soul" and (on the other hand) the humanistic view "that the heart is the core of our existence." How does this conflict influence our struggle to understand the relationship between life and death?

PUTTING IT ALL TOGETHER

15. How does the story of "Patient H" frame a complex argument about the line between life and death? Explain how Roach arranges her sources and evidence to create a coherent relationship between her ideas and the supporting evidence.

IDEAS IN AMERICAN CULTURE
Criticism and Critique

In the second half of the twentieth century, Cold War anxieties and complex global turmoil led to many earnest reactions, such as nationalism, the peace movement, religious fervor, and pleas for common humanity. But it also led to ironic responses, as many saw the absurdity of living in the modern world. The fiction of writers like Kurt Vonnegut, Flannery O'Connor, and Ken Kesey; the songs of Bob Dylan and the poems of Allen Ginsburg; popular television shows like *The Twilight Zone*, all drew on incongruity, hyperbole, irony, and other satirical elements to offer a dark — and darkly comic — commentary in an era that seemed increasingly dangerous. As television brought images of Vietnam home to Americans, many viewers saw a stark disparity between American ideals and the horrors of a remote and confusing war. Indeed, the war itself was steeped in multiple ironies. The consequences were both tragic and tragically absurd: as casualties mounted, the most powerful nation in the world won most of the battles but proved incapable of either winning — or extricating itself — from the war.

Not surprisingly, perhaps, comedy became explicitly social and "serious," as satirists, comedians, cartoonists, and others directed their irony at American life. For example, anthropologist Horace Miner's 1956 essay "Body Ritual among

IDEA BANK

Absurdity
Apathy
Change
Civility
Comedy
Contrast
Corruption
Criticism
Critique
Hypocrisy
Incongruity
Influence
Insight
Irony
Parody
Power
Reflection
Ridicule
Satire
Subversion
Tragedy

Nightbucks, by Barry Kite/Aberrant Art

Nightbucks is a parody: a humorous imitation of a serious work. In this case, artist Barry Kite revises Edward Hopper's famous 1942 painting *Nighthawks*. Kite's parody juxtaposes the old and new "hangouts." The original artwork shows patrons in a diner, which now sits empty across from the crowded Starbucks.

What does the painting's juxtaposition suggest? How does the irony communicate a message about contemporary society?

the Nacirema" (p. 663) compares the daily rituals of two cultures viewed through the social scientific lens of anthropology. The satirical *MAD* magazine, founded in 1952, ridiculed every aspect of American life and questioned every source of traditional authority. Comedians such as Lenny Bruce, George Carlin, and Richard Pryor turned their wit on previously taboo subjects such as race, sex, and patriotism. In the 1970s, the Watergate scandal pulled back the curtain on deeply flawed government officials and public institutions. It also provided more material for sharp-eyed comedy writers, like the ones who created NBC television's *Saturday Night Live* in 1975, which remains popular today.

That show is now, itself, a respectable institution. But its subversive influence, along with the legacy of American irony and comedy of the last sixty years, is now second nature to us. We see that irony in films, such as *Scary Movie*, mockumentaries, or even comedy shows like *The Daily Show with Trevor Noah*, *The Tonight Show with Jimmy Fallon*, and *Full Frontal with Samantha Bee*. We hear it in the understatement of "Wealthy Teen Nearly Experiences Consequences" (p. 669) from the parody news site The Onion, as well as in the article's point about wealth and privilege. Other sites, such as The Hard Times, ClickHole, and The Babylon Bee use similar tools — incongruity, understatement, sarcasm, and clever juxtapositions — to puncture self-importance, hypocrisy, and corruption. Irony has its limitations, of course — especially when it leads to apathy in the face of injustice. Used well, however, the anarchic power of irony and satire remains an essential weapon in defense of liberty, justice, and civil society.

▲

This photo features writer and comedian Amber Ruffin in a 2018 sketch called "Liberty" on NBC's *Late Night with Seth Meyers*. Ruffin was the first African American woman to be a writer for a late-night network talk show. In 2020, Ruffin became the host of her own late-night talk show, *The Amber Ruffin Show*, which streams on the Peacock network.

How do comedians and comedy writers use humor to criticize serious contemporary subjects? Do you think they perform an important role in keeping Americans informed about social and political issues? Do they encourage active participation in politics? Should they? Why or why not?

Body Ritual among the Nacirema
Horace Miner

THE TEXT IN CONTEXT

American anthropologist Horace Miner (1912–1993) served on the faculty of the University of Chicago (where he earned his doctorate), Wayne State University, and the University of Michigan. As a Fulbright Scholar, he also taught in Uganda and other parts of Africa and South America. His books include *Culture and Agriculture* (1949) and *City in Modern Africa* (1967). In the following 1956 satirical article published in the scholarly journal *American Anthropologist*, Miner observes the practices of the Nacirema tribe as a study in anthropology.

The anthropologist has become so familiar with the diversity of ways in which different peoples behave in similar situations that he is not apt to be surprised by even the most exotic customs. In fact, if all of the logically possible combinations of behavior have not been found somewhere in the world, he is apt to suspect that they must be present in some yet undescribed tribe. This point has, in fact, been expressed with respect to clan organization by Murdock (1949: 71). In this light, the magical beliefs and practices of the Nacirema present such unusual aspects that it seems desirable to describe them as an example of the extremes to which human behavior can go.

Professor Linton first brought the ritual of the Nacirema to the attention of anthropologists twenty years ago (1936: 326), but the culture of this people is still very poorly understood. They are a North American group living in the territory between the Canadian Cree, the Yaqui and Tarahumare of Mexico, and the Carib and Arawak of the Antilles. Little is known of their origin, although tradition states that they came from the east. According to Nacirema mythology, their nation was originated by a culture hero, Notgnihsaw, who is otherwise known for two great feats of strength—the throwing of a piece of wampum across the river Pa-To-Mac and the chopping down of a cherry tree in which the Spirit of Truth resided.

Nacirema culture is characterized by a highly developed market economy which has evolved in a rich natural habitat. While much of the people's time is devoted to economic pursuits, a large part of the fruits of these labors and a considerable portion of the day are spent in ritual activity. The focus of this activity is the human body, the appearance and health of which loom as a dominant concern in the ethos of the people. While such a concern is certainly not unusual, its ceremonial aspects and associated philosophy are unique.

The fundamental belief underlying the whole system appears to be that the human body is ugly and that its natural tendency is to debility and disease. Incarcerated in such a body, man's only hope is to avert these characteristics through the use of the powerful influences of ritual and ceremony. Every household has one or more shrines devoted to this purpose. The more powerful individuals in the society have several shrines in their houses and, in fact, the opulence of a house is often referred to in terms of the number of such ritual centers it possesses. Most houses are of wattle and daub construction, but the shrine rooms of the more wealthy are walled with stone. Poorer families imitate the rich by applying pottery plaques to their shrine walls.

While each family has at least one such shrine, the rituals associated with it are not family ceremonies but are private and secret. The rites are normally only discussed with children, and then only during the period when they are being initiated into these mysteries. I was able, however, to establish sufficient rapport with the natives to examine these shrines and to have the rituals described to me.

The focal point of the shrine is a box or chest which is built into the wall. In this chest are kept the many charms and magical potions without which no native believes he could live. These preparations are secured from a variety of specialized practitioners. The most powerful of these are the medicine men, whose assistance must be rewarded with substantial gifts. However, the medicine men do not provide the curative potions for their clients, but decide what the ingredients should be and then write them down in an ancient and secret language. This writing is understood only by the medicine men and by the herbalists who, for another gift, provide the required charm.

The charm is not disposed of after it has served its purpose, but is placed in the charm-box of the household shrine. As these magical materials are specific for certain ills, and the real or imagined maladies of the people are many, the charm-box is usually full to overflowing. The magical packets are so numerous that people forget what their purposes were and fear to use them again. While the natives are very vague on this point, we can only assume that the idea in retaining all the old magical materials is that their presence in the charm-box, before which the body rituals are conducted, will in some way protect the worshipper.

Beneath the charm-box is a small font. Each day every member of the family, in succession, enters the shrine room, bows his head before the charm-box, mingles different sorts of holy water in the font, and proceeds with a brief rite of ablution. The holy waters are secured from the Water Temple of the community, where the priests conduct elaborate ceremonies to make the liquid ritually pure.

In the hierarchy of magical practitioners, and below the medicine men in prestige, are specialists whose designation is best translated "holy-mouth-men." The Nacirema have an almost pathological horror of and fascination with the mouth, the condition of which is believed to have a supernatural influence on all social relationships. Were it not for the rituals of the mouth, they believe that their teeth would fall out, their gums bleed, their jaws shrink, their friends desert them, and their lovers reject them. They also believe that a strong relationship exists between oral and moral characteristics. For example, there is a ritual ablution of the mouth for children which is supposed to improve their moral fiber.

The daily body ritual performed by everyone includes a mouth-rite. Despite the fact that these people are so punctilious about care of the mouth, this rite involves a practice which strikes the uninitiated stranger as revolting. It was reported to me that the ritual consists of inserting a small bundle of hog hairs into the mouth, along with certain magical powders, and then moving the bundle in a highly formalized series of gestures.

In addition to the private mouth-rite, the people seek out a holy-mouth-man once or twice a year. These practitioners have an impressive set of paraphernalia, consisting of a variety of augers, awls, probes, and prods. The use of these objects in the exorcism of the evils of the mouth involves almost unbelievable ritual torture of the client. The holy-mouth-man opens the client's mouth and, using the above mentioned tools, enlarges any holes which decay may have created in the teeth. Magical materials are put into these holes. If there are no naturally occurring holes in the teeth, large sections of one or more teeth are gouged out so that the supernatural substance can be applied. In the client's view, the purpose of these ministrations is to arrest decay and to draw friends. The extremely sacred and traditional character of the rite is evident in the fact that the natives return to the holy-mouth-men year after year, despite the fact that their teeth continue to decay.

It is to be hoped that, when a thorough study of the Nacirema is made, there will be careful inquiry into the personality structure of these people. One has but to watch the gleam in the eye of a holy-mouth-man, as he jabs an awl into an exposed nerve, to suspect that a certain amount of sadism is involved. If this can be established, a very interesting pattern emerges, for most of the population shows definite masochistic tendencies. It was to these that Professor Linton referred in discussing a distinctive part of the daily body ritual which is performed only by men. This part

of the rite involves scraping and lacerating the surface of the face with a sharp instrument. Special women's rites are performed only four times during each lunar month, but what they lack in frequency is made up in barbarity. As part of this ceremony, women bake their heads in small ovens for about an hour. The theoretically interesting point is that what seems to be a preponderantly masochistic people have developed sadistic specialists.

The medicine men have an imposing temple, or *latipso*, in every community of any size. The more elaborate ceremonies required to treat very sick patients can only be performed at this temple. These ceremonies involve not only the thaumaturge but a permanent group of vestal maidens who move sedately about the temple chambers in distinctive costume and headdress.

The *latipso* ceremonies are so harsh that it is phenomenal that a fair proportion of the really sick natives who enter the temple ever recover. Small children whose indoctrination is still incomplete have been known to resist attempts to take them to the temple because "that is where you go to die." Despite this fact, sick adults are not only willing but eager to undergo the protracted ritual purification, if they can afford to do so. No matter how ill the supplicant or how grave the emergency, the guardians of many temples will not admit a client if he cannot give a rich gift to the custodian. Even after one has gained admission and survived the ceremonies, the guardians will not permit the neophyte to leave until he makes still another gift.

The supplicant entering the temple is first 15 stripped of all his or her clothes. In everyday life the Nacirema avoids exposure of his body and its natural functions. Bathing and excretory acts are performed only in the secrecy of the household shrine, where they are ritualized as part of the body-rites. Psychological shock results from the fact that body secrecy is suddenly lost upon entry into the *latipso*. A man, whose own wife has never seen him in an excretory act, suddenly finds himself naked and assisted by a vestal maiden while he performs his natural functions into a sacred vessel. This sort of ceremonial treatment is necessitated by the fact that the excreta are used by a diviner to ascertain the course and nature of the client's sickness. Female clients, on the other hand, find their naked bodies are subjected to the scrutiny, manipulation and prodding of the medicine men.

Few supplicants in the temple are well enough to do anything but lie on their hard beds. The daily ceremonies, like the rites of the holy-mouth-men, involve discomfort and torture. With ritual precision, the vestals awaken their miserable charges each dawn and roll them about on their beds of pain while performing ablutions, in the formal movements of which the maidens are highly trained. At other times they insert magic wands in the supplicant's mouth or force him to eat substances which are supposed to be healing. From time to time the medicine men come to their clients and jab magically treated needles into their flesh. The fact that these temple ceremonies may not cure, and may even kill the neophyte. in no way decreases the people's faith in the medicine men.

There remains one other kind of practitioner, known as a "listener." This witch-doctor has the power to exorcise the devils that lodge in the heads of people who have been bewitched. The Nacirema believe that parents bewitch their own children. Mothers are particularly suspected of putting a curse on children while teaching them the secret body rituals. The counter-magic of the witch-doctor is unusual in its lack of ritual. The patient simply tells the "listener" all his troubles and fears, beginning with the earliest difficulties he can remember. The memory displayed by the Nacirema in these exorcism sessions is truly remarkable. It is not uncommon for the patient to bemoan the rejection he felt upon being weaned as a babe, and a few individuals even see their troubles going back to the traumatic effects of their own birth.

In conclusion, mention must be made of certain practices which have their base in native esthetics but which depend upon the pervasive aversion to the natural body and its functions. There are ritual fasts to make fat people thin and ceremonial feasts to make thin people fat. Still other rites are used to make women's breasts larger if they are small, and smaller if they are large. General dissatisfaction with breast shape is symbolized in the fact that the ideal form is virtually outside the range of human variation. A few women afflicted with almost inhuman hypermammary development are so idolized that they make a handsome living by simply going from village to village and permitting the natives to stare at them for a fee.

Reference has already been made to the fact that excretory functions are ritualized, routinized, and relegated to secrecy. Natural reproductive functions are similarly distorted. Intercourse is taboo as a topic and scheduled as an act. Efforts are made to avoid pregnancy by the use of magical materials or by limiting intercourse to certain phases of the moon. Conception is actually very infrequent. When pregnant, women dress so as to hide their condition. Parturition takes place in secret, without friends or relatives to assist, and the majority of women do not nurse their infants.

Our review of the ritual life of the Nacirema 20 has certainly shown them to be a magic-ridden people. It is hard to understand how they have managed to exist so long under the burdens which they have imposed upon themselves. But even such exotic customs as these take on real meaning when they are viewed with the insight provided by Malinowski when he wrote (1948: 70):

> Looking from far and above, from our high places of safety in the developed civilization, it is easy to see all the crudity and irrelevance of magic. But without its power and guidance early

man could not have mastered his practical difficulties as he has done, nor could man have advanced to the higher stages of civilization.

References Cited

Linton, Ralph

1936 *The Study of Man.* New York, D. Appleton-Century Co.

Malinowski, Bronislaw

1948 *Magic, Science, and Religion.* Glencoe, The Free Press.

Murdock, George P.

1949 *Social Structure.* New York, The Macmillan Co.

This political cartoon was created by Patrick Chappatte and published in the *New York Times*. It comments on Amazon's purchase of the Whole Foods company. ▶

How does the cartoon use both exaggeration and understatement to criticize Amazon's effect on small businesses in America?

Reprint of a cartoon by Chappatte: © Chappatte in The New York Times

RHETORICAL SITUATION

1. How does the **writer** provide **context** in the **introduction**? How does he address the needs of the **audience**?

2. The **conclusion** offers a broad, universal message. What is that **message**? How might it resonate with the intended audience?

3. Explain the multiple **audiences** for the text. Who are they? How do they contribute to the complexity of Miner's argument?

CLAIMS AND EVIDENCE

4. How is Miner's **evidence** relevant to his claim? Find two examples of evidence and explain their relevance.

5. How does Miner strategically select the **evidence** to appeal to the audience? Choose two pieces of evidence. Then explain how the evidence might **appeal** to the audience and strengthen their relationship with the writer.

6. Select a piece of **evidence** that Miner uses for a comparison. Then explain how this evidence contributes to the comparison and the overall argument.

REASONING AND ORGANIZATION

7. What is Miner's **method of development** in this argument? In other words, how does he organize and divide text? What makes this division ironic and humorous?

8. As Miner **divides** the characteristics of the Nacirema, he often includes **process** analysis. Choose one of these processes and explain how it contributes to the writer's message.

9. How does Miner organize the text: **inductively** or **deductively**? How does this organization contribute to the purpose and the message of the argument?

LANGUAGE AND STYLE

10. How does Miner create an **incongruity** of ideas in the first paragraph? What examples of **irony** can you find in the text? Choose one and explain how it contributes to Miner's message.

11. How do Miner's **syntax** and **diction** contribute to his overall argument? Do they seem suitable to his subject, or do they seem **incongruous** with his subject? Explain.

12. While **satire** offers social or political criticism, it usually does so indirectly. How is this argument satirical? What is Miner criticizing? What are the implications of that criticism?

IDEAS IN AMERICAN CULTURE

13. While it was written in the 1950s, Miner's parody remains relevant. How might you adapt his satirical strategy to describe "rituals" among Americans? What common activities or practices might appear especially incongruous if they were presented in the voice of a social science researcher?

PUTTING IT ALL TOGETHER

14. Identify two or three key rhetorical choices that help Miner achieve his purpose in examining rituals of the Nacirema tribe. How do they contribute to the purpose?

Wealthy Teen Nearly Experiences Consequence

The Onion

THE TEXT IN CONTEXT

The Onion is an online parody newspaper that tackles current events, sports, entertainment, and countless other media topics with a biting satirical tone and perceptive eye for incongruity. In this 2008 satirical article, The Onion addresses the culture of entitlement among privileged teens.

SOMERSET, NJ—In what local authorities are calling a "near tragedy," Charles Wentworth, a 17-year-old Rutgers Preparatory senior and member of the affluent Wentworth family, came perilously close to suffering a consequence resulting from his own wrong-doing Saturday.

Wentworth made his senior photo shoot even after coming within inches of an actual repercussion from the accident.

Wentworth, reportedly ignoring the protests of his classmates, got behind the wheel of his turbocharged Supra 2000GT after consuming half the contents of a bottle of Goldschläger at a friend's party. While driving westbound on Route 27, a disoriented Wentworth drifted across two lanes of traffic and collided with a minivan carrying a family of four, bringing the teen face-to-face with a potentially life-altering lesson.

Wentworth escaped unscathed and unpunished, however, when his airbags deployed and a team of high-powered attorneys rushed to the scene and rescued him from the brink of personal responsibility.

"Amazingly, Mr. Wentworth did not experience a single repercussion for consuming alcohol under age or operating a motor vehicle while intoxicated, and is furthermore completely unaware that he did anything wrong," local police chief Marvin Taylor said. "He is a very lucky boy.

"If he had been driving just 5 mph faster, or if his parents hadn't had the influence to keep the matter out of court and the endless financial resources to lease a car of the exact same make and model to prevent him from having to face even the relatively trivial humiliation of being taunted by his peers for driving a slightly less expensive vehicle—my God, who knows what could have happened?" Taylor added. "He could have died or, worse, been held accountable for his actions."

The Accident

According to police reports that have since been shredded and stricken from Wentworth's permanent record, when briefly taken into custody, the privileged teenager began swearing, vomiting, and kicking at the windows of the squad car in which he was momentarily placed following the collision. Wentworth later said the only thing that got him through that dark time was thinking of his rich, well-connected loved ones. With them in mind, he repeatedly shouted, "Don't you know who I am?" and summoned the strength to refuse a field sobriety test.

"A lot of kids in Charles' situation would have confessed and accepted punishment for their mistake, but my son is strong," said Wentworth's father, aluminum magnate Herman Wentworth, who after arriving at the crash site told his son that "everything is taken care of," and while Charles sat in his father's BMW texting his friends, loudly threatened to call the police commissioner if any charges were pressed. "Charles would never allow himself to give up and gain valuable insight into the way things work in the real world without a fight."

District Judge and close friend of the Wentworth family Donald Lamb agreed.

"Charles is very lucky to be alive and well-off," Lamb told reporters. "The fact that he was able to walk away from this crash with no injuries, zero remorse, and his skewed priorities in one piece is a miracle." 10

Despite returning to the safety of his $2.3 million home, Wentworth's harrowing brush with consequence was not over.

A week after the near ordeal, Wentworth was again put in jeopardy of learning a lesson when he was nearly sentenced to 50 hours of community service. Tragedy was averted, however, when his mother paid a consultant to testify before the judge that Wentworth had suffered emotional trauma. Further, during this time, Wentworth was forced to put his video game on pause for several seconds in order to sign affidavits stating that the Breathalyzer was administered improperly.

"To think that I was that close to seeing that there is an entire society with its own laws and standards outside my protected sphere of wealth and privilege—it's frightening," Wentworth said. "It almost makes you consider your actions and their impact on others. Almost.

"I'm just grateful I can finally get back to my life as a self-centered prick who believes the entire world revolves around him," Wentworth added. "After all, I was just admitted to Columbia despite almost failing out of high school because I rarely attended class, and it would have been a shame to have had to defer for a semester just because of some legal . . . unpleasantry."

At press time, Wentworth is resting comfortably on a six-figure inheritance in a chaise lounge by his backyard pool. The other four victims of the crash remain in intensive care at St. Peter's University Hospital, suffering from conditions ranging from poor to lower-class. 15

▲

The long-running *Saturday Night Live* is famous for its political satire. In this still image from the show, Jim Carrey impersonates President Joe Biden and Maya Rudolph impersonates Vice President Kamala Harris.

How do shows like this, along with internet memes and other contemporary social comedy, shape public perceptions of politics? On the whole, do you think they lead to a more informed and engaged electorate? Why or why not?

RHETORICAL SITUATION

1. The writers assume that they share beliefs and values with their **audience**. What are some of those shared beliefs? How do they affect the writers' **rhetorical choices**?

2. Identify two rhetorical choices in the text that help connect it with its intended **audience**. How might they be interpreted differently by an unintended audience?

3. What is the **message** in the **conclusion**? What does that message imply?

CLAIMS AND EVIDENCE

4. Identify a moment in the text when the writers make a **concession** and then explain how that concession contributes to the message of the text.

5. What functions as "**evidence**" in the article? What effect does this evidence create? Does this evidence support the claim of the text? Explain.

6. How is the selection of the **evidence** targeted for a specific **audience**? How does the evidence contribute to the message of the text?

REASONING AND ORGANIZATION

7. What is the **method of development**? How does this method reflect the purpose of the text?

8. What is the tension or **incongruity** in the text? How does it contribute to the **purpose** of the argument?

9. How do the writers use verbs or **transitions** to indicate the **cause-and-effect** relationships within the **evidence**?

LANGUAGE AND STYLE

10. There are many instances of **hyperbole** and **exaggeration** throughout the text. Choose one example of each. Then discuss how each choice contributes to the message of the text.

11. How do the writers use quotation marks to create **tone** in the text?

IDEAS IN AMERICAN CULTURE

12. We live in a world full of internet memes, mocking videos, and countless other forms of comedy. Can you think of a serious issue in your school or community that could be addressed ironically? How might irony communicate the seriousness of the message? How could humor reinforce the relationship between the writer and the audience?

PUTTING IT ALL TOGETHER

13. The writers use understatement and irony to discuss a serious issue. How do these elements contribute to the purpose of the text?

COMPOSITION WORKSHOP
Writing an Evaluation Argument: Proposing a Solution

In Unit 7, you practiced writing an evaluation argument organized by comparison/contrast. In this workshop, you will build on that knowledge to write a second type of evaluation argument organized by the problem-solution mode of development.

We don't have to look very far to identify problems in our community, our country, and our world. In most cases, they are complex issues that require careful consideration and may have a number of possible solutions. So we must evaluate these possibilities based on a goal or a criterion for success, which will help us identify a solution that will best address the problem while aligning with our purpose. For example, your school administrators may wish to reduce excessive classroom tardiness among students. Their goal is to encourage promptness so that no valuable in-class learning time is lost. Therefore, as the administrators consider solutions, they must evaluate their alternatives with this central goal — maximizing learning time — in mind.

In this workshop, you will develop a problem-solution argument. First, you will identify and describe a problem, including its causes and effects. Then you will present possible solutions based on your goal or success criterion. In your conclusion, you will propose a solution that best aligns with your goal.

> **KEY POINT**
> Writers organize proposal arguments by first explaining the problem or issue and establishing a goal. Then they evaluate the pros and cons of different options. Finally, they propose a solution with the best chance of achieving their goal.

Self-Care Alone Will Not Fix the System
Walter Li

The following example was written by high school student Walter Li. The essay was a runner-up in the *New York Times* 2019 Student Editorial Contest.

Mental health is entering the mainstream. The conversation has opened up as more high-profile individuals talk about their mental health struggles. As a mental health activist, I am thrilled at the momentum, yet I have reservations about the dominant focus of the conversation. Those reservations surfaced recently when I was posting a self-care tip about the value of journaling on the Instagram of my school's mental health club. Something felt off; telling people to journal felt like putting a band-aid on a broken arm.

re-examines his own claim from an earlier post

analogy suggests that self-care is not enough

analogy conveys a sarcastic attitude

refutes previous
solutions that over-
simplify the issue

cause (media atten-
tion) and effect
(oversimplifying
treatment)

solutions based upon
the goal: accessible
and comprehensive

Like my post, mainstream conversations oversimplify mental
health. Self-care (meditation, mindfulness, and other self-help
methods) have dominated current narratives. Media profiles of
athletes or celebrities accessing treatment miss a crucial fact:
treatment is still too expensive and stigmatized for the vast majority.
Self-care tips are not enough. It is time for mainstream conversations
to address how the mental health treatment system is fundamentally
broken. It is time we talk about how to fix the system to offer accessible,
comprehensive care for everyone.

analogy emphasizes
the importance of
seeking solutions

The default in society is to deal with your mental illness alone:
according to Mental Health America, 56.4 percent of adults struggling
with a mental illness never get help. Imagine if 56.4 percent of adults
with a broken arm never saw a doctor. How did we get here? After
psychiatric asylums were closed in the United States, the goal was
to replace them with a more supportive alternative. That alternative
never came to fruition, meaning a comprehensive mental health
system was never put in place.

The debate over solutions has some consensus: according to the
New York Times Editorial Board, no one "wants to return to the era of
'insane asylums,' . . . Nor does anyone disagree that the 'system' that
replaced them is a colossal failure." The core components of a working system include overall higher quality care with more treatment
options and a greater bandwidth of medical programs including integrated and preventive care. This system must be paired with insurance parity and a culture that makes accessing care clear, affordable,
and de-stigmatized for everyone. According to Mental Health America, this new system must "support individuals at all stages of their
recovery." Many people have promoted ideas for the exact details of

concession: self-care
not the only solution

reiterates problems
with current system

claim: current
treatments must be
re-evaluated

call to action

this new system; however, these ideas cannot coalesce unless a discussion occurs in mainstream circles.

I do not write this editorial to say that self-care is less important.
I write it to say that the status quo of the current mental health
system must be challenged. This system is not working: it is too
expensive, too inaccessible, and too stigmatized. We cannot go
forward unless we carefully examine and alter mental health
treatment. Now is the time to have that conversation.

 YOUR ASSIGNMENT

Your local newspaper has invited high school students to share their perspectives by
contributing to the annual "Year in Review" issue that will focus on the major local and
national events of the year. Your editorial must identify a current problem and propose
a solution to that problem. Think of a local, state, or national issue that is important to

you. Then write an evaluation argument that explains the problem and discusses possible solutions by judging their effectiveness based on your goal for success. Finally, convey your perspective to your audience by proposing the best solution.

Your problem-solution argument should include:

- An introduction that explains both the problem and the consequences of ignoring it
- A thesis statement that makes a claim (perspective + unifying idea) and establishes the goal or success criterion
- A line of reasoning that presents possible solutions in relation to your goal
- Evidence to prove your reasoning, qualify your argument, and demonstrate the complexity of the problem and solution
- A conclusion that proposes and justifies the solution
- Stylistic strategies, especially comparisons, ironic perspectives, or parenthetical elements, that appeal to your audience

Potential Subjects

- Distracted driving
- Rising college costs
- Cancel culture
- Rising high school dropout rate
- Food deserts
- Teen substance abuse
- Technology addiction

RHETORICAL SITUATION Addressing Complexity

AP® Enduring Understanding (RHS-1)

Individuals write within a particular situation and make strategic writing choices based on that situation.

As you begin to plan your problem-solution argument, carefully consider how you will describe the complexity of the problem and the validity of your proposed solution to your intended audience. Before you can begin evaluating possible solutions, you must describe the problem clearly and concisely. Where do we see evidence of the problem? What caused the problem? What are its effects? Remember: In most problem-solution arguments, you must first convince your audience that the problem is real, urgent, and likely to lead to unwanted consequences if not addressed. So your introduction should briefly contextualize the problem using this information.

For an audience to accept your proposal, they must see you as credible (i.e., knowledgeable and fair). Therefore, you must consider the perspectives, contexts, and needs of your intended audience when making your rhetorical choices. To make this connection, begin with your syntax and diction, which contribute to your credibility with the audience. These choices are your main tools for conveying your attitude toward various solutions and delivering your message to the audience. In earlier units, we practiced the syntactical choices of subordination and qualification, which signal that you are addressing the complexity of the issue and considering different perspectives. This is another chance to put those skills into practice.

Additionally, you can unravel complexity and relate to your audience by using rhetorical comparisons, such as analogies, extended metaphors, and allusions. In other words, when a problem is unfamiliar or challenging to an audience, you can often find an analogy or metaphor that helps explain it in more familiar terms. Consider the following example of an analogy:

> *Arriving to class late is like missing the beginning of a movie: everyone else knows what is going on while you feel lost.*

In this example, the audience may not fully appreciate the importance of the first few minutes of a classroom lesson, but they may have experienced the confusion of missing the beginning of a movie — or even annoyance at constant questions from a latecomer. The analogy, then, helps the audience connect a familiar experience to a less familiar idea in your argument — and understand the importance of that idea.

Because evaluation arguments are comparative, writers often juxtapose (or place side by side) ideas or evidence to facilitate these comparisons. In your problem-solution argument, for example, you will present possible solutions and their related pros and cons in close proximity. That will allow the audience to notice the distinctions between them, more clearly understand your evaluation, and consider accepting your proposal.

Try to incorporate some of the following types of rhetorical comparisons when developing your argument.

RHETORICAL COMPARISONS	
Organizational Choice	**Description**
Analogy	Presents two things as similar based on common attributes and then draws an inference, hypothesis, or conclusion about a similarity that has yet to have occurred or been observed
Extended Metaphor	Establishes a comparison between two unlike things throughout the text and focuses on the shared characteristics to emphasize an idea critical to the writer's claim
Allusion	Refers to history, pop culture, literature, or art that the audience knows as a way of illustrating a similarity

Comparisons should be familiar to the intended audience. When incorporating analogies, extended metaphors, allusions, or other rhetorical comparisons, you should choose objects of comparison that are known to the intended audience. Otherwise, you will not achieve the intended effect because your audience does not understand the reference.

 RHETORICAL SITUATION
Addressing Complexity

Begin planning your problem-solution argument by considering the following:

- What **problem** would I like to solve?
- What are the **causes** and **effects** of the problem?
- What are the **consequences** if the problem goes unsolved?
- Who is my **audience**?
- What **alternative perspectives** should be addressed?
- What **solution** will I recommend to my audience in the **conclusion**?

REASONING AND ORGANIZATION | Justifying a Claim

 Enduring Understanding (REO-1)

Writers guide understanding of a text's line of reasoning and claims through that text's organization and integration of evidence.

After considering the rhetorical situation and the complexity of solving the problem, you are ready to write your claim and plan the line of reasoning that justifies your claim. As you know from prior workshops, your claim includes a controlling or unifying idea and your perspective. For the proposal argument, your controlling idea corresponds to the goal or the success criterion used to evaluate the possible solutions. For example, in addressing student tardiness, the administration determines that the ultimate goal of the new policy is to maximize learning time in the classroom. The idea of learning time is the driving force for improving the policy. Therefore, the solutions in the line of reasoning will be measured by their contribution to learning time.

Idea: *Learning time*

Perspective: *Maximize time for learning*

Claim: *When students arrive to class on time, schools can maximize the learning time.*

Thesis: *Because student tardiness reduces learning time in the classroom, the administration should implement practical and systematic changes to facilitate students' on-time arrival.*

You will establish your line of reasoning by identifying possible solutions to the problem — each developed in a body paragraph that includes evidence and evaluation. To address tardiness, for example, we might consider several options: adjusting the school schedule, implementing stricter consequences for students, and making systematic changes during passing periods.

We will explore each possible solution in a body paragraph. Each paragraph will use evidence to examine the pros and cons of a possible solution and evaluate that solution based on our goal of maximizing learning time. For example, if we consider the option of adjusting the school schedule to lengthen the time between classes, we can determine that this solution takes time away from class; therefore, it does not meet the established success criterion.

In your argument, the final body paragraph will reveal your proposed solution. You will support this proposal with evidence that justifies it based on the success criterion. Then you can write a conclusion that describes the solution's outcomes and calls the audience to action.

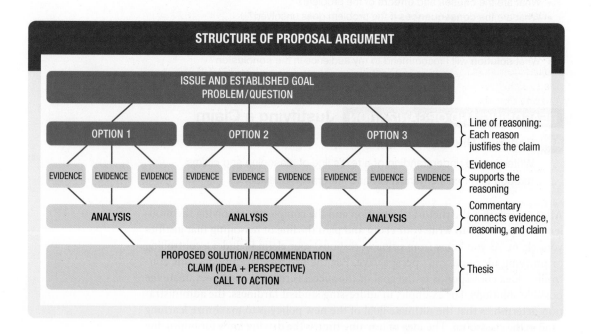

STRUCTURE OF PROPOSAL ARGUMENT

In this workshop, we have been exploring the sample problem of habitual tardiness. In the following outline, observe how the writer's planned introduction establishes the context of the problem and asserts a claim (unifying idea + perspective). Next, the line of reasoning supports the claim by listing possible solutions that the writer will develop and evaluate based on the success criterion. Then, the writer reveals the proposed solution and justifies the choice while also acknowledging its limitations. Finally, the writer prepares to call the audience to action in the conclusion.

Problem: *Excessive tardiness in school is disrupting the learning environment*

Introduction

- Hook the audience:

  Startling statistic of the total number of tardies recorded in a school year and the resulting time lost

- Describe and contextualize the problem:

  Some students are habitually late to class, tardiness is increasing

  Causes: *Crowded hallways, loitering, lack of consequences, apathy*

- Establish success criterion:

  Idea: *Learning time*

  Perspective: *Maximize learning time in the classroom*

  Question: *What changes will facilitate and encourage students to be on time to class while protecting instructional time in the classroom?*

Option One	Option Two	Option Three
Adjust the school schedule to allow more time for passing periods.	*Implement a no-tolerance policy that requires students to go directly to detention for the class period.*	*Strategize better and more logical hallway traffic patterns.*

Proposed Solution

Implement proactive measures such as redesigning traffic patterns and posting principals and teachers in hallways to encourage students to keep moving.

- Clear and sufficient justification:

  Reduce the barriers that keep students from arriving on time and then focus specifically on positive reinforcement to change the behavior and the culture.

- Limitations (concession or qualifying language):

  While no solution can eliminate tardiness altogether . . .

  Granted, some students will be late no matter what strategies are in place . . .

- Thesis: Claim (unifying idea + perspective + a goal or success criterion):

  To maximize learning time in the classroom, school administration should implement practical and systematic changes to facilitate students' on-time arrival.

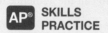 **SKILLS PRACTICE** | REASONING AND ORGANIZATION
Justifying a Claim

As you begin drafting your problem-solution argument, complete the following steps:

1. Review your notes for context, complexity, and audience before crafting your introduction.
2. Write a thesis statement that includes a claim and identifies your goal.
3. Generate possible solutions for your line of reasoning.

Problem
Introduction
Describe and contextualize the problem:
Establish Success Criteria:

Option One	Option Two	Option Three (optional)

Proposed Solution

Thesis: (unifying idea + perspective) + a goal or success criterion

---

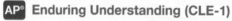 **CLAIMS AND EVIDENCE** **Developing a Counterargument**

AP® Enduring Understanding (CLE-1)

> Writers make claims about subjects, rely on evidence that supports the reasoning that justifies the claim, and often acknowledge or respond to other, possibly opposing, arguments.

To support your claim and line of reasoning, you must provide evidence and commentary to evaluate the possible solutions presented in the body of your argument. This involves weighing options against one another and choosing the best solution for your final proposal. To complete a fair and successful evaluation, you must consider different perspectives and alternative solutions. This evaluation takes place in the body paragraphs as you examine the advantages of each solution (pros) and raise any potential problems (cons). Remember to unify your argument by anchoring your evaluations to the goal established in your claim.

WAYS TO JOIN THE CONVERSATION THROUGH CORROBORATION, REFUTATION, REBUTTAL, AND CONCESSION

	Agree with source information and justify your response	Refute or rebut source information and justify your response	Concede, in part, to source information and justify your response	Acknowledge the limitations of your own argument and offer explanation
Responding to a Claim	_____ makes an accurate claim that _____ which is important to note because _____.	The claim from _____ is inaccurate/ irrelevant/outdated because _____.	Although _____ makes a strong point that _____, the claim fails to address _____.	Admittedly, the claim that _____ is not always the case because _____. However, _____ is still an important consideration because _____.
Responding to Qualitative Evidence	It is important to consider _____'s evidence that _____ because it supports the idea that _____.	While not inaccurate, _____'s evidence that _____ does not address the central issue of _____ because _____.	While it is true that the evidence suggests _____, we must also consider _____ because _____.	Evidence that _____ may not apply in all situations; however, within the current context this evidence _____.
Responding to Quantitative Evidence	The data reported from _____ that suggests _____ reveals _____.	The data that suggests _____ is misleading in that _____. One should instead consider data from _____ that suggests _____ because _____.	The data is accurate in that _____; however, anecdotal evidence contradicts these conclusions and suggests that _____.	Since the data that suggests _____ may be outdated/ inconclusive/ limited, we must also consider _____ which confirms that _____.

Some opposing solutions might seem like viable options, but you will need to **refute** them (prove them wrong) if they are based on questionable or invalid evidence. Or, if you simply disagree with some opposing solutions or decide that they fail to address your goal, you can offer a **rebuttal** (argue against them) from your own perspective. In these cases, you should address opposing evidence first and then follow with your own evidence and commentary. This will give you the last word.

Finally, you may find that some opposing solutions have valid ideas or even valid objections to your solution. You can address these differing perspectives by offering a **concession** — that is, acknowledging the validity of opposition or the limitations of your own argument. Because most problems are complex, you may even need to make concessions when you justify your final proposal. Remember, though, valid concessions contribute to your ethos. They indicate to the audience that you are fair, trustworthy, and open to considering other perspectives.

Use counterarguments strategically, however. Concessions, rebuttals, and refutations can strengthen your credibility and address an audience's concerns. But you should deploy them wisely. If your concessions outweigh the reasons and evidence for your proposal, you may sound indecisive and unconvincing.

Whatever method of counterargument you choose, remember that you must support your reasons with relevant and sufficient evidence. As you select evidence, keep your audience and your goal in mind. Remember as well that you will need to include commentary to connect the evidence to your line of reasoning (and your claim). Finally, use helpful transitions both to connect the solutions to your goal and signal any shifts in perspective. These transitions will guide the reader through your argument.

Rhetorical Move	Example
Refutation	Some teachers argue that if the consequences were more severe, students would arrive to class on time. _However_, in recent studies, researchers reported that schools with lenient tardy policies and those with strict policies had roughly the same number of tardies per student.
Rebuttal	Typical schools address the problem of tardiness by focusing their efforts on punishments for students. _In contrast_, innovative schools stress the benefits of punctuality by offering incentives for students.
Concession	_It is true that_, for some students who are habitually late, no punishments or incentives will change their behavior. Schools _regrettably_ cannot eliminate tardiness altogether.

Review the following graphic organizer. It shows a plan for developing the line of reasoning through evidence and commentary. Note that refutation and rebuttal express cons or objections to possible solutions. In contrast, concessions acknowledge the benefits of an opposing solution or the limitations of your proposal.

Problem: _Excessive tardiness_		
Question: _What changes will facilitate and encourage students to be on time to class while protecting instructional time in the classroom?_		
Solution One	**Solution Two**	**Solution Three**
Lengthen the time between classes	_Send students directly to detention for the class period when they arrive late_	_Strategize better and more logical traffic patterns_

Pros	Pros	Pros
Allows students time to navigate crowded hallways and to take care of personal business	*Late students will not disrupt the class already in session if they go to an alternate location*	*Opening up traffic space allows students to move swiftly in the hallway*
Cons/Objections	**Cons/Objections**	**Cons/Objections**
More time in passing periods reduces the instructional time for everyone; students who are "hanging out" may just do so longer	*Students who are tardy would miss all of the instruction for the class period*	*Does not address the problem of loitering*
Evaluation Based on the Goal	**Evaluation Based on the Goal**	**Evaluation Based on the Goal**
Takes away learning time in every class daily, but this is minimal and is not interruptive	*Protects learning time for students who arrive on time but removes late students from the learning environment*	*Could potentially promote timeliness and protect learning time*

Proposed Solution

Implement a two-fold solution: Strategize effective traffic flow and increase faculty presence in the hallway to keep students not only moving but also moving in the right direction.

Clear and sufficient justification:

Data from schools and teacher feedback suggest that punishment does not significantly decrease tardiness; observations of model schools suggest that an adult presence in the hallways reduces loitering and encourages people to move more swiftly, which protects the learning time for students.

Limitations (concession or qualifying language):

While no solution can eliminate tardiness altogether, . . .

Granted, some students will be late no matter what policies are in place . . .

Conclusion

Description of outcomes and implications:

When students see faculty involvement, as well as the school's efforts to address the causes of tardiness, these measures can cause a cultural change — one that protects learning time.

Thesis:

To maximize learning time in the classroom, the school administration should implement physical and systematic changes to facilitate students' on-time arrival.

Call to action:

Urge audience to consider adopting the proposal.

AP® SKILLS PRACTICE

CLAIMS AND EVIDENCE
Developing a Counterargument

Using the thesis and line of reasoning (i.e., possible solutions) you developed earlier, choose your evidence and plan your commentary. For each solution, address the alternative perspectives by examining pros and cons; then, conclude the paragraph with an evaluation of the solution based on your goal. Address alternate perspectives in your argument by using counterarguments: concession, rebuttal, or refutation.

Introduction
Explain and contextualize the problem:

Question (establish goal or success criteria):

Option One	Option Two	Option Three
Pros	Pros	Pros
Cons/Objections	Cons/Objections	Cons/Objections
Evaluation Based on Goal	Evaluation Based on Goal	Evaluation Based on Goal

Proposed Solution
Clear and sufficient justification:

Limitations (concession or qualifying language):

Conclusion
Description of outcomes and implications:

Thesis:

Call to action:

LANGUAGE AND STYLE **Connecting with an Audience through Stylistic Choices**

AP **Enduring Understanding (STL-1)**

The rhetorical situation informs the strategic stylistic choices that writers make.

In addressing the complexity of arguments, we have discussed how rhetorical comparisons can connect to your audience and help them understand the problem or possible solutions. But you can also help achieve these goals with syntactical stylistic strategies, such as dashes, parenthetical asides, and quotation marks. These choices clarify ideas, add details, or suggest an attitude or tone.

Some writers find it helpful to set up contrasts that highlight, emphasize, or create interest. Contrasts might be created by juxtaposing evidence, examples, or even perspectives. In terms of language or diction, some writers use hyperbole and understatement to connect with their audience and create familiar associations. At the same time, you may find it effective to emphasize contrasts or incongruities with irony, puns, exaggerations, sarcasm, and satire. These rhetorical choices can help you connect to your audience and advance your purpose. But you must use them thoughtfully: some issues are ill-suited to sarcasm. Likewise, make sure that irony fits the audience and the context.

Finally, your stylistic choices engage an audience. Even if your argument is not satirical, you may use contrast and incongruity to connect with an audience. Your diction and syntactic choices can create comic effects, reveal your attitude, and prepare the audience to hear your message. In some circumstances, you may wish to incorporate **irony** into your problem-solution argument to create emphasis, interest, or humor. While it may seem strange to claim the opposite of what you really mean, your audience is likely familiar with this rhetorical strategy. In fact, most of us use irony and sarcasm naturally in our daily conversations. For example, if your teacher assigns a lot of reading over the weekend, you might say to a friend, "Great: I didn't have anything to do this weekend, anyway." Your friend will understand your attitude and see that you mean the opposite of your claim: you have plans, and the heavy reading assignment may ruin them. The ironic tone lightens the mood and may even elicit sympathy from the listener.

	Example
Irony	*Tougher punishments for tardiness may result in apathy or even outright defiance from students, which leads to even more tardy violations.*
Sarcasm	*Well, at least punctuality isn't important in the real world, right?*
Juxtaposition	*Before the tardy bell rings, the hallways are crowded with students dodging their way through the masses. Meanwhile, the classrooms remain almost deserted except for the teachers eagerly awaiting the last-minute rush.*

(continued)

	Example
Pun	*If you are considering revising your school's tardy policy, it's about time.*
Hyperbole	*Students move about the hallways, sloth-like, even after the tardy bell has rung.*
Understatement	*As a majority of students are now regularly late to classes, we appear to have a small problem with our tardiness policies.*

 **SKILLS PRACTICE** | LANGUAGE AND STYLE
Connecting with an Audience through Stylistic Choices

As you write your problem-solution argument, include a variety of stylistic choices, such as comparison, irony, and parenthetical elements.

Highlight and label these choices on your draft and then explain the effects you are trying to create.

 **SKILLS PRACTICE** | PUTTING IT ALL TOGETHER
Revising and Editing a Problem-Solution Argument

Peer-Revision Checklist: Revising and Editing a Problem-Solution Argument		
Revising and Editing Checklist	**Unit 8 Focus Skills**	**Comment on the Effectiveness and/or Make a Suggestion**
Does the claim in the introduction or conclusion connect the subject to a perspective?	*Problem-solution argument*	
Has the writer explained the problem and connected the solutions to his or her perspective? Are these choices effective for the specific audience and purpose?	*Addressing complexity*	
Is the evidence and commentary organized by the possible solutions to the problem? Does the writer evaluate the solutions based on a goal and make a recommendation to the reader?	*Justifying a claim*	

Has the writer evaluated the solutions and employed rebuttal, refutation, and/or concession when appropriate?	*Developing a counterargument*	
Is the writing clear and specific? Does the word choice convey the writer's attitude toward the subject? Does the writer employ rhetorical comparisons or express irony or incongruity?	*Connecting with an audience through stylistic choices*	
Is the writing free of errors in spelling, usage, punctuation, capitalization, and agreement?	*Writing conventions*	

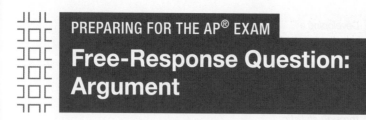

Free-Response Question: Argument

Acknowledging and Responding to Opposing Arguments

In this final workshop for the AP® free-response argument question, you will continue practicing the skills required to make a claim, establish a line of reasoning, support your claim, and develop commentary. As you recall, in Unit 5, you practiced creating coherence in your argument. Now, you will work on including commentary in your argument. Commentary adds complexity and sophistication to your text. It also allows you to respond to opposing arguments and strengthen your claim.

Read the following practice prompt, which is like one you may see on the AP® English Language and Composition Exam.

Prompt:
Playwright Henrik Ibsen (1828–1906) once wrote, "Money may be the husk of many things, but not the kernel. It brings you food, but not appetite, medicine, but not health, acquaintances, but not friends, servants, but not loyalty, days of joy, but not peace or happiness."

Write an essay that argues your position on the relationship between money and happiness.

In your response, you should do the following:

- Respond to the prompt with a thesis that presents a defensible position.
- Provide evidence to support your line of reasoning.
- Explain how the evidence supports your line of reasoning.
- Use appropriate grammar and punctuation in communicating your argument.

→ **Step One: Determine Your Unifying Idea and Perspective and Brainstorm Potential Examples**

Take some time to plan. The suggested time to complete the argument question on the AP® Exam is forty minutes. You should dedicate a few minutes at the beginning of your allotted time for planning so that you can develop a solid claim and choose the best evidence in the steps that follow.

As we have practiced before, read the prompt carefully so that you can identify a unifying and controlling idea to guide your argument. Use the quotation or other information provided in the prompt to generate this unifying idea. Next, determine your perspective about the idea and begin brainstorming potential examples to develop your argument.

In the sample prompt, the question requires you to discuss the relationship between money and happiness. Your unifying idea, then, could be prompted by the keyword "happiness." You might think of synonyms for your idea (e.g., joy, pleasure, contentment, cheerfulness). Because you are determining the relationship between money and happiness, you will ultimately need to answer these questions: Can money buy happiness? Why or why not?

Next, think of examples from your reading, observation, or experience that may help you develop an argument on this subject. You might quickly create a T-chart with opposing perspectives (e.g., yes/no, for/against) on each side and list possible examples that you might incorporate into your argument. Your examples may come from your own experiences or observations, from pop culture, history, sociology, science, entertainment, or other sources.

To address complexity, make sure that you consider the argument from other perspectives as well. Think of your argument as a two-sided coin. If you want to claim that money can buy happiness because buying things brings joy and satisfaction, consider the other side of the coin. How would someone who disagrees with you respond? What evidence could your opponent offer? For example, someone with an opposing perspective might argue that many lonely, unhappy people have enough money to buy the things that they want. These considerations will help you as you develop your thesis, line of reasoning, and commentary.

→ **Step Two: Develop a Defensible Claim and Unified Line of Reasoning**

In prior workshops, you have learned to develop a thesis statement that makes a claim. This claim conveys a unifying idea and your perspective (and perhaps position) on the question in the prompt. Here is an example of thesis development for our sample prompt about the relationship between money and happiness.

Subject:	*Relationship of Money and Happiness*
Idea:	*Contentment*
+	
Perspective:	*Lasting Contentment*
Thesis:	*Those who desire lasting contentment should prioritize human interactions over financial transactions.*

This thesis statement makes a concise claim: lasting contentment does not depend on accumulating money; it depends on investing in relationships. Now, try to expand on this thesis statement by adding complexity.

A complex thesis statement leads to a more nuanced and sophisticated argument because it suggests that you have considered other perspectives. To include other viewpoints, but still emphasize your own perspective and claim, you can use subordination in a complex sentence for your thesis. Express the opposing perspective in a subordinate clause beginning with a subordinating conjunction (e.g., while, although, since). Next, include your defensible claim in the independent clause to give it the proper emphasis. This structure will signify that the nuanced argument to follow accounts for the complexities and tensions of the subject.

Complex Thesis: *While it may be true that having enough money to make a comfortable living can provide temporary moments of happiness, those who desire lasting contentment should prioritize human interactions over financial transactions.*

Once you have written your complex thesis, you can develop your line of reasoning. Recall from earlier units that your argument should have multiple supporting reasons. To support your claim, you should have two or more reasons, each developed with supporting evidence and commentary. Generally, these reasons are developed in separate body paragraphs that demonstrate a logical progression of thought supporting your claim and unifying idea.

You may wish to organize your body paragraphs by providing reasons in support of your claim stated in the main clause. You may also organize your paragraphs by addressing the opposing perspective from the subordinate clause in your thesis and then writing one or more paragraphs addressing your claim in the main clause (see the following example).

Writing a Claim and Planning a Line of Reasoning

Introduction: Context

Distinguish between temporary happiness and lasting contentment

Thesis: (unifying idea + perspective)

While it may be true that having enough money to make a comfortable living can provide temporary moments of happiness, those who desire lasting contentment should prioritize human interactions over financial transactions.

Reason 1	Reason 2	Reason 3
Money can provide some form of happiness, but this superficial happiness <u>does not last.</u> (acknowledges opposing point of view and then counters it)	*Those who focus on serving others rather than gaining wealth report a deeper sense of satisfaction <u>throughout their lives.</u>*	*Those who prioritize personal relationships over material possessions find contentment that <u>sustains</u> them and brings joy.*

A complex thesis does not always lead to a complex argument. Briefly addressing another perspective in your thesis may make it complex. To create a complex argument, you must explain that other perspective through refutation, concession, and rebuttal within your argument.

→ **Step Three: Choose Relevant Evidence**

For every reason in your line of reasoning, you must choose relevant and specific evidence from your list of possibilities that exemplifies each reason and connects it to your unifying idea. We learned in Unit 5 that evidence can come from a variety of sources and that the examples should work together in a coherent way to support your claim.

When including your evidence as support, present it as specifically as you can. Hypothetical or vague references do not support your reasons as effectively as precise examples. You can achieve this specificity by avoiding overly general or collective nouns (e.g., one, people, teenagers, everyone) whenever possible. Instead, choose either specific people or precise groups of people (e.g., Elon Musk, lottery winners, my father).

While you must generate relevant and specific evidence to develop your claim and support your reasons, this evidence cannot stand alone. You must explain how the evidence supports each reason and connects to your claim's controlling and unifying idea. In each body paragraph, introduce your reason and then provide your specific evidence. Write several sentences to develop the example using precise details.

Finally, in addition to choosing evidence that supports your claim, review your list of possible evidence and choose examples that support other perspectives as well. Doing so will allow you to present a nuanced argument that addresses the complexity of the subject. In your presentation of evidence, you may respond to these ideas in your commentary either through concession, rebuttal, or refutation.

Choosing Relevant Evidence		
Reason 1	**Reason 2**	**Reason 3**
Money can provide some form of happiness, but this superficial happiness does not last.	*Those who focus on serving others rather than gaining wealth report a deeper sense of satisfaction in life.*	*Those who prioritize relationships over material possessions find contentment that sustains them and brings joy.*
Evidence	**Evidence**	**Evidence**
Buying a new game system made me very happy for a time (concession). *Winners of big lottery jackpots report that the money brought complications and hardship (refutation).*	*Personal anecdote of positive feelings after volunteering for a local charity*	*Research reports of members of poorer cultures who spend more time with family and have fewer mental health issues* *Reference to Thoreau to "simplify"*

→ Step Four: Develop Your Commentary

Commentary is the most important part of your argument. It's where you explain how and why your evidence supports your reason, as well as its significance to the unifying idea in your claim. Too often, writers present relevant and sufficient evidence but then fail to explain the significance or relevance of that evidence. In contrast, effective writers use commentary to explain their reasoning. But developing insightful commentary isn't easy; it takes practice.

Commentary may be developed by

- explaining the significance of the evidence,
- explaining the relevance of the evidence,
- explaining insightful and relevant connectors,
- explaining how the evidence corroborates, or
- qualifying or modifying an argument by considering alternative perspectives.

Next, you develop commentary by explaining how the example supports the reason, as well as how that reason develops the claim and connects to the unifying idea.

Similarly, a sophisticated argument contains commentary that articulates the complexities and tensions of a subject by responding to opposing arguments. You may wish to acknowledge the validity of an opposing idea or the limitations of your own argument through concession. You may also wish to refute (disagree with) or offer rebuttal (prove wrong) evidence from opposing arguments.

Even when you are addressing the opposition, your commentary should support your own line of reasoning. You can strengthen your argument by considering differing perspectives, especially if doing so makes you seem fair, reasonable, and, most importantly, credible.

To appear fair, you should use language that conveys a respectful tone when addressing opposing ideas. While you may be passionate about your position on a subject, you should demonstrate fairness and civility when responding to other points of view. Harsh or insulting language (e.g., ridiculous, stupid, evil) and absolute language that bars any exceptions (e.g., never, none, always, all) suggest that you may not understand the complexity of the subject. It may also indicate that you are unwilling to consider other perspectives and engage in a conversation. This is not to say that you should give in to your opposition. In fact, you may wish to follow a concession with a strong claim of your own.

The following chart demonstrates the relationship between a reason, a piece of evidence, and the commentary that explains it. Note that without the commentary, the audience would have no idea how the example of purchasing a new game system applies to the relationship between money and happiness.

Writing Commentary

Reason 1

Money can provide some form of happiness, but this superficial happiness does not last.

Evidence

For example, in ninth grade, I got money for my birthday and was thrilled to get to buy a new game system (concession).

Commentary

I did, in fact, feel quite happy for a few months. Playing new games with my friends and spending hours immersed in new challenges was exhilarating. However, just like my old game systems, this one eventually bored me. I realized that the happiness it brought was temporary, and what I really enjoyed was being with my friends, no matter what we were doing. While I don't regret spending my money on something that was fun, I understand that the expensive video game system did not bring me lasting happiness, or contentment, which is much deeper and dependent on other factors.

Conclusion

Once you have connected your evidence to your reasons in the body of your argument, you will need to write a conclusion that will reiterate your line of reasoning and bring your argument to a unified end. Your final commentary in your conclusion then connects your reasons one final time to your claim and unifying idea.

PREPARING FOR THE AP® EXAM

The following is an example of an argument free-response question. Practice the skills you have learned in this workshop to write an argument in response to the prompt.

Prompt:

In his 1841 essay "Self-Reliance," Ralph Waldo Emerson writes, "It is easy in the world to live after the world's opinion; it is easy in solitude to live after our own; but the great man is he who in the midst of the crowd keeps with perfect sweetness the independence of solitude."

Write an essay that argues your position on the relationship between the individual and society.

In your response, you should do the following:

- Respond to the prompt with a thesis that presents a defensible position.

- Provide evidence to support your line of reasoning.

- Explain how the evidence supports your line of reasoning.

- Use appropriate grammar and punctuation in communicating your argument.

Tear Down This Wall
Ronald Reagan

Where four decades ago there was rubble, today in West Berlin[1] there is the greatest industrial output of any city in Germany — busy office blocks, fine homes and apartments, proud avenues, and the spreading lawns of parkland. Where a city's culture seemed to have been destroyed, today there are two great universities, orchestras and an opera, countless theaters, and museums. Where there was want, today there's abundance — food, clothing, automobiles — the wonderful goods of the Ku'damm.[2] From devastation, from utter ruin, you Berliners have, in freedom, rebuilt a city that once again ranks as one of the greatest on earth. The Soviets may have had other plans. But my friends, there were a few things the Soviets didn't count on — *Berliner Herz, Berliner Humor, ja, und Berliner Schnauze.*[3]

In the 1950s, Khrushchev[4] predicted: "We will bury you." But in the West today, we see a free world that has achieved a level of prosperity and well-being unprecedented in all human history. In the Communist world, we see failure, technological backwardness, declining standards of health, even want of the most basic kind — too little food. Even today, the Soviet Union still cannot feed itself. After these four decades, then, there stands before the entire world one great and inescapable conclusion: Freedom leads to prosperity. Freedom replaces the ancient hatreds among the nations with comity and peace. Freedom is the victor.

And now the Soviets themselves may, in a limited way, be coming to understand the importance of freedom. We hear much from Moscow about a new policy of reform and openness. Some political prisoners have been released. Certain foreign news broadcasts are no longer being jammed. Some economic enterprises have been permitted to operate with greater freedom from state control.

Are these the beginnings of profound changes in the Soviet state? Or are they token gestures, intended to raise false hopes in the West, or to strengthen the Soviet system without changing it? We welcome change and openness; for we believe that freedom and security go together, that the advance of human liberty can only strengthen the cause of world peace. There is one sign the Soviets can make that would be unmistakable, that would advance dramatically the cause of freedom and peace.

General Secretary Gorbachev,[5] if you seek peace, if you seek prosperity for the Soviet Union

---

[1]Between 1961 and 1989, the city of Berlin was split between democractic West Germany and Communist East Germany. The city became a symbol of the tensions between Communist countries and the "free world."

[2]Kurfürstendamm — One of the most famous avenues in Berlin: lined with shops, houses, hotels, and restaurants.

[3]Translation from German: The heart of Berlin, the humor of Berlin, yes, and the rough talk/lip of Berlin.

[4]Soviet politician who led the Soviet Union and the Communist Party during part of the Cold War from 1953 to 1964.

[5]The eighth and last leader of the Soviet Union and the Communist Party from 1985 until 1991.

and Eastern Europe, if you seek liberalization: Come here to this gate! Mr. Gorbachev, open this gate! Mr. Gorbachev, tear down this wall!

I understand the fear of war and the pain of division that afflict this continent — and I pledge to you my country's efforts to help overcome these burdens. To be sure, we in the West must resist Soviet expansion. So we must maintain defenses of unassailable strength. Yet we seek peace; so we must strive to reduce arms on both sides.

Beginning 10 years ago, the Soviets challenged the Western alliance with a grave new threat, hundreds of new and more deadly SS-20 nuclear missiles, capable of striking every capital in Europe. The Western alliance responded by committing itself to a counter-deployment unless the Soviets agreed to negotiate a better solution; namely, the elimination of such weapons on both sides. For many months, the Soviets refused to bargain in earnestness. As the alliance, in turn, prepared to go forward with its counter-deployment, there were difficult days — days of protests like those during my 1982 visit to this city — and the Soviets later walked away from the table.

But through it all, the alliance held firm. And I invite those who protested then — I invite those who protest today — to mark this fact: Because we remained strong, the Soviets came back to the table. And because we remained strong, today we have within reach the possibility, not merely of limiting the growth of arms, but of eliminating, for the first time, an entire class of nuclear weapons from the face of the earth.

6

7

8

1. In the first paragraph, the dependent clause at the beginning of the first sentence primarily
   (A) introduces criticism of East Berlin and the conditions of the people there.
   (B) refutes any initial counterarguments that might be made for why West Berlin should not be considered a great city.
   (C) emphasizes the growth and development of West Berlin.
   (D) defines the conflict between the Soviets and the United States.
   (E) appeals to the rational minds of the audience to establish trust.

2. In the first paragraph, the writer's statement that "you Berliners have, in freedom, rebuilt a city that once again ranks as one of the greatest on earth" (sentence 4) accomplishes which of the following?
   (A) It refers to a prediction that both East and West Berlin would eventually fail.
   (B) It refutes the notion that a free society can thrive.
   (C) It specifies the type of city that West Berlin has become because of the freedom and prosperity of the people.
   (D) It defends the choice of West Germany and West Berlin to ally with the United States and other Western countries.
   (E) It qualifies comments about the differences between East and West Berlin.

3. In the first sentence of the second paragraph, the speaker quotes the statement "We will bury you" to
   (A) remind the audience of a more frightening past in comparison to this moment.
   (B) establish the conflict between the Soviets and the United States and the countries of Western Europe.
   (C) appeal to the humanity of the audience and their willingness to forgive.
   (D) create a comparison between the early days of the Cold War and the failures of the Soviet Union.
   (E) contextualize the lives of the German people who were so greatly affected by the Berlin Wall.

4. In the third paragraph, the speaker's use of
    the words "may," "some," and "certain" and
    the phrase "in a limited way" display his
    (A) naive simplicity.
    (B) reluctant optimism.
    (C) neutral position.
    (D) ironic perspective.
    (E) sense of resentment.

5. In the context of the excerpt as a whole, the
    speaker uses paragraph 3 to
    (A) question the intention of the Soviets and
        their leaders.
    (B) transition from a historical explanation
        of the Soviet Union to criticism of
        their treatment of people under their
        governance.
    (C) draw attention to evidence of
        communists' failures as social and
        political leaders.
    (D) point out a flaw in the line of reasoning
        of those who disagree with him.
    (E) transition from establishing the
        historical and political context of the
        speech to an illustration of the changes
        underway in the Soviet Union.

6. In the fourth paragraph, the semicolon in
    the third sentence ("We welcome . . . world
    peace.") serves which of the following
    purposes?
    (A) It connects what people in Western
        countries fear with what they need to be
        secured against.
    (B) It creates a distinction between freedom
        and the need for security to restrict
        freedoms.
    (C) It creates a suggestion that the "change
        and openness" will result in "freedom
        and security."
    (D) It sets apart the two clauses about
        "change" and "security" because those
        are conflicting ideas in his argument.
    (E) It suggests more "openness" in the Soviet
        society so that people can feel more
        secure.

7. In the context of the sixth paragraph, the
    speaker uses the clause "Yet we seek peace" to
    (A) affirm the intentions of the America
        people.
    (B) qualify the developing claim about
        strength and nuclear arms.
    (C) refute claims that America wants to
        destroy the Soviets.
    (D) explain his purpose for speaking in
        Berlin.
    (E) control perspectives about the Soviets
        and their allies.

8. In the second sentence of the eighth para-
    graph, the speaker uses the parenthetical
    element "I invite those who protest today" to
    help emphasize which part of his message?
    (A) Western countries allowed the Soviets
        to dictate what was acceptable and what
        was not in the resistance to Soviet rule.
    (B) There are parallels between the pain
        of the people of Berlin and that of the
        average Soviet citizen.
    (C) Protests against nuclear weapons
        ultimately have no effect on the growth
        of nuclear arsenals around the world.
    (D) The current protests and those of the
        past are part of a tradition of strength
        that the Soviets could not defeat.
    (E) Only the most recent protests by people
        and policies of Western countries have
        pushed the Soviets "back to the table."

9. In the context of the eighth paragraph, the
    speaker uses the phrase "within reach" to
    (A) indicate his skeptical perspective about
        recent Soviet actions.
    (B) illustrate just how near the world has
        come to nuclear war.
    (C) specify the limited possibilities of a free
        world.
    (D) limit the claims he is making about
        eliminating certain nuclear weapons.
    (E) refute Soviet claims about the need for
        nuclear weapons.

PREPARING FOR THE AP® EXAM
Multiple-Choice Questions: Writing

The passage below is a draft.

(1) During the Russian campaigns against Germany in World War II, Major Marina Raskova was able to convince her Russian commanders to allow women to form their own combat units. (2) Unlike other allied forces, women played active combat roles in the Russian military throughout the war, fighting alongside men, as well as in their own units. (3) A group of bombers, one of these units was the 588th Air Regiment, assigned to purely nighttime attacks on German forces.

(4) Using U-2 biplanes, the exclusively female air regiment flew thousands of bombing raids between 1942 and 1945. (5) Where most Russian military planes could carry dozens of bombs, the obsolete U-2 was so small that it could only carry two bombs at a time. (6) To account for this, each pilot would do numerous bombing runs per night. (7) These numerous runs were further complicated by how pitifully slow the planes were. (8) If a pilot was heard and then spotted by a German searchlight, then the Germans would easily shoot her down with their antiaircraft guns. (9) Essentially, these women were helpless in the slowest and weakest planes in the Russian military.

(10) Though harrowing, these circumstances helped the women of the 588th Air Regiment show that heroism sometimes requires both genius and bravery. (11) To approach their targets without being heard, as each pilot descended toward her target, the "Night Witches" — as the Germans came to call them — developed a near-suicidal strategy: they would turn off her motor and glide silently. (12) Once close enough, they would restart her motor in time to drop the bombs and then fly away before being seen. (13) Sometimes they would even fly in pairs, making use of the same technique but having one pilot distract the Germans by flying in a different direction with her motor on while another silently glided to her target and dropped her bombs unseen.

(14) Eventually, 23 of the 261 women who served in the regiment were recognized as "heroes of the Soviet Union," including Flight Commander Irina Sebrova, who flew 1,008 missions, more than any other Russian woman. (15) While 32 of these women died during the war, the regiment embraced them all and continues to stand as a historical example of ingenuity in the face of adversity.

1. The writer wants to reduce ambiguity in sentence 3 (reproduced below) by changing the placement of the underlined text, adjusting punctuation and capitalization as needed.

   A group of bombers, one of these units was the 588th Air Regiment, assigned to purely nighttime attacks on German forces.

   Which of the following is the most reasonable placement for the underlined text?

   (A) Before "A group"
   (B) After "group"
   (C) After "assigned"
   (D) After "attacks"
   (E) After "forces"

2. The writer is considering deleting the underlined portion of sentence 5 (reproduced below), adjusting the capitalization as necessary.

Where most Russian military planes could carry dozens of bombs, the obsolete U-2 was so small that it could only carry two bombs at a time.

Should the writer keep or delete the underlined clause?

(A) Keep it, because it better defines the roles of these pilots in the Russian Military Air Corps.
(B) Keep it, because it introduces a comparison that allows the audience to better understand the circumstances faced by the women.
(C) Delete it, because it introduces unnecessary information about the performance of faster planes.
(D) Delete it, because it draws the attention of the audience away from the achievement of these women and makes the passage about Russian airpower in general.
(E) Delete it, because it fails to provide enough specific information to be useful in the passage.

3. The writer is considering replacing the underlined portion of sentence 7 (reproduced below).

These numerous runs were further complicated by how pitifully slow the planes were.

Which of the following versions of the underlined text most closely fits the style and tone of the entire passage?

(A) (as it is now)
(B) absurdly
(C) absolutely
(D) deceptively
(E) concerningly

4. The writer is considering deleting sentence 9 (reproduced below).

Essentially, these women were helpless in the slowest and weakest planes in the Russian military.

Should the writer keep or delete the sentence?

(A) Keep it, because it helps the reader better understand why the writer is focusing on this group of female pilots.
(B) Keep it, because it introduces a counterargument to the idea that these were brave and intelligent women and then allows the reader to transition into the next paragraph with more skepticism toward their achievements.
(C) Keep it, because it synthesizes the problems these women faced, asserts the attitude toward the absurd conditions these women faced, and helps to transition to their solutions in the next paragraph.
(D) Delete it, because the problems faced by these women are made clear enough by other details earlier in the paragraph and including this sentence may make the reader numb to the pilots' circumstances.
(E) Delete it, because it does not contribute to the argument being made about the hard work and intelligence of these pilots.

5. Which of the following versions of sentence 11 (reproduced below) is the clearest?

To approach their targets without being heard, as each pilot descended toward her target, the "Night Witches"—as the Germans came to call them—developed a near-suicidal strategy: they would turn off her motor and glide silently.

(A) (as it is now)

(B) The "Night Witches"—as the Germans came to call them—to approach their targets without being heard, came up with a near-suicidal strategy: as each pilot descended toward her target, she would turn off her motor and glide silently.

(C) As each pilot descended toward her target, she would turn off her motor and glide silently to approach her target without being heard: the "Night Witches"—as the Germans came to call them—came up with a near-suicidal strategy.

(D) To approach their targets without being heard, the "Night Witches"—as the Germans came to call them—came up with a near-suicidal strategy: as each pilot descended toward her target, she would turn off her motor and glide silently.

(E) To approach their targets without being heard, as each pilot descended toward her target, she would turn off her motor and glide silently: and so the "Night Witches"—as the Germans came to call them—came up with a near-suicidal strategy.

6. In sentence 15 (reproduced below), the writer wants to leave the reader with clear knowledge of the long-term recognition the women of the regiment have received.

While 32 of these women died during the war, the regiment embraced them all and continues to stand as a historical example of ingenuity in the face of adversity.

Which of the following revisions to the underlined portion of the sentence best accomplishes this goal?

(A) (as it is now)

(B) not all of those died in battle but the regiment

(C) that is nothing compared to the 8.7 million total Russian military dead throughout the regiment and

(D) the entire regiment has been memorialized and immortalized in books and film and

(E) and several of them died of disease and accidents, the regiment

UNIT

9

Joining the Conversation

By now you've come to understand that arguments are part of ongoing conversations. We develop arguments to share our ideas about important issues. By adding our voices, we join a conversation that may affirm our existing perspectives or challenge them. This is true for writing in the classroom, as well as writing in our daily lives.

In the image, a woman is viewing modern contemporary artwork created by Kehinde Wiley, a contemporary artist who painted Barack Obama's 2018 portrait, which hangs in the national portrait gallery. Wiley's work (center) is displayed between two other works at the gallery. Viewers at the museum, like the one pictured, may consider these works part of a conversation. How might these pieces of art and their creators be speaking to one another in the context of a larger conversation?

One thing is for certain: arguments can change the world. Writers use their own voices and the power of argument to make a difference.

UNIT GOALS

	Unit Focus	Reading, Analyzing, and Interpreting	Writing
Big Idea: Rhetorical Situation	**Understanding the Rhetorical Situation**	Explain how a writer's argument responds to other arguments and contributes to ongoing conversations.	Analyze positions and perspectives in an argument that have already been considered.
Big Idea: Claims and Evidence	**Biases, Limitations, and Implications**	Explain the significance and relevance of an argument.	Synthesize evidence to corroborate an argument and respond to counterarguments.
Big Idea: Reasoning and Organization	**Multimodal Arguments**	Explain how writers develop ideas through multiple modes of development.	Write an argument developed through two or more modes of development.
Big Idea: Language and Style	**Voice and Complexity**	Explain how stylistic choices contribute to the writer's message.	Employ stylistic choices to convey a message to an audience.
Ideas in American Culture	• **Truth and Consequences** • **Technology and Globalization**	Explain how the ideas of truth, consequences, technology, and globalization are reflected in classic, as well as contemporary, texts.	
AP® Exam Preparation	• **Free Response: Synthesis** • **Multiple Choice**	Analyze rhetorical choices in classic and contemporary nonfiction texts.	Synthesize ideas from multiple sources and perspectives to develop a complex argument.

Understanding the Rhetorical Situation

 Enduring Understanding (RHS-1)

Individuals write within a particular situation and make strategic writing choices based on that situation.

KEY POINT

Arguments are part of ongoing conversations about important issues. They have real-world implications. When you enter a conversation, you must examine the positions and perspectives of others as you add your own voice.

From the first unit of this book, you've examined arguments based on the context in which they were written. You've considered what may have inspired or provoked a writer to create an argument, and you've analyzed how writers appeal to their audiences to achieve their purposes. All of these factors are important as you read to understand the writer's message.

Arguments Are Part of an Ongoing Conversation

Now, you can reflect more broadly on how a particular rhetorical situation fits into a larger conversation about a subject. For example, citizens, experts, and policy officials all over the world were already having a conversation about effective public health strategies before the emergence of COVID-19 in 2019–2020. When the scope and implications of the pandemic began to change, so did the rhetorical situation. In the United Kingdom, to take one instance, the rise in both the number of cases and the mortality rate prompted Queen Elizabeth to speak directly to the public and add her voice to the conversation (see p. 7).

Of course, different individuals and audiences respond to arguments in different ways. After the Queen's speech, Britons and Americans alike took to Twitter to applaud her. By doing so, they added their own voices to the conversation as well.

 Rebecca Reid
Just wept my way through the Queen.

 Tom McTague
Eesh, I found that surprisingly moving.

 Nicola Swanson
I welled up at the Queen's speech. I've officially lost it. #EmotionalWreck

 Timothy Burke
93-year-old Queen Elizabeth II just delivered a more inspiring display of leadership than I've seen from any federal American politician. sheesh.

These conversations occur simultaneously in different contexts across time and space. A particular response can contribute to prior conversations or even spark new ones. For example, the global health insurance company Zurich produced a 2020 report called "COVID-19: The Interconnected Consequences." This study evaluated political and economic responses to the pandemic, among its other ramifications. In other words, the company responded to the ongoing conversation around the pandemic and spawned a new conversation about its economic and political implications.

Arguments Have Real-World Implications

An argument is more than a paper you write for a class. Arguments — and the rhetorical choices writers use to make them — have real-world consequences. Look carefully at the following examples:

Writer	Strategy and Appeal	Audience and Goal	Real-World Implication/ Consequence
A high school senior	writes a descriptive and insightful personal essay that	causes a college admission officer to accept the student for	admission to the student's top-choice college.
A defense attorney	develops reasoning with evidence and a closing argument that	moves a jury to deliver a not guilty verdict	which leads to an acquittal and protects the defendant's freedom.
A political candidate	creates an ad campaign and delivers speeches addressing local issues that	convinces a majority of voting citizens	to elect the candidate to office.
An international nonprofit human rights organization	presents personal testimony and video footage in a digital program that	persuades individuals to sponsor a child in need,	providing essential food and health care.

As you analyze arguments about an important subject, you must place those arguments within the context of the broader, ongoing conversation about that subject.

INSIDER AP® TIP

Understand perspectives; don't just know them.
Understanding an argument requires knowing others' perspectives. But effective writers go beyond summarizing and paraphrasing the ideas of others. They connect other arguments to their own through corroboration, refutation, concession, and rebuttal as they convey their own original perspective.

JOINING THE CONVERSATION: UNDERSTANDING PERSPECTIVES

	Questions to Consider
Subject	What is the topic or issue?
Significance	Who cares about it? Why?
Perspective	What perspective does the writer have about the subject?
	Why does he or she have that perspective?
	What biases might he or she have?
Other Perspectives	What other positions and/or perspectives exist about the subject?
	What are others' arguments about the subject?
	Has this subject been addressed before? When? Where?
Position	What is the writer's claim (position, perspective, and idea) about the issue or subject?
Response	Who corroborates or agrees with the writer's claim? Why?
	Who doubts — or disagrees with — the writer's claim? Why?
	Who doesn't care either way?
Implications	How could the writer's claim or conclusion affect others?
	How will the writer's response affect future audiences?
	What are the short- and long-term consequences of the writer's claim or conclusion?

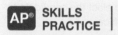 **SKILLS PRACTICE** | **RHETORICAL SITUATION** **Understanding an Issue**

Think of an existing conversation about an issue that is important to you. In this context, *issues* are problems or questions within a broader subject: Should we raise the minimum wage? Should college athletes be paid? How should we protect endangered animal species? How much weight should be given to standardized test scores in the college admissions process? Of course, many others have addressed these questions before you, so you are joining a conversation already in progress. Choose an issue that is important to you. Then use the following graphic organizer to help deepen your understanding of both the issue and the wider conversation.

Joining the Conversation: Understanding an Issue

	Questions to Consider	Your Notes and Comments
Subject	What is the topic or issue?	
Significance	Who cares about it? Why?	

Perspective	What perspective do you currently have about the subject or issue?	
	Why do you have that perspective?	
	What biases do you have?	
Other Perspectives	What other positions and/or perspectives exist about the subject?	
	What are others' arguments about the subject?	
	Has this subject been addressed before? When? Where?	
	Which arguments do you agree with? Why?	
	Which ones do you disagree with? Why?	
Position	What is your position and perspective about the subject?	
Response	Who will agree with you?	
	Who will corroborate your position?	
	Who will be the skeptics or disagree with your position? Why?	
Implications	How will your position affect others?	
	How will this response affect future audiences?	
	What are the short- and long-term consequences?	

Five Lessons That Veterans Can Teach Us
Dan Crenshaw

REUTERS/Kevin Lamarque/Newscom

THE TEXT IN CONTEXT

Daniel Reed Crenshaw (b. 1984) is a Republican U.S.
Representative for Texas's second congressional district.
Prior to joining Congress, he served in the navy as a SEAL, part of the elite naval special
operations unit, with deployments in both Iraq and Afghanistan. Crenshaw lost his right
eye in 2012 when he was hit by an improvised explosive device in Afghanistan. He is the
recipient of two Bronze Star Medals, the Purple Heart, and other military honors. In this
2020 Veterans Day speech given at the Ronald Reagan Presidential Library in Simi Valley,
California, Crenshaw pays tribute to the American veterans who have sacrificed and
served our country. But he also highlights the lessons that they can teach us.

AP® SKILLS PRACTICE	RHETORICAL SITUATION **Understanding the Rhetorical Situation**

As you read Crenshaw's Veterans Day address, consider how he reveals his
understanding of different perspectives. Use the following graphic organizer to
record textual evidence.

Joining the Conversation: Understanding Perspectives		
	Questions to Consider	**Evidence from the Text**
Subject	What is the topic or issue?	
Significance	Who cares about it? Why?	
Perspective	What perspective does the writer have about the subject? Why does he or she have that perspective? What biases might he or she have?	
Other Perspectives	What other positions and/or perspectives exist about the subject? What are others' arguments about the subject? Has this subject been addressed before? When? Where?	

Position	What is the writer's claim (position, perspective, and idea) about the subject?	
Response	Who corroborates or agrees with the writer's claim? Why?	
	Who disagrees with or is a skeptic of the writer's claim? Why?	
	Who doesn't care either way?	
Implications	How could the writer's claim or conclusion affect others?	
	How will the writer's response affect future audiences?	
	What are the short- and long-term consequences of the writer's claim or conclusion?	

Five Lessons That Veterans Can Teach Us

It's an important day for the obvious reason: to honor our vets and honor their sacrifice, the sacrifice of their families, and to tell them that we not only thank them for their service, but that we will never forget. Let's see. That's just the start. It seems to me we have grown accustomed to the ritual of thanking our veterans, and this is a good thing, no doubt. But I worry that we have also grown forgetful about the principles the same veterans stand for.

I think on this veterans day that it might be worth remembering what it is veterans fight for in the first place. Of course, it's this—it's all of this. It's all of you and not just the beautiful hills you see here. America is much more than her physical landscapes, as majestic as they are. It's the American spirit: this great American experiment. America is the greatest idea in human history: a republic constructed upon the principle that government exists to protect your God-given rights. America is your freedom to speak freely, your freedom to pursue your happiness, your freedom to take risks unburdened by the whims of a select elite few and government bureaucracy.

Preserving the legacy that is the American spirit is no easy task. We pretend it is self-sustaining. In fact, it is not. President Reagan famously warned us that freedom is never more than one generation away from extinction. I think there are many who rightfully fear that that moment is closer than we might have imagined.

It's surprisingly easy these days to lose gratitude for the miracle that America is. It is easier for many to embrace self-pity, resentment, and envy of another. It's always easier to demand more of others than it is yourself, easier to feel like a victim instead of a victor. Accountability and personal responsibility are hard things, after all.

Maybe it's here that veterans have something to teach us. So on this veterans day, I'll give you five lessons that we can learn from our veterans. These are five lessons in fortitude.

5

Number one: Seek perspective. When I was hit by an IED in 2012 in Afghanistan, I was left blind for weeks. I was unsure if I'd ever see again. My doctor certainly did not think I would see again. This was perhaps the hardest physical trauma I'd ever dealt with. But it wasn't the hardest thing anyone had dealt with. Many of my teammates had paid a far greater price. Many gold star wives—my dear friends—were still without their soul mates.

I laid there and I thought of my own mother: a young woman in her 30s with two small children who battled cancer for five long years before she lost that battle when I was ten. She didn't partake in self-pity. She dealt with her suffering with grace, humor, and grit. See, there's a hard truth that we must live by: Whatever you're going through, you've probably been through something harder so you can deal with this too. And if this is indeed the hardest moment of your life, then consider this truth: Someone else has dealt with something harder and they dealt with it better than you are dealing with it now.

This is perspective in the most fundamental sense. And this seems like an especially important lesson in the year 2020. Times are hard for many this year, no doubt about it. But if we're being honest, this is not our country's darkest times. Far from it. It behooves us to put our hardships in perspective. From perspective comes gratitude, and from gratitude comes hope, and from hope comes perseverance.

We are a people that does not wallow in despair but overcomes. We do so because there is no other choice.

Lesson number two: Do something hard. 10 Modern society has fooled people into thinking the purpose of life is to end all suffering, make all hardships go away, seek comfort and pleasure—as if these things are the ultimate goal, as if living your best life is nothing more than indulging the pleasures of modern times.

Many in our country have come to believe that what doesn't kill you makes you weaker. There is a belief that all opposing opinions are harmful to one's health, that safe spaces must be sought out to protect you from harm. But this is not true. The best things in life must be worked for. They must be sacrificed for. The truth is that suffering must not be avoided but embraced. It is unavoidable, after all, because we live in the real world, not the world we wish were real.

Veterans—and the vast majority of Americans, for that matter—know there are no safe spaces in the real world. We know that true purpose true happiness is achieved through hardship. We know that in order to live your purpose, you must challenge yourself willingly. For the hardships that are imposed upon you, well, you must "embrace the suck," as we say in the seal teams. You embrace it because you have no choice. You tell yourself a story of overcoming your hardship, not falling victim to it.

There's value in our suffering. You punish yourself in the gym because it makes you stronger. You put in extra hours at work because it makes you more competitive. You train longer. You wake up earlier and try to be kinder to those you might despise. These things are good because they are hard. You overcome your pain because to do so builds character. It builds fortitude, so do something hard.

Lesson number three: No plan B. In BUDS (Basic Underwater Demolition School), the six-month basic training that SEALS go through to prove themselves worthy, the only men that make it are those who never gave themselves a choice. This is a deeper concept than just not quitting. It is living according to the purpose, according to the mission, that you set out for yourself.

Those who ring the bell three times to signal that they have dropped out of training—they gave themselves a choice. They allowed themselves to have a plan B. I don't mean "plan B" as a contingency. Everyone has a backup plan—or at least you should. If you want to be an artist but you can't paint, and you change career paths as a result, I don't think that makes you a quitter.

Quitting is something that happens deep within, when you know you gave up on the best version of yourself. It happens when you don't live according to the purpose, according to the mission, that you knew that you could. Purpose is your plan A. It's giving 110 percent. Plan B is cutting corners. Plan B is doing just enough to get by. Plan B lands you in mediocrity. But living plan A elevates you above your current self.

The comforts of modern society allow many of us to make those excuses to live a lesser version of our best self. We must avoid this temptation and live with no plan B.

Lesson number four: The right sense of shame. In the SEAL teams, we often say don't be "that guy." This means exactly what it sounds like: Don't be the guy who forgets the right piece of gear on a mission. Don't be the guy who is late to muster. Don't be the weakest link. Others' lives are depending on it, so it's a pretty important principle to live by.

Shame is good. Shame is accountability. Shame means you actually feel bad about your shortcomings instead of lazily accepting them. Too often these days, we become obsessed with living our own truth. Our institutions—instead of forming our future generations into tough courageous Americans—have instead stopped to coddle our youth, tell them they are never wrong, never in need of

self-improvement. Self-esteem becomes a goal in itself, without consideration for virtue or moral strength.

But here's the hard truth: None of us are fine the way we are. That's okay. We all have work to do. But that work will never get done, we will never hold ourselves accountable, we will never know what to strive for if we do not feel a sense of shame when we have done wrong.

What's number five? A sense of duty. The whole point of feeling shame is not just to make you feel bad. It is to pave the way for doing what is right. To live with duty. In the military the concept of duty is so deeply ingrained that it becomes self-evident one does the right thing because it is the right thing. End of story. To do otherwise is to betray your flag and your teammates.

Sure there are orders, rules in place to direct one's actions. No one is perfect, after all. But for the most part, this sense of duty must be self-actualizing. You have a duty to ensure your gear is squared away, your batteries charged, your magazines loaded. You will not be the weakest link. This has practical value but also deeper moral value. To be a dutiful citizen is no different. At least it shouldn't be.

We should strive to do the simplest of things right: be on time, work hard, do what it takes, help our neighbors before demanding that government does it for us. This has always been a key pillar of American exceptionalism.

Pope John Paul II—Saint John Paul II, for you Catholics in the audience—said that freedom consists not in doing what we like, but in having the right to do what we ought. Fundamentally, what does this mean? It means that our country, our great republic, is centered around this concept of a dutiful citizen. Freedom is not unbridled hedonism. It is ordered liberty. Only a moral, dutiful people can be trusted with freedoms. Otherwise, we are nothing but a society in turmoil and chaos. Laws can be enforced after they are broken, but it takes a good and moral people to avoid breaking them in the first place.

The proper sense of duty comes from a proper sense of moral truth. In the House of Representatives, the words "In God We Trust" are inscribed above the chair of the Speaker of the House. Our laws, our country's founding were based in absolute truth derived from God. This anchors us. And it's more important than I think people realize. We avoid duty, we avoid truth, at our own peril. 25

Our society—our country—cannot survive an increasing number of citizens that wish only to survive off the work and ingenuity of others. We have a duty to be stronger citizens if our great American experiment is to survive. And veterans have long sought to protect these values, to impart these lessons, because American values aren't necessarily self-sustaining. Personal responsibility, mental fortitude, moral truth, gratitude for our nation, liberty to pursue our happiness—these things must be taught and passed down.

Our institutions must rediscover their purpose in molding our future generations instead of simply reflecting the emotional whims of a restless youth. We can only embark upon such a journey if we rediscover some gratitude for the foundations that make our country the miracle that indeed it is.

This place, this idea, is built upon the greatest ideas that humankind ever had. From Jerusalem, we learned moral truth. From Athens we discovered philosophy. And from Rome the rule of law and the structures of a republic. And from London the first elements of the free market, common law, and the revelation from the Magna Carta: that even kings must be subject to laws. We wrote these ideas down in Philadelphia.

This grand experiment has created more good and more prosperity than any other in human history. Our story is unparalleled. It is one of true exceptionalism. It is why Reagan called us the last best hope on earth and paved the way for us to live up to that hope.

To persevere—and I think we can, I think we must—I think the next century will be America's best and brightest if we only believe it is our duty to live up to our greatest ideals. God bless you, God bless our veterans, and God bless our great country. 30

Thank you so much.

RHETORICAL SITUATION

1. What subject does Crenshaw focus on? How does the subject contribute to the **message** of the text?

2. Other politicians have delivered speeches that recognize the service of veterans. What are some of these other **perspectives**? How have other perspectives informed and influenced Crenshaw's argument?

3. Who are the intended and unintended **audiences** for this text? Explain the possible **perspectives**, **positions**, and **biases** of these different **audiences**?

4. What is the writer's **claim**? How does the **conclusion** convey the consequences of the subject for both the current audience and for future audiences?

CLAIMS AND EVIDENCE

Biases, Limitations, and Implications

AP **Enduring Understanding (CLE-1)**

Writers guide understanding of a text's lines of reasoning and claims through that text's organization and integration of evidence.

As you learned in the previous unit, subjects are rarely as clear-cut as they appear on the surface. Whether you're examining arguments in class, debating informally among friends, or evaluating ideas later in your professional career, subjects will become more complex as you explore different perspectives.

Moreover, you will often discover that different — even opposing — viewpoints on a subject can be "true" or valid simultaneously. For example, assess the validity of the following perspectives:

- Getting a job over the summer is a rite of passage for young people, which allows them to practice workplace skills.

- Getting a job over the summer is a necessity for young people: it lets them practice financial independence and helps them pay for personal and family expenses.

- Getting a job over the summer is outdated and impractical: young people are better served by participating in exploratory college programs and camps that improve their chances of earning scholarships.

Each perspective considers different aspects of summer jobs: immediate practicality, long-term benefits, individual families' circumstances, and students' interests.

KEY POINT

Entering ongoing conversations requires writers to engage with other perspectives—even those viewpoints that have already been discussed many times by others.

Effective Arguments Consider the Perspectives of Others

Remember that in the context of arguments, evidence is not necessarily "neutral" or unbiased. Indeed, the evidence writers use to **corroborate** (or support) their arguments may reflect their own **biases**, as well as the limitations of their chosen sources. You can often judge a source's bias by looking carefully at how it presents competing perspectives.

These same biases influence a writer's willingness — or ability — to evaluate competing perspectives fairly. But recall that the term *biased* is not synonymous with *dishonest* or *incompetent*. All writers have biases: assumptions, values, attitudes, and other factors that shape their viewpoints.

Effective writers recognize the limitations of their sources and viewpoints. Most often, they present competing perspectives fairly and then address them through **refutation**, **concession**, and/or **rebuttal**.

USING EVIDENCE PURPOSEFULLY		
Purpose of Evidence	Definition	Effect
Corroboration	Uses evidence or sources that complement or support an argument	Draws upon the perspectives of others to support the writer's argument and contribute to the writer's credibility
Refutation	Demonstrates with evidence that all (or a portion) of a competing claim is invalid	Illustrates the weaknesses of another perspective while implying that the writer's own argument is more valid
Concession	Accepts all (or a portion) of a competing claim as correct or correct under different circumstances	Acknowledges the validity of another's argument (in part) and the limitations of the writer's own argument, which strengthens the writer's credibility (*ethos*)
Rebuttal	Offers a contrasting perspective on an argument and its evidence or provides alternative evidence to propose that all (or a portion) of a competing claim is invalid	Acknowledges and counters an opposing point of view in relation to the writer's perspective while providing a counterclaim or supporting evidence for a counterclaim

Not All Evidence Is Equal

Writers use evidence both to support their own arguments and challenge the arguments of others. But remember that not all pieces of evidence are equally relevant, sufficient, or compelling to different audiences.

Even the most up-to-date research, articles, documentaries, and eyewitness accounts have limitations. Indeed, facts themselves have limitations: we may only know some of the facts or one piece of information. We may not be certain that our data is correct. In such cases, we must connect this evidence to other information, which will give us a more complete and accurate picture of a subject.

Several different factors can limit a writer's choice of evidence, including

- the subject,
- the writer's purpose,
- the source's biases,
- the credibility of the source,
- the accessibility of the source, and
- a source's publication or broadcast date.

To some extent, the text's audience affects the **limitations** of the evidence. For example, if the audience does not know a historical or literary reference, or is unaware that the evidence is out of date or from a biased source, then the evidence is not received as the writer intended.

Writers and audiences must also be open to new information that changes the conversation about a subject. This emerging evidence, which may not have been available at the time the writer was writing, can require a writer to adjust a thesis or related claim. In other words, to remain part of the conversation, writers must remain open to revisiting their arguments based on new information.

Arguments Affect Our Lives

Arguments are not just academic texts that you read in class and then move on. In fact, the best writers make and support claims about issues that matter. Arguments have real-world **implications** — and they can even change the world around you. Think about the following scenarios:

- A coach motivates an underdog soccer team with a persuasive speech, which inspires them to win the tournament.
- A community member convinces others to fundraise for the local animal shelter, which saves the lives of rescued animals.
- A YouTube channel influences a viewer to purchase a new piece of technology.
- A proposed piece of legislation becomes a law and provides economic stimulus to citizens in need.

Every day, writers make arguments about subjects that directly affect your life, along with the lives of your neighbors, friends, and family. In fact, your own arguments may have effects beyond the page — and outside your original rhetorical situation.

Regardless of the context, writers must understand the complexities of the conversation that they are entering. If they do not, their arguments can reveal a lack of understanding. In turn, that lack of understanding can lead to oversimplification and overgeneralization. Both will undermine the writer's credibility.

 **INSIDER AP TIP**

Summary is not analysis. Analytical writers must be able to explain how sources and evidence relate to each other, as well as how they function together within the argument.

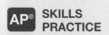 **AP SKILLS PRACTICE** | **CLAIMS AND EVIDENCE**
Responding to Others' Arguments

Consider the following claim: "To ensure the safety and privacy of our students, minors should have absolutely no unmoderated access to the internet (including use of social media, streaming videos, online gaming, and chat rooms)."

Identify examples of evidence you could use to corroborate, refute, rebut, or concede to the preceding claim.

(continued)

Purpose of Evidence	Definition	Examples of Evidence
Corroboration	Uses evidence or sources that complement or support an argument	
Refutation	Demonstrates with evidence that all (or a portion) of a competing claim is invalid	
Concession	Accepts all (or a portion) of a competing claim as correct or correct under different circumstances	
Rebuttal	Offers a contrasting perspective on an argument and its evidence, or provides alternative evidence to propose that all (or a portion) of a competing claim is invalid	

Are Space Habitats the Way of the Future?

Matthew S. Williams

Matthew Williams

THE TEXT IN CONTEXT

Novelist and science writer Matthew S. Williams is the author of the science fiction novels *The Cronian Incident* (2017), *The Jovian Manifesto* (2018), and *The Frost Line Fracture* (2020). He also writes about a broad range of science topics for publications such as *Popular Mechanics*, *Business Insider*, and *Gizmodo*. Currently, he curates "Universe Today's Guide to Space" at Universe Today, a popular astronomy website. In this 2019 article from the online publication Interesting Engineering, Williams explores the future of space habitats and the prospects for private companies that want to make space travel available to ordinary citizens.

 **SKILLS PRACTICE**

CLAIMS AND EVIDENCE
Analyzing the Purpose and Effect of Evidence

As you read Williams's argument, record specific moments when he uses evidence to address the perspectives of others. After identifying these examples, explain the effects of each piece of evidence within his argument.

Analyzing the Purpose and Effect of Evidence		
Purpose of Evidence	Example(s) from the Text	Effect of Evidence
Corroboration		
Refutation		
Concession		
Rebuttal		

Are Space Habitats the Way of the Future?

According to some, humanity's future lies in space. In addition to the proposals from nations like China, which have announced plans to establish an outpost on the Moon in the next decade, some private aerospace companies are looking to make regular trips to the Moon and beyond a reality.

Someday, this could lead to ventures like space tourism—where customers can book a trip to orbit, the Moon, and even Mars—and even the creation of commercial space stations and lunar and Martian colonies.

For generations, human beings have fantasized about the day when people could live on the Moon or Mars. With all the developments that have happened in the past decade or so, we are coming to the point where some of these ideas are starting to look more feasible.

This begs the question: how will human beings live in space over the long haul? Should we be planting our roots in the soil of other planets and altering them (and/or ourselves) to ensure our survival? Or should we look to

creating orbiting habitats with microclimates and artificial gravity?

In terms of resources, time, effort, and accommodation, are space habitats the way to go? And from a strictly cost/benefit analysis, is it a better option than colonizing planets, moons, and other celestial objects?

Colonizing Space

During the Planetary Science Vision 2050 Workshop, which took place in February of 2017 at NASA's Headquarters in Washington, DC, scientists from all over the world came together to share research and presentations about the future of humanity in space.

It was here that Valeriy Yakovlev—an astrophysicist and hydrogeologist from the Laboratory of Water Quality in Kharkiv, Ukraine—presented a paper titled "Mars Terraforming—the Wrong Way."

Rather than colonizing and transforming the various bodies of the Solar System, he argued, humanity should instead construct space habitats. Addressing the idea of establishing a permanent colony on Mars, he claimed that:

"[A] radical obstacle to this is the unavailability of human beings to live in conditions of the reduced gravity of the Moon and Mars, being in their earthly bodies, at least in the next decades."

"If the path of space exploration is to create 10 a colony on Mars and furthermore the subsequent attempts to terraform the planet, it will lead to the unjustified loss of time and money and increase the known risks of human civilization."

The reason for this, according to Yakovlev, is because surface habitats and terraforming do not address the main challenges of colonizing space. His concern is that, rather than focusing on how to get there or how we intend to go about creating the necessary infrastructure, the main challenge of living in space comes down to the difficulty of having babies in space.

The Hazards of Living in Space

Let's face it, there are no shortages of hazards when it comes to living in space. Besides the danger of living in a sealed, pressurized tin can that is the only thing between the occupants and the vacuum of space, there's also all manner of things that can kill you.

Micrometeoroids are one danger. These small particles of space debris can pose a threat to spacecraft operations in Earth's orbit. While tiny and weighing less than a gram (0.035 ounces), they can reach tremendous speeds and generate a significant force of impact.

The average velocity of micrometeoroids relative to a spacecraft in orbit is about 10 km/s (6.2 mi/s), which works out to 36,000 km/h (22,500 mph). While individual impacts are not likely to rupture a spacesuit or the hull of

a spacecraft or space station, long-term exposure can cause significant wear and tear.

Then there is the danger posed by radiation 15 in space. Thanks to Earth's atmosphere and its protective magnetic field, human beings in developed nations such as the United States are exposed to 0.31 rem (3.1 mSv) of background radiation, with another 0.31 rem (3.1 mSv) per year from artificial sources.

However, beyond our atmosphere and magnetosphere, astronauts are exposed to much higher levels of solar radiation and galactic cosmic rays (GCR). There's also the elevated radiation that comes with solar particle events (SPE).

According to NASA studies, astronauts aboard the International Space Station (ISS) for six months are exposed to doses of ionizing radiation in the range of 50 to 2,000 mSv.

These and other studies have established an upper limit of 500 mSv per year for astronauts, which is the highest annual dose for which there was no observed increase in the rate at which cancer occurs in humans.

However, prolonged exposure dramatically increases the risk of acute radiation sickness, cancer, damage to the central nervous system, increased risk of degenerative disease, genetic damage, and even death.

Long-Term Effects of Low Gravity

On Earth, the force of gravity is equal to 9.8 20 meters per second per second (9.8 m/s^2). This means that any object in freefall towards the surface accelerates at a rate of 9.8 meters (32 feet) for every second it is falling.

Long-term exposure to microgravity (which astronauts experience in orbit), or lower levels of gravity, can have detrimental effects on all living creatures that have evolved in "Earth-normal" gravity (or 1 g). Multiple studies have been conducted into this phenomenon, largely aboard the ISS.

This includes NASA's seminal Twins Study, where astronauts Scott and Mark Kelly were used for comparative analysis. While Scott Kelly acted as a test subject and spent a year aboard the ISS, Mark Kelly remained on Earth and acted as the control.

Multiple physicals were conducted on both astronauts after Scott Kelly returned to Earth. In addition to muscle and bone density loss, the studies showed that long-duration missions to space led to diminished organ function, eyesight, and even genetic changes. Re-adapting to Earth-normal gravity can also be arduous and painful for astronauts.

At present, it is entirely unknown whether or not medical advances can counteract these effects. It is also unknown whether or not rehabilitation strategies, such as those that involve centrifuges, will be effective over long periods of time.

This raises the question, why not simply establish habitats that are able to simulate Earth-normal gravity? Not only would inhabitants have no need for medical intervention to prevent physical degeneration, but they would also possibly be able to have children in space without additional worries about the effects of microgravity. As for what kind of space habitats we could build, there are a number of options, all of which have been explored in science fiction and official studies.

History of the Concept

Much like research into rocketry and space exploration, the idea of creating habitats in Earth orbit or space predates the Space Age and goes back to the beginning of the 20th century.

It is also here that a great debt is owed to Konstantin Tsiolkovsky (1857–1935), one of the founding fathers of rocketry and aeronautics. In 1903, he published a study titled "Investigation of Outer Space Rocket Devices," where he suggested using rotation to create artificial gravity in space.

In 1928, Sloven rocket engineer Herman Potočnik released his seminal book *Das Problem der Befahrung des Weltraums der Raketen-Motor* (*The Problem of Space Travel—the Rocket Motor*). Here, he suggested building a spinning, wheel-shaped station with a 30-meter (~100 foot) diameter that could be placed in geostationary orbit.

In 1929, Irish scientist John Desmond Bernal wrote "The World, the Flesh & the Devil: An Enquiry into the Future of the Three Enemies of the Rational Soul" in which he described a hollow spherical space habitat measuring 16 km (10 miles) in diameter, filled with air, and able to accommodate a population of 20,000 to 30,000 people.

In the 1950s, German-American rocket scientists Wernher von Braun and Willy Ley updated the idea as part of an article and spread for *Colliers Magazine*—titled "Man Will Conquer Space Soon!"

Von Braun and Ley envisioned a 3-deck, rotating wheel with a diameter of 76 meters (250 feet). This wheel would revolve at 3 rpm to provide artificial gravity (one-third of Earth's gravity), and act as a staging point for spacecraft headed to Mars.

In 1954, the German scientist Hermann Oberth described the use of massive, rotating cylinders for space travel in his book *People into Space—New Projects for Rockets and Space Travel* (*Menschen im Weltraum—Neue Projekte für Raketen-und Raumfahrt*).

In 1975, NASA's Ames Research Center and Stanford University jointly held the first annual NASA Summer Study. This ten-week program saw professors, technical directors and students come together to create a vision of how people might someday live in a large space colony.

The result of this was the Stanford Torus Space Settlement, a design for a wheel-like space station that would house 10,000 people and would rotate to provide the sensation of either Earth-normal or partial gravity.

In 1974, while teaching at Princeton University, physicist Gerard K. O'Neill proposed the concept of a rotating cylinder in outer space, which was detailed in a September 1974 article of *Physics Today*—titled "The Colonization of Space."

This idea was the result of a cooperative study where O'Neill's students were tasked with designing stations that would allow for the colonization of space by the 21st century, using materials extracted from the Moon and Near-Earth Asteroids (NEAs).

O'Neill expanded on this in his 1976 book, *The High Frontier: Human Colonies in Space*, emphasizing how these types of "islands in space" could be built using existing technology.

"We now have the technological ability to set up large communities in space," he wrote, "communities in which manufacturing, farming, and all other human activities could be carried out."

According to his description, this cylinder would consist of two counter-rotating cylinders measuring 8 km in diameter and 32 km long. This would provide artificial gravity while also canceling out any gyroscopic effects.

During the 1990s, several updated versions of these concepts were proposed, thanks in large part to the Space Settlement Contest launched by NASA and the NSS in 1994.

These included updated versions of O'Neill cylinders, Bernal Spheres, and wheel stations that would take advantage of the latest developments in technology and materials science.

In 2011, Mark Holderman and Edward Henderson—of NASA's Technology Applications Assessment Team (TAAT)—designed a concept for a rotating wheel space station. This was known as the Non-Atmospheric Universal Transport Intended for Lengthy United States Exploration (Nautilus-X).

The concept was originally proposed for long-duration missions (1 to 24 months) to limit the effects of microgravity on human health. More recently, the idea was explored as a possible sleep quarters module that would be integrated with the ISS.

This would make it possible to experiment with artificial gravity without destroying the usefulness of the ISS for experiments in microgravity. The research could also help refine concepts for spacecraft that are able to simulate gravity using a centrifuge.

In 2010, NASA began working to fulfill their vision for the future of human space exploration, now known as their "Moon to Mars" program. This program envisioned the development of a new generation of heavy launch vehicles, spacecraft, and space stations that would allow for human exploration beyond Earth.

A central part of the mission architecture is the Deep Space Gateway, an orbiting habitat which would be built in cis-lunar space. This habitat would facilitate future missions to the Moon for NASA, other space agencies, and commercial partners, while also serving as a staging point for missions to Mars.

In 2018, the proposed habitat was renamed the Lunar Orbital Platform-Gateway (LOP-G)— or just the Lunar Gateway. The proposed configuration calls for the creation of a modular station consisting of eight elements, contributed by NASA and international partners.

This station will serve as a stopover point where crews launched from Earth—using the Space Launch System (SLS) and the Orion space capsule—will be able to dock and resupply. Astronauts and commercial crews will be able to travel to the lunar surface [and] will do so using a reusable lunar lander.

For missions headed to Mars, NASA plans on adding another spacecraft element—the

Deep Space Transport. This reusable spacecraft will rely on Solar-Electric Propulsion (SEP) to make trips between the Lunar Gateway and another station in orbit around Mars.

This station is known as the Mars Base Camp, another modular station that will allow for astronauts to dock and resupply before going down to the Martian surface. This will be accommodated by the Mars Lander, another reusable spacecraft.

In January of 2016, the Keck Institute for Space Studies hosted a presentation at Caltech titled "Building the First Spaceport in Low-Earth Orbit." The lecture was presented by members of the Gateway Foundation, a non-profit organization dedicated to creating the world's first spaceport.

The Gateway's design consists of two con-centric inner rings fixed by four spokes to an outer ring. The inner rings make up the Lunar Gravity Area (LGA), where tourists will be able to dine and play and the station's rotation will simulate lunar gravity.

The outer ring (LGA Habitation ring) is where habitation modules are placed. The outer ring, known as the Mars Gravity Area (MGA), experiences faster rotation and pro-vides an artificial gravitational environment similar to what people would experience on the surface of Mars.

The core of the station is where the Hub and Bay would reside. This is where the Gate-way's traffic control and operations would be coordinated from. The Hub will also have an observation lounge where guests can watch incoming shuttles.

The Gateway concept is one of many indi-cations of the growing relevance and presence of the commercial aerospace industry in space. The Foundation also envisions that commercial launch providers like SpaceX will be invaluable in sending the Gateway's modules to orbit (using the Starship/Super Heavy launch system).

Benefits over Surface Colonies

Space colonies have their fair share of upsides and downsides. But compared to establishing colonies on planets, moons, and asteroids, there are a number of really favorable trade-offs.

For one, rotating space stations—whether they take the form of O'Neill Cylinders, Von Braun Wheels or Stanford Torii—can be spun up to the point that they can mimic Earth-normal gravity.

This would eliminate concerns about the long-term health effects of low-g, and allow colonists a better chance of having children without the need to rely on medical treat-ments or artificial methods.

Radiation protection could also be provided by ensuring that the stations' outer walls are reinforced with radiation-resistant material (like lead, depleted uranium, or wastewater). Additional shielding could possibly be pro-vided by generating a magnetic field.

Space habitats could also allow for a great deal of flexibility when it comes to where to locate the colony. They could be built in orbit around Earth, the Moon, Mars, or possibly even other planets and major bodies in the Solar System.

They could also be positioned at any or all of the Lagrange Points throughout the Solar System. These are locations where the grav-itational forces of a two-body system (like the Sun and the Earth) produce regions of enhanced equilibrium, where a spaceship can be "parked."

Challenges of Making Space Habitats

Of course, no discussion about space habitats would be complete without mentioning the many challenges they present. Much like any effort to colonize beyond Earth, the most obvi-ous one is cost.

To build a single habitat in orbit around Earth would require a considerable amount of building materials, fuel, and construction robots. As it stands, SpaceX's *Falcon 9* and *Falcon Heavy* can deliver payloads to LEO at a rate of $2,719 and $1,410 per kg, respectively.

While the development of fully reusable vehicles—as well as smallsat launch services and single-stage-to-orbit (SSTO) rockets—has led to a significant reduction in launch costs, sending all the necessary materials and equipment into orbit would still be a monumental expenditure.

A possible solution would be to extract materials from NEAs or the Moon using robotic spacecraft and haulers. These could then be brought to Earth orbit to be processed into building materials and assembled using construction robots.

65

However, this would still require that a megatons worth of material and machinery be sent into space to build these robots and facilities. The costs become even more prohibitive the farther away these habitats are being built.

Way of the Future?

However, this is another advantage of creating space habitats. While the initial investment to create them in orbit around Earth or in cislunar space would be immense, these habitats could serve as stepping stones to more distant locations.

Basically, having these habitats in place between Earth and the Moon would mean that spacecraft could be assembled in orbit using materials harvested from space. They would also be able to launch from these stations, rather than having to take off from Earth.

This would mean significant reductions in terms of the number of launches from Earth, not to mention the amount of fuel needed to mount deep-space missions.

From the Earth-Moon system, robotic spacecraft and crews could potentially be sent to Mars, the Asteroid Belt, and to the outer and inner Solar System to build additional habitats using materials harvested locally.

70

The more locations we have "colonized" with space habitats, the easier it will be to expand humanity's presence across the Solar System. However, it is unlikely that future generations would choose one option over the other.

In the end, it seems more realistic to assume that space habitats could facilitate the spread of human beings through space, which includes allowing for settlements on other planets. So in addition to "Martians" and the like, there would also be "Lagrangians" (or whatever name they go by).

CLAIMS AND EVIDENCE

1. Find two examples of different **perspectives** presented in the text. How is each one related to Williams's perspective?

2. Williams uses evidence for a variety of purposes. Identify a moment in the text when Williams uses evidence to **corroborate** his own perspective. Then explain how that evidence contributes to his argument.

3. Throughout the text, Williams responds to different perspectives with **refutation**, **concession**, and **rebuttal**. Give an example of each, and then explain how it contributes to his argument.

4. What is Williams's **thesis**? What are the **implications** of his claim?

REASONING AND ORGANIZATION
Multimodal Argument

 Enduring Understanding (REO-1)

Writers make claims about subjects, rely on evidence that supports the reasoning that justifies the claim, and often acknowledge or respond to other, possibly opposing, arguments.

Throughout this book, you've read many arguments by writers who have different ideas and different purposes. Some have tried to influence public policy. Others have aimed to get an audience to accept their way of thinking. Still others have written to make the audience laugh or to show different, sometimes marginalized, perspectives. But all these writers have one thing in common: they use their words, their arguments, and their voices to make a difference in the world around them.

KEY POINT

Writers strategically make rhetorical choices and employ multiple methods of development within a single argument to connect with audiences and achieve their goal(s).

Conversations Are Transactional

When you enter a **conversation**, you join a transactional exchange with other people: a give-and-take of claims, evidence, and ideas with both their sources and their audience. In other words, conversations require writers to synthesize sources, incorporate various multiple modes, and use multiple methods of development strategically to achieve their purpose with the largest audience.

Arguments May Have Multiple Purposes

In Unit 4, you learned that a writer may have more than one purpose for an argument. Similarly, in a larger or even more transactional argument, a writer may draw upon those different purposes to support the overall argument. Each of these sections contributes to the writer's overall purpose. In the "Reasoning and Organization" in each unit of this book, you have considered a specific purpose and the **method of development** to achieve that purpose. For example, a writer who is proposing a solution to address safety in public parks may draw upon multiple methods to develop that argument. While the writer's overall goal is problem-solution, he or she may draw upon narration, compare and contrast, definition, cause and effect, and process to develop and justify the argument. The following example demonstrates how an essay on the safety of public parks may be arranged to achieve the writer's purpose.

Writer's Rhetorical Choice	Method of Development	Intended Effect
Begins with an anecdote that **illustrates** the problem	Narration	Hooks the reader and appeals to the audience's emotions
Describes safety issues at parks in **similar** communities	Compare and Contrast	Explains similarities and differences of subjects to determine which options may be applicable
Identifies and describes the **characteristics** or elements of safety	Definition	Establishes the writer's goal, which can be used to evaluate the potential solutions
Explains possible **options** and their potential **effects**	Cause/Effect	Provides the opportunity to analyze the pros and cons of the option in light of the goal established in the question or claim
Concludes with a description of the **steps** that should be taken	Process	Provides a recommendation that meets the goal established in the claim

JOINING THE CONVERSATION

Strategy	Definition	Effect	Example
Synthesizing Sources	Incorporating the ideas and perspectives of others	Enhances the writer's credibility through corroboration, concession, refutation, and rebuttal	A review of a new messaging app incorporates the testimony of early adopters, information from the manufacturer, and the experience of the writer.
Incorporating Multiple Modes of Communication	Embedding different media such as charts, tables, illustrations, photographs, and videos into written arguments	Increases the likelihood that the writer's message will be received by audiences who have different media preferences and prefer different types of appeals	An entrepreneur makes a product pitch in a "shark tank" and incorporates a short video from a user, graphs that show recent sales, illustrations that explain how the product is made, and a written marketing plan.
Drawing upon Elements of Design	Incorporates elements of design such as typography (e.g., bold, italics, font style and size) and other visual elements (e.g., color, pull quotes, white space)	Emphasizes key ideas and draw attention to important information	An online article about time management uses a numbered list, with each paragraph as a recommendation; the topic sentence of each new paragraph is in bold type; paragraph headers are in color.
Using Multiple Methods of Development	Arranges smaller claims and purposes that support the larger argument and overall purpose	Meets the needs of the audience by guiding readers to the writer's conclusion in a clear and logical way	A true-crime podcast begins with a vivid description of the crime scene, explains the investigation process, and compares and contrasts potential suspects.

INSIDER TIP

Writers develop their arguments to meet their specific goals. As you analyze arguments, you'll want to describe how writers combine and arrange multiple methods of development to justify their claims. More importantly, you must also explain how the arrangement and development contribute to the writer's overall purpose, as well as how they may impact his or her audience.

METHODS OF DEVELOPMENT AND ORGANIZATION		
Method of Development and Purpose		**Organization/Line of Reasoning**
Narration (illustration)		Beginning (exposition) — conflict initiated Middle (climax) — moment of truth End (resolution) — illustrates the claim
Persuasion (call to action or change)		• Inductive reasoning • Deductive reasoning
Exposition (informational/ explanatory)	Definition (what something is)	• Characteristics • Traits • Attributes • Components
	Classification/Division	
	Process Analysis (how something works/functions or how to do something)	• Steps • Stages • Phases
	Cause/Effect (why something came about OR the impact of something)	• Causes • Effects • Link cause to effect
Evaluation (recommend or propose)	Comparison/Contrast	• Subject by subject • Point by point
	Problem/Solution	• Describe problem • Analyze: compare/contrast options • Propose a solution

AP® SKILLS PRACTICE | REASONING AND ORGANIZATION
Determining a Rhetorical Strategy

Think of a conversation about an important subject that you've had recently or would like to have. You can also choose one of the following:

- Working a summer job while in high school
- Using the ACT or SAT as part of the college admissions process
- Reducing your carbon footprint
- Playing a sport or being active in a club while in high school
- Participating in a service-learning initiative
- Spending time with (or caring for) family members

Identify your claim (idea + perspective). Then use the following organizer to outline a possible argument that draws upon multiple methods of development to connect with your audience, justify your claim, and achieve your purpose.

Subject:		
Claim:		
Your Strategy	Method of Development	Intended Effect

It's All a Part of the Game
John Barry

THE TEXT IN CONTEXT

Originally intending to become a historian, John M. Barry (b. 1947) dropped out of his PhD program to work as a high school football coach and teacher. Barry ultimately moved to the college level, working as an assistant coach at Tulane University. After publishing his first article in a specialized coaching journal, he began working as a freelance writer for outlets such as *Sports Illustrated*, the *New York Times*, the *Washington Post*, *Fortune*, and *Newsweek*. Today, he is a *New York Times* best-selling author whose books have won multiple awards.

Alex Wong/Getty Images

Barry covers a range of topics, from politics and medicine to coastal protection and public policy. The National Academies of Sciences named his book *The Great Influenza: The Story of the Deadliest Pandemic in History* (2004), a study of the 1918 flu pandemic, the outstanding book on science or medicine for 2005. The following is an excerpt from his first book, *Power Plays: Politics, Football, and Other Blood Sports* (1991), which examines the nature of power in different contexts. In the excerpt, Barry draws on his experience as a football coach.

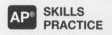 **SKILLS PRACTICE** | REASONING AND ORGANIZATION
Analyzing the Organization and Development of an Argument

As you read "It's All a Part of the Game," use the following table to capture how Barry arranges and organizes his argument. Then explain how these strategic choices contribute to his purpose and justify his claim.

Analyzing the Organization and Development of an Argument		
Claim:		
Writer's Strategy	**Method of Development**	**Intended Effect**

It's All a Part of the Game

Recently I watched New England Patriots quarterback Jim Plunkett, the former Heisman trophy winner, go down with an injury that required surgery, and then listened as another Patriots player was asked about it. "It's part of the game," he said. "You know? You can't worry about going down. It's part of the game."

Football coaches become inured to players getting hurt, even though the coaches are as vulnerable to injuries as the players. After all, it can mean coaches' jobs and coaches' careers. When I coached, I waved aside images of players going under the knife. I had to. But now,

when a player lies on the ground I go get a hot dog, or turn away from the television set for one or two or three minutes, and try not to think about the one boy I saw get really hurt. I'm not a coach anymore and I do think about it.

I went down myself as a player; pain shot up my leg and I was wincing instead of running. My recovery progressed slowly. I believed the coaches all thought I was dogging it, but, damn it, I wasn't. At first the sideways glances the coaches shot at me made me feel guilty, but later I grew so angry that I decided never to play again.

The next season found me in the stands, but watching gnawed and gnawed at me. Not so much the not playing. It was more that I felt like a quitter, which is far worse than being just a loser. That feeling continued to haunt me after graduation until I scrapped my Ivy League degree and graduate-school fellowship and nascent doctoral dissertation to coach a high school team. Of course, I swore always to give a player the benefit of the doubt on any injury.

Like every other high school coach, when a boy went down I would run onto the field and order players to move back and ask, "Where's it hurt?" and hope someone who actually knew something about injuries would come out on the field. Quick.

During one game at a private school in the South the smallest player on the field, one of those fast, tough kids with a great heart you always see in high school athletics, the kind of kid you love, went down. Out cold. I ran out there with a doctor. The boy was not badly hurt, the doctor said, and could even return to the game, so after he rested I sent him back in. We needed him in there.

But in the locker room after the game the boy collapsed. He lay on the floor unconscious, his eyes glassy, sweating profusely.

I raced out of the locker room to find the doctor. While waiting for the ambulance—the one at the game had left already—I slammed my fist against the lockers and shouted, "That doctor said he could play! Where's that doctor?" I felt guilt and wanted to transfer that guilt to him. I felt hate and wanted to kill him. The boy, as it turned out, was fine and later in the season even played again.

I was successful enough in high school, then coached football at a small college and finally joined the staff at Tulane University. Fantasy land for someone who didn't even play three years of Ivy League football. But it wasn't the sauna in the locker room or the 80,000-seat home stadium that struck me as so different. It was the zippers. So many athletes had zippers down the side of their knee, or knees, they thought nothing of it and called this or that a "Band-Aid" operation. I just kept looking at where the knife had cut and shaking my head. There were so many who had had surgery.

In college the coaches don't deal directly with injuries. There are trainers for that. In college the coaches receive injury reports and worry about them. "Oh, Christ," they mutter when someone lies a little too long on the ground. "Get up. You're not hurt. Damn it, don't be hurt."

"It's not too bad," the trainer says. "Have to cut sometime, but not right now. You never know. He might make it through the whole season."

When the season ends, those injured players who did make it through the year check into the hospital for surgery. The sooner the better for all concerned. The players are as anxious as the coaches; spring practice is not that far away. I remember thinking how odd one thing was: one freshman had made the varsity that more than half a million adults had paid to cheer. He was under eighteen so the hospital put him in the "kiddies' ward" and decorated his walls with floppy-eared elephants. He did not take kindly to his surroundings. He's an orthopedic surgeon himself now.

It's a cold business all right. In preseason we were running a game-type scrimmage inside our huge empty stadium, referees and all. A wide receiver runs an out. The quarterback ducks a rushing linebacker and starts to run, is chased, crosses the line of scrimmage. The receiver's eyes gleam, a pursuing defensive tackle all picked out, and he sets himself to unload a blind-side shot, to clean that guy's clock. Except it isn't blind side. The defensive tackle sees him coming and—WHAM!—he does the unloading on the receiver, running full-speed at him, and the receiver goes down, stumbles to his feet, goes down again and stays on the ground. Out run the trainers. Out runs a substitute receiver. The boy went down in front of the defensive bench. The defensive coaches ignore him. Hell, he's a receiver. He's not one of theirs. The offensive coaches are huddled, engrossed in play selection. The trainers help the boy off the field.

The head coach, Benny Ellender, approaches the offensive coaches, beckons one of them closer.

"Don't you *ever*," he says, "don't you *ever* let 15 a boy lie on the ground again without a coach going over to him."

The season started and the team was doing well, winning games and staying pretty healthy. One starter did get hurt, though, and had to have his knee operated on, for the third time. He'd have been a pro prospect but for those operations. A couple of days after the surgery we were playing a night game at home. I knew no players would visit him that day—on game days the players had to stay in the athletic dorm for meetings and taping and eating and just being together. I thought the player would feel like the forgotten man, so in the afternoon, when I had nothing to do really but watch whatever game was on TV, I decided to visit him myself. Another visitor was there when I arrived. The head coach, Ellener. You wouldn't catch many head coaches out visiting a player, except maybe a high school All-American, the day of a game. I always liked that man.

When I think of football injuries I like to think of incidents like that, like Ellender on game day visiting the boy in the hospital. And to forget a day I can't forget. I was coaching the defense at Providence College, very small-time football. (Big-time basketball; the PC basketball team went to the Final Four that year, but small-time football.) But for our level the team was excellent. Even though it was November,

we had not lost a game. Naturally the team we were playing was up, whooping and hollering and jumping up and down on each other's toes and in general doing all sorts of carrying-on before the game. We went through our warm-ups with a minimum of screeching, poised as always. The other team was screaming louder than ever at the opening kickoff, on which our two-hundred-pound return man took the ball out to about the 30, near our sideline. I saw the hit that brought him down. It was not a particularly hard tackle, but the other team shouted, "Good stick! Good stick!" just the same, and a couple of their players hustled over to pat the tackler as he got up. Except he didn't get up. He had gone down.

Their trainer ran out there, with the other team's coaches, talking to him. He wasn't moving. Our trainer ran out.

"For Chrissakes," I was thinking. "Get up, kid."

Our head coach came over to me. "Really 20 playing the role out there, huh!"

"Yeah."

Then the other team's trainer yelled for the doctor.

The doctor! Maybe the kid was hurt after all. We looked for the doctor. No doctor. The boy had been on the field for close to five minutes now. The trainer asked a cop to call the rescue squad. Where the hell was an ambulance? No doctor, no ambulance.

The doctor arrived. We weren't paying him. He was a volunteer. He thought it was a 2:00 game, not 1:30. Sorry.

Now rumors spread along our bench that 25 the kid was dead. I turned around and tongue-lashed a player who said that. "Don't be a jerk. Look at him. He's talking to the doctor."

Sirens. The rescue truck digging tracks in the moist field. Ten minutes had passed since the kid went down. I finally decided to join the huddle around the boy and see if we could get things moving.

With his helmet off, he looked shrunken and fragile in his equipment, his head sticking out of the massive shoulder pads like that of a small boy from his father's much-too-large jacket. He looked frightened. The doctor leaned over him.

"Am I going to be all right? I'm going to be all right, aren't I?"

"Just relax now."

"I can't feel anything. My legs. I can't feel anything." His voice, a scared child's voice. A lost child's voice. Wanting to be found. His face was handsome, almost pretty. The trainer took the boy's cleats and socks off. [30]

"Can you move your toes!"

The boy's face strained and tensed, his teeth grated and his eyes closed as be bore down, and a little sweat appeared on his face. The toes did not move.

"Can you feel this!" The trainer jabbed a scissors' tip into his foot.

"What did you say!" the boy asked.

The trainer looked up, as if appealing to me. "Oh . . . nothing," he told the boy. [35]

As all the people bustled around the boy, he asked again, "Am I going to be all right! I can't feel my legs."

The doctor said they were taking him to the hospital, that one of the best neurosurgeons in the country, from Brown University, would see him, as if the boy should feel honored, as if the fact that the neurosurgeon taught at Brown University made him omniscient and omnipotent.

Our offensive team was on the field running through plays. Their defense was doing calisthenics. It was not cold for the season, but it was November, and they had to stay warm or risk muscle pulls. I looked at the boy's face, at the wonderment in it, and felt sick. Sick of football. It couldn't be worth it. His eyes were open wide, as if absorbing this world never seen before. They started cutting off his equipment and he closed his eyes briefly, then reopened them.

"Am I going to be all right!" he asked the doctor one last time.

"Yes," the doctor answered him, "you're going to be fine." [40]

Although he was already lying flat on the ground he seemed to lean back then, or sort of settle. I stood off to the side with our head coach, watching knives slash through pads. We had loaned our opponents some equipment before the game; their managers had screwed up their preparations and had forgotten to pack some pads. "With our luck," somebody said, "those are our pads they're cutting through."

I laughed. It was funny. I turned away from the semicircle of people gathered around the boy and tried not to laugh, put my hand over my mouth and still laughed. It was funny. We had had budget problems all year.

They weren't our pads. We won the game easily, our filth shutout of the season. The boy was paralyzed. I continued to coach for another three years before I quit. During that time I had players in the hospital and never got around to visiting them. Too busy planning practices. And after all, you can't worry about going down. It's part of the game.

REASONING AND ORGANIZATION

1. What is Barry's **purpose** in this argument? Does he have multiple purposes? If so, what are they?

2. How does Barry **arrange** his argument to achieve his **purpose(s)**?

3. How does Barry's **method of development** help communicate his message to his **audience**?

Voice and Complexity

AP® **Enduring Understanding (STL-1)**

The rhetorical situation informs the strategic stylistic choices that writers make.

KEY POINT

A writer's rhetorical choices are part of his or her strategy to communicate a message to an audience.

If you asked your friends to describe your style, what do you think they would say? Preppy? Hipster? Grunge? Retro? Athletic? How would they describe you, and why would they choose that description? They might start with your clothes, your makeup, your accessories, your hair — as they look at the choices you have made to create your look. Whether you intend them to or not, all of these elements make up your style. Indeed, that style shapes how other people identify you as a person.

The same principles apply to writing style: all a writer's rhetorical choices help identify the writer's style. Make sure that you develop your style strategically; that is, use it to connect with your audience and send a deliberate message.

Often, writers employ similar rhetorical choices (e.g., creating long sentences, using anecdotes and stories, incorporating scientific and technical vocabulary, using personal pronouns) over the body of their work. When these rhetorical choices become a pattern, they begin to define a writer's style.

Style Enhances Meaning

When we refer to the *style* of writers, we usually mean the combination of word choice, syntax, and writing conventions. **Style** may also include their choice of subjects, their chosen methods of development, and even the kind of characters they tend to write about. If you are familiar with specific writers, you might be able to identify them by style alone. You may even gravitate to a favorite writer because of his or her subjects, characters, or voice.

If you can identify a writer's style, discussing its elements will add more complexity to your analysis of arguments and texts.

Some building blocks of style are more obvious choices, such as the use of

- connotative and denotative meaning of words,
- subordination and coordination,
- modifiers, and
- parenthetical elements (parentheses, dashes, commas).

But other, more subtle, factors can contribute to a writer's style. For example, a writer may continually return to ideas like psychology and horror in Stephen King's writings, or a region like Mark Twain's writings about the Mississippi River,

STYLISTIC CHOICES THAT ENHANCE THE WRITER'S MESSAGE		
Element of Style	Rhetorical Choice	Possible Effect
Diction	Connotation	Creates specific emotional connections with the audience
	Precise Word Choice	Contributes to a specific tone
	Type of Diction (e.g., jargon colloquialism, informal, formal, technical)	Addresses a particular audience
Syntax	Independent Clause • Simple sentence • Fragment • Rhetorical question	Creates emphasis Calls for reflection or action
	Subordination	Illustrates an imbalance or inequality of ideas
	Coordination	Illustrates balance or equality of ideas
	Modifier • Adjective • Adverb • Appositive	Reduces ambiguity through description, clarification, qualification, or specification
	Parenthetical Element • Parentheses • Dash • Comma	Offers clarification, description, or insight
Punctuation	Comma Colon Semicolon Dash Hyphen Parentheses Quotation mark Period	Clarifies, organizes, emphasizes, indicates purpose, supplements information, or contributes to tone
Design Features	Italics Boldface	Creates emphasis

LANGUAGE AND STYLE

or a Mary Roach's writings about the social implications of science. Other writers may adopt a distinctive rhythm or pacing in their writing.

A Writer's Voice Emerges from Style

You may want to focus on a writer's **voice** when analyzing his or her style. This voice on the page — its "sound," choices of words, syntactical pacing, and figures of speech — can give readers a strong sense of the writer's perspective and attitude toward the subject. A more subjective way to consider voice is the soul of the text that connects with the audience — the writer's unique fingerprint embedded within the text.

Voice is an effect of a writer's style. But remember that style and voice serve a larger aim: to support the writer's purpose with the audience. For example, a writer may use parenthetical elements to allude to an idea that he or she shares with readers. The interruption created by these parenthetical elements draws attention to additional information that may address an audience's needs or advance the writer's purpose. This can create a subtle, implicit connection with the audience and reinforce the meaning of the text. So, style and voice emerge from many smaller choices in diction, syntax, structure, punctuation, and design.

INSIDER AP® TIP

Stylistic choices are rhetorical choices. If you become engrossed in a text, figure out *why* you are engrossed in that text. Pay close attention to the writer's choices that created that style and explain how those choices engage the audience.

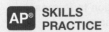 **AP® SKILLS PRACTICE** | **LANGUAGE AND STYLE**
Analyzing a Writer's Style

Find an advertisement (either digital or print) that draws upon the elements of style discussed in this chapter. Then describe the details of the ad and explain how the rhetorical choice contributes to the purpose of the text and the audience's understanding of the message.

Element of Style	Detail from the Ad	Explain How the Rhetorical Choice Contributes to Purpose and Meaning
Diction		
Syntax		
Punctuation		
Design Features		

Once Upon a Falling October

Ingrid Marie Geerken

THE TEXT IN CONTEXT

As a high school senior, Ingrid Marie Geerken submitted the following personal statement when she applied for admission at University of North Carolina at Chapel Hill. Identified as exemplary by college admissions counselors, "Once Upon a Falling October" was featured in *Essays That Worked* (1986), an anthology of outstanding college application essays. She is now a highly regarded psychotherapist.

 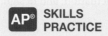 **SKILLS PRACTICE** | LANGUAGE AND STYLE
Analyzing How Stylistic Choices Enhance Meaning

As you read Geerken's essay, pay attention to her rhetorical and stylistic choices. Use the organizer to identify some of the ways that her style contributes to her purpose.

Analyzing How Stylistic Choices Enhance Meaning		
Element of Style	Examples from the Text	Contribution to Purpose and Message
Diction		
Syntax		
Punctuation		
Design Features		

Once Upon a Falling October

Once upon a falling October, screech-ingly close to when all post secondary applications were due, a girl in red hightops, (preferring to write in the third person), sat down to explain who she was (who *was* she?) on a blank, square piece of paper. She thought (this was done with an alarming frequency) how she yearned to fling herself across that little, but, oh, so very demanding, white essay space, seal herself up snugly in a rectangular envelope—lift the gooey flap before it slammed shut, slide her arm out the back, and stamp it right in the corner. If her mom were home—she'd ask her politely to address the envelope and send it off to the Undergraduate Admissions, Monogram Building 153-A, Country Club Road, Chapel Hill, NC 27514.

On second thought (something she also did with an alarming frequency) she thought that writers are so temperamental that she would probably crumple up and throw herself away.

"Where are they when I need them!?" she cried in delirious desperation, groping for the heroes living on her shelves, loung-ing luxuriously inside her books, rooming comfortably with their settings, characters, plots, themes, styles, tones, ironies and symbolisms.

"Certainly their words chiseled a glimpse of human nature into a monument of truth. Surely, they could write a classic—but, the question is—could they write a college essay?"

If you wish, use the following space to provide information about yourself which you think may help us in making our decision. Please add extra sheets if necessary. 5

What would Hemingway write? I mused.

My name is Ernest. I am a man. I am a writer. I would like to attend the University of North Caro-lina. At Chapel Hill.

Presenting Faulkner.

The name given to me at the moment of glorious birth when the fruits of the conception that were created through the guiding hands of the most Holy Being through the act of ultimate love between those who gave me life is the striking and most beautiful appellate of William Faulkner.

e.e. cummings in the Spotlight: 10

> mY (N)a(ME !!! E.?e. (is)
> sgnimmuC.
> 1 a m. a
> (poet.)(.)
> i.

Though he claimed that brevity was the soul of wit, Shakespeare always had a way with words:

The wheel of fortune hath spun—that errant whore bestowed upon me the most wretched of inquiries. Thy wit shalt not go slipshod. Here me committee—set less than thou trowest. I owest thou naught my name. Go to, have thy wisdom; it is William Shakespeare.

J. D. Salinger is a favorite of mine:

Damn it! Why the hell are you asking my name? Phonies are always asking crap like that. I don't know why, but they get a goddamn kick out of asking people who they are and what their names are and if they have a permanent mailing address. Those phony bastards really kill me. They want to know what your goddamn address is so that they can send you a god-damn letter saying that you're not good enough for them. Things like that really depress me.

David Thoreau meditates: 15

*Why was I named David Thoreau. With respect-
ful civil disobedience, I must defer this question
until I have gone into the woods and contemplated
the matter more thoroughly. (thoreau-ly.) UNC.
"There I might live, I said . . ."*

Freud insists:

*My identification is goal-oriented with a small
tendency toward narcissism. My Id, Ego, and
Superego are all fully developed and the most
predominant defense mechanism of my ego is
projection. (For example, if I am not accepted into
the University of North Carolina At Chapel Hill,
I will utilize my ability to blame it on outside or
extenuating circumstances, and I will say, They
don't know a good essay when they see one.)
Because of my pleasure derived from relieving
myself during the Anal stage of development, I am
basically an outgoing person. I chew on my pen
caps because some of my libido was stunted in the
oral stage of development.*

Arthur Miller dramatizes:

BEN: *Why, boys, when l was seventeen I*   20
*walked into the University of North Carolina
at Chapel Hill and when I was twenty-one
I walked out. He laughs. And by God I was
wise!*
WILLY: *You see what I been talking about? The
greatest things can happen.*

I say, (says she, switching from third to
first person) that my name is Ingrid. I think
too much, I laugh too loud, I live intensely.
Heaven for me would be to be locked up in a
small room with stacks and piles and reams
of blank paper; Hell for me would be to be
locked up in a small room with stacks and
piles and reams of blank sheets of white
paper, without a pencil, pen, typewriter,
piece of chalk, crayon, carbon, paint, or any
other type of writing utensil. It's equivalent
to locking Michaelangelo up in a room with
thousands of pure marble blocks and refusing
to give him a chisel. (The situations are equivalent—not the artists.)

When I go to college, (Will UNC have anything to do with me?), I have decided that I
will bring forth from my room these things:
l) The complete works of J. D. Salinger, 2)
A Separate Peace by John Knowles, 3) *A Winter's
Tale* by Mark Helprin, 4) Poetry by Carl Sand-
burg and T. S. Eliot, 5) My poster of the statue
of David by Michelangelo, 6) Mickey Mouse
and my Teddy Bear, 6) My watercolors, 7) My
Talking Heads Albums, 8) My newspapers, my
yearbook (My unsigned yearbooks. I always
hated signing them) 9) My English teacher's
address. 10) Myself. My name is Ingrid and
more than anything else in the world right
now, I want to become a part of the University
of North Carolina at Chapel Hill.

LANGUAGE AND STYLE

1. Geerken uses **parenthetical elements** throughout the text. Choose three examples and explain how each addresses the audience's needs and advances the writer's purpose.

2. Geerken imitates the style of several famous writers. Explain how these imitations contribute to Geerken's own **style** and message.

3. How does the writer consider the context and needs of the intended audience through her choices of **diction**?

4. Who is her unintended audience? How do her **rhetorical choices** affect that audience?

Modeled Text

Be Your Own Story

Toni Morrison

Boston Globe/Getty Images

THE TEXT IN CONTEXT

Toni Morrison (1931–2019) was one of the major American writers of the last century. Born in Ohio, Morrison attended Howard University as an undergraduate and then studied literature at Cornell University as a graduate student. In the 1960s, Morrison became an editor at Random House, where, as the publisher's first African American woman fiction editor, she helped raise the profile of African American writers such as Wole Soyinka, Chinua Achebe, Toni Cade Bambara, and Angela Davis. Morrison published her first novel, *The Bluest Eye*, in 1970. Over the next several decades, she explored race, American history, family, community, and other themes in novels such as *Sula* (1973), *Beloved* (1987), *Jazz* (1992), and *Home* (2012). She also taught at several universities, including Howard University, Yale University, and Princeton University. In 1993, she became the first African American to win the Nobel Prize in Literature. Morrison gave the following commencement address at Wellesley University, an all-female liberal arts college in Massachusetts, in 2004.

Unifying Idea	Be Your Own Story	Rhetorical Choices	Effects of Choices
self-actualization	I have to confess to all of you, Madame President, Board of Trustees, members of the faculty, relatives, friends, students. I have had some conflicted feelings about accepting this invitation to deliver the Commencement Address to Wellesley's Class of 2004. My initial response, of course, was glee, a very strong sense of pleasure at, you know, participating personally and formally in the rites of an institution with this reputation: 125 years of history in women's education, an enviable rostrum of graduates, its	method of development: narration writer's credibility	uses anecdote of personal experience to establish credibility reveals her ambivalence (pleasure and misgiving)

Unifying Idea	Be Your Own Story	Rhetorical Choices	Effects of Choices
	commitment sustained over the years in making a difference in the world, and its successful resistance to challenges that women's colleges have faced from the beginning and throughout the years. An extraordinary record—and I was delighted to be asked to participate and return to this campus.		
self-actualization	But my second response was not so happy. I was very anxious about having to figure out something to say to this particular class at this particular time, because I was really troubled by what could be honestly said in 2004 to over 500 elegantly educated women, or to relatives and friends who are relieved at this moment, but hopeful as well as apprehensive. And to a college faculty and administration dedicated to leadership and knowledgeable about what that entails. Well, of course, I could be sure of the relatives and the friends, just tell them that youth is always insulting because it manages generation after generation not only to survive and replace us, but to triumph over us completely.	audience and exigence	offers an example of self-awareness
self-actualization	And I would remind the faculty and the administration of what each knows: that the work they do takes second place to nothing, nothing at all, and that theirs is a first order profession. Now, of course to the graduates I could make reference to things appropriate to your situations—the future, the past, the present, but most of all happiness. Regarding the future, I would have to rest my case on some bromide, like the future is yours for the taking. Or, that it's whatever you make of it. But the fact is it is not yours for the taking. And it is not whatever you make of it. The future is also what other people make of it, how other people will participate in it and impinge on your experience of it.	refutation	on the road to self-actualization, one may encounter obstacles

Unifying Idea	Be Your Own Story	Rhetorical Choices	Effects of Choices
self-actualization	But I'm not going to talk anymore about the future because I'm hesitant to describe or predict because I'm not even certain that it exists. That is to say, I'm not certain that somehow, perhaps, a burgeoning *ménage a trois* of political interests, corporate interests and military interests will not prevail and literally annihilate an inhabitable, humane future. Because I don't think we can any longer rely on separation of powers, free speech, religious tolerance or unchallengeable civil liberties as a matter of course. That is, not while finite humans in the flux of time make decisions of infinite damage. Not while finite humans make infinite claims of virtue and unassailable power that are beyond their competence, if not their reach. So, no happy talk about the future.		
self-actualization	Maybe the past offers a better venue. You already share an old tradition of an uncompromisingly intellectual women's college, and that past and that tradition is important to both understand and preserve. It's worthy of reverence and transmission. You've already learned some strategies for appraising the historical and economical and cultural past that you have inherited. But this is not a speech focusing on the splendor of the national past that you are also inheriting.	direct address	understanding the past, present, and future of audiences
self-actualization	You will detect a faint note of apology in the descriptions of this bequest, a kind of sorrow that accompanies it, because it's not good enough for you. Because the past is already in debt to the mismanaged present. And besides, contrary to what you may have heard or learned, the past is not done and it is not over, it's still in process, which is another way of saying that when it's critiqued, analyzed, it yields new information about itself.		

Unifying Idea	Be Your Own Story	Rhetorical Choices	Effects of Choices
	The past is already changing as it is being reexamined, as it is being listened to for deeper resonances. Actually it can be more liberating than any imagined future if you are willing to identify its evasions, its distortions, its lies, and are willing to unleash its secrets.		
self-actualization	But again, it seemed inappropriate, very inappropriate, for me to delve into a past for people who are in the process of making one, forging their own, so I consider this focusing on your responsibility as graduates—graduates of this institution and citizens of the world— and to tell you once again, repeat to you the admonition, a sort of a wish, that you go out and save the world. That is to suggest to you that with energy and right thinking you can certainly improve, certainly you might even rescue it. Now that's a heavy burden to be placed on one generation by a member of another generation because it's a responsibility we ought to share, not save the world, but simply to love it, meaning don't hurt it, it's already beaten and scoured and gasping for breath. Don't hurt it or enable others who do and will. Know and identify the predators waving flags made of dollar bills. They will say anything, promise anything, do everything to turn the planet into a casino where only the house cards can win—little people with finite lives love to play games with the infinite. But I thought better of that, selecting your responsibilities for you. If I did that, I would assume your education had been in vain and that you were incapable of deciding for yourself what your responsibilities should be.	use of parenthetical	dashes amplify the message that self-actualization requires connecting to the world

Unifying Idea	Be Your Own Story	Rhetorical Choices	Effects of Choices
self-actualization	So, I'm left with the last thing that I sort of ignored as a topic. Happiness. I'm sure you have been told that this is the best time of your life. It may be. But if it's true that this is the best time of your life, if you have already lived or are now living at this age the best years, or if the next few turn out to be the best, then you have my condolences. Because you'll want to remain here, stuck in these so-called best years, never maturing, wanting only to look, to feel and be the adolescent that whole industries are devoted to forcing you to remain.	method of development: definition	define happiness and continual growth and maturity
self-actualization	One more flawless article of clothing, one more elaborate toy, the truly perfect diet, the harmless but necessary drug, the almost final elective surgery, the ultimate cosmetic—all designed to maintain hunger for stasis. While children are being eroticized into adults, adults are being exoticized into eternal juvenilia. I know that happiness has been the real, if covert, target of your labors here, your choices of companions, of the profession that you will enter. You deserve it and I want you to gain it, everybody should. But if that's all you have on your mind, then you do have my sympathy, and if these are indeed the best years of your life, you do have my condolences because there is nothing, believe me, more satisfying, more gratifying than true adulthood. The adulthood that is the span of life before you. The process of becoming one is not inevitable. Its achievement is a difficult beauty, an intensely hard won glory, which commercial forces and cultural vapidity should not be permitted to deprive you of.	method of development: comparison/contrast

parenthetical | contrasts happiness to stasis to encourage self-actualization

inserts "believe me" to create an intimate bond with the audience |

Unifying Idea	Be Your Own Story	Rhetorical Choices	Effects of Choices
self-actualization	Now, if I can't talk inspiringly and hopefully about the future or the past or the present and your responsibility to the present or happiness, you might be wondering why I showed up. If things are that dour, that tentative, you might ask yourself, what's this got to do with me? What about my life? I didn't ask to be born, as they say. I beg to differ with you. Yes, you did! In fact, you insisted upon it. It's too easy, you know, too ordinary, too common to not be born. So your presence here on Earth is a very large part your doing.		
self-actualization	So it is up to the self, that self that insisted on life that I want to speak to now—candidly—and tell you the truth that I have not really been clearheaded about, the world I have described to you, the one you are inheriting. All my ruminations about the future, the past, responsibility, happiness are really about my generation, not yours. My generation's profligacy, my generation's heedlessness and denial, its frail ego that required endless draughts of power juice and repeated images of weakness in others in order to prop up our own illusion of strength, more and more self congratulation while we sell you more and more games and images of death as entertainment. In short, the palm I was reading wasn't yours, it was the splayed hand of my own generation and I know no generation has a complete grip on the imagination and work of the next one, not mine and not your parents', not if you refuse to let it be so. You don't have to accept those media labels. You need not settle for any defining category. You don't have to be merely a taxpayer or a red state or a blue state or a consumer or a minority or a majority.	method of development: comparison/contrast	compares and contrasts to other generations to illustrate that self-actualization is individual for each person

Unifying Idea	Be Your Own Story	Rhetorical Choices	Effects of Choices
self-actualization	Of course, you're general, but you're also specific. A citizen and a person, and the person you are is like nobody else on the planet. Nobody has the exact memory that you have. What is now known is not all what you are capable of knowing. You are your own stories and therefore free to imagine and experience what it means to be human without wealth. What it feels like to be human without domination over others, without reckless arrogance, without fear of others unlike you, without rotating, rehearsing and reinventing the hatreds you learned in the sandbox. And although you don't have complete control over the narrative (no author does, I can tell you), you could nevertheless create it.	writer's message	self-actualization requires action: to be the story and the author of it
self-actualization	Although you will never fully know or successfully manipulate the characters who surface or disrupt your plot, you can respect the ones who do by paying them close attention and doing them justice. The theme you choose may change or simply elude you, but being your own story means you can always choose the tone. It also means that you can invent the language to say who you are and what you mean. But then, I am a teller of stories and therefore an optimist, a believer in the ethical bend of the human heart, a believer in the mind's disgust with fraud and its appetite for truth, a believer in the ferocity of beauty. So, from my point of view, which is that of a storyteller, I see your life as already artful, waiting, just waiting and ready for you to make it art. Thank you.	message/ implication for present and future audiences	every life has the potential to be an expression of art

IDEAS IN AMERICAN CULTURE
Truth and Consequences

News and information are everywhere: on-screen at a gas station pump, beeping at us on our smartphones. However, we seem caught in an irony: we have more access to information than ever, yet we still struggle to stay informed about what matters.

From the broadsides of the Revolutionary period to the muckraking exposés of the Progressive Era, newspapers have played a significant role in U.S. culture. They are even enshrined in the Constitution's First Amendment, which forbids the government from "abridging the freedom of speech, or of the press."

But does this mechanism of truth and consequences still function? In the United States, the regulation of the press has largely been left to the free market. Private companies own publications, broadcast stations, cable outlets, and streaming services; they compete with each other for advertising or subscriptions. But the press has also relied on self-regulation, including ethical standards established for professional journalism as illustrated in "Truth in Journalism" (p. 749), an 1853 *Scientific American* editorial.

Of course, those standards have changed over the years with the growth of various media forms. But the most fundamental shifts from "newspapers" to "media" have occurred in the last seventy years. So has our conception of "journalism." For much of the country's history, newspaper work was not a profession.

IDEA BANK

Accountability
Balance
Belief
Bias
Cancel Culture
Code
Consequences
Disinformation
Freedom of Speech
Information
Investigation
Issue
Knowledge
Media
Opinion
Reality
Standards
Truth

This image was created by artist Alex Nabaum to accompany an article on how artists comment on current events, and journalists rely on artistry to engage audiences and get their message across.

Consider the various images that make up the work and how they are arranged. What message might this artwork present about truth in journalism? What might it imply about the balance between information and opinion?

Alex Nabaum

743

That began to change in the early twentieth century as journalism became a specialized field of expertise: the University of Missouri opened the first U.S. college of journalism in 1908, with Columbia University in New York following in 1912.

Broadcast journalism on radio and later television came to prominence in the 1940s and 1950s. The "New Journalism" of the 1960s deployed literary techniques in reporting — especially a subjective perspective that emphasized the writer's skills, perceptions, and personality. We can see this tradition in the experiential, first-person reporting of Barbara Ehrenreich's "In America, Only the Rich Can Afford to Write about Poverty" (p. 745). As news has evolved into entertainment, large corporations — AT&T, CBS, Comcast, Fox, Viacom, and the Walt Disney Company — now own 90 percent of the news outlets in the United States. Likewise, national newscasters and cable television talk show hosts have become wealthy celebrities. Meanwhile, local newspapers, which rely on dwindling subscribers and diminishing advertising revenue, are languishing.

Not surprisingly, then, the U.S. media has been subject to criticism. For example, the political left has traditionally disliked corporate media, which privileges profits over news standards and leaves private interests to hold themselves accountable. The political right has long accused the American press of having a "liberal bias." But the emergence of the internet over the last two decades has, in some ways, democratized news reporting. The prevalence of social media and smartphone cameras allow *anyone* to report as a citizen journalist. However, with no editorial oversight "fake news" can spread and take hold.

Similarly, social media sites such as Facebook and Twitter have acknowledged their role in contributing to misinformation by instituting stricter fact-checking standards. In turn, these protocols have led some to accuse these sites of bias and even censorship. Regardless, Americans remain hungry for news and information. But consumers must evaluate sources — and take into account their own biases.

This shot from San Francisco, California, shows street-side newspaper vending machines that have been removed from service as print circulation declines.

What perspective does this image communicate about the newspaper industry? Many people believe that the newspaper industry is dying. Do you agree? What is the value of local reporting and local newspapers? When these outlets close, what are the consequences for communities?

Justin Sullivan/Getty Images

In America, Only the Rich Can Afford to Write about Poverty

Barbara Ehrenreich

Tom Williams/Getty Images

THE TEXT IN CONTEXT

Barbara Ehrenreich (b. 1941) is an American author and political activist. Her writing has appeared in the *New York Times*, the *Atlantic Monthly*, the *Nation*, the *Washington Post*, and other publications. Ehrenreich views her work in the tradition of Progressive Era "muckraking" journalism: reporting that aimed to expose injustice, corrupt institutions, and other social problems. She is best known for her 2001 book *Nickel and Dimed: On (Not) Getting By in America*. The book documents Ehrenreich's three-month experiment surviving on minimum wage as a waitress, hotel maid, house cleaner, nursing home aide, and Wal-Mart clerk. In the following 2015 online article for *TheGuardian.com*, she explores the changing role of journalists.

Back in the fat years—two or three decades ago, when the "mainstream" media were booming—I was able to earn a living as a freelance writer. My income was meager and I had to hustle to get it, turning out about four articles—essays, reported pieces, reviews—a month at $1 or $2 a word. What I wanted to write about, in part for obvious personal reasons, was poverty and inequality, but I'd do just about anything—like, I cringe to say, "The Heartbreak Diet" for a major fashion magazine—to pay the rent.

It wasn't easy to interest glossy magazines in poverty in the 1980s and 90s. I once spent two hours over an expensive lunch—paid for, of course, by a major publication—trying to pitch to a clearly indifferent editor who finally conceded, over decaf espresso and crème brulee, "OK, do your thing on poverty. But can you make it upscale?" Then there was the editor of a nationwide, and quite liberal, magazine who responded to my pitch for a story involving blue-collar men by asking, "Hmm, but can they talk?"

I finally got lucky at *Harper's*, where fabled editor Lewis Lapham gave me an assignment that turned into a book, which in turn became a bestseller, *Nickel and Dimed: On (Not) Getting By in America*. Thanks to the royalties and subsequent speaking fees, at last I could begin to undertake projects without concern for the pay, just because they seemed important to me. This was the writing life I had always dreamed of—adventurous, obsessively fascinating and sufficiently remunerative that I could help support less affluent members of my family.

Meanwhile, though I didn't see it at first, the world of journalism as I had known it was beginning to crumble around me. Squeezed to generate more profits for new media conglomerates, newsrooms laid off reporters, who often went on to swell the crowds of hungry freelancers. Once-generous magazines shrank or slashed their freelance budgets; certainly there were no more free lunches.

True, the internet filled with a multiplicity of new outlets to write for, but paying writers or other "content providers" turned out not to be part of their business plan. I saw my own fees at one major news outlet drop to one third of their value between 2004 and 2009. I heard from younger journalists who were scrambling for adjunct jobs or doing piecework in "corporate communications." But I determined to carry on writing about poverty and inequality even if I had to finance my efforts entirely on my own. And I felt noble for doing so.

Then, as the kids say today, I "checked my privilege." I realized that there was something wrong with an arrangement whereby a relatively affluent person such as I had become could afford to write about minimum wage jobs, squirrels as an urban food source or the penalties for sleeping in parks, while the people who were actually experiencing these sorts of things, or were in danger of experiencing them, could not.

In the last few years, I've gotten to know a number of people who are at least as qualified writers as I am, especially when it comes to the subject of poverty, but who've been held back by their own poverty. There's Darryl Wellington, for example, a local columnist (and poet) in Santa Fe who has, at times, had to supplement his tiny income by selling his plasma—a fallback that can have serious health consequences. Or Joe Williams, who, after losing an editorial job, was reduced to writing for $50 a piece for online political sites while mowing lawns and working in a sporting goods store for $10 an hour to pay for a room in a friend's house. Linda Tirado was blogging about her job as a cook at IHOP when she managed to snag a contract for a powerful book entitled *Hand to Mouth* (for which I wrote the preface). Now she is working on a "multi-media mentoring project" to help other working-class journalists get published.

There are many thousands of people like these—gifted journalists who want to address serious social issues but cannot afford to do so in a media environment that thrives by refusing to pay, or anywhere near adequately pay, its "content providers." Some were born into poverty and have stories to tell about coping with low-wage jobs, evictions or life as a foster child. Others inhabit the once-proud urban "creative class," which now finds itself priced out of its traditional neighborhoods, like Park Slope or LA's Echo Park, scrambling for health insurance and childcare, sleeping on other people's couches. They want to write—or do photography or documentaries. They have a lot to say, but it's beginning to make more sense to apply for work as a cashier or a fry-cook.

This is the real face of journalism today: not million dollar-a-year anchorpersons, but low-wage workers and downwardly spiraling professionals who can't muster up expenses to even start on the articles, photo-essays and videos they want to do, much less find an outlet to cover the costs of doing them. You can't, say, hop on a plane to cover a police shooting in your hometown if you don't have a credit card.

This impoverishment of journalists impov- 10 erishes journalism. We come to find less and less in the media about the working poor, as if about 15% of the population quietly emigrated while we weren't looking. Media outlets traditionally neglected stories about the downtrodden because they don't sit well on the same page with advertisements for diamonds and luxury homes. And now there are fewer journalists on hand at major publications to arouse the conscience of editors and other gatekeepers. Coverage of poverty accounts for less than 1% of American news, or, as former *Times* columnist Bob Herbert has put it: "We don't have coverage of poverty in this country. If there is a story about poor people in the *New York Times* or in the *Washington Post*, that's the exception that proves the rule. We do not cover poverty. We do not cover the poor."

As for commentary about poverty—a disproportionate share of which issues from very well paid, established, columnists like David Brooks of the *New York Times* and George Will of the *Washington Post*—all too often, it tends to reflect the historical biases of economic elites, that the poor are different than "we" are,

less educated, intelligent, self-disciplined and more inclined to make "bad lifestyle choices." If the pundits sometimes sound like the current Republican presidential candidates, this is not because there is a political conspiracy afoot. It's just what happens when the people who get to opine about inequality are drawn almost entirely from the top of the income distribution. And there have been few efforts focused on journalism about poverty and inequality, or aimed at supporting journalists who are themselves poor.

It hurts the poor and the economically precarious when they can't see themselves reflected in the collective mirror that is the media. They begin to feel that they are different and somehow unworthy compared to the "mainstream." But it also potentially hurts the rich.

In a highly polarized society like our own, the wealthy have a special stake in keeping honest journalism about class and inequality alive. Burying an aching social problem does not solve it. The rich and their philanthropies need to step up and support struggling journalists and the slender projects that try to keep them going. As a self-proclaimed member of the 0.01% warned other members of his class last year: "If we don't do something to fix the glaring inequities in this economy, the pitchforks are going to come for us."

Black, white and Hispanic Americans give very different reasons for why they feel the news media don't understand them

Among U.S. adults who say news organizations do not understand people like them, % who say ___ is what news organizations misunderstand the most about them

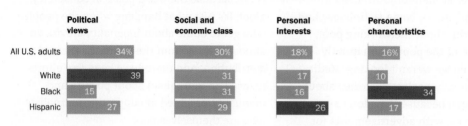

Note: Those who did not provide an answer not shown. White and Black adults include those who report being one race and are non-Hispanic. Hispanics are of any race.
Source: Survey of U.S. adults conducted Feb. 18-March 2, 2020.

PEW RESEARCH CENTER

"Black, white and Hispanic Americans give very different reasons for why they feel the news media don't understand them," Pew Research Center, Washington D.C., June 25, 2020, https://www.pewresearch.org/fact-tank/2020/06/25/black-hispanic-and-white-adults-feel-the-news-media-misunderstand-them-but-for-very-different-reasons/ft_2020-06-25_misunderstood_02b/

A study by the Pew Research Center and the Knight Foundation found that American news consumers don't feel that the news media represents the diversity of America.

The chart captures diverse responses to the question of why the news media does not represent most Americans. Review the data and then explain the relationships that exist among the various groups.

RHETORICAL SITUATION

1. What is Ehrenreich's **message**? Who might corroborate her claim? Who might be skeptical of it?

2. What is the writer's **perspective** on the subject? Why does she have this perspective? Explain any limitations or biases to this perspective.

3. What does Ehrenreich's **conclusion** imply about the future of journalism?

CLAIMS AND EVIDENCE

4. Ehrenreich offers multiple perspectives. Which perspectives are adequately supported? Which ones are not? How does their inclusion reflect Ehrenreich's **bias** or the **limitations** of her argument?

5. What are the implications of Ehrenreich's **evidence**? How might emerging evidence challenge the validity of her argument in the future?

REASONING AND ORGANIZATION

6. What is the overarching purpose of the text? Does it have more than one purpose? Explain how Ehrenreich uses **methods of development** to achieve multiple purposes.

7. Is the argument arranged **inductively** or **deductively**? How does this arrangement strengthen the argument?

LANGUAGE AND STYLE

8. Ehrenreich addresses counterarguments throughout the text. How does she **transition** to these concessions and rebuttals? Do her responses to these other views strengthen her argument? Why or why not?

9. Choose two **syntactical** structures (e.g., subordinate clauses) and then explain the effect of these elements on both the **tone** and the message of the text.

10. How would you describe Ehrenreich's **style**? Which rhetorical choices contribute to that characterization?

IDEAS IN AMERICAN CULTURE

11. Ehrenreich describes contemporary journalism in terms of "low-wage workers and downwardly spiraling professionals." She claims, "This impoverishment of journalists impoverishes journalism." Do you agree with her? Explain.

PUTTING IT ALL TOGETHER

12. Why is Ehrenreich's argument complex? Explain how her rhetorical choices contribute to the complexity of her argument.

Truth in Journalism
Scientific American

THE TEXT IN CONTEXT

Scientific American is a popular science magazine first published in 1845 by inventor Rufus Porter. Today, the magazine reaches over five million people internationally each month. Over its history, *Scientific American* has published over 200 Nobel Laureate authors. In the following 1853 article, the magazine's editors offer their perspective on the importance of truth in journalism.

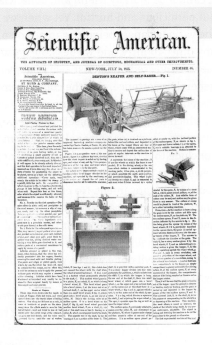

One of the daily papers of this city, while descanting recently on the *Newspaper Press*, placed its influence far above that of the pulpit, and its usefulness far above that of general book literature. The influence of the newspaper press, at the present day, is indeed very great, either for good or evil. Its influence is great for good, according to its truthfulness; for evil, according to its disregard of truth. The promulgation of truth in discreet and prudent language never can do evil, but good, and the influence for good of a newspaper which makes truth its aim and object, is in proportion to its circulation. On the other hand, the influence for evil of a newspaper which does not respect truth, is evil only and that continually. Editors should therefore be exceedingly careful of what they say in order that they may not mislead and deceive, and thereby avoid doing injury to the community. Truth should be their idol, their first and last consideration always, for unless truth is the leading characteristic of the newspaper press, it cannot be morally useful and beneficial, but pernicious and hurtful. Yet when we read the various papers belonging to our own, or any other country, and witness the various views expressed on almost every subject of general importance, also the contradictory statements in them respecting many events in which the papers themselves have peculiar interests—party or personal—we cannot but conclude that truth is not yet the idol of the newspaper press, and that there is still great room for improvement. No editor is perfect, and no paper can be utterly free from error and mistakes; but where truth is the rule of conduct, although every essential error must do evil, the evil done will be greatly mollified by astern anxiety always to be right. . . .

The most absurd and dangerous views upon any subject will find believers; no limit can be assigned to the credulity of man, nor the evil to be apprehended from the propagation of falsehood and error. "Error of opinion may indeed be safely tolerated while reason is left free to combat against it," because any other course of conduct towards errorists, would be injurious to society, still neither errors of opinion, nor erroneous statements are safe in themselves, they are dangerous and should be guarded against with the most sleepless vigilance, especially by the newspaper press. The poet Editor, W. C. Bryant, than whom there is no better judge, asserted that the literature of the *Daily Press* was, in many respects, superficial, and the reason of this is obvious. Readers of daily papers expect editors to present their views on the subjects of the day—passing events of the moment—hence there is often much inconsiderate haste displayed, on the very questions which require the most research and caution, viz., those of deep and exciting general importance. Much evil is done by taking up a position—sides—hastily upon any new question, and in expressing opinions favorable or unfavorable, which future developments may prove to be wrong. There is a natural vanity in man which tempts him, after he has committed himself to wrong views, ignorantly though it may be, to confess an error, even after he becomes perfectly convinced of the same. This is the reason why so many errors, by the influence of the press, roll on through space and time, accumulating and propagating evil. Every editor should therefore be exceedingly cautious of what he says, for the evil that men do, especially through the influence of the press, is not confined to our own day and generation. These remarks have been elicited by those in the paper referred to; also, in consequence of seeing in another of our daily papers, a few days ago, statements respecting a certain inventor known to us, which were the very opposite of truth, and of this the author of the statements could not have been ignorant. The V press is indeed a mighty engine for good or evil; but it has not yet, we believe, reached its climax of influence, dignity, and usefulness; and will not, until truth in journalism becomes its guide and its glory.

▲

In this political cartoon by Jimmy Margulies, he focuses on the importance of the First Amendment. The First Amendment protects freedom of speech, the press, assembly, and the right to petition the government.

How valuable is the First Amendment to the Constitution to democracy? Do you believe that the press is a pillar of democracy? Explain.

RHETORICAL SITUATION

1. Who is the intended **audience** for this article? Who might be the unintended audience? Explain how the editors take into account the beliefs, values, and needs of both the intended and unintended audience.

2. What is the subject of this article? What **perspective** do the writers convey about the subject? Explain why the writers have this perspective.

3. What is the **purpose** of this text? If it has more than one purpose, identify the main one, and then identify the other purposes.

CLAIMS AND EVIDENCE

4. Identify both a **refutation** and a **concession**. Explain how they function within the argument.

5. How does the **evidence** offer multiple perspectives on the issue? Explain how these perspectives affect the argument.

REASONING AND ORGANIZATION

6. What **method of development** do the writers use? Explain how this method of development contributes to their writing purposes.

7. Who may **corroborate** the writers' perspective? Who might be skeptical about it? How do these responses contribute to an ongoing conversation?

LANGUAGE AND STYLE

8. How are dashes used in this article? Give two examples of the use of other **parenthetical elements** in the text. Explain how each contributes to the writers' message.

9. Focus on the **syntax** of the text. Give an example of two or more sentences that include intentional punctuation that contributes to the message.

IDEAS IN AMERICAN CULTURE

10. Is this 1853 text on journalism still relevant now? Why or why not? Explain the issues that resonate in journalism today.

PUTTING IT ALL TOGETHER

11. The writers select evidence and offer multiple perspectives to explain the responsibility of journalists. Explain how these rhetorical choices contribute to the purpose and help develop a message about journalism.

IDEAS IN AMERICAN CULTURE
Technology and Globalization

In the excerpt from Thomas Friedman's *The World Is Flat* (p. 755), you might notice that Friedman travels to Bangalore, India: that country's "Silicon Valley" (in his words). It is not a coincidence that his argument about globalization focuses, in large part, on technology. These two ideas have long been connected. Even Christopher Columbus's expeditions to the Americas were enabled by contemporary innovations in ship design and navigational tools. Today, however, the pace of technological progress is much faster, as the technology itself makes the world seem "smaller." While it took Columbus two months to travel from Spain to the American continent, air travel now makes that voyage possible in about seven hours, and with supersonic travel (the *Concorde* in the 1970s and 1980s), even shorter. Technological advances, like Google Earth, GPS, and public surveillance systems, allow quick access of information and convenience of travel while raising concerns about privacy.

The upsides of technology are obvious. We now have instant access — to information, ideas, experiences, products, entertainment, faraway places, and social interaction, among other things. For those born after the 1980s, that

IDEA BANK

Connection
Convenience
Disruption
Ethics
Exceptionalism
Globalization
Influence
Innovation
Intelligence
Isolation
Nationalism
Native
Network
Opportunity
Populism
Privacy
Sovereignty
Technology
Terrorism

This image, taken from a promotional video, depicts two Boston Dynamic robots and one dog-like robot dancing to the 1962 Motown hit "Do You Love Me" by The Contours. The video shows impressive achievements in mobility and artificial intelligence.

When you think about advancements in robotics and artificial intelligence, are you excited and hopeful about the future role of robots in human life? Are you pessimistic, or even frightened? Explain.

connectivity is just a given: these "digital natives" have only known a highly connected world. But downsides of technology are often apparent too. For example, smartphones can be distracting, isolating, and addictive experiences. Increased connectivity creates more opportunities for hackers, as well as the growing problem of cyber warfare. New developments in genetic engineering, artificial intelligence, and machine learning also raise complex questions. For example, if a driverless car strikes a pedestrian, who is responsible?

Like technology, globalism is a double-edged sword. It has led to the spread of knowledge, lower costs for many products, and increased cooperation between many nations. But it has also come under much scrutiny and criticism, as Fareed Zakaria writes in "Everyone Seems to Agree, Globalization Is a Sin. They're Wrong." (p. 763).

Indeed, these problems are significant: lost jobs as corporations seek the cheapest workers, the exploitation of labor in countries with low wages and few regulations, theft of proprietary technologies, the rapid spread of novel viruses, the empowerment of unaccountable non-state actors — from corporations and individuals to terrorists — to shape events and policies. We can understand the recent history of both Brexit and Donald Trump's "America First" themes in this context. In both cases, populist nationalism expressed anger and concern: about lost national sovereignty, porous national borders, and a weakened economy. But if globalization, like technological progress, is inevitable, we need to learn how to maximize its benefits while managing its disruptions.

Mural by Amandine Lesay, Anadolu Agency/Getty Images

▲

During the COVID-19 pandemic, people celebrated frontline workers, many of whom risked their lives to ensure the safety of others. This mural is one among many other creative gestures of appreciation.

How did science, medical, and health organizations work together in response to this devastating virus?

from The World Is Flat

Thomas Friedman

ullstein bild Dtl./Getty Images

THE TEXT IN CONTEXT

Pulitzer Prize–winning journalist and author Thomas Friedman (b. 1953) studied at Brandeis University, Oxford University, and the American University in Cairo. After graduation, he began his journalism career at the United Press International before becoming the Jerusalem bureau chief of the *New York Times* in 1984. In 1995, he became the *New York Times* foreign affairs columnist. Regarding his international reporting, Friedman has stated, "I am a big believer in the saying 'If you don't go, you don't know.'" His books include *From Beirut to Jerusalem* (1989), *The Lexus and the Olive Tree: Understanding Globalization* (1999), and *The World Is Flat: A Brief History of the Twenty-First Century* (2005). In the following excerpt from *The World Is Flat*, Friedman reflects on a new era of globalization.

> *Your Highnesses, as Catholic Christians, and princes who love and promote the holy Christian faith, and are enemies of the doctrine of Mahomet, and of all idolatry and heresy, determined to send me, Christopher Columbus, to the above-mentioned countries of India, to see the said princes, people, and territories, and to learn their disposition and the proper method of converting them to our holy faith; and furthermore directed that I should not proceed by land to the East, as is customary, but by a Westerly route, in which direction we have hitherto no certain evidence that anyone has gone.*
>
> —Entry from the journal of Christopher Columbus on his voyage of 1492

No one ever gave me directions like this on a golf course before: "Aim at either Microsoft or IBM." I was standing on the first tee at the KGA Golf Club in downtown Bangalore, in southern India, when my playing partner pointed at two shiny glass-and-steel buildings off in the distance, just behind the first green. The Goldman Sachs building wasn't done yet; otherwise he could have pointed that out as well and made it a threesome. HP and Texas Instruments had their offices on the back nine, along the tenth hole. That wasn't all. The tee markers were from Epson, the printer company, and one of our caddies was wearing a hat from 3M. Outside, some of the traffic signs were also sponsored by Texas Instruments, and the Pizza Hut billboard on the way over showed a steaming pizza, under the headline "Gigabytes of Taste!"

No, this definitely wasn't Kansas. It didn't even seem like India. Was this the New World, the Old World, or the Next World?

I had come to Bangalore, India's Silicon Valley, on my own Columbus-like journey of exploration. Columbus sailed with the *Niña*, the *Pinta*, and the *Santa María* in an effort to discover a shorter, more direct route to India by heading west, across the Atlantic, on what he presumed to be an open sea route to the East Indies—rather than going south and east around Africa, as Portuguese explorers of his day were trying to do. India and the magical Spice Islands of the East were famed at the time for their gold, pearls, gems, and silk—a source of untold riches. Finding this shortcut by sea to India, at a time when the Muslim powers of the day had blocked the overland routes from Europe, was a way for both Columbus and the Spanish monarchy to become wealthy and powerful. When Columbus set sail, he apparently assumed the earth was round, which was why he was convinced that he could get to India by going west. He miscalculated the distance, though. He thought the earth was a smaller sphere than it is. He also did not anticipate running into a landmass before he reached the East Indies. Nevertheless, he called the aboriginal peoples he encountered in the new world "Indians." Returning home, though, Columbus was able to tell his patrons, King Ferdinand and Queen Isabella, that although he never did find India, he could confirm that the world was indeed round.

I set out for India by going due east, via Frankfurt. I had Lufthansa business class. I knew exactly which direction I was going thanks to the GPS map displayed on the screen that popped out of the armrest of my airline seat. I landed safely and on schedule. I too encountered people called Indians. I too was searching for the source of India's riches. Columbus was searching for hardware—precious metals, silk, and spices—the sources of wealth in his day. I was searching for software, brainpower, complex algorithms, knowledge workers, call centers, transmission protocols, breakthroughs in optical engineering—the sources of wealth in our day. Columbus was happy to make the Indians he met his slaves, a pool of free manual labor.

I just wanted to understand why the Indians I met were taking our work, why they had become such an important pool for the outsourcing of service and information technology work from America and other industrialized countries. Columbus had more than one hundred men on his three ships; I had a small crew from the Discovery Times channel that fit comfortably into two banged-up vans, with Indian drivers who drove barefoot. When I set sail, so to speak, I too assumed that the world was round, but what I encountered in the real India profoundly shook my faith in that notion. Columbus accidentally ran into America but thought he had discovered part of India. I actually found India and thought many of the people I met there were Americans. Some had actually taken American names, and others were doing great imitations of American accents at call centers and American business techniques at software labs.

Columbus reported to his king and queen that the world was round, and he went down in history as the man who first made this discovery. I returned home and shared my discovery only with my wife, and only in a whisper.

"Honey," I confided, "I think the world is flat."

• • •

How did I come to this conclusion? I guess you could say it all started in Nandan Nilekani's conference room at Infosys Technologies Limited. Infosys is one of the jewels of the Indian information technology world, and Nilekani, the company's CEO, is one of the most thoughtful and respected captains of Indian industry. I drove with the Discovery Times crew out to the Infosys campus, about forty minutes from the heart of Bangalore, to tour the facility and interview Nilekani. The Infosys campus is reached by a pockmarked road, with sacred cows, horse-drawn carts, and motorized rickshaws all jostling alongside our vans. Once you enter the gates of Infosys, though, you are in a different world. A massive resort-size swimming pool nestles amid boulders and manicured lawns, adjacent to a huge putting green. There are multiple restaurants and a fabulous health club. Glass-and-steel buildings seem to sprout up like weeds each week. In some of those buildings, Infosys employees are writing specific software programs for American or European companies; in others, they are running the back rooms of major American- and European-based multinationals — everything from computer maintenance to specific research projects to answering customer calls routed there from all over the world. Security is tight, cameras monitor the doors, and

if you are working for American Express, you cannot get into the building that is managing services and research for General Electric. Young Indian engineers, men and women, walk briskly from building to building, dangling ID badges. One looked like he could do my taxes. Another looked like she could take my computer apart. And a third looked like she designed it!

After sitting for an interview, Nilekani gave   10 our TV crew a tour of Infosys's global conferencing center — ground zero of the Indian outsourcing industry. It was a cavernous wood-paneled room that looked like a tiered classroom from an Ivy League law school. On one end was a massive wall-size screen and overhead there were cameras in the ceiling for teleconferencing. "So this is our conference room, probably the largest screen in Asia — this is forty digital screens [put together]," Nilekani explained proudly, pointing to the biggest flat-screen TV I had ever seen. Infosys, he said, can hold a virtual meeting of the key players from its entire global supply chain for any project at any time on that supersize screen. So their American designers could be on the screen speaking with their Indian software writers and their Asian manufacturers all at once. "We could be sitting here, somebody from New York, London, Boston, San Francisco, all live. And maybe the implementation is in Singapore, so the Singapore person could also be live here . . . That's globalization," said Nilekani. Above the screen there were eight clocks that pretty well summed up the Infosys workday: 24/7/365. The clocks were labeled US West, US East, GMT, India, Singapore, Hong Kong, Japan, Australia.

"Outsourcing is just one dimension of a much more fundamental thing happening today in the world," Nilekani explained. "What happened over the last [few] years is that there was a massive investment in technology, especially in the bubble era, when hundreds of millions of dollars were invested in putting broadband connectivity around the world, undersea cables, all those things." At the same time, he added, computers became cheaper and dispersed all over the world, and there was an explosion of software—email, search engines like Google, and proprietary software that can chop up any piece of work and send one part to Boston, one part to Bangalore, and one part to Beijing, making it easy for anyone to do remote development. When all of these things suddenly came together around 2000, added Nilekani, they "created a platform where intellectual work, intellectual capital could be delivered from anywhere. It could be disaggregated, delivered, distributed, produced, and put back together again—and this gave a whole new degree of freedom to the way we do work, especially work of an intellectual nature . . . And what you are seeing in Bangalore today is really the culmination of all these things coming together."

We were sitting on the couch outside Nilekani's office, waiting for the TV crew to set up its cameras. At one point, summing up the implications of all this, Nilekani uttered a phrase that rang in my ear. He said to me, "Tom, the playing field is being leveled." He meant that countries like India are now able to compete for global knowledge work as never before—and that America had better get ready for this. America was going to be challenged, but, he insisted, the challenge would be good for America because we are always at our best when we are being challenged. As I left the Infosys campus that evening and bounced along the road back to Bangalore, I kept chewing on that phrase: "The playing field is being leveled."

What Nandan is saying, I thought to myself, is that the playing field is being flattened . . . Flattened? Flattened? I rolled that word around in my head for a while and then, in the chemical way that these things happen, it just popped out: My God, he's telling me the world is flat!

Here I was in Bangalore—more than five hundred years after Columbus sailed over the horizon, using the rudimentary navigational technologies of his day, and returned safely to prove definitively that the world was round—and one of India's smartest engineers, trained at his country's top technical institute and backed by the most modern technologies of his day, was essentially telling me that the world was flat—as flat as that screen on which he can host a meeting of his whole global supply chain. Even more interesting, he was citing this development as a good thing, as a new milestone in human progress and a great opportunity for India and the world—the fact that we had made our world flat!

In the back of that van, I scribbled down   15
four words in my notebook: "The world is flat." As soon as I wrote them, I realized that this was the underlying message of everything that I had seen and heard in Bangalore in two weeks of filming. The global competitive playing field was being leveled. The world was being flattened.

As I came to this realization, I was filled with both excitement and dread. The journalist in me was excited at having found a framework to better understand the morning headlines and to explain what was happening in the world today. Clearly, it is now possible for more people than ever to collaborate and compete in real time with more other people on more different kinds of work from more different corners of the planet and on a more equal footing than at any previous time in the history of the world—using computers, email, networks, teleconferencing, and dynamic new software. That is what Nandan was telling me. That was what I discovered on my journey to India and beyond. And that is what this book is about. When you start to think of the world as flat, a lot of things make sense in ways they did not before. But I was also excited personally, because what the flattening of the world means is that we are now connecting all the knowledge centers on the planet together into a single global network, which—if politics and terrorism do not get in the way—could usher in an amazing era of prosperity and innovation.

But contemplating the flat world also left me filled with dread, professional and personal. My personal dread derived from the obvious fact that it's not only the software writers and computer geeks who get empowered to collaborate on work in a flat world. It's also al-Qaeda and other terrorist networks. The playing field is not being leveled only in ways that draw in and superempower a whole new group of innovators. It's being leveled in a way that draws in and superempowers a whole new group of angry, frustrated, and humiliated men and women.

Professionally, the recognition that the world was flat was unnerving because I realized that this flattening had been taking place while I was sleeping, and I had missed it. I wasn't really sleeping, but I was otherwise engaged. Before 9/11, I was focused on tracking globalization and exploring the tension between the "Lexus" forces of economic integration and the "Olive Tree" forces of identity and nationalism—hence my 1999 book, *The Lexus and the Olive Tree*. But after 9/11, the olive tree wars became all-consuming for me. I spent almost all my time traveling in the Arab and Muslim worlds. During those years I lost the trail of globalization.

I found that trail again on my journey to Bangalore in February 2004. Once I did, I realized that something really important had happened while I was fixated on the olive groves of Kabul and Baghdad. Globalization

had gone to a whole new level. If you put *The Lexus and the Olive Tree* and this book together, the broad historical argument you end up with is that there have been three great eras of globalization. The first lasted from 1492—when Columbus set sail, opening trade between the Old World and the New World—until around 1800. I would call this era Globalization 1.0. It shrank the world from a size large to a size medium. Globalization 1.0 was about countries and muscles. That is, in Globalization 1.0 the key agent of change, the dynamic force driving the process of global integration was how much brawn—how much muscle, how much horsepower, wind power, or, later, steam power—your country had and how creatively you could deploy it. In this era, countries and governments (often inspired by religion or imperialism or a combination of both) led the way in breaking down walls and knitting the world together, driving global integration. In Globalization 1.0, the primary questions were: Where does my country fit into global competition and opportunities? How can I go global and collaborate with others through my country?

The second great era, Globalization 2.0, lasted roughly from 1800 to 2000, interrupted by the Great Depression and World Wars I and II. This era shrank the world from a size medium to a size small. In Globalization 2.0, the key agent of change, the dynamic force driving global integration, was multinational companies. These multinationals went global for markets and labor, spearheaded first by the expansion of the Dutch and English joint-stock companies and the Industrial Revolution. In the first half of this era, global integration was powered by falling transportation costs, thanks to the steam engine and the railroad, and in the second half by falling telecommunication costs—thanks to the diffusion of the telegraph, telephones, the PC, satellites, fiber-optic

20

cable, and the early version of the World Wide Web. It was during this era that we really saw the birth and maturation of a global economy, in the sense that there was enough movement of goods and information from continent to continent for there to be a global market, with global arbitrage in products and labor. The dynamic forces behind this era of globalization were breakthroughs in hardware—from steamships and railroads in the beginning to telephones and mainframe computers toward the end. And the big questions in this era were: Where does my company fit into the global economy? How does it take advantage of the opportunities? How can I go global and collaborate with others through my company? *The Lexus and the Olive Tree* was primarily about the climax of this era, an era when the walls started falling all around the world, and integration, and the backlash to it, went to a whole new level. But even as the walls fell, there were still a lot of barriers to seamless global integration. Remember, when Bill Clinton was elected president in 1992, virtually no one outside of government and the academy had email, and when I was writing *The Lexus and the Olive Tree* in 1998, the internet and e-commerce were just taking off.

Well, they took off—along with a lot of other things that came together while I was sleeping. And that is why I argue in this book that right around the year 2000 we entered a whole new era: Globalization 3.0. Globalization 3.0 is shrinking the world from a size small to a size tiny and flattening the playing field at the same time. And while the dynamic force in Globalization 1.0 was countries globalizing and the dynamic force in Globalization 2.0 was companies globalizing, the dynamic force in Globalization 3.0—the force that gives it its unique character—is the newfound power for *individuals* to collaborate and compete globally. And the phenomenon that is enabling,

empowering, and enjoining individuals and small groups to go global so easily and so seamlessly is what I call the flat-world platform, which I describe in detail in this book. Just a hint: The flat-world platform is the product of a convergence of the personal computer (which allowed every individual suddenly to become the author of his or her own content in digital form) with fiber-optic cable (which suddenly allowed all those individuals to access more and more digital content around the world for next to nothing) with the rise of workflow software (which enabled individuals all over the world to collaborate on that same digital content from anywhere, regardless of the distances between them). No one anticipated this convergence. It just happened—right around the year 2000. And when it did, people all over the world started waking up and realizing that they had more power than ever to go global as individuals, they needed more than ever to think of themselves as individuals competing against other individuals all over the planet, and they had more opportunities to work with those other individuals, not just compete with them. As a result, every person now must, and can, ask: Where do I fit into the global competition and opportunities of the day, and how can I, on my own, collaborate with others globally?

But Globalization 3.0 not only differs from the previous eras in how it is shrinking and flattening the world and in how it is empowering individuals. It is different in that Globalization 1.0 and 2.0 were driven primarily by European and American individuals and businesses. Even though China actually had the biggest economy in the world in the eighteenth century, it was Western countries, companies, and explorers who were doing most of the globalizing and shaping of the system. But going forward, this will be less and less true. Because it is flattening and shrinking the world, Globalization 3.0 is going to be more and more driven not only by individuals but also by a much more diverse—non-Western, nonwhite-group—of individuals. Individuals from every corner of the flat world are being empowered. Globalization 3.0 makes it possible for so many more people to plug in and play, and you are going to see every color of the human rainbow take part. . . .

Needless to say, I had only the vaguest appreciation of all this as I left Nandan's office that day in Bangalore. But as I sat contemplating these changes on the balcony of my hotel room that evening, I did know one thing: I wanted to drop everything and write a book that would enable me to understand how this flattening process happened and what its implications might be for countries, companies, and individuals. So I picked up the phone and called my wife, Ann, and told her, "I am going to write a book called *The World Is Flat*." She was both amused and curious—well, maybe more amused than curious! Eventually, I was able to bring her around, and I hope I will be able to do the same with you, dear reader. Let me start by taking you back to the beginning of my journey to India, and other points east, and share with you some of the encounters that led me to conclude the world was no longer round—but flat.

▲

This photograph of the historic DongMen District of Shenzhen, China, suggests globalization is often associated with American brands and products such as the American fast-food chains shown here.

Consider the juxtaposition of cultures in the photograph. What does this implied contrast suggest about globalization today?

Stephen Lioy/Alamy Stock Photo

RHETORICAL SITUATION

1. Who is Friedman's intended **audience**? Who is the unintended audience? What assumptions does he make about his audiences?

2. What is Friedman's **perspective** on the subject? What are some other perspectives on it? How do these views affect Friedman's perspective?

3. What is the **exigence** and **context** of the text? Why is Friedman invested in this issue?

CLAIMS AND EVIDENCE

4. What is Friedman's **thesis**? What perspectives corroborate his claim? What perspectives are skeptical of his claim?

5. Look closely at the **evidence** in the text. Find an example of limited or biased evidence and then explain how it affects Friedman's argument.

6. Give an example of **evidence** in the text that supports or complements Friedman's argument. Then explain how this evidence affects the argument.

7. How do the **counterarguments** contribute to Friedman's argument? Choose two examples of counterarguments (concession, refutation, or rebuttal) and then explain how they function in the argument.

REASONING AND ORGANIZATION

8. How does Friedman use multiple **methods of development** to convey the purpose? Identify his overarching purpose. Then explain how his methods of development contribute to that purpose.

9. How does Friedman arrange the **line of reasoning** for his argument? What effect does this arrangement have on his purpose, message, and audience?

LANGUAGE AND STYLE

10. Look closely at Friedman's **syntactical choices**. Identify and describe two examples from the text. Then explain how they contribute to the writer's message.

11. Friedman's **voice** is clear throughout his argument. Use specific examples from the text to explain how Friedman achieves this distinctive voice.

12. Friedman uses punctuation to illustrate relationships within the text. Choose one **syntactical** example that reveals the equality of ideas and one that illustrates the inequality of ideas.

IDEAS IN AMERICAN CULTURE

13. Globalization, as Friedman states, has been around since Christopher Columbus. Explain why Friedman titled his book *The World Is Flat* and consider the implications of the message. Why, as Friedman suggests, does the concept bring us to a conflicted conclusion? Is his outlook optimistic? Pessimistic? Both? Explain.

PUTTING IT ALL TOGETHER

14. Friedman takes a debunked scientific idea — that the world is flat — and uses it to point out that people around the world are closer and more connected than is generally understood. How does Friedman strategically employ both rhetorical and stylistic choices to connect with his audience and convey his message?

Everyone Seems to Agree, Globalization Is a Sin. They're Wrong.

Fareed Zakaria

Joe Kohen/Getty Images

THE TEXT IN CONTEXT

Fareed Zakaria (b. 1964) is an Indian-American journalist, author, and political commentator. He is the host of CNN's *Fareed Zakaria GPS* and writes a weekly column for the *Washington Post*. Born and raised in Mumbai, India, he received his undergraduate degree from Yale University in 1986 and his PhD from Harvard University. Zakaria began his career in journalism as an editor at *Foreign Affairs* magazine and joined ABC News as an analyst in 2002. He now hosts *Fareed Zakaria GPS*, a weekly public affairs show on CNN. In addition to his broadcast journalism, Zakaria has written for the *New York Times*, the *Wall Street Journal*, the *New Yorker*, and other publications. He has also written several books, including *The Post-American World* (2008) and *Ten Lessons for a Post-Pandemic World* (2020). In the following 2017 *Washington Post* column, Zakaria considers the future of globalization.

The World Economic Forum this year feels like an exercise in ritual self-flagellation, which—as with the old Christian practice of fasting and whipping one's own body—is supposed to purify the sinful nature of man. The sin, of course, is globalization, which everyone now seems to agree has been lopsided, inequitable and dangerous. In fact, most of the flaws attributed to globalization are actually mistakes in national policy that can be corrected.

It took a Chinese billionaire to speak frankly on this topic. Jack Ma, the founder of the e-commerce giant Alibaba, estimated that over the past three decades the U.S. government spent $14.2 trillion fighting 13 wars. That money could have been invested in America, building infrastructure and creating jobs. "You're supposed to spend money on your own people," he said. He pointed out that globalization produced massive profits for the U.S. economy but much of that money ended up on Wall Street. "And what happened? Year 2008. The financial crisis wiped out $19.2 trillion [in the] U.S.A. alone. . . . What if the money [had been] spent on the Midwest of the United States developing the industry there?" he asked. "It's not [that] the other countries steal jobs from you guys—it is your strategy," he concluded.

You don't have to accept Ma's specifics and statistics to recognize the validity of his general point. Globalization created huge opportunities for growth, many of which were taken by U.S. companies. The global economy is still dominated by large American firms; 134 of Fortune's Global 500 are American. And if you look at those in cutting-edge industries, the vast majority are American. These companies have benefited enormously by having global supply chains that can source goods and services around the world, either to lower labor costs or to be close to the markets in which they sell. Since 95 percent of the world's potential consumers live outside the United States, finding ways to sell to them will have to be a core strategy for growth, even for a country with a large domestic economy such as the United States.

Obviously globalization has large effects on national economies and societies, and it produces some significant problems. What complex phenomenon does not? But it also generates opportunities, innovation, and wealth for nations that they can then use to address these problems through good national strategies. The solutions are easy to state in theory—education, skills-based training and retraining, infrastructure. But they are extremely expensive and hard to execute well.

It is much easier to rail against foreigners and promise to fight them with tariffs and fines. But the cost of addressing these problems at the global level is massive. *The Economist* reports, in a survey on globalization, that in 2009 the Obama administration punished China with a tariff on its tires. Two years later, the cost to U.S. consumers was $1.1 billion, or $900,000 for every job "saved." The impact of such tariffs is usually felt disproportionately by the poor and middle class because they spend a larger share of their income on imported goods, such as food and clothing. That same *Economist* survey points to a study that calculated that, across 40 countries, if transnational trade ended, the wealthiest consumers would lose 28 percent of their purchasing power, but the poorest tenth would lose a staggering 63 percent.

Perhaps most important, the key driver depressing wages and eliminating jobs in the industrialized world is technology, not globalization. For example, between 1990 and 2014, U.S. automotive production increased by 19 percent, but with 240,000 fewer workers.

Even when manufacturing comes back to the United States, it is high-end manufacturing. It's not just new Intel plants that have few workers anymore. Adidas has set up a new shoe factory in Germany that is run almost entirely by robots. It will open a similar one near Atlanta later this year. And the few workers in these factories tend to be highly skilled technicians and software engineers.

You can't turn off technological revolutions. Nor is there a quick fix to stop business from going to other countries. Tariffs on China will simply mean that production will come from some other developing country.

The best approach to the world we are living in is not denial but empowerment. Countries should recognize that the global economy and the technological revolution require large, sustained national efforts to equip workers with the skills, capital and infrastructure they need to succeed. Nations should embrace an open world, but only as long as they are properly armed to compete in it. And that requires smart, effective—and very expensive—national policies, not some grand reversal of globalization.

World Map of Economic Growth
Predicted Growth Rate (%) Annually to 2024

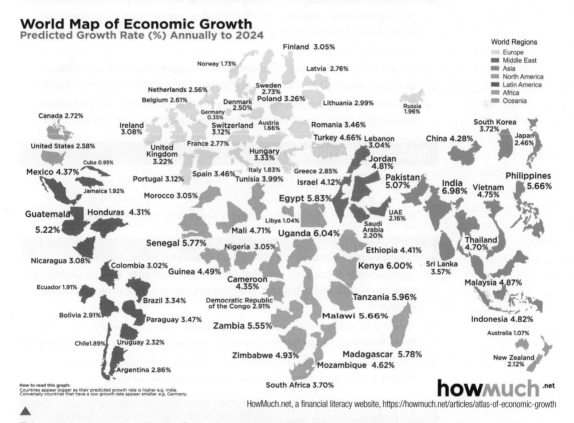

HowMuch.net, a financial literacy website, https://howmuch.net/articles/atlas-of-economic-growth

▲

This scaled map produced by the Center for International Development at Harvard University (CID) represents the forecasted economic growth for countries around the world. The map shows that South Asia and East Africa have the greatest potential for growth. The CID predicts that the countries that can diversify their production knowledge and increase productivity will see the most future gains.

What growth does this map forecast for the United States? What factors might affect the accuracy of that prediction? Do you think the well-being of a country's population is determined by economic growth? Why or why not?

RHETORICAL SITUATION

1. What is the **subject**? What is Zakaria's **perspective** on the subject? How does his argument contribute to a larger **conversation**?

2. What other **perspectives** does the writer include in the argument?

3. Who is the **audience** for this argument? What assumptions does Zakaria make about them? How does he address the **audience's** beliefs, values, and needs?

CLAIMS AND EVIDENCE

4. What is the writer's **thesis**? What is his **call to action**? Explain some of the implications of Zakaria's argument. For example, what does he imply in the conclusion?

5. Zakaria uses **refutation** and **concession** throughout the argument. Give an example of each. Then explain how they contribute to the message of the text.

6. How does the writer select his **evidence** to address the multiple perspectives surrounding this subject? How could emerging evidence affect his argument?

REASONING AND ORGANIZATION

7. What is Zakaria's **line of reasoning**? What are his reasons?

8. Identify at least two **purposes** of the text. How do they reinforce his **line of reasoning**? How does he **organize** his **reasoning** to achieve his **purpose(s)**?

LANGUAGE AND STYLE

9. Look carefully at Zakaria's use of **parenthetical elements**. Find an example of parenthetical dashes in the text. Then explain how the dashes function in the argument.

10. How does Zakaria **transition** to address opposing arguments? Explain how these transitions reveal the function of the evidence within the overall argument?

11. Describe Zakaria's **style**. How does he create this style? Give an example of diction, syntax, or another writing move that illustrates his style.

IDEAS IN AMERICAN CULTURE

12. Zakaria's thesis suggests that technology and education will help advance our society in a global context. Do you agree or might other factors complicate the writer's argument? Explain.

PUTTING IT ALL TOGETHER

13. Zakaria considers multiple audiences and various perspectives. He also offers a solution to some of the problems caused by globalization. Explain how the argument's organization and the writer's inclusion of different perspectives contribute to both the purpose and the message.

COMPOSITION WORKSHOP
Writing a Multimodal Argument

Throughout this book, you have learned about the different methods of development that writers choose to create their arguments. So far, you have explored these methods one at a time. Now, you will discover how different methods can work together in an argument.

Writers may use more than one method of development to serve different purposes within their larger argument. For example, a writer may begin an argument by narrating a brief story, transition to a description of a problem, and then offer a solution. Or, perhaps a writer needs to define important concepts or terms before comparing and contrasting them to make a claim. To determine the best methods of development for an argument, writers must consider their audience's knowledge and values, along with their own purpose.

Like all other arguments, the multimodal argument focuses on a unifying idea and develops a thesis that expresses a perspective on that idea. The line of reasoning, again, as in other arguments, draws upon strategically chosen methods and modes of communication while presenting relevant and sufficient evidence and includes helpful commentary to connect the evidence to the thesis.

In this workshop, you will develop an argument using two or more methods of development that you have practiced in Units 1 through 8. To support your claim, you should draw upon a variety of research, sources, and evidence. You should also become familiar with — and incorporate — multiple perspectives on your subject, not just your own.

KEY POINT

Multimodal arguments are strategically created by using multiple modes of communication, methods of development, and elements of design to communicate your message and achieve your purpose.

Quiet Confidence: Introverts and the Power of Silence

Nati Duron

The following argument by student writer Nati Duron appeared in the December 20, 2017, issue of *The Chant*, a publication from North Cobb High School in Kennesaw, Georgia.

Solitude, the state or situation of loneliness, plays a role in society. For introverts, it becomes the air that they breathe. Introverts possess the most powerful intellect, but their mind fails to believe it.

}— begins with definitions of key terms

establishes a comparison/ contrast between introverts and extroverts

In today's society, an extrovert possesses the characteristics of *intelligence*, *happiness*, and *charisma*. On the other hand, an introvert comes off as scared, timid, and not trying hard enough. The extent to which we falsely speculate a person's exterior, based on society's labels, ruins the beautiful idea of introverts. The world subjects to the misconception that if you hold outgoing, extroverted characteristics, one will achieve success.

exemplifies the perception of introversion over time

Introversion, or the intense feeling of the need for privacy and satisfaction from one's own thoughts, presents itself throughout historic figures. The greatest leaders, quoted and lauded for their traits, Rosa Parks, Abraham Lincoln, Mahatma Gandhi, and Sir Isaac Newton, each possessed introverted characteristics, even though they believed that they would never amount to anything. In the end, all of these leaders impacted the world, despite their characteristics of shyness and timidness.

Extroverts crave attention. They crave constant motion or enjoyment, whereas an introvert finds happiness in quiet and calm places. This bias of extroverted success appears at workplaces and especially in schools. Today, a teen who does not talk in class, raises his or her hand, or fails to speak in group works, comes off as lazy or frightened to share his or her thoughts.

claim refutes common misperceptions about introverts

In reality, introverts do pay attention in class, and they would love to express their feelings. The anxiety of answering incorrectly or other students judging their answer stops them. As a growing society, we must teach students and the children in this generation that working alone relaxes the mind, and that being independent helps students grow.

Reality shows that out of every two or three people, one would classify themselves as an introvert.

transition introduces evidence that will follow

To three female high schoolers who identify as introverts, though they know they exist everywhere, they feel as though people choose to ignore them.

Sonia Jorge-Gonzalez, a sophomore at NC, identifies as an introvert. She always knew that she seemed more shy than the other students, but she never allowed her characteristic to impact her academic life. Gonzalez feels like her silence and what some would identify as antisocial behavior affects her life, and it makes her an introvert. When she sees or hears an extrovert, she likes to listen to how they speak and finds the difference between her and the extrovert intriguing. Although Gonzalez rarely speaks in class, she does not become bothered when others call her "shy."

In the midst of all her school work, Gonzalez discovered her passion for travel and the importance of learning new languages. Her friends know well about this affinity of hers, but sometimes fail to recognize it. At school, Gonzalez loves working in groups, but she does not prefer participating in class discussions.

"I don't like teachers calling on me at all. It's not where I don't know the answer. I just don't like [the concept of calling on random students]. Depending on the class, I'll sometimes like it," Gonzalez said.

quotes directly from the source to include the first perspective

Whenever she presents a project in class, she feels a wave of nervousness standing in front of a room with all eyes on her. Along with this nervous feeling, she feels afraid of social events when her friends do not attend.

Her friends support her, lift her spirits, and encourage her to love herself. Without a friend at the party or in the class, Gonzalez feels excluded and alone. She finds solace in her friends when she hangs out with them. With her peers, however, she feels as if they see her as someone else.

To prevent this misunderstanding, Gonzalez believes that people must teach others that quietness does not make a person any less better or capable than those who tend to speak more. The loud mind of an introvert does not compare to the loud mouth of an extrovert.

includes the repetition of loud to emphasize a contrast

"I feel like there's a lot to me, to my personality that they don't know. I just don't feel comfortable acting like that around others yet," Gonzalez said.

On social media, Gonzalez does not express herself because of what her peers will think. In a society of free-thinking and prosperity, Gonzalez does not want to feel afraid of her peers or of school. Gonzalez, who loves to travel and explore the world, feels like that would not fit in society. She possesses the potential to visit any city or country with her passion and wants society to see that.

Imagine feeling anxious when in the center of attention; feeling like the world will cave in at any moment.

This feeling affects junior Moya Perez because of her introversion. She calls herself an introvert because of her quiet mouth and loud thinking. Academically, Perez cares about mistakes but does not feel motivated enough to better herself. She finds her peers that act sociable appealing.

repeats the descriptive word "loud" to amplify the message

"I love them. I believe that we all balance each other out, and in today's society, we all just need to accept everyone for who they are, so I appreciate listening [to them]," Perez said.

quotes directly from the source to include the second perspective

In class, Perez rarely speaks, and when a teacher calls on her, she tries to bat her eyes and not make eye contact. She finds this situation awkward; it makes her anxious. She also hates to present projects because it arouses her anxiety.

"Presenting is the worst. I get shaky hands and start to stutter. It's just not fun for me to publicly speak," Perez said.

Perez finds happiness in loving and helping others. She wants to study the art of helping others in college, and while her best friends know this, others do not ask Perez about her passion. She finds it extremely annoying when others call her shy since she does not agree with labeling others just from what they show on the outside. From the people around her in school, she troubles herself with anxiety from the crowding.

"Crowded rooms give me terrible anxiety. Especially since I'm kind of short, people tower over me and it's a lot. For example, malfunction junction is just a big mess of anxiety for me," Perez said.

Perez feels that others need to learn that to respect students with anxiety and introversion, rather than trying to change them, to better the overall school environment.

uses narration to engage audience and establish credibility

To her friends and family, she acts like her true self. Alyssa Sidler, Perez's best friend for over 11 years, believes Perez should never feel shy because of her astonishing personality.

"I love every single thing about Moya, and how beautiful she is, and how she cares for others more than she cares about herself, and [especially] how selfless she is," Sidler said.

further develops contrasts between introverts and extroverts

Sophomore Maddie Sullivan includes herself in the introvert category because of her focus on her own thoughts and lack of comfort around people she does not know, especially in crowds at school. Despite this, she never let her introspective personality come between her academic life. In class, around extroverted people, Sullivan finds them overshadowing her and frequently talk over her.

She loves animals and plans to become a veterinarian. She hopes to inspire others with this passion, but believes most of her peers do not know nor care.

In certain social events, Sullivan finds herself clinging onto her friends as large groups scare her and intensify her anxiety. Situations like this stress her out, along with silly mistakes, because she feels all eyes on her.

Sullivan prefers to participate as the leader in situations where she must contribute to group work. This type of behavior usually appears in introverts, as sometimes introverts like to lead groups and then watch the others talk.

Social media affects the way people express their thoughts, especially for introverts and extroverts.

"Posting on social media depends. I'm sometimes worried about what I post because I don't want to offend anyone," Maddie said. To Sullivan, people misunderstand the personality of an introvert.

"The biggest misunderstanding to me is that we can't be loud or outgoing all the time. Because even the quietest people get their loud moments, and it's stupid words that categorize people that ruin how people see each other, because it's more than what they think. Because everyone is more than just being quiet or shy," she said.

> quotes directly from the source to include the second perspective

Sullivan believes that all introverts, including herself, want to attend school without the stress of a teacher calling on them, or presenting a project. The teachers need to show more respect to the shy students, to further support their mentality of silence.

Instead of calling an introvert "shy," "fragile," or "scared," try calling an introvert "determined," "bright," or "brilliant." Instead of forcing a student to work with a group of people in class, allow him or her to work independently.

> thesis demonstrates the writer's claim that quietness (idea) may contain power (perspective)

Misunderstanding an introvert became one of society's gravest mistakes, as these quiet, powerful intellectuals contain the mind of a leader.

Look beyond the label of "quiet" or "antisocial" to meet a curious traveller, a kind-hearted, soft-spoken communicator, and a devoted veterinarian.

> call to action persuades the reader to change an attitude about introverts

 ## YOUR ASSIGNMENT

A national current affairs and culture magazine is celebrating its one-hundredth year in publication with a series of special editions focused on contemporary issues. To include the perspective of younger readers, they are seeking submissions from high school students. You have decided to submit an essay. Research a subject that is important to you. Then write an argument that explores the evolution of your issue over time and conveys your perspective. Include at least two different methods of development within your argument.

Your multimodal argument should include:

- A thesis statement that makes a claim (unifying idea + perspective)
- A line of reasoning that supports your claim, established with multiple methods of development
- Evidence from research, observation, and/or experience to prove your reasoning
- Commentary that connects your evidence to your thesis and your argument to a wider conversation
- Rhetorical strategies that appeal to your audience and represent your voice and style

Potential Subjects:

- Artificial intelligence
- Biometrics
- Business start-ups
- Cancel culture
- Community policing
- Distance learning
- Engineering solutions
- Food deserts
- Income gap
- Mental health
- Mob mentality
- Renewable energy
- Standardized testing

RHETORICAL SITUATION ## Acknowledging Multiple Perspectives

 Enduring Understanding (RHS-1)

Individuals write within a particular situation and make strategic writing choices based on that situation.

Before you write your argument, you must consider the real-world implications of your subject and examine the perspectives, contexts, and needs of your intended audience. Your subject is likely to have been part of an ongoing conversation over time. You should use your introduction to provide the necessary background information so that your audience can understand the complexity of both the issue and your argument. Whether you are organizing deductively or inductively, your perspective and unifying idea should be clear in your introduction.

In the body of your argument, you will develop your thesis while acknowledging alternative perspectives through your evidence and commentary. To examine and address alternative perspectives, you need to consider a number of questions.

Review the following model for exploring multiple perspectives in preparation to develop your argument.

Sample Responses
Joining the Conversation: Understanding the Issue of Online Learning

	Questions to Consider	Notes and Comments
Subject	What is your topic or issue?	*Does a fully online learning experience in college offer the same quality of education as in-person learning?*
Significance	Who cares about it? Why?	*College administrators: adapting schedules, reducing staff, reducing budgets, increasing enrollment*
		College students: missing the "college experience," enjoying flexibility, gaining access to education
		Parents: determining the value of the investment, savings
		Future employers: evaluating the preparedness of the workforce, development of "soft skills"
Perspective	What is your current perspective on the subject? Why do you have that perspective? What are your biases?	*I believe that taking some classes online may save time and money but that students should be required to attend some face-to-face instruction.*
		My positive experiences interacting with other students and working collaboratively contribute to my perspective.
		I have the means to pursue an in-person degree. I come from a family with experience attending large universities.
Other Perspectives	What other positions and/or perspectives exist about the subject? What are others' arguments about the subject? Has this subject been addressed before? When? Where? Which arguments do you agree with? Why?	*Student athletes and student workers benefit from the scheduling flexibility offered by the online program.*
		Some professors develop their online courses to use repeatedly and can spend more time engaging individually with students during virtual office hours.
		Other professors question the engagement of the students and cite examples of those who do fail because they fall behind.
		Online education is not new. Several schools have extensive online programs.

(continued)

	Questions to Consider	Notes and Comments
Other Perspectives (*continued*)	Which ones do you disagree with? Why?	*Administrators see it as a way to save money on facilities and staffing.* *I disagree with the decision to go online to save money.* *I do see the benefits for students with special circumstances, such as working mothers.* *Flexibility may open up opportunities to underrepresented groups of people.*
Position	What is your position and perspective about the issue or subject?	*Taking classes online may save time and money, but students should be required to attend some face-to-face instruction to ensure they are gaining the necessary knowledge and skills.*
Response	Who will agree with you? Who will corroborate your position? Who doubts or disagrees with your claim? Who doesn't care either way? Why?	(Refutation, Concession, Rebuttal) *Those who have had positive experiences with in-person learning or challenges with online learning will agree.* *Those who have successfully completed an online degree may disagree because they value their experience.*
Implications	How will your claim or conclusions affect others? How will your response affect future audiences? What are the short- and long-term consequences?	*My position challenges fully online programs by inserting a requirement that some of the interactions should be live or face-to-face. In the long term, however, programs may be able to use technology for students to collaborate with each other in synchronous time but from a distance.*

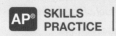 **SKILLS PRACTICE** | RHETORICAL SITUATION
Acknowledging Multiple Perspectives

Consider the specific rhetorical situation of your argument. Then answer the following questions about your issue as you prepare to write your multimodal argument.

Joining the Conversation: Understanding an Issue		
	Questions to Consider	**Notes and Comments**
Subject	What is your topic or issue?	
Significance	Who cares about it? Why?	

Perspective	What is your current perspective on the subject?	
	Why do you have that perspective?	
	What biases do you have?	
Other Perspectives	What other positions and/or perspectives exist about the subject?	(Summarize, Paraphrase, Quote)
	What are others' arguments about the subject?	
	Has this subject been addressed before? When? Where?	
	Which arguments do you agree with? Why?	
	Which ones do you disagree with? Why?	
Position	What is your position and perspective about the issue or subject?	
Response	Who will agree with you?	(Refutation, Concession, Rebuttal)
	Who will corroborate your position?	
	Who will doubt or disagree with your position? Why?	
Implications	How will your position affect others?	
	How will this response affect future audiences?	
	What are the short- and long-term consequences?	

REASONING AND ORGANIZATION ## Unifying Your Argument across Multiple Methods of Development

 Enduring Understanding (REO-1)

Writers guide understanding of a text's line of reasoning and claims through that text's organization and integration of evidence.

Writers can have more than one purpose and more than one audience in mind when they develop an argument. Still, they unify their argument by focusing on a unifying and controlling idea and perspective. In other words, they have a purpose in mind and consider what an audience needs to understand that purpose. Writers also choose methods of development based on the audience's needs.

For example, a writer may introduce an argument about the value and convenience of an online education by using narration to tell a brief story about a student's experiences with a specific online class. Or perhaps the writer may begin by defining key terms for the issue like "courseware" and "synchronous learning." Next, the writer may develop the argument by one or more of the following:

- comparing and contrasting online- and classroom-based classes,
- classifying different types of online experiences,
- examining the causes and effects of the shift from in-person to online classes, or
- describing a problem related to the shift in formats and then offering a solution.

The following chart reviews the methods of development that you have learned in Units 1 through 8. When you carefully reflect on the audience, context, and message of your argument, you may determine the most effective method (or combination of methods) of development to achieve your purpose.

METHODS OF DEVELOPMENT AND ORGANIZATION

Method of Development and Purpose		Organization/Line of Reasoning
Narration (illustration)		Beginning (exposition) — conflict initiated Middle (climax) — moment of truth End (resolution) — illustrates the claim
Persuasion (call to action or change)		• Inductive reasoning • Deductive reasoning
Exposition (informational/ explanatory)	Definition (what something is)	• Characteristics • Traits
	Classification/Division	• Attributes • Components
	Process Analysis (how something works/functions or how to do something)	• Steps • Stages • Phases
	Cause/Effect (why something came about OR the impact of something)	• Causes • Effects • Link cause to effect
Evaluation (recommend or propose)	Comparison/Contrast	• Subject by subject • Point by point
	Problem/Solution	• Describe problem • Analyze: compare/contrast options • Propose a solution

Sample Line of Reasoning Considerations

Part of the Argument	Method(s) of Development	Purpose or Desired Effect
Introduction Context of the argument	**Narration** *Begin with a narrative about one student's struggle to pass an online class*	*The anecdote personalizes the issue and provides some context for the argument.*
Multiple perspectives	*Review existing perspectives of college administrators, professors, parents, and students*	*A review of different perspectives establishes the complexity of the argument.*
Thesis or question to consider	*Do online college programs offer the same quality of education as face-to-face programs?*	*This argument will be organized inductively so that the thesis will be in the conclusion.*
Body Paragraph Reason 1	**Comparison/Contrast** *(quality of instruction)* *Evidence for both in-person and online programs* *data, examples, and observations*	*Organizing by categories of comparison emphasizes the important factors and allows the audience to understand the writer's evaluation.*
Body Paragraph Reason 2	**Comparison/Contrast** *(quality of interaction)* *Evidence for both in-person and online programs* *data, examples, and observations*	
Body Paragraph Reason 3	Evaluation of Evidence	*This paragraph evaluates the comparisons by category of instruction and interaction and includes further commentary.*

(continued)

Part of the Argument	Method(s) of Development	Purpose or Desired Effect
Conclusion Thesis (idea + perspective)	Implications Idea — *Quality* Perspective — *Collaboration increases quality* Thesis: *Online degree programs may be of equitable quality to in-person programs when they create opportunities for meaningful collaboration and interaction*	*Based on the evidence, the writer will concede that the quality of instruction is equitable but that the interaction is lacking; this leads to a nuanced conclusion, including consideration for both learning formats with an established condition.*
Call to Action	*Colleges and universities should design online degree programs for students that include requirements for direct interaction and collaboration with classmates and instructors*	

 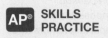 **SKILLS PRACTICE**

REASONING AND ORGANIZATION
Unifying Your Argument across Multiple Methods of Development

To achieve your purpose, you will need to determine the needs and values of your audience. Then you will need to meet those needs. Use the following chart to plan your line of reasoning. Include at least two different methods of development and explain your choices.

Part of the Argument	Method(s) of Development	Purpose or Desired Effect
Introduction: Context of the argument: Multiple perspectives: Thesis or question to consider:		
Reason 1: Body Paragraph:		

(continued on next page)

Reason 2: Body Paragraph:		
Reason 3: Body Paragraph:		
Conclusion:		

CLAIMS AND EVIDENCE Synthesizing Evidence

AP® Enduring Understanding (CLE-1)

Writers make claims about subjects, rely on evidence that supports the reasoning that justifies the claim, and often acknowledge or respond to other, possibly opposing, arguments.

If you have ever tried to talk to people who dominate conversations or only talk about themselves, you know that it is frustrating when you have no opportunity to speak. Perhaps you did have a chance to speak, but the others responded entirely in clichés or only half-listened and just repeated your own words back to you. No doubt, these experiences would discourage you from seeking further conversations with such disengaged people.

In contrast, when you join a conversation with people who share their ideas, listen to others, and thoughtfully consider perspectives different from their own, you feel satisfied that a meaningful exchange has taken place. You have shared ideas and likely emerged with a deeper understanding of the subject of that conversation.

Writing an argument is like joining an ongoing conversation and engaging with other perspectives. Your job is not simply to push one side of an issue while ignoring all other considerations. Likewise, your job is not to merely summarize well-known evidence without adding anything new. Instead, you should discuss this evidence in a fresh way that supports your perspective.

Of course, you will be **biased** toward your own perspective. Your research sources will have biases of their own. As you explore the issue, you will agree with some sources of evidence and disagree with others. But you must acknowledge other perspectives — both to demonstrate the complexity of the issue and to show your audience that you are being thorough and fair. By doing so, you will create an argument that is strong but also nuanced and complex.

In Unit 8, you learned how to develop a counterargument through refutation, rebuttal, and concession. We also discussed the value of revealing the limitations of your own argument. Review the following transitions to help you introduce a counterargument as you support your claim with evidence and commentary. Then review the sentence stems to help you develop your commentary so you can join the conversation.

INSIDER AP TIP

Synthesizing is more than quoting, summarizing, or paraphrasing. Synthesis requires you to connect information from others' arguments by explaining the relationship and relevance of those perspectives to your own argument.

TRANSITIONS TO JOIN THE CONVERSATION

Corroboration	Counterargument		
Agreement (include evidence that supports or complements your claim)	**Rebuttal** (offer a contrasting perspective to a competing claim)	**Refutation** (demonstrate a competing claim is invalid)	**Concession** (agree in part to a competing claim or acknowledge the limitations of your own argument)
Additionally	Alternatively	Although	Admittedly
As a matter of fact	Besides	But	Certainly
Certainly	Conversely	In contrast	Even though
For example	In reality	In spite of	Granted
Furthermore	On the contrary	Instead	It is true that
In addition	On the other hand	Nevertheless	Of course
Likewise	Unlike	Still	
Not only, but also	Whereas		
Similarly	While		
To illustrate			

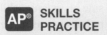

AP SKILLS PRACTICE | CLAIMS AND EVIDENCE **Synthesizing Evidence**

- Prepare to write your multimodal argument by selecting evidence that supports your line of reasoning and your claim.
- Include evidence for corroboration, as well as refutation, rebuttal, and/or concession. (Note: you may not have a counterargument in every body paragraph.)
- Record your choices in the following chart. When you have completed your outline, evaluate any apparent biases and limitations of your argument.

(continued on next page)

Thesis (idea + perspective):		
Reason 1:	**Reason 2:**	**Reason 3:**
Evidence for support	Evidence for support	Evidence for support
Commentary	Commentary	Commentary
Evidence from alternative perspective	Evidence from alternative perspective	Evidence from alternative perspective
Commentary	Commentary	Commentary

LANGUAGE AND STYLE Establishing a Voice

AP® Enduring Understanding (STL-1)

The rhetorical situation informs the strategic stylistic choices that writers make.

Throughout this book, we have explored how a writer's language choices contribute to the effect of the argument. Not only do these choices create clarity and fluency in the language itself, but they also reveal the writer's attitude and voice. In turn, these stylistic qualities help the writer connect to the audience. This connection occurs when a writer controls the tone of the argument (e.g., serious, humorous, matter of fact) or chooses an appropriate voice (e.g., personal, academic, empathetic). The writers' choices contribute to the effectiveness of the argument when they are appropriate for the subject, purpose, audience, and context.

Effective writers express tone and voice through language that is strategically chosen for a desired effect. This often recognizable series of stylistic choices (diction, syntax, and design) is known as the writer's **style**.

The goal of creating different sentence types and using different syntactical techniques is not to achieve variety. Rather, a writer's goal is to create sentence types that show the relationship of ideas to one another. While variety may be achieved along the way throughout the text, it is not the writer's primary goal to "vary their sentence structure."

STYLISTIC CHOICES THAT ENHANCE THE WRITER'S MESSAGE

Element of Style	Rhetorical Choice	Possible Effect
Diction	Connotation	Creates specific emotional connections with the audience
	Precise Word Choice	Contributes to a specific tone
	Type of diction (e.g., jargon, colloquialism, informal, formal, technical)	Addresses a particular audience
Syntax	Independent Clause • Simple sentence • Fragment • Rhetorical question	Creates emphasis Calls for reflection or action
	Subordination	Illustrates an imbalance or inequality of ideas
	Coordination	Illustrates balance or equality of ideas
	Modifier • Adjective • Adverb • Appositive	Reduces ambiguity through description, clarification, qualification, or specification
	Parenthetical Element • Parentheses • Dash • Comma	Offers clarification, description, or insight
Punctuation	• Comma • Colon • Semicolon • Dash • Hyphen • Parentheses • Quotation mark • Period	Clarifies, organizes, emphasizes, indicates purpose, supplements information, or contributes to tone
Design Features	• Italics • Boldface	Creates emphasis

Review the following examples of sentences that have been edited to include more effective language choices.

Original Sentence	Stylistic Choice	Edited Sentence
In-person classes have better participation.	Diction	*In-person classes encourage more meaningful interactions between students.*
	Syntax (rhetorical question)	*Can students interact meaningfully if they are logging in from different locations at different times?*
	Modifiers	*Even though online classes may have some virtual discussion requirements, in-person classes encourage more meaningful interaction between students.*
	Parenthetical elements	*In-person classes (those that require students to be face-to-face with instructors and each other) encourage more meaningful interactions between students.*

 SKILLS PRACTICE | LANGUAGE AND STYLE
Establishing a Voice

Revise your multimodal argument to incorporate your own style and voice (diction, syntax, and other rhetorical choices).

1. Plan a pattern of diction to express your attitude toward the subject. Make a list of connotative words that help establish your desired tone. Identify this language if it is already in your argument. If it is not, revise to incorporate your list of connotative words.

2. Identify syntactical choices within your argument and their desired effects. Establish a pattern of sentence structures that represent your desired cadence and tone.

 SKILLS PRACTICE | PUTTING IT ALL TOGETHER
Revising and Editing a Multimodal Argument

Peer-Revision Checklist: Revising and Editing a Multimodal Argument

Questions to Consider	Unit 9 Focus Skills	Comment on the Effectiveness and/or Make a Suggestion
Does the introduction address multiple perspectives or changing perspectives over time? Does the claim in the introduction or conclusion connect the subject to the writer's perspective?	*Acknowledging multiple perspectives*	
Has the writer used two or more methods of development in the argument? Are these choices effective for the specific audience and purpose?	*Multimodal argument*	
Questions to Consider	Unit 9 Focus Skills	Comment on the Effectiveness and/or Make a Suggestion
Does the writer incorporate multiple sources of evidence that support the argument? Has the writer included evidence from alternative perspectives by employing rebuttal, refutation, and/or concession when appropriate?	*Synthesizing evidence*	
Is the writing clear and specific? Does the word choice convey the writer's attitude toward the subject? Does the writer employ patterns of diction, syntax, or other rhetorical choices to create a style?	*Employing voice and style*	
Is the writing free of errors in spelling, usage, punctuation, capitalization, and agreement?	*Writing conventions*	

Free-Response Question: Synthesis

Demonstrating Complexity

In Unit 6, you worked on synthesis — that is, how to choose and combine relevant evidence to support your thesis and line of reasoning. Now, take this process one step further by learning how to enter a conversation with differing perspectives. To synthesize effectively, you include alternate perspectives and evidence from a variety of sources, even as you effectively support your own thesis.

→ **Step One: Determine a Unifying Idea and Position and Evaluate Sources**

As you begin, remember to read the introductory material, which includes helpful context and introduces the specific writing task in the exam prompt. You are provided fifteen minutes of reading time (in addition to the suggested forty minutes for writing) to evaluate the six provided sources. As you read and evaluate the written and visual sources, consider their individual positions, claims, and perspectives. Also, note any evidence from the sources that you might connect to your unifying and controlling idea and perspective.

When you read through multiple sources, think of them as part of a larger conversation about the subject: try to determine what each participant in the conversation is saying. In other words, you are not only including your own response to the source information; you are also suggesting how the sources might respond to each other.

- What differing perspectives are represented in the sources?
- Which sources agree with your perspective? How?
- Which sources contradict your perspective? How?
- Which sources complement each other? How?
- Which sources contradict each other? How?

Evaluating Visual Sources: Quantitative Sources

In addition to the written sources, you will also be provided with at least two visual sources for the synthesis question: one **qualitative** source, as we practiced in Unit 6, and one **quantitative** source.

Recall that qualitative sources provide evidence that can be observed or described but not necessarily measured or expressed in numbers. These sources include photographs, cartoons, illustrations, artwork, diagrams, advertisements, infographics, and other visual representations of information.

In contrast, quantitative sources, as the name suggests, provide numerical or statistical data: information that can be measured in numbers. These sources include statistics, percentages, and ratios that are represented visually in tables, bar graphs, line graphs, pie charts, map charts, and infographics. When visual quantitative sources are effective, they make information accessible and clear for the audience.

Here are guidelines for evaluating the information in a **quantitative source**:

- Read the title and subtitle carefully to determine the purpose of the data.
- Read all column headings, labels, and footnotes provided on the visual to understand what is being measured.
- Note the context, origin, and date of the information to determine its relevance and timeliness.
- Identify the specific data being compared in the chart or graph and consider the implications of the comparison.
- Determine whether the visual features, the ranges of time, or the presentation of numbers manipulate or distort the data in any way.

ANALYZING QUANTITATIVE DATA

Quantitative Data Source	Purpose(s)	Questions to Consider
Table	To organize large amounts of data so that readers can process it more easily	What patterns or trends are apparent in the data set? How are the data presented? Is the presentation accurate? Is the presentation misleading?
Pie Chart	To measure and compare parts of a whole (usually through percentages)	How do the sections of the pie chart compare? Are they evenly or unevenly distributed? What do these comparisons suggest?
Bar Charts and Graphs	To compare data among categories. To compare data between different groups. To compare data over time	What value is expressed in each bar? How are the data compared? What are the implications of these comparisons?
Line Graph	To track changes in data over time. To compare data from two or more groups over time	What values are represented on each axis? How do the data change? How do the numbers compare across different groups?
Map Chart	To show data on a geographical background that demonstrates relationships and highlights comparisons	What do the colors on the map chart represent? How do the data compare across locations? What are the implications of the similarities and differences in the data?

→ **Step Two: Develop a Defensible Claim and Unified Line of Reasoning**

Before you begin to write your argument, you will develop your defensible thesis and identify the reasons for supporting your position on the subject. As you learned in Unit 6, your thesis statement must make a claim that establishes your line of reasoning.

To add complexity within your argument, you might write a nuanced thesis that states your claim but acknowledges other perspectives or even notes the limitations of your own argument.

Consider the following sample synthesis subject and model thesis statements. All of them make a defensible claim. But when writers include a limitation or qualification in the thesis, they signify that they are entering a wider conversation about the subject.

Subject:	*Value of fine arts education*
Unifying Idea:	*Creativity*
+	
Perspective:	*Fosters growth*

Thesis with position and claim	*Funding fine arts programs in public schools nurtures creativity (**position**), fostering growth in students (**claim**).*
Thesis with position, claim, and line of reasoning	*Fine arts education should be fully funded in public schools (**position**) because the creativity it develops in students helps them to grow (**claim**) socially, emotionally, and academically (**line of reasoning**).*
Thesis that acknowledges limitations of the argument	*Even if budget cuts reduce available income (**limitation**), public schools should provide adequate funding to fine arts programs because participation in the arts nurtures creativity that fosters growth in students.*
Thesis that acknowledges other perspectives	*While schools may feel the pressure of more testing and less funding (**other perspectives**), fine arts programs should remain a priority because participation in the arts nurtures creativity that fosters growth in students.*

After you establish your thesis, you will plan a logical line of reasoning that justifies your claim. Most often, synthesis arguments are organized deductively, with the thesis at the end of the introduction. You then support the thesis with reasons and evidence from a variety of sources and perspectives.

Your topic sentences must provide reasons that support your perspective. You may demonstrate complexity in your argument by rebutting or refuting claims of the opposition, or even a combination of both. You develop your line of reasoning by considering the issue, your perspective, and the needs and values of your audience. Look closely at the following outline for an argument. You may include alternative perspectives within each of your paragraphs or include them in a paragraph of their own.

PLANNING A SYNTHESIS ARGUMENT: CHOOSING RELEVANT EVIDENCE

Introduction to subject with context

Defensible thesis with position and claim (idea + perspective)

Reason One	Reason Two	Reason Three
Supporting evidence and commentary (idea)	Supporting evidence and commentary (idea)	Supporting evidence and commentary (idea)
Supporting evidence and commentary (idea)	Supporting evidence and commentary (idea)	Supporting evidence and commentary (idea)
Alternative perspective or connection to another source (when appropriate)*	Alternative perspective or connection to another source (when appropriate)*	Alternative perspective or connection to another source (when appropriate)*

Conclusion

Discussion of your claim's implications

*Note: Some writers may choose to address counterarguments in a separate paragraph.

→ Step Three: Choose Relevant Evidence

As you have learned in prior units, you must choose evidence from sources to support your thesis and then arrange that evidence within your line of reasoning. Remember, you want to demonstrate to your audience that you understand the complexities of the issue. This requires you to examine the issue from multiple perspectives. As you build your argument, you can show this understanding by including both evidence that supports your claim and evidence from alternative perspectives when appropriate. Generally, you should include more than one source to support each reason in your line of reasoning. Note, as well, how these sources talk to one another: Do they agree with each other? Disagree? Both? You will be joining this conversation when you write your commentary.

When you introduce evidence from sources effectively, you demonstrate your control of language, as well as your understanding of the issue. But remember that information from sources only becomes evidence when you explain how it relates to your argument. One way to do this is through the verb you choose to introduce that evidence. Choosing a strong verb for argument conveys perspective as well. For example, the verbs *insists*, *states*, *believes*, and *reports* all carry different connotations and suggest your attitude or perspective. Review the following precise verbs for presenting and explaining source evidence.

VERBS FOR INTRODUCING EVIDENCE FROM SOURCES

Relating a Perspective	Agreeing/Conceding	Disagreeing/Refuting
Argues	Acknowledges	Argues
Asserts	Adds	Avoids
Avows	Admits	Cautions
Believes	Affirms	Challenges
Claims	Agrees	Complains
Concludes	Clarifies	Contrasts
Declares	Compares	Corrects
Explains	Concedes	Denies
Expresses	Continues	Denounces
Implies	Defends	Disagrees
Indicates	Emphasizes	Juxtaposes
Insists	Illustrates	Objects
Notes	Maintains	Protests
Observes	Relates	Qualifies
Offers	Reminds	Questions
Points out	Restates	Rebuts
Presents		Rejects
Proclaims		Retorts
Proposes		Stipulates
Reports		Warns
Reveals		
Speculates		
States		
Thinks		

For this free response, you must synthesize at least three sources from the six that are provided for you. But avoid simply dedicating a paragraph to each source or perspective. Instead, try to juxtapose evidence from sources that complement each other or even contradict each other, arranged strategically to support your reasons and your claim. Keep in mind that you do not need to cite from all of the sources. Likewise, you can cite the same source more than once in your argument. Remember, however, you should only include evidence that will contribute to the development of your claim and unifying idea.

→ **Step Four: Develop Your Commentary**

In earlier units, you practiced explaining how the evidence supports your claim. To write a more sophisticated argument, your commentary must also explain how the evidence and reasoning contribute to a larger conversation. Remember that you control the argument, so your arrangement and presentation of reasons and evidence will lead your audience to understand your claim. Your thesis statement, line of reasoning, and selection of evidence contribute to the conversation, but your commentary actually *creates* the conversation.

Joining the conversation involves more than just quoting from a few select sources to support your position. Rather, you must also convey the complexity of the issue, respond to a variety of sources, and explain how the sources respond to one another. In these sentences of explanation, you make your perspective clear to your audience as well. Without this commentary, your synthesis argument will become merely a paraphrase or summary of the sources or a list of evidence.

Your commentary connects your evidence to your line of reasoning and unifying idea. It creates that connection in several ways:

- It provides context for your evidence.
- It explains how the source evidence justifies your claim.
- It explains how qualitative or quantitative data justifies your claim or disproves your opposition.
- It explains the limitations of other perspectives or your own claim.
- It questions the validity of an opposing claim.

If you include quantitative data as evidence, make sure to add commentary. In other words, do not depend upon the data to speak for itself. You must explain not only how the numbers are represented but also what the numbers mean. Use the following questions to help generate commentary:

- Is there an increase or decrease in the numbers?
- What does this change in value imply?
- Do you see contrasts in data across groups, time, or location?
- What does this contrast suggest?
- What factors prompt the change in data over groups, time, or location?
- How do these numbers and statistics support your claim or refute another source?

WAYS TO JOIN THE CONVERSATION THROUGH CORROBORATION, REFUTATION, REBUTTAL, AND CONCESSION

	Agree with Source Information and Justify Your Response	Refute or Rebut Source Information and Justify Your Response	Concede, in Part, to Source Information and Justify Your Response	Acknowledge the Limitations of Your Argument and Offer an Explanation
Responding to a Claim	_____ makes an accurate claim that _____, which is important to note because _____.	The claim from _____ is inaccurate/ irrelevant/ outdated because _____.	Although _____ makes a strong point that _____, the claim fails to address _____.	Admittedly, the claim that _____ is not always the case because _____. However, _____ is still an important consideration because _____.
Responding to Qualitative Evidence	It is important to consider _____'s evidence that _____ because it supports the idea that _____.	While not inaccurate, _____'s evidence that _____ does not address the central issue of _____ because _____.	While it is true that the evidence suggests _____, we must also consider _____ because _____.	Evidence that _____ may not apply in all situations; however, within the current context, this evidence _____.
Responding to Quantitative Evidence	The data reported from _____ that suggests _____ reveals _____.	The data that suggests _____ is misleading in that _____. One should instead consider data from _____ that suggests _____ because _____.	The data is accurate in that _____; however, anecdotal evidence contradicts these conclusions and suggests that _____.	Since the data that suggests _____ may be outdated/ inconclusive/ limited, we must also consider _____ which confirms that _____.

INSIDER AP® TIP

Information from sources is not your explanation. Developing a nuanced argument requires you to explore complexities and discuss the implications of the argument in a broader context. Therefore, you must present evidence, respond to multiple perspectives, and convey your own perspective throughout your argument.

PREPARING FOR THE AP® EXAM

The following prompt is an example of a synthesis free-response question. As in Unit 6, you will be given a complete prompt that includes six sources, two of which are visual. Use what you have learned in this workshop to respond to the following prompt and join the conversation.

Prompt:

Recent increases in college costs have ignited the debate about which course of studies offers the greatest opportunities for college graduates: STEM disciplines (science, technology, engineering, math) or liberal arts (social sciences, literature, fine arts). Some argue that the STEM focus prepares students for practical jobs available in our increasingly technological world. Others contend that liberal arts students experience a more comprehensive education, which develops their communication, problem-solving, and leadership skills.

Carefully read the following **six** sources, including the introductory information for each. Write an essay that synthesizes material from at least three of the sources and develops your position on the best academic path for success in a changing world.

Source A (Pasquerella)

Source B (Reich)

Source C (Bortz)

Source D (Vedder et al.)

Source E (table)

Source F (infographic)

In your response, you should do the following:

- Respond to the prompt with a thesis that presents a defensible position.
- Select and use evidence from at least three of the provided sources to support your line of reasoning. Indicate clearly the sources used through direct quotation, paraphrase, or summary. Sources may be cited as Source A, Source B, etc., or by using the description in parentheses.
- Explain how the evidence supports your line of reasoning.
- Use appropriate grammar and punctuation in communicating your argument.

Source A

Pasquerella, Lynn. "Yes, Employers Do Value Liberal Arts Degrees." *Harvard Business Review*, 19 Sept. 2019, hbr.org/2019/09/yes-employers-do -value-liberal-arts-degrees.

The following excerpt was published in an online magazine focused on general management.

It's no secret that American higher education is under siege, with public confidence in the entire system in rapid decline. Politicians have fueled this by proposing legislation that would base funding for public colleges and universities exclusively on job acquisition for college graduates or stripping out so-called educational "frills," such as "the search for truth," "public service," and "improving the human condition" from their university system's mission statements. . . . A liberal education, they would have us believe, is reserved for those within the ivory tower, reflecting a willful disconnect from the practical matters of everyday life. This positioning fosters the image of a liberal education as a self-indulgent luxury — an image that has led to the excising of humanities programs, especially in public institutions, in favor of vocational and pre-professional programs that are regarded as singularly capable of responding to demands for economic opportunity.

The positing of a false dichotomy between a liberal arts education and preparation for work and life has contributed to a decoupling of higher education from the American Dream, obscuring the reality that colleges and universities continue to represent powerful institutional forces in catalyzing individual and societal transformation. However, it is not enough to decry the skeptics of higher education as misguided. Instead, those of us in academia do need to respond to their overarching concerns that higher education is too expensive, too difficult to access, and doesn't teach people 21st-century skills.

This call to action was part of the impetus behind the Association of American Colleges and Universities' (AAC&U's) most recent round of employer research . . . aimed at assessing the extent to which business executives and hiring managers believe that a college education is important and worthwhile. . . .

. . . . The 501 business executives at private sector and nonprofit organizations and 500 hiring managers, whose current job responsibilities include recruiting, interviewing, and hiring new employees, expressed greater confidence in colleges and universities than the American public does. Sixty-three percent noted having either "a lot of confidence" or "a great deal of confidence" in American higher education. Business executives (82%) and hiring managers (75%) also agree upon the value of college, maintaining that it is an essential and worthwhile investment of time and money. In addition to the potential for increased earnings, both groups cited the benefits of the accumulation of knowledge, the development of critical and analytical skills, and the ability to focus on a goal — in this case, earning a degree — as being especially meaningful. . . .

. . . It is precisely because employers place a premium on innovation in response to rapid change that they emphasize these student experiences rather than narrow technical training. Therefore, the dominant narrative that one's undergraduate major is all that matters and that only some majors will prepare students for success in the workplace doesn't match the reality. A student's undergraduate experience, and how well the experience advances critical learning outcomes (knowledge of human cultures and the physical and natural world, intellectual and practical skills, personal and social responsibility, integrative and applied learning), is what matters most, with 80% of employers agreeing that all students need a strong foundation in the liberal arts and sciences. Indeed, in the global knowledge economy, employer demand for graduates with a liberal education is growing. . . .

. . . Given that students today will experience an average of 11.9 career changes over their lifetimes, half of which will occur between the ages of 18–24, colleges and universities must partner with business and industry to develop the skills that will prepare our students not only for a wide range of workplace options, but that will also equip them to deal with a future none of us can fully predict.

In short, we need to push back against the narrative that a liberal arts education is "useless." That type of thinking simply doesn't bear out in the real world.

Source B

Reich, Robert. "A Four-Year College Degree Is Not Preparing People for Today's Jobs." Edited by Noël Merino, Greenhaven Press, 2016. At Issue, https://link .gale.com/apps/doc/EJ3010971205/OVIC?u=j021901003&sid=OVIC&xid= f992966d. Accessed 30 Sept. 2020.

The following blog was posted by the chancellor's professor of Public Policy at the University of California at Berkeley and former U.S. secretary of labor.

This week [September 1–5, 2014], millions of young people head to college and universities, aiming for a four-year liberal arts degree. They assume that degree is the only gateway to the American middle class.

It shouldn't be.

The Problems with College

For one thing, a four-year liberal arts degree is hugely expensive. Too many young people graduate laden with debts that take years if not decades to pay off.

And too many of them can't find good jobs when they graduate, in any event. So they have to settle for jobs that don't require four years of college. They end up overqualified for the work they do, and underwhelmed by it.

Others drop out of college because they're either unprepared or unsuited for a four-year liberal arts curriculum. When they leave, they feel like failures.

We need to open other gateways to the middle class.

Jobs That Do Not Require Four Years

Consider, for example, technician jobs. They don't require a four-year degree. But they do require mastery over a domain of technical knowledge, which can usually be obtained in two years.

Technician jobs are growing in importance. As digital equipment replaces the jobs of routine workers and lower-level professionals, technicians are needed to install, monitor, repair, test, and upgrade all the equipment.

Hospital technicians are needed to monitor ever more complex equipment that now fills medical centers; office technicians, to fix the hardware and software responsible for much of the work that used to be done by secretaries and clerks.

Automobile technicians are in demand to repair the software that now powers our cars; manufacturing technicians, to upgrade the numerically controlled machines and 3-D printers that have replaced assembly lines; laboratory technicians, to install and test complex equipment for measuring results; telecommunications technicians, to install, upgrade, and repair the digital systems linking us to one another.

Technology is changing so fast that knowledge about specifics can quickly become obsolete. That's why so much of what technicians learn is on the job.

But to be an effective on-the-job learner, technicians need basic knowledge of software and engineering, along the domain where the technology is applied — hospitals, offices, automobiles, manufacturing, laboratories, telecommunications, and so forth.

The Community College System

Yet America isn't educating the technicians we need. As our aspirations increasingly focus on four-year college degrees, we've allowed vocational and technical education to be downgraded and denigrated.

Still, we have a foundation to build on. Community colleges offering two-year degree programs today enroll more than half of all college and university undergraduates. Many students are in full-time jobs, taking courses at night and on weekends. Many are adults.

Community colleges are great bargains. They avoid the fancy amenities four-year liberal arts colleges need in order to lure the children of the middle class.

Even so, community colleges are being systematically starved of funds. On a per-student basis, state legislatures direct most higher-education funding to four-year colleges and universities because that's what their middle-class constituents want for their kids.

American businesses, for their part, aren't sufficiently involved in designing community college curricula and hiring their graduates, because their executives are usually the products of four-year liberal arts institutions and don't know the value of community colleges.

The German System

By contrast, Germany provides its students the alternative of a world-class technical education that's kept the German economy at the forefront of precision manufacturing and applied technology.

The skills taught are based on industry standards, and courses are designed by businesses that need the graduates. So when young Germans get their degrees, jobs are waiting for them.

We shouldn't replicate the German system in full. It usually requires students and their families to choose a technical track by age 14. "Late bloomers" can't get back on an academic track.

But we can do far better than we're doing now. One option: Combine the last year of high school with the first year of community college into a curriculum to train technicians for the new economy.

Affected industries would help design the courses and promise jobs to students who finish successfully. Late bloomers can go on to get their associate degrees and even transfer to four-year liberal arts universities.

This way we'd provide many young people who cannot or don't want to pursue a four-year degree with the fundamentals they need to succeed, creating another gateway to the middle class.

Too often in modern America, we equate "equal opportunity" with an opportunity to get a four-year liberal arts degree. It should mean an opportunity to learn what's necessary to get a good job.

Source C

Bortz, Daniel. "Skills Employers Look for in College Graduates," n.d.
    Monster.com, Monster Worldwide, www.monster.com/career-advice
    /article/5-skills-employers-want-in-new-grads-and-arent-finding.

The following is an article posted on a job and career website.

All set to land your first job out of college? Get ready to put your talent to the test. According to the National Association of Colleges and Employers' Job Outlook 2020 survey, there are a handful of specific skills employers look for in new grads.

Below you'll find the top 10 most sought-after attributes and skills to put on a résumé that hiring managers want from this year's graduating class. So if you're on the hunt for an entry-level job, read on to learn what these skills are and how to master them, and be sure to check out Monster's grad site for more great info.

Ten Skills Employers Look for in New Grads

1. Problem-solving skills

Nine in ten employers (91.2%) want to see new college graduates tout excellent problem-solving skills. Many hiring managers use behavioral interview questions — phrases such as "tell me about a time when" or "give me an example of" — to assess a job candidate's problem-solving ability. Thus, you'll want to prepare anecdotes that paint you as a solution finder.

You don't need job experience to provide proof that you're a problem solver, says Los Angeles-based career coach Nancy Karas. "Think about times where you were proactive, innovative, or highly responsive to a challenge," like that time you helped solve a customer complaint while working at the campus coffee shop, Karas says. Even better: Show that you took the initiative to *identify* a problem and then solved it.

2. Ability to work in a team

It goes without saying that nobody likes the employee who wants to hog the spotlight. But unlike your career as a student, where you're really the only one who can make or break your success, the workplace depends on teams of people to get the job done. No surprise, then, that 86.3% of hiring managers want to know you can collaborate well with lots of different personalities.

You'll need to learn how to delegate, take direction, value differences of opinion, and play to your and your co-workers' strengths and weaknesses. "Being a team player is all about being reliable and trustworthy," says career coach Denise Dudley, author of *Work It! Get In, Get Noticed, Get Promoted*.

3. Strong work ethic

You need to be committed to your job responsibilities and understand that performing your role is more than just means to a paycheck — after all, a company stands for something beyond business and so should you. That's why 80.4% of hiring managers want to see new hires demonstrate a strong work ethic. Show up on time, be engaged in your work, and act with integrity.

4. Analytical skills

Eight in ten hiring managers (79.4%) want to hire entry-level workers who possess analytical skills, meaning they're searching for critical thinkers — people who know how to gather and evaluate information and then make good decisions based on that intel.

5. Written communication skills

Good communication is always going to be among the top skills employers look for. The survey found that 77.5% of managers feel writing proficiency is the most desirable hard skill among recent college graduates. Therefore, submitting a well-crafted cover letter is crucial.

You'll want to highlight experiences on your résumé that demonstrate your writing skills. If you volunteered to be the scribe for a group project in college, for example, include that on your résumé, advises Dawn Bugni, a professional résumé writer in Atkinson, North Carolina. And depending on the nature of the industry — marketing, communications, or journalism to name a few — you might also submit writing samples with your application. "A writing portfolio speaks for itself," Bugni says.

6. Leadership skills

It's a tall order: 72.5% of hiring managers want potential hires with great leadership skills. Believe it or not, there are ways you can show possible employers that you have leadership potential before you even enter the workforce.

If you held a leadership role in college (e.g., president of the French club), highlight it on your résumé. If you emerged as the informal leader on a group project, talk about the experience during the job interview.

Also, get letters of recommendation from former internship managers that speak to your leadership skills. "Glowing references can solidify a job offer," says Stefanie Wichansky, CEO at Randolph, New Jersey, management consulting and staffing firm Professional Resource Partners.

7. Verbal communication skills

Seven in ten hiring managers (69.6%) surveyed said good verbal communication skills are a must-have for new grads. Communication skills set the tone for how people perceive you and help you build relationships with co-workers.

Verbal communication prowess is best demonstrated during job interviews. Presenting answers to interview questions clearly goes a long way. You should also ask job interviewers open-ended questions to show that you're engaged.

8. Initiative

Tied with verbal communication skills, 69.6% of hiring managers reported they want newly minted college graduates who know how to take initiative. This is where the maxim "Show them, don't just tell them" applies. In the experience section of your résumé, cite an example of a time when you deal with a difficult situation in a direct way or a time when being proactive enabled you to head off a problem.

9. Detail-oriented

According to the survey, 67.6% of managers are looking for new grads that have meticulous attention to detail. As a result, make sure your résumé is impeccable, free of typos and grammatical errors, and organized with the use of clear, concise, and effective language. As Monster's résumé expert Kim Isaacs puts it: "You want your résumé to be as perfect as humanly possible."

10. Technical skills

Many industries, not just jobs in the technology sector, call for professionals with technical abilities. Case in point: 65.7% of hiring managers said new grads should possess technical skills. Describe how you applied your technical skills in the past. For instance, if your résumé lists that you have Java experience, it should also describe how YOU utilized the program on a particular project in college.

Highlight Your Skills on Your Résumé

Now that you know which skills employers look for in new grads in order to turn heads, you'll want to feature them prominently on your résumé, in addition to your quantifiable achievements. Need help with that? Get a free résumé evaluation today from the experts at Monster's Résumé Writing Service. You'll get detailed feedback in two business days, including a review of your résumé's appearance and content, and a prediction of a recruiter's first impression. Let Monster's experts show you how you can use your résumé to signal to hiring managers that you've got what they're looking for.

Source D

Vedder, Richard, et al. "The Value of a College Degree Is Diminishing Over Time." *How Valuable Is a College Degree?*, edited by Noël Merino, Greenhaven Press, 2016. At Issue. *Gale in Context: Opposing Viewpoints*, https://link.gale.com/apps/doc/EJ3010971209/OVIC?u=j021901003&sid =OVIC&xid=6da94000.

The following excerpts are from an article published by an organization dedicated to researching public policy and economic issues relating to postsecondary education.

The mismatch between the educational requirements for various occupations and the amount of education obtained by workers is large and growing significantly over time. The problem can be viewed two ways. In one sense, we have an "underemployment" problem: College graduates are underemployed, performing jobs which require vastly less educational tools than they possess. The flip side of that, though, is that we have an "overinvestment" problem: We are churning out far more college graduates than required by labor-market imperatives. The supply of jobs requiring college degrees is growing more slowly than the supply of those holding such degrees. . . .

The Wisdom of College for All
. . . That suggests the earnings advantage associated with a bachelor's degree will change over time. By one way of looking at it, the college degree becomes less worthwhile financially: If one compares earnings of those with bachelor's degrees with that of all workers (not merely high-school graduates), the day may come when the bachelor's degree will pay less than that of all workers, as the proportion of workers with more than bachelor's degrees comes close to approximating that of those with less than a four-year diploma. . . .

. . . All of this calls into question the wisdom of the "college for all" movement. Does it make sense to become the world's leader again in the proportion of young adults with college degrees? . . .

A Shielded Overinvestment
. . . That raises questions that go beyond higher education. As the number of years of education of workers rises in virtually all non-professional and technical jobs, is the reason ultimately that really it takes, say, 14 or 15 years of schooling to offer the same learning that previously was accomplished in 12 years? Is the deterioration in the quality of our primary and secondary education a contributing factor in the credential inflation obvious at the postsecondary level? That suggests there may be two major economic issues facing higher education. First, it is too costly, too inefficient, too shielded from the useful market forces of "creative destruction." Second, because of massive overinvestment reflecting indifference to labor-market realities, we are vastly wasting scarce resources, both public and private. . . .

. . . Economists for generations have long accepted the law of diminishing returns—when one adds more and more resources, at some point the marginal contribution to output falls. The law applies to education as to almost everything in life. One manifestation of it in American university life is the underemployment of college graduates; we might be seriously overinvested in higher education. . . .

Source E

"High-Impact, Applied Learning Practices." *Association of American Colleges and Universities*, Association of American Colleges and Universities, www .aacu.org/sites/default/files/files/LEAP/2HIPS.pdf.

The following data is published on a website dedicated to research for colleges and universities.

EMPLOYER RESEARCH SUPPORTS
HIGH-IMPACT, APPLIED LEARNING PRACTICES

• **93%** of executives and **94%** of hiring managers say that they would be *more likely to hire a recent graduate who has held an internship or apprenticeship* with a company or organization, including 52% of executives and 60% of hiring managers who would be *much more likely* to do so.

• **76%** of executives and **87%** of hiring managers rate it *very important that recent graduates demonstrate the ability to apply knowledge and skills in real-world settings,* yet only 33% of executives (43-point gap) and **39%** of hiring managers (48-point gap) think that recent graduates are well prepared in this area.

More likely to hire employees with these experiences:	Executives	Hiring Managers
Internships/apprenticeship with company/organization	93%	94%
Multiple courses requiring significant writing assignments	82%	72%
Research project done collaboratively with peers	81%	81%
Advanced, comprehensive senior project/thesis	80%	76%
Field-based project in diverse community	72%	83%
Service Learning project with community organization	71%	78%
Study Abroad program	54%	47%

Association of American Colleges and Universities

Source: Hart Research Associates. *Fulfilling the American Dream: Liberal Education and the Future of Work* (Washington, DC: AAC&U, 2018) www.aacu.org/leap/public-opinion-research.

1818 R St. NW, Washington, DC 20009   202.387.3760   www.aacu.org

LEAP

Source F

"Business: Supporting College- and Career-Readiness." *Committee for Economic Development.* http://www.ced.org/projects/single/k-12/all.

The following infographic was created by the Committee for Economic Development.

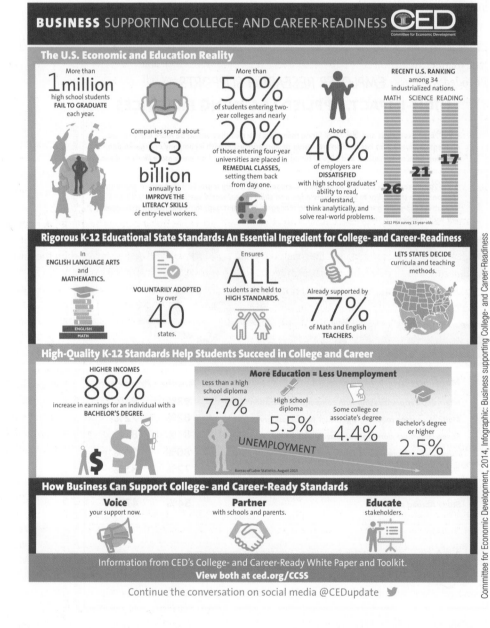

BUSINESS SUPPORTING COLLEGE- AND CAREER-READINESS **CED**
Committee for Economic Development

The U.S. Economic and Education Reality

More than
1 million
high school students
FAIL TO GRADUATE
each year.

Companies spend about
$3 billion
annually to
IMPROVE THE LITERACY SKILLS
of entry-level workers.

More than
50%
of students entering two-year colleges and nearly
20%
of those entering four-year universities are placed in **REMEDIAL CLASSES**, setting them back from day one.

About
40%
of employers are **DISSATISFIED** with high school graduates' ability to read, understand, think analytically, and solve real-world problems.

RECENT U.S. RANKING among 34 industrialized nations.
MATH SCIENCE READING
26   21   17
2012 PISA survey, 15-year-olds

Rigorous K-12 Educational State Standards: An Essential Ingredient for College- and Career-Readiness

In **ENGLISH LANGUAGE ARTS** and **MATHEMATICS**.
ENGLISH
MATH

VOLUNTARILY ADOPTED by over
40
states.

Ensures
ALL
students are held to **HIGH STANDARDS**.

Already supported by
77%
of Math and English **TEACHERS.**

LETS STATES DECIDE curricula and teaching methods.

High-Quality K-12 Standards Help Students Succeed in College and Career

HIGHER INCOMES
88%
increase in earnings for an individual with a **BACHELOR'S DEGREE.**

More Education = Less Unemployment

Less than a high school diploma
7.7%

High school diploma
5.5%

Some college or associate's degree
4.4%

Bachelor's degree or higher
2.5%

UNEMPLOYMENT

Bureau of Labor Statistics, August 2015

How Business Can Support College- and Career-Ready Standards

Voice
your support now.

Partner
with schools and parents.

Educate
stakeholders.

Information from CED's College- and Career-Ready White Paper and Toolkit.
View both at ced.org/CCSS

Continue the conversation on social media @CEDupdate

PREPARING FOR THE AP® EXAM
Multiple-Choice Questions: Reading

The Bird of Paradise
E.O. Wilson

Consider one such bird for a moment in the analytic manner, as an object of biological research. Encoded within its chromosomes is the developmental program that led with finality to a male *Paradisaea guilielmi*.[1] The completed nervous system is a structure of fiber tracts more complicated than any existing computer, and as challenging as all the rain forests of New Guinea surveyed on foot. A microscopic study will someday permit us to trace the events that culminate in the electric commands carried by the efferent neurons to the skeletal-muscular system and reproduce, in part, the dance of the courting male. This machinery can be dissected and understood by proceeding to the level of the cell, to enzymatic catalysis, microfilament configuration, and active sodium transport during electric discharge. Because biology sweeps the full range of space and time, there will be more discoveries renewing the sense of wonder at each step of research. By altering the scale of perception to the micrometer and millisecond, the laboratory scientist parallels the trek of the naturalist across the land. He looks out from his own version of the mountain crest. His spirit of adventure, as well as personal history of hardship, misdirection, and triumph, are fundamentally the same.

Described this way, the bird of paradise may seem to have been turned into a metaphor of what humanists dislike most about science: that it reduces nature and is insensitive to art, that scientists are conquistadors who melt down the Inca gold. But bear with me a minute. Science is not just analytic; it is also synthetic. It uses artlike intuition and imagery. In the early stages, individual behavior can be analyzed to the level of genes and neurosensory cells, whereupon the phenomena have indeed been mechanically reduced. In the synthetic phase, though, even the most elementary activity of these biological units creates rich and subtle patterns at the levels of organism and society. The outer qualities of *Paradisaea guilielmi*, its plumes, dance, and daily life, are functional traits open to a deeper understanding through the exact description of their constituent parts. They can be redefined as holistic properties that alter our perception and emotion in surprising and pleasant ways.

There will come a time when the bird of paradise is reconstituted by the synthesis of all the hard-won analytic information. The mind, bearing a newfound power, will journey back to the familiar worlds of seconds and centimeters. Once again, the glittering plumage takes form and is viewed at a distance through a network of leaves and mist. Then we see the bright eye open, the head swivel, the wings extend. But the familiar motions are viewed across a far greater range of cause and effect. The species is understood more completely; misleading illusions have given way to light and wisdom of a greater degree. One turn of the cycle of intellect is then complete. The excitement of the scientist's search for the true material nature of the species recedes, to be replaced in part by the more enduring responses of the hunter and poet.

What are these ancient responses? The full answer can only be given through a combined idiom of science and the humanities, whereby the investigation turns back into itself. The human being, like the bird of paradise, awaits our examination in the analytic-synthetic manner. As always by honored tradition, feeling and myth can be viewed

[1]Scientific name for the bird of paradise.

at a distance through physiological[2] time, idiosyncratically, in the manner of traditional art. But they can also be penetrated more deeply than ever was possible in the pre-scientific age, to their physical basis in the processes of mental development, the brain structure, and indeed the genes themselves. It may even be possible to trace them back through time past cultural history to the evolutionary origins of human nature. With each new phase of synthesis to emerge from biological inquiry, the humanities will expand their reach and capability. In symmetric fashion, with each redirection of the humanities, science will add dimensions to human biology.

1. The writer's description of the bird of paradise in the first paragraph serves primarily to
   (A) examine the complexities of life on many different levels.
   (B) demonstrate the different scales of perception that laboratory scientists experience in their studies.
   (C) display what makes each different species unique on both physiological and atomic levels.
   (D) emphasize the importance of maintaining different environments for a diversity of animals.
   (E) explain why naturalists care so much about the physiology of certain animals.

2. In paragraph 2, sentence 1 ("Described . . . Inca gold."), the writer mentions "what humanists dislike most about science" primarily to
   (A) provide supporting evidence for the claims made later in the same paragraph.
   (B) rebut the opposing viewpoint of those who would disagree with him.
   (C) concede the perspective of a portion of his audience.
   (D) suggest a way for humanists and scientists to better cooperate.
   (E) make a claim about the role of science in the humanities.

3. In paragraph 2, the colon in sentence 1 ("Described . . . Inca gold.") serves which of the following purposes?
   (A) To indicate that what follows the colon will clarify "what humanists dislike most about science"
   (B) To create separation between the metaphors of the bird and the conquistadors on the different sides of the colon
   (C) To draw attention to the comparisons being made on each side of the colon
   (D) To break up the sentence so the reader can better understand the relationship between the bird of paradise and the Inca gold
   (E) To signal the description that is indicated by the first word in the sentence

4. In the third paragraph, the semicolon in the sixth sentence ("The species . . . greater degree.") serves which of the following purposes?
   (A) It connects two different descriptions of the bird of paradise into a single idea about that bird as a metaphor.
   (B) It combines the two independent clauses about the species being "understood more completely" to demonstrate the larger idea about the power of scientific analysis to enhance appreciation of nature.
   (C) It allows a single sentence to demonstrate two different views on the relationship between science and the humanities without sounding contradictory.
   (D) It prevents the reader from being misled by assumptions about the entire bird of paradise species by connecting a clarifying clause.
   (E) It distinguishes between the humanistic and scientific understanding of the species by combining the separate clauses into one sentence.

[2]Pertaining to physiology, the branch of biology that deals with the normal functions of living organisms and their parts.

5. In paragraph 4, sentence 6 ("It may . . . nature."), the pronoun "them" refers to
   (A) "the evolutionary origins of human nature" (sentence 6).
   (B) "mental development, the brain structure, and indeed the genes themselves" (sentence 5).
   (C) "science and the humanities" (sentence 2).
   (D) "ancient responses" (sentence 1).
   (E) "feeling and myth" (sentence 4).

6. In the fourth paragraph, the last two sentences helped to conclude the passage by
   (A) summarizing the perspectives of scientists and humanists to clarify that they are more closely related than they perceive.
   (B) circling back to the metaphor of the bird of paradise to bring the argument of the passage full circle.
   (C) explaining how both science and the humanities will continue to benefit from their mutual development.
   (D) describing how the relationship between the humanities and science is deeply rooted in the human brain.
   (E) combining the unique perspectives of the humanities and science to emphasize the important work of both.

7. Which of the following adjectives reveals the most about the writer's perspective on the relationship between science and the humanities?
   (A) "enduring" (paragraph 3)
   (B) "symmetric" (paragraph 4)
   (C) "analytic" (paragraph 2)
   (D) "hard-won" (paragraph 3)
   (E) "artlike" (paragraph 2)

8. Of the following statements from the passage, which one best considers the perspectives, contexts, and needs of the intended audience?
   (A) "personal history of hardship, misdirection, and triumph, are fundamentally the same" (paragraph 1).
   (B) "the most elementary activity of these biological units creates rich and subtle patterns at the levels of organism and society" (paragraph 2).
   (C) "misleading illusions have given way to light and wisdom of a greater degree" (paragraph 3).
   (D) "with each redirection of the humanities, science will add dimensions to human biology" (paragraph 4).
   (E) "to their physical basis in the processes of mental development, the brain structure, and indeed the genes themselves" (paragraph 4).

9. In the passage, the perspectives examined by the writer reflect the ongoing conversations between which of the following?
   (A) scientists and humanists
   (B) zoologists and scientists
   (C) hunters and poets
   (D) historians and evolutionists
   (E) intellectuals and Philistines

The passage below is a draft.

(1) Most Americans know the name Rosa Parks, the forty-two-year-old African American woman from Montgomery, Alabama, arrested because she refused to give up her bus seat to a white man. (2) While her arrest led to the 381-day boycott of the city bus system and eventually to the integration of those buses, a pivotal moment in the history of civil rights and nonviolent protest in the United States.

(3) Nearly no one knows the name Claudette Colvin.

(4) Nine months before Parks's arrest, the fifteen-year-old Colvin was removed from a Montgomery bus and arrested for the exact same reason. (5) In her segregated school, they had been studying African American leaders who struggled against slavery and for equal rights. (6) Later in her life, Colvin explained that "my head was just too full of black history, you know, the oppression that we went through. (7) It felt like Sojourner Truth was on one side pushing me down, and Harriet Tubman was on the other side of me pushing me down. (8) I couldn't get up."

(9) Ironically, she was shunned by parts of her community. (10) Instead of the eventual hero that Parks would become, Colvin said she was viewed as a troublemaker who was only making things worse for her community. (11) No leaders came to her aid or threatened to boycott due to her arrest. (12) She withdrew from her community and eventually got pregnant before moving to Brooklyn, New York, in 1958.

(13) Rosa Parks, on the other hand, had been the long-time secretary for the local chapter of the National Association for the Advancement of Colored People (NAACP), so local civil rights leaders knew her and trusted her reputation. (14) Colvin felt that Parks had a certain look that leaders found more appropriate for the media attention that would come. (15) "Her skin texture was the kind that people associate with the middle class," said Colvin, "she fit that profile."

(16) These leaders knew that to have a figure-head in the fight against segregation, it needed to be a person beyond reproach. (17) Someone who people could see and empathize with immediately. (18) The modest and reliable Parks, not the troubled and unpredictable Colvin, would become the catalyst for change in Montgomery. (19) While Colvin should be respected for her bravery as a teenage girl, she must also be seen as another victim of the conditioned prejudice that requires people of color to meet higher standards than their white peers.

1. The writer is considering revising the underlined portion of sentence 2 (reproduced below) to more clearly indicate the relationship between the bus boycott and integration of the buses.

   While her arrest led to the 381-day boycott of the city bus system and eventually to the integration of those buses, a pivotal moment in the history of civil rights and nonviolent protest in the United States.

   Which of the following revisions best accomplishes this goal?

   (A) (as it is now)
   (B) Her arrest
   (C) Despite her arrest, her treatment
   (D) Regardless of her arrest, it
   (E) In fact, her arrest

2. The writer is considering moving sentence 3 (reproduced below) to a position in the passage that would better indicate that Colvin is often forgotten in the historical context of the argument.

Nearly no one knows the name Claudette Colvin.

What is the best location for this sentence?

(A) (where it is now)
(B) Before sentence 1
(C) Before sentence 9 and in the same paragraph
(D) After sentence 18
(E) After sentence 19 as its own paragraph

3. The writer wants to combine sentences 14 and 15 (reproduced below) in a way that indicates that the information in sentence 15 is intended to explain the statement in sentence 14.

Colvin felt that Parks had a certain look that leaders found more appropriate for the media attention that would come. "Her skin texture was the kind that people associate with the middle class," said Colvin, "she fit that profile."

Which of the following revisions best achieves this goal?

(A) Colvin felt that Parks had "skin texture [that] was the kind that people associate with the middle class."
(B) Colvin felt that "her skin texture was the kind that people associate with the middle class," and that "she fit that profile."
(C) Colvin felt that Parks had a certain look that leaders found more appropriate for the media attention that would come: "Her skin texture was the kind that people associate with the middle class," said Colvin, "she fit that profile."
(D) Colvin felt that Parks had a certain look that leaders found more appropriate for the media attention that would come, "her skin texture was the kind that people associate with the middle class," said Colvin, "she fit that profile."
(E) Colvin felt that Parks had a certain look that leaders found more appropriate for the media attention that would come ("Her skin texture was the kind that people associate with the middle class," said Colvin, "she fit that profile").

4. To enhance the credibility of the argument, the writer is considering adding the following sentence immediately before sentence 16 and in the same paragraph.

    It would be easy to look at this profile of Colvin and blame the leaders of her community for turning their backs, but that fails to consider the broader context.

    Should the writer make this change?

    (A) Yes, because it expands on the relationship between the leaders of the African American community and Colvin.
    (B) Yes, because it refutes the argument that a reader may offer in judgment of the community leaders' actions.
    (C) No, because it introduces a claim that is not addressed elsewhere in the passage.
    (D) No, because it fails to consider Rosa Parks's perspective on the incidents involving both her and Colvin.
    (E) No, because there is never any blame assumed in the passage.

5. The writer wants to replace the underlined adjectives in sentence 18 (reproduced below) with more precise language, taking into account the context of the passage.

    The modest and reliable Parks, not the troubled and unpredictable Colvin, would become the catalyst for change in Montgomery.

    Which of the following choices best accomplishes this goal?

    (A) (as it is now)
    (B) hushed and awkward
    (C) silent and reserved
    (D) dependable and well-known
    (E) insistent and committed

6. To better relate to the ongoing conversation about race and the historical context of that conversation, the writer is considering including the following quote from Rosa Parks in the passage.

    "People always say that I didn't give up my seat because I was tired, but that isn't true. I was not tired physically. . . . No, the only tired I was was tired of giving in."

    Should the writer include this quote somewhere in the passage?

    (A) Yes, because it makes Parks's motivations for her refusal very clear in the context of the Montgomery bus and the larger context of racial segregation in the United States.
    (B) Yes, because it refutes the assumptions made by many detractors that she was not a person being wronged but only physically tired.
    (C) Yes, because including a statement from Rosa Parks will increase the credibility of the argument.
    (D) No, because Colvin and Parks were clearly different people, and including Parks would only take away from Colvin's statements.
    (E) No, because the passage is not directly focused on Parks or her experience and this would considerably shift the passage toward her.

Guide to MLA, APA, and CSE Documentation Styles

The purpose of documentation is to provide thorough, accurate, and quick information about your sources when you give credit for words and ideas that are not your own. Make sure to check with your teacher or instructor about which style guide he or she prefers.

Modern Language Association (MLA), American Psychiatric Association (APA), and the Council of Science Editors (CSE) are three organizations that provide consistent documentation and publication style guidelines for academic disciplines. Generally speaking, MLA is used when working in English and in the arts; APA is used when working in the social sciences, such as psychology, education, and economics; and CSE is used when writing in the sciences.

All three style guides use in-text citations that are set off by parentheses. Generally, the MLA conventions provide the name of the author and the page numbers of the publication where the source material first appeared. The APA and CSE rules add the year of publication to the citation. Note that different types of sources may require additional information in citations, such as the line numbers of a play or the name of a specific television episode.

IN-TEXT CITATIONS

MLA	APA	CSE
Jessica Mitford refers to the "intractable reticence" of morticians (302).	According to Mitford (1963), most morticians have an "intractable reticence" (p. 302).	According to Mitford (1963), most morticians have an "intractable reticence" (p. 302).
Morticians have an "intractable reticence" (Mitford 302).	Morticians often have an "intractable reticence" (Mitford, 1963, p. 199).	

Each style guide has its own rules for works cited (MLA), reference lists (APA), and references (CSE). However, the basic source information will remain consistent across different formatting conventions. Each entry should include the author, the title of the source, the place of publication, the name of the publisher, and the date of publication. Depending on the type of source (e.g., essay in an edited anthology, a video on YouTube, or an article in an online magazine), you may need to include additional or different information as well.

BASIC STYLE GUIDELINES FOR A LIST OF WORKS CITED

MLA	APA	CSE
• Begin the works-cited list on a new page after the last page of your text.	• Begin each entry flush with the left-hand margin; indent subsequent lines one-half inch.	• The reference list should begin on a new page titled "References" or "Cited References" (do not underline this heading or place it in quotation marks).
• Begin each entry flush with the left-hand margin; indent subsequent lines one-half inch.	• Italicize the titles of books and periodicals; do not italicize article titles or place them within quotation marks.	• Only works cited in your paper should appear in the reference list.
• List references alphabetically by the author's last name (or by the first major word of the title, if no author is identified).	• List references alphabetically by the author's last name (or by the first major word of the title, if no author is identified).	• List references alphabetically by the author's last name (or by the first major word of the title if no author is identified).
• Double-space the list of entries.	• Use initials for authors' first and middle names.	• Use initials for authors' first and middle names.
	• If the list includes two or more sources by the same author, list them in order of year of publication.	

GUIDELINES FOR A LIST OF WORKS CITED

	MLA Works Cited	APA Reference List	CSE References (or Cited References)
BOOKS			
Book by one author	Verma, Neil. *Theater of the Mind: Imagination, Aesthetics, and American Radio Drama*. University of Chicago Press, 2012.	Verma, N. (2012). *Theater of the mind: Imagination, aesthetics, and American radio drama*. University of Chicago Press.	Verma N. 2012. Theater of the Mind: Imagination, Aesthetics, and American Radio Drama. Chicago (IL): The University of Chicago Press. 305 p.
Book by two authors	Levitt, Steven D. and Stephen J. Dubner. *Freakonomics: A Rogue Economist Explores the Hidden Side of Everything*. William Morrow, 2020.	Levitt, S. D., & Dubner, S. J. (2020). *Freakonomics: A rogue economist explores the hidden side of everything*. William Morrow.	Levitt SD, Dubner S. 2020. Freakonomics: A Rogue Economist Explores the Hidden Side of Everything. New York (NY): William Morrow. 352 p.
Book by three or more authors	Hand, Cynthia, et al. *My Lady Jane*. HarperTeen, 2017.	Hand, C., Ashton, B., & Meadows, J. (2017). *My lady Jane*. HarperTeen.	Hand C, Ashton B, Meadows J. 2017. My Lady Jane. New York (NY): HarperTeen. 512 p.

	MLA Works Cited	APA Reference List	CSE References (or Cited References)
Edited book	Pollack, Harriet, editor. *New Essays on Eudora Welty, Class, and Race.* University Press of Mississippi, 2019.	Pollack, H. (Ed.). (2020). *New essays on Eudora Welty, class, and race.* University Press of Mississippi.	Pollack H, editor. 2020. New Essays on Eudora Welty, Class, and Race. Jackson (MS): University Press of Mississippi. 246 p.
Essay in an edited book or anthology	Vernet, Mark. "Film Noir on the Edge of Doom." *Shades of Noir*, edited by Joan Copjec, Verso, 1996, 1–31.	Vernet, M. (1996). Film noir on the edge of doom. In J. Copjec (Ed.), *Shades of noir* (pp. 1–31). Verso.	Vernet M. 1996. Film Noir on the Edge of Doom. In: Copjec J, editor. Shades of Noir. New York (NY): Verso. P. 1–31.
Translation	Simenon, Georges. *Maigret in New York.* Translated by Linda Coverdale, Penguin, 2016.	Simenon, G. (2016). *Maigret in New York* (L. Coverdale, Trans.). Penguin.	Simenon G. 2016. Maigret in New York. Coverdale L, translator. New York (NY): Penguin. 192 p.
Poem (in a book)	Oliver, Mary. "The Dog Has Run Off Again." *New and Selected Poems*, Beacon Press, 2005, p. 123.	Oliver, M. (2005). *New and selected poems.* Macmillan.	
Short story (in an anthology)	Minot, Susan. "Lust." *The Compact Bedford Introduction to Literature*, edited by Michael Meyer, Bedford/St. Martin's, 2012, pp. 279–286.	Minot, S. (2012). Lust. In M. Meyer (Ed.), *The compact introduction to literature* (pp. 279–286). Bedford/ St. Martin's.	
PERIODICALS			
Article in a journal (print)	Landon, Philip J. "From Cowboy to Organization Man: The Hollywood War Hero, 1940–1955." *Studies in Popular Culture*, vol. 12, no. 1, 1989, pp. 28–41.	Landon, P. J. (1989). From cowboy to organization man: The Hollywood war hero, 1940–1955. *Studies in Popular Culture*, *12*(1), 28–41.	Landon PJ. 1989. From Cowboy to Organization Man: The Hollywood War Hero, 1940–1955. Studies in Popular Culture. 12(1): 28–41.
Article in a magazine (print)	Mallon, Thomas. "Weegee the Famous, the Voyeur and Exhibitionist," *The New Yorker*, 28 May, 2018, pp. 64–70.	Mallon, T. (2018, May 28). Weegee the Famous, the voyeur and exhibitionist. *The New Yorker*, 64–70.	Mallon T. 2018 May 28. Weegee the Famous, the Voyeur and Exhibitionist. The New Yorker. 97(15): 64.
Article in a newspaper (print)	Shearer, Lloyd. "Crime Certainly Pays Onscreen." *The New York Times*, 5 Aug. 1945, p. 77.	Shearer, L. (1945, August 5). Crime certainly pays onscreen. *The New York Times*, 77.	Shearer L. 1945 Aug. 7. Crime Certainly Pays Onscreen. The New York Times; p. 77.

	MLA Works Cited	APA Reference List	CSE References (or Cited References)
Letter to the editor	Sorin, Martin. Letter. *The New York Times*, 31 Jan. 1973, p. 42.	Sorin, M. (1973, January 31). Another view of the Nixon record [Letter to the editor]. *The New York Times*, 12. https://timesmachine .nytimes.com /timesmachine/1973/02 /08/79841060.html ?pageNumber=42	
Anonymous articles (print)	"The Complex Legacy of Thomas Becket's Life and Death." *The Economist*, 15 May 2021, p. 34.	Anonymous. (2021, May 15). The complex legacy of Thomas Becket's life and death. *The Economist*, 34. Print.	The Complex Legacy of Thomas Becket's Life. 2021 May 15. The Economist; p. 34.
INTERNET SOURCES			
Book on a website	Chesnutt, Charles W. *The Colonel's Dream*. Doubleday, Page, & Co., 1905. *The Literature Network,* http://www .online-literature.com /charles-chesnutt /colonels-dream.	Chesnutt, C. W. (1905). *The colonel's dream*. The Literature Network. http:// www.online-literature .com/charles-chesnutt /colonels-dream	Chesnutt CW. 1905. The Colonel's Dream. [Internet]. Garden City (NJ): Doubleday, Page & Company; [cited 2021 May 16]. Available from: http:// www.online-literature .com/charles-chesnutt /colonels-dream.
E-book	Ruefle, Mary. *The Most of It*. E-book ed., Wave Books, 2008.	Ruefle, M. (2008). *The most of it* [Apple Books edition]. Wave Books.	Ruefle M. 2008. The Most of It. [Internet; Apple Books edition]. Seattle (WA): Wave Books; [cited 2021 May 16].
Website	"Writing Center Commitment to Antiracism, Inclusion, and Equity." The Writing Center at Franklin and Marshall College, https:// www.fandm.edu/writing -center. Accessed 11 May 2021.	The Writing Center at Franklin and Marshall College. (2021, May 11). *Writing Center commitment to antiracism, inclusion, and equity.* https:// www.fandm.edu /writing-center/writing -center-commitment-to -antiracism-inclusion -and-equity2	The Writing Center at Franklin and Marshall College [Internet]. Lancaster (PA): Franklin and Marshall College; [updated 2020 Jan 28; cited 2021 May 16]. Available from: https://www .fandm.edu/writing-center.

	MLA Works Cited	APA Reference List	CSE References (or Cited References)
Article from an online database	Griffith, Robert. "The Selling of America: The Advertising Council and American Politics, 1942-1960." *The Business History Review*, vol. 57, no. 3, 1983, 388–412. JSTOR, doi:10.2307/3114050.		
Article in an online magazine	Epstein, David. "General Education Has a Bad Rap." *Slate*, 17 April 2021, https://slate.com /human-interest/2021/04 /vocational-training -general-education -debate-research-range -david-epstein.html.	Epstein, D. (2021, April 17). General education has a bad rap. *Slate*. https://slate.com /human-interest/2021/04 /vocational-training -general-education -debate-research-range -david-epstein.html	Epstein D. 2021. General Education Has a Bad Rap [Internet]. New York (NY): Slate; [cited 2021 May 16]. Available from https://slate.com /human-interest/2021/04 /vocational-training-general -education-debate-research -range-david-epstein.html.
Article in an online journal	Laine, Tarja. "Traumatic Horror Beyond the Edge: *It Follows* and *Get Out*." *Film-Philosophy*, vol. 22, no. 1, 2019, https://doi.org/10.3366 /film.2019.0117.	Laine, T. (2019). Traumatic horror beyond the edge: *It Follows* and *Get Out*. *Film-Philosophy*, 22(1). https://www .euppublishing .com/doi/10.3366 /film.2019.0117	Laine T. 2019. Traumatic Horror Beyond the Edge: It Follows and Get Out [Internet]. Edinburgh (SCT): Film-Philosophy 22(1). Retrieved from https://www .euppublishing.com /doi/10.3366/film.2019.0117.
Email	O'Brien, Kate. Email to Sam Hoffman. 1 Feb. 2021.	Emails are not included in an APA® list of references. Instead, parenthetically cite them in your main text: (K. O'Brien, personal communication, February 1, 2021)	E-mails are not included in a CSE list of references. Instead, parenthetically cite them in your main text: (2021 e-mail from K O'Brien to S Hoffman)
YouTube videos	"What Is Literature For?" YouTube, uploaded by The School of Life, 18 Sep. 2014, https:// www.youtube.com /watch?v=4RCFLobfqcw.	The School of Life. (2014, September 18). What is literature for? [Video]. YouTube. https:// www.youtube.com /watch?v=4RCFLobfqcw	The School of Life. 2014. What Is Literature For? [Internet]. YouTube.com; [cited 16 May 2021]. Available from: https:// www.youtube.com /watch?v=4RCFLobfqcw.

	MLA Works Cited	APA Reference List	CSE References (or Cited References)
Blog post	Mike H [Mike Howlett]. "Tried and True and Something New." *Hit Me With Your Nature Stick*, 24 April 2021, https://hitmewithyournaturestick.blogspot.com/2021/04/tried-and-true-and-something-new-april.html.	Howlett, M. (2021, April 24). Tried and true and something new. *Hit Me With Your Nature Stick*. https://hitmewithyournaturestick.blogspot.com/2021/04/tried-and-true-and-something-new-april.html	Howlett M. 2021 April 24. Tried and True and Something New. Hit Me With Your Nature Stick Blog [Internet]. Boston [MA]: hitmewithyournaturestick.blogspot.com. [Cited 16 May 2021]. Available from: https://hitmewithyournaturestick.blogspot.com/2021/04/tried-and-true-and-something-new-april.html.
Streaming television show (specific episode)	"Port in a Storm." Directed by Robert F. Colesberry. *The Wire*, Season 2, episode 12, HBO, 12 May 2021. *Netflix Video* app.	Simon, D. (Writer) & Colesberry, R. F. (Director). (2003, Aug. 24). Port in a Storm (Season 2, Episode 12) [TV series episode]. In D. Simon, R. F. Colesberry, & N. K. Noble (Executive Producers), *The Wire*. HBO Entertainment.	Simon D (Writer-executive producer). 2003, August 24. Episode 12 [Television series episode]. In *The Wire*. New York, NY, HBO.
Painting (or other art work) on the internet	Hassam, Childe. *At Dusk (Boston Common at Twilight)*. 1886. Boston Museum of Fine Arts. https://collections.mfa.org/objects/32415.	Hassam, C. (1886). *At dusk (Boston Common at twilight)* [Painting]. Museum of Fine Arts, Boston, MA, United States. https://collections.mfa.org/objects/32415	Hassam C. At Dusk (Boston Common at Twilight) (oil on canvas). Boston (MA): Collection.mfa.org; [accessed 2021 May 15]. Located in the Suzanne and Terrence Murray Gallery (Gallery 226) Museum of Fine Arts, Boston. https://collections.mfa.org/objects/32415.
Photograph on the internet	Leifer, Neil. *Muhammad Ali vs. Sonny Liston*. 1965. "*Time* 100 Photos," http://100photos.time.com/photos/neil-leifer-muhammad-ali-sonny-liston.	Leifer, N. (1965). *Muhammad Ali vs. Sonny Liston* [Photograph]. *Time* 100 Photos. http://100photos.time.com/photos/neil-leifer-muhammad-ali-sonny-liston	Leifer N. Muhammad Ali vs. Sonny Liston (photograph). New York (NY): Time 100 Photos [accessed 2021 May 16]. https://www.wnycstudios.org/podcasts/radiolab/episodes/217555-when-brains-attack.

	MLA Works Cited	APA Reference List	CSE References (or Cited References)
Podcast	"When Brains Attack!" *Radiolab*, hosted by Jad Abumrad and Robert Krullwich, season 10, episode 9, 12 June 2012. https://www .wnycstudios.org /podcasts/radiolab /episodes/217555-when -brains-attack.	Lechtenberg, S. (Executive Producer). (2002– present). When brains attack! [Audio podcast]. WNYC. https://www .wnycstudios.org /podcasts/radiolab /episodes/217555-when -brains-attack	Abumrad J, Krulwich R. When Brains Attack! [podcast]. Radiolab. WNYC. 2012 Jun 12, 60 minutes. [Accessed 2021 May 16]. https://www.wnycstudios .org/podcasts/radiolab /episodes/217555-when -brains-attack.

Glossary/Glosario

A	
English	**Español**
accurate evidence Verifiable information or data that can be confirmed by other credible sources.	**evidencia certera** Información o datos verificables que se pueden confirmar con otras fuentes confiables.
allusion An indirect or implied reference to literature, culture, religion, or history that connects a writer's subject to a larger idea or meaning.	**alusión** Referencia literaria, cultural, religiosa o histórica que hace el escritor de manera indirecta o implícita para relacionar su tema con una idea o significado más amplio.
ambiguity Language or writing that is imprecise or vague, either intentionally or unintentionally.	**ambigüedad** Lenguaje o texto que es impreciso o vago de manera intencional o no.
analogy The presentation of two things as similar based on common attributes, often used to explain an unfamiliar subject using objects and concepts that are more familiar to an audience.	**analogía** Presentación de dos cosas como semejantes sobre la base de los atributos que tienen en común. Se suele usar para explicar un tema poco conocido a través de objetos y conceptos más conocidos por el público.
anecdote A brief account of a particular incident.	**anécdota** Breve recuento de un incidente particular.
antecedent The original noun that is replaced by a pronoun.	**antecedente** Sustantivo original que se reemplaza con un pronombre.
antithesis A contrast of ideas presented in parallel grammatical structure.	**antítesis** Contraste de ideas que se presenta en una estructura gramatical paralela.
appeal A rhetorical strategy used to influence an audience.	**apelación** Estrategia retórica que se usa para influir en el público.
argument A claim justified through a unified line of reasoning that is supported with evidence.	**argumento** Proposición justificada a través de un razonamiento que está respaldado por evidencia.
arrangement The ordering of reasons and evidence within an argument.	**organización** Orden de los razonamientos y de la evidencia en un argumento.
attribution The explicit acknowledgment or credit given to a source of evidence.	**atribución** Reconocimiento o crédito explícito que se da a una fuente de evidencia.
audience The people who read or hear a text.	**público** Personas que leen o escuchan un texto.

B	
English	**Español**
bias The assumptions, values, attitudes, and other (often unexamined) factors that shape a person's viewpoints.	**sesgo** Supuestos, valores, actitudes y demás factores (a veces no examinados) que forman los puntos de vista de una persona.

C

English	Español
call to action The part of a persuasive text that asks the audience to take action or change their thinking.	**llamado a la acción** La parte de un texto persuasivo con la que se le pide al público que entre en acción o cambie su manera de pensar.
causal argument A method of development that explains how a result or effect came about, or that explains the short- or long-term effects that result from causes.	**argumento causal** Método de desarrollo que explica cómo se dio un resultado o efecto, o que explica los efectos a corto o largo plazo que se derivan de ciertas causas.
chronological order A method of arrangement based on time order or a sequential series of steps.	**orden cronológico** Método organizativo que toma en cuenta el orden temporal o una secuencia de pasos.
citation A formal attribution to the author or other source of evidence.	**cita** Atribución formal a un autor u otra fuente de evidencia.
claim A writer's defensible position that includes a unifying idea and perspective about the subject.	**proposición** Posición defendible de un escritor, que incluye una idea unificadora y una perspectiva sobre el tema.
classification argument A method of development that places objects or concepts into categories.	**argumento de clasificación** Método de desarrollo que pone los objetos o conceptos en categorías.
clause A group of words that includes a subject and a verb.	**cláusula** Grupo de palabras que incluye un sujeto y un verbo.
coherence A writer's strategy to illustrate the relationship between sentences, paragraphs, information, and ideas within a text.	**coherencia** Estrategia de un escritor para ilustrar la relación que hay entre las oraciones, los párrafos, la información y las ideas de un texto.
commentary A writer's explanation that connects evidence to a line of reasoning and the unifying idea of a claim.	**comentario** Explicación de un escritor que conecta la evidencia con un razonamiento y con la idea unificadora de una proposición.
comparison/contrast A method of development or arrangement that evaluates two or more subjects by analyzing their similarities and their differences.	**comparación/contraste** Método de desarrollo u organización que evalúa dos o más temas al analizar sus semejanzas y diferencias.
concession Acknowledging the limitations of one's own argument by accepting all or a portion of a competing claim as correct, or correct under different circumstances.	**concesión** Reconocer las limitaciones de un argumento al aceptar por completo o en parte una proposición contraria que es correcta o al menos correcta en otras circunstancias.
conclusion The ending of an argument that brings unity and closure to the reasoning.	**conclusión** Final de un argumento. Cierra y le da unidad al razonamiento.
connotation The sensory, emotional, or cultural associations of a word.	**connotación** Asociaciones sensoriales, emocionales o culturales de una palabra.
context The time, place, and occasion that a text was created, delivered, or read.	**contexto** Tiempo, lugar u ocasión en que se creó, narró o leyó un texto.
coordination A grammatical and rhetorical structure within a sentence that indicates equality or balance between ideas and elements.	**coordinación** Estructura gramática y retórica dentro de una oración que indica una igualdad o equilibrio entre ideas y elementos.

English	Español
corroboration The use of evidence or sources to complement or support an argument.	**corroboración** Uso de evidencia o fuentes para complementar o respaldar un argumento.
counterargument A response by a writer to an opposing claim or argument.	**contraargumento** Respuesta de un escritor a una proposición o argumento contrario.
credibility The audience's trust in the writer's authority, honesty, and perspective.	**credibilidad** Confianza que pone el público en la autoridad, honestidad y perspectiva del escritor.

D

English	Español
deductive reasoning An organizational strategy that begins with a broad generalization and moves to specific observations.	**razonamiento deductivo** Estrategia organizativa que comienza con una generalización y sigue con observaciones específicas.
definition argument A method of development that explains a word, subject, or concept.	**definición** Método de desarrollo que explica una palabra, tema o concepto.
denotation The relatively neutral dictionary definition of a word.	**denotación** Definición relativamente neutra de una palabra en un diccionario.
description A method of development that presents details and sensory language to depict a subject.	**descripción** Método de desarrollo que presenta detalles y lenguaje sensorial para describir un tema.
design feature A way of presenting a text through the use of typography (e.g., bold, italics, font style and size) and other visual elements (e.g., color, pull quotes, white space) that emphasize or convey information.	**característica de diseño** Manera de presentar un texto mediante el uso de tipografía (p. ej., negrita, cursiva, estilo y tamaño de letra) y otros elementos visuales (p. ej., colores, citas destacadas, espacio en blanco) que hacen énfasis o transmiten información.
detail A specific piece of information about a subject that can function as evidence.	**detalle** Información específica sobre un tema, que puede servir como evidencia.
device See *rhetorical device*.	**figura** Ver *recurso retórico*.
diction The specific word choices writers make to convey their ideas.	**dicción** Palabras específicas que escoge un escritor para expresar sus ideas.
division argument A method of development that explains a subject or concept by breaking it down or dividing it into its component parts.	**división** Método de desarrollo que explica un tema o concepto al desglosarlo o dividirlo en partes.

E

English	Español
effect The intended or unintended impact of a rhetorical choice on an audience.	**efecto** Repercusión, intencional o no, que tiene un recurso retórico en el público.
element of design See *design feature*.	**elemento de diseño** Ver *característica de diseño*.
epiphany A moment of sudden revelation, insight, or awareness.	**epifanía** Momento de revelación, introspección o conciencia repentina.

ethos An appeal that helps establish a writer's credibility by building rapport and earning the trust of an audience.

ethos Apelación que permite establecer la credibilidad del escritor al crear afinidad con el público y ganarse su confianza.

evaluation An argument whose purpose is to make a judgment or present a recommendation.

evaluación Argumento cuyo objetivo es dar una opinión o presentar una recomendación.

evidence Information, details, and/or data used to support a reason within an argument.

evidencia Información, detalles y datos que se usan para respaldar una razón dentro de un argumento.

example A type of evidence that illustrates the specific characteristics of a subject by presenting a representative instance.

ejemplo Tipo de evidencia que ilustra las características específicas de un tema al presentar un caso típico.

exigence The part of a rhetorical situation that inspires, stimulates, or provokes a writer to create a text.

exigencia Parte de una situación retórica que inspira, estimula o incita al escritor a crear un texto.

experiment A type of evidence generated from the observation of phenomena under controlled conditions, especially in a scientific context.

experimento Tipo de evidencia generada a partir de la observación de fenómenos en condiciones controladas, sobre todo en un contexto científico.

expert opinion A type of evidence that presents testimony from credible sources in a particular field.

opinión de un experto Tipo de evidencia que presenta un testimonio de fuentes verosímiles en un campo específico.

exposition A rhetorical purpose that gives an explanation of a subject, often through definition, process, or causality.

exposición Recurso retórico que da una explicación de un tema, por lo general, a través de una definición, proceso o causalidad.

extended metaphor A comparison that is sustained throughout a text.

metáfora extendida Comparación que se hace a lo largo de un texto.

F

English	Español

fact A type of evidence that presents a truth known by actual experience or empirical observation.

hecho Tipo de evidencia que presenta una verdad conocida a través de una experiencia real u observación empírica.

figurative language Comparisons (analogies, metaphors, similes, personifications) that draw upon concrete objects to represent abstract ideas.

lenguaje figurado Comparaciones (analogías, metáforas, símiles, personificaciones) que se valen de objetos concretos para representar ideas abstractas.

fragment A broken thought or idea, or an incomplete part of a sentence used intentionally for emphasis.

fragmento Pensamiento o idea truncada, o una parte incompleta de una oración, que se usa intencionalmente para hacer énfasis.

G

English	Español

genre The type or classification of a text, such as a graduation speech, an executive summary, or a personal essay.

género Tipo de clasificación de un texto, como un discurso de graduación, un resumen ejecutivo o un ensayo personal.

H

English	Español
hook A strategy that engages an audience at the beginning of a text.	**gancho narrativo** Estrategia para captar la atención del público al comienzo de un texto.
hyperbole An exaggeration that is not meant to be taken literally, but instead used for comparison, emphasis, or humor.	**hipérbole** Exageración que no debe entenderse literalmente, sino que sirve para comparar, hacer énfasis o agregar humor.

I

English	Español
idea An abstract concept that presents a writer's unique stance and serves to unify an argument.	**idea** Concepto abstracto que transmite la postura particular de un escritor y que sirve para unificar el argumento.
illustration A type of evidence such as a photograph, cartoon, chart, artwork, infographic, or other visual support for an argument.	**ilustración** Un tipo de evidencia, como una fotografía, una tira cómica, una tabla, una pieza de arte, una infografía u otro recurso visual que respalde al argumento.
image A sensory detail of a subject, such as its sound, sight, smell, touch, or taste.	**imagen** Detalle sensorial de un tema, como su sonido, apariencia, olor, textura o sabor.
imagery The written expression of a sensory experience, such as sound, sight, smell, touch, or taste.	**imaginería** Expresión escrita de una experiencia sensorial, como un sonido, visión, olor, textura o sabor.
implication An intended or unintended consequence of a claim or argument, either real or hypothetical.	**implicación** Consecuencia, intencionada o no, de una proposición o argumento, que puede ser real o hipotética.
importance (order of) A method of arrangement that presents reasons and information from least significant to the most significant, or vice versa.	**importancia (orden de)** Método organizativo que presenta razones e información desde la menos importante hasta la más importante o viceversa.
incongruity A revealing contrast that runs counter to expectations.	**incongruencia** Contraste revelador que va en contra de las expectativas.
inductive reasoning An organizational strategy that moves from specific observations to broad generalizations.	**razonamiento inductivo** Una estrategia organizativa que va de observaciones específicas a grandes generalizaciones.
intellectual property The ownership and rights to any written or creative product.	**propiedad intelectual** Propiedad y derechos sobre cualquier escrito o producto creativo.
introduction The opening of an argument that engages the audience, establishes the writer's purpose, and provides context for the subject.	**introducción** Apertura de un argumento que capta la atención del público, establece el objetivo del escritor y ofrece el contexto del tema.
irony An effect that results from the difference between an argument's claim or conclusion and the readers' expectations or values.	**ironía** Efecto que se obtiene de la diferencia entre la proposición o conclusión de un argumento y las expectativas o valores del lector.

J

English	Español
juxtaposition The presentation of evidence or examples side by side to emphasize similarities or differences, often in the context of ideas or values.	**yuxtaposición** Presentación lado a lado de evidencia o ejemplos para hacer énfasis en las semejanzas o diferencias, por lo general, en el contexto de ideas o valores.

L

English	Español
line of reasoning The sequence of reasons that work together to support the unifying idea and perspective of a writer's argument.	**línea de razonamiento** Secuencia de razones que funcionan juntas para apoyar la idea unificadora y perspectiva del argumento de un escritor.
logos An appeal to an audience's sense of reasoning or logic.	**logos** Apelación al sentido racional o lógico del público.

M

English	Español
message The writer's claim (idea and perspective) that is developed with reasoning and evidence.	**mensaje** Proposición del escritor (idea y perspectiva) que se desarrolla con razonamientos y evidencia.
metaphor A comparison of two unrelated objects that assigns ideas to the points of comparison.	**metáfora** Comparación de dos objetos sin relación, que asigna ideas a los puntos de comparación.
method of development A rhetorical strategy, such as definition or cause and effect, that a writer uses to achieve a purpose and establish a line of reasoning.	**método de desarrollo** Estrategia retórica, como la definición o causa y efecto, que usa el escritor para lograr un objetivo y establecer una línea de razonamiento.
mode of communication The medium (e.g., speech, text, podcast, video, etc.) that a writer chooses to convey a message.	**modo de comunicación** El medio (p. ej., discurso, texto, podcast, video, etc.) que escoge el escritor para transmitir su mensaje.
modifier Any word, phrase, or clause that qualifies, clarifies, or specifies another word, phrase, or clause.	**modificador** Toda palabra, frase o cláusula que califique, aclare o especifique a otra palabra, frase o cláusula.
motif A series of recurring, related symbols or images that create a pattern to reinforce an idea.	**motivo** Serie de símbolos o imágenes recurrentes y relacionadas, que crean un patrón para reforzar una idea.
multimodal argument An argument that draws upon multiple modes of communication or methods of development.	**argumento multimodal** Argumento que recurre a varios modos de comunicación o métodos de desarrollo.

N

English	Español
narrative distance The amount of time and space between the writer and the writer's subject.	**distancia narrativa** Cantidad de tiempo y espacio entre el escritor y el tema del escritor.

English	Español
narration A rhetorical purpose that draws upon story-telling and details to convey a message.	**narración** Propósito retórico que se vale de cuentos, historias y detalles para transmitir un mensaje.
negation A strategy for definition that uses contrast to explain what something is not.	**negación** Estrategia de definición que se vale del contraste para explicar que algo no es tal cosa.

O

English	Español
organization The structural form (including the method of development, arrangement, and logic) in which claims, reasoning, and evidence are presented in an argument.	**organización** Forma estructural (incluidos el método de desarrollo, la organización y la lógica) en la que las proposiciones, el razonamiento y la evidencia se presentan en un argumento.

P

English	Español
parallel structure The repetition words or phrases in similar syntax (or word order) to emphasize the equality between words, subjects, and ideas.	**estructura paralela** Repetición de palabras o frases con una sintaxis (u orden de las palabras) parecida para hacer énfasis en la igualdad entre palabras, temas e ideas.
paraphrase A restatement of a source's evidence or ideas that maintains the original intention and emphasis, but rephrases the source's language.	**paráfrasis** Repetición de la evidencia o ideas de una fuente, que mantiene la intención y el énfasis original, pero que reformula el lenguaje de la fuente.
parenthetical element A pause or interruption within a sentence where the writer provides additional information for the audience, or advances his or her purpose.	**elemento parentético** Pausa o interrupción dentro de una oración en la que el escritor ofrece información adicional para el público, o propone su intención.
pathos An emotional appeal in an argument that attempts to move an audience toward a specific action or belief.	**pathos** Apelación emocional en un argumento que trata de conmover al público hacia una acción o creencia específica.
personal experience A type of evidence based on the writer's firsthand encounters and direct observations of a subject.	**experiencia personal** Tipo de evidencia fundamentada en los encuentros de primera mano y en las observaciones directas de un tema por parte del escritor.
personal observation A type of evidence based on elements of the writer's subject that he or she has seen directly.	**observación personal** Tipo de evidencia fundamentada en los elementos del tema del escritor que este ha visto directamente.
perspective A writer's stance about an idea related to a subject; the lens through which a subject is viewed.	**perspectiva** La postura del escritor en relación con un tema; lente por el cual se ve el tema.
persuasion A rhetorical purpose that asks the audience to think or act in a specific way.	**persuasión** Recurso retórico con el que se le pide al público que piense o actúe de una manera específica.
position The side that a writer takes on the subject of an argument.	**posición** El lado que toma el escritor hacia el tema de un argumento.

problem/solution argument A method of development that identifies a problem, evaluates potential solutions, and recommends a response.

argumento de problema y solución Método de desarrollo que identifica un problema, evalúa las posibles soluciones y recomienda una respuesta.

process analysis argument A method of development that explains how something works, how to do something, or how something is/was done.

argumento de análisis del proceso Método de desarrollo que explica cómo funciona algo, cómo hacer algo o cómo se hace o se hizo algo.

purpose The goal that a writer hopes to accomplish within a text (e.g., to persuade, narrate, explain, evaluate).

propósito Objetivo que el escritor quiere lograr con un texto (p. ej., persuadir, narrar, explicar, evaluar).

Q

English

Español

quantitative source or evidence Information that presents numerical data, facts, and statistics which comes from surveys, polls, charts, and graphs.

fuente o evidencia cuantitativa Información que presenta datos numéricos, hechos y estadísticas que provienen de encuestas, sondeos, tablas y gráficas.

R

English

Español

reason A sub-claim that justifies and validates an argument's claim.

razón Subproposición que justifica y valida la proposición de un argumento.

rebuttal A contrasting perspective on the evidence or claims of an opposing argument.

impugnación Perspectiva contrastante de la evidencia o proposiciones de un argumento contrario.

refutation A demonstration (with evidence) that all or a portion of a competing claim is invalid.

refutación Demostración (con evidencia) de que una proposición (en su totalidad o parcialmente) es inválida.

relevant evidence Information that directly supports the reasons and claims of an argument.

evidencia relevante Información que respalda directamente las razones y proposiciones de un argumento.

repetition A rhetorical strategy in which a writer uses a word, phrase, sentence, or other element two or more times for effect or emphasis.

repetición Estrategia retórica en la que el escritor usa una palabra, frase, oración u otro elemento dos o más veces para producir un efecto o hacer énfasis.

rhetoric A message created to appeal to a specific audience.

retórica Mensaje creado para apelar a un público en particular.

rhetorical choice The strategic and intentional decisions a writer makes to achieve specific effects.

elección retórica Decisiones estratégicas e intencionales que hace el escritor para producir ciertos efectos.

rhetorical device A concrete choice or method that a writer uses for effect, such as metaphor, allusion, or repetition.

recurso retórico Elección o método concreto que usa el escritor para producir un efecto, como una metáfora, alusión o repetición.

English	Español
rhetorical question A syntactical device that a writer uses to compel the audience to pause and reflect rather than respond with a literal answer.	**pregunta retórica** Recurso sintáctico que usa el escritor para obligar al público a hacer una pausa y reflexionar en vez de simplemente responder a una pregunta literal.
rhetorical strategies The techniques (e.g., comparison, balance, contrast) that a writer uses to achieve an intended effect.	**estrategias retóricas** Técnicas (p. ej., comparación, balance, contraste) que usa el escritor para lograr un efecto intencionado.

S

English	Español
shift The writer's change, qualification, or reconsideration of a perspective.	**cambio** Reconsideración de una perspectiva por parte del escritor.
simile A comparison of two unrelated objects using *like* or *as* that assigns ideas to the point of comparison.	**símil** Comparación de dos objetos no relacionados en la que se usa *como* para asignarle ideas al punto de comparación.
simple sentence An independent clause that expresses a complete thought (subject and verb) and often emphasizes a writer's main idea.	**oración simple** Cláusula independiente que expresa un pensamiento completo (sujeto y verbo) y que por lo general hace énfasis en la idea principal del escritor.
sophistication A complex understanding of the rhetorical situation that might include an analysis of a subject's tensions or implications, along with a vivid and persuasive style.	**sofisticación** Comprensión compleja de la situación retórica, que podría incluir un análisis de las tensiones o implicaciones del tema, junto con un estilo vívido y persuasivo.
source A person or organization from which information is taken and used to support or refute reasons in an argument.	**fuente** Persona u organización a partir de la cual se toma información que sirve para respaldar o refutar las razones de un argumento.
spatial (order) A method of arrangement that presents information and reasoning in terms of relative location, space, or geography, such as nearest to farthest, or vice versa.	**espacial (orden)** Método de organización que representa información y razonamientos en términos de ubicaciones relativas, espaciales o geográficas, como de más cerca a más lejos o viceversa.
speaker The writer or creator of a text (see *writer*).	**orador** Escritor o creador de un texto (ver *escritor*).
specificity (order of) A method of arrangement that presents information from least specific to most specific or vice versa.	**especificidad (orden de)** Método de organización que presenta información de la menos específica a la más específica o viceversa.
statistic A type of evidence such as numerical facts or quantitative data.	**estadística** Tipo de evidencia, como datos numéricos y datos cuantitativos.
strategy See *rhetorical strategies*.	**estrategia** Ver *estrategias retóricas*.
style The cumulative effect of a writer's choices, including diction, syntax, tone, and other elements of writing.	**estilo** Efecto cumulativo de las elecciones de un escritor, incluida la dicción, la sintaxis, el tono y otros elementos de la escritura.
subject The literal topic or issue addressed in a text.	**tema** Asunto que se toca en un texto.

English	Español
subordination A grammatical and rhetorical structure that indicates the inequality or imbalance of ideas and elements.	**subordinación** Estructura gramática y retórica que indica la desigualdad o desbalance de las ideas o elementos.
sufficient evidence The inclusion of enough relevant information and data to support a line of reasoning.	**evidencia suficiente** Inclusión de suficiente información relevante y datos para respaldar una línea de razonamiento.
summary A brief account of a subject or text that distills the main idea for the reader.	**resumen** Breve recuento de un tema o texto, que le presenta la idea principal al lector.
syntax The specific selection and arrangement of sentences within a text.	**sintaxis** Selección y orden específico de las oraciones de un texto.
synthesis An argument that integrates multiple sources to support a claim.	**síntesis** Argumento que integra varias fuentes para respaldar una proposición.

T

English	Español
testimony Evidence in the form of statements made by others who may be experts, or who may just have relevant experiences with a subject.	**testimonio** Evidencia en forma de afirmaciones que hacen otras personas, que pueden ser expertos, o que tienen la experiencia relevante sobre el tema.
text A writer's creation that conveys a message for an audience.	**texto** Creación del escritor, que le transmite el mensaje al público.
thesis statement The formal expression of a writer's claim (idea and perspective) about a subject.	**tesis** Expresión formal de la proposición del escritor (idea o perspectiva) sobre un tema.
tone A writer's attitude toward the subject expressed through diction, syntax, and other elements of style.	**tono** Actitud del escritor en cuanto al tema expresado mediante la dicción, la sintaxis y otros elementos de estilo.
transitions Words, phrases, clauses, sentences, or paragraphs that illustrate relationships among ideas and contribute to coherence.	**transiciones** Palabras, frases, oraciones o párrafos que ilustran las relaciones que hay entre las ideas y que generan coherencia.
typical evidence Evidence that is representative of a population or issue.	**evidencia típica** Evidencia que es representativa de una población o tema.

U

English	Español
understatement The presentation of claims or ideas as having less importance than they actually have for effect (the opposite of *hyperbole*).	**subestimación** Disminuir la importancia de proposiciones o ideas para producir un efecto (es lo contrario de la *hipérbole*).
unifying idea A single abstract concept that controls a line of reasoning.	**idea unificadora** Concepto abstracto que controla una línea de razonamiento.

English	Español
unity A writer's strategy that connects various reasons and supporting evidence to one controlling idea within an argument.	**unidad** Estrategia del escritor en la que se conectan varias razones y pruebas con una idea imperante dentro del argumento.

V

English	Español
validity The outcome that results when all of the reasons justify a claim within an argument.	**validez** Resultado de cuando todas las razones justifican una proposición dentro de un argumento.
visual source Any graphic source of evidence, such as artwork, photography, images, illustrations, charts, or graphs.	**fuente visual** Cualquier fuente de evidencia gráfica, como obras de arte, fotografías, imágenes, ilustraciones, tablas o gráficas.
voice The distinctive sound and identity that emerges from a writer's word choice, syntax, and tone.	**voz** Sonido e identidad particular que surge de las palabras, la sintaxis y el tono que escoge el escritor.

W

English	Español
writer The author of a text who presents a perspective shaped by his or her background and context (sometimes called the *speaker*).	**escritor** El autor de un texto, quien presenta una perspectiva a partir de sus circunstancias o contexto (a veces se llama *orador*).

Text Credits

Kareem Abdul-Jabbar, "Op-Ed: Don't Understand the Protests? What You're Seeing is People Pushed to the Edge," *Los Angeles Times*, May 30, 2020. Copyright © 2020 by Kareem Abdul-Jabbar. All rights reserved. Used with permission.

Chimamanda Ngozi Adichie, "The Danger of a Single Story" by Chimamanda Adichie. Copyright © 2009 by Chimamanda Ngozi Adichie, used by permission of The Wylie Agency LLC.

Jerald Bachman, "Working A Lot in High School Can Shortchange a Student's Future," University of Michigan Institute for Social Research. Copyright © 2020 by Jerald Bachman. Used with permission.

Dan Barber, "What Farm to Table Got Wrong," *New York Times*, May 17, 2014. Copyright © 2014 The New York Times Company. All rights reserved. Used under license. https://www.nytimes.com/

John Barry, "It's All Part of the Game," *Power Plays: Politics, Football, and Other Blood Sports*. Copyright © 2001 by John Barry. All rights reserved. Used with permission.

Wendell Berry, "The Agrarian Standard," *Orion Magazine*. Copyright © 2002 by Orion Magazine. Used with permission.

Alyssa Biederman, Melinda Walling, and Sarah Siock, "Meet Gen Z Activists," *Bucks County Courier Times*, September 29, 2020. Copyright © 2020, by Bucks County Courier Times– USA TODAY NETWORK. All rights reserved. Used with permission.

Daniel Bortz, Excerpt from "Skills Employers Look for in College Graduates," *Monster*. Copyright © 2020 by Monster. Used with permission.

Suzanne Britt, "Neat People vs. Sloppy People" from *Show and Tell* (1982). Reprinted by permission of the author.

Business Supporting College and Career Readiness. Copyright © 2018 Association of American Colleges and Universities. Republished with permission of Association of American Colleges and Universities. Permission conveyed through Copyright Clearance Center, Inc.

Josh C., "A Massacre of Art" from *Student Voice: 100 Argument Essays by Teens on Issues That Matter to Them*. Copyright © 2020 by W. W. Norton and Company. Used with permission.

Rachel L. Carson, "The Obligation to Endure" from SILENT SPRING by Rachel Carson. Copyright © 1962 by Rachel L. Carson, renewed 1990 by Roger Christie. Reprinted by permission of Houghton Mifflin Harcourt Publishing Company and Frances Collin, Trustee. All copying, including electronic, or redistribution of this text, is expressly forbidden.

Grace Chen, "Should Public Schools Provide Students with Vocational Opportunities?" *Public School Review*, June 25, 2019. Copyright © 2019 by Public School Review. Used with permission.

Durga Chew-Bose, "Tan Lines," *Matter* (the original flagship publication of *Medium*), August 17, 2015, https://medium.com/matter/tan-lines-55b7b4753703

Emma Chiu, "Driving: It's Going Out of Style" from *Student Voice: 100 Argument Essays by Teens on Issues That Matter to Them*. Copyright © 2020 by W. W. Norton and Company. Used with permission.

Christian Cooper, "Why Poverty is Like a Disease," *Nautilus*, no. 47 (April 20, 2017), accessed at http://nautil.us/issue/47/consciousness/why-poverty-is-like-a-disease

Christopher B. Daly, "How the Lawyers Stole Winter," originally published in *The Atlantic*, March 1995. Used with permission.

Kalindi Desai, "Phones Create Barriers Between Peers," *The Catamount Newspaper* 4, no. 5 (April 2016): 6. Copyright © 2016 by College Station High School. Used with permission.

Jennifer Dickler, "Why so few teenagers have jobs anymore," *CNBC*, October 6, 2019. Copyright © 2019 by CNBC.

Narain Dubey, "Breaking the Blue Wall of Silence: Changing the Social Narrative about Policing in America" from *Student Voice: 100 Argument Essays by Teens on Issues That Matter to Them*. Copyright © 2020 by W. W. Norton and Company. Used with permission.

Nati Duron, "Quiet Confidence: Introverts and the Power of Silence," *The Chant*, December 20, 2017, https://nchschant.com/11851/investigative/quiet-confidence-introverts-and-the-power-of-silence/

Brighton Earley, "Finding the Flexibility to Survive," from *This I Believe: Life Lessons*, 176–178. Copyright © 2013 by John Wiley & Sons, Inc. Used with permission.

Barbara Ehrenreich, "In America, Only the Rich Can Afford to Write about Poverty" by Barbara Ehrenreich. First published in *The Guardian* on August 6, 2015. Copyright © 2015 by Barbara Ehrenreich. Reprinted by permission of ICM Partners.

Ralph Ellison, "Hidden Name and Complex Fate," copyright © 1964 and renewed 1992 by Ralph Ellison; from THE COLLECTED ESSAYS OF RALPH ELLISON by Ralph Ellison. Used by permission of Modern Library, an imprint of Random House, a division of Penguin Random House LLC. All rights reserved.

Index